Aircraft Leasing and Financing

Aircraft Leasing and Financing

Tools for Success in International Aircraft Acquisition and Management

Vitaly S. Guzhva
Embry-Riddle Aeronautical University, Daytona Beach, FL, United States

Sunder Raghavan
Embry-Riddle Aeronautical University, Daytona Beach, FL, United States

Damon J. D'Agostino
Zephyrus Aviation Capital, Fort Lauderdale, FL, United States

ELSEVIER

Elsevier
Radarweg 29, PO Box 211, 1000 AE Amsterdam, Netherlands
The Boulevard, Langford Lane, Kidlington, Oxford OX5 1GB, United Kingdom
50 Hampshire Street, 5th Floor, Cambridge, MA 02139, United States

British Library Cataloguing-in-Publication Data
A catalogue record for this book is available from the British Library

Library of Congress Cataloging-in-Publication Data
A catalog record for this book is available from the Library of Congress

ISBN: 978-0-12-815285-0

For Information on all Elsevier publications
visit our website at https://www.elsevier.com/books-and-journals

Publisher: Joe Hayton
Acquisition Editor: Brian Romer
Editorial Project Manager: Thomas Van Der Ploeg
Production Project Manager: Anusha Sambamoorthy/Anitha Sivaraj
Cover Designer: Mark Rogers

Typeset by MPS Limited, Chennai, India

Contents

About the Authors

Vitaly S. Guzhva

Dr. Guzhva is a Professor of Finance in the College of Business of Embry-Riddle Aeronautical University where he teaches Aviation Finance courses. He holds BS in Aeronautical Engineering, MS in Military Science, MBA in Aviation, and Ph.D. in Finance degrees as well as the Chartered Financial Analyst (CFA) and Accredited Senior Appraiser (ASA) with an aircraft specialty designation. As a military and corporate pilot, Dr. Guzhva has logged more than 5000 flight hours primarily in high-performance jet aircrafts. Dr. Guzhva's work appeared in various peer-review journals including *Journal of Economics and Finance*, *Journal of Air Transport Management*, *Journal of Public Budgeting, Accounting and Financial Management*, *Transportation Research Record, Risk Management*, and others. Dr. Guzhva's research related to the United States airlines' losses following September 11, 2001, and the financial health of United States general aviation airports was widely discussed in national business and aerospace press. Dr. Guzhva is a professional member of multiple Finance and Aviation associations. His applied research and consulting projects included industry assessments and market analyses for major aircraft manufacturers, benefit-cost analyses of Operational Improvements for NextGen Air Transport Management system, assessments of major investments in aviation infrastructure, and others. His current research interests include analysis of airline bankruptcies, development of dynamic fuel and currency hedging strategies for domestic and international airlines and investment performance of Aircraft ABS and EETCs.

Sunder Raghavan

Dr. Raghavan is a Professor of Finance, a Fulbright Scholar, and an ISTAT U program coordinator at the College of Business at the Daytona Beach campus of Embry-Riddle Aeronautical University. He received his PhD from Washington State University and is an Accredited Senior Appraiser (ASA) with an aircraft specialty designation. His research interests are in the area of aircraft finance and leasing, international aviation finance, fuel price hedging, exchange rate modeling, financial distress and bankruptcy, functioning of financial markets in developing countries and theoretical application of finance to the airline industry. Dr. Raghavan has published various articles in journals including Elsevier's *Journal of Air Transportation Management*. He has authored two case study books in aviation finance. He has served as a consultant to the Reserve Bank of India (India's Central Bank) and his report on the Corporate Bond Market Developments in India was published by the Reserve Bank of India. He has served as an external thesis examiner for doctoral dissertations in finance and has reviewed textbooks in finance. Dr. Raghavan has international teaching and research experience in the United States, Canada, China, India, and the Middle East. Currently, and as part of his Fulbright grant, Dr. Raghavan would be researching innovative aircraft financing methods used by Middle Eastern Airlines.

Damon J. D'Agostino

Damon J. D'Agostino is the President and CEO of Zephyrus Aviation Capital—a leasing platform focusing on mid- to late-life aircraft. Prior to Zephyrus, he spent majority of his career at CIT Aerospace, one of the world's leading aircraft-leasing companies. His last role at CIT was chief commercial officer, where he was responsible for all aspects of CIT's commercial strategy and execution including aircraft sale and lease transactions, airline relationship management, contract negotiation, restructurings, and new aircraft and engine acquisitions. Prior to that role, he served as chief sales officer, with global responsibility for marketing CIT's owned and managed aircraft portfolio which, by 2017, exceeded 350 aircraft and was valued at eleven billion dollars. Starting his career in the early 1990s, D'Agostino held a succession of sales and marketing roles and responsibilities with his personal transaction success including the sale, lease, and financing of over 170 aircraft. D'Agostino is a graduate of Embry-Riddle Aeronautical University, where he received a Bachelor of Science Degree in Aviation Business Administration, with a concentration in Finance. He also received an MBA in international business from the University of Miami where he was summa cum laude and valedictorian of his graduating class.

Acknowledgments

Any long and demanding project has a trigger that makes a need for such a project evident and persuades participating parties to invest their time and effort toward worthwhile goals. The International Society of Transport Aircraft Trading (ISTAT) Foundation created this trigger for the development of this book by launching the ISTAT University (ISTAT U) program in 2015 in conjunction with Embry-Riddle Aeronautical University (ERAU). The ISTAT U curriculum has been developed in partnership with ISTAT industry professionals and specifically tailored to prepare graduate students for careers in the exciting field of aircraft financing, leasing, and trading. After teaching ISTAT U courses for several semesters, we realized the need for organizing our lecture notes, PowerPoint presentations, collections of articles, and transcripts of our interviews with ISTAT industry experts into a book that can be used by ISTAT U students as well as students and professionals looking to expand their knowledge in the field of aviation finance. We have been overwhelmed by the level of encouragement and assistance from so many individuals whom we would like to gratefully recognize for their contribution to this book.

We would like to thank ISTAT and the ISTAT Foundation for providing us with relevant topics and ideas and for organizing industry expert interviews at the various ISTAT conferences. We are also grateful to numerous ISTAT industry experts who advised us on curriculum development and interviewed with us discussing important industry issues. In particular, we would like to thank Shannon Ackert, Bob Agnew, Goran Avdicevic, Peter Barret, Leo Burrell, Peter Chang, Kristen Chmielewski, Geoff Deal, George Dimitroff, Mark Ditto, Robert Fanning, John Feren, Dick Forsberg, Todd Freeman, Robert Gates, Richard Genge, Dean Gerber, Simon Goodson, Sergio Guedes, Christine Hafner, Stuart Hatcher, Joel Hussey, Danielle Kaskel, Doug Kelly, Tobias Konrad, Harold Kugelman, Gerry Laderman, Bryan Lange, Gene Levitin, Matthew Little, Tim Lynes, Robyn Mandel, Andy Mansell, Paul Mason, Steve Mason, Ryan Mckenna, Don Mitchell, Bryson Monteleone, Robert Neal, Dan Pietrzak, Mike Platt, Olga Razzhivina, Doug Runte, Brian Rynott, Stuart Schwartzberg, Phil Seymour, Carl Shephard, Betsy Snyder, David Swan, Caroline Vandedrinch, Haseem Vazhayil, Madhu Vijay, Jose Vincente, Eddo Weijer, Warren Willits, Barry Wolf, David Yu, Yunda Zapatero, and Kostya Zolotusky. As a small token of our gratitude to the ISTAT members, who shared with us their invaluable time and expertise, we are donating our share of the proceeds from the sale of this book to the ISTAT foundation.

Also, we would like to thank all our students at ERAU who helped us with the research and writing of this book. We are grateful to Hua Chai, Sloane Churchill, Thomas Garnier, James Joseph, Ali Mazhar, Viraj Oza, Sharath Sashikumar, Nathan Schnitzlein Michael Welch, Gabriel Wiscombe, and Dawei Yu.

We particularly acknowledge our families who supported us in this endeavor. Finally, with so many people contributing to this book, we probably missed somebody and profoundly apologize for that.

Vitaly S. Guzhva
Embry-Riddle Aeronautical University, Daytona Beach, FL, United States

Sunder Raghavan
Embry-Riddle Aeronautical University, Daytona Beach, FL, United States

Damon J. D'Agostino
Zephyrus Aviation Capital, Fort Lauderdale, FL, United States

Foreword

When I started in aviation in the early 1980s, it was common for airlines either to own their aircraft or to lease them through a long-term finance lease with a purchase option. Today, almost 40 years later, and having spent most of my career in the financing and leasing of commercial aircraft, I have witnessed many changes in the aviation industry. When asked who owns the airplanes that the airlines fly, the response will most likely be, "the airlines, of course." While it is true that airlines own a majority of their aircraft on average, what many people don't realize is that more than 40% of the world's fleet is leased—and that figure continues to rise. Commercial aircraft cost tens of millions of dollars each, sometimes in the hundreds of millions of dollars, resulting in the need to finance the purchase of an aircraft, whether it be by an airline for its own use or by a lessor to lease the aircraft to an airline.

Aircraft Leasing and Financing: Tools for Success in International Aircraft Acquisition and Management captures these changes in the aviation industry by providing a comprehensive overview of the commercial aircraft industry and explains in detail how both airlines and leasing companies finance the purchase of these capital intensive assets. This book will serve as an excellent text and reference for students planning for a career in aviation. In addition, experienced professionals will find herein the means to familiarize themselves with aspects of the industry that may be outside their area of expertise.

Various chapters cover why and how airlines select certain types and models of aircraft for their fleets and how to decide whether it's better to lease or own the aircraft. Legal and regulatory issues, insurance, aircraft valuation, and taxation are also explained, all of which are critically important to the overall financing aspect of an aircraft. Chapters regarding leasing explain how lease rates and maintenance reserves are calculated and the mechanics behind engine leasing.

Over the years, the main sources of finance have shifted from banks to nonbank financing such as capital markets, private equity, export credit agencies, and others. In many cases, tax considerations can be the decisive factors when weighing whether to purchase or lease aircraft. Aircraft lessors have moved their main presence from the United States to hubs in Ireland, Singapore, and Hong Kong. New leasing companies are growing rapidly in China and Europe, and consolidation among lessors is becoming increasingly common. *Aircraft Leasing and Financing* provides a comprehensive overview of the evolution of many types of financing in use today, as well as the growth of cross-border leasing and the additional burdens imposed by the requirement for lessors to be aware of laws and regulations imposed in different jurisdictions.

Two professors from Embry-Riddle and a senior executive from the aircraft leasing industry—with input from experienced industry experts—have coauthored what serves as an excellent resource for everyone in the commercial aviation industry.

C. Jeffrey Knittel

Chairman and Chief Executive Officer of Airbus Americas, Inc.,
Herndon, VA, United States

Foreword

The commercial aviation industry is big business, generating over $700 billion of annual contribution to global GDP, making it larger than some G20 countries. Passenger demand continues to grow at more than 5% per annum, a trend that has been sustained, virtually unabated, for half a century. Some 500 airlines now carry more than 4 billion passengers every year on a fleet of 25,000 jet airliners and 4000 turboprop aircraft.

A total of 40,000 new commercial jet aircraft are expected to deliver over the next 20 years, 60% of which will be needed for airline growth requirements, with the balance replacing existing, aging fleets. These deliveries will require $6 trillion of financing, sourced through a combination of secured and unsecured bank debt, bonds, portfolio securitizations, and other capital markets products, equity investors, and cash flows from retained profits. Up to 50% of the total funding requirement will be channeled through operating lessors that already own and manage over 40% of the world fleet, valued at close to $300 billion.

For airlines, the selection of aircraft to operate their future networks is typically focused on performance capabilities and measured by payload, range, fuel burn, and other operating costs, as well as ownership cost. For operating lessors and other investors in aircraft, the analysis is quite different. Whilst the benefit accruing to the airline operators is a critical part of the analysis, the long-term value retention of these high-cost assets and their liquidity (how many airlines will continue to want to operate the aircraft and how many investors will continue to want to acquire them) are the most significant considerations and understanding these requires specialist skills and extensive industry experience gained over several industry cycles.

Sustainable success for an aircraft investor will be driven by two factors—securing the lowest possible acquisition prices for the assets and ensuring that sufficient liquidity is always available to finance those assets at the lowest possible blended cost of capital. Delivering these core elements and then selecting the right aircraft for long-term investment, knowing the "right" price to pay, protecting the asset's value through its economic life, and achieving the desired sale price on exit are not determined by luck.

This book provides a step-by-step guide through all of the key considerations and processes required to undertake a successful aircraft acquisition and financing assignment as well as negotiating the subsequent lease agreement and dealing with the ongoing risk and portfolio management and asset value considerations that will be needed in order to achieve the expected economic returns from the initial investment. The global nature of the industry is also reflected in the book's coverage of issues such as taxation, accounting treatment, and cross-border transactions, which will become ever more relevant as emerging leasing jurisdictions such as Hong Kong and Singapore extend their influence.

The authors combine real-world aircraft leasing, financing, and investment experience with the knowledge of what is needed to deliver relevant information and knowledge to students in an academic environment as well as to current practitioners who wish to expand their existing knowledge of the sector. As such, it fills an important gap in the market and will be an invaluable text and reference source for a wide audience, adding to the range of tools available to prime future generations of aviation industry professionals and investors.

Dick Forsberg
Head of Strategy, Avolon, Dublin, Ireland

CHAPTER

1

OVERVIEW OF THE AIRCRAFT-LEASING INDUSTRY AND MARKET ENVIRONMENT

CHAPTER OUTLINE

Aircraft Leasing and Financing. DOI: https://doi.org/10.1016/B978-0-12-815285-0.00001-8

STATE OF THE AIRLINE INDUSTRY

Out of all the alternatives to travel, air transportation is one of the fastest and one of the most expensive ones. What we call the airline industry today can be traced back to 1925 when the Air Mail Act in the United States facilitated the development of commercial air transportation by allowing the postmaster to contract private airlines to deliver mail. The Air Commerce Act in 1926 provided the Secretary of Commerce with the power to establish airways, license pilots, certify aircraft, and issue and enforce air traffic regulations. The Civil Aeronautics Act of 1938 created the Civil Aeronautics Board, the regulatory body that among other functions was charged with determining airline routes and regulating passenger airfares. However, the two most significant events that led to the airline industry as we know it today were the development of the Boeing 707, the first widely produced commercial aircraft powered by a jet engine, in 1957 and the Airline Deregulation Act of 1978. Jet-powered aircraft became the primary mode of long-distance travel in the world. The deregulation started the era of innovation and free-market competition in the airline industry and made airline travel affordable.

While air transportation used to be accessible only to wealthy individuals after deregulation, more airlines joined the competition putting downward pressure on airfares. The low-cost business model, pioneered by Southwest Airlines, made air travel even less expensive. Middle class became the driving force of the industry. Economic growth in developing nations in Asia, the Middle East, and South America resulted in the emergence of the middle class, which propelled the global air transportation industry even further. Also, the air service liberalization, such as "open-skies" agreements increased competition, improved incentives for airline efficiency, and provided substantial benefits to consumers.

With a growing world population and historically low oil prices in recent years, the demand for air travel is increasing exponentially. As presented in Fig. 1.1, the number of airline passengers

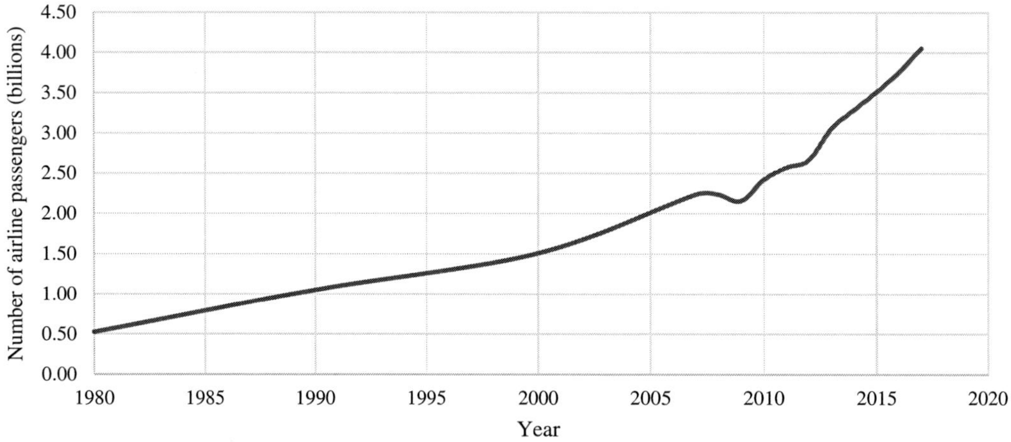

FIGURE 1.1

Total number of airline passengers.

Compiled by authors using ICAO Data+.

increased eightfold from 1980 to 2017 and almost doubled from 2007 to 2017 exceeding 4 billion passengers per year.

One common statistic that is used in the airline industry is revenue passenger miles (RPMs) (or kilometers). For airlines, it is important to know how many revenue passengers they carried for a mile or kilometer, because each of those passengers generates revenue. This measure combines the distance flown by aircraft, their capacity, and load factor. As presented in Fig. 1.2, measuring global airline industry performance using RPMs also demonstrates a tremendous growth in the last 10 years with RPMs in 2017 more than double their 2007 levels. Fig. 1.3 shows that this growth in RPMs was not only fueled by just increased capacity but also by higher utilization of airline fleets globally. From 1980 to 2017, the airline average annual load factor went from about 60% to more than 80%.

Today, after decades of low (or negative) profitability, the airline industry is performing well. Airlines have learned how to control costs and capacity, optimize their networks, minimize distribution costs, generate significant amounts of ancillary revenues, and efficiently finance their fleets. For example, in baggage fees alone, American Airlines collected almost $1.2 billion in 2017, which was the highest amount among the US airlines. Delta Air Lines and United Airlines were in the second the third place with $900 and $800 million, respectively. The International Air Transport Association estimates $38.4 billion of net profit for the global airline industry (IATA, 2017).

The growth and success of the airline industry has translated into robust demand for commercial aircraft. Fig. 1.4 presents the total dollar value of aircraft delivered by major commercial aircraft manufacturers from 1958 to 2017. The graph shows an exponential increase after 1980 with the dollar value of deliveries reaching $110 billion in 2015.

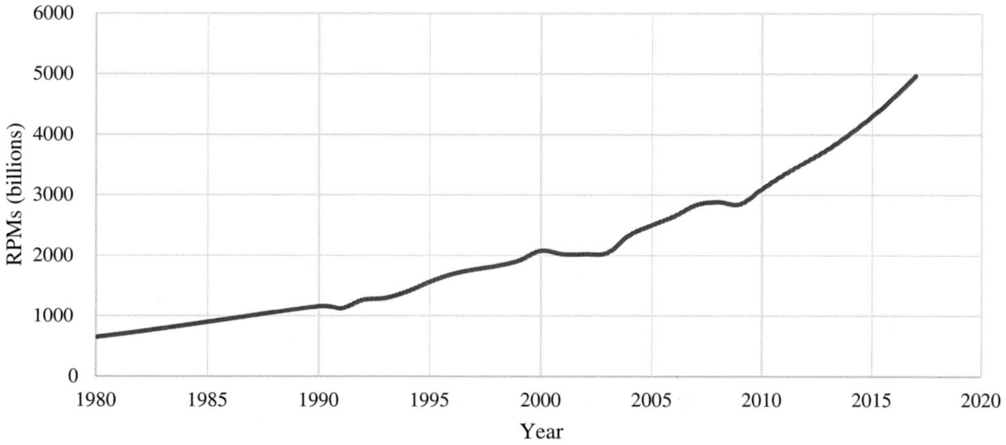

FIGURE 1.2

Global annual RPMs. *RPM*, Revenue passenger miles.

Compiled by authors using the Airline Monitor data.

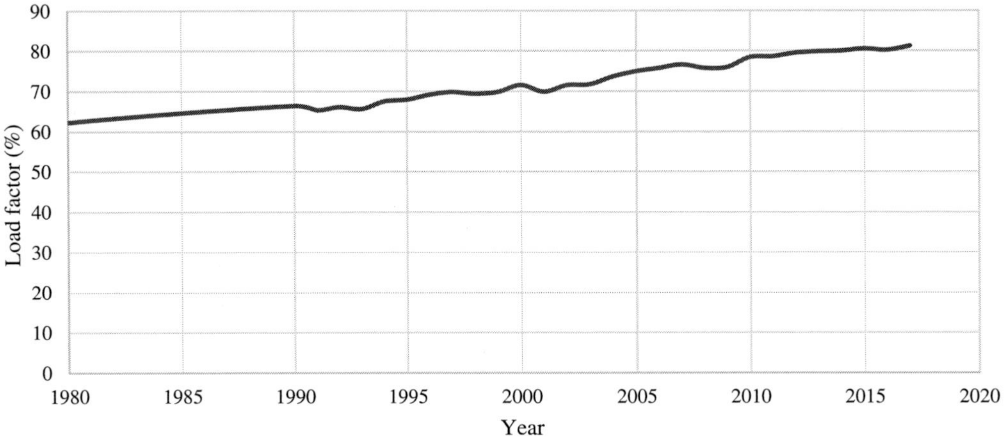

FIGURE 1.3

Global airlines load factor.

Compiled by authors using the Airline Monitor data.

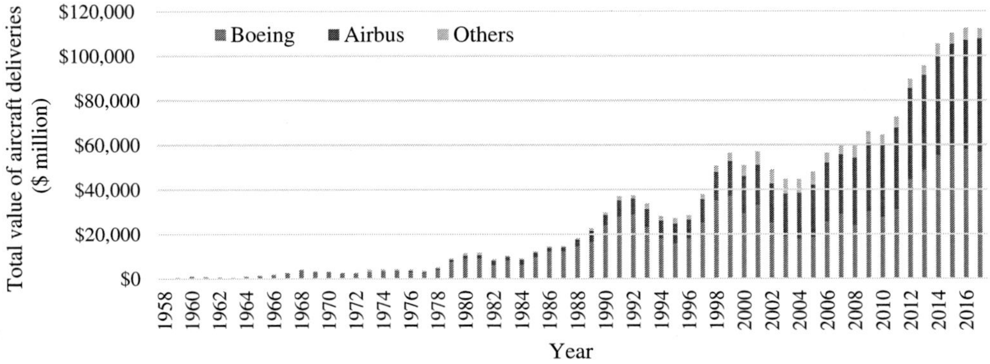

FIGURE 1.4

Annual value of aircraft delivered.

Compiled by authors using the Airline Monitor data.

THE MARKET FOR COMMERCIAL AIRCRAFT

According to the Airline Monitor, as of December 2017, there were more than 28,307 aircraft delivered globally (Fig. 1.5). Boeing still has the major share with almost 50% of the world fleet (including the remaining McDonnell Douglas aircraft). A relative newcomer, Airbus is not too far behind manufacturing 35% of the total number of aircraft in the world. Based on Airline Monitor data, between 2002 and 2011, Airbus delivered more aircraft than Boeing. However,

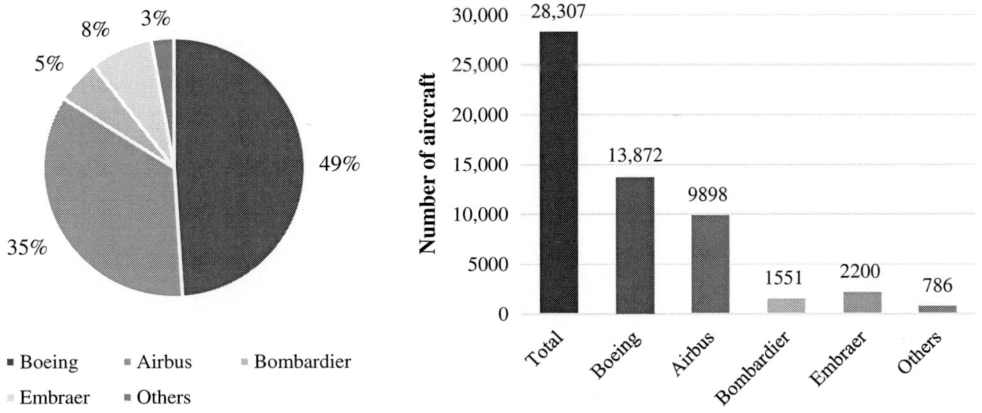

FIGURE 1.5

Commercial aircraft manufacturer market share as of December 31, 2017.

Compiled by authors using the Airline Monitor data.

in 2012, Boeing reclaimed the lead back. Thus, in 2017, Boeing delivered 763 aircraft versus 718 deliveries for Airbus. It is remarkable that both manufacturers have considerably ramped their production capacity, but both still have astonishing backlogs that keep increasing every year. As of December 2017, Boeing has a backlog of approximately 5900 aircraft, while Airbus's backlog is approaching 7300 aircraft. Even though Boeing has delivered more airplanes than Airbus in recent years, as reflected in the backlogs, Airbus is outperforming Boeing with new orders.

FORECAST

The major factors that influence demand for new aircraft are the need for more fuel efficient aircraft when fuel costs are high, the replacement cycle of the aircraft and global economic growth that creates a requirement for more capacity, especially in emerging markets. On average, commercial jets have a useful economic life of 25 years, with widebody aircraft typically being on the longer end of the range and narrowbody aircraft being on the shorter end. However, the optimal economic life depends on many internal and external factors: interest rates, fuel prices, availability of new technology, and others. When airlines operate aircraft, they balance capital and direct operating costs. Capital costs include depreciation and amortization that are large for new aircraft and then decrease with aircraft age. Aircraft acquisition and financing costs or lease payments (for leased aircraft) contribute to the capital costs and are highly dependent on the level of interest rates. In a low-interest rate environment, capital costs tend to be relatively lower leading to shorter economic lives of capital assets. Direct operating costs include fuel, maintenance, crew, and insurance costs. When aircraft age, maintenance costs drive the direct operating costs up. Also, fuel costs are higher for older aircraft compared to modern new technology aircraft. Therefore, higher fuel prices and low-interest rates accelerate the aircraft replacement

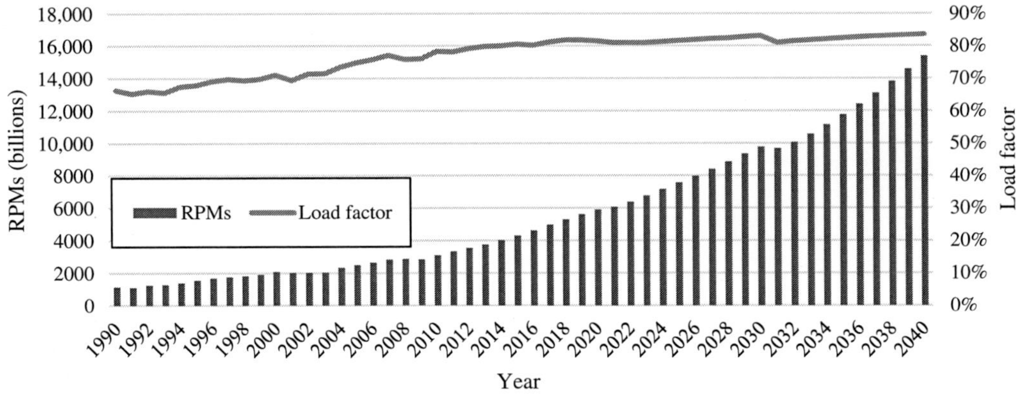

FIGURE 1.6

Historical data and forecast for RPMs and load factor. *RPMs*, Revenue passenger miles.

Compiled by authors using the Airline Monitor data.

cycle, while high interest rates and low fuel prices tend to extend economic lives of commercial aircraft.

All major forecasts indicate significant growth in air traffic for the next 20 years with a reasonably high and constant load factor. Fig. 1.6 presents a forecast by the Airline Monitor, but both Airbus and Boeing project similar growth. Airbus predicts an average air traffic growth of 4.4% per year with 35,000 new passenger and freighter aircraft delivered by 2036 with an estimated value of US$5.3 trillion (Airbus, 2017). Airbus anticipates 60% of new aircraft will be delivered to meet the growing demand and 40% to replace existing fleets. Boeing expects an annual air traffic growth of 4.7% with which approximately 41,000 new deliveries at an estimated market value of US$6.1 trillion by 2036 (Boeing, 2017). The forecasts by Airbus and Boeing included passenger aircraft with 100 or more seat capacity. The Airline Monitor's forecast presented in Figs. 1.7 and 1.8 considers all commercial passenger and cargo aircraft increasing the number of estimated aircraft deliveries to more than 56,000 units. Almost 90% of the in-service aircraft in 2040 would consist of aircraft delivered after 2017.

AIRCRAFT FINANCING

With such a large number of aircraft to be delivered after 2017, airlines and leasing companies will need to finance more than $5 trillion worth of aircraft. Since we will discuss the sources of aircraft financing in details in Chapter 6, we only briefly mention them here. Three decades ago, cash and equity financing were the primary sources of aircraft funding. Now, the aircraft financing landscape is quite complex and includes bank and capital market debt, manufacturer and export credit agency financing, insurance, revolving credit, warehouse facility, and other sources of funding. Probably, the most significant development, however, is an increased share of leased aircraft in the airline fleets that currently is more than 40% of the global fleet and more than 50% of the new deliveries.

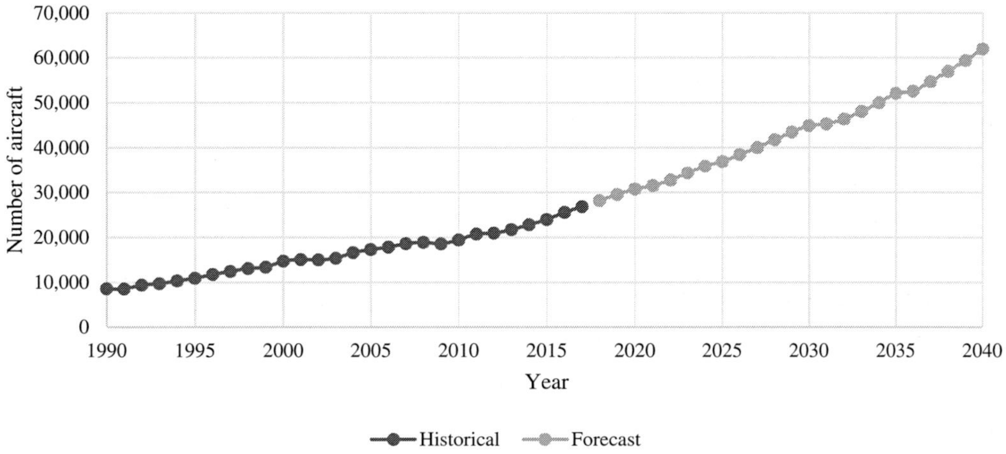

FIGURE 1.7

Historical data and forecast of aircraft deliveries.

Compiled by authors using the Airline Monitor data.

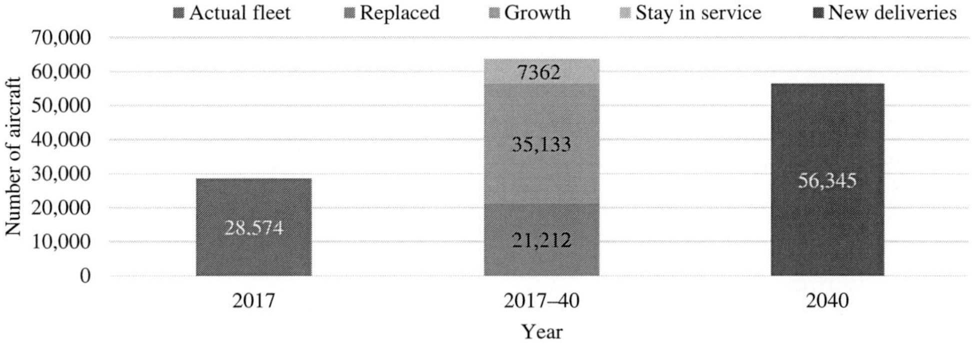

FIGURE 1.8

Current and forecasted in-service aircraft and deliveries.

Compiled by authors using the Airline Monitor data.

Fig. 1.9 presents the sources of funds for global aircraft and Boeing deliveries in 2017. Lessors accounted for approximately 51% of aircraft deliveries in 2017 with the majority of funding coming from bank debt and capital markets. Airlines used more bank debt than capital markets in 2017 because banks were offering very attractive financing deals to the airlines. However, for aircraft lessors, the capital markets were the primary source of financing with 65% of aircraft deliveries financed using secured or unsecured capital market debt. Between 2016 and 2017, the capital market financing increased from $63.2 to $65.4 billion with aircraft lessors accounting for 36.7% and 65% of this number, respectively (Boeing, 2018).

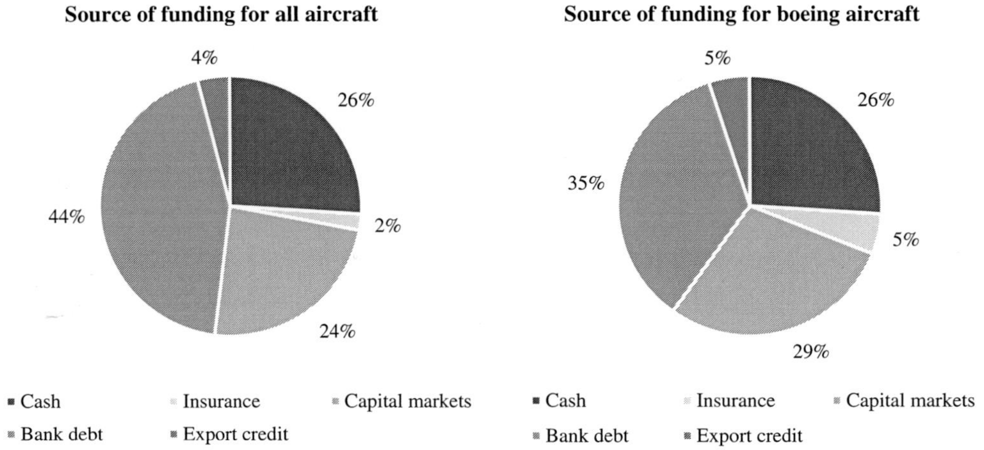

FIGURE 1.9

Source of funding for aircraft deliveries in 2017.

2018 Boeing Finance Market Outlook.

AIRCRAFT-LEASING INDUSTRY

Forty years ago, the aircraft-leasing industry was virtually nonexistent and accounted for less than 2% of the global aircraft fleets. This percentage remained small until the early 1990s, which was around 15%, then it jumped to 25% in 2000, and finally over 40% in 2017 (Kaplan, 2017).

Fig. 1.10 depicts the progression in the number of aircraft leased in 10-year increments. There were only 17 aircraft leased in 1970 and 100 in 1980.

As of December 2017, there were more than 50 lessors with aircraft portfolio values $1 billion or more. Table 1.1 presents the top 20 lessors based on portfolio values. These 20 lessors have combined portfolio values of more than $220 billion and 7208 aircraft. Even more impressive, the top three lessors manage almost 3000 aircraft with a combined fleet value of $76.7 billion! The aircraft-leasing industry has been going through consolidation with mergers and acquisitions. Thus, AerCap acquired International Lease Finance Corporation in December 2013. Avolon had a strong organic growth from 2010 to 2016, and then it merged with Hong Kong Aviation Capital in 2016 and acquired CIT Aerospace in 2017. AWAS sold 40 aircraft to Macquarie in 2015 ahead of its acquisition by DAE Capital in 2017. The industry consolidation will likely continue as larger lessors are better positioned to take advantage of their low cost of capital and the attractive deals available in the strong market (Wood, 2018).

Fig. 1.11 presents lessors' fleets by operating regions as of June 2018. Asia and the Southwest Pacific region are ahead of the rest of the world regarding the number of leased aircraft and their value, followed by Europe and North America. A higher value of leased aircraft operating in Asia and the Southwest Pacific implies that lessors deploy more new and more expensive, such as wide-body, aircraft in this region compared to Europe and North America.

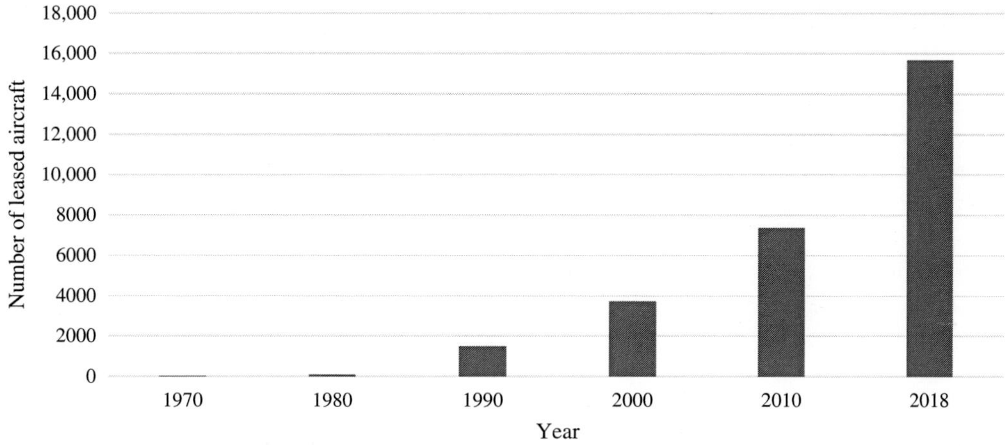

FIGURE 1.10

Number of leased aircraft.

Compiled by authors using CAPA and Ascend data.

Table 1.1 Top 20 Lessors Based on Fleet Value

2017 Rank	Lessor	Total Fleet Value ($ million)	Total Number of Aircraft
1	AerCap	31,944	1076
2	GECAS	25,760	1324
3	Avolon	19,038	585
4	SMBC Aviation Capital	15,808	450
5	BBAM LLC	15,523	324
6	ICBC Leasing	13,931	323
7	BOC Aviation	13,890	326
8	Air Lease Corporation	12,896	293
9	DAE Capital	10,536	349
10	Aviation Capital Group	7340	273
11	CDB Aviation Lease Finance	6915	198
12	BoCom Leasing	6671	165
13	Jackson Square Aviation	6305	152
14	ORIX Aviation	6219	227
15	Nordic Aviation Capital	5865	416
16	Macquarie AirFinance	4955	204
17	Standard Chartered Aviation Finance	4913	136
18	Aircastle Limited	4659	191
19	Goshawk	3668	93
20	China Aircraft-Leasing Limited	3593	103

From Flight Global.

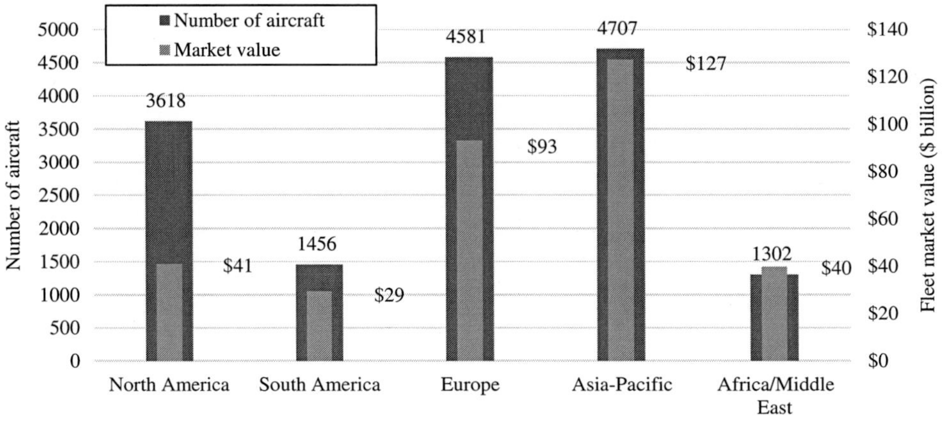

FIGURE 1.11

Lessor fleets by operating regions as of June 2018.

Compiled by authors using CAPA data.

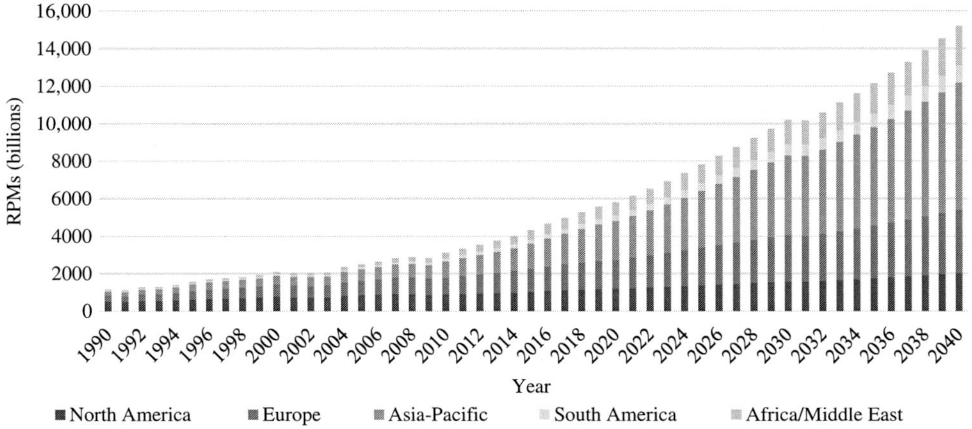

FIGURE 1.12

Historical data and forecast of RPMs by region. *RPMs*, Revenue passenger miles.

Compiled by authors using the Airline Monitor and ICAO data.

REGIONAL MARKETS

While world air traffic has been growing and forecasted to continue its growth at about 4.5% in the future, the regional growth is disparate. Fueled by an emerging middle class, traffic growth in the Asia/Pacific region is outperforming developed markets of North America and Europe. As presented

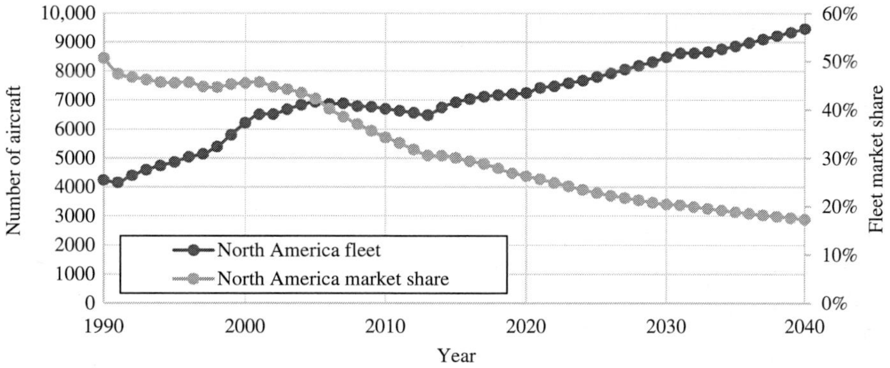

FIGURE 1.13

North American fleet and market share.

Compiled by authors using the Airline Monitor and ICAO data.

in Fig. 1.12, the Asia/Pacific region will represent about 50% of world traffic by 2040. Also, in the same year of 2040, Africa and the Middle East will reach the traffic level of North America.

NORTH AMERICA

Based on the International Monetary Fund 2017 data, North America included three countries that ranked the 1st, 10th, and 15th based on their GDPs: United States, Canada, and Mexico. The North American air transportation industry went through consolidation and is very mature. North America accounts for about 30% of the world commercial fleet and will require a large number of replacements over the next 20 years. Boeing expects an annual air traffic growth of 3%, with the fleet growth of 1.8%, including 8640 aircraft deliveries with a market value of US$1.04 trillion (Boeing, 2017). Airbus forecasts a bit slower annual air traffic growth or 2% for 2018–36 (Airbus, 2017). Fig. 1.13 presents historical data and forecast for North American fleets and market share. While the number of aircraft in North America will steadily increase, higher growth in Asia/Pacific and Africa/Middle East regions will reduce North American fleet market share to under 20% by 2040.

SOUTH AMERICA

South American countries have faced economic difficulties, but the economic reforms in the region are expected to stimulate the markets, especially in Brazil and Argentina that are the two largest countries in South America. In its market outlook, Boeing expects an annual air traffic growth of 6.1% in Latin America that includes Central and South American region. This growth will result in a 4.4% annual increase in the number of aircraft in the region, with more than 3000 deliveries valued at $350 billion (Boeing, 2017). Similarly, Airbus projects 2720 new aircraft deliveries in Latin America in the next 20 years (Airbus, 2017) (Fig. 1.14).

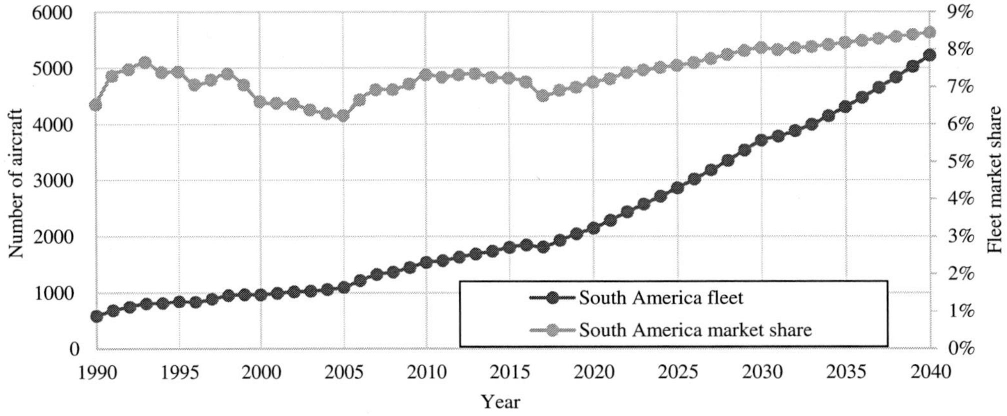

FIGURE 1.14

South American fleet and market share.

Compiled by authors using the Airline Monitor and ICAO data.

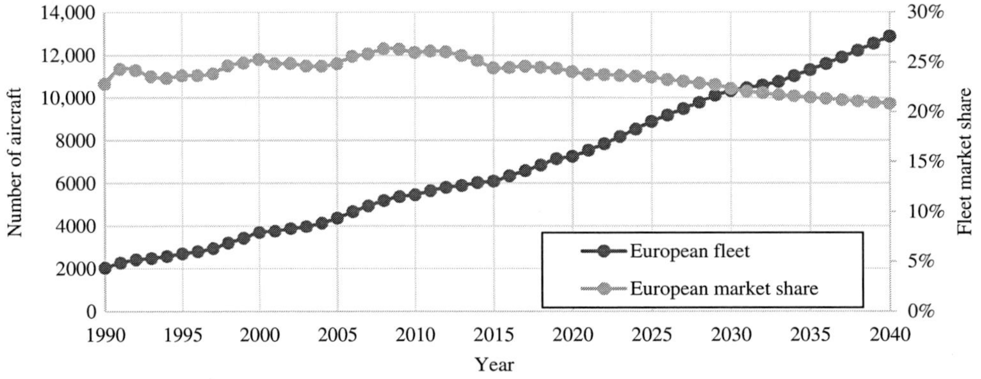

FIGURE 1.15

European fleet and market share.

Compiled by authors using the Airline Monitor and ICAO data.

EUROPE

With more than 50 countries and over 200 different languages, Europe is very diverse in terms of the strength of local economies, cultures, and transportation preferences. Despite being a mature industry and the presence of competition from the well-developed railway system, European air transport industry continues to grow. Over the next 20 years, Boeing projects 3.7% annual growth in traffic and 2.7% in fleets with 7530 aircraft deliveries valued at more than $1.1 trillion

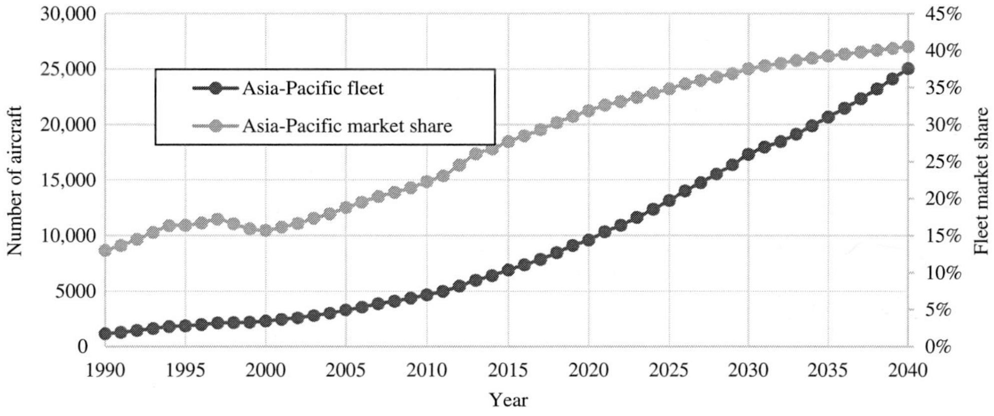

FIGURE 1.16

Asia and Pacific fleet and market share.

Compiled by authors using the Airline Monitor and ICAO data.

(Boeing, 2017). Airbus also expects 7175 commercial aircraft deliveries to European airlines by 2037 (Airbus, 2017) (Fig. 1.15).

ASIA AND SOUTHWEST PACIFIC

The Asia-Pacific region has been and will continue to be the most dynamic region in the world. The economic expansion in India and China leads to the rapid development of a middle class that is the primary driver of air traffic growth. Through 2036, Boeing expects an annual air traffic growth of 5.7% in the region, with 4.8% annual growth in fleets and 16,050 deliveries of new commercial aircraft valued at $2.5 trillion (Boeing, 2017). Airbus has a similar forecast of 15,895 deliveries in the Asia-Pacific region by 2037 (Airbus, 2017) (Fig. 1.16).

AFRICA AND THE MIDDLE EAST

Africa is a large and diverse continent with an abundance of natural resources such as metals, oil, and minerals. While the continent has many tourist and business destinations, the air transport industry still has room to grow before it reaches maturity similar to North America or Europe. For Africa, Boeing expects an annual air traffic growth of 5.9% and fleet growth of 4.1% with 1220 aircraft deliveries valued at $180 billion over the next 20 years (Boeing, 2017). Airbus forecasts 1154 deliveries over the same period (Airbus, 2017).

The Middle East is known for its petroleum resources and its location between Asia, Africa, and Europe that offers convenient connections among these regions. For this region, Boeing projects an annual air traffic growth of 5.6% and fleet growth of 5.1% with 3350 aircraft deliveries valued at $730 billion over the next 20 years (Boeing, 2017). Similarly, Airbus forecasts 2879 deliveries in the region for the same period (Airbus, 2017) (Fig. 1.17).

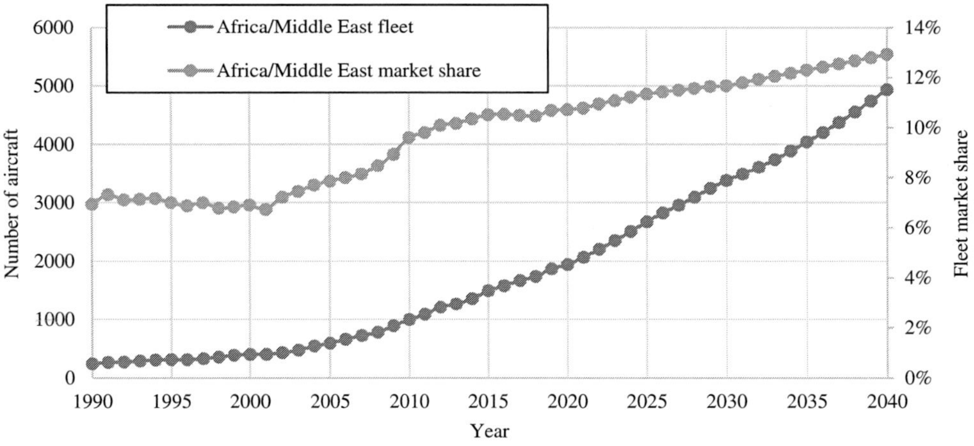

FIGURE 1.17

Africa and Middle East fleet and market share.

Compiled by authors using the Airline Monitor and ICAO data.

CURRENT STATE OF AIRCRAFT FINANCING AND LEASING INDUSTRY

Even though world GDP has been growing at a suboptimal rate, airline traffic, measured by RPMs, continues to grow at almost 8% annually indicating the robustness of the industry (Wood, 2018). Robust growth of RPMs supports adding capacity through new aircraft deliveries to airlines and lessors. Improved airline profits, availability of liquidity in global financial markets, and historically low oil prices help to create a favorable environment for the aircraft-leasing industry. The fact that the recent airline bankruptcies in Europe (Alitalia, Airberlin, and Monarch) did not have a severe adverse effect on the industry also demonstrates the resilience. Most of the affected aircraft were quickly remarketed and released to other airlines. While air transportation is a cyclical industry, the current growth phase of the cycle seems more prolonged than in the past and does not show signs of slowing down, and the industry remains attractive for investors. New capital has flooded the industry in recent years, which compressed the lease rates and resulting margins. Compressed margins may serve as a leading indicator of the approaching end of the expansion phase, but the majority of industry players expect the expansion to continue through 2018 and 2019 (Wood, 2018).

Several areas of concern are increasing fuel prices and interest rates, intense competition among airlines, and the relative strength of the US dollar (for those airlines that have large portions of revenues denominated in foreign currencies). Also, geopolitical developments, such as the departure of the United Kingdom from the European Union, and economic sanctions of Russia, Iran, and North Korea may also impact the future of the industry.

Attracted by potential returns, new investors, such as banks, private equity firms, and hedge funds, are still entering the industry through mergers and acquisitions, which is the fastest way to obtain technical and marketing expertise in the aircraft-leasing industry. There are no signs that the industry consolidation will stop any time soon, as the low cost of capital (that is correlated with the credit rating of the lessors) is a prerequisite for acceptable returns in the low margin environment. Industry insiders blame the new entrants and enhanced competition for compressed lease rate factors, especially in the sale-leaseback market for new aircraft. In some instances, the lease rate factor in the sale-leaseback market for new narrowbody aircraft have reached the low .50 seconds, which are not sustainable for lessors in the longer term.

Capital markets currently dominate aircraft lessor financing with both unsecured issues and aircraft asset-based securities (ABS). While bank financing is also available, Basel III and upcoming Basel IV are limiting traditional balance sheet financing, and most of the bank deals are in the structured finance space. The demand for funding has led to the emergence of new capital sources, such as Aircraft Finance Insurance Consortium (that will be further discussed in Chapter 6), crowdfunding as a source of equity, and others. More new sources of capital will definitely appear in the near future to finance large fleets projected to be produced by aircraft manufacturers.

TOPICS DISCUSSED IN THE BOOK

This book presents a collection of topics and insights that are essential for professionals working in the aircraft-leasing and financing industry as it has grown into one of the most distinctive and important industries in the world. While facts and discussions included in the book are known to seasoned aircraft financing specialists, young professionals entering the industry or professionals moving into the aircraft financing and leasing field from different industries will find that the book will accelerate their learning and help in understanding a wide variety of topics that make this industry unique.

FLEET PLANNING

We start with aircraft selection strategy basics in Chapter 2 which discusses how airlines and aircraft-leasing companies select aircraft to include in their fleets and how aircraft manufacturers decide which aircraft to manufacture. The aircraft selection decisions are crucial for these companies as they involve hugely capital intensive assets that are at the core of their businesses. Also, the aircraft selection decisions are complex and influenced by multiple variables, including global economic conditions, company strategies, technological innovations, air transport market developments, decision-maker influence, and others. Fleet planning involves multiple functions of an airline or lessor: *financial*—acquisition, ownership, and financing costs; *operational*—flight and cabin crew training, passenger experience, etc.; *engineering*—technical crew training, maintenance intervals, engine commonality, investment in tooling, projected dispatch reliability, etc.; *strategic planning*—how the aircraft fits in an airline network or lessor portfolio; and *strategic vision*—how the potential market, technological, and macroeconomic developments change the outlook for this aircraft.

Chapter 2 provides fleet-planning perspectives from an airline, lessor, and manufacturer point of view that are related but may have different goals and measures of success. Understanding the wants and needs of all industry players will lead to a greater understanding of effective aircraft selection decision-making.

PRINCIPLES OF AIRCRAFT LEASING VERSUS OWNERSHIP

Chapter 3 discusses lessees' and lessors' decision-making process. Specifically, we focus on leasing or purchasing aircraft as a lessee's financing decision that involves a selection of the lowest cost alternative to use the aircraft. However, leasing also provides flexibility for an airline in its fleet decisions, access to current aircraft technology, and helps transferring aircraft residual value risk to the lessor. From a lessor's perspective, leasing an aircraft is a capital budgeting or investment decision when the lessor is assessing whether the income stream from the lease would generate an adequate return on their investment. Chapter 3 numerically demonstrates how to calculate a Net Advantage to Leasing and a range of lease payments that would satisfy both the lessee and the lessor, as well as the process associated with evaluating the criteria involved in the lease versus buy decisions.

AVIATION LEGAL AND REGULATORY FRAMEWORK

Aircraft financing and leasing is an industry governed by unique rules and regulations. The mobile nature of aircraft assets creates complicated multijurisdictional issues. Moreover, high equipment value and interchangeable components lead to increased legal, political, and collateral risk. Chapter 4 addresses legal and regulatory matters specific to aircraft financing. Particular topics include applicable governing law, conventions and treaties (Chicago, Warsaw, Montreal, Geneva, Cape Town), aircraft registration and ownership, recordation of interest in aircraft, Section 1110 of the US Bankruptcy code, liens, regulatory considerations, jurisdictional review, lessor and operator liability, and multilateral agreements.

AVIATION INSURANCE

Insurance is a risk-management technique that reflects the need to protect property interests in the event of property damage. It involves a contractual agreement between an individual or entity seeking protection and an insurance company that is providing protection. As part of this agreement, the insurer charges the premium in exchange for the promise to cover losses that may result from an accident. Airlines, leasing companies, and other aircraft owners (e.g., aircraft investors) all seek protection against the risks associated with operating aircraft. Insurance is a critical sector of the aviation industry. Before writing an insurance policy, the underwriter carefully evaluates each risk, and it is this process that determines the premium. Chapter 5 will help with understanding the types of coverage, factors that affect the premium, and the legal regulations of the airline business and the overall process of drafting an effective insurance policy.

AIRCRAFT FUNDING—DEBT, EQUITY, AND THE CAPITAL MARKETS

In Chapter 6, we discuss how airlines and leasing companies raise funds to finance their fleets. Chapter 6 focuses on various aspects of equity and debt financing, as well as on national and international organizations that facilitate aircraft financing for airlines and leasing companies. It also provides a brief overview of the pecking-order theory of capital structure, describes major debt instruments used in fleet financing by airlines and leasing companies, reviews the role of rating and export credit agencies, and discusses significant innovations in aircraft financing. Special considerations are given to enhanced equipment trust certificates, ABS, and predelivery payments financing.

AIRLINE CREDIT ANALYSIS

In leasing, risk underwriting is the process of assessing risks faced by a lessor in order to decide whether or not to originate a lease. The risks are not limited to creditworthiness. The process also involves a thorough analysis of the lessee's ability and willingness to meet the lease requirements. In Chapter 7, we discuss how lessors conduct airline credit analysis. Specific topics include assessing airline business models, strategy, and ownership structures; airline ability to generate revenues and its sources (business travel mix, cargo, etc.); airline yield and load factor; airline cost structure; key industry-specific credit/leverage metrics and coverage ratios; cash balance and sources of potential liquidity; debt and lease maturity profiles; availability of funding for aircraft; balance sheet strength; and airline risk-management practices.

LEASING PORTFOLIO MANAGEMENT AND RISK MANAGEMENT

Purchasing the right aircraft at the right price, managing them well, and selling (or disposing) them at the right price are essential for a leasing company's success. A small mistake at any stage (purchasing, managing, or disposing of aircraft) may reduce a leasing transaction return to an unsustainable level. Risk management and portfolio management discussed in Chapter 8 are critical for a leasing company's survival. We start with a brief overview of aircraft acquisition channels and risks inherent with the business of leasing aircraft. While risk and portfolio management are overlapping concepts, we present them in two different subsections: understanding and mitigating risks on asset and liability sides and then managing lessors' portfolios by diversifying their exposure to substantial individual risks. We describe major risks faced by aircraft-leasing companies and the techniques used to mitigate them. Interest rate risk management is discussed at length as it is critical for lessors that manage the spreads between the cost of funds and return on assets.

PRINCIPLES OF MAINTENANCE RESERVE DEVELOPMENT AND MANAGEMENT

Chapter 9 provides an overview of aircraft technical conditions and maintenance reserves and their application in the world of aircraft leasing. Since regular and proper maintenance is crucial for safe aircraft operation and maximum value preservation, leasing companies expect the airlines to maintain assets according to manufacturer's recommendations and regulatory requirements. Charging airlines a maintenance reserve is one way to ensure that maintenance costs are accounted for even if an airline defaults on its lease. The chapter describes major maintenance events, determining proper maintenance reserve rates, reserve rate escalation, and other related topics. The chapter contains examples of relevant documents as well as a mini case to practice maintenance reserve rate calculations and maintenance reserve cash flow forecasting.

TRANSACTION COST MODELING

In Chapter 10, we discuss the critical variables in an aircraft lease transaction and how to model the lease cash flows. Some of the key factors that affect a lease transaction include the purchase price, rent (lease rates), maintenance reserves, residual values, and transaction costs. All of these factors will impact the lessor's return calculations. Modeling a lease transaction, therefore, involves taking into account the above cash flows to determine the purchase price that the lessor should pay in order to get a fair and adequate return on their investment using capital budgeting tools such as net present value and internal rate of return. Case studies and examples are used to show how to model the different factors and stress test the model and identify the key drivers that drive the returns for a lessor.

LEASE AGREEMENT AND NEGOTIATION

Chapter 11 focuses on the lease negotiation and the key elements of a lease contract. From a lessor's perspective, a lease serves two primary purposes: First, to structure an economic return and second, to manage asset and credit risk. The key elements contained in a lease include the acquisition price in the case of a sale and leaseback, lease term, lease rental, technical specification of the aircraft being delivered, technical return conditions and details on how deviations from these conditions will be compensated, security deposits, maintenance reserves, other risk mitigants and covenants, restrictions on quiet enjoyment, which may include limitations on subleasing or operation in restricted jurisdictions, provisions for maintaining airworthiness and cost sharing, both during and after the end of the lease and restrictions on changes to aircraft specification, and the use of parts manufacturer approval parts. Lease negotiations are both an art and a science. For a lessor, the aircraft acquisition price and the lease rate are the elements of science, as both these factors are linked to financing costs and the return requirements for the business. While the art aspects of a lease negotiation depend on the individual lessor, lessee, and particular transaction, generally, the negotiations are structured around the risk mitigants (maintenance reserves, security deposits, and return conditions) as areas that may require compromise. The extent of the compromise from a lessor's perspective typically depends on factors such as lessee's track record of performance under previous leases, additional protection that the lessee can provide, or if the lessee is located in a country which is a signatory to the Cape Town Convention.

AIRCRAFT VALUATION AND APPRAISALS

An appraisal, in essence, is an opinion of value derived based on a systematic process. Determining the value of an aircraft is important for different stakeholders such as leasing companies, financial institutions, aircraft brokers, airlines/operators, insurers and manufacturers. The valuation process is a systematic procedure used by appraisers to provide answers to a client's question about value and value-related issues. In this process, it is essential to identify the client and other intended users, the use of the appraisal opinion and conclusion, and the type and definition of value required as of a particular date. Two major organizations provide guidelines to appraise aircraft. These are the International Society of Transport Aircraft Trading (ISTAT) and the American Society of Appraisers (ASA). While ISTAT has focused on commercial aircraft appraisals, ASA has focused mainly on business and general aviation appraisals. In Chapter 12, we address the main elements of the appraisal process and discuss the different approaches to value and various publications and sources providing aircraft values. We also include two case studies to outline the process of appraising a business and a commercial aircraft.

TAXATION AND CONSIDERATIONS FOR CROSS-BORDER TRANSACTIONS

Leasing transactions typically have multiple tax implications for both lessors and lessees. Since the transaction's economics to a considerable degree are based on tax benefits, tax considerations are critical for lease structures, particularly for cross-border transactions. Chapter 13 provides an overview of different taxes applicable to lease transactions for both domestic and cross-border leases. We start with general concepts of aircraft lease-related taxes and then look at the country and regional markets and associated considerations for cross-border transactions in those markets. Over the past few decades, the popularity of leasing transactions has been growing steadily partially due to the tax advantages that come with leasing, especially for operating leases, as opposed to conventional financing for asset acquisition. Recent changes in the accounting treatment that require firms to show operating leases on their balance sheet may lead to a reexamination of the continued benefits of operating leases compared to other sources of financing. Further, diversity among countries' tax laws may amplify these tax advantages, creating opportunities for new leasing structures to maximize the allocation of the available tax allowances.

ENGINE LEASING

Chapter 14 provides an overview of the leading engine OEMs and their products in the narrowbody and widebody aircraft market. Topics include engine maintenance, engine leasing, and aftermarket service programs. Initially, an engine might be worth 30% of the total aircraft value. However, with the correct maintenance, the same engine could retain 70% of its value, whereas the airframe is likely to depreciate by 80%–90% over a 20-year utilization. This is why airlines and lessors are so focused on engine maintenance. Since the aircraft is the critical tool which airlines use to generate profit, they must have access to spare engines either by purchasing the spare engine from an OEM or by leasing from an engine lessor or through hourly agreements that provide access to a spare engine pool to cover the engine shop visit period. There are also aftermarket service programs available from the OEMs to help airlines maximize engine value and maintain a more accurate forecast of future-maintenance events and expenses.

REFERENCES

Airbus. (2017). *Global market forecast 2017–2036*. Retrieved from Aircraft Market: <http://www.airbus.com/aircraft/market/global-market-forecast.html>.

Boeing. (2017). *Current market outlook*. Retrieved from Commercial Market: <https://www.boeing.com/commercial/market/current-market-outlook-2017/>.

Boeing. (2018). *Current aircraft finance market outlook 2018*. Retrieved from Boeing Capital Corporation: <https://www.boeing.com/resources/boeingdotcom/company/capital/pdf/2018_cafmo.pdf>.

IATA. (2017, December). *Strong airline profitability continues in 2018*. Retrieved from IATA pressroom: <http://www.iata.org/pressroom/pr/Pages/2017-12-05-01.aspx>.

Kaplan, T. (2017, March). *Mid-life aircraft trading patterns and the impact of lessors*. (Flight Global) Retrieved from FlightAscend Consultancy: <https://www.flightglobal.com/asset/16191>.

Wood, T. (2018, January). *Lessors*. Retrieved from KPMG in Ireland: <https://home.kpmg.com/ie/en/home/insights/2018/01/lessors.html>.

CHAPTER

PRINCIPLES OF AIRCRAFT SELECTION

2

CHAPTER OUTLINE

Aircraft Leasing and Financing. DOI: https://doi.org/10.1016/B978-0-12-815285-0.00002-X

FLEET PLANNING

When considering the selection of an aircraft, whether it be by a lessee or a lessor, there are many factors that go into the choice of the proper aircraft. These factors may include global economic forces, company strategy, and decision-maker influence. It is essential that all of these elements flow together in order to maintain a successful business moving forward. Fleet planning is a continuous exercise that normally looks at least 15 years into the future (Clark, 2007). Because the future can be very uncertain, in particular with respect to commercial aviation, it is very important to choose the right aircraft at the right time.

Aircraft selection is incredibly risky because the wrong decisions can mean the downfall of a firm. The wrong fleet, in the best case, can greatly impede the profitability of an airline or lessor, and in the worst case, it can lead to bankruptcy. Aircraft are high-cost assets and airlines, and lessors around the world collectively hold billions of dollars' worth of aircraft on their balance sheets. As aircraft usually comprise the largest part of a firm's balance sheet, the strategy behind what type of aircraft to buy or lease, the number of units, and the negotiated price per unit can be a politicized event. It is important to note, however, that due to the politically sensitive nature and size of an aircraft order, sometimes the best decision for fleet strategy is not taken because of economic or other factors. For instance, due to political reasons a state-owned airline may be pressured by its government to purchase a Boeing aircraft versus a Airbus aircraft despite Airbus aircraft being the better solution to its fleet needs. In this chapter, our focus is on other factors that are important in the aircraft-selection process, but political pressure should be recognized as a wildcard influence in the fleet decision-making process.

ORGANIZATION STRUCTURE

Where should fleet planning fit in a corporate environment?

Fleet planning brings together multiple functions of an airline or lessor to decide on the best aircraft and quantities to acquire. Each function must work together in order to find the most appropriate option (Clark, 2007). The key functions are listed in the following sections.

Financial

How much does the aircraft cost? What is the total cost of ownership? Just like any major asset purchase, the purchase price can heavily influence the decision to acquire an aircraft. Boeing and Airbus list prices for new aircraft coming off the production line are shown in Tables 2.1 and 2.2. List prices, however, are often not the final prices paid by either an airline or a lessor. Depending on bulk order sizes, strategic importance to the manufacturer, and customer relationships, operators and financiers can receive discounts of over 50%.

In addition to price, the cost of ownership influences the decision to purchase an aircraft greatly. Aspects such as maintenance, financing, insurance, crew costs, fuel burn, and many other costs and expenses will be discussed in the following chapter outlining an aircraft's overall cost of ownership.

Table 2.1 Boeing and Airbus List Prices (2018)

Boeing	List Price (USD Millions)	Airbus	List Price (USD Millions)
737-700	85.8	A318	75.9
737-800	102.2	A319	90.5
737-900ER	108.4	A320	99.0
737 MAX 7	96.0	A321	116.0
737 MAX 8	117.1	A319neo	99.5
737 MAX 200	120.2	A320neo	108.4
737 MAX 9	124.1	A321neo	127.0
737 MAX 10	129.9	A330-200	233.8
747-8	402.9		
747-8 Freighter	403.6	A330-200 Freighter	237.0
767-300ER	209.8	A330-300	259.0
		A330-800(neo)	254.8
767-300 Freighter	212.2	A330-900(neo)	290.6
777-200ER	295.2	A350-800	275.1
777-200LR	334.0	A350-900	311.2
777-300ER	361.5	A350-1000	359.3
777 Freighter	339.2	A380	436.9
777-8	394.9		
777-9	425.8		
787-8	239.0		
787-9	281.6		
787-10	325.8		

Data from *Boeing and Airbus website.*

Table 2.2 Boeing Forecasted Global Aircraft Deliveries by Category (2017–36)

Category	New Airplanes	Value (USD Billions)
Regional jet	2370	$110
Single aisle	29,530	$3180
Small widebody	5050	$1340
Medium/Large widebody	3160	$1160
Freighters	920	$260

Boeing (2017).

Operational

How will the pilots and flight attendants be able to operate this new aircraft? Will they need additional training and/or be able to fly other aircraft or just this type exclusively (Clark, 2007)? A common rating allows an airline to utilize fewer pilots and thus save money on training and labor cost. How will the passenger's experience relate in the aircraft under evaluation versus aircraft in the airline's or competitor's fleet? It may not be evident to all passengers which type and variant of aircraft they may be flying on, and not every aircraft provides the same passenger experience in terms of comfort, but what is common amongst passengers is the desire for a smooth and comfortable experience to entice them to return. Some aircraft have a smoother flight than others, some are quieter than others, and some newer technology aircraft have the ability to reduce the effects of jetlag. For example, the Airbus 350 and Boeing 787 have been designed to pump small amounts of water vapor throughout the cabin during flight, have in-cabin altitudes of 6000 ft, and feature light-emitting diode (LED) mood lighting to match the time of day throughout the different phases of the flight so that the passenger feels refreshed after a long flight. Boeing and Airbus also have different flight controls and cockpit layouts, and the two manufacturers have different ideas for cabin layouts, which will have an effect on the passenger experience. Since the majority of above the wing labor is unionized, their input is sought and in some cases required as part of the selection process. Physical characteristics of commercial aircraft will be further outlined in the following pages.

Engineering

What do the maintenance intervals look like for an aircraft? Does the airline have the proper equipment (tooling) and training to perform maintenance on the aircraft? How does the maintenance cost compare with competing aircraft when new but also as it ages? These questions are essential for carriers to answer before making a decision on an aircraft type (Clark, 2007). Whether the airline provides their own maintenance in-house or outsources it to third-party providers, these topics could have significant cost or operational impact, which need to be factored into the selection process. Lessors and smaller carriers who outsource maintenance may not be as concerned with the tooling and training because they will seek maintenance providers with the necessary capability, but the other factors are just as relevant regardless as to the source of the maintenance provider. The fleet-planning department must work closely with the maintenance and engineering departments to confirm that they have the capabilities to service a particular aircraft. For example, if an airline only operates CFM (manufactured by CFM International, the designation of which is derived from the two parent companies' commercial engine designations: GE's, "CF" and Snecma's, "M") engines, it will likely increase costs to add an aircraft with Pratt and Whitney engines or vice versa. Tooling, training, updated manuals and software would be needed to make that transition. Maintenance costs will be further analyzed in Chapter 9.

Strategic planning

How does this aircraft fit in an airline's network both presently and within a forecasted operational timeframe? Will the aircraft support the routes that the airline intends to fly in terms of capability and profitability? Is the market over or undersaturated with this aircraft? These questions will narrow down the list of potential aircraft to purchase very quickly. Smaller airlines will typically not operate large widebodies, while low-cost carriers (LCCs) usually operate either Airbus or Boeing aircraft exclusively which provide appropriate returns and fleet standardization, both of which are key for an LCC's success. Aspects such as range and payload capabilities and network analysis will be discussed in the following pages.

Strategic vision

Is the airline upgauging? Is the airline in a growth phase and considering new routes? What is the macroeconomic outlook for demand of each aircraft type? Aircraft are purchased or committed to be leased at a minimum of months and more commonly years in advance. A fleet type decision may span a decade or more and often take place when the aircraft technology is still on the drawing board as little more than a sales pitch and a promise from the aircraft manufacturer. The person or team responsible for the fleet type selection must have the foresight to know where the aircraft selected will fit in the strategic vision over that horizon. As if that is not enough of a burden, they also have to have the fortitude to trust their assumptions on the global market in terms of both aircraft values and expected passenger demand (Clark, 2007). Aircraft orders are frequently measured in billions of dollars, so it is imperative that the correct decision is made. Simply put, there is no room for error. The right or wrong fleet for an airline or lessor can sink or propel them relative to their competitors.

AIRCRAFT CATEGORIES

Aircraft come in many shapes, sizes, and prices. Flag carriers, LCCs, and network carriers usually operate a mix of aircraft, which can either be multiple types and variants of narrow and widebody aircraft or both size categories. Regional airlines tend to operate turboprops and smaller regional jets, which are more right-sized and economical for the shorter routes they operate. Fuel efficiency per seat is generally correlated to aircraft size, which means that seat cost decreases as aircraft get larger, but the trip and ownership costs are higher for larger aircraft. Several types of aircraft are described below.

Turboprop aircraft utilize gas-turbine engines, each connected to a gearbox that turns a propeller(s) to move the aircraft on the ground and in the air. They have a maximum cruise speed of around 400 mph and typically seat between 25 and 90 passengers. When used by commercial airlines, turboprops typically fly very short routes (usually less than 1 hour) or routes with low or inconsistent passenger demand. While turboprop aircraft can be inefficient on longer routes, due to their slower speed compared to jets, these types of aircraft are especially effective at reaching smaller cities that connect to a hub airport. Table 2.3 shows some of the popular turboprops.

Regional Jets are short-to-medium—haul single aisle turbofan-powered aircraft. These aircraft cruise at around 600 mph and typically seat between 50 and 125 passengers. Similar to turboprops, airlines use these aircraft to fly between small and medium-sized cities to hub airports or on thin routes in terms of passenger demand. By using more regional jets on a route, an airline can increase frequency while maintaining similar seat supply for a given city pair. Due to their size and cost

Table 2.3 Examples of Turboprop Aircraft Flown by Airlines

Aircraft	Max Seats	MTOW (lb/kg)	Range (nm/km)	Max Speed (km/h)	Length (ft in./m)	Wingspan (ft in./m)
ATR 72-600	70	50,706/23,000	825/1528	509	89 ft 2 in./27.17	88 ft 9 in./27.05
Bombardier Q400	90	67,200/30,481	1100/2040	667	107 ft 9 in./32.8	93 ft 3 in./28.4
Embraer 120	30	26,433/11,500	945/1750	552	65 ft/20.00	64 ft 10 in./19.78
Saab 2000	58	50,265/22,800	1549/2869	665	89 ft 6 in./27.28	81 ft 3 in./24.76
Cessna 402	9	6850/3107	1273/2360	428	36 ft 5 in./11.09	44 ft 2 in./13.45

MTOW, *Maximum take-off weight.*
Data gathered from different manufacturers' websites.

Table 2.4 Examples of Regional Jet Aircraft Flown by Airlines

Aircraft	Max Seats	MTOW (lb/kg)	Range (nm/km)	Max Mach Number	Length (ft in./m)	Wingspan (ft in./m)
ARJ21-900	105	96,157/43,616	1200/2200	M0.82	119 ft 3 in./36.35	89 ft 6 in./27.28
Bombardier CRJ 700	78	75,000/34,019	1400/2593	M0.83	106 ft 7 in./32.3	76 ft 3 in./23.2
Embraer 145	50	48,501/22,000	1550/2873	M0.78	98 ft 0 in./29.87	65 ft 9 in./20.04
Embraer 170	72	85,098/38,600	2150/3982	M0.82	98 ft 1 in./29.9	85 ft 4 in./26
Embraer 190	100	114,199/51,800	2450/4537	M0.82	118 ft 11 in./36.24	94 ft 3 in./28.72
Sukhoi SSJ 100	108	101,150/45,880	1894/3048	M0.81	98 ft 3 in./29.94	91 ft 2 in./27.8

Data gathered from Bombardier (2017), Embraer (2018) and other manufacturers' websites.

relative to the passenger count, regional jets typically have a higher seat cost than larger narrowbody aircraft, but a lower trip cost. Table 2.4 shows details of some of the major regional aircraft.

Narrowbody aircraft are single-aisle aircraft with a maximum width of six seats abreast. Narrowbody jets are capable of flying transcontinental and shorter transatlantic flights. They cruise at about 620 mph and typically seat between 120 and 240 passengers. Narrowbodies make up a larger percentage of the world's commercial airlines fleet, thus making them the most liquid from an owner and financier's perspective. Current technology aircraft are extremely fuel efficient and manufacturers are consistently upgrading and improving these aircraft to meet the requirements of the airlines and the market. They offer an airline a great deal of flexibility and can be used efficiently for dense flights of less than 1 hour and as long as 6–7 hours. Airbus and Boeing are the two primary manufacturers for narrowbody aircraft, but recently Bombardier in Canada (the Bombardier C Series aircraft have now been redesignated as the Airbus A220 due to Airbus taking a majority stake in the C Series program), Irkut in Russia, and COMAC in China have also entered the market. Table 2.5 compares the technical details of a number of popular narrowbody aircraft, including the two most popular types, the B737–800 and A320ceo.

Intermediate Widebody aircraft have two aisles with seven or more seats abreast in the economy class. These are typically long haul aircraft that cruise at around 650 mph and typically seat between 200 and 400 passengers. Most international flights that operate transcontinental routes are usually operated by a widebody aircraft. However, even some densely populated city pairs in the same country will use widebody aircraft due to the high volumes of passenger traffic. This is predominantly the case in Asia where large populations of people tend to move between select city pairs. Airbus and Boeing are the two primary manufacturers for commercial widebody aircraft (Table 2.6).

Large Widebodies are widebody aircraft which typically accommodate more than 400 seats. Similar to intermediate widebodies, large widebodies cruise around 650 mph. These aircraft are best utilized on very densely populated city pairs across continents or city pairs that are separated by a significant distance. These aircraft are the most expensive from an acquisition or capital cost and trip cost perspective but have the lowest seat mile costs. They are the most volatile aircraft with respect to residual value due to very few airlines having the route network and passenger movements that can support them (Table 2.7).

Freighters are aircraft that carry cargo rather than passengers. They can be either narrowbody or widebody in guage. One of the most popular freighters has been the 747F due to its ability to carry a large volume of cargo over a long distance. However, the 777 freighter has quickly replaced the 747 due to its greater fuel efficiency and the reduction of volume (size) in air movements. Freighters can either be purchased brand new directly from the original equipment manufacturer (OEM) or be converted from older passenger aircraft. Since a freighter typically flies fewer hours and cycles per day than a passenger aircraft, they typically have a longer operational life. This is one reason that it makes financial sense to convert a passenger aircraft that is partially or fully depreciated—in order to extend the useful economic life of the asset (Table 2.8).

Table 2.5 Examples of Narrowbody Aircraft Flown by Airlines

Aircraft	Max Seats	MTOW (lb/kg)	Range (nm/km)	Max Mach Number	Length (in./m)	Wingspan (in./m)
Airbus A320ceo	186	172,000/ 78,000	3300/ 6100	M0.82	123 ft 3 in./ 37.57	117 ft 5 in./ 35.8
Boeing 737-800	189	174,200/ 79,016	29,35/ 5436	M0.82	129 ft 6 in./ 39.5	117 ft 5 in./ 35.8
Boeing 757-200	239	255,000/ 11,5660	3915/ 7250	M0.86	155 ft 3 in./ 47.3	124 ft 10 in./ 38.0
Airbus A220	160	149,000/ 67,585	3300/ 6112	M0.82	127 ft 0 in./ 38.7	115 ft 1 in./ 35.1
COMAC C919	168	159,835/ 72,500	2200/ 4075	M0.785	127.6 ft/38.9	117.5 ft/35.8

Data gathered from different manufacturers' websites.

Table 2.6 Examples of Intermediate Widebody Aircraft Flown by Airlines

Aircraft	Max Seats	MTOW (lb/kg)	Range (nm/km)	Max Mach Number	Length (in./m)	Wingspan (in./m)
Airbus A330-300	440	533,500/ 242,000	6350/11,750	M0.86	208 ft 10 in./ 63.66	197 ft 10 in./ 60.3
Airbus A350-900	400	617,290/ 280,000	8100/15,000	M0.89	219 ft 2 in./ 66.08	212 ft 5 in./ 64.75
Boeing 767-400ER	409	450,000/ 204,116	5625/10,415	M0.86	201 ft 4 in./ 61.37	170 ft 4 in./ 51.92
Boeing 787-9	406	560,000/ 254,011	6430/11,908	M0.90	224 ft/68.28	197 ft 3 in./ 60.12
Ilyushin II-96M	420	595,000/ 270,000	6907/12,800	M0.84	212 ft 3 in./ 64.7	197 ft 3 in./ 60.12

Data gathered from different manufacturers' websites.

Table 2.7 Examples of Large Widebody Aircraft Flown by Airlines

Aircraft	Max Seats	MTOW (lb/kg)	Range (nm/km)	Max Mach Number	Length (in./m)	Wingspan (in./m)
Airbus A350-1000	440	679,000/ 308,000	7950/14,750	M0.89	242 ft 1 in./ 73.79	212 ft 5 in./ 64.75
Airbus A380	853	1268,000/ 575,000	8200/15,200	M0.89	238 ft 7 in./ 72.2	261 ft 8 in./ 79.75
Boeing 747-8	605	987,000/ 447,696	8000/14,816	M0.90	250 ft 2 in./ 76.3	224 ft 5 in./ 68.4
Boeing 777-300ER	396	775,000/ 351,533	7370/13,649	M0.89	242 ft 4 in./ 73.9	212 ft 7 in./ 64.8

Data gathered from different manufacturers' websites.

Table 2.8 Examples of Freighter Aircraft Flown by Airlines

Aircraft	Max Capacity (lb/kg)	MTOW (lb/kg)	Range (nm/km)	Max Mach number	Length (ft in./m)	Wingspan (ft in./m)
Boeing 747-400ERF	274,100/ 124,330	875,000/ 396,890	4985/ 9230	M0.92	231 ft 10 in./ 70.66	211 ft 5 in./ 64.44
Boeing 777F	224,900/ 102,010	766,800/ 347,815	4970/ 9200	M0.89	209 ft 1 in./ 63.73	199 ft 11 in./ 60.93
Airbus A330F	154,324/ 70,000	513,677/ 233,000	4000/ 7400	M0.82	193 ft/58.82	198 ft/60.3

Data gathered from different manufacturers' websites.

OPERATING WEIGHTS AND PAYLOAD CAPABILITY

Over time, new aircraft that are being manufactured will be able to fly further and longer while also weighing less and consuming less fuel. The goal of selecting the right aircraft means choosing the most optimal plane for the mission it needs to fly. It is important to understand the terminology and driving factors behind an aircraft's performance characteristics. The following section will outline these features.

The first is *weight*, which directly impacts the performance of an aircraft during flight, with different weight categories having maximum limits which should not be exceeded. There are different weight definitions that are important to understand when selecting an aircraft with an optimal weight. It is best to think of the different aircraft weight measures as building blocks from manufacturer's empty weight to maximum taxi weight as we go through the definitions illustrated in Table 2.9 (Ackert, 2013).

Following weight is *range*. How far can the aircraft fly at a given weight? There are trade-offs between weight and range. Range decreases as weight increases, all else held constant. Fig. 2.1 describes the trade-off between weight and range for a B777. This is very important because a single aircraft type can have range differences of over 3000 mi (5556 km) with payload capabilities separated by over 200,000 kg (about 441,000 lb). As noted in the chart, range increases as weight decreases but only to a certain extent. After a certain point, range will no longer increase as weight drops because the aircraft is operating at its maximum efficiency.

Table 2.9 Weight and Payload Terminology

Illustration	Term	Definition
Taxi fuel	MTW	The maximum weight for ground maneuver as limited by airplane strength and airworthiness requirements
Trip fuel	MDTOW or MTOW	The maximum certified weight at which the aircraft can takeoff as limited by airplane strength and airworthiness requirements
Reserve fuel	MLW	The maximum weight for landing as limited by airplane strength and airworthiness requirements
Cargo + passengers + baggage	Maximum payload	MZFW minus OEW
	MZFW	The maximum weight permitted before usable fuel and other specified items are loaded
Aircraft structure + systems + propulsion + operators items	OEW	The weight of the aircraft prepared for service and is composed of the MEW plus operator items
	MEW	The weight of the aircraft as it has been built by the manufacturer. Excluding operator items

MTW, *Maximum taxi weight;* MDTOW, *Maximum designed takeoff weight (generally referred to as MTOW, maximum take-off weight);* MLW, *Maximum landing weight;* MZFW, *Maximum zero-fuel weight;* OEW, *Operator empty weight;* MEW, *Manufacturer's empty weight.*
Ackert (2013).

The range-payload trade-off is described in Fig. 2.1. There are four pivot points on this chart where the trade-off between payload and range occurs (Ackert, 2013):

- *Point A* represents the aircraft at maximum zero-fuel weight. Since the aircraft has no fuel, its range is 0 mi.
- *Point B* is the maximum range the aircraft can fly with a maximum payload. So, to fly further distances, payload must be reduced.
- *Point C* is at a weight where maximum fuel is being used with reasonable payload. This is where the aircraft is most efficient in regards to the payload-range trade-off.
- *Point D* is the operator empty weight or "ferry weight." It represents maximum fuel with minimum payload. The movement from point C to D is achieved through exclusively reducing payload.

Fig. 2.2 is specifically arranged for different B777 variants. It outlines specific weights at each trade-off point. Note how passenger configuration will change the range of an aircraft by over 1000 NM. For example, a B777-300ER can fly similar ranges to the B777-200 at maximum payload. However, as weight decreases, the B777-200LR has the ability to fly further distances. Knowing the size of payload expected and the route distance is essential in choosing the best possible aircraft.

Flight performance and capability are essential in choosing the correct aircraft, but the way an aircraft is operated on the ground is very important as well. Ground handling speed and seating styles can reduce or increase turnaround times for an aircraft, which will decrease or increase the cost for an airline.

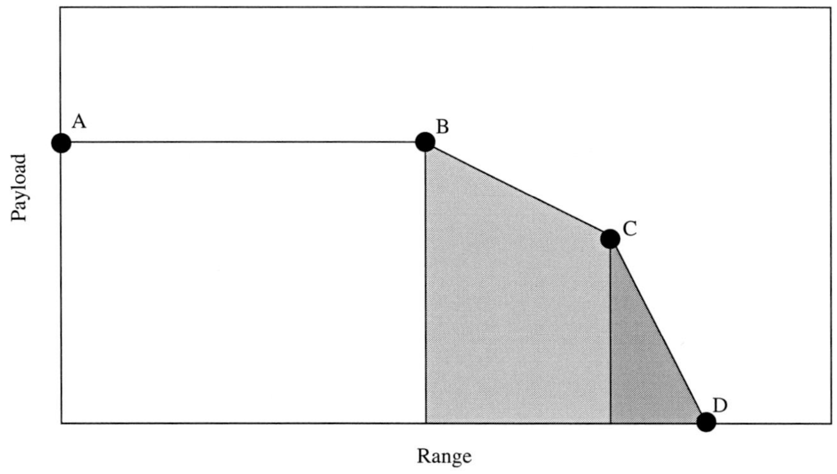

FIGURE 2.1

Range and payload trade-off.

Ackert (2013).

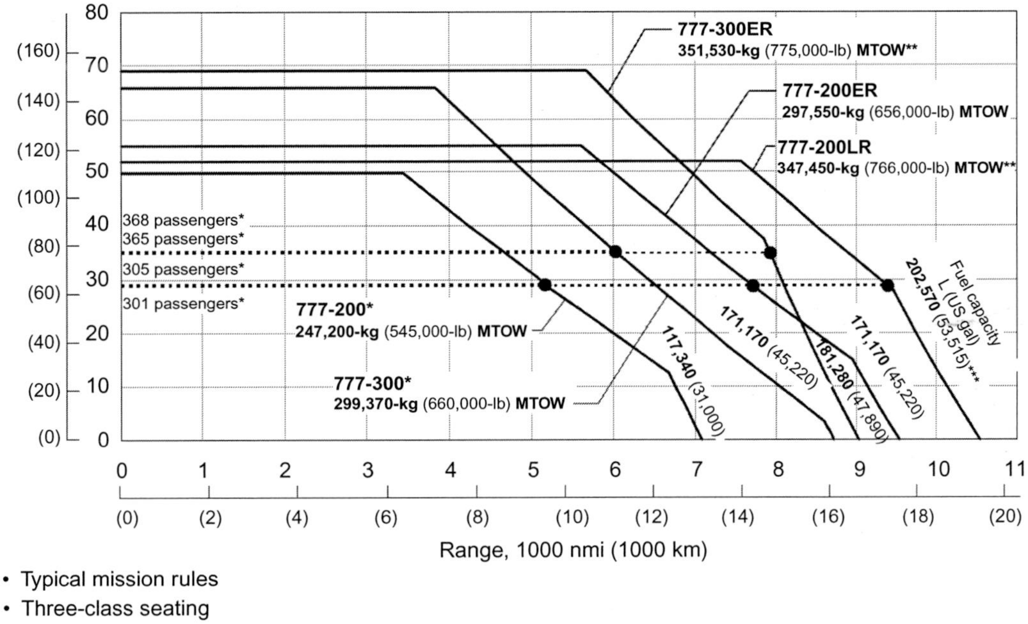

FIGURE 2.2

B777 payload and range.

Ackert (2013).

REVENUE AND COST COMPONENTS

In essence, an aircraft is a revenue generating machine that is the largest, if not singular generator of cash for airlines. While it is very important to examine and reduce costs, it is equally important to maximize revenue for an airline to be successful. Airline profitability depends on the ability to manage costs and improve revenue. The following terms are important in understanding how lessors and airlines calculate revenue components for both the aircraft and airline as a whole.

Available Seat Mile (ASM) is a measure of capacity. It is calculated by

$$ASM = Seats \times Miles\ Flown$$

One seat (whether occupied or not) flying 1 mi is an ASM. For example, a 200-seat aircraft flying 500 mi has 100,000 ASMs. This can be measured at the aircraft level or at the airline level when aggregating the entire fleet. ASM can also be calculated as ASKs, or available seat kilometers, simply replacing miles flown with kilometers flown in the above calculation.

Revenue per ASM (RASM) is also called unit revenue and is calculated by

$$RASM = Revenue\ /\ Available\ Seat\ Mile$$

RASM is an effective tool in determining the revenue generated for one seat (empty or filled) flying 1 mi. Some airlines price the same seat at drastically different rates, and some airlines price all seats at relatively the same rate. RASM is a good way of smoothing out these variances and determining the appropriate revenue for an aircraft or an airline. RASK is the revenue per ASK and can be calculated using ASK in the above equation.

Cost per ASM (CASM) is a measure of unit cost and is calculated by

$$CASM = Direct\ Operating\ Cost\ /\ Available\ Seat\ Mile$$

CASM identifies how much it costs to fly one seat (empty or filled) 1 mi. Direct operating costs include pilot pay, flight attendant pay, aircraft ownership costs, maintenance, insurance, and sometimes fuel. Fuel can either be included or excluded from CASM because of its volatility, which may not accurately reflect an airline's true operating costs. CASM can change within the same aircraft type depending on its configuration. Seat density is a key in reducing CASM. LCCs generally have a lower CASM than legacy carriers because of their higher seat densities. Similar to revenue per available seat kilometer (RASK), cost per available seat kilometer (CASK), or, can be calculated using ASK in the above equation.

The Load Factor (LF) is the ratio of revenue passengers or freight to available seats or freight capacity, expressed as a percentage.

$$Load\ Factor = Total\ Passenger\ Count\ /\ Available\ Seats$$

To present the LF calculation, consider a B737-800 with 189 seats that carries an average of 150 passengers on an established city pair of 1500 NM. The passenger LF is calculated as 150/189 = 79.37%.

When deciding which aircraft to buy, it is important to factor in the seat density in which it will be flying. As seats increase, all else equal, CASM and RASM both decrease. Thus, there is a trade-off that must be taken into consideration. Table 2.10 demonstrates this trade-off. However, with more seats typically comes an increase in revenue, so in this case, CASM will decrease and RASM may increase as well.

ADDITIONAL CONSIDERATIONS

Noise and CO_2 pollution

In addition to weight and payload capabilities, there are additional financial considerations that could be determinants in selecting an aircraft. First, there are environmental considerations. Fuel consumption and the size of the carbon dioxide footprint of an aircraft can be scrutinized by the public. In many countries, especially in Europe, aircraft are charged a tax to fly through their airspace or land at their airports based on the level of an aircraft's CO_2 emissions. Fortunately, less fuel burn leads to not only lower fuel costs but fewer CO_2 emissions, and therefore a lower financial penalty. Aside from the financial and public relations impact, it is a good policy for an airline to take pride in the environment they operate in, and where possible, select aircraft that can minimize the carbon dioxide released into the atmosphere.

Next to CO_2 pollution is noise pollution. Through technological advances over the past several decades, jet engines are now much quieter than they once were. EASA and the FAA have strict guidelines for noise regulations which airlines must adhere to. Currently, there are four stages of jet noise, with stage 1 being the loudest and stage 4 being the quietest. Currently, neither EASA nor the FAA allows stage 1 or 2 aircraft to fly commercially in the United States and Europe. It is expected that within a few years, stage-3 aircraft will be required to be modified to become quieter

Table 2.10 CASM

CASM Example			
Direct operating cost	$100,000.00	$100,000.00	$100,000.00
Revenue	$150,000.00	$150,000.00	$150,000.00
Stage length (mi)	3500	3500	3500
Seats	150	175	200
ASM	$525,000.00	$612,500.00	$700,000.00
CASM	$0.19	$0.16	$0.14
RASM	$0.29	$0.24	$0.21

ASM, *Available Seat Mile;* CASM, *Cost per available seat mile;* RASM, *Revenue per available seat mile.*

or they too will be restricted from flying in many countries. Presently there are some airports that will restrict the operation of stage-3 aircraft to certain times of the day, or to certain runways. These restrictions can impact an airline's ability to freely schedule an aircraft, and therefore impact the airline's ability to generate the level of revenue they would otherwise have without a restriction. There are also airports that will levy penalties and fines for airlines that do not meet the most stringent stage-4 noise restriction, leading to higher landing fees and usage charges.

For example, the UK Department for Transport has created a Quota Count (QC) system that determines how much noise airports can emit at night. Different types of aircraft are then assigned to a noise band for takeoff and landing, ranging from QC/0.5 to QC/16, with a certain amount of points. Once an airport has reached their allocated points for the night, no more night flights are allowed at that airport without severe penalty. London Heathrow Airport (2018) does not allow any noise band above QC/2 to land between 11:30 p.m. and 6:00 a.m. and charges smaller landing fees to airlines using their quietest planes during those hours.

Maintenance cost considerations

Aircraft maintenance can weigh heavily on an aircraft's cost of ownership. If an aircraft is purchased new, it is important to understand the aircraft's warranty both in terms of length and items covered. Generally speaking, as part of the purchase agreement, the buyer will negotiate terms over the warranty and certain maintenance cost guarantees. This is important, especially for a new aircraft type that is in the "launch" phase and without any operational experience. Since a new aircraft type is not proven until it has had significant experience flying in real world operations, it is difficult to know exactly how much maintenance will be required.

If an aircraft is used, it is important to know where it is in its maintenance interval, and if there is a maintenance reserve account attached to the aircraft to cover the cost of the maintenance life that has been previously consumed. Airframe heavy checks and large maintenance events like engine performance restorations can cost millions of dollars, so it is essential to include these assumptions in a cost of ownership model. In Chapter 9, we cover maintenance reserves and cost calculations in greater detail. Another important consideration is to determine if there are any pending regulatory requirements or airworthiness directives that will require compliance in the near future.

Crew cost considerations

Other variable costs which fluctuate based on the aircraft type are flight crew costs. Before a purchase decision is made, one must determine how much training will be required for pilots to operate a particular model. For instance, if an airline currently operates a Boeing 737NG fleet, their pilots can quickly transition to the 737 MAX with only minor differences in training. However, if the same airline were to switch to an Airbus 320 fleet, much costlier and more time-consuming training would be required, and vice versa. At the same time, there is also the concept of a common cockpit rating which can not only save an airline training costs but also reduce the total number of crews an airline needs to have on its payroll. A common cockpit rating allows a pilot to move from one aircraft variant to another. For instance, a pilot can fly the Airbus 319 one day and fly the Airbus 330 the next. Cabin crew training and staffing is another consideration when evaluating the type and layout of an aircraft. Each country's regulatory authority sets a minimum number of flight attendants for every increment of seats. For example, the FAA requires one flight attendant for every 50 passenger seats on board an aircraft (regardless if those seats are filled or not). So a cabin layout of 148 seats compared with 152 can increase cabin crew costs considerably with only a small increase in potential revenue.

Other cost considerations

There are many other fees and expenses that go along with an aircraft operation. We mentioned earlier about fees for carbon emissions and noise pollution that some countries or airports levy. In addition, every airport charges landing fees which are based on weight of the aircraft. Likewise, navigation fees, also known as overflight fees are charged by most countries when an aircraft passes through that country's airspace. Most countries calculate this charge based on the weight of the aircraft as well. It is therefore important to be aware of where the aircraft will be flying and what third-party fees will be charged on such aircraft.

AIRCRAFT VALUES

We discuss aircraft values and valuation methodology in greater detail in Chapter 12. We introduce the concepts here as they are essential for an understanding of the aircraft selection process.

The value of an aircraft is driven by multiple factors. First, like any asset, the greatest factor in setting an aircraft's value is supply and demand. In other words, the market will set the value for different aircraft variants based on the market forces at play at any given point in time. Total cost of ownership, age, and revenue-generating potential are also factors that the market weighs in setting the price of an aircraft. Second, the maintenance status of an individual aircraft will either raise or lower that market value depending on where the aircraft is in its maintenance interval. For instance, if an aircraft is due for a heavy check or engine performance restoration, that cost could be in the millions of dollars, and the value of that aircraft will reflect the maintenance yet to be performed. Also, if the aircraft has a cockpit or interior configuration that is uncommon or is in need of updating or replacement, that too will impact the value of a particular aircraft. Finally, the pedigree or operating history is a variable that can improve or take away from the value of an aircraft. An aircraft that has operated in a harsh environment like the Middle East, India, or China will be prone to higher maintenance costs, even if it no longer operates in that environment. On the other hand, an aircraft that has operated in a very benign environment, like a cool sea level climate, should have a lower maintenance burden, all else being equal. These factors, along with other negotiable items, are what may make two seemingly similar aircraft valued differently in a sale.

Valuation methodology

Base Value (BV) is the ideal dollar amount set for an aircraft transaction between a willing and informed buyer and seller in a competitive and balanced market where supply and demand are relatively equal. It is based on historical values and trends as well as projections of future trends. BV does not take into consideration short-term fluctuations and volatility in the market such as political instability, fuel prices, or economic events. It should be noted that the BV assumes the aircraft is at the halfway point between all of its maintenance events, known as "half-life" condition. In reality, this is a fictional reference, as an aircraft is rarely ever in a state where every maintenance item is actually midway through its maintenance interval. However, aircraft appraisers have agreed that this is the best theoretical reference point to use as a baseline for aircraft value. BV almost never represents the actual price at which an individual aircraft is traded (ISTAT Appraisers' Program, 2013).

Current Market Value (CMV) is the actual trading price at which an aircraft is appraised. This takes into consideration short-term political changes, fuel prices, and economic events. The aircraft is also valued at half-life condition for CMV.

BV and CMV can be equal if market conditions are balanced. The following illustration shows how the market may affect CMV.

CMV = BV	Market conditions are in equilibrium
CMV > BV	Market conditions support higher prices due to a shortage of supply or an excess in demand
CMV < BV	Market conditions support lower prices due to an excess in supply or a shortage of demand

CMV, *Current market value;* BV, *base value.*

In addition to CMV and BV, there are additional terms that include forecasted assumptions to derive an estimated price for an aircraft.

Future BV is the appraiser's forecasted future aircraft value from an initial starting point that is generally its BV. A curve is then generated using normalized data points derived from the aircraft's BV, and an extension of that curve produces the future BV curve for an aircraft type. Future values are normally projected in current dollars and, as such, entail inflation assumptions. Appraisers often forecast future values assuming current inflation rates (ISTAT Appraisers' Program, 2013).

Adjusted Market Value indicates that the market value of the aircraft has been adjusted from half-life condition to account for the actual maintenance status. The maintenance performed on an aircraft has an impact on its value. Therefore, it is important to quantify in monetary terms the maintenance status of aircraft involved in transactions, since a strong correlation exists between the cost of conducting maintenance and value enhancement (ISTAT Appraisers' Program, 2013).

Table 2.11 displays aircraft values for several Boeing, Airbus, and Embraer aircraft. This is the average CMV for each aircraft variant. Notice the size and age trade-off between the aircraft variants listed below. For example, the B767-300ER is a long range widebody, but the younger and newer technology of the B737-800, along with the higher demand, gives the narrowbody a higher

Table 2.11 Aircraft Current Market List Prices (2018)

Aircraft	2018 Base Value (Millions USD)	Aircraft Vintage (Year)
A319-100	17.0	2008
A320-200	22.0	2008
A321-200	24.5	2008
A330-200	39.5	2008
A330-200F	53.0	2010
A350-900	101.4	2013
A380-800	75.5	2008
B737 MAX 8	44.3	2016
B737-800	24.1	2008
B737-900ER	24.3	2008
B747-8	76.9	2011
B747-8F	84.9	2009
B767-300ER	20.0	2008
B777-200ER	48.8	2008
B777F	87.4	2008
B787-9	99.9	2013
E190	14.5	2008

Avitas Jet Aircraft Values (2017—37) (Avitas (2017).

value. Also, narrowbodies are more liquid and can be easily remarketed, so often a smaller and younger aircraft will bring a higher CMV versus an older and out of production widebody.

THE LESSOR'S PERSPECTIVE ON AIRCRAFT SELECTION

An operating lessor does not operate the aircraft, and therefore it is important that the lessor have aircraft in its portfolio or on order that meet the requirements of an airline. Lessors look at a number of different aspects when assessing which aircraft to select and which aircraft to order including market analysis, aircraft liquidity, production stages of aircraft, and various risks.

MARKET ANALYSIS

For a lessor there are two major questions to answer regarding market analysis: What aircraft are needed and how many aircraft does the market require today? Where will the demand be in the future with respect to various aircraft types? With respect to where the market will be in the future, the first thing to examine is the technical aspects or capability of the aircraft. This means looking into the future to understand market trends and developments. This analysis allows one to forecast where the market is heading and what aircraft will be required to operate various routes and missions. As an example, if there is passenger growth expected in Asia that will predominantly move passengers on long haul routes; that will mean that more aircraft which can fly large numbers of passengers over longer distances will be needed. If growth is in areas where there are short sector stage lengths or the trend is moving toward more hub and spoke frequencies, that will mean more narrowbody aircraft may be needed. Matching growth areas with appropriate aircraft is the foundation of a lessor's business model.

Second, lessors look at the current state of the market. In other words, what has already been ordered by the airlines. Just because there may be requirements for a large number of long haul widebody aircraft it does not necessarily mean all lessors will purchase that specific type of aircraft. It is essential for lessors to find gaps in the market. These gaps come from the difference between what the airlines have in their existing fleet and on order from the manufacturers and what lessors forecast the airlines will require. This exercise is done at both a macro and a micro level, starting with the global universe of airlines, and then drilling down to the micro level which entails determining which airlines would meet a lessor's criteria for entering into a transaction.

Also, for any particular aircraft, it is important for the lessor to see the revenue generating potential of the aircraft over its economic life and not just when the aircraft is placed into service. For example, the Airbus A380 was in high demand when it was launched, and airlines found an aircraft that could fly long distances and carry a large amount of passengers and freight to combat the high fuel prices of the time. Therefore, there was an initial requirement for a large number of aircraft that would have a great first home. However, from an operating lessor's perspective, the aircraft is not expected to have a very deep secondary market. In other words, at the end of its first lease (typically 12–15 years), there may be limited opportunity to re-lease that airplane or transition that airplane to a second operator. It is important therefore for an operating lessor to think about an aircraft through its entire aircraft life cycle, not just where it will be leased in the first instance but where will it be leased in the second and third instance ideally through a period of time of about 25 years.

AIRCRAFT PLACEMENT

Lessors can place aircraft in four main areas of the market: new markets, replacements/retirements, natural growth, and right-sizing.

New Markets are simply markets that have not existed before or have not shown maturity yet. Greater liberalization of aviation markets is often a driver for aviation growth and the development of new markets through the opening of new air routes between growing numbers of origins and destinations. The impact of liberalization is particularly dramatic in the case of low-cost airlines, which are stimulating air travel by lowering fares and opening new markets. Examples of current new markets include Latin America, India, and Southeast Asia. Most airlines in these markets do not have the necessary capital to purchase an aircraft, so leasing is very prevalent. However, developing nations contain imperfect legal systems that could result in financial losses for lessors if an emerging airline should default.

Replacements/Retirements are a key part of any forecast, as the time at which aircraft leave passenger service to retire or be converted for other uses has an impact on the level of demand of new aircraft deliveries. High fuel costs and the need to meet new environmental regulations are compelling airlines to accelerate the replacement of older and inefficient airplanes. Replacement needs are higher with established airlines in mature economies. Further, the higher the utilization of an aircraft, the higher the need for replacements.

Natural Growth is the driver behind Boeing and Airbus' large order books. Worldwide economic activity is the most powerful driver of natural growth in commercial air transport and the resulting demand for airplanes. World GDP is expected to grow at about 2.8%, with emerging economies such as India and China leading the way with growth exceeding 6.1% and 4.9%, respectively, over the same time span (Boeing, 2017).

Right-Sizing is a balancing mechanism in the market. When bubbles of demand and supply form, they will naturally be smoothed out by the market. Using right-sized equipment allows airlines to maximize operational efficiency and profitability by optimizing capacity to demand. For example, the Embraer E190 provides operators with an optimally designed aircraft for targeting routes/frequencies where regional jets are too small and the standard B737/A320 family of aircraft is too large. Fears of a pilot shortage have led many airlines, especially in the United States, to up-gauge (move from regional jets up to 100 plus seat narrowbodies) their fleets.

VALUE RETENTION AND LIQUIDITY

Following the initial operating lease of an aircraft, it is essential for that aircraft to hold the necessary residual value that will allow the lessor to either sell or release the asset at a profitable rate. In essence, the retained value and liquidity of the aircraft can single handedly determine if a transaction was profitable or not. Limited geographical and global fleet spread will limit secondary market prospects, so aircraft investors almost always focus on popular, liquid aircraft that are well dispersed amongst customers and regions.

Generally, lessors prefer very liquid aircraft. For example, the B737-800 is currently one of the best selling, most liquid aircraft in production with over 150 customers and 3910 firm orders globally dispersed amongst all regions. Therefore, it is one of the most preferred aircraft by the lessors. Although most investors tend to focus primarily on liquid aircraft, there are a number of lessors who will invest in specialized/niche aircraft, or those considered to have poor residual value prospects. They will generally do so by either buying these aircraft at low market values, charging premium rents, or a combination of the two. Examples of specialized aircraft today are the B777-200LR and the A380.

PRODUCTION STAGES

Aircraft with sustained production runs have greater market share and geographical spread than those with shorter product life cycles. More importantly, aircraft that are still in production tend to retain their values and lease rates to an even greater degree than those that have ceased production.

What phase an aircraft is in its production cycle also influences its value retention. More often, early production units tend be heavier, have lower maximum gross weights and thrust, and incur higher direct operating costs when compared to mid-to-later built higher specification units. In contrast, aircraft manufactured at the tail end of a production cycle tend to experience higher declines in future values given these aircraft are competing against newer technology aircraft that often offer significant improvements in operating efficiency.

Let us illustrate the B787 as an example. The B787 program was launched with three variants (the B787-3, B787-8, and the B787-9). The B787-3 was meant to be a short range aircraft predominantly for the intra-Asia market. It never received any customer acceptance, and ultimately it was never built and the variant was dropped. Most of the orders focused on the B787-8. When Boeing booked most of these orders in 2008, fuel prices were on the rise, so airlines were focusing on the right size and the gauge of aircraft to combat the rising fuel prices. Then, the production program was delayed and fuel prices continued to rise significantly. As airlines looked at competing aircraft, specifically the A350-XWB, they realized the A350 was more efficient. Boeing's response was to try and direct customers toward the B787-9 instead of the B787-8 in a head-to-head competition with the A350. Customers began converting their orders from the B787-8 to the B787-9, and as more airlines placed new orders (orders that were not previously on the books with Boeing), Boeing started focusing on the B787-9 variant. Operating lessors acted similarly. By watching the dynamics of the market evolve and airlines move from the B787-8 to the B787-9, lessors needed to make sure that they had the aircraft that the airlines would want as well. Since then, Boeing has introduced an even larger variant, the B787-10. The B787-10 is an airplane that is meant to fly the same range as the B787-9 but with more passengers. Right now, only a few airlines have ordered that aircraft. If that aircraft also has the same market acceptance, or a broader market acceptance similar to the B787-9, it can be assumed that lessors will order the B787-10 or convert some of the positions in their order book to the larger B787-10. In summary, lessors need to follow the market for the airlines and be aware of the factors which may cause changes to or shifts in orders. They need to make sure that they have the aircraft in their portfolios that the airlines want to lease.

LEASE RATE FACTOR

A lease rate factor is essentially a monthly rent payment that is a percentage of the overall purchase price of the aircraft. The industry refers to lease rates in terms of lease rate factor. In general, there are two different ways an airline can enter into an operating lease of an aircraft. The first is through a sale and leaseback. In a sale and leaseback process, an airline has already purchased their aircraft from the manufacturer, but they have made the decision that they want to finance the airplane through an operating lease structure. The airline in the sale and leaseback agreement will sell the aircraft to the lessor and immediately lease it back. In this transaction, an airline will prescribe a price and see what type of lease rates and terms any lessor will offer them. Lessors will bid that in terms of the lease rate and then a lease rate factor. The airline will then assess the lease rate, term, and lease rate factor of the competing lessors, and, all else held constant, they would choose the operating lessor who could provide the lowest lease rate factor to the airline or the lowest net lease rate with the most desirable lease term.

Second, a lessor can lease an aircraft from their forward order book. In this type of transaction, the lessors do not disclose their lease rate factor. If they did, the airline would quickly be able to back into the lessor's purchase price. Again, as in the case of the sale and leaseback transaction, lease rate factor is a function of the cost of the aircraft as well as the monthly lease rate.

$$\textit{Lease Rate Factor} = \textit{LeaseRate} \; / \; \textit{Acquisition Price of Aircraft}$$

In addition, it is important to understand the market lease rate. A market lease rate is driven by supply and demand in the market. For example, if a lessor has a B787 on order and one for delivery in 2018 and two other leasing companies have aircraft that are also available in 2018, the market lease rate will be determined by the lessor's view of the market. If the competing lessors each lease their aircraft at the same lease rate, then that is where the lease rate for that market would settle. If, however, one of the three lessors in this instance sets the lease rate differently, the other lessors will likely offer a higher or lower lease rate which might be due to differences in purchase price, cost of capital, or return criteria of the lessor. Lessors essentially set the market lease rate by charging rates higher or lower than the current market rate. If one lessor charges a lower rate, it can drive market rates down as others will need to do so to remain competitive, but if collectively they can charge a higher rate, it drives the market lease rate up. Market lease rates on forward order books, therefore, are very much driven by supply and demand factors. Every lessor has their own view and requirements in terms of residual value and in terms of return on investment or equity. Each lessor might see the market slightly differently, and that is what could cause some variance in market lease rates as well. Table 2.12 displays current lease rates for different vintage aircraft. Lease rate factors fluctuate based on the age, size, and residual value risk of an aircraft. A low lease-rate factor can be attributed to a small or narrowbody aircraft (such as the A319) in high demand. Lessors will receive a higher rate of return on large aircraft like the A380 and B747-8 because they hold the residual value risk of the aircraft. Older aircraft already have a low residual value with minimal risk because the part out value is almost equal to the CMV of the aircraft. Generally, as an aircraft ages over the course of the lease, the lease rate factor will gradually increase due to the fixed lease payment compared to the decreasing market value of the aircraft.

Table 2.12 Major Aircraft Lease Rates (2018)

Aircraft	Aircraft Age	Lease Rate ($ Per Month)
A318-100	10	90,000
A319-100	10	135,000
A320-200	10	195,000
A321-200	10	210,000
A330-200	10	300,000
A330-300	10	340,000
A340-600	10	300,000
A380-800	10	745,000
717-200	10	130,000
737NG	10	215,000
747-400	10	328,000
767-300	10	295,000
777-200	10	550,000
777-300	10	550,000
777F	10	705,000
EMB145	10	35,000

CAPA (2018).

CURRENT TRENDS

In assessing how current trends would affect their business models, lessors look at what those trends are with respect to production of newer aircraft as well as airline's need in the future. Analyzing the recent trends, one can see that there is currently a noticeable trend toward production of fuel efficient aircraft due to the volatility of fuel prices. From an airline perspective, airlines want to make sure they remain competitive and profitable and seek out the aircraft they want in their portfolio to remain competitive. One key determinant of an airline's competitive strength is to have the right aircraft in terms of fuel efficiency, whether it be less fuel efficient planes in a low-fuel-price environment or more fuel efficient planes in a high-fuel-price environment, operating the routes in their network. Current new technology aircraft available on the narrowbody side are the Airbus A320neo family and the Boeing 737 MAX family. As fuel price have been rising, airlines are starting to update their fleet from the current versions of the A320 and the B737-NG to the newer narrowbody versions. On the wide body side, airlines are upgauging their B787, A350, and A330neo aircraft to the larger variant of the widebody. Lessor's therefore have to carefully evaluate what aircraft airlines are looking at operating in the future and accordingly adjust their future plans to order aircraft from the manufacturer or obtain in the secondary market.

AIRLINE'S PERSPECTIVE ON AIRCRAFT SELECTION

An airline's aircraft selection process has important differences from that of a lessor because an airline, unlike a lessor, is more concerned with the total cost of ownership of the aircraft rather than liquidity or residual value. This is because a lessor typically plans on leasing an aircraft multiple times over its life and then selling it, while an airline typically intends to operate a new aircraft for the duration of its 25–30 year life. Therefore, while it is possible that residual value may be a crucial determining factor in an airline's decision to lease or buy (discussed in Chapter 3), it is not their primary reason for selecting an aircraft. Since aircraft represent a large cost to an airline, the selection process is critical. The factors involving aircraft selection for airlines include mission capability, strategic goals, availability, aircraft economics, and the availability of funding.

MISSION CAPABILITY

Airlines look for an aircraft with the minimum range and payload requirements to fly the desired mission for the planned routes. Knowing what routes the aircraft will be placed on is essential in determining which aircraft type to buy or lease. In addition to range and payload, environmental factors and altitude of airports are critical in the selection process. Higher altitudes combined with hot environments (hot and high airports, such as Las Vegas) will require more exertion from an aircraft, thus reducing its range, payload, and takeoff capabilities.

Table 2.13 shows the maximum range and typical seat counts for Boeing and Airbus aircraft. A typical range for a narrow body such as the B737 MAX or the A320neo family is about 3500–4000 nm (5400–7500 km) and for a typical intermediate widebody aircraft such as the A330 is about 6350–7500 nm (11,750–12,130 km).

Table 2.13 Maximum Range

Aircraft	Max Range (nm)	Max Range (km)	Max Seats
A319neo	3750	6950	160
A320neo	3500	6500	165
A321neo	4000	7400	244
A330-200	7250	13,450	406
A330-300	6350	11,750	440
A330-800neo	7500	13,900	406
A330-900neo	6550	12,130	440
A350-800	8245	15,270	276
A350-900	8100	15,000	400
A350-1000	7950	14,750	440
A380	8000	14,800	800
737 MAX 7	3850	7130	172
737 MAX 8	3550	6570	210
737 MAX 9	3550	6570	220
737 MAX 10	3300	6110	230
777-200LR	8555	15,843	317
777-300ER	7370	13,649	396
777-8	8700	16,110	375
777-9	7600	14,075	425
787-8	7355	13,620	242
787-9	7635	14,140	290
787-10	6430	11,910	330

From Airbus, Boeing websites.

Fleet Composition

There are two main ways in which an airline can structure its fleet: standardized or diversified fleet. Some airlines, most notably Southwest and Ryanair, find it more economical to fly a standardized fleet with the same aircraft even though it may not be the best one for every mission. Southwest and many others believe that saving costs on crew training and route modeling (amongst a host of other savings) by flying only B737s will benefit the airline as a whole. Other airlines, such as Delta or United, purchase or lease aircraft to fit a complex hub and spoke model that services unique city pairs with uneven demand. This allows the airline more flexibility in choosing routes, schedule times, and a wide range of stage lengths. Whether an airline chooses a standardized fleet or a diversified fleet is also representative of their specific business models. For instance, an airline with a standardized fleet will be more focused on frequency of flights and turnover times at the gate, while an airline with a diversified fleet will have more of a focus on CASM and fitting the aircraft perfectly to the mission. Tables 2.14–2.17 outline Ryanair, Emirates, United, and China Eastern Airline's fleet types for both in service and on order aircraft. United uses aircraft from two different

Table 2.14 Ryanair Airlines Fleet (2018)

Ryanair Aircraft	In Service	On Order	On Option
B737-800	397	34	0
B737 MAX	0	110	100
Total	*397*	*144*	*100*

CAPA different years.

Table 2.15 Emirates Fleet (2018)

UAE Aircraft	In Service	On Order
A330-200	1	0
A340-300X	2	0
A340-500	0	0
A380-800	85	57
B777-200ER	3	0
B777-200LR	10	0
B777-300	10	0
B777-300ER	124	28
B777-8X	0	35
B777-9X	0	115
B777F	13	0
Total	*248*	*235*

CAPA different years.

Table 2.16 China Eastern Fleet (2018)

CES Aircraft	In Service	On Order
A319-100	37	0
A320-200	165	0
A321-200	61	0
A330-200	30	0
A330-300E	9	0
A330-300X	6	0
A350-900XWB	0	20
B737 MAX	0	60
B737-300	0	0
B737-700	46	0
B737-800	79	71
B777-300ER	15	5
B787-9	0	15
CRJ200ER	0	0
C919	0	5
EMB-145LI	0	0
Total	*448*	*176*

CAPA different years.

Table 2.17 United Airlines Fleet (2018)

UAL Aircraft	In Service	On Order
A319-100	56	0
A320-200	97	0
A350-1000XWB	0	35
B737-700	38	61
B737-700(ETOPS)	2	0
B737-800	105	9
B737-800(ETOPS)	31	0
B737-9	0	99
B737-900	12	0
B737-900ER	131	6
B747-400	21	0
B757-200	11	0
B757-200(ETOPS)	44	0
B757-300	11	0
B757-300(ETOPS)	10	0
B767-300ER	35	0
B767-400ER	16	0
B777-200(ETOPS)	19	0
B777-200ER	55	0
B777-300ER	0	14
B787-10	0	14
B787-8	12	0
B787-9	18	10
Total	*724*	*248*

CAPA different years.

manufacturers that include narrowbody, widebody, and regional jets. This is costlier than Ryanair's all Boeing 737 fleet because of crew training and added maintenance spares provisioning costs. However, United is able utilize the best aircraft for each route because of their diverse fleet. Ryanair may fly routes at times where the 737 is too big or small to capture the appropriate demand or their fleet may lack the range required for new routes that could be profitable. Generally, the larger the airline, the more likely it is to have a diversified fleet.

AVAILABILITY

Even if an airline has the perfect aircraft in mind and is willing to pay a market price, it still may not be available in the timeframe the airline requires as lead times on new aircraft can be more than 5 years. For example, if an airline ordered a B787 in 2018, they might be able to take delivery from Boeing in 5–7 years at a production rate of 14 per month. Due to demand and production lead times, new aircraft must be ordered well in advance of expected delivery. Airlines and lessors, can however work together to reduce the lead time. Lessors can focus on market expectations, take greater risk than airlines, and place large orders with OEMs, while airlines, in turn, can avail the opportunity to lease these aircraft from the lessors with a shorter lead time.

On the used aircraft front, availability becomes an issue if the airline is looking for multiple aircraft with similar specifications and pedigree. It is very costly for an airline to reconfigure an aircraft and provision spare parts, making large orders of used aircraft quite rare. Airlines ideally try to get as close of a match to their existing fleet as possible. Another feature of the used aircraft market is maintenance. Knowing where the particular aircraft is in its maintenance cycle is essential in order to get the correct price.

Overall, the availability issue is more significant for smaller airlines. Large airlines have the luxury of placing large aircraft orders well in advance because they have the capital to do so and are able to take on more risk than smaller airlines. Smaller or undercapitalized airlines do not have wide access to capital and are required to place smaller orders on a shorter time horizon. This is where lessors, who have large forward order books, can find their greatest opportunities to transact.

Aircraft availability for airlines goes hand in hand with the aircraft's liquidity characteristics. As discussed before, lease rates are a function of the market. If an aircraft type is widely unavailable and sought after, according to the principles of supply and demand, the market lease rate will increase for these aircraft in high demand.

ECONOMICS

Aircraft economics includes not only the acquisition cost but also the cost of ownership. Major airlines tend to purchase and acquire aircraft with the intent of operating them for their entire useful lives. This is where the business model of a lessor and an operator (airline) differ, as lessors are most concerned about liquidity and future remarketability of the aircraft (residual value), whereas the operator is most concerned with the total cost of ownership.

Every airline wishes they could have the fastest and most fuel efficient plane at the cheapest price on the market. However, there are trade-offs that come with acquiring old versus new planes in terms of fuel price, maintenance cost, passenger comfort, and payload range. An airline must assess what factors are most important for their particular business model prior to making a decision.

In terms of leasing, LCCs generally prefer newer and more fuel efficient narrowbody aircraft. LCCs do not always have the capital to purchase new and expensive aircraft, so they often lease a large portion of the aircraft in their fleet. However, when LCCs decide to lease versus buy an aircraft, they consider all of the cost factors, including capital and operating costs, among others. The lease versus buy decision as well as leasing trends among different types of carriers is discussed further in Chapter 3.

Legacy carriers generally purchase and operate new aircraft and hold onto the aircraft for the full duration of its useful life. This is because legacy airlines tend to borrow at a very low-interest rate and have the cost structure to withstand fuel price volatility and an increased maintenance cost burden as the aircraft ages. Legacy carriers are interested in finding the lowest total cost of ownership throughout the life of the aircraft, considering purchase price, maintenance costs, capital costs, etc., as opposed to the lowest cost per flight. For example, if an airline owns its aircraft outright with no outstanding debt during a downturn in the economy, the airline could park that aircraft and not worry about having to make monthly lease payments or mortgage payments while the asset is not utilized. In this way, legacy carriers have the advantage of taking higher risks to benefit from market changes.

In addition, the more an airline utilizes the aircraft, the lower the cost of operating the aircraft. Fig. 2.3 outlines the profit contribution based on fuel cost and utilization.

As fuel prices rise, the airlines benefit from higher utilization of a more fuel-efficient aircraft. Thus, when making the decision to purchase a newer aircraft, airlines must consider planned utilization and estimated fuel prices over the course of the aircraft's life.

Finally, noise and carbon dioxide (CO_2) emissions also contribute to an aircraft's total cost of ownership. There are currently 309 airports around the world which contribute to 32% of the world's departures and have some type of noise restriction. These airports impose a fee based on noise emitted at takeoff and landing. For example, the Airbus A320neo is expected to save $60,000 per month on noise charges compared to the A320ceo. Newer technology can also reduce an operator's environmental fees. However, the low price of older aircraft still may outweigh additional costs. Modeling these trade-offs therefore is imperative in selecting the right aircraft.

Beginning in the 2010s, there has been a trend toward airlines upgauging in order to reduce cost. Upgauging is the process by which an airline increases the size of an aircraft on a given route while simultaneously reducing the frequency of the route. This keeps capacity constant while

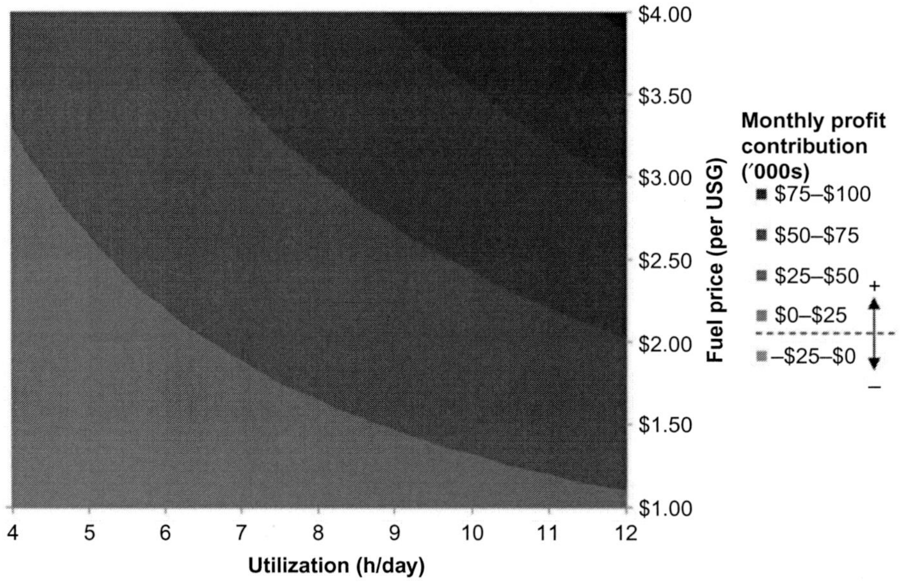

FIGURE 2.3

Utilization and fuel relationship.

CIT.

Table 2.18 Bombardier Fleet Forecast

World	2013 Fleet	2033 Fleet	Increase/Decrease (%)
20–59 seat aircraft	3400	1000	– 340
60–99 seat aircraft	2750	6850	40
100–149 seat aircraft	4650	8450	55
Total	*10,800*	*16,300*	*66*

Bombardier.

reducing labor, fuel, and other costs. The trend towards upguaging can be seen in Table 2.18 that describes Bombardier's regional fleet forecast.

The table shows a strong decrease in projected demand for small regional jets. Upgauging will be a common trend to analyze in the years to come, not just for regional jets but also for narrowbody and widebody aircraft.

FINANCING

The type of aircraft an airline wishes to acquire and the quantity of aircraft they want to order depends greatly on its credit rating and its ability to raise funds. Since the purchase price of new and used aircraft varies greatly, some airlines are limited to their balance sheet capabilities in their selection of an aircraft.

An airline has the option to either purchase or lease an aircraft. When the aircraft is leased, there are a series of monthly payments the operator pays to the lessor and a defined timeframe of the lease, along with other factors that will be discussed in more depth in later chapters. The airline also has an option to pay for the aircraft with cash or debt. There are several types of financing mechanisms an airline can pursue which include unsecured debt, Enhanced Equipment Trust Certificates, capital/finance leases, and bank loans. All of these strategies will be discussed further in Chapter 6.

MANUFACTURER'S PERSPECTIVE ON AIRCRAFT SELECTION

Since the Wright Brothers took flight in 1903, companies across the world began to rapidly research and develop aircraft. After more than a century of consolidation, the primary commercial aircraft manufacturers are Boeing, Airbus, Embraer, and Bombardier, which produce the majority of commercial aircraft today. However, Airbus has now taken a majority stake in Bombardier's CSeries commercial jet program and Boeing is expected to shortly finalize an 80% majority stake in a joint venture with Embraer's commercial aircraft and services business. In addition, other manufacturers, such as COMAC in China, are likely to increase in presence in the coming years as air traffic, and thus demand for aircraft will continue to increase, especially in Asia. The following

Table 2.19 World GDP Growth

World GDP Growth	
Region	**2017–36 Growth (%)**
Asia	3.90
Middle East	3.50
Africa	3.50
World	2.80
Latin America	3.00
CIS	2.00
North America	2.10
Europe	1.70
India	6.1
China	4.9

Boeing (2017).

section will analyze how aircraft manufacturers decide which aircraft to produce and how many to build in a rapidly changing global economy.

The process for the developing the next aircraft program starts with an understanding of the underlying demand for air travel. Aircraft manufacturers have forecasted long-term air travel demand for almost 60 years. They forecast air travel demand in global as well as regional markets and then subdivide that demand forecast into what types of aircraft the airlines will require to carry the anticipated traffic. Both regional and global demands drive the requirement for aircraft. Tables 2.19–2.21 show the projected world GDP growth in different world regions as well as the forecasted aircraft deliveries for such regions through 2036. It is standard practice to align air travel demand with growth in GDP in a particular region. However, with GDP growth, one must also take into account the various economic stages, spending power and current aircraft placement in a given region. Note that Airbus has a weaker outlook than Boeing in terms of forecasted units and value. Airbus forecasts a total of 34,166 new aircraft for the forecast period with a value of $5137 billion compared to Boeing's forecast of 41,030 new aircraft with a total value of $6100 billion for the same period.

Note that strong GDP growth in Asia leads to a strong order book outlook for that region. However, regions such as Africa have a strong GDP growth forecast, but that does not translate into demand for more aircraft because of low spending power in that region along with inadequate aviation governance. Further, geographical diversity of demand has improved greatly over time. In the early 1970s, the US market was the only market demand that was significant. Later it was the United States and Europe. Today there is a solid four-legged regional demand, namely, United States/Europe, Asia/Middle East, Africa, and Latin America that is tracked and forecasted by manufacturers. If growth or passenger demand in one region of the world is slowing, there is an opportunity for Boeing or Airbus to sell assets to another region that may be experiencing higher growth. Boeing, Airbus, and others use forecasted macro demand data and have detailed discussions with

Table 2.20 Boeing Demand Forecast

Boeing Delivery Demand Forecast		
Region	**New Airplanes (2017–36)**	**Value ($B)**
Asia	16,050	2500
North America	8640	1040
Europe	7530	1110
Middle East	3350	730
Latin America	3010	350
Africa	1220	180
CIS	1230	140
Total	*41,030*	*6100*

Boeing Global Market Outlook 2017–36 (Boeing, 2017).

Table 2.21 Airbus Demand Forecast

Airbus Delivery Demand Forecast		
Region	**New Airplanes (2016–35)**	**Value ($B)**
Asia	14,280	2271
North America	5620	689
Europe	6820	968
Middle East	2530	564
Latin America	2670	350
Africa	1050	144
CIS	1200	151
Total	*34,166*	*5137*

Airbus Market Forecast 2017–36 (Airbus, 2017).

individual airlines across regions to find solutions for the needs of future aircraft. In effect, the goal of an aircraft manufacturer is to produce aircraft programs that address the general global demand sufficiently rather than focus on producing niche aircraft for a highly specialized market.

COMPETITION AND FUTURE OF COMMERCIAL AIRCRAFT MANUFACTURING

In order to understand the duopoly of today's aircraft manufacturing industry, it is important to take a look at the history of today's two major commercial aircraft manufacturers: Airbus and Boeing (Figs. 2.4 and 2.5).

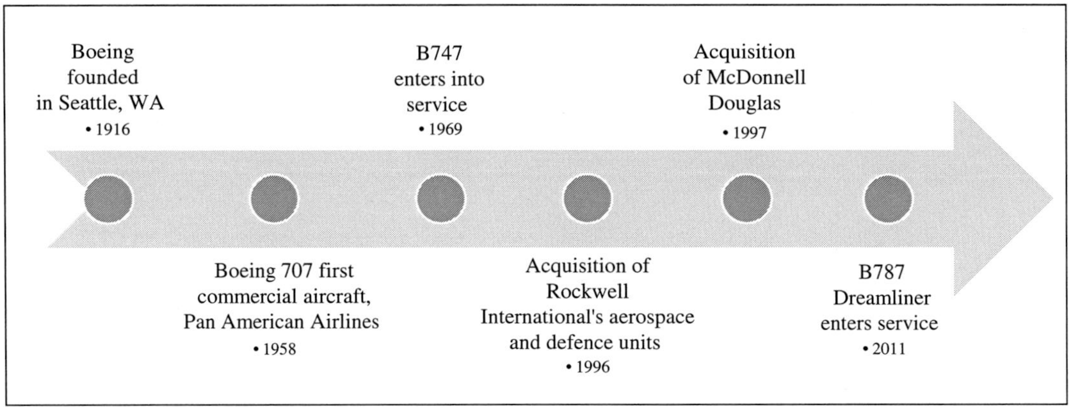

FIGURE 2.4

Boeing timeline.

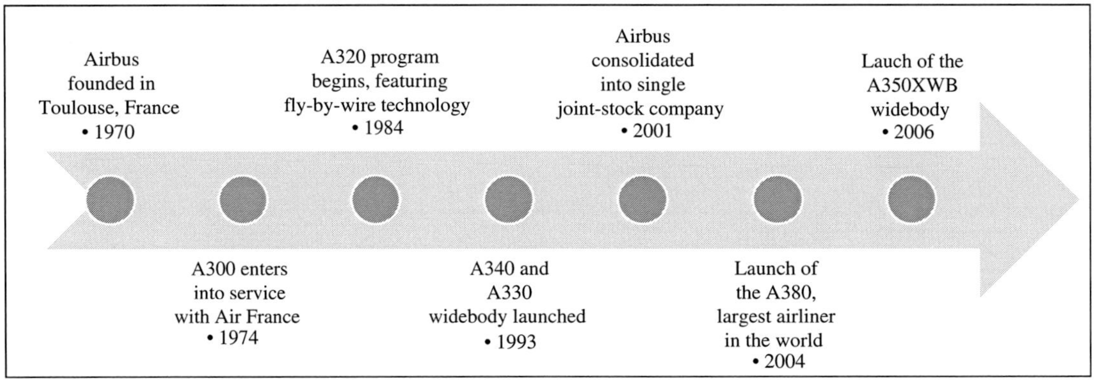

FIGURE 2.5

Airbus timeline.

Boeing

Boeing was started in 1916 in Seattle, WA, United States focusing on defense aircraft until after World War II, when it began introducing its first commercial aircraft, the Boeing 707, which went into service with Pan American in 1958. The Boeing 737 with twin jet engines entered into service in 1968 and would became the best selling commercial aircraft in the world. Updated versions of the 737 are still being produced today. Boeing introduced its first passenger widebody aircraft, the B747, in 1969 and later produced a smaller widebody, the B767, in 1982, which was followed the next year by the narrowbody B757. What was unique about these two aircraft was that they featured the same flight deck, meaning pilots and crew could fly both aircraft with only one type certification, which served to reduce costs for airlines. In 1994, Boeing introduced the B777 twin engine widebody, which was designed and engineered entirely on computers without even creating a mockup of the aircraft. Boeing's most recent development, the B787 Dreamliner, was first delivered in 2011 and was built of a composite material, which drastically reduced the weight of the aircraft and increased fuel efficiency to combat rising fuel costs which were in the forefront of every airline Chief Financial Officer (CFO)'s decision criteria at the time. In 1996, Boeing acquired Rockwell International's aerospace and defense units, as Rockwell intended to continue focusing on avionics and automation, and in 1997, Boeing also acquired the failing military and commercial US aircraft manufacturer McDonnell Douglas. By acquiring its competition in both the military and commercial industries, Boeing essentially competed in a duopoly with Airbus who started to gain traction in the market in the 1980s and has since proved itself a worthy competitor (Weiss & Amir, 2018a).

Airbus

Airbus was founded in 1970 outside of Toulouse, France, and originally consisted of several European aviation and aerospace companies as an attempt to compete with the Boeing Company. Its focus was in the short-to medium-range jetliners, eventually expanding to the widebody jet, helicopter, and defense markets as well. In 2001, Airbus consolidated from a consortium to a single joint-stock company and is owned 80% by European Aeronautic Defence and Space Company and 20% by BAE Systems (British Aerospace). Airbus' first aircraft, the A300, entered service with Air France in 1974 featuring 250 seats and two engines. Initially, it did not sell well due to the company's youth and inexperience until 1977 when Eastern Air Lines leased the aircraft type. Shortly thereafter the smaller A310 entered service in 1985, designed to compete against Boeing's 767. The A320 program began in 1984 featuring the world's first viable fly-by-wire technology and computer-based controls. The A320 family was born, expanding to the A318, A319, and A321 via lengthening or shortening the fuselage. In 1993, the A340 was delivered with four engines and the A330 with two engines later that year. In 2007, Airbus delivered the largest airliner in the world, the A380. This aircraft features two decks with a standard capacity of 555 passengers in a multi-class configuration and up to 853 passengers in an all economy configuration. The aircraft was so large that it required airports around the world to update terminals and taxiways to be able to accommodate it in commercial operation. In 2004, Airbus launched the widebody A350 as a redesigned A330 but with updated engines to compete with the Boeing 787. Unfortunately, sales floundered and Airbus was forced to redesign the aircraft. In 2006, it was relaunched as the A350XWB (for extra widebody). Designed to be slightly larger than the Boeing 787, it is also constructed with composite materials and new technology engines for better economics (Weiss & Amir, 2018b).

Possibility of new competitors?

When investigating the nature of the commercial aircraft-manufacturing business, it is important to understand their true business models. What is the airplane business? Is it product strategy? Engineering? Large scale manufacturing? Ability to certify? Ability to support? Ability to finance? The answer is that it is all of them. Not only figuring out all of those aspects of the business but also doing them all well is very difficult. Therefore, developing a reliable aircraft takes decades and a lot of advanced technologies. This imposes a high barrier to entry for new manufacturers, such as COMAC, wishing to enter the aircraft manufacturing market to produce reliable aircraft and convince the lessors and airlines to invest in them. Over time, new entrants may pose a credible threat to the Airbus and Boeing duopoly, but for now Airbus and Boeing continue to dominate the market. Despite the fact that Boeing and Airbus have a duopoly in the commercial aircraft market, the industry has been extremely competitive, which has put a lot of pressure on Airbus and Boeing to continuously innovate and improve the value proposition and drive prices down.

PRIMARY MARKET

Aircraft customers come in two categories: the customers that operate airplanes and customers that buy airplanes as an investment. Sometimes they are one and the same; however, many times they are not. Airlines are the customers that operate the airplane. There is also a whole set of bankers and lessors who actually pay for those airplanes, and their interest is very different from the interest of the airlines. Lessors view airplanes as investments and airlines view airplanes as their main, if not only, revenue-generating assets. Table 2.22 outlines the delivery demand for the major types of aircraft categories. Airlines will purchase aircraft directly from OEMs to generate income by operating the aircraft to fly passengers and cargo, whereas lessors purchase aircraft as an investment to earn income by leasing them to airlines. The table below represents only new aircraft; replacement aircraft will be discussed later in this section.

CUSTOMER NEEDS AND PREFERENCES

It is important to understand the customer needs and preferences in the market to know what investors and operators are willing to pay for an aircraft. Macroeconomic factors should not be the sole determining factor in the decision to develop and produce an aircraft as it can sometimes lead to wrong decisions. For example, fuel prices rose drastically in the late 1990s through 2008, and airlines and lessors demanded more fuel-efficient aircraft as well as larger aircraft to reduce frequency and CASM. Airbus and Boeing thought it best to focus primarily on fuel efficient aircraft such as the A320neo and the B737 MAX, as well as large aircraft such as the A380 due to the facts at the time. After fuel prices dropped, airlines found they could continue to operate their older, less fuel-efficient aircraft economically, and demand for new, more fuel efficient aircraft softened.

Table 2.22 Aircraft Delivery Forecast

Delivery Demand Forecast		
Aircraft Type	**New Airplanes (2017–36)**	**Aircraft Value (USD Billion)**
Regional jets	2370	$110
Single aisle	29,530	$3180
Widebody	5050	$1340
Large widebody	3160	$1160
Freighters	920	$260
Total	*41,030*	*$6050*

Boeing (2017).

In addition, after the introduction of the A380, it was discovered that there are limited markets for an aircraft of this size, as passengers prefer higher frequencies on smaller aircraft than the lower frequency of a larger aircraft.

Lessors and investors will focus on asset liquidity in connection with yield. Liquidity is almost synonymous with risk. If the aircraft is very liquid, risk is much lower, which therefore means the investor may be satisfied with a lower return. If a lessor is seeking higher returns, they should invest in less liquid assets to receive a premium. For example, the B737-800 is considered a highly liquid aircraft. However, the returns on this aircraft for a lessor tend to be lower due to large numbers of financiers who are offering creditworthy airlines low-interest rates to finance the aircraft, forcing lessors to offer low lease rates to compete. Widebodies such as the A380 or B777 have a much narrower customer base, making it much more difficult to redeploy the airplane and lessors face additional risk resulting from the costs associated with reconfiguration. The number of routes and operating customers is smaller, so the risks are much higher and few parties are willing to invest, generating seemingly higher returns assuming the investor's residual value assumption plays out as expected. When examining today's investment profile, almost half of the narrowbody fleet is owned by investors rather than the airlines, whereas only 30% of widebodies are owned by financial investors, and the remaining 70% are owned by airlines due to the higher risk associated with widebodies and the secondary market.

Another example of a category of aircraft which customers have expressed an interest in is what is referred to as the "middle of the market" aircraft. The gap between the A321 and the B787-8 in terms of size is wide enough to warrant an aircraft similar to, or slightly larger than, the B757. Airlines have the requirement, but manufacturers are hesitant to produce it because of the significant development cost associated with designing and producing a new aircraft type. Thus, manufacturers are not willing to commit to a new airframe program without a solid economic case, and that means enough demand to far exceed the development costs, leading to a profitable program.

MACROECONOMIC INFLUENCES

Recent trends in the market, as well as demand-management strategies, have helped aircraft manufacturers better manage short-term macroeconomic disruptions to their production process. First, manufacturers' production plans take into account the airline's fleet-planning processes (typically over a 15–20-year time horizon) rather than short-term fluctuations in macroeconomic variables such as fuel price, interest rates, or exchange rates. Further, there has been a significant change in aircraft manufacturing business models that in many ways are adapted or learned from their customers. Airlines have long realized that their seats are a perishable product, and the best way to fill them is to oversell (which is referred to as the over-book rate). The manufacturers have started following a similar type of production-management process where they sell more than their planned production because they know that historically, based on various market fluctuations (fuel, interest rates, GDP, etc.), some customers will cancel or defer their orders. This production-management process has helped the manufactures create the needed flexibility to shift different customers and keep their production rates fairly consistent.

Second, airlines have started ordering aircraft on a much longer horizon. Historically, aircraft order backlogs were 2–3 years. Now it is not unusual to have 5–7 years backlogs. This helps

Table 2.23 Demand Type

Delivery Demand Forecast	
Need Type	**New Airplanes (2017–36)**
Growth	22,030
Replacement	12,870
Retained	7630
Total	*42,530*

Airbus (2017).

Table 2.24 Aircraft Retirements

Aircraft	Number Delivered	Average Age at Retirement	Retired (%)
Bae 146	217	19.7	42
MD-80	1191	22.4	42
Boeing B737	1988	21.8	33
Fokker 70/100	322	17.2	25
MD-90	116	12.5	17
Bae Avro RJ	170	16.0	12
Boeing B757	1048	23.4	9
Airbus A300	559	22.8	51
Airbus A310	253	22.2	51
Boeing B747–400	690	20.5	17
Boeing B777	1053	22.6	14
MD-11	198	19.2	14
Total	*7805*	*21.7*	*27*

Frosberg (2015, March).

dampen the cyclicality of the market whether it is political or economic turmoil that causes volatility.

The third dynamic that helps smooth out manufacturing demand is that there has always been a replacement requirement. The installed fleet has gotten so large that replacement demand has grown to about 37% of aircraft being delivered. So, with such a large installed fleet, there is a continuous demand to update and renew the installed fleet. Table 2.23 shows the forecast for replacement aircraft along with growth of aircraft that will continue to stay in an operator's fleet.

Over 16,000 aircraft are forecast to be replaced over the next 20 years. Table 2.24 outlines aircraft types, delivery totals, average ages at retirement, and the percentage that have been retired as of 2015 (Frosberg, 2015).

Finally, another important dynamic, which has helped smooth out the demand and the production for aircraft, has been the diversification in airline business models. As recently as 2001, roughly 90% of the traffic was carried by "network carriers" such as Lufthansa, United Airlines, and Delta with regional networks and global international connections. The proliferation of the LCCs such as Ryanair, EasyJet, and others in the early 2000s lead to the diversification of the business model where both the "network carriers" and the LCCs have coexisted. This diversified business model has helped smooth the production process. This is because, the economic life cycle causes varying peaks and troughs in the demand for airlines with differing airline business models. For example, in a weak economy causing network carriers to struggle, the LCCs are counter cyclical and their demand grows as passengers look for cheaper ways to travel. As the economy improves, network carriers perform better as passengers become less price sensitive, counterbalancing the demand for aircraft.

ENGINE MANUFACTURERS

Apart from airframe manufacturers such as Boeing and Airbus, it is important to understand the dynamics that drive the engine manufacturers such as GE, Rolls Royce and Pratt & Whitney. This is because since Boeing and Airbus do not manufacture the engines, they have to partner with various engine manufacturers, to supply their aircraft. A commercial aircraft is typically operated with a turbofan jet engine. A jet engine is the most efficient type of aircraft engine currently developed and can propel commercial aircraft from speeds of 310 to 620 mph. The turbofan engine market is dominated by Pratt & Whitney, Rolls Royce, and General Electric. These three major engine manufacturers make engines for both Airbus and Boeing. Table 2.25 outlines the different engine types and manufactures for each major aircraft type. Note that some aircraft have two or more engine options while others have just one. On the one hand, an aircraft, with more than one engine option, may improve the bargaining power of the buyer. On the other hand, fragmentation among multiple engine manufacturers may make remarketing of the aircraft difficult for an investor, potentially leading to reduction in future values for aircraft with multiple engine options.

In addition to engine options, aircraft also come with a range of thrust ratings which affects the value of the aircraft purchased. According to Ackert (2012), the value difference between a 737NG equipped with CFM56-7B26 engine rated at 26,300 lb versus a CFM56-7B24 rated at 24,200 lb is about \$1.7–\$1.8 million.

Finally, as the aircraft ages, the value of the aircraft switches from the airframe to the engines and may be a crucial determining factor in an airline's decision to purchase an aircraft and hold it for the long-term to leverage the available green time left on the engine.

TRANSPARENCY OF AIRCRAFT VALUES

Aircraft values tend to vary greatly from one buyer to another and from one appraiser to another. There currently exists no system for mass marketing of aircraft such as the multiple listing service (MLS) used in real estate. Manufacturers' sell aircraft directly to airlines and lessors at discounts of up to 50% from their list price. Manufacturers' explain these deep discounts by pointing out that every aircraft is unique and configured differently which results in a broad range of prices for each aircraft variant. Airlines often tend to get lower prices, because each tends to buy aircraft in bulk

Table 2.25 Engines

Aircraft Type	Manufacturer
Airbus A320	CFM
	Pratt & Whitney
Airbus A330	GE
	Pratt & Whitney
	Rolls Royce
Airbus A340	GE
	Rolls Royce
Airbus A350	Rolls Royce
Airbus A380	GE/Pratt & Whitney engine alliance
	Rolls Royce
Boeing B737	CFM
Boeing B747	GE
	Pratt & Whitney
	Rolls Royce
Boeing B757	Pratt & Whitney
	Rolls Royce
Boeing B767	GE
	Pratt & Whitney
	Rolls Royce
Boeing B777	GE
	Pratt & Whitney
	Rolls Royce
Boeing B787	GE
	Rolls Royce

From Airbus, Boeing websites.

with the same configuration. On the other hand, when a manufacturer sells airplanes to a leasing company, they sell an enormous amount of flexibility to that lessor. The lessor can require different configurations for different customers raising their cost of purchasing each aircraft. Another reason for the variability in the price is due to the time lag, from the time an aircraft is ordered, to the time it is ultimately delivered. The manufactures price their aircraft in the year of the contract and then escalate the purchase price for inflation and other factors, up to the time of delivery. Manufactures also tend to sell aircraft with different optionality and value. Therefore, to get a true sense of the value of the aircraft, one must ask, when does the airplane deliver? What are the weights? What are the thrusts? What is the configuration? What was the flexibility that the customer had prior to the delivery of that airplane? All those factors are important to understand the range of prices for a given aircraft. Aircraft values and valuation will be explored in greater detail in Chapter 12.

SUMMARY

Fleet-planning decisions require a lot of research and are different for airlines and a leasing company. The decision to purchase a particular aircraft depends greatly on a firm's capital structure, maintenance abilities, and strategic goals. In addition to a firm's constraints, collaboration among engineers, network planners, financial analysts, and senior level management is essential in choosing the best possible aircraft for all the firm's needs.

For a lessor, fleet planning falls into two categories: the current market and the future market. Since aircraft lessors do not operate the asset, they must source an aircraft that airlines want to lease and operate. For a lessor, widebody aircraft tend to produce a higher return but are riskier. On the other hand, narrowbody aircraft are more liquid but can produce lower returns. Further lessors must take into consideration lease issues like maintenance reserves, residual values, and return conditions among many others to create a mutually beneficial scenario for both parties.

For an airline, the total cost of ownership is the main decision driver in selecting an aircraft. For an airline purchasing or leasing an aircraft, there is not as much concern with the residual value of the aircraft as their lessor counterparts. Airlines should view aircraft as a cost, not an investment, and seek to minimize the cost by acquiring fuel efficient aircraft at favorable prices through bulk orders.

Finally, aircraft and engine manufacturers are the group that makes the whole story possible. It takes decades to research, design, and build a new aircraft or engine variant. Manufacturers are tasked with predicting not only where the market is heading but also to provide a product incorporating the latest technology that customers (lessors or airlines) will buy. At the same time, they must manage their production process to produce and deliver aircraft and engines in a reliable and timely manner.

APPENDIX 2A: MINI CASE STUDY A

AIRCRAFT SELECTION (AIRLINE)

Spirit Airlines is an LCC based out of Fort Lauderdale, Florida. Their fleet composition consists entirely of Airbus A320 family variants. As an LCC, Spirit Airlines is most concerned with reducing costs including fuel, labor, and fleet costs. The A320 has proven to be a reliable and fuel efficient aircraft that is capable of most domestic missions in the United States. The aircraft seats up to 186 passengers and has a range of over 3000 NM.

Spirit Airlines has entered into a growth phase and is in the market to acquire more aircraft. The main goal is to examine the total cost of ownership for various aircraft and make a purchase decision based on reducing that ownership cost.

As Spirit's CFO, you are choosing between two aircraft to purchase: the A320ceo (current engine option) and A320neo (new engine option). Fuel prices have been volatile over the previous decade and having a fuel efficient aircraft in the A320neo would be most ideal but it comes with a cost. This particular aircraft will be used on missions that average 1000 mi and will be utilized approximately five times a day.

The following table outlines some important features of the two options.

	A320ceo	A320neo
Price	$25,000,000.00	$40,000,000.00
Age (years)	7	0
Gallons of fuel used per trip	4000	3500
Retirement age	25	N/A
Seats	186	186
Average mission distance (mi)	1000	1000
Missions per day	5	5
Maintenance costs per year (increases by $25,000 per year)	$325,000.00	$200,000.00
Service days per year	320	320

In addition to the aircraft specifics listed above, fuel prices are expected to range between $2 and $5/gal over the life of both aircraft. The A320ceo will also incur an estimated noise surcharge of $500 per mission.

Conduct an investigation into the decision criteria for the selection of the best possible aircraft to add to Spirit's fleet. The below guidelines should be used as a basis of consideration in the aircraft-selection process and presented in a thorough analysis supporting your decision.

Aircraft-selection guidelines:

Airline type

The structure and business model of an airline will have an effect on its aircraft-selection decisions. The factors of consideration for LCCs will differ from those of legacy and network carriers. In considering the airline type, factors to evaluate during the aircraft-selection process are as follows: Does the airline have an older or younger fleet profile? Does the airline operate short or long-haul flights? Does the airline predominately own or lease its fleet?

Mission capability

Ensuring the correct aircraft is selected as an appropriate fit for the missions of the airline is a crucial point. Considerations for payload and range, destination airport characteristics, noise/emission impacts, as well as configuration standardization should all be evaluated.

Fleet commonality

Additional aircraft entering an airline's fleet have the capacity to impact a variety of costs. How additional aircraft fit into the fleet family should be considered (standardization of the fleet for all missions versus operating a diversified fleet specific to each mission). The effects this decision will have on both tooling and training for mechanics as well as those associated with crew training should also be examined.

New technology implication

Advanced technology on new aircraft can provide revenue generating and cost-reducing opportunities. In evaluating the benefits of new technology aircraft, factors to consider are increased costs of ownership for that technology, and fuel savings and pricing opportunities resulting from that technology (Mason & Morrison, 2016). The downside risk of being the initial operator of an initial new generation aircraft versus a later vintage model which is likely to have benefitted from service bulletins and manufacturer troubleshooting needs to be studied.

New network opportunities

Increased utilization is accretive to an airline's profitability. Whether the aircraft under evaluation has the capability to create additional network expansion opportunities based on its age, technologies, and operational specification to increase utilization ought to be researched.

Availability

Time sensitivity for the need of additional aircraft should be weighed in the selection process. Typically, new and more popular aircraft have longer lead times for delivery, whereas older/in-service aircraft can be available earlier. Thus, time constraints can play a factor in decision-making. Cabin and galley configurations, as well as buyer-furnished equipment (which if needing to be reconfigured) can also have an impact on how quickly an aircraft can be ready for delivery to an airline.

Economic considerations and availability of financing

The value of aircraft, both initial purchase prices and resale values, can be considerably high. Given the cost, credit markets are instrumental in the acquisition. Airlines need to be aware of the how credit markets are evaluating specific aircraft models and variants, and if the markets are liquid and financing is available. The credit worthiness of an airline also plays a factor affecting the access to and the eventual cost of financing.

APPENDIX 2B: MINI CASE STUDY B

AIRCRAFT SELECTION (LESSOR)

University leasing company (ULC) is a leading global aircraft lessor with over 415 owned and managed commercial aircraft leased to approximately 90 airlines in over 40 countries. ULC's fleet consists of both single and twin-aisle aircraft, and their order book is currently one of the industry's largest.

As a provider of high valued in-production assets to its global customer base, ULC is looking to purchase a 737NG or a 737 MAX currently on lease to Mayil Airlines, Indonesia.

As Vice President—marketing Asia Pacific, you must make a determination of which aircraft that ULC must purchase from Mayil Airlines. The current market environment is stable, and there are no extraneous factors influencing the selection decision.

The following table outlines some important features of the two options:

	737 NG	737 MAX
Base value—current market value	$27,700,000	$54,000,000
Age (years)	5	0
Proposed lease term	8 Years	8 Years
Flight hours/flight cycles	16,500/11,000	0/0
Engines	CFM56–7	CFM LEAP-1B
Next maintenance overhaul	2 Years	5 Years
Maintenance costs per year (Increases by $25,000 per year)	$325,000.00	$200,000.00
Standard seating configuration	189	189
Missions per day	6	6
Service days per year	320	320

Conduct an investigation into the decision criteria for the best possible aircraft to purchase for ULC from Mayil Airlines. The below factors should be considered in the aircraft-selection process and presented in a thorough analysis supporting your decision.

Aircraft-selection guidelines:

Aircraft price

For a lessor, the price of an aircraft is a key factor in the selection process. Industry appraisers evaluate aircraft values in the form of BVs and CMVs which take into consideration the maintenance status of an aircraft, similar transaction types, availability, and the views of additional industry sources.

Aircraft lease rate

The aircraft lease rate along with price is an important consideration for you to take into account. Additional consideration such as maintenance reserve payments, return conditions, and security deposits are also important considerations in a lease, and we will discuss this in later chapters but are beyond the scope of this case study.

Residual value

Asset risk is a key factor assessing a lease transaction. If an aircraft is easily financeable, has a strong market presence, and a low probability of obsolescence, the residual value should track inflation over the course of its economic life, thereby allowing the transaction to add value to a lessor's portfolio. The economics of the transaction will be an underlying determinant for moving forward, and the ability to forecast if the aircraft will generate value over its economic life will determine if it will be a good candidate for an operating lease in the lessor's portfolio.

Aircraft order book

An aircraft's order book with a manufacturer serves as a clear indication of both its market share and its ability to hold its value over time. When evaluating aircraft alternatives, lessors should focus on the number of firm orders, deliveries, and the firm backlog to obtain a clear picture of the aircraft's future outlook.

Market penetration

Researching the regions where an aircraft has been deployed, the types of carriers that currently operate it, and the circumstances for which the aircraft was deployed are helpful tools in assessing the current and future value/need of an aircraft.

Production stage

Where an aircraft stands in its production cycle, and the level of sustained production can influence an aircraft's competitiveness in the market. Evaluating global capacity and room for growth provides insight into the future value of the aircraft.

Capital market outlook

Access to the capital markets and credit is crucial to the ability to finance and lease aircraft. A lessor needs to evaluate the lessee's credit worthiness, the aircraft's residual and future value, as well as the pricing of the aircraft prior to approaching the capital markets for funding. Given the lessor is not operating the aircraft, keeping the airline's needs top of mind ensures the right aircraft are ordered/funded to meet an airline's mission criteria.

Aircraft remarketability

Evaluating how an aircraft will progress through its economic life provides insight into the overall value generation of an asset. For an operating lessor, understanding the ability of an aircraft to be placed in the secondary market after the expiration of its initial lease offers key information necessary in the decision-making process. Points for consideration are the remarketability of the aircraft to second or third tier operators, the potential for cargo conversion as the aircraft ages, or the ability to part-out the aircraft should it become operationally or economically obsolete.

Aircraft transition and reconfiguration costs

Consider also the transition and reconfiguration cost in the event the aircraft is returned or needs to be repossessed. These costs are often very significant and might have an important bearing on the type of aircraft selected.

Jurisdictional and tax consideration

Consider the jurisdiction of the lessor and lessee and the role that will play in structuring the lease to protect the rights of the lessor and any additional cost that it may impose on the lessor. You should also consider tax implications of the lease rentals and ensure that the lease is structured in a manner that minimizes the tax burden for both parties.

Aircraft performance

How an aircraft will perform on the missions it is intended to fly and the specification options attached to the aircraft will help keep demand for that aircraft high during its life cycle. Recognizing engine configurations, certified capabilities, and where equipment sits in its maintenance cycle can aid in the conclusion to lease an aircraft.

New technology implication

Technology impacts performance; therefore, first generation versus second generation technologies on an aircraft should be measured. Understanding where the market is trending, and what airlines are requesting for future deliveries needs to be reviewed against current aircraft availability/specifications. Is current technology sufficient, is added longevity and value gained from newer technology, and will step-changes toward more cutting edge technology by competitors create functional obsolescence for a new generation aircraft are all questions that should be studied.

Fleet commonality

Business models of lessors vary, and determining if the aircraft available for acquisition and placement fits within that model should be evaluated. Is the lessor focused on maintaining a fleet commonality of widebody or narrowbody aircraft, or is the lessor's portfolio made up of a mix of both single and twin-aisle aircraft?

Global demand—aviation value cycle

The aviation industry tends to track global economic activity. At a given point in time, understanding where in the economic life cycle the placement of an aircraft falls can offer insight into both current and future airline needs as well as demand for an aircraft and its residual value.

ACKNOWLEDGMENTS

We would like to thank Dan Pietrzak of Delta Air Lines and Kostya Zolotusky of Boeing Capital Corporation for providing guidance and background information in the development of this chapter.

REFERENCES

Ackert, S. (2012). *Basics of aircraft market analysis*. Retrieved from Aircraft Monitor: <http://www.aircraft-monitor.com/>.

Ackert, S. (2013). *Aircraft payload-range analysis for financiers*. Retrieved from Aircraft Monitor: <www.aircraftmonitor.com>.

Airbus. (2017). *Global market forecast: 2017–2036*. Retrieved from Airbus.com: <http://www.airbus.com/aircraft/market/global-market-forecast.html>.

AVITAS. (2017). *Blue book of jet aircraft values*. Chantilly: AVITAS.

Boeing. (2017). *Current market outlook*. Retrieved from Boeing.com: <http://www.boeing.com/commercial/market/current-market-outlook-2017>.

Bombardier. (2017). *Q series*. Retrieved from Bombardier.com: <https://commercialaircraft.bombardier.com/content/dam/Websites/bombardiercom/supporting-documents/BA/DDBC0275_Factsheet-Q400_EN_V8.pdf>.

CAPA. (2018). *CAPA Fleet Data*. Retrieved from centerforaviation.com: <https://centreforaviation.com/data/fleet>.

Clark, P. (2007). *Buying the big jets: Fleet planning for airlines* (2nd ed.). Hampshire: Ashgate Publishing Limited.

Embraer. (2018). *Commercial aviation*. Retrieved from embraercommericalaviation.com: <https://www.embraercommercialaviation.com/commercial-jets/e190/>.

Frosberg, D. (2015, March). *Aircraft retirement and storage trends: Economic life analysis reprised and expanded*. Retrieved from Avolon: <http://avolon.aero/wp/wp-content/uploads/2015/03/Avolon-White-Paper-FInal-30-March-2015.pdf>.

Heathrow Airport. (2018). *Night flights*. Retrieved from heathrow.com: <https://www.heathrow.com/noise/heathrow-operations/night-flights>.

ISTAT Appraisers' Program. (2013, January). *Handbook ISTAT appraisers' program*. Retrieved from International Society of Transport Aircraft Trading (ISTAT): <https://www.istat.org/Appraisers>.

Mason, S., & Morrison, J. (2016). *The value of new-technology single-aisles*. Retrieved from cit.com: <https://www.cit.com/assets/0/74/83/350/4294967336/351/db6c88a6-d02f-4c14-8ba9-1a28bc679ea7.pdf>.

Weiss, S., & Amir, R. (2018a). *Airbus industrie*. Retrieved from Encyclopaedia Britannica: <https://www.britannica.com/topic/Airbus-Industrie>.

Weiss, S., & Amir, R. (2018b). *Boeing company*. Retrieved from Encyclopaedia Britannica: <https://www.britannica.com/topic/Boeing-Company>.

CHAPTER

PRINCIPLES OF AIRCRAFT LEASING VERSUS OWNERSHIP

3

CHAPTER OUTLINE

Aircraft Leasing and Financing. DOI: https://doi.org/10.1016/B978-0-12-815285-0.00003-1

AIRCRAFT LEASING

INDUSTRY LANDSCAPE

In the early days of aircraft leasing, airlines entered into long-term finance leases with financial institutions, and usually purchased the aircraft at the end of the lease. In the United States, banks were prohibited by the Federal Reserve from entering into operating leases as they were viewed as risky. Many leasing companies were subsidiaries of banks and were subject to the Federal Reserve laws. That started to change when private companies began leasing aircraft to airlines. One of the early pioneers was George Batchelor who founded Arrow Air as a cargo airline and International Air Leases, an aircraft leasing company based in Miami. Batchelor made a fortune leasing old aircraft in risky third world countries. In 1973 Steven Udvar-Házy, along with father and son, Leslie and Louis Gonda founded International Lease Finance Corporation (ILFC) in Los Angeles, California. Steven Udvar-Házy, is credited with creating the modern concept of the operating lease after the realization that airlines needed fleet and financial flexibility as they evolved from propeller powered aircraft to jet engine-powered aircraft. ILFC's initial lease of a Douglas DC-8 to Aeromexico spawned a dynamic global industry that is projected to be valued at over $300 billion by 2020. The North American aircraft leasing market is one of the world's most active and is home to some of the industry's largest companies by fleet size, including General Electric Capital Aviation Services (GECAS), BBAM Aircraft Leasing and Management, Aviation Capital Group, Aircastle and Air Lease Corporation. While operations of these companies are headquartered in the United States, many of their lease transactions involve an Irish subsidiary to capitalize on favorable tax treatment and treaties.

In the 1980s, Tony Ryan (founder of the Ryanair) launched Guinness Peat Aviation in Ireland. Ryan saw an opportunity to place surplus or underutilized aircraft "on lease" to be used in areas around the globe where there was a requirement or shortage of aircraft. This allowed airlines to improve their returns and have the flexibility to operate aircraft tailored to their missions. Favorable legal, financing, and tax regulations soon placed Ireland as the global hub for aircraft financing, aiding in attracting the world's largest aircraft-leasing companies to domicile operations in the country.

With the growth of global demand pivoting to Asia, many of the top global lessors have opened operations in Singapore and/or Hong Kong where similar regulatory advantages have helped in establishing the industry in the region. The growth of the aviation industry in China, fueled by the expected increase in the number of airports in the country to 240 by 2020 (Reuters, 2015), is driving the demand for added capacity. The forecasted need of 7240 aircraft over the next 20 years (Boeing, 2017) will provide an opportunity for airlines to continue to grow their fleets. Through acquisition, capital market access, and purchases, Chinese leasing companies are growing their presence in meeting this demand in the region as well as around the globe.

The current industry landscape, which comprises strong commercial aircraft fundamentals along with innovative funding options, has prompted the interest of new and experienced investment professionals and financiers to the aircraft finance industry. The International Air Transport Association (IATA) reports the growth in air traffic demand, load factors, lower oil prices, and utilization has increased projected airline profits to around $38.4 billion in 2018 (IATA, 2016). As a result, the demand for both new and replacement aircraft is strong as airlines look to meet the growing demand. According to FlightGlobal (2017), the number of aircraft operating through lease financing has steadily increased over time, from less than 2% of the global aircraft fleet in 1980 to around 40% in 2017 (Fig. 3.1).

The growth in global aircraft demand along with the trend of airlines to move more toward the use of operating leases presents a cautionary landscape of opportunity for the industry as lessors, and financial institutions look to capitalize on growth in addition to building in protection from

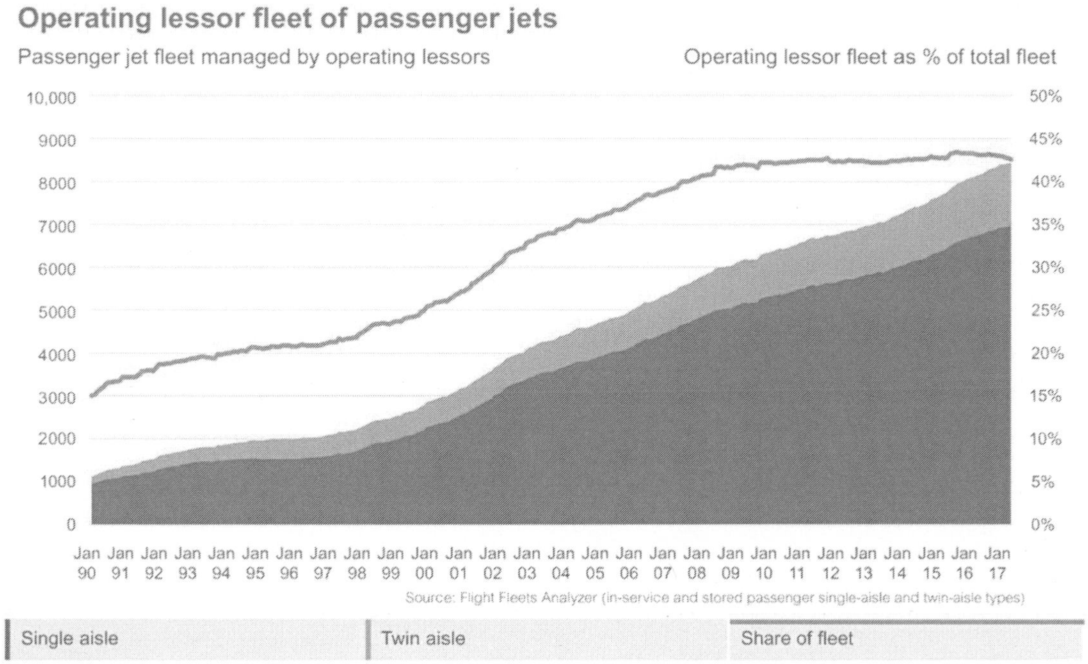

FIGURE 3.1

Proportion of total world fleet owned by lessors.

FlightGlobal (2017).

market risks. Funding aircraft requires access to the capital markets, and with an estimated $172 billion in new aircraft deliveries over the next 5 years, the monitoring of risk will be essential in maintaining the industry's development. Global and regional demand shocks as well as sustained order backlogs will be key barometers in defining the landscape and direction of the industry into the future.

The industry's top 10 lessors manage 15% of the global fleet of all aircraft (Fig. 3.2). While the fleet profiles are composed predominately of narrowbodies and widebodies, some lessors do hold regional jets and turboprop aircraft in their portfolios. Having a diversified portfolio of aircraft provides a hedge against technological obsolescence, fuel price volatility, as well as residual value and replacement risk. While new technology in airframes and engines is constantly evolving, certain market developments can renew interest in older and previously out-of-favor aircraft.

Strong industry fundamentals continue to drive airline growth, aircraft demand, and leasing industry prospects (Hallfors & Riggi, 2016). With lessors expected to account for 50% of the market by 2020 (Avolon, 2017), diverse funding sources will provide opportunities as new deliveries increase. Combined with a healthy aircraft-financing market and the growth in popularity of operating leases, the aircraft-leasing industry is likely to see the strength of commercial aircraft as an asset class become more widely recognized. As this recognition unfolds, the industry could face

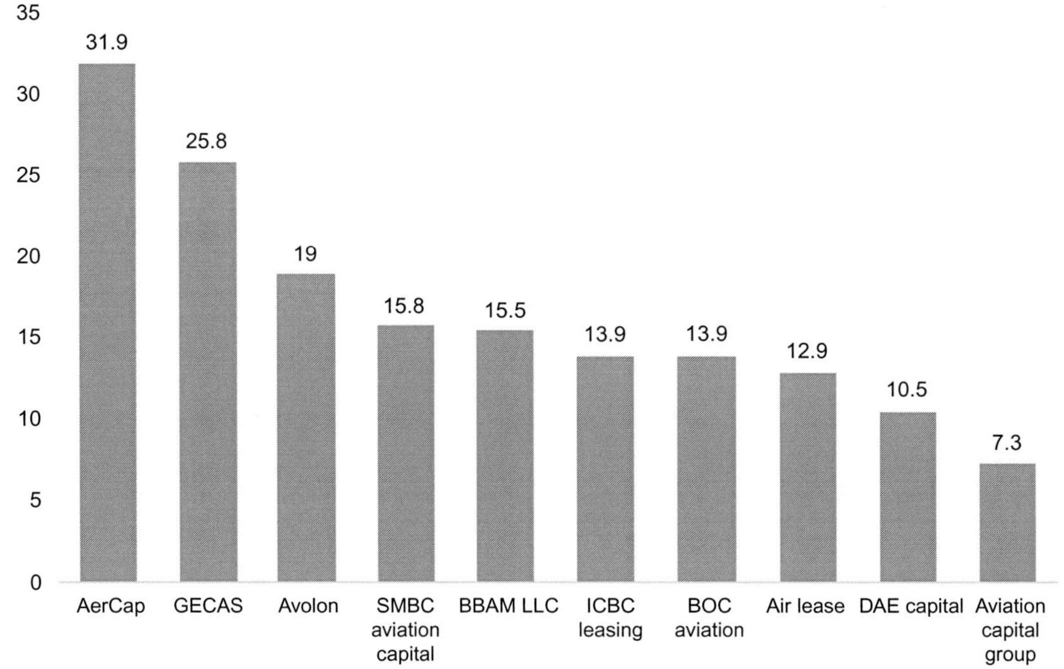

FIGURE 3.2

Top 10 aircraft lessors by fleet value (USD billions).

FlightGlobal (2018).

further consolidation along with growth in the remarketing and trading of aircraft. These activities will allow established lessors to free up capital for purchases of newer technology aircraft while at the same time allowing new lessors to enter the industry and build their fleets.

New entrants, strategic alliances, growing demand, and the retirement of older aircraft has opened the door for a shift in the aircraft-acquisition process for airlines. As many embark on expansion and re-fleeting, the buy and hold strategy undertaken in the past has evolved to include the use of shorter term leases, which offer more flexibility. As technology continues to advance, operating leases are an avenue that airlines will continue to pursue to prevent technological obsolescence and to capitalize on the benefits of maintaining a younger fleet. As global airlines focus on improving their operating performance and growing profits, short-term operating leases offer an airline more flexibly in their fleet to more quickly react to changes in demand.

For airlines, although purchase prices for newer aircraft are high, younger fleets can be advantageous due to their increased fuel efficiencies and lower maintenance costs. In certain economic or operating environments, the benefits of older aircraft could outweigh the benefits of purchasing a new aircraft; however, meeting passenger demands with a modernized fleet and maintaining an efficient cost structure often serve as important functions in the longevity of the organization.

DRIVING FORCES OF GROWTH

Increased access to capital and capital flexibility will help maintain demand for commercial aircraft leasing. The three main funding sources in the industry are lessors, commercial banks, and capital markets. With an ability to access diverse channels of liquidity, lessors can offer airlines competitive pricing and lease rates, as well as financing alternatives. Low-interest rates have given rise to high volumes of secured and unsecured debt as lessors have been able to take advantage of low-interest rates.

Passenger growth is forecasted to grow at roughly 5% over the next 20 years, with the key drivers being sustained globalization of world economies, increases in global tourism, continued deregulation in the air-travel markets, and decreasing airfares. Capitalizing on anticipated growth, lower oil prices, and improved incumbent airline profitability, new airlines will likely continue to emerge. The low-cost carrier (LCC) business model has experienced significant growth over the previous two decades and is positioned to offer practitioners growth going forward. The LCC's, through the introduction of lower fares, open up access to travelers that otherwise would not have been able to fly in the past and create repeat passengers who will continue to travel with these airlines in the future. Typically, smaller airlines are cost conscious and have more limited access to capital. In order to grow their fleets, these new carriers largely depend on financing, more specifically operating leases, for fleet expansion.

The long-term demand for new and replacement aircraft remains strong, and aircraft backlogs are at historically high levels, which offer attractive investment opportunities for investors. In 2017, Boeing had a backlog of 5864 aircraft, and Airbus had a backlog of 6691 aircraft (Airbus, 2018). Boeing expects that by 2036, there will be demand for 41,030 new airplanes, with a regional composition split between Europe (19%), North America (17%), Asia (40%), Latin America (6%), Middle East (13%), and Africa (3%). The order backlog, coupled with expected demand and financing flexibility, is increasing the incentive for airlines, lessors, and banks to place the to-be-delivered aircraft on operating leases (Deloitte, 2016).

In the wake of the 2008–09 financial crisis, when traditional bank lending was scarce, Export Credit Agencies (ECAs) offered a guaranteed backstop for debt to increase lending and drive growth. With a lower risk and the guarantee to cover any losses, banks and capital markets became more willing to provide debt and price aircraft more competitively. As liquidity returned to the market and rates reset to market-adjusted levels, a 2013 aircraft-sector understanding was released to level the premiums on ECA financing. While ECAs offered advantageous financing, the rising costs and increasing bank regulations have since made alternate sources of funding more attractive, placing lessors in a strong position to offer operating leases at competitive rates to airlines looking to grow their fleets.

BENEFICIAL MARKET DYNAMICS

IATA (IATA, 2018) forecasts suggest annual passenger traffic will grow to 7.2 billion by 2035, an average of 3.7% growth per year. The main driver of growth in passenger traffic is expected to come from the Asia-Pacific region. IATA anticipates that the size of China's aviation market will surpass the United States by 2024.

In the Asia-Pacific region, China is expected to be the fastest growing nation year over year; however, any slowdown in China's growth can detract from the region's overall growth prospects. Southeast Asia, Latin America, and the Middle East are also expected to have rapid growth due to increased accessibility to air travel and economic expansion. Strikingly, Africa hosts seven of the ten fastest growing markets, each of which are expected to grow by 7%–8% annually for the next several decades, albeit from a relatively low baseline. The table below presents a 20-year forecast of the growth in global GDP, cargo traffic, airline traffic, and passenger growth. It is interesting to note that cargo, airline, and passenger growth are all expected to grow at a faster pace than global GDP (Boeing, 2017) (Fig. 3.3).

In response to aging aircraft fleets, volatility in fuel prices, and technological obsolescence, the demand for next-generation aircraft has increased to record levels. The desire to operate more fuel-efficient aircraft has increased as aircraft and engine manufacturers have made significant design improvements to help realize operating efficiencies (DVB Bank SE, 2018). In addition, technological advances have increased, allowing for an improved passenger and crew experience during flight. According to Boeing's Current Market Outlook 2017, the global commercial fleet is expected to grow at an average pace of 3.5% per year, which is also expected to double by 2036. Fig. 3.4 shows the projected levels of narrowbody and widebody aircraft by 2036.

The sustainability of the trend of 6–10 years of production backlog relies on continued globalization, the continued growth of emerging markets, and the rise of new carriers offering service. Shifts in the regional dominance of air traffic from North America and Europe to Asia-Pacific is evidenced by Fig. 3.5 which shows the projected new delivery profile by region into the future.

As low-cost operators expand their presence in emerging markets, the opportunity exists to take a growing number of passengers to a growing number of destinations. In addition, with an expanding product offering with next-generation technology, new carriers' demand to increase their fleet sizes to compete in long-haul markets previously controlled by foreign carriers is also growing. Both scenarios will drive the new delivery growth in the next 20 years.

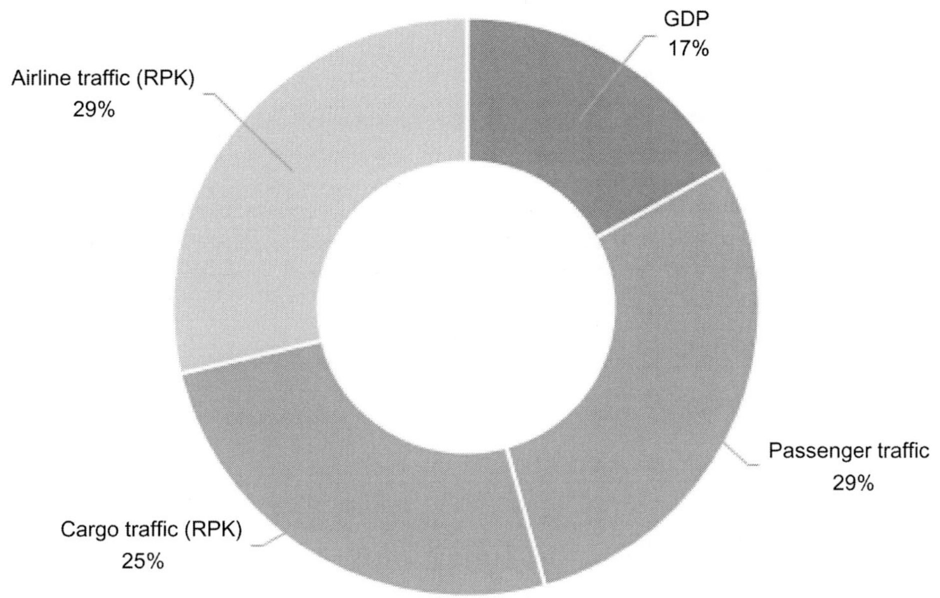

FIGURE 3.3

20 year market growth forecast (2017–36).

Boeing Current Market Forecast (2017).

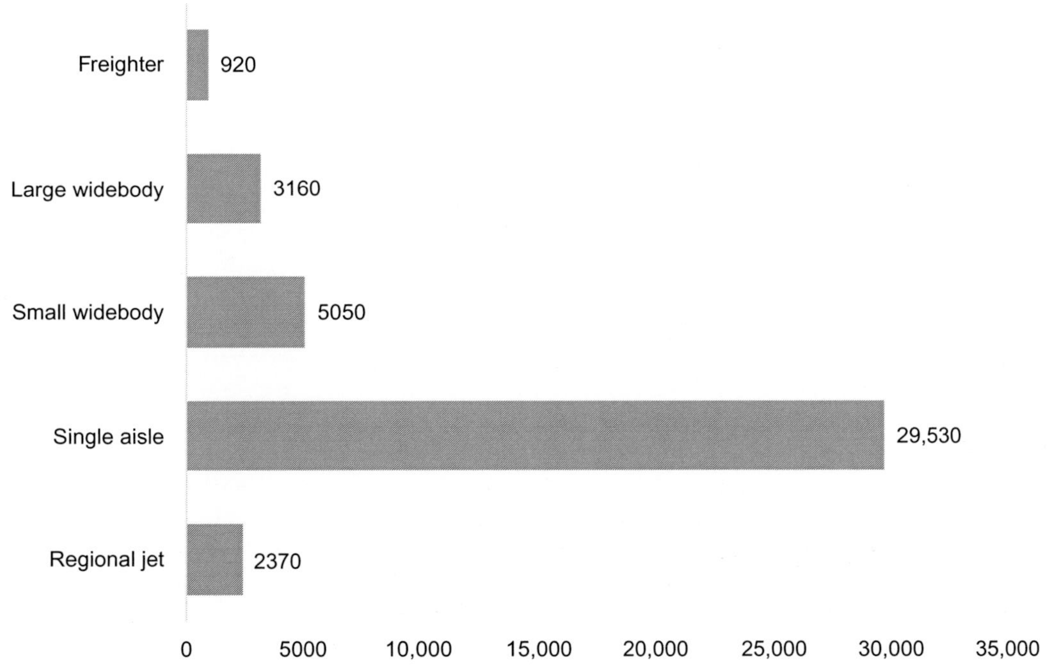

FIGURE 3.4

Forecasted new aircraft deliveries by type (2017–36).

Boeing Current Market Outlook (2017).

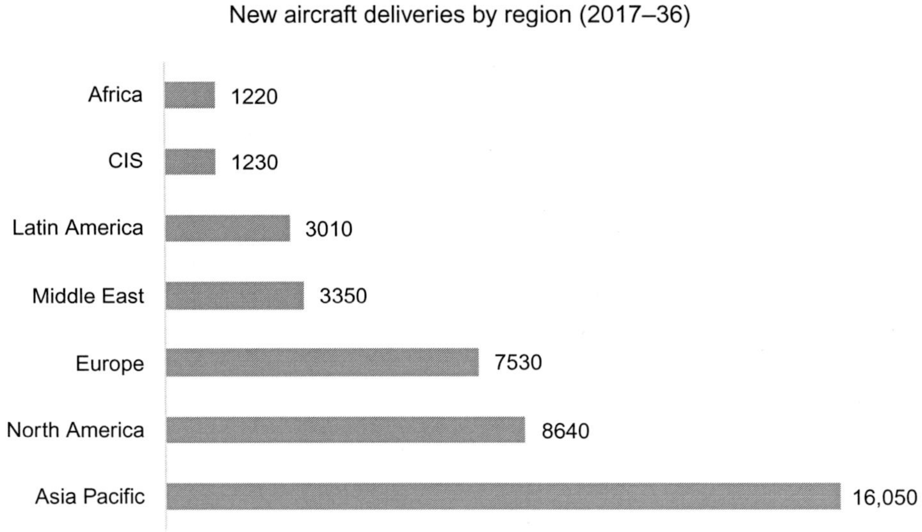

FIGURE 3.5

Forecasted new aircraft deliveries by region (2017–36).

Boeing Current Market Outlook (2017).

WORLD AIRCRAFT FLEET ON LEASE

Airlines all over the world take advantage of the benefits of leasing, albeit at different levels. LCCs tend to lease at higher levels than full-cost carriers (FCCs) and legacy carriers. Younger airlines, regardless of whether they are an LCC or an FCC, also tend to lease at higher rates than the well-established legacy carriers. In the North America, for example, as of 2018, Delta Air Lines, a legacy carrier, leased about 25% of its fleet while Frontier airlines, an LCC, leased 94% of its fleet. In addition, leasing rates differ regionally. FCCs in Asia consistently lease below 30% of their fleets, while FCCs in the Americas and Europe consistently lease 25%–50% of their fleets (CAPA, 2018). Trends in leasing change over time and with developments in the market, so it is important for lessors, manufacturers, and airlines to keep track of market developments to ensure proper fleet management.

SOURCES OF FINANCING

The continued evolution of innovative capital-market lending solutions has created a diverse range of choices for lessors and lessees to evaluate for individual transactions. In addition to the capital markets, transaction funding is seeing growth in unsecured debt, private placements, asset-backed securities (ABSs), enhanced equipment trust certificates (EETCs), and recently the Aircraft Finance Insurance Consortium (AFIC). These innovative solutions are offered at attractive rates and have increased the strength of the sector as well as attracted new investor attention. Fig. 3.6 shows the

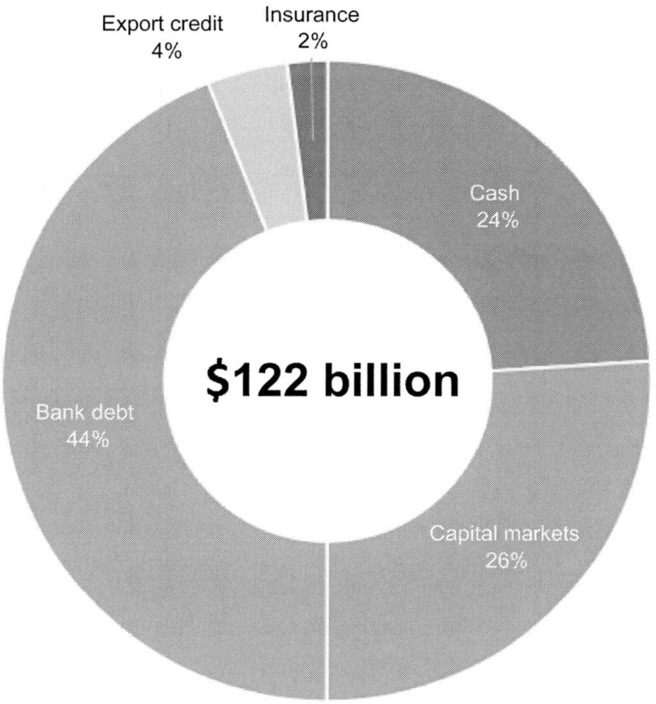

FIGURE 3.6

Actual aircraft industry financing sources 2017.

Boeing Current Aircraft Finance Market Outlook 2018 (Boeing, 2017).

breakdown of funding sources for the $122 billion in financing that was required to finance the new deliveries in 2017.

The generation of cash flows, access to capital markets, and bank debt are the predominant sources of funding needs for the lessors and lessees. While the largest source of funding for the lessors remains secured debt, the financial and operational flexibility of the unsecured debt markets is leading to an increase in its use. For the airlines or lessees, the three important sources of funding are leasing companies, along with commercial banks and capital markets.

We discuss below some of the important sources of funding for the lessors and lessees.

SECURED DEBT

This form of financing is a loan, typically from a bank, that is secured by collateral. In the case of using secured debt to finance the purchase of an aircraft, the aircraft contractually becomes the asset backing to secure the loan. When the asset is the collateral backing of the debt, the bank can seize the asset in the event the borrower defaults on its payment obligations. At this point, after repossessing the asset, the bank could then sell the asset to recover any balance owed. Secured, or collateralized, debt is seen as a way to reduce the risks associated with lending and is a favored form of lending when the borrower has poor credit. For a borrower with poor credit, secured debt is a strategy to pivot a lender's focus from their credit worthiness to the liquidation of the asset.

UNSECURED DEBT

Unsecured debt financing is a loan, also typically from a bank, that is not contractually backed (secured) by an underlying asset or collateral. Since there is no asset securing the financing, the loan is issued and supported based on an analysis and evaluation of the borrower's creditworthiness. Given the risk associated with this form of financing, borrowers must have a high credit rating. Due to high risk for the lender, unsecured debt obligations typically come with higher interest rates than other forms of secured loans, which can place increased financial burden on the borrower.

PRIVATE PLACEMENTS

A private placement is the sale of a security that is not listed on a public exchange. This type of security issuance is typically made to a small number of selected, qualified investors and is a way for a firm to raise capital. The investor base for a private placement tend to be large banks, mutual funds, insurance companies, pension funds, and, in some cases, high net worth individuals. Given the nature of the placement, the security is not required to be registered with the Securities and Exchange Commission, leaving the financial details of the transaction undisclosed. Typically, private placements take the form of bond issuances and do not require credit agency ratings. Due to the private nature of the securities, issuers tend to offer higher rates of interest to entice and compensate investors for added risk.

ENHANCED EQUIPMENT TRUST CERTIFICATES

An Equipment Trust Certificate (ETC) is a form of aircraft financing where a trust certificate is sold to an investor group, typically by an airline, to finance the purchase of an aircraft. The trust is managed on behalf of the investors and is used to lease an aircraft to an airline, with all lease rental payments being passed through the trust before being distributed to investors. Similar to secured debt financing, the aircraft is owned by the trust until the maturity date of the loan where the airline will then receive title to the aircraft.

An EETC is an extension of the above, involving multiple aircraft that are divided into two or more classes of securities with different payment priorities and claims on the assets. The EETC has a similar structure to that of a securitization, in that ownership of the asset does not lie with the operator but rather with a separate entity, which in this case is a trust. The main goal of EETC is to achieve credit protection and ratings that are potentially well above the corporate credit rating on the issuing airline. EETCs tend to have the following key features:

1. A pass-through certificate structure, in which each aircraft is secured by debt and a pass-through trust, collects the payments on the debt and allocates them to one or more classes of certificates. This two-level structure allows for defaults and remedies on individual aircraft debt

without necessarily triggering a default on the certificates because interest is paid when due and principal is not due until the final legal maturity date (but it is paid as available).

2. Credit tranching, which includes a senior class of certificates and one or more junior classes, and a priority of payments.
3. A dedicated liquidity facility, which is usually sized to cover 18 months of interest payments on the certificates. If an airline enters bankruptcy and stops paying on an EETC, the liquidity facility would be drawn to pay interest while the certificate holders are negotiating with the airline or are repossessing and selling the aircraft collateral to pay off the debt.
4. A legal framework that allows aircraft lenders or lessors (and thus indirectly the EETC holders) to repossess the aircraft collateral on a timely and predictable basis if a bankrupt airline ceases payments on its EETCs.

EXPORT–IMPORT BANK

The Export–Import Bank, or EXIM Bank, is an independent US federal agency chartered in 1934 whose purpose is to assist companies in exporting goods from the United States. EXIM Bank services include finance lease guarantees, foreign loan guarantees, protection against buyer nonpayment, export credit insurance, and other export-supportive activities (see Export-Import Bank of the United States (n.d.)). In aircraft leasing, transactions completed through the EXIM Bank are structured as capital leases and are typically performed via a special purpose company to allow foreign companies to more easily purchase or lease American aircraft. It is important to note that according to OECD Arrangement Guidelines, an EXIM Bank–supported loan cannot exceed 85% of the net invoice price of the aircraft. The remainder of the purchase price is typically obtained through a loan from a non-EXIM Bank–guaranteed commercial loan or funds from the airline directly.

ASSET-BACKED SECURITIES

A commercial Asset-Backed Security (ABS) is a financial security, notably a bond or a note, backed by cash flows from the receivables of a portfolio of assets. In an ABS, the underlying assets have limited liquidity and are individually difficult to sell. A firm holding multiple leases associated with multiple aircraft can increase their marketability by pooling a group of aircraft together into a portfolio to then be sold to investors in the market through a process known as securitization. Boeing's Aircraft Finance Market Outlook from 2018 notes that the ABS market is an important alternative for lessors to sell and/or finance a portfolio of aircraft. ABS has helped create new structures that will facilitate portfolio liquidity and create more efficient risk management of aircraft-residual values.

Aircraft-backed ABS financing has proven to be a viable and attractive funding option for lessors. Aircraft portfolio sales have been instrumental in assisting lessors in keeping their fleets young while generating revenue from asset management for third-party funds. Due to growing strength of the US dollar against major Asian currencies, aircraft lessors have remained in high demand by Asian investors. These investments provide a perfect gateway for Asian investors to enter into the aircraft-leasing industry.

AIRCRAFT FINANCE INSURANCE CONSORTIUM

Boeing recently announced that it has helped form an alliance of insurers to provide lenders with loan and bond guarantees for jet sales. An initial consortium of four insurers—Allianz AG, Axis capital, Endurance/Sompo international, and Fidelis SA—has been assembled to provide guarantees that loans or bonds are paid. Aircraft Finance Insurance Consortium (AFIC) issues an aircraft non-payment insurance (ANPI) policy to cover a lender's credit, aircraft residual, and jurisdiction risks. More than $1 billion of new airplane deliveries in 2017 were supported by the AFIC (Boeing, 2018). This is expected to fill a gap in aircraft financing created by the closure of ECAs in the United States and Europe. Recently, Apple Bank Inc., used the AFIC structure to arrange the purchase of a B747-8 freighter for Intrepid Aviation which is leasing the plane to Russia based AirBridgeCargo.

LEASING

According to the Boeing Aircraft Finance Market Outlook for 2018, aircraft leasing continues to grow in absolute size with a global market share close to 40%. The report expects good prospects in 2018 for the lessors due to strong demand and liquidity in the market.

TYPES OF LEASES

WHAT IS A LEASE?

A lease is a contract or agreement between a lessee, a lessor, and sometimes a third-party financier, where the lessor grants the lessee the use of an asset for a designated amount of time in exchange for predetermined and regular rental payments. Lease agreements in the aviation industry generally include the term of the lease, the monthly lease payments, the required maintenance and return condition for the aircraft, termination conditions, and whether or not there is an option for the lessee to purchase the aircraft for a discounted price at the end of the lease term. The chart below describes some basic lease terminology necessary to understand the components of a lease agreement. Chapter 11 of this text goes into greater detail about lease agreements and negotiations (Table 3.1).

There are two general classes of leases: operating leases and capital (financial) leases, which differ in their terms and accounting and tax treatments. Within operating leases in the aviation industry are wet and dry leases. Each type of lease is discussed in greater detail below.

OPERATING LEASE

An operating lease is defined as a contract between a lessor and a lessee of an asset for its use over a particular period of time (Vasigh, Taleghani & Jenkins, 2012). Operating leases have a duration that is shorter than the economic life of the asset, are not fully amortized, and do not include the transfer of any ownership rights from the lessor to the lessee at the end of the lease term. Throughout the term of the lease, regular lease payments (typically monthly rentals) are made to the lessor for the right to use the asset. In aircraft leasing, operating leases range in duration from 3

Table 3.1 Basic Structure of Leases—Definitions	
Asset	Subject of Lease
Lessor	Leases the asset to a lessee
Lessee	Obtains right to use the asset by entering into a lease agreement with a lessor
Lease term	Period of time for which the asset is leased
Lease rental payment	Periodic payments made by the lessee to lessor
Termination clauses	Condition under which either party can cancel the lease
Purchase option	Option for the lessee to purchase the asset at the end of the lease term
Return condition	Condition of the asset is required to be in at the time of return

to 12 years, and the level of monthly rental payments is unique to each lease transaction and is a function of the purchase price, lease term, and other market factors.

For a lessee, a major benefit of utilizing an operating lease is the flexibility it provides to operate an aircraft without a large up-front capital investment. In this scenario, a lessor or a bank purchases the aircraft from the manufacturer and leases the aircraft to an airline via an operating lease. Similar to renting an apartment or a car, the airline pays a security deposit (usually 2–3 times the monthly rental amount) to be held until the termination of the lease. The airline makes monthly lease rental payments to the lessor as well as a monthly maintenance reserve payment, if required, to cover the utilization costs of the aircraft.

Lessees do not hold any residual value risk associated with the aircraft and are not obligated to renew the lease at the end of the term. Currently classified as an off-balance sheet transaction, the monthly payments made during the term of a lease can be used as a tax shield in the form of an operating expense tax-write off for the lessee. However, a new law in the United States will be in effect from the beginning of January 2019 requiring operating leases to be held on the balance sheet, which will effectively eliminate the difference between an operating lease and a short-term finance lease. This topic will be discussed in depth in Chapter 13 concerning leasing and taxation. If the airline were to purchase the aircraft, they could take advantage of depreciation of the asset for tax purposes, which is often a larger benefit than writing off lease payments. For a clearer presentation of an airline's operating lease obligations, additional information is presented in the footnotes of their respective financial statements.

For the lessor, because they are the owner of the asset and bear the residual value risk, protecting the asset during the term of the lease is extremely important. Lessors include sections in the lease agreement to mitigate risks associated with the nature of an operating lease, such as maintenance reserve payments and redelivery/return conditions. These requirements are some of the ways the lessor attempts to keep the aircraft in optimal operational condition during the life of the lease and to moderate the aircraft's residual value risk upon redelivery. The regulations of the aviation authority will require the operator of a leased aircraft to maintain its maintenance records the same as if the operator owned the aircraft. However, in the case of a leased aircraft, the lease agreement may require the lessee to maintain even more records than those required by regulations and those records must be turned over to the lessor at redelivery. Lessors often include periodic inspections into the lease agreements as well to ensure the aircraft is being maintained as agreed upon. As the owner of the asset, the lessor can fully depreciate the aircraft over the term of a lease, offsetting the depreciation expense against revenues, reducing taxable income, and is also entitled to the after-tax residual value upon sale of the aircraft. The table below outlines the essential features of different types of operating leases. (Table 3.2).

Dry lease

A dry lease is the common type of operating lease. In a dry lease, the lessor provides an aircraft without the crew and maintenance obligations and passes all operational control over to the lessee. Under a dry lease, the lessee must include the aircraft on its operating certificate and maintain all required registrations and insurances. In a dry lease, the lessee will remit the monthly rental payments and maintenance reserves to the lessor for the use of the aircraft and will also have to provide crew, maintenance, and insurance for the aircraft.

Wet lease

In a wet lease, in addition to an aircraft, the crew, maintenance, and insurance are also provided by the lessor. Under a wet-lease arrangement, the lessee will still remit monthly payments to the lessor; however, in the case of a power by the hour type lease, these payments are made on the basis of hours operated. In addition, the lessee is responsible for fuel, fees, and taxes associated with their use of the aircraft. This type of lease can be seen in a sublease agreement between one airline (the lessor, who maintains the aircraft on their operating certificate) and another airline (the lessee) during times of peak operations or between maintenance events. Sublease agreements can also be included when a leasing company owns the aircraft but may require the lessor's prior consent.

CAPITAL/FINANCIAL LEASE

A capital lease or a financial lease is a long-term lease agreement that allows the lessee to hold the asset on their balance sheet at the present value of the lease payments and depreciate the asset as if they owned it. In this way, lessees can take advantage of some tax benefits of ownership, such as depreciation and interest expense, while maintaining the reduced residual value risk of leasing. Capital leases are not cancellable and usually contain a bargain purchase option at the end of the lease where the lessee can purchase the aircraft for less than current market value (CMV). This bargain purchase option is typically presented in the form of a balloon payment at the end of the lease.

Table 3.2 Types of Operating Leases

Lease Features	Dry Lease	Wet Lease ACMI	Damp Lease	Moist Lease
Aircraft	Yes	Yes	Yes	Yes
Crew	No	Yes	Limited crew	No crew
Maintenance	No	Yes	Yes	Yes
Insurance	No	Yes	Yes	Yes
Lease duration	Long term	Short term	Short term	Short term
Aircraft operators certificate	Lessee	Lessor	Lessor	Lessor

ACMI, *Aircraft Crew Maintenance Insurance*

In order to be classified as a capital lease, the lease agreement must meet one of four requirements as presented by the Financial Accounting Standards Board (FASB), to be discussed in the tax implications section later in the chapter.

LEVERAGED LEASE

A key characteristic of this type of lease is the involvement of three parties: a lessee, a lessor, and a long-term creditor. The lessee is typically the end user of the asset and should have a strong credit rating. The lessor, otherwise known as the equity investor, invests funds that are less than the full value of the aircraft. Although the amount can vary from transaction to transaction, lessors can invest from 10% to 50% of the value of the aircraft. Investing funds in the transaction places the lessor (leasing company) in an ownership position which allows it to then capitalize on the tax benefits from the depreciation of the asset. The long-term creditor is the final party and will fund the remaining cost of the aircraft. Given the level of the cost associated with the purchase of an aircraft, it is not uncommon to have more than one long-term creditor participating in a leveraged lease transaction. For the long-term creditors, this type of lease is a nonrecourse lease, and their lien on the equipment value precedes that of the lessor in the event of default, where they would then take ownership of the asset.

The leverage effect of borrowing creates multiple benefits in the transaction that can be passed through to the parties involved. Through the lessor's ability to depreciate the value of the asset and deduct interest payments made to the lender, they are able to pass the economic benefits down to the lessee in the form of lower lease rates. Under a leveraged lease, the lease payments made by the lessee are funneled through the lessor and go directly to the lender; the lessor then has a claim on any surplus remaining once both principal and interest payments have been covered.

SALE AND LEASEBACK

Under a sale and leaseback transaction, an airline, as owner of an aircraft, will sell its aircraft to a third party at an agreed-upon price, usually an aircraft-leasing company or a bank, and immediately undertake an agreement to lease that aircraft back on previously agreed-upon terms. The third-party purchaser then becomes the owner and lessor, while the airline that sold the aircraft becomes the lessee. The airline therefore gets an infusion of cash upfront from the sale of the aircraft while making rental payments over time and retaining the use of the aircraft for its operations. Further by transferring ownership through the sale of the asset, the airline effectively transfers the residual value risk at the end of the lease to the lessor.

A sale and leaseback transaction will allow for both parties to take advantage of the tax benefits. The lessor as the current owner of the aircraft is able to avail the tax reductions from depreciation and interest expenses incurred. The lessee on the other hand, who no longer owns the asset, is able to remove a substantial portion of debt from its balance sheet while making lease rental payments, which are treated as current expenses, and therefore subject to tax deductions.

Airlines typically place orders for large quantities of aircraft with a manufacturer when expanding or re-fleeting, which allows for substantial discounts off published list prices. To secure their orders, an airline may be required to fund up to 30% of their purchase price and make predelivery payments to the manufacturer. An airline looking to enter a sale and leaseback transaction close to the delivery of the aircraft may have the opportunity to sell the same aircraft to a third party at a higher price than was contracted for during their initial negotiations with the manufacturer. This provides the airline an opportunity to make a profit and deploy the capital back into the organization to fund operations. This aircraft arbitrage is an added benefit of the sale and leaseback transaction for lessees. One point that should be considered, however, is the effect the higher purchase price may have on the subsequent monthly lease payments being made to the lessor as lease rates are a function of the purchase price.

FACTORS AFFECTING AIRCRAFT LEASING

PROS AND CONS OF LEASING FOR AN AIRLINE

Airlines who are young, have a low credit rating, or do not have access to the capital necessary to purchase aircraft might find leasing an aircraft a better option. For an experienced full-service carrier, leasing provides fleet flexibility and helps with fleet planning. Leasing therefore has its benefits and drawbacks, several of which will be discussed (Conklin & Decker, 2010) and is summarized in Table 3.3 below.

Pros to leasing for an airline

1. *Reduced capital investment*

   When an airline purchases an aircraft, it is required to make a large down payment to the manufacturer. In addition, prior to taking delivery of a new aircraft, the airline must make predelivery payments to the manufacturer. If the airline is financing the purchase of the new aircraft via a third-party financier, there are interest payments to make in addition to repaying the principal borrowed to purchase the aircraft. By leasing as opposed to purchasing, the lessee avoids large down payments, predelivery payments, or interest payments for a new aircraft, by transferring that financial burden to the lessor.
2. *Increased fleet flexibility*

   Leasing gives the airline more flexibility with fleet planning because it makes it easier for lessees to keep their fleets young and technologically advanced. When purchasing an aircraft,

Table 3.3 Advantages and Drawbacks of Leasing for Airlines

Advantages	Drawbacks
Reduced capital investment requirement	Exposure to lease rate fluctuations
Increased fleet plan flexibility	Reduced tax benefits
Earlier delivery may be available	Difficulty financing aircraft which are not in high demand
Payments can be fixed or floating depending on lessee requirements	Conditions of return and penalties
No residual value risk	Operating restrictions

many airlines keep aircraft for a majority of its operating life. Over that time, new technology will have superseded the current technology, making the airline's fleet less efficient. By leasing new aircraft for less than its operating life, lessees can continuously update their fleet as new, more efficient technology becomes available.

3. *No residual value risk*

   By leasing an aircraft, the lessee is not exposed to residual value risk of the aircraft. Lessors are highly concerned with maintaining the residual value of the aircraft because they have to either re-lease or sell the aircraft after each lease agreement and would like to recoup as much of the initial investment in purchasing the aircraft as possible. A lessee does not have to worry about re-leasing or selling the aircraft at the end of the lease agreement, and thus it is not concerned with the residual value of the aircraft.

4. *Off-balance sheet financing*

   One of the more dubious reasons why operating leases are preferred is because they are considered off-balance sheet financing. Currently, operating lease payments are considered an expense on the income statement and not a liability on the balance sheet. This can paint a much more robust picture for the lessee, than warranted, by improving their financial ratios. However, it is important to note, currently the details of any operating leases must be disclosed in the notes to the financial statements, and financial analysts often adjust the balance sheet to reflect this liability. Off-balance sheet financing will no longer be an option for airlines, as a new FASB codification will become effective on January 2019 requiring all leases to be shown on the balance sheet.

Cons to leasing for an airline

1. *Reduced tax benefits*

   An airline that owns an aircraft has the right to claim depreciation expense, which is a benefit that reduces the airline's taxable income. In addition, interest expenses paid on loan repayments from financing an aircraft are tax deductible. Airlines who lease an aircraft cannot take advantage of any depreciation tax deductions of ownership in an operating lease but can take lease expenses as a deduction for tax purposes. However, in a financial lease, since the lease is held on the balance sheet, the lessee can take advantage of depreciation deductions for tax purposes, as well as deduct a portion of the lease payment as interest expense. Overall, the tax benefits of ownership are greater than that of leasing for an airline.

2. *Difficulty financing aircraft not in high demand*

   Aircraft-leasing companies perform market analyses to understand the types of aircraft demanded by airlines all over the world. Lessors then purchase the aircraft they feel will be the easiest to market, lease out, and finance. Narrowbody aircraft, such as the Boeing 737 or the Airbus A320, are highly liquid and thus make up a majority of most lessor's portfolios. Due to the liquidity of narrowbody aircraft, financing is relatively easy and inexpensive for the lessors, so lease rates are relatively minimal for lessees. If a lessee wants to lease a widebody aircraft, such as the Boeing 787 or Airbus A380, which are significantly more difficult to market, lease, and finance for a lessor, the lessee should expect difficultly finding these aircraft available to lease as well as higher lease rates than a narrowbody.

3. *Return conditions and penalties*

   Lease agreements for aircraft contain return conditions and penalties relating to the state of the aircraft upon return to the lessor at the end of the lease agreement. These return conditions usually relate to aircraft and engine maintenance, utilization limits, and general wear and tear. Conditions are agreed upon in the lease agreement, and if the aircraft is returned to the lessor in less than required condition, the airline will have to pay penalties to the lessor and will risk forfeiting their security deposit. Additional penalties would be incurred by the lessee if the lessee broke the lease and returned the aircraft prior to the end of the lease.
4. *Operating restrictions*

   Operating restrictions for the aircraft are negotiated between lessee and lessor and are a part of the lease agreement. Some of these restrictions can include how the aircraft is operated, utilization or cycle limits, maintenance requirements, and where the aircraft can travel or be stored. These restrictions may make it more difficult for lessees to operate the aircraft as part of their normal operations, as they need to consider these operating restrictions when utilizing the aircraft on a particular mission. Instead if an airline were to purchase the aircraft, they can operate the aircraft, however, they choose with no restrictions.

LEASING AND DEBT DISPLACEMENT

Leasing an asset, both operating (under the new leasing rules set to take effect) and financial leases, shares several similarities to financing the purchase of an asset. A lease agreement creates a liability for a company similar to that of debt. Every month, the lessee is required to make a payment to the lessor for the use of the asset, similar to the monthly repayment of a loan to finance the asset. Whether the airline leased or financed the purchase of an aircraft, it would have full use of the asset as well as receive all benefits of operating the asset, making leasing and financing comparable. Leasing an asset therefore is similar to debt and reduces the ability of the airline to take on additional debt, thereby reducing its debt capacity. This reduces the benefits the firm could receive from leveraging, including interest expense deductions for taxes. Since leasing and financing have similar effects on the airline, leasing calculations utilize the firm's after-tax cost of debt to discount future cash flows.

OPTIMAL LEVEL OF LEASING

Leasing an aircraft is more expensive in the long run than purchasing it, but the costs associated with leasing also come with reduced risk and increased fleet flexibility for the airline. A study conducted by Bourjade, Huc & Muller-Vibes (2017) concluded that the optimal level of leasing for the airline industry is 53.4%. However, the industry overall, including both LCCs and FCCs or legacy carries, is operating at about a 40% lease ratio, which is below the estimated optimum. The leasing industry has been growing significantly in the past several years, which could be attributed to airlines attempting to reach this optimal level of leasing in their fleets.

Airlines with low lease ratios who lease an additional aircraft will experience marginally higher return on investment than an airline currently operating closer to their optimal lease ratio due to decreasing marginal returns to leasing in the airline industry (Bourjade et al., 2017). As airlines lease above this optimal level, however, leasing could actually harm the airline's operating profits as the cost of leasing begins to outweigh the benefits of increased flexibility.

LEASING AND AIRLINE BUSINESS MODELS

The effect of leasing on an airline also depends on the business model of the airline. LCCs and FCCs are both most profitable when operating at their optimal level of leasing. LCCs, however, are significantly more sensitive to changes in the leasing ratio than FCCs due to their smaller fleet size and increased risk. FCCs typically have larger, more diverse fleets, which makes it easier for them to switch aircraft around to react to changes in demand on certain routes. Many LCCs have fewer types and amounts of aircraft in their fleets, making them much more sensitive to changes in their leasing ratio. Fig. 3.7 shows the economic profit of selected airlines in millions of USD from 2002 to 2009. Fig. 3.8 shows the lease ratio for the same airlines over the same period. These two figures together show the relationship between an airline's economic profit against its strategy for leasing. For example, Air Arabia, an LCC in the United Arab Emirates, has relatively low economic profit and the highest lease rate (86%) of the airlines shown. Air Arabia therefore may benefit from reducing the percentage of leased aircraft in their fleet as they are well above the optimal level of leasing. On the other hand, Ryan Air, another LCC, leases only 13% of their fleet, and it can probably increase its profitability by increasing the percentage of its fleet leased.

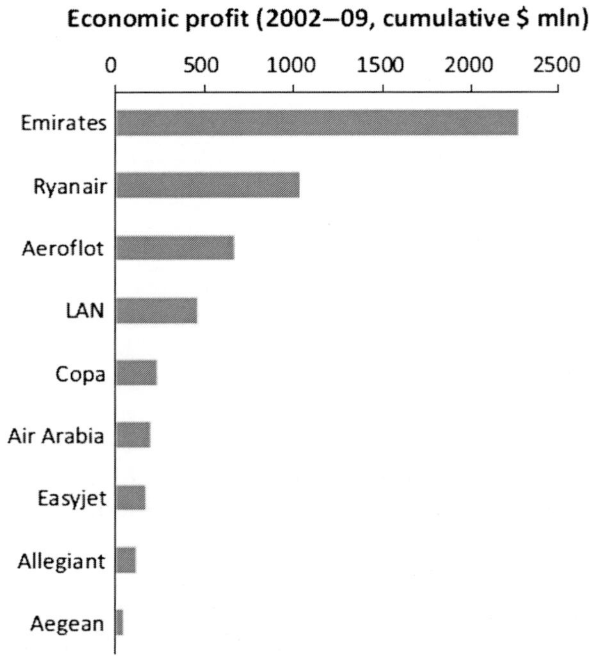

FIGURE 3.7

Cumulative economic profit of Select World Airlines (2002–09).

Bourjade et al. (2017).

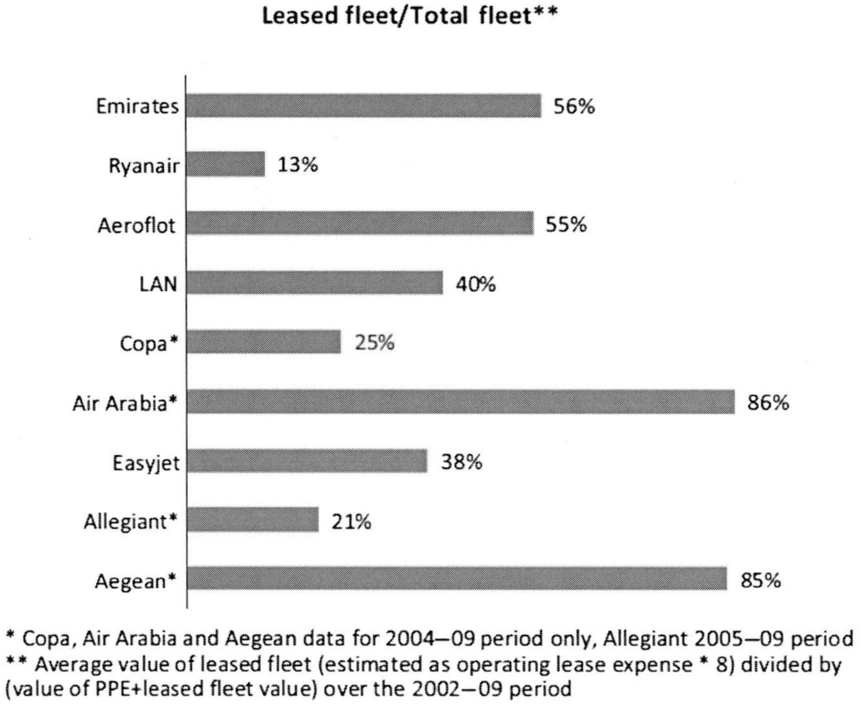

FIGURE 3.8

Fleet lease ratio of Select World Airlines (2002–09).

Bourjade et al. (2017).

AIRLINE EXPERIENCE AND LEASING

The age and experience of the airline also has a role in the effects of leasing on the airline's operating profit. The trade-off between the cost of leasing and the benefits of flexibility is different depending on the age and experience of the airline. The study from Bourjade et al., (2017) shows that leasing is less profitable for older, more well-established airlines because long-term debt is cheaper for them than leasing. This is due to the fact that FCCs typically have developed relationships with manufacturers and financial institutions and are able to negotiate better deals than with leasing companies due to their age and reputation. Whereas older airlines are able to adjust to changes in demand more readily with their own diverse fleets, younger airlines need to use leasing to create that fleet flexibility. Essentially, the cost of flexibility is less to a younger airline and more for an established airline. Fig. 3.9 shows the average age of FCCs and LCCs in the industry. It is important to note that while the study showed that age and business model were unrelated variables, most FCCs are above the age of 40, while most LCCs are below the age of 40.

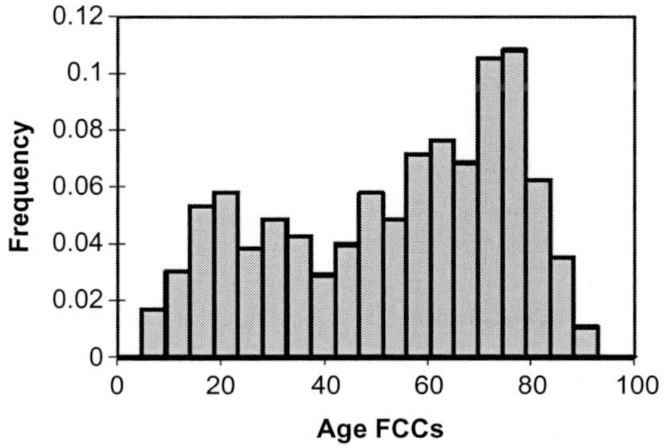

FIGURE 3.9

Average age of FCCs and LCCs. *FCC*, Full-cost carrier; *LCC*, low-cost carrier.

Bourjade et al. (2017).

ACCOUNTING IMPLICATIONS OF LEASING

When a business, or individual, purchases an asset, the IRS allows for tax deductible benefits to be realized on the asset's depreciation and interest payments made on the loan. The added benefits of depreciation can also be realized at the time of sale of the asset if the market value of the asset is below the depreciated book value.

One reason, for the growth of the leasing industry, has been the tax differential that exists between highly profitable leasing companies, compared to the low profits, in the airline industry. As the owner of the asset, lessors get a bigger tax deduction from depreciation and interest expenses and are able to pass on that benefit to airlines in terms of lower lease payments. This has made leasing attractive to airlines compared to purchase, because in addition to the flexibility, it provides for fleet management; often due to their low profitability, airlines are unable to fully use the tax benefit of depreciation and interest tax deduction from owning the aircraft.

Operating leases

As previously discussed, operating leases are currently not held on the lessee's balance sheet, as they do not own the aircraft and thus are not able to take advantage of tax benefits of ownership. Lessees report lease rental payments as an expense on the income statement and for tax purposes. However, details of operating leases are voluntarily disclosed in the footnotes to the financial statements. Not having operating leases on the balance sheet for airlines made balance sheets and financial ratios look more robust, as they did not reflect all liabilities of the airline.

A new financial accounting standard (FAS), issued by the FASB, will make it a requirement that all leases less than 12 months must be held on the company's balance sheet, effective January 1, 2019 for all companies. This has been done in an attempt to make companies' balance sheets more accurately reflect short and long-term liabilities. This FAS will be discussed fully in Chapter 13.

Table 3.4 Comparison of Operating and Finance Leases

Operating Lease	Finance Lease
Only annual-operating lease rental payments are reported as operating expenses on the income statement	Present value of future minimum lease payment is recorded as an asset in the balance sheet
This kind of financing completely bypasses balance sheet	An equal amount is recorded as a liability in the balance sheet to represent the lease obligation
The tax benefits of depreciation deductions belong to the owner of the asset, the lessor	Minimum lease payment is reported as interest and depreciation expenses in the income statement
Efforts are underway to better reflect operating leases on the firm's balance sheet	The tax benefits of depreciation deductions belong to the lessee

Financial leases

Financial leases are held on the company's balance sheet, making the company effectively the owner of the asset for accounting and tax purposes. Airlines are able to take advantage of depreciation expense and interest expense on lease payments as a tax deduction. The amount of the liability recorded on the balance sheet is equal to the present value of all of the lease payments to be made during the course of the lease, which is then depreciated, typically using modified accelerated cost-recovery system (MACRS) or the straight-line method. Table 3.4, summarizes and compares the accounting and tax implication of an operating vs. a financial lease.

In order to be classified as a financial lease, FAS 13 states that one of the four following requirements must be met in the lease:

1. The present value of lease payments must be 90% or more of the total asset value.
2. The lease transfers ownership of the asset.
3. The lease term is 75% or more of the estimated economic life of the asset.
4. The lessee has the option to purchase the asset at a price below fair market value at the end of the lease (bargain purchase option).

REAL WORLD APPLICATION

Lease Versus Buy Decisions at United Airlines

How does United Airlines make decisions on whether to lease or buy? What are the departments and personnel involved in the decision process? Does United Airlines lease or own most of its aircraft? In other words, what percentage of United Airlines's fleet is on lease? Does their decision to own versus lease differ for new versus old aircraft? We explore these ideas in this real world application of the lease versus buy decision at United Airlines.

The process for lease versus buy decisions at United Airlines starts in the fleet planning and management department which then coordinates with different departments at United Airlines such as technical operations, network planning, marketing, flight operations, inflight, and finance on United Airlines long-term fleet plan which then leads to a decision on what aircraft to order from the major manufacturers such as Boeing and Airbus. United Airlines owns both Boeing and Airbus aircraft, and currently its order book comprises predominantly Boeing Aircraft with some Airbus 350 aircraft on order from Airbus. The order book typically goes out somewhere between 5 and 10 years with firm orders as well as options to purchase aircraft. United Airline's fleet planning therefore is a long-term process. The next step in the process is to finance the aircraft, and the corporate finance team is brought into the decision-making

(Continued)

(CONTINUED)

process at this stage to decide the optimal way to finance the aircraft. United Airlines typically finances every new aircraft it acquires rather than paying cash upfront to purchase the aircraft. United Airlines thinks of their new aircraft as a very good collateral to leverage and get inexpensive financing and lease rates in a sale and leaseback transaction.

An important consideration in the process of lease versus buy decision for United Airlines is their decision as to how long they want to keep their aircraft. United Airlines believes that an important reason for leasing is that it allows the flexibility for an airline to exit the aircraft after the first lease term (which is usually 10–12 years). United Airlines, however, prefers to own most of its aircraft because they acquire new aircraft which they consider "core aircraft," which they expect to operate for their entire useful life (which is usually 25–30 years). United Airline's most recent fleet plan calls for its mainline operation to grow from 744 aircraft at the end of 2017 to 768 by end of 2018. The carrier has a new-order backlog of 220 aircraft, consisting of 160 737 MAX family models (Aviation Week, March 19, 2018).

In making the lease versus buy decision, United Airlines compares the cost of financing the aircraft to lease rates they would obtain from a sale and leaseback transaction. One of the major factors that drive the decision for United Airlines is the residual value of the aircraft at the end of the expected lease term. The fleet group would determine based on past experience what the break-even residual value would be for popular aircraft such as the B737 or the A320. According to United Airline's calculation, this break-even point is about 29% of the original price of the aircraft. In other words, if United Airlines feels that the aircraft will retain more than 29% of its initial value, they would purchase the aircraft, if not they would lease the aircraft. United Airline's analysis leads them to conclude that owning is better than leasing for United Airlines, especially for new aircraft as new aircraft rarely lose more than 29% of the value at the end of the lease term. United Airlines currently owns about 78% of their fleet with 22% of their fleet on lease.

What about used aircraft? Does United Airlines still prefer to own rather than lease? Here the answer is not that clear. United Airlines prefers to lease its used aircraft fleet to give it some flexibility and supplement their purchase of new aircraft for their core aircraft fleet. Further, most of the used aircraft lease market is dominated by leasing companies, and United Airlines feels that its options are limited to purchase them. However, United Airlines has been recently purchasing leased used aircraft from their own fleet. In 2017, it purchased 46 aircraft from its own fleet and plans to purchase additional aircraft from the 60 aircraft with leases that will expire in 2018 (Aviation Week, March 2018).

United Airline's strategy, however, may not work for all airlines. Airlines with weaker credit or a low-cost business model may prefer the added flexibility of leasing to ownership. Further, other airlines may not necessarily have the access to capital that United Airlines has, making leasing their only option. Leasing companies are also willing to take more credit risk and lease to airlines with lower credit, making leasing a more viable option for these carriers.

This analysis is based on an interview with United Airlines Chief Financial Officer, Gerry Laderman and data from Aviation Week.

DECISION TOOLS FOR ANALYSIS OF LEASE VERSUS BUY DECISIONS

In their analysis, firms looking to fund capital expenditures with today's dollars evaluate all future cash flows in comparison to the initial investment outflow. When airline management or a lessor is evaluating their fleet-planning options, several tools exist for calculating the impact of their decisions. The considerations however are different when you look at it from an airline perspective versus a lessor perspective. An airline, as the operator of the aircraft, is looking to minimize the cost of financing the aircraft from either purchase or lease of the aircraft. Therefore, for an airline, lease versus buy is a financing decision (Economist, 2012). The lessor, as the investor, is interested in maximizing returns from leasing the aircraft to the lessee. For a lessor, therefore, this is an investment decision.

CASH FLOWS FROM LEASE VERSUS BUY OPTION FOR A LESSEE

If a lessee decides to lease the aircraft, the relevant cash flows for evaluation is the lease payment for the lease and any associated tax benefits from the lease (Table 3.5). The lessee may also be required to make maintenance reserve payments, but we discuss maintenance reserve payments in a later (Chapter 9) chapter to keep the analysis simple here.

For the purchase option, the lessee can either finance the initial upfront payment of the aircraft with a cash payment or finance it via a loan. If the lessee purchases the aircraft and finances it with a loan, then the lessee gets depreciation tax benefit as well as the interest expense on the loan is tax deductible. Finally, since the lessee owns the aircraft, the lessee is entitled to the after tax residual value of the aircraft (Table 3.6).

The final step in this process is to compare the current cost or present value cost of purchase versus lease. If the present value cost of leasing is lower than the present value cost of purchase, then there is a net advantage to leasing (NAL), and therefore leasing is preferred to purchase. If on the other hand the present value cost of purchase is lower than the present value of leasing, purchasing is preferred.

In other words, the

$$\text{NAL} = \text{Present Value}_{\text{Lease}} - \text{Present Value}_{\text{Purchase}}$$

$$\text{If NAL} > 0,\ \text{leasing is preferred}$$
$$\text{If NAL} < 0,\ \text{purchase is preferred}$$

In order to get to the present value of the purchase and lease, however, one has to use a discount rate to discount the present value of the future cash flows, and next we discuss what should be the relevant discount rate.

Table 3.5 Cash Flow of a Lease to a Lessee

Lease Option	Net Impact
Initial investment	Cash outflow
Lease payments	Cash outflow
Lease payment tax deduction	Cash inflow

Table 3.6 Cash Flow of Purchase to a Lessee

Buy/Purchase Option	Net Impact
Loan payments	Cash outflow
Loan interest tax deduction	Cash inflow
Depreciation tax deduction	Cash inflow
Residual value	Inflow/outflow based on salvage value

DISCOUNT RATE

The lessee and the lessor have to make decisions today based on cash flows they expect in the future. Therefore, the future cash flows need to be discounted to the present using a discount rate. The discount rate reflects the level of risk associated with the cash flows and can be thought of as rate of return required by shareholders, the firm's cost of borrowing funds, or a combination of the two. In general, the discount rate and the present value of future cash flows have an inverse relationship. As discussed previously, leasing is similar to debt financing, and therefore the relevant discount rate for a lessee making a lease versus buy decision is the after-tax cost of debt.

$$\textit{After-Tax Cost of Debt} = \textit{Before-Tax Cost of Debt} \times (\textit{1} - \textit{incremental tax rate})$$

The after-tax cost of debt is the interest rate that a firm will pay on borrowed funds, less the impact of their incremental income tax rate. A firm's after-tax cost of debt can vary, depending on a firm's profitability. If profits are low, a firm's marginal tax rate will also be low; therefore, the after-tax cost of debt and hence the discount rate will be high. Conversely, as the firm generates more profits, it will incur a higher tax rate, which will cause its after-tax cost of debt and the discount rate to decline.

DEPRECIATION TAX BENEFIT

One of the benefits of a purchase is the depreciation tax benefit from owning an aircraft. One can either use the MACRS or a straight-line method to depreciate the asset. Under MACRS, the cost of the aircraft is recovered over a 7-year period (due to the half-year convention, however, this extends to the 8th year). The IRS publishes the percentages to depreciate each year and the total percentage adds up to 100% or the asset is assumed to be fully depreciated (e.g., an asset depreciated over 7 years would be depreciated each year as follows: 14.29%, 24.49%, 17.49%, 12.49%, 8.93%, 8.92%, 8.93%, and 4.46%).

Under the straight-line method, the cost of the asset less salvage value is depreciated equally over the life of the asset. Thus, if the initial investment in the aircraft is $1,000,000 with a salvage value of $50,000 and asset has an expected life of 5 years, the straight-line depreciation would be

$$\text{Straight-line depreciation} = (\$1,000,000 - \$50,000)/5 = \$190,000 \text{ depreciation each year}$$

Once the amount of depreciation is determined for each year using either the MACRS or straight-line methods, this amount would be multiplied by the firm's corporate tax rate to show the tax benefit due to depreciation.

In the above example, assuming a tax rate of 35% and a depreciation of $190,000 each year, the tax benefit would be

$$\text{Tax benefit} = 0.35 \times \$190,000 = \$66,500$$

RESIDUAL VALUE OF AIRCRAFT

A key driver of the lease vs buy decision is the residual value of the aircraft. Ensuring an aircraft retains the best possible value during the lease term is of utmost importance to the aircraft owner (airline, lessor or bank). For loan and lease modeling purposes, the aircraft trading market values used aircraft based on the CMV of the asset, assuming the aircraft has no leases or additional encumbrances attached to it. Appraisers may adjust the base value to aid in determining the CMV for a given transaction under the prevailing market conditions. Forecasting an accurate residual value of an aircraft is important for both an airline and a lessor in order to understand when to add incremental aircraft to a fleet or a portfolio. In addition, it is also of significant importance in structuring financing packages, as the tax implications on the residual values at the termination of a lease or sale can influence the NPV analysis determining the viability of the loan or lease. The below chart from PK AirFinance presents resale values for commercial jet aircraft as a function of their age from 1974 to 1998, illustrating the volatility and uncertainty that can exist in the market (Fig. 3.10).

Many factors affect the residual value including age, production status, supply/demand, performance, configuration, maintenance status, as well as a host of additional factors.

From a lease versus buy analysis, as mentioned previously, as the owner of the aircraft, the purchaser is entitled to the after-tax cash flow from the sale of the asset at the end of the comparable lease period. For aircraft that have better value retention (such as the A320neo or 737 MAX), this may sway the lessee to purchase the aircraft than opt for leasing.

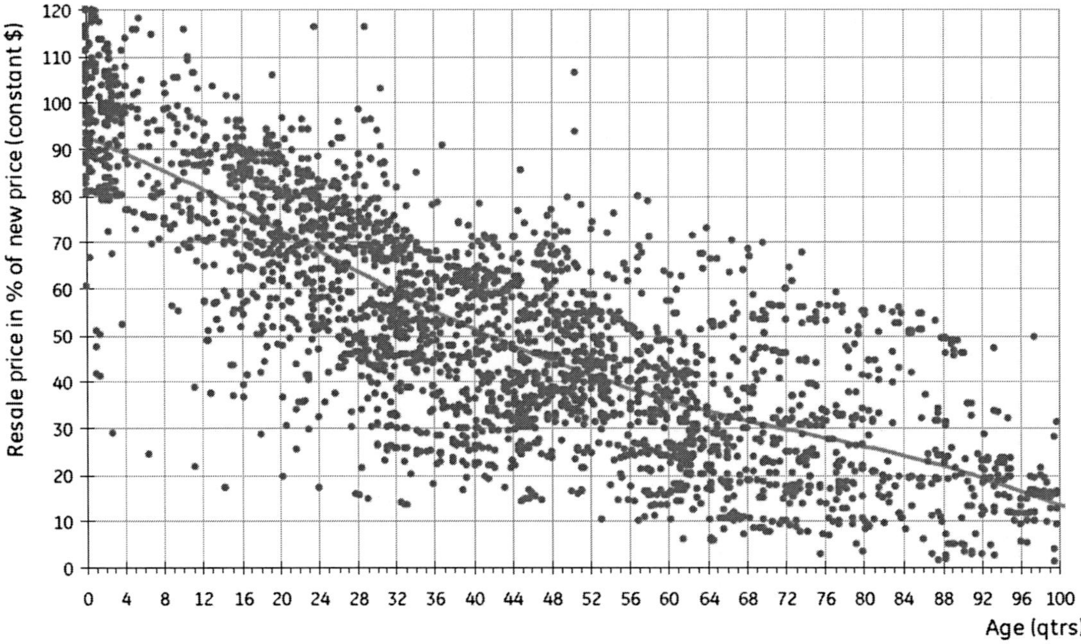

FIGURE 3.10

Volatility of residual values of aircraft

PK Airfinance (2017).

CASH FLOWS FOR A LESSOR'S INVESTMENT DECISION

The evaluation of undertaking a lease transaction for a lessor is a capital-budgeting decision, as the asset is an investment and needs to generate a return and add value to the organization over time. The question to be considered from the lessor's viewpoint is "Does it make economic sense to purchase the aircraft and lease it to the lessee (airline)?" The value generated over the term of the lease should be evaluated by performing an NPV analysis of the costs and benefits of undertaking the lease. When building the NPV analysis, the cash flow drivers that should be considered are the aircraft cost, residual value/sale proceeds, lease payments, depreciation, taxes, transaction costs, and after-tax cost of debt. Table 3.7 summarizes the cash flows of the lease option for the lessor, assuming no initial payments are required, and there are no monthly maintenance payments being made.

From a lessor's evaluation perspective, the initial investment and cash outflow is the purchase of the asset. When the asset is on lease to an airline (lessee), the scheduled lease payments made are inflows to the lessor. These inflows are also taxed at the firm's corporate tax rate. As previously mentioned above in the lessee purchase option, when a lessor owns an asset, they benefit from the tax depreciation of that asset over its economic life. The depreciable value per period will be calculated similar to the lessee example through the use of either straight line depreciation or the MACRS method of depreciation. The tax shield will then be calculated from the periodic deduction at the rate of the firm's corporate tax rate. Finally, if at the end of the lease period, the asset is sold, a cash inflow equal to the resale value less any tax (on resale value above book value) would accrue to the lessor.

Once the full-term cash flows have been calculated, the lessor should then evaluate the NPV of the overall transaction. If the NPV is positive, it means that the lease will add value to a firm over time, while a negative NPV will lead to a deterioration of the value of the firm over time.

INTERNAL RATE OF RETURN

Another tool used for investment decision analysis is an internal rate of return (IRR) calculation in order to rank the project based on the returns the lease is expected to generate. If the IRR generated by the cash flows is greater than the firm's discount rate, the lease transaction will add value to the firm, and if the IRR is less than the discount rate, the lessor is better off pursuing alternative investment opportunities.

Table 3.7 Lease Cash Flows to a Lessor

Initial investment	Cash outflow
Lease payments	Cash inflow
Tax on lease payments	Cash outflow
Depreciation tax deduction	Cash inflow
Residual value (less taxes)	Cash inflow

PAYBACK

The payback method looks at how long it would take for an initial investment to be recovered. In this analysis, the cash flows generated from the investment is compared to the original investment to determine the amount of time it takes to recover the initial investment. The payback method, while useful from a timing and investment recovery perspective, however, does not take into consideration the time value of money or any cash flows beyond the cutoff date. Further, the cutoff date for the payback period is an essentially arbitrary decision by management and not based on strong theoretical background. Therefore, the payback method is often used as a rough guideline, and not as a tool to make investment decisions.

RETURN ON ASSETS AND RETURN ON EQUITY

Finally, two important measures of profitability for an airline or lessor are return on assets (ROA) defined as ROA = net income/total assets and return on equity (ROE) defined as ROE = net income/total equity. While ROA is a measure of profit per dollar of assets, ROE measures the return for every dollar in equity, which goes to the shareholder. While these two measures are popular and often cited, it should be remembered that these are accounting rates of return and are often affected by changes in the accounting rules and regulations and should therefore be used cautiously. For example, the recent accounting change to show operating leases on the balance sheet may increase the total assets at an airline and therefore reduce the ROA for an airline. One, however, needs to realize that this is merely an accounting change and not a material change for the airline as analysts were already adjusting airline balance sheets by including the operating leases.

ACCEPTABLE RANGE OF LEASE PAYMENTS

Once the lessor and lessee have completed their independent assessment, a lease would be executed if both parties feel that it would be beneficial for them. However, there is not necessarily one lease payment that would make both the lessee and the lessor willing to transact. Typically, there is a range of lease payments that will make the lease viable, and therefore attractive, to both parties. The minimum lease payment is the lowest lease payment the lessor would be willing to accept for the lease, while the maximum lease payment is the largest lease payment the lessee would be willing to make for the lease.

LEASE VS BUY DECISION EXAMPLE

We will now look at a basic example of a lease vs buy decision from both the lessee's and lessor's perspectives. The example for Magna Charter is presented in the box below.

> Magna Charter has been asked to operate a Beaver bush plane for a mining company exploring north and west of Fort Liard. Magna will have a firm 1-year contract with the mining company and expects that the contract will be renewed
>
> *(Continued)*

(CONTINUED)

for the 7-year duration of the exploration program. Magna can either purchase the necessary plane for $1,000,000 or arrange for a 7-year operating lease from Stellar Leasing Company. Maintenance and insurance will be borne by Magna. Lease payments will be of equal amounts each year due at the beginning of the year. The plane falls in the 5-year MACRS depreciation class and will have a salvage value of $50,000 at the end of the 7 years. Magna's pretax cost of debt is 10% with a marginal tax rate of 20%. Stellar Leasing Co. can earn a pretax rate of return of 10% on investments of similar risk and has a marginal tax rate of 40%.

We will now evaluate the lease between Magna Charter and Stellar Leasing Company assuming a lease payment of $180,500 per year.

LESSEE PERSPECTIVE

As discussed previously, evaluating a lease from the lessee's perspective is a multistep process that begins with calculating the cost of ownership and comparing it to the cost of leasing, resulting in the NAL. If the NAL is positive, Magna will choose to lease the plane, and if the NAL is negative, Magna will choose to purchase the plane.

First we evaluate Magna's present value cost of purchasing the plane. Using the 5-year MACRS schedule, we can determine the depreciation expense and, therefore, the depreciation tax shield, for both the lessee and the lessor.

Depreciation Schedule				**Dep Tax Savings**	
Year	**MACRS Rate (%)**	**Dep Exp ($)**	**End of Year Book Value ($)**	**Lessee ($)**	**Lessor ($)**
1	20	200,000	800,000	40,000	80,000
2	32	320,000	480,000	64,000	128,000
3	19	190,000	290,000	38,000	76,000
4	12	120,000	170,000	24,000	48,000
5	11	110,000	60,000	22,000	44,000
6	6	60,000	0	12,000	24,000

MACRS, *Modified accelerated cost-recovery system.*

The $1,000,000 cost of the aircraft is multiplied by the MACRS rate to produce the depreciation expense for each year. The end-of-year book value is the purchase price less the accumulated depreciation. The depreciation tax savings (shield) is the depreciation expense multiplied by each company's respective tax rates. For instance, the lessee's depreciation tax savings in year 1 equals the depreciation expense of $200,000 multiplied by Magna's tax rate of 20% to get the $40,000 depreciation tax savings.

Next, we evaluate the cash flows from the purchase of the bush plane.

Cost of Owning:								
	Year 0	**Year 1**	**Year 2**	**Year 3**	**Year 4**	**Year 5**	**Year 6**	**Year 7**
Equip cost ($)	(1,000,000)							
Dep tax sav ($)		40,000	64,000	38,000	24,000	22,000	12,000	
Maintenance ($)	0	0	0	0	0	–	–	–
Main tax sav ($)	0	0	0	0	0	–	–	–
Residual val ($)								50,000
Res val tax ($)								(10,000)
Net CF ($)	(1,000,000)	40,000	64,000	38,000	24,000	22,000	12,000	40,000
PV cost of owning ($)		(814,412)						

CF, *Cash Flow;* PV, *Present Value*

The equipment cost of $1,000,000 is a cash outflow at year 0, which is followed by cash inflows from the depreciation tax savings in years 1 through 6 calculated above. At the end of the project (year 7), Magna will receive the residual value from selling the plane at $50,000. However, Magna has to pay taxes of 10% on the residual value received, producing a cash inflow of $40,000 at year 7. It is important to note that the appropriate discount rate for this calculation is Magna's after-tax cost of debt as leasing is similar to debt for a company. The net cash flows calculated above for each year are discounted at Magna's after-tax cost of debt of 8%, resulting in a present value cost of purchasing of $814,412.

Now that we have the present value cost of purchasing, we evaluate Magna's present value cost of leasing the bush plane in order to calculate the NAL.

Cost of Leasing:								
	Year 0	**Year 1**	**Year 2**	**Year 3**	**Year 4**	**Year 5**	**Year 6**	**Year 7**
Lease pmt	($180,500)	($180,500)	($180,500)	($180,500)	($180,500)	($180,500)	($180,500)	$0
Pmt tax sav	36,100	36,100	36,100	36,100	36,100	36,100	36,100	0
Net CF	($144,400)	($144,400)	($144,400)	($144,400)	($144,400)	($144,400)	($144,400)	$0
PV cost of leasing		($811,944)		**NAL**	**$2469**			

CF, *Cash Flow;* PV, *Present Value*

The lease payments are a yearly outflow for Magna of $180,500(since lease payments are usually at the beginning of the period it starts from year 0 rather than year 1). Since the lease payments Magna makes to Stellar are tax deductible, we add back $36,100 of tax savings due to lease payments each year. The net cash flows are discounted at Magna's after-tax cost of debt of 8% to produce the present value cost of leasing the plane of $811,944. To calculate the NAL, subtract the cost of purchasing the plane from the cost of leasing the plane, resulting in an NAL of $2469 for Magna. Since the NAL is positive, Magna would prefer to lease the plane.

Lessor perspective

Now we will evaluate the net present value of this transaction from Stellar Leasing Company's perspective. Referring to the lessor section of the depreciation schedule above, we find the depreciation tax savings that Stellar will receive from purchasing the aircraft. The depreciation tax savings are different for Magna and Stellar because they fall into different marginal tax brackets with different tax rates. Stellar receives a larger tax benefit from purchasing the plane because of its higher tax rate of 40%.

	Year 0	Year 1	Year 2	Year 3	Year 4	Year 5	Year 6	Year 7
Equip cost ($)	(1,000,000)							
Dep tax sav ($)		80,000	128,000	76,000	48,000	44,000	24,000	–
Maintenance ($)	0	0	0	0	0	–	–	–
Man tax sav ($)	0	0	0	0	0	–	–	–
Lease pmt ($)	180,500	180,500	180,500	180,500	180,500	180,500	180,500	–
Pmt tax ($)	(72,200)	(72,200)	(72,200)	(72,200)	(72,200)	(72,200)	(72,200)	–
Residual val ($)								50,000
Res val tax ($)								(20,000)
Net CF ($)	(891,700)	188,300	236,300	184,300	156,300	152,300	132,300	30,000
NPV of lease ($)		1819						
IRR of lease (%)		6.07						

CF, *Cash Flow*; NPV, *Net Present Value*; IRR, *Internal rate of return.*

In addition to the depreciation tax savings, other cash inflows for Stellar include the yearly lease payments of $180,500 and the residual value of $50,000 from selling the aircraft at the end of the project. Cash outflows for Stellar include taxes paid on the lease payments, as well as taxes paid on the residual value received. The net cash flows are then discounted at Stellar's after-tax rate of return of 6% to produce an NPV of $1819 and an IRR of 6.07%. The NPV is positive, so Stellar should choose to purchase the plane and lease it to Magna. In addition, the IRR of 6.07% is above the after-tax rate of return of 6%, further supporting Stellar's decision to engage in the transaction.

Maximum and minimum lease payments

Once we have calculated the base case scenario, we can find the range of lease payments that would appeal to both the lessee and the lessor. The minimum lease payment is the smallest lease payment the lessor would be willing to accept. The maximum lease payment is the largest lease payment the lessee would be willing to pay. Any lease payment within the minimum and maximum would be acceptable to both parties in the transaction.

In order to calculate minimum and maximum lease payments, it is most practical to use the Goal Seek function in Microsoft Excel. By setting up calculations in Excel similar to the setup in the tables above using formulas and referenced cells wherever possible, it is simple to manipulate the calculations. In order to calculate the minimum lease payment, refer to the lessor's NPV analysis. In Goal Seek, set the NPV cell to 0 by changing the lease payment. The result is the minimum lease payment. To calculate the maximum lease payment, refer to the lessee's NAL calculation. In Goal Seek, set the NAL to 0 by changing the lease payment. The result is the maximum lease payment. In the case of Magna Charter and Stellar Leasing Co., the minimum lease payment is $179,998 and the maximum lease payment is $181,049. In negotiations between the two companies, the agreed-upon lease payment should fall within this range, or the transaction may not occur.

This example demonstrates the difference in the types of decisions lessees and lessors make when deciding whether or not the lease transaction is beneficial for them. For the lessee, it is a financing decision to find the best option to fulfill its need as economically as possible, whether that be to buy or lease the aircraft. From the lessor's perspective, it is an investment decision as the lessor has to determine whether or not it makes sense to purchase the aircraft and lease it to the lessee.

CHAPTER CONCLUSION

This chapter outlined the lease decision-making process from a lessee and a lessor's perspective. Specifically, for a lessee this is a financing decision, or a lease versus buy decision where the lessee is trying to choose the lowest cost alternative, between purchase and lease, to operating the aircraft. Leasing also provides flexibility for an airline in its fleet decisions, access to current technology, and helps transfer residual value risk to the lessor. From a lessor's perspective, this is a capital-budgeting decision or investment decision in which the lessor is deciding whether the income stream from the lease would generate an adequate return on their investment in an aircraft. A numerical example was used to show how to calculate a range of lease payments which would appeal to the lessee and the lessor. Appendix 3A to the chapter contains a mini case study for you to practice the lease versus buy decisions using the tools discussed in this chapter.

APPENDIX 3A: CASE STUDY: LEASE VERSUS BUY DECISION AT AEROMEXICO

Aeromexico is Mexico's flag carrier with operations based in Mexico City, Mexico. The airline serves more than 80 destinations throughout the Americas, the Caribbean, Europe, and Asia through the operation of an all-Boeing fleet. Aeromexico currently has 70 aircraft in service with an additional 65 on order and options for 34 more (CAPA, March 2017). Aeromexico's current in-service fleet is composed of 77% narrowbodies and 23% widebodies; and their future orders and options are also heavily weighted toward narrowbody aircraft (B737 MAX 8) which make up 91% of future deliveries.

The decision to operate a single fleet type offers efficiencies from both a passenger and an operational perspective. With cabin configuration options for 184 and 162 passengers in single and double cabin configurations, respectively, the B737 MAX 8 offers an in-flight experience that is comfortable, relaxing, and consistent with other aircraft in Aeromexico's fleet. Operationally, the addition of the B737 MAX 8 will eliminate the added maintenance costs required in the setup of maintaining a second aircraft type. In addition, the MAX 8 is also designed to reduce direct airframe maintenance costs by 6%. With fuel and dispatch reliability being substantial costs, the MAX 8 will also bring an 8% fuel efficiency savings along with a 99.7% schedule reliability level which will provide savings in the form of reduced flight cancellation costs and passenger goodwill. Single fleet type operations do have a downside; it that can inhibit an airline from being able to properly adjust to demand changes in their route network. Fortunately, the B737 family has wide passenger capacity and range availabilities which allow airlines to up-gauge or perform cabin reconfigurations to match supply to demand.

Aeromexico is a legacy FCC, whose management evaluates the decision to acquire a new aircraft differently than the management of a startup or LCC. The decision to either lease or purchase a new aircraft by Aeromexico will consider factors such as fleet flexibility and total aircraft ownership, impact on operating margins, and their costs of borrowing.

Leasing an aircraft through a short-term lease for 7 years, offers the airline the ability to shift resources in the event of a change in market dynamics. Should modifications in the network range be needed, leasing would allow the airline the ability to match short-haul routes with narrowbodies and long-haul routes with widebodies more efficiently through the fleet flexibility associated with leasing an aircraft. In addition, should forecasted capacity levels on individual Aeromexico routes change positively or negatively, responses to these changes through the increase or decrease of capacity can be made more quickly through leased aircraft and the nonrenewal of existing lease agreements. Under an operating lease, the lease payments that would be made to the lessor would be tax deductible. Lastly, should Aeromexico not wish to operate the aircraft over the entirety of its useful life, leasing shifts the residual value risk from Aeromexico to the lessor at the end of the lease term.

As a legacy FCC and the flag carrier of Mexico, Aeromexico may have incentives to favor a cash purchase or a purchase through long-term debt financing to own its new delivery aircraft outright. The optimal level of leased aircraft for an airline, where operating margins are maximized, is 53.4% (Bourjade et al., 2017). With roughly 84.2% of its current fleet leased (CAPA, March 2017), the incremental benefits of leasing an additional aircraft may be marginal. As the research suggests, it could be time for the management of Aeromexico to begin to evaluate diversifying away from lease transactions and move toward owning or debt finance the purchase of their additional aircraft. Through favorable relationships with banking institutions, the airline could benefit from lower interest rates which, all things being equal, would favor long-term debt as being less expensive than leasing. In addition, with a growing network and the proven ability of the B737 family to efficiently operate Aeromexico's routes, the benefits of owning the aircraft over its full useful life through a purchase or loan option should be considered. Owning the aircraft removes any negative financial impact of an aircraft being out-of-service and rental payments still needing to be made to the lessor. Finally, acquiring aircraft through long-term financing and utilizing the aircraft over its economic useful life allows the airline to benefit from the treatment of aircraft depreciation. Depreciating an owned aircraft will allow Aeromexico to tax-deduct the yearly depreciation balances from their income, leading to a positive impact on earnings.

Taking these into consideration, the following section presents details related to the acquisition decision of Aeromexico for a 2019 delivery of one of its B737 MAX 8 aircraft. Review the details and complete the required analysis.

AEROMEXICO'S DECISION

Aeromexico is evaluating the financing options for one of its scheduled 2019 aircraft deliveries of a new B737 MAX 8 aircraft. The decision options available to Aeromexico are to (1) purchase the aircraft with an 8-year loan, (2) purchase the aircraft with cash-on-hand, or (3) enter into a sale and leaseback transaction with a lessor to lease the aircraft for 7 years. Through negotiations with the manufacturer, the airline has come to a purchase price of $60 million for the aircraft, and it is estimated that the residual value will be $43.7 million at the end of the 7-year term. Aeromexico can borrow funds to finance the purchase of the aircraft at 6% (assume that entire amount can be borrowed at this rate), and the company has a corporate tax rate of 40%. For depreciation purposes, Aeromexico will depreciate the aircraft to a zero-value using a 7-year MACRS depreciation schedule. Exhibit 3.1 provides additional details related to the lease transaction for the aircraft.

Exhibit 3.1: **Asset:** One new Boeing 737 MAX 8, to be delivered in 2019.

Base Lease Term: 7-year operating lease with right to buy option for the lessee at the end of the lease term

Aircraft Purchase Price: $60,000,000 USD

Lease Rate Factor (LRF): Assume a LRF of 0.70%

Basic Rent: Monthly payment of $420,000 paid at the beginning of each month.

Security Deposit: First 2 months of rent paid up front and will be returned at the end of lease term

Maintenance Reserve: Assuming that Aeromexico does not pay any maintenance reserves

Lessor Cost of Capital: Assume cost of debt of 5%

Loan Rate: Annual rate of 6%

7-Year MACRS Depreciation Schedule: 7-year property, half-year convention

MACRS Schedule	
Year	**7 Years (%)**
1	14.29
2	24.49
3	17.49
4	12.49
5	8.93
6	8.92
7	8.93
8	4.46

Investigate the buy vs lease decision of a B737 MAX 8 aircraft for Aeromexico.

1. From the standpoint of Aeromexico, develop an excel spreadsheet to present the transaction details and model:
   a. An NPV analysis of leasing the aircraft for 7 years.
   b. An NPV analysis of purchasing the aircraft with cash on hand.
   c. An NPV analysis of purchasing the aircraft through a 7-year loan.
2. In addition, model the analysis from the standpoint of the lessor, and evaluate the range of lease payments for this transaction from both the lessor's and Aeromexico's perspective.

REFERENCES

Airbus. *Orders and deliveries*. (2018, January 31). Retrieved from <http://www.airbus.com/aircraft/market/orders-deliveries.html>.

Aircraft Leasing Buy or Rent? (2012, January 21). *The Economist*. Retrieved from <http://www.economist.com/node/21543195>.

Avolon. (2017, October 30). *World Fleet Forecast*. Retrieved from Avolon.aero: <https://cms.avolon.aero/wp-content/uploads/2018/07/Avolon_White-paper_Digital-27.10.17.pdf>.

Boeing. (2017). *Current aircraft finance market outlook 2018*. Boeing.

Boeing. *2018 Orders and deliveries*. (2018, January 31). Retrieved from <http://www.boeing.com/commercial/#/orders-deliveries>.

Bourjade, S., Huc, R., & Muller-Vibes, C. (2017). Leasing and profitability: Empirical evidence from the airline industry. *Transportation Research Part A*, 30–46.

CAPA Centre for Aviation. Global fleet summary. *Global Fleet Database*. (2018, February). Retrieved from <https://centreforaviation.com/data/fleet>.

Conklin, & de Decker. *Lease pros and cons: The things you should know*. (2010). Retrieved from <https://www.conklindd.com/t-leaseprosandcons.aspx>.

Deloitte. *Global commercial aerospace industry aircraft order backlog analysis*. (2016, July). Retrieved from <https://www2.deloitte.com/content/dam/Deloitte/us/Documents/manufacturing/us-manufacturing-aircraft-order-backlog-analysis.pdf>.

DVB Bank SE. (2018). *An overview of commercial aircraft 2018–2019*. DVB Bank SE.

Export-Import Bank of the United States. (n.d.). EXIM Bank: What we do. *EXIM Bank*. Retrieved from <https://www.exim.gov/what-we-do>.

FlightGlobal (2018). (2018, January – February). Finance and Leasing 2018. *FlightGlobal Airline Business*, pp. 1–3.

FlightGlobal. (2017, April). *Commercial operating leasing market dynamics*.

Hallfors, L., & Riggi, M. (2016). Aircraft leasing industry: Recap of 2015 & outlook for 2016. *Kroll bond rating agency research report*.

IATA. *IATA forecasts passenger demand to double over 20 years*. (2016, October 18). Retrieved from <http://www.iata.org/pressroom/pr/Pages/2016-10-18-02.aspx>.

IATA. *Strong airline profitability continues in 2018*. (2017, December 5). Retrieved from <http://www.iata.org/pressroom/pr/Pages/2017-12-05-01.aspx>.

PK AirFinance. *Modeling aircraft loan & lease portfolios*. (2017, October). Retrieved from <http://www.pkair.com/common/docs/modeling-aircraft-loan-and-lease-portfolios.pdf>.

Reuters. (2015, June 26). *China's Airport Boom drives airport building frenzy*. Retrieved from Rueters.com: https://www.reuters.com/article/us-china-aviation/chinas-aviation-boom-drives-airport-building-frenzy-idUSKBN0P60F220150626.

Vasigh, B., Taleghani, R., & Jenkins, D. (2012). Aircraft Leasing and Finance. In: *Aircraft Finance: Strategies for Managing Capital Costs in a Turbulent Industry* (pp. 269–297). Fort Lauderdale: J. Ross Publishing.

CHAPTER

AVIATION LEGAL AND REGULATORY FRAMEWORK

4

CHAPTER OUTLINE

Aircraft Leasing and Financing. DOI: https://doi.org/10.1016/B978-0-12-815285-0.00004-3

Aircraft financing and leasing is an industry governed by unique rules and regulations. The mobile nature of aircraft assets creates complicated multijurisdictional issues. Moreover, high equipment value and interchangeable components lead to increased legal, political, and collateral risk. In this chapter, we address legal and regulatory issues specific to aircraft financing, most of which stem from several key historic conventions. Thus, we address the modern implication of these events through further discussion on registration/ownership, jurisdictional review, bankruptcy, and open skies policy. The chapter includes the following sections.

INTRODUCTION TO AVIATION LAW

Aviation dates back thousands of years from the development of kites in China to hot air balloons in France during the late 1700s. While the concept of air rights was noted in medieval Roman property law, the first applicable aviation laws were enacted as local ordinances in France just prior to the Revolution. Balloons were used a century later during the Franco–German War, and the subsequent Hague Conference of 1899 was among the first attempts to establish international treaties regarding laws of war. Specifically, this conference included a discussion about the use of projectiles from hot air balloons.

As air transportation evolved externally during the 1900s, global leaders began seeing the need to establish international standards. The concept of airspace regulation first surfaced when German balloons began flying over France.[1] As a result, 18 European nations gathered at a conference in Paris in 1910 to discuss solutions and establish rules for aerial navigation. Following the first international flights during World War I, the conference reconvened in 1919, and participants agreed that each nation should have exclusive sovereignty over the airspace above its land and adjacent waters.[2] 38 countries ratified this agreement, which initiated the development of the International Commission for Air Navigation (ICAN).

With the high number of aircraft in service today, uniformity is important both operationally and financially. Many countries, including the United States and much of Europe, govern air transportation at the federal level. Moreover, due to the nature of commercial air travel, most nations around the world consider aviation law a matter of international law. The multilateral movements of the early 20th century ultimately paved the way for further treaties that helped shape the legal and regulatory framework of the industry today.

OVERVIEW OF LEGAL TERMS

International agreements involve a variety of "instruments," most of which exist as written documents. So, before we get into detail about the history of aviation law, it is important to understand the meaning behind the various instruments and legal terms that are referenced throughout this chapter:

[1] *The International Declaration Prohibiting the Discharge of Projectiles and Explosives from Balloons*, The Hague, Jul 29, 1899.

[2] *Convention Relating to the Regulation of Aerial Navigation (Paris Convention)*, Oct 13, 1919, ch 1, art 1.

- *State (sovereign state):* A nation, country, or territory with one central government that has independent control over its geographic area and population. A sovereign state can create relations with another state, but it is not subject to any powers of that state.
- *Treaty:* An agreement made under international law between sovereign nations and international organizations. A treaty may be bilateral (between two states) or multilateral (between more than two states) and is often referred to as an agreement, convention, or protocol.
- *Convention:* The definition of this term is twofold. It refers to an international gathering of delegates, but as mentioned above, it is also used as another word for treaty.
- *Article:* A rule or "term" of a treaty.
- *Amendment:* An official alternation of the terms of a treaty. A formal amendment applies to all members, except when an original provision dictates otherwise.
- *Adoption:* This is a formal act that establishes the proposal and content of a treaty. Adoption does not automatically put the agreement in effect.
- *Entry into force:* The official date that a treaty takes effect for current participants or the official date that a treaty takes effect for each new participant. Most treaties specify the exact day, month, and year that the agreement is to enter into force following adoption, whereas some treaties are more provisionally based. For example, a treaty may enter into force as soon as all negotiating states have signed or satisfied certain conditions.
- *Signature:* A signature is a preliminary endorsement, but it does not establish any consent nor does it obligate a state to the bounds of an agreement. It simply represents a state's consideration of the treaty. However, a signatory is typically required to refrain from any act that goes against the purpose of the treaty.
- *Ratification:* This process represents a state's decision to participate in a treaty for which it has already provided a preliminary signature. Ratification is the formal agreement to be bound by the terms of a treaty. It requires the state to officially implement the terms into its domestic legislation and to formally declare the intent to participate. In most cases, ratification occurs before a treaty enters into force.
- *Accession:* Legally, accession has the same effect as ratification, but there is no preliminary signature. Accession signifies a state's official acceptance of an existing treaty that has already been negotiated by other states. This usually occurs after the treaty has entered into force, either by all members approving the new member or by the new member simply binding himself/herself to the existing terms. A treaty may instead reference the terms *acceptance*, *approval*, or *adherence*. These have the same meaning and are sometimes used at the national level when a constitution does not require ratification.
- *Contracting state:* A state that has ratified or acceded a treaty.
- *Declaration:* An official statement regarding a state's position or opinion. This is a rather loose term that usually does not involve a binding agreement. For example, a state may simply declare its goal to ratify a treaty in the future. Alternatively, a declaration may serve as clarification, a recommendation, or an informal agreement. Context is important, as some declarations do create legally binding terms.
- *Denunciation:* A state's withdrawal from a treaty. This requires a formal declaration and usually involves a waiting period before the state is officially released from the terms.
- *Perfection:* The process of making a security interest valid or enforceable against a third party, namely, in the event of default.
- *Choice of law:* The decision on which jurisdictional laws to apply to a case involving parties from different states or sovereign nations.

We will refer back to these terms as we discuss how treaties develop among an initial set of nations. In some cases, a state may choose to sign but not initially ratify. This is often the result of concern for a domestic market. Over time and through the adoption of protocols and adjustments, more states may join the agreement, which effectively gives it more international power. It is important for industry financiers to understand these distinctions, particularly when it comes to foreign jurisdictions that are selective about their level of compliance. The following section discusses the development and practice of the fundamental conventions in modern aviation.

CONVENTION
POUR
L'UNIFICATION DE CERTAINES RÈGLES
RELATIVES AU
TRANSPORT AÉRIEN INTERNATIONAL,
PROTOCOLE ADDITIONNEL
ET
PROTOCOLE FINAL
Adoptés par la IIe Conférence Internationale de Droit Privé Aérien réunie à Varsovie du 4 au 12 Octobre 1929

ICAO.int.

WARSAW CONVENTION

The year 1914 is often cited as the year of the first commercial air service, but the industry did not pick up speed until after World War I. Recalling the chapter introduction, we know that world leaders had already initiated the concept of airspace rights. Unlike the Paris conference, the Warsaw Convention was the first major effort to address the mobile nature of aircraft from both a safety and financial standpoint. Specifically, delegates at this event focused on their growing concern for the innate liability of commercial air travel. Several attempts had already been made to convene such a conference, but all were deferred until the late 1920s. The Warsaw Convention, also known as the Convention for Unification for Certain Rules Relating to International Carriage by Air, was signed in Warsaw, Poland on October 12, 1929. It went into effect on February 13, 1933 and explicitly addresses liability issues related to the

> international carriage of persons, luggage or goods performed by aircraft for reward [and] to gratuitous carriage by aircraft performed by an air transport undertaking.[3]

[3]*Convention for the Unification of Certain Rules Relating to International Carriage by Air*, Oct 12, 1929, art. 1, Stat. 1.

The Warsaw Convention consists of 41 articles outlined in five separate chapters. First and foremost, Chapter 1 officially defined international air transport as any carriage between a departure point within a contracting state and a destination point within a second contracting state, regardless of any connection or break in service. The origin and destination points can also be within the same state, but there must be an agreed-upon stopover in another state (contracting or noncontracting). For example, a flight from Hamburg to Frankfurt is not considered international carriage. But if the plane makes a stop in Amsterdam along the way, then it is classified as international carriage.

Chapter 2 of the convention addresses specific rules for documentation. Perhaps the most notable of these is the requirement that all carriers provide a passenger ticket and a luggage ticket. Each must indicate the origin and destination of the carriage and, if there is a connection, at least one of the stopover points. Essentially, the purpose of the ticket is to legally constitute the conditions of carriage. Another key mandate of the convention relates to cargo and requires that all packages include an air consignment note that was issued by the consignor and contain all the details of a particular package.

Initially, the Warsaw agreement simply referenced "the carrier," but this led to confusion about which party was actually liable. Specifically, was it only the carrier that concluded the contracted service? Or, did liability also extend to any carrier that took part in the service? Chapter 4 of the convention addresses the issue of combined carriage. The Guadalajara Supplementary Convention of 1961 eventually expanded the definition of "carrier" to "actual carrier," effectively extending the rules and liability to contractors and codeshares. This means, for example, that if luggage is transferred to another carrier during a connecting flight, then the carriage by both carriers is considered a single, undivided carriage.

Chapter 3 is arguably the most important contribution of the Warsaw treaty, as it deals specifically with liability and monetary limits. According to Article 17,

> The carrier [actual carrier] is liable for the damage sustained in the event of the death or wounding of a passenger or any other bodily injury suffered by a passenger, if the accident which caused the damage so sustained took place on board the aircraft or in the course of any of the operations of embarking or disembarking.

During the years between World War I and World War II, the industry made a number of significant advancements in aircraft technology. The conventional biplane eventually evolved into a more high-powered, aluminum-encased aircraft with a single wing. Likewise, it was during this time period that engineers began to develop the jet engine. Ultimately, as planes began flying longer distances and with more passengers on board, regulators grew more concerned about safety and legality. The Warsaw Convention created a uniform body of rules and remedies for passenger accidents and damages on commercial flights between treaty members. Chapter 3 established a presumption of law, which means that a carrier is held liable for damages without the need for a passenger to prove the carrier's fault or negligence. However, these remedial provisions are also designed to protect the operator. Suppose an aircraft loses power mid-flight, plummets to the ground, and kills all passengers on board. Such a catastrophe could easily bankrupt an airline. Therefore, the Warsaw Convention put a monetary cap on the amount of restitution that passengers (or families of passengers) can claim from any one carrier. Officially, damages for bodily injury and death were limited to 125,000 gold francs (roughly $8300).[4] However, if a carrier can prove that the damage was actually the result of a passenger's negligence, then it may be cleared of any liability claim to the extent that the negligent acts contributed to the damage. Furthermore, the treaty holds carrier's responsible for any damage to cargo and passengers' baggage while in transit, unless the airline can prove that the damage was the result of an inherent defect, an act of war, or the actions of a public authority figure who handled the items during entry, exit, or transit. The liability limit for cargo was set at approximately $20/kg.

Ultimately, the purpose of the Warsaw Convention was twofold. Members wanted international uniformity in daily operations, but they also wanted a flexible liability system that could sustain future growth and change. For the airlines, presumed liability was essentially exchanged for limited liability. It is worth noting that the Warsaw treaty was primarily a product of Europe; the United States did not ratify the agreement until October 29, 1934. This was the midpoint of the Great Depression when liability provisions had the potential to benefit airlines, customers, and cargo shippers. For an infant industry, the provisions worked reasonably well. But, as living standards increased and more people began flying, the original per-passenger liability limit proved insufficient.

Therefore, there have been several key amendments to the Warsaw Convention, the first being the Hague Protocol, which was signed on September 28, 1955. This amendment raised the damages-per-passenger limit to 250,000 Francs, an equivalent of roughly $16,600. Once again, the United States signed but did not ratify, arguing that the limit was still too low for its domestic market. In fact, Congress suggested implementing a supplemental domestic insurance program that would raise the figure to $66,600. However, due to considerable opposition, the proposal never made it to the court. Congress then attempted to secure a voluntary agreement from all the US airlines to raise the amount to $100,000. This strategy also failed, which led the United States to file for denunciation of the Warsaw Convention. It was this act that prompted international action, and in 1966, Congress reluctantly accepted a proposal by which all member states agreed to increase the limit to $75,000 on all flights to and from the United States (Boyle, 1973).

Nonetheless, the $75,000 limit was more of an interim agreement, and delegates continued to argue over what permanent limit would actually meet public interest. From the US perspective, the objective was for a passenger to achieve certainty, speed, and sufficiency in recovery from a traffic incident (Boyle, 1973). The problem was that the sum of limited liability in one country might equate to unlimited liability in another country. The other problem was concern for willful misconduct on the part of the carrier. In the end, an unbreakable limit was set to $100,000 as amended by the Guatemala Protocol of 1971. This amendment established strict liability, which meant that carriers are held responsible regardless of the actual intent or any negligent behavior (Figs. 4.1–4.3).

Special drawing rights

The Warsaw treaty initially expressed all amounts in gold francs, but additional protocol in 1975 changed the figures to Special Drawing Rights (SDR). The International Monetary Fund established the SDR in 1969 to supplement national reserves of member states. It can be exchanged for any useable currency. SDR value is based on the weighted average of five currencies: Euro, US Dollar, Japanese Yen, British Pound, and Chinese Renminbi [International Monetary Fund (IMF), 2016].

---

[4] *Id.*, art. 22, Stat 1.

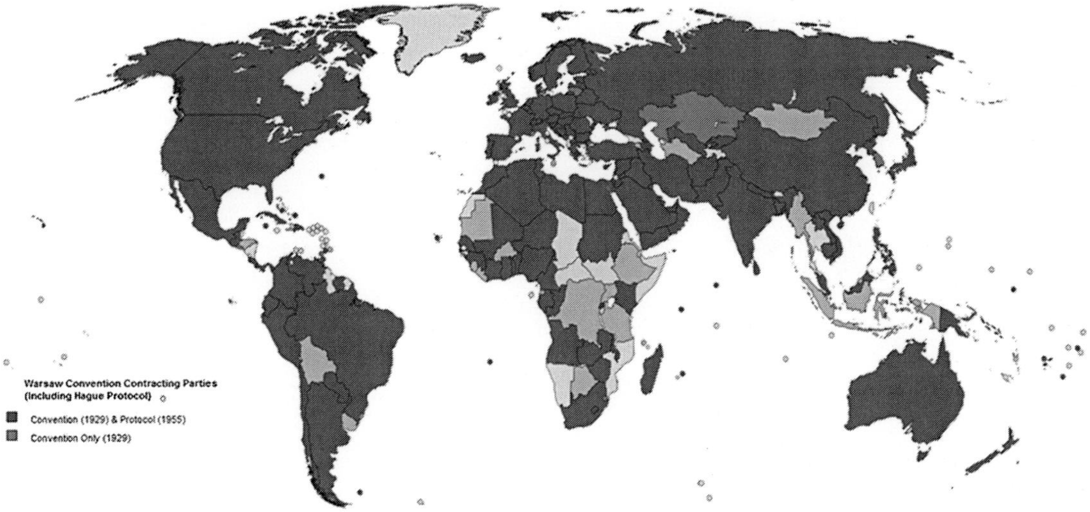

FIGURE 4.1

Warsaw Convention participating countries.

FIGURE 4.2

Sample Air Waybill.

US Postal Service (USPS) (2017).

FIGURE 4.3

Montreal Convention participating countries.

Thus, the passenger liability limit officially changed to $16,600 SDR. Likewise, the limit for baggage and cargo was recorded at 17 SDR/kg. These limits specified in the Warsaw Convention remained in effect until the Montreal Convention in 1999.

MONTREAL CONVENTION

The Montreal Convention was signed on May 28, 1999 and went into force on November 4, 2003. This treaty, known as MC99, reaffirmed the call for orderly development in the industry, but more importantly, it reestablished strict liability and recognized

> the need to modernize and consolidate the Warsaw Convention and related instruments [and] the importance of ensuring protection of the interests of consumers in international carriage by air and the need for equitable compensation based on the principle of restitution.[5]

Ultimately, MC99 updated the Warsaw limits on liability to adjust for inflation. The amount was initially set at 100,000 SDR, but this is subject to a review every 5 years. As of 2016, damages for passenger injury and death increased by roughly 13% to a minimum of 113,100 SDR (roughly $160,000).[6] Furthermore, unlike Warsaw, the Montreal Convention based baggage liability on

[5] *Convention for the Unification of Certain Rules for International Carriage by Air*, opened for Montreal Convention, May 28, 1999 (ICAO Doc No 4698), Introduction.

[6] US Department of Transportation, *Inflation Adjustments to Liability Limits Governed by the Montreal Convention*, 74 FR 59017, Nov 16, 2009.

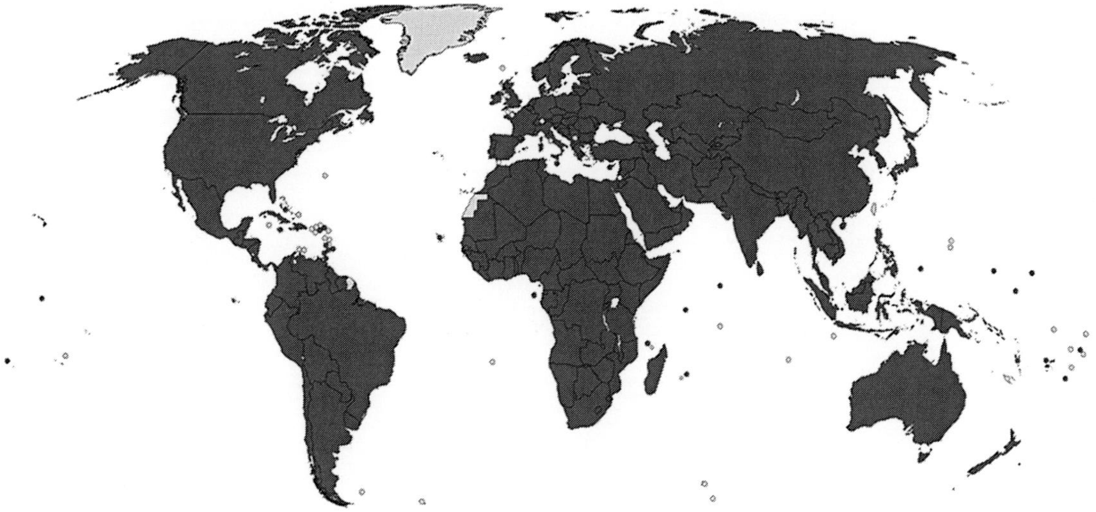

FIGURE 4.4

Geneva Convention participating countries.

possession rather than just negligence. As such, carriers are strictly liable for up to 1131 SDR (updated) for the destruction, loss, damage, or delay of passenger baggage.[7]

The Montreal Convention also restructured the rules for cargo, and the associated liability amount has been updated to 19 SDR/kg. Another MC99 contribution replaced the air consignment note with the air waybill (Fig. 4.4). This was primarily meant to streamline trade, and it now provides shippers with more accurate documents, easier customs compliance, enhanced security, and faster shipping times. The standardized process also lowers costs for the airlines. Finally, MC99 expanded the Warsaw provisions such that carriers are now required to hold an approved insurance policy.

The Montreal agreement is considered to be the updated standard, but as of 2016, it has only been ratified by 122 (60%) of all Warsaw Convention members. In many cases, this has been due to the complexity of the transitioning process, but it has nevertheless led to considerable confusion over which regime to apply. At the 39th International Civil Aviation Organization (ICAO) assembly in October 2016, all remaining states were urged to adopt MC99 as soon as possible [International Air Transport Association (IATA), 2016].

CHICAGO CONVENTION

The Chicago Convention is a product of World War II and remains one of the most well-known treaties in aviation. Commercial air transportation accelerated rapidly after this point, particularly in terms of product development. Flight technology had already improved, and production was set

[7] *Montreal Convention*, 1999, Art 22, Stat 2.

to increase. During the last stage of the war, delegates from 55 states gathered in Chicago to discuss how all nations might benefit from the growing air transport industry. The goal was to promote peace and cooperation at the global level. On December 7, 1944, 52 of the attending members signed the convention on International Civil Aviation, otherwise known as the Chicago Convention. This proved to be one of the most successful international initiatives in history. Specifically, the treaty seeks to create a collective understanding.

ICAO.int.

> in order that international civil aviation may be developed in a safe and orderly manner and that international air transport services may be established on the basis of equality of opportunity and operated soundly and economically.[8]

The event also led to the creation of the ICAO, a United Nations–specialized agency charged with promoting global cooperation and governing standards, regulations, and procedures in civil aviation. ICAO oversees the Chicago Convention and eventually took over the ICAN office in Paris in 1947.

The Chicago agreement officially established international rules for airspace rights, regulation, and safety measures, but it applies only to civil aircraft (not military, customs, or other). Its first and foremost principle reiterates the Paris agreement that every state should have exclusive sovereignty over the airspace above its territory. Accordingly, territory is deemed to be the *land areas and territorial waters adjacent thereto under the sovereignty, suzerainty, protection or mandate of such State*.[9] Furthermore, every state has the right to regulate air services and cabotage within its borders. Cabotage refers to the right to conduct point-to-point service within a foreign territory. For

[8] *Convention on International Civil Aviation*, Dec 7, 1944, Preamble.
[9] *Id.*, art. 1 & 2, 61 Stat. at 1180.

example, if the United States prohibits cabotage, then an Emirates-based airline may not operate a flight from New York to Los Angeles.

Essentially, the articles in the first part of the convention grant individual states the power to make decisions regarding foreign carriers. Local authorities have the right to deny airspace access, designate specific customs/entry airports, and perform a search of any incoming or outgoing aircraft. However, Article 12 requires all members to strive for uniformity. In other words, each country should keep its domestic rules as closely aligned to the rules of the convention as possible. Additional protocol added in 1984 also prevents the use of weapons against any civil aircraft.[10]

The second half of the agreement addresses aircraft registration and operator documentation. While the Chicago Convention affects the industry at all levels, it draws particular interest from aviation financiers and lessors who deal with the nationality of aircraft. According to the agreement, aircraft have nationality of the state in which they are registered and *cannot be validly registered in more than one state.*[11] However, Article 1 allows registration to be transferred to another state according to the laws of that state. Registration is typically made in the name of the owner or the operator. In the United States, for instance, the Federal Aviation Act imposed an owner-based system.

Maintenance and airworthiness of an aircraft are primarily governed by the rules of the country where it is currently registered. Furthermore, all carriers are required to operate with certificates on board, including airworthiness, registration, crew licenses, logs, manifests, and any radio licenses.

Another area of interest for financiers and lessors is deregistration of aircraft, which is required for any cross-border lease transfer. As per the Chicago Convention, an aircraft can only be registered under one jurisdiction, so it must be deregistered and then reregistered in order to legally operate in another country. Without going through the full process, a lessor or owner of an aircraft registered in one jurisdiction is unable to remarket and deliver the asset to a potential lessee or buyer located in a different jurisdiction. This is precisely what occurred following Kingfisher Airlines' suspension of operations in October 2012. Disputes over competing claims and confusion regarding the power balance between international agreements and local courts hampered the efforts of various foreign lessors who tried to repossess over a dozen Airbus jets parked in airports across India.

The Chicago Convention has gone through several revisions. Today, all member states have agreed to over 12,000 international standards and recommended practices as outlined through a series of annexes (ICAO, 2017). In addition, the original air rights were expanded to cover nine Freedoms of Air, which are discussed in detail toward the end of this chapter.

GENEVA CONVENTION

The Geneva Convention is another treaty that was established shortly after World War II, but it was the first attempt to address jurisdictional differences regarding aircraft security interests. After the war, aircraft manufacturing nations became concerned about the reluctance of financial institutions to invest in aircraft without assurance that their interests were secure, especially when the equipment was outside the state of registry. As a remedy, the Geneva Convention (not to be

[10]*Id*, art 3 bis.
[11]*Id*, art. 17 & 18, 61 Stat. at 1185.

confused with the Geneva Conventions of global war law) was signed on June 19, 1948 and went into force on September 17, 1953. It is officially known as the Convention on the International Recognition of Rights in Aircraft and is meant to facilitate financing and to recognize property basis and conditions for aircraft sales. Specifically, Article I of the agreement recognizes the following rights:

1. Rights of property in aircraft;
2. Rights to acquire aircraft by purchase coupled with possession of the aircraft;
3. Rights to possession of aircraft under leases of 6 months or more;
4. Mortgages and similar rights in aircraft which are contractually created as security for payment of an indebtedness;

    Provided that such rights

    a. have been constituted in accordance with the law of the Contracting State in which the aircraft was registered as to nationality at the time of their constitution and
    b. are regularly recorded in a public record of the Contracting State in which the aircraft is registered as to nationality.[12]

A right is often referred to as an interest, which essentially means an advantage, a share, or a legal title to a piece of property. Under the Geneva Convention, property refers to "aircraft," which includes the airframe, engines, propeller, and radio apparatus.[13] The treaty also recognizes recorded interests in spare parts.

The Geneva Convention established the concept of aircraft registration, but it is not just about who owns the equipment. Rather, the important question is who can exercise control over its domestic and international operation? This question usually arises during a financial event such as a sale or credit dispute, and the Geneva Convention essentially allows for the international choice of law regarding ownership. In general, aircraft interests coincide with registration. According to Article II, any effects of the rights mentioned above are to be determined and governed by the laws of the state where the aircraft is currently registered, not necessarily where the aircraft is physically located. For example, if a plane is registered in Brazil but located in France, the rights recorded with its registration take priority over any third-party rights from European stakeholders or any other foreign entity. Furthermore, the Brazilian government can choose whether or not to recognize these outside claims.

In general, rights of the Geneva Convention should have priority over the rights recognized by any contracting state. As such, aircraft financiers may assert recognition of rights, as constituted under the laws of the state of registry, and establish a commitment on the part of the contracting nations to recognize and enforce such rights. For example, if a Federal Aviation Administration (FAA)-registered aircraft is seized by its financier within the borders of another contracting nation, the contracting nation has agreed that any conflict of interest regarding the aircraft will be resolved according to the US law.

When it comes to selling the asset, the rules are slightly different. Any proceedings during the sale of an aircraft must be undertaken according to the laws of the contracting nation where these proceedings are brought. There is also a mandatory notice period (of at least 6 weeks) for the date

[12]*Convention on the International Recognition of Rights in Aircraft*, June 19, 1948, art. I.
[13]*Id*, art. XVI.

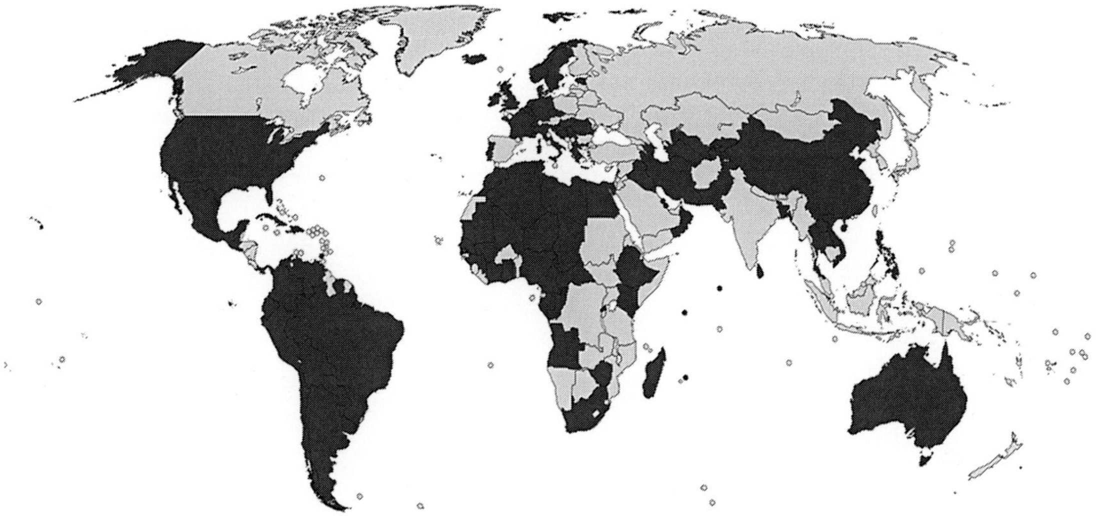

FIGURE 4.5

Chicago Convention participating countries.

and place of the sale. Unfortunately, this is not always a viable option for a creditor who requires prompt enforcement. Also, no change in registration may occur unless *all holders of recorded rights have been satisfied or consent to the transfer*, thereby protecting other financiers who may have recorded interests.

The Geneva Convention is recognized by 89 countries (Fig. 4.5). However, the major disadvantage is that it only applies if both the registry country and the location country are participating members. As a further restriction, the last article allows a participant to formally exclude another territory. Exclusions are recorded at the time of ratification or adherence and can be declared against both member and nonmember nations. For example, Mexico and The Netherlands ratified the convention in 1950 and 1959, respectively. Both were original signatories. However, The Netherlands deposited its instrument of ratification along with a specific declaration that it would not recognize the treaty with Mexico. Kuwait submitted a similar declaration against Israel, which is not a convention participant.

These provisions have generated a lot controversy, mostly due to the fact that several prominent nations did not and still have not ratified the Geneva Convention. As of the time of the writing of this text, current nonmembers include Japan, United Kingdom, Canada, and Austria, all of which cited specific conflicts with their own legal structures. In addition, even if a nonmember state agrees to recognize an aircraft mortgage, the convention does not provide a solution for cases that involve debtor default.

CAPE TOWN CONVENTION

Even before the Geneva Convention took effect, many viewed it as insufficient to the evolving needs of aircraft investors and financial institutions. The industry was already in full swing. On top of that, the US Airline Deregulation Act of 1978 further liberalized aviation in the United States. While the government continued to maintain control over safety and operational elements, the US airlines were finally free to fly any route and charge any price. This legislation had both domestic and international impacts, and the industry continued to evolve. During the 1990s, Boeing and Airbus both projected the demand for thousands of B747 and A340 aircraft over the following decades. At a unit cost well above $150 million, this meant billions of dollars in assets that were to be scattered around the globe.

In retrospect, one major flaw of Geneva comes from Article I: *provided that such rights (i) have been constituted in accordance with the law of the Contracting State*. Not all states uphold the same choice of law rules, so this raises the immediate question as to which regime applies—a state's domestic law or its private international law. In addition, in many jurisdictions, unpaid customs and landing charges often take priority over recorded interests. Perhaps the main flaw from a financier's perspective is, again, the fact that the Geneva provisions provide no useful measure for handling conflicts regarding insolvency.

These issues were the focal point at the later Cape Town Convention, which is arguably the most successful treaty in aviation. While Geneva merely recognizes aircraft interests, Cape Town actually creates international interests. The main treaty is formally known as the Convention on International Interests in Mobile Equipment and was signed in South Africa on November 16, 2001. Broadly speaking, it serves to standardize the process for sales contracts, security interests, leases, and defaults involving moveable property (rail, air, and space). The associated protocol on matters specific to aircraft equipment went into force in 2006 and is the only protocol still in effect. This part of the treaty serves to trump inconsistent national law. Ultimately, it is designed to meet the demands of financiers for a unified set of legal rules to facilitate aircraft financing, leasing, and sales.

Aircraft objects

The rules and benefits of the Cape Town protocol apply exclusively to "aircraft objects," which the agreement defines as any one of the followings:

- Airframes that are type certified to transport at least eight persons.
- Engines having at least 1750 lbs of thrust in the case of jet propulsion and the in case of turbine-powered or piston-powered aircraft engines having at least 550 rated takeoff shaft horsepower.
- Helicopters that are type certified to transport at least five persons.[14]

International interests and registry

Cape Town's first major contribution was the launch of a web-based international registry for aircraft objects. Again, the key was to *create* international interests, all of which are compulsorily recorded and can be verified at any time. According to Article VII, aircraft objects are referenced by manufacturer, the manufacturer's serial number, and the equipment's model number. Once an asset is recorded, the registered owner can exercise his/her interest in any contracting state or under any jurisdiction that applies the treaty. Unlike the Geneva Convention, rules under the Cape Town

[14]Protocol to the Convention on International Interests in Mobile Equipment on Matters Specific to Aircraft Equipment, November 16, 2001. Art 1, Stat 1.

Convention supersede local laws when it comes to recognizing international interests. However, contracting states are permitted to make a declaration via which national law can supersede the registry. In such cases, international interests and the terms under the convention do not, in any way, affect the actions specified in the declaration.

To qualify as an international interest under the Cape Town protocol, the interest must be associated with the actual aircraft object. Furthermore, it must be

1. granted by a chargor under a security agreement,
2. vested in a person who is the conditional seller under a title reservation agreement, or
3. vested in a person who is the lessor under a leasing agreement.[15]

   In addition, according to convention Article 7 and protocol Article V,

4. the transaction must be in writing,
5. the charger, conditional seller, lessor, or seller must have power (not just the right) to dispose of the aircraft object,
6. the aircraft object must be referenced by the manufacturer's name, serial number, and model number.

Just to recap, a leasing agreement is a contract whereby a lessor grants a lessee the right to possess and control an aircraft object in return for rental payments. A security agreement refers to a contract by which a chargor (lender/lessor) grants or agrees to grant to the chargee (lessee/debtor) an interest in an aircraft object for the purpose of securing the performance of an existing or future obligation (Gerber, 2012). Finally, under a title reservation agreement, ownership does not transfer until certain conditions are met.

One notable feature of the international registry is that each interest is granted a priority status. In general, a registered interest takes precedence over an unregistered interest and over any subsequent registered interest. In other words, first come, first served. It is important to note that while registration is necessary to establish priority, it is not necessary for the creation of the interest.

If an aircraft is sold, the agreement must be in the form of an official contract for the outright sale of the object. As such, ownership immediately passes from the seller to the buyer, subject to deregistration. The buyer also assumes all associated rights, including payments from a debtor, as well as all international interests and priorities of the assignor. The Cape Town Convention does not initially account for the location of the asset, so a "contract of sale" prevents the issue of *lex situs*, which is the legal doctrine stating that title transfers are dependent upon the location of the property. In addition, any contracting state may designate an authority or entry point through which information required for international interest registration may be transmitted. In the United States, this is the FAA Aircraft Registration Branch located in Oklahoma City.

Choice of law

The Cape Town Convention also allows parties to choose which laws will govern their lease contract and any future disputes, regardless of whether or not the parties have a "reasonable relationship" to the chosen jurisdiction (Vedder Price, 2017).[16] However, as we learned with Geneva Convention, not all states have the same choice of law rules.

---

[15]Convention on International Interests in Mobile Equipment, art 2(2) (a,b,c).

[16]A reasonable relationship must exist for contracts subject to the Uniform Commercial Code (UCC).

Under New York law, for example, an aircraft lease may be re-characterized as a security interest, in which case the lessor would have to perfect the interest. Such risk does not exist under English law. In addition, while many foreign jurisdictions recognize judgments issued by New York courts, the United States has not signed any treaties that specifically address the recognition of foreign judgments. Instead, this recognition is determined on a case by case basis. Conversely, English law coincides with several regulations that enforce judgments between EU states,[17] as well as additional bilateral agreements with non-EU states. Furthermore, the two laws differ in terms of how they recognize and handle contract breach and damage claims (Vedder Price, 2017).

Most lessors prefer to use either New York or English law, as these have the most international credibility and provide the highest level of certainty and stability when it comes lease enforcement. However, it is important for lessors to understand these differences and tailor their lease agreements accordingly.

Default remedies

Another primary goal of the Cape Town treaty is to protect the rights of creditors in cases involving debtor default. This protection includes a range of basic default remedies, and when there is evidence of default, a means of obtaining an efficient interim relief, pending final determination of a claim on assets. The idea is to give financiers greater confidence in their client decisions, enhance the credit rating of equipment receivables, and reduce borrowing costs to the advantage of all interested parties.

Basic measures depend on the role of the creditor. A chargee (lender or lessor) may take control of the aircraft object, sell or grant lease over the object, or collect any income resulting from the use or management of the object. A conditional seller or lessor may do the same, or they may apply for the assistance of a court order.[18] In addition, Article XI of the protocol provides two alternatives:

1. Allows the creditor to take possession of the aircraft object within a specified time period—until the debtor cures all defaults and agrees to fulfill their future obligations.
2. Allows the debtor to either cure all defaults and agree to fulfill future obligations or to give possession of the aircraft object to the creditor.

States such as China, India, and Russia adopted the first insolvency remedy, since it seems more favorable for creditors. We will come back to these remedies when we discuss bankruptcy later in the chapter.

Regarding deregistration for default or export purposes, the convention provides the legal framework and the export power of attorney—more commonly known as IDERA (irrevocable deregistration and export request authorization). The debtor must submit this form for record to the relevant civil authority. In the United States, IDERAs were approved for use by the federal government, which subsequently transferred the duty to the FAA.

The fundamental rule of Cape Town is that it applies only when the debtor is situated in a contracting state, whereas the creditor's location does not matter. Clearly, the main drawback occurs when foreign legislation fails to recognize securities (including mortgages), retention of title

[17]Given the UK's exit from the European Union, future applicability remains in question.
[18]*Id Protocol*, art. 10.

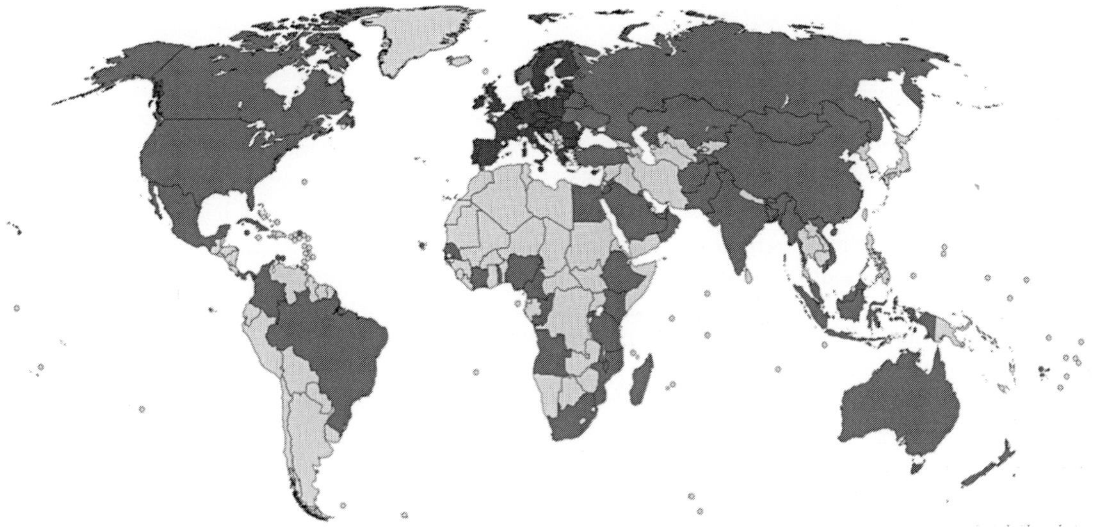

Afghanistan
Albania
Angola
Australia
Bangladesh
Belarus
Brazil
China
Cameroon
Canada
Cape Verde
Colombia
Cuba
Egypt
Ethiopia
European Union
Fiji
India
Indonesia
Ireland
Ivory Coast
Latvia
Luxembourg
Jordan
Kenya
Madagascar
Malawi
Malaysia
Malta
Mexico
Moldova
Mongolia
Mozambique
Myanmar
New Zealand
Netherlands Antilles
Nigeria
Norway
Oman
Pakistan
Panama
Russia
Rwanda
San Marino
Saudi Arabia
Senegal
Sierra Leone
Singapore
South Africa
Spain
Sweden
Tajikistan
Tanzania
Togo
Turkey
Ukraine
United Arab Emirates
United Kingdom
United States
Vietnam

FIGURE 4.6

Cape Town Convention participating countries, 2017.

(conditional sale agreements), equipment leases, and bankruptcy, all of which are critical for negotiation and repossession. As of January 2017, 60 countries participate in the Cape Town agreement (Fig. 4.6). However, ratifying states have the freedom to customize the convention, so to speak. In fact, members are free to deviate from most of the treaty's provisions, namely, when it comes to default/insolvency remedies, interim remedies, and the priority level of unpaid local charges. For states that opt to maintain their own insolvency laws, the associated rights to the lessor will depend on how favorable that country's regime is. For example, civil law jurisdictions tend to favor the debtor, whereas common law jurisdictions tend to favor the creditor.

Ultimately, if a state judicial system is not equipped to meet modern commercial requirements and it allows operators to initiate legal proceedings to prevent an international interest from exercising remedies, then repossession could take years. As such, the creditor would have no perceived benefits under the Cape Town Convention. For example, India, although a Cape Town signatory, does not explicitly address aircraft repossession by a lessor in its civil aviation regulations. Until a clear clause is added, there will be further challenges to aircraft repossession in India, which demonstrates the need for active involvement by countries party to the convention. For India, the first step occurred in March 2017 when the country's Directorate General of Civil Aviation published an amendment to the original Aircraft Rules of 1937. According to Rule 30 (7), registration of an aircraft registered in India, to which the provisions of the Cape Town Convention or Cape Town Protocol apply, shall be cancelled by the Central Government, **within five working days** ....

Furthermore, newly added Rule 32(A) states that upon cancellation of the registration, the government is required to facilitate the export and physical transfer of the aircraft within 5 working days. The new deadline provision provides some hope for financiers, although it remains unclear as to how exactly the Indian government will "facilitate" these transfers.

Overall, the purpose of Cape Town is to make aircraft financing and leasing easier, more available, and less uncertain. It also greatly reduces financing costs for operators, which, after all, was the underlying motivation behind the treaty. Although it can be ratified in different ways as we saw in the Kingfisher case, most jurisdictions do so in way that benefits financiers attempting to reclaim their assets.

We now move into the second part of the chapter, which deals with the applicability of the conventions discussed thus far. Much of the discussion centers on the Cape Town provisions, as they are not only the most recent but also arguably the most complex.

US REGISTRATION AND OWNERSHIP

This section focuses on aircraft registration specifically in the United States, providing an example of the various ways that a prominent Cape Town party may choose to exercise the treaty.

As mentioned earlier, the FAA is the industry governing body in the United States and maintains its own international registry to facilitate aircraft registration, certify aircraft worthiness, approve specialized maintenance programs for airlines, and record security interest relating to a particularly aircraft. The FAA will not register any aircraft that is already registered in another country. Moreover, the asset must be owned by a US citizen or foreign national lawfully admitted for permanent residence, or by a US corporation that does business under the US law. After meeting these requirements, an applicant must prepare FAA Form 8050-1 (Fig. 4.7). Apart from the original, two copies must be made: a green copy is submitted along with the original to the FAA, while a pink copy must be carried on board the aircraft to be used as a temporary authority until the actual certificate is received. If a sale or aircraft ownership transfer occurs, the original Certificate of Aircraft Registration must be returned to the FAA by the seller or transferor within 21 days from the date of sale or transfer.

Initially, aircraft registration was considered a onetime process, but this resulted in records containing erroneous information for almost one-third of all FAA-registered aircraft. Therefore, as of October 1, 2010, a registered owner is required to reregister the aircraft once every 3 years by completing and submitting an FAA Form 8050-1B.[19]

Pursuant to the Aircraft Registration and Recordation Processes issued by the FAA Aircraft Registration Branch AFB-710 in June 2018 an individual can register an aircraft with the FAA if he/she is a citizen of the United States or one of its possessions or has been lawfully granted

[19]Re-registration and Renewal of Aircraft Registration, 75 Fed. Reg. 41, 968 (July 20, 2010).

UNITED STATES OF AMERICA – DEPARTMENT OF TRANSPORTATION
FEDERAL AVIATION ADMINISTRATION – MIKE MONRONEY AERONAUTICAL CENTER
AIRCRAFT REGISTRATION APPLICATION

UNITED STATES REGISTRATION NUMBER **N**	TYPE OF REGISTRATION (Check one box.) ☐ 1. Individual ☐ 2. Partnership ☐ 3. Corporation ☐ 4. Co-Owner ☐ 5. Government ☐ 7. Limited Liability Company (LLC) ☐ 8. Non-Citizen Corporation ☐ 9. Non-Citizen Corporation Co-Owner
AIRCRAFT MANUFACTURER AND MODEL	
AIRCRAFT SERIAL NUMBER	

NAME(S) OF APPLICANT(S) [Person(s) shown on evidence of ownership. If individual, give last name, first name and middle initial.]

TELEPHONE NUMBER: ( )

MAILING ADDRESS (Permanent mailing address for first applicant on list.)

NUMBER AND STREET: ______

RURAL ROUTE: ______ P.O. BOX ______

CITY: ______ STATE: ______ ZIP: ______

PHYSICAL ADDRESS/LOCATION IF P.O. BOX OR RURAL ROUTE BOX USED FOR MAILING ADDRESS

NUMBER AND STREET: ______
DESCRIPTION OF LOCATION: ______

CITY: ______ STATE: ______ ZIP: ______

☐ ***CHECK HERE IF YOU ARE ONLY REPORTING A CHANGE OF ADDRESS***

CERTIFICATION

I/WE CERTIFY:

(1) That the above aircraft is owned by the undersigned applicant who is: **(MUST CHECK AND/OR COMPLETE a, b, c, or d)**

☐ a. A citizen of the United States as defined by 49 USC 40102(15);

☐ b. A resident alien with alien registration (Form 1-551) No. ______

☐ c. A non-citizen corporation organized and doing business under the laws of (state) ______ and said aircraft is based and primarily used in the United States. Records of flight hours are available for inspection at **(provide complete physical address)**: ______

☐ d. A corporation using a voting trust to qualify. Enter name of trustee ______

(2) If box c or d above is checked, I, the below signed, certify that I am authorized, by the applicant shown above, to sign corporate documents and to seek aircraft registration on behalf of the entity and that I will provide the same authorization if requested;

(3) That the aircraft is not registered under the laws of any foreign country; and

(4) That legal evidence of ownership is attached or has been filed with the Federal Aviation Administration.

ANY AND ALL SIGNATORIES OF THIS APPLICATION MUST READ THE FOLLOWING AND UNDERSTAND THAT, BY APPLYING A SIGNATURE TO THIS DOCUMENT, THEY ARE SUBJECT TO THE REFERENCED STATUTES AND ASSOCIATED PENALTIES.

I hereby certify that the information provided herein and in any attachments to the application for aircraft registration is true, accurate and correct to the best of my knowledge and belief. I understand that the information provided by me will be relied on by the FAA administrator in his/her determination of qualification for aircraft registration. I understand that whoever, in any matter within the jurisdiction of any department or agency of the United States, knowingly and willfully falsifies, conceals or covers up (by any trick, scheme or device) a material fact or who makes any false, misleading or fraudulent statements or representations or entry, may be fined up to $250,000 or imprisoned not more than five (5) years or both (18 U.S.C. Sections 1001 and 3571). I understand that, should I intentionally provide any inaccurate or false information, registration of the subject aircraft may be revoked.

NOTE: If executed for co-ownership, all applicants must sign. Use next page and add page(s) if necessary.

1	SIGNATURE:	DATE:
	TYPED/PRINTED NAME:	TITLE:
2	SIGNATURE:	DATE:
	TYPED/PRINTED NAME:	TITLE:

NOTE: Except when the most recent registration of the subject aircraft is expired or cancelled, 14 CFR 47.31(c) provides for an airworthy U.S. aircraft to be operated for up to 90 days within the United States when a copy of the signed application for its registration is carried in the aircraft while awaiting issuance and receipt of the new registration certificate.

AC Form 8050-1 (10/18)

FIGURE 4.7

FAA Aircraft Registration Application.

FAA Website, Form AC 8050-1.

permanent residence. In the case of partnerships, all partners must be citizens of the United States. A resident alien cannot be a member of such a partnership. Specific rules apply with respect to a corporation, Limited Liability Corporation, or other legal entity. A possible workaround, if one or more of the partners is a nonindividual, is registration under a trustee who is bound by a trust agreement. A corporation becomes eligible to register an aircraft if it is organized under the US law, its president and at least two-thirds of its board of directors and managing officers are US citizens, and if it has a minimum of 75% of the voting interest owned and controlled by US citizens. Likewise, an LCC is eligible to register an aircraft in its name as long as it was created and organized under the US law and satisfies the corporate criteria mentioned just above (Gerber, 2012).

Regarding non-US citizens, there are only three ways to register an aircraft: through an owner trust, through a voting trust, or by basing and primarily operating the aircraft in the United States and under the US law. An owner trust allows a grantor trust to hold legal title to the aircraft on behalf of one or more beneficiaries. A voting trust, on the other hand, can be used by corporations that do not fall under the required regulations. In both cases, the trustee needs to ensure that at least 75% of the trust members are US citizens and that the remaining 25% non-US citizens will have no influence on the decisions made by the trust. In order to register under the last option, at least 60% of the total flight hours must be flown in the Unites States. However, flight hours accumulated in the Unites States are counted only if they are nonstop flights, with the exception of stops made due to an emergency.

It is vitally important that an aircraft owner maintains his/her US citizenship. Loss of citizenship implies that the aircraft's registration will lapse; thus, the owner is required to return the registration certificate immediately.

For a newly manufactured aircraft or for an aircraft previously registered in the United States, a registration application and aircraft bill of sale (Fig. 4.8) need to be submitted in proper form. In addition, any owner wishing to reregister in the United States must provide adequate proof of and information about previous ownership and transactions.

If an aircraft was previously registered in a foreign country, deregistration of the aircraft must have been verified and fully completed in compliance with the terms of both the Geneva Convention and the Cape Town Convention. Pursuant to § 47.37 of 14 CFR Part 47, the FAA requires submission of evidence satisfactory to the FAA that foreign registration has ended or is invalid before the aircraft can be resistered with the FAA. Following verification, a new application form as stated above must be submitted to proceed with registration.

The last possible type of aircraft acquisition is by repossession or foreclosure. In such cases, the repossessor must submit a repossession certificate (Fig. 4.9), a certified copy of the applicable security agreement, and a bill of sale (in cases where repossession was conducted via a sale).

In addition, a transfer statement along with the certificate of repossession is required to complete the ownership transfer.

Registration for aircraft not previously registered in a foreign country takes effect at the date and time the FAA Aircraft Registry receives the documents required to complete registration. For an aircraft previously registered in a foreign country, registration comes into effect only when the registration certificate is issued.

Again, the FAA requires all aircraft to be registered under the owner, which broadly speaking, is the person or entity holding title to the asset. Conversely, some countries, such as the United Kingdom, use operator-based registries. Given the security benefits (discussed later), many owners

UNITED STATES OF AMERICA
U.S. DEPARTMENT OF TRANSPORTATION FEDERAL AVIATION ADMINISTRATION

OMB Control No. 2120-0042
Exp. 09/30/2020

AIRCRAFT BILL OF SALE

FOR AND IN CONSIDERATION OF $ THE UNDERSIGNED OWNER(S) OF THE FULL LEGAL AND BENEFICIAL TITLE OF THE AIRCRAFT DESCRIBED AS FOLLOWS:

UNITED STATES REGISTRATION NUMBER **N**

AIRCRAFT MANUFACTURER & MODEL

AIRCRAFT SERIAL NO.

DOES THIS DAY OF ,
HEREBY SELL, GRANT, TRANSFER AND DELIVER ALL RIGHTS, TITLE, AND INTERESTS IN AND TO SUCH AIRCRAFT UNTO:

Do Not Write In This Block
FOR FAA USE ONLY

PURCHASER

NAME AND ADDRESS
(IF INDIVIDUAL(S), GIVE LAST NAME, FIRST NAME, AND MIDDLE INITIAL.)

DEALER CERTIFICATE NUMBER

AND TO EXECUTORS, ADMINISTRATORS, AND ASSIGNS TO HAVE AND TO HOLD SINGULARLY THE SAID AIRCRAFT FOREVER, AND WARRANTS THE TITLE THEREOF:

IN TESTIMONY WHEREOF HAVE SET HAND AND SEAL THIS DAY OF

SELLER

NAME(S) OF SELLER (TYPED OR PRINTED)	SIGNATURE(S) (IN INK) (IF EXECUTED FOR CO-OWNERSHIP, ALL MUST SIGN.)	TITLE (TYPED OR PRINTED)

ACKNOWLEDGMENT (NOT REQUIRED FOR PURPOSES OF FAA RECORDING: HOWEVER, MAY BE REQUIRED BY LOCAL LAW FOR VALIDITY OF THE INSTRUMENT.)

ORIGINAL: TO FAA:

AC Form 8050-2 (10/18)

FIGURE 4.8

FAA Aircraft Bill of sale format.

FAA Website, Form AC 8050-2.

OMB Control No. 2120-0042
Exp. 09/30/2020

PRA Public Burden Statement: A federal agency may not conduct or sponsor, and a person is not required to respond to, nor shall a person be subject to a penalty for failure to comply with a collection of information subject to the requirements of the Paperwork Reduction Act unless that collection of information displays a currently valid OMB Control Number. The OMB Control Number for this information collection is 2120-0042. Public reporting for this collection of information is estimated to be approximately 30 minutes per response, including the time for reviewing instructions, searching existing data sources, gathering and maintaining the data needed, completing and reviewing the collection of information. All responses to this collection of information are required to show evidence of ownership to register an aircraft or hold an aircraft in trust in accordance with 14 CFR Part 47. Send comments regarding this burden estimate or any other aspect of this collection of information, including suggestions for reducing this burden to: Information Collection Clearance Officer, Federal Aviation Administration, 10101 Hillwood Parkway, Fort Worth, TX 76177-1524.

U.S. DEPARTMENT OF TRANSPORTATION FEDERAL AVIATION ADMINISTRATION

Aircraft Registration Branch
PO Box 25504
Oklahoma City, Oklahoma 73125-0504

CERTIFICATE OF REPOSSESSION OF ENCUMBERED AIRCRAFT

The undersigned hereby certifies that they are the true and lawful holder of a note or other evidence of indebtedness secured by a

________________________ on the following described aircraft:
(Type of Security Agreement)

Aircraft Manufacturer and Model ________________________

Aircraft serial number ____________ FAA registration number ____________

Said Security agreement on the above aircraft bears the date of ____________ and was executed by

________________________ to ________________________

and assigned to ________________________. This Security agreement was

recorded under Title 49, United States Code, Section 44107, on the ______ day of ________, ______,

and was entered in the Civil Aviation Registry as document no. ____________.

On the ______ day of ________, ______, the aforesaid ____________ breached the obligations and promises contained in the Security agreement. The undersigned certifies that the secured party has performed all obligations imposed on it by the security agreement and applicable local laws; that in accordance with the terms of said security agreement, and pursuant to the pertinent laws of the state of ____________, the undersigned repossessed the aircraft described above and foreclosed on the ______ day of ________, ______, and that pursuant to local law, divested the said debtor, and any and all persons claiming by, through or under them, of any and all title they had or may have had, and the secured party now owns the aforesaid aircraft, or the aircraft has been sold.

NOTE: If the agreement involved was not recorded with the Aircraft Registration Branch, the original or certified true copy should accompany this certificate of repossession

____
NAME OF HOLDER OF SECURITY AGREEMENT

____
SIGNATURE (IN INK)

____
TITLE

____
ACKNOWLEDGMENT (Not required for purposes of FAA recording; however, may be required by local law for validity of the instrument.

AC FORM 8050-4 (10/18)

FIGURE 4.9

Repossession form, FAA.

FAA Website, Form AC 8050-4.

and operators choose to register their aircraft in the United States. However, some lessors opt to register overseas to enjoy tax deductibility or easier access to registry authorities. In any case, the registry nation is responsible for complying with all international standards and airworthiness directives, and lessors can exercise rights under the Chicago Convention according to the laws of the state registry.

LIENS

Another element of the Cape Town convention relates to the security and filing of liens. A lien is a legal hold placed on an object (by a party) until all debts are cleared by the debtor. In the United States, the Uniform Commercial Code (UCC) governs the process of commercial transactions and is one of many uniform acts meant to harmonize state laws. Specifically, Article 9 of the UCC governs security interests in debt collateral, including how such interests are created (attached) and when they become enforceable (perfected). This is important for aircraft-related liens, because UCC filings function on a first-come, first-served basis. In other words, the first lender to file a UCC lien on an aircraft object will have the "first rights" to collect on the asset. Filing under Article 9 of the UCC is essentially the same as filing with the FAA, but "to the extent that the Federal Aviation Act does not regulate the rights of parties to and third parties affected by such transactions, security interests in aircraft remain subject to this Article, pending passage of federal legislation."[20]

In aviation, liens are broadly classified as consensual (with the consent of the owner or operator) or nonconsensual (without the consent of the owner or operator).

Consensual liens are filed mainly on instruments or parts used in an aircraft. These include airframes, engines, propellers, and spare parts. The FAA requires consensual liens to be filed in a certain manner as a recordation of conveyances, which refers to instruments or objects that may affect the interests in an aircraft. For instance, the laws pertaining to airframes are much broader than those pertaining to engines and propellers, which have certain prerequisites. Liens for spare parts can be recorded only if they are being maintained for the benefit of a certified air carrier. Thus, consensual security interests are perfected through recordation with the FAA.

Registration of *nonconsensual liens* is a more complicated issue. Charges to mechanics, material men, and repairmen are all regarded as nonconsensual liens. These liens mainly arise from aircraft parts supply or from unpaid labor put into aircraft repair and can only be filed if the claimant is in the contracting state, as provided for by FAA rules. The other types of nonconsensual liens are judgment liens and tax liens. Judgment liens can be filed against airframes, engines, propellers, and spare parts under the FAA. However, only state tax liens can be filed with the FAA. The Internal Revenue Code requires all federal tax liens to be filed elsewhere.

Prior to 1981, the FAA accepted all mechanics' liens for recordation from lien claimants in all the 50 states. However, in 1981, the Aeronautical Center Counsel (ACC) took the position that mechanics' liens over aircraft can only be recorded on the FAA Aircraft Registry if the state law creating the lien allows for the creation or perfection of such liens. The ACC currently maintains a

[20]UCC Section 9-104(a).

list of the 37 jurisdictions that maintain recording statutes that satisfy the ACC's criteria. It is important to emphasize that the Federal Aviation Act preemption for the mechanics' lien laws for those 37 jurisdictions is very limited—only the *location* for filing a lien statement is preempted.

The Federal Aviation Act does not preempt other aspects of state law regarding the creation, nature, perfection, or priority of such liens. Filing a lien outside one of the jurisdictions on the ACC's list makes the lien imperfect and renders it unenforceable against third parties. However, filing with the FAA Aircraft Registry alone does not ensure that a mechanic's lien is enforceable. This is because state law still governs the enforceability of mechanics' liens; thus, depending on the state's law and recording a mechanic's lien on the FAA Aircraft Registry may be insufficient to render it enforceable.

A floating mechanic's lien attaches to equipment that comes into possession of a mechanic who has not been paid for work previously performed on other property belonging to the debtor. The debtor needs not be the owner of the equipment. At least one jurisdiction, Georgia, recognizes floating mechanics' liens over aircraft equipment. Floating mechanics' liens are noteworthy because of their potential to pose a much greater threat to interests involving aircraft equipment in states where they are recognized over other types of mechanics' liens. A floating lien, for an amount representing every dollar that a debtor owes a mechanic, could attach to a single piece of aircraft equipment, which in turn, could potentially wipe out the security interest of a prior-perfected mortgagee. This creates a major problem for secured lenders, particularly when a specific mechanic regularly performs work on a debtor's fleet.

Liens pose considerable risk for lessors attempting to repossess aircraft. For example, the borrower may owe back taxes on the asset, which may also carry an additional lien for repairs. Likewise, airports can hold liens on landing charges or unpaid fines. Depending on the circumstances, these liens may attach to a specific debt or extend to other assets in the borrower's fleet. In general, liens associated with operation are not typically attached to the aircraft. For example, airport charges are typically owned by the aircraft operator rather than owner (Narayanan, 2013, p. 5). This was the case in Aer Lingus Limited v. Airport Authority of India.[21] The court ruled that any dues owed by Aer Lingus to the airport would not prevent the aircraft owner from deregistering or repossessing his asset.

JURISDICTIONAL REVIEW FOR CROSS-BORDER TRANSACTIONS

The Cape Town Convention makes foreign leasing much more feasible, but there are still considerable risks involved with financing or leasing aircraft outside the United States. Ideally, foreign jurisdictions should provide the financier with rights and remedies substantially similar to those he/she might receive domestically. There are also minimum criteria that need to be met in order to take part in cross-border financing. First and foremost, the country of registry should be a party to the Chicago Convention. This ensures that registration, maintenance, and operations are carried out accurately according to standards. The favorability of local laws and customs in the jurisdiction where the aircraft will be primarily operated is of vital importance to the financier. For instance, the financier should verify beforehand whether or not the aircraft can be deregistered. Also, choice of law in the jurisdiction can prove to be a determining factor in many situations.

[21]Writ Petition No. 618 of 1997 & Notice of Motion No. 586 of 1997. Decided March 9, 2011.

Ideally, the aircraft is registered in the jurisdiction where it is primarily operated, but as we learned earlier, there is also an option to register the aircraft in the United States. A financier should state such interest in the documentation within the foreign aircraft registry, even though the aircraft is owned by the operator.

In the case of operator default, the financier should be able to deregister the aircraft and repossess its rights. However, the foreign jurisdiction must be a Chicago Convention signatory and agree to the procedure. Again, the Kingfisher case proves that repossession alone is insufficient. Full deregistration is required before the aircraft can be reregistered or sold (Gerber & Walton, 2014). Furthermore, it is imperative that the financier obtains an irrevocable power of attorney from the operator that grants him/her the authority to seek such action. This should be provided at the time the aircraft is delivered to the lessee.

Unfortunately, the presence of a lien on leased equipment deprives the financier from realizing its full value upon exercising any remedy. Recall the lien risks mentioned earlier. Apart from standard types of liens—mechanic or tax—the operation of an aircraft in a foreign jurisdiction can result in aircraft-specific liens. Under local statutory rights of detention, a foreign aviation authority could detain or even sell the aircraft to compensate for unpaid air navigation fees. Again, these charges may be levied on a leased asset or on any aircraft in the operator's fleet. To avoid such issues, a lessor should state in the lease that these charges are to be paid promptly. In fact, most financiers require their lessees to provide a monthly or quarterly report proving payment of such charges. Alternatively, lessors also have the right to obtain this information directly from the respective authority.

LIABILITY

The Warsaw Convention laid much of the groundwork related to liability in aviation. From a lessor's perspective, it is important to understand the level of exposure resulting from an airline-operated aircraft. Who is responsible for damage to the asset? What about damage to passengers? In the United States, liability laws and limits are governed at both the state and federal level.

LESSOR/OWNER LIABILITY

Most states impose strict liability on the owner (including the lessor) for harm resulting from the use or operation of equipment. For manufacturers, this means product liability, particularly when a sale is made with the knowledge of a defect that can negatively impact the operation of an aircraft. Similarly, the lessor can be held liable based on the theory of negligence, as it is his/her duty to know that the equipment sold was unsafe to operate. In court, however, negligence theories are commonly overlooked on the grounds that lessors are merely financiers who need not know the mechanical details of operation. This is supported by the fact that the lessor does not make any representation of the product to the lessee or to the public in general. Another factor protecting the lessor from liability is that the financier is not directly involved in any of the manufacturing processes. Thus, the lessor has no control over the quality of the product being delivered.

A few states do still impose strict liability on owners, even though the owners are only holding the title of lessor under a financial lease. To further protect such lessors, US Federal Statute 49 preempts any contrary state laws that impose liabilities on lessors or passive owners. The statute states that financial lessors, passive owners, and lenders of aircraft are not held responsible for any personal injury, death, or property damage caused by an aircraft. However, the lessor can still be held liable if there is any damage to life or property resulting from aircraft that is "actually possessed or controlled" by the lessor. A financier is further guarded from potential liabilities by naming them as indemnities under the general indemnity provision in the lease.

OPERATOR LIABILITY

In general, lessees are required to operate and maintain aircraft in a locally and federally lawful manner. The operation must comply with all regulatory requirements in the given jurisdiction. Likewise, the lessee is responsible to maintain such aircraft pursuant to a maintenance program approved by the respective national aviation authority (NAA) using NAA approved parts and qualified NAA licensed mechanics. These provisions mean limited liability for the lessor, who typically has "no duty to inspect [aircraft] and shall not incur any liability or obligation by reason of not making any such inspection" [Securities and Exchange Commission (SEC), 2012, art 3.7].

When it comes to distress situations, a lease will typically provide the lessor with comprehensive protection against damages resulting from operation or maintenance of the aircraft. This is assuming that the lessee has adequate insurance (Shupe & Buhler, 2004).

AVIATION INSURANCE

One of the key takeaways from the Montreal Convention was the requirement that all airlines carry liability insurance for passenger death and injury. Similar in other industries, this is a contract whereby an airline or operator (the insured) pays a qualifying insurer for indemnity against certain operational risks. The concept stems from 15th century sea trade, but the first policy for air transport was written in 1911.

Today, coverage is available to both the commercial and general sectors, but when it comes to leasing, it makes the most sense for airlines and operators to assume and control this risk. Therefore, it is the lessee/borrower, rather than the financier/lessor, who is responsible for maintaining a policy on each aircraft. Policies vary according to the nature of the operation but generally fit into one of several categories:

- *Hull Insurance* covers all aircraft parts against physical damage that occurs whether the aircraft is parked or in motion, where the cost to correct such damage is in excess of a significant deductible amount. In the event of a total loss, the insurer will pay the insured value regardless of the aircraft's current market value. Total airframe loss is considered a total aircraft loss, with the insurer having salvage rights on all equipment including engines, but excluding spare parts. Agreed value does not require proof of loss and is a common practice in commercial aviation. See Chapter 5 for consent requirements and hull coverage variations.
- *Liability Insurance* covers physical injury to passengers as well as any damage to public (third-party) persons or property resulting from an aircraft's operation. However, this coverage is capped and limited to claims arising from a single occurrence. As such, an airline may be left to handle additional losses that were caused by a particular event. Most underwriters use combined

single limit policies (Chapter 5) to provide airlines and operators with more flexibility when handling major losses.

- *War and Allied Peril Insurance* protects against risks such as war, hostile detonation of atomic weapons, strikes, riots, civil commotion, terrorist acts, and hijacking. This category is explicitly omitted from hull coverage policies. Similar to liability insurance, war and peril coverage is limited to fixed amounts per occurrence. However, after the 9/11 terrorist attacks, the US Government stepped in with dedicated loans, bailouts, and compensation funds to assist operators and private insurers.
- *Political Risk Insurance* extends to government action or inaction in the aircraft's registry state. However, it is the lessor who is responsible for purchasing and maintaining this type of policy. Such coverage is primarily used for financiers who are unable to repossess or recover their assets. It also extends to tax risks, currency inconvertibility, trade issues, confiscation, and government refusal of deregistration (Gerber, 2012).

Aviation insurance is a broad market with considerable variability. Therefore, we discuss the evolution and application of these concepts in greater detail in Chapter 5.

BANKRUPTCY AND SECTION 1110

Recall our previous discussion on Cape Town remedies. The ultimate goal was to standardize aviation law as it applies to financiers, particularly when it comes to foreign insolvency procedures with weak protection for creditors. Alternative A of the convention offers substantial support to capital markets and essentially parallels the same protections outlined in Section 1110 of the US Bankruptcy code, provided the creditor has a registered interest. In this section, we discuss bankruptcy proceedings, reorganization, and protection.

LIQUIDATION VERSUS REORGANIZATION

Financial distress can lead an airline to bankruptcy, but it does not always mean imminent demise. In many cases, the firm will be forced into a financial restructure after defaulting on its contracts. This process typically begins by reducing capital spending and/or selling off assets. Another option is to merge. Conversely, liabilities restructuring involves issuing new securities, negotiating with creditors, exchanging debt for equity, and worst case, filing for bankruptcy.

Filing for the US Bankruptcy under Chapter 7 means terminating the firm as a going concern. In this situation, either the firm or one of its creditors files a court petition, after which an elected trustee starts liquidating or salvaging the assets. Payments are then prioritized according to claim. After administrative fees, back wages, consumer claims, and, taxes, proceeds then go toward paying off creditors. Any remaining amount gets distributed first to preferred shareholders and then to common stock shareholders.

Alternatively, a firm that files under Chapter 11 remains a going concern. This type of bankruptcy is commonly called reorganization and may involve issuing new securities. After the court approval of a voluntary or involuntary petition, the firm is given 120 days to submit a reorganization plan, which must be approved by at least half of the creditors who claim two-thirds of the debt. Payments begin once the plan is accepted and confirmed in court.

AIRLINE BANKRUPTCIES

Nearly 200 airline bankruptcies have been filed in the United States since 1978. Some of the most notable cases are also the most recent:

American Airlines, 2011 (Chapter 11)
Delta Airlines, 2005 (Chapter 11)
Northwest Airlines, 2005 (Chapter 11)
US Airways, 2002, 2004 (Chapter 11)
United Airlines, 2002 (Chapter 11)
Aloha Airlines, 2008 (Chapter 7)
Midway Airlines, 2003 (Chapter 7)
Southeast Airlines, 2004 (Chapter 7)

Europe tells a similar story, as the market continually draws in new carriers while driving out others. In fact, the famous Swiss Air Grounding of 2001 proved that no carrier is too big to fail. So, why do so many airlines struggle? The simple answer is leverage. Airlines naturally operate with fixed costs that are much higher than their variable costs. Such high operating leverage can lead to cash flow problems (flow-based insolvency), particularly amidst a recession, a fuel price increase, a terrorist event, or other external shock. Airlines also operate under high financial leverage, meaning they are financing most of their assets with debt. This leads to stock-based insolvency.

We mentioned earlier that merging is one solution to financial distress. Mergers often go hand in hand with bankruptcy because airlines can save cash when creditors are paid in goods or services, and the process also opens up special provisions for fleet upgrades. Furthermore, the Justice Department usually tries to mitigate antitrust issues for airlines that merge after declaring bankruptcy.

PROTECTION FOR FINANCIERS

Section 1110 of the US Bankruptcy code includes special security measures for aircraft financiers and applies to leases, conditional agreements, and conditional sales contracts. These protections are designed to help lessors obtain their assets immediately following a default. 1110 (a) 1 of the code states:

> Except as provided in paragraph (2) and subject to subsection (b), the right of a secured party with a security interest in equipment described in paragraph (3), or of a lessor or conditional vendor of such equipment, to take possession of such equipment in compliance with a security agreement, lease, or conditional sale contract, and to enforce any of its other rights or remedies, under such security agreement, lease, or conditional sale contract, to sell, lease, or otherwise retain or dispose of such equipment, is not limited or otherwise affected by any other provision of this title or by any power of the court.[22]

However, a lessor's right to practice remedies is subject to an automatic stay provision in Section 362, which gives debtors the chance to "cure" all existing default obligations within 60 days of the order being filed. If the airline/lessee refuses to make such a court-approved agreement or fails to seek an extension, then the automatic stay no longer applies and the lessor can

[22]Chapter 11, U.S. Bankruptcy Code § 1110—*Aircraft equipment and vessels.*

commence foreclosure or repossess the aircraft. Essentially, the 60-day window is an opportunity for the airline to "reorganize." Thus, protection does not apply to Chapter 7 default cases. Ultimately, a debtor has three options:

1. Make a Section 1110(a) agreement to perform all current and future obligations under the existing finance agreement and cure all default within 60 days.
2. Negotiate to extend the 60-day stay under 1110(b).
3. Refuse to make an agreement, thereby terminating the automatic stay and relinquishing lease rights to the asset.

Debtors/airlines typically exercise 1110 on aircraft in which they have equity value, for equipment that is critical to operations or to renegotiate financing terms for aircraft that are not yet in default. For deficit-value aircraft, the debtor may make an election if the curing costs are minimal. Alternatively, the carrier may decline both elections if the asset is not critical to operations and if the company does not believe that the creditor will enforce repossession remedies. This is known as going naked.

On the other end, the code extends to all lessors and secured creditors, but it does not apply to non-purchase money security interests on any aircraft that was put into service before October 22, 1994. The following requirements apply to all financiers seeking protection under 1110:

1. The debtor must be subject to a Chapter 11 Bankruptcy case.
2. Equipment (asset) is defined as aircraft, engine, propeller, appliance, or spare part.[23]
3. The asset must be under an official lease, conditional agreement, or conditional sales contract.
4. The operative agreement must provide a remedy for default under the 60-day stay (usually implied).
5. The debtor must possess an air-carrier operator certificate issued by the US Department of Transportation under Chapter 447 of title 49 for aircraft capable of carrying 10 or more passengers or at least 6000 lbs of cargo.

If a lessor is unsure whether or not a particular transaction is covered under 1110, he/she should consult the bankruptcy court before attempting to repossess an asset. For example, if there is an excess market supply of a particularly aircraft, the lessor may have less negotiating leverage over the 1110 election. Moreover, the lessor should thoroughly evaluate existing security deposits, maintenance reserves, and the full cost of remarketing the aircraft after exercising these remedies.

DUE DILIGENCE

Today, successfully leasing or financing an aircraft is much more feasible than it was 20 years ago. Nonetheless, it is not without financial and legal risk. Many business professionals have heard of or utilized the process known as Know Your Customer. The central idea behind this philosophy is due diligence. By investigating the identity of a potential client, companies are more likely to avoid loss and corruption. Likewise, it is imperative that aircraft lessors practice due diligence not only just on potential clients but also on existing clients. For example, leasing companies should perform

[23] *Id*, (a)(2)(A).

an annual audit of current accounts. Airlines are highly volatile, so it is wise to consider how operating environments or business models might have changed. In addition, lessors should know shareholders, board members, and other parties that the company may be working with. This information should also be cross-checked with the EU and US consolidated lists.

SANCTIONS

Lessors should also consider any legal restrictions on trade activity with specific countries or individuals. In the United States, for example, the government maintains sanctions and embargoes on several nations, namely, those considered to be state sponsors of terrorism or those with questionable or poor human rights activity. The Treasury Department's Office of Foreign Assets Control (OFAC) also maintains a list of Specially Designated Nationals (SDN) and Blocked Persons. SDNs are individuals or entities that the OFAC has determined to be "owned or controlled by, or acting for or on behalf of targeted countries or groups."[24] It also includes persons or organizations involved in terrorism, rough diamond trade, and drug trafficking. The US citizens are legally prohibited from dealing with assets owned or operated by SDNs. In fact, even the facilitation or consideration of a deal may result in liability.

The situation is similar for lessors in Europe. In 2014, for example, the European Union ordered sanctions against Dobrolet, the Russian-based low-cost subsidiary of Aeroflot. All EU citizens were prohibited from providing any economic resources. As a result, lessors were forced to cancel their agreements with Dobrolet, payments were frozen, and the airline eventually ceased operation in 2014.

It is important to note that while a sanction may be lifted, a government may still require a license to conduct business with the individual or entity in question. Ultimately, it is the lessor's responsibility to practice due diligence. Moreover, they should be reasonably confident that a client is operating within the laws of its jurisdiction.

MULTILATERALISM AND OPEN SKIES

Up to this point, we have discussed the modern applicability of aviation conventions, but one main concept that has surfaced throughout is the idea of multiple states acting collectively on cross-border issues. Chicago, Warsaw, and Cape Town all established one or more bilateral or multilateral treaties. By nature, aviation is a global industry and operates under policies and authorities that were created at these conventions. In this final section, we outline these principles as they exist today and follow with a brief overview of the key international organizations that continue to oversee and advocate for global aviation.

FREEDOMS OF THE AIR

After World War I, many state-owned airlines stood as symbols of national pride, hence the term "legacy carrier." As mentioned earlier, it was the Chicago Convention that ultimately set the stage for liberalization in the civil sector, where bilateral and multilateral agreements were developed to

[24]U.S. Department of the Treasury Resource Center, *Specially Designated Nationals (SDN) and the SDN List.*

facilitate passenger service between different countries. As part of this effort, the convention established distinct freedoms that grant scheduled airlines the privilege to enter and land in a foreign airspace. These rights, eventually expanded to nine Freedoms of the Air, are as follows [International Civil Aviation Organization (ICAO), 2004]:

- *First Freedom*—The right or privilege to fly over a foreign territory without landing. Nearly all countries, including non-signatories, grant this right, although some charge a fee based on the distance traveled.

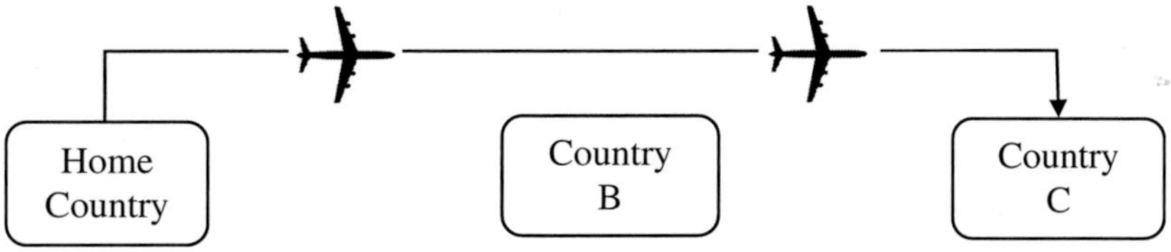

- *Second Freedom*—The right or privilege to make a technical stop in another country without disembarking. This typically means refueling or maintenance. While this right was heavily utilized during the 20th century, technical stops are less common with today's high-tech aircraft.

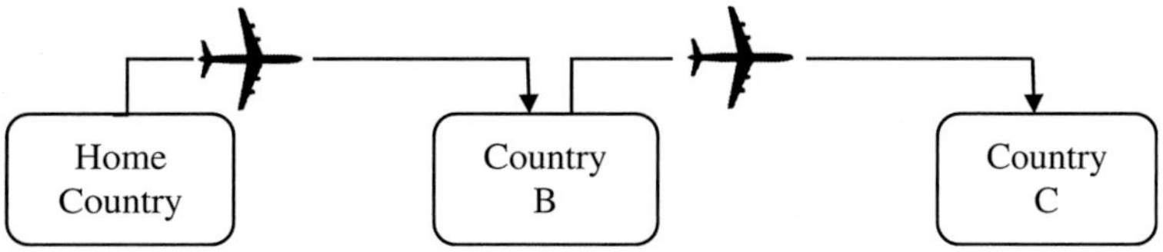

- *Third Freedom*—The right or privilege to land and disembark in a foreign country. This is typically granted in conjunction with the fourth freedom below. Moreover, some states may only allow access to certain routes, airports, or city pairs.

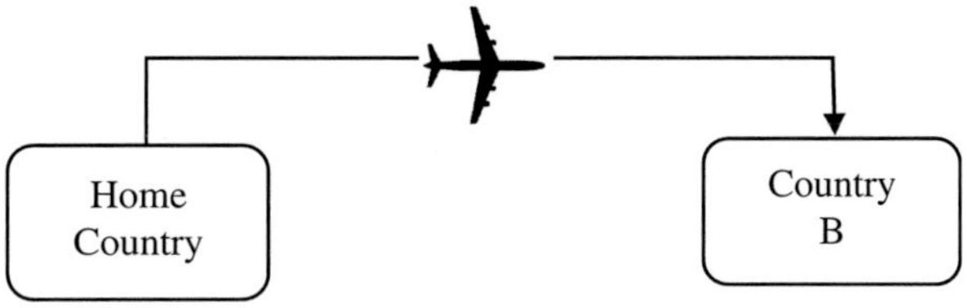

- *Fourth Freedom*—The right or privilege to fly from a foreign country back to the carrier's home country.

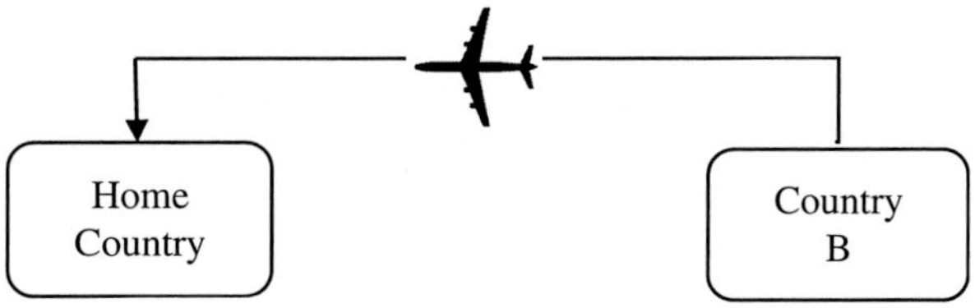

- *Fifth Freedom*—The right or privilege to fly to and disembark passengers in a foreign country and then continue on to a third destination. All three countries must be in agreement.

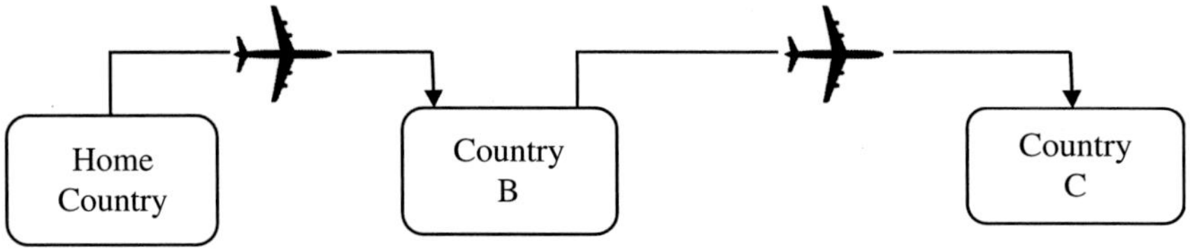

- *Sixth Freedom*—The right or privilege to fly between two foreign countries but, on the way, make a full stop in the carrier's home country. This is common on flights from the United States to Africa via Europe and from Europe to South America via the United States.

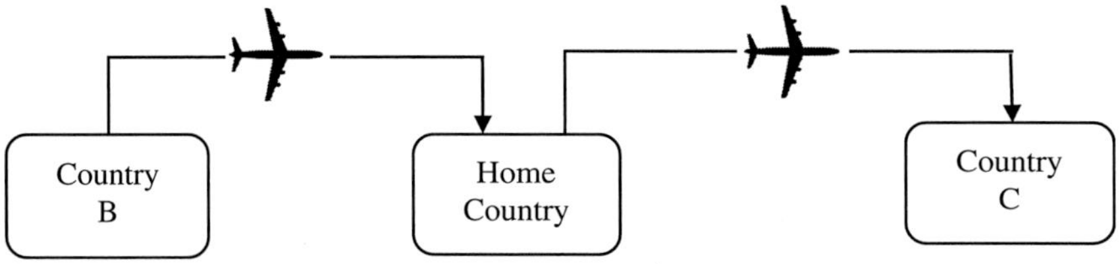

- *Seventh Freedom*—The right or privilege to fly between two foreign countries without touching down in the carrier's home country. Initially, this freedom was practiced almost exclusively in Europe, but other countries have opened up such access, namely, for cargo.

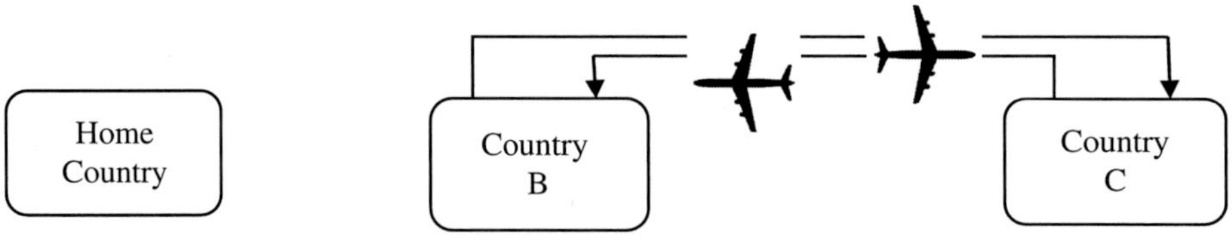

- *Eighth Freedom*—The right or privilege to fly between two points within a foreign country on a service that originates in the carrier's home country (cabotage).

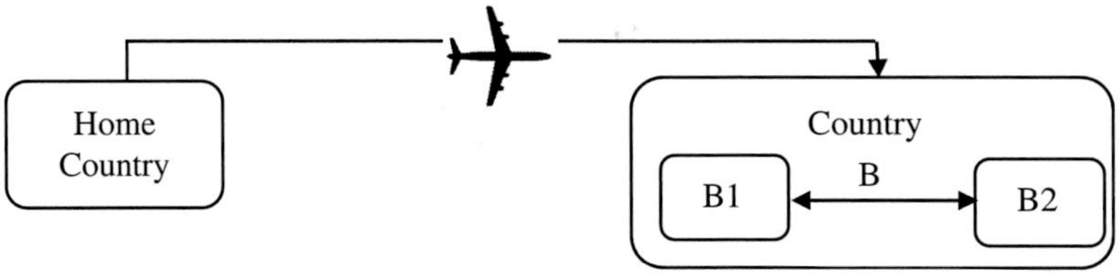

- *Ninth Freedom*—The right or privilege to fly between two points within a foreign country on a service that originates in that foreign country (stand-alone cabotage).

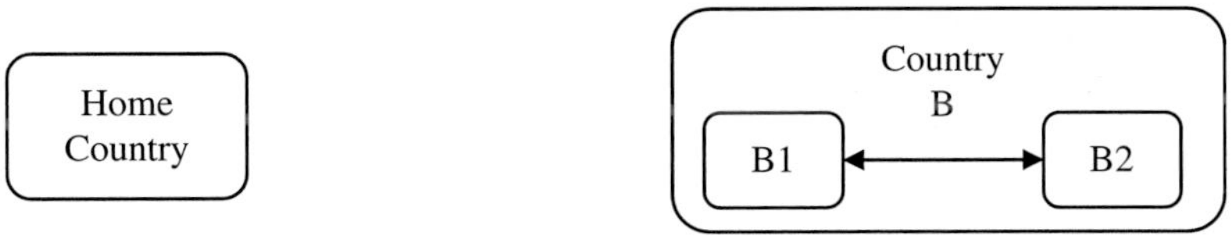

Most nations recognize the first two freedoms through the Chicago Convention. The remaining rights are usually recognized through bilateral or multilateral service agreements. Furthermore, the last four rights are commonly referred to as unofficial or so-called freedoms, as they remain heavily debated among governments and regulators. This is especially true for rights involving cabotage, which is still rarely practiced outside of Europe.

OPEN SKIES

Aviation continued to liberalize into the 21st century, and Open Skies is a term that refers to this very concept—limiting government intervention and opening up markets for international passenger and cargo traffic. The following introduction comes from the current US model for Open Skies agreements:

The Government of the United States of America and the Government of [country] (hereinafter, "the Parties");

Desiring to promote an international aviation system based on competition among airlines in the marketplace with minimum government interference and regulation;

Desiring to make it possible for airlines to offer the traveling and shipping public a variety of service options, and wishing to encourage individual airlines to develop and implement innovative and competitive prices;

Desiring to facilitate the expansion of international air transport opportunities;

Desiring to ensure the highest degree of safety and security in international air transport and reaffirming their grave concern about acts or threats against the security of aircraft, which jeopardize the safety of persons or property, adversely affect the operation of air transportation, and undermine public confidence in the safety of civil aviation; and

Being Parties to the Convention on International Civil Aviation, done at Chicago December 7, 1944;

Have agreed as follows (US State Department, Bureau of Economic and Business Affairs, 2017).

The United States has been the front-runner of the Open Skies movement, having had initiated over 20 bilateral arrangements by the early 1980s. Europe followed suit over the following decade. In 2001, the United States signed the industry's first multilateral agreement with four other countries—Brunei, Chile, Singapore, and New Zealand. Likewise, the EU–US Open Skies agreement of 2008 allows any EU- or US-based airline to fly between any point in the United States and any point within a European Union country.

Since 1992, the United States has adopted 120 Open Skies partnerships with nations of all economic levels (Table 4.1), and these partner destinations account for 70% of the current international departures from the United States. In 2015 and 2016, the State Department announced finalized arrangements with seven additional countries.

Today, Open Skies service agreements initiated between two countries typically increase air traffic by approximately 17% (InterVISTAS, 2015). Such arrangements not only make air service more efficient and affordable, but they also stimulate trade, job creation, and overall economic growth. According to the US State Department, Bureau of Economic and Business Affairs (2017), estimates on the recent impact of Open Skies include the following:

- $4 billion annually in economic consumer gain
- Over $1 billion in US air freight to the Middle East, India, and Africa (2013)
- A 938% increase in the number of Brazilian visitors to Orlando, Florida
- $720 million in annual economic activity from a new US–EU direct route

INTERNATIONAL CIVIL AVIATION ORGANIZATION

Recalling our introduction on conventions, ICAO is a UN-specialized agency established in 1944. This organization continues to administer and govern the Convention on International Civil Aviation (Chicago). ICAO currently works with industry leaders and the convention's 191 signatories to *reach consensus on international civil aviation Standards and Recommended Practices (SARPs) and policies in support of a safe, efficient, secure, economically sustainable and environmentally responsible civil aviation sector.*[25] Member states use these standards and policies to ensure that local operations and regulations are conducive to those in other countries. An elected council governs the organization, while an assembly of state representatives meets every 3 years. In addition, the Secretariat consists of five bureaus: air navigation, air transport, technical cooperation, legal, and administration and services.

ICAO also provides safety audits, performance reports, and local assistance for global-development projects. At the 38th assembly, for example, all members agreed to create a market-based measure on emissions by 2016. *The work being done on a global solution to deal with emissions makes an even bigger statement about the enduring relevance of inclusive thinking* (IATA, 2014).

INTERNATIONAL AIR TRANSPORT ASSOCIATION

International Air Transport Association (IATA) is the world airline trade association. It represents 83% of global traffic and 265 member carriers in 121 countries. Montreal serves as headquarters, but the association operates 63 separate offices around the world. The association's core mission is to lead and serve the industry, with a vision *to be the force for value creation and innovation driving a safe, secure, and profitable air transport industry that sustainably connects and enriches our*

[25] www.icao.int/about-icao/Pages/default.aspx.

Table 4.1 US Open Skies Partners (2017)

Partner	Status/Date		Partner	Status/Date		Partner	Status/Date		Partner	Status/Date	
Netherlands	In force	1992	Romania	In force	1998	Madagascar	Provisional	2004	Croatia	In force	2008
Belgium	Provisional	1995	Italy	Provisional	1998	Gabon	In force	2004	Kenya	In force	2008
Finland	In force	1995	UAE	In force	1999	Indonesia	C&R[a]	2004	Laos	In force	2008
Denmark	In force	1995	Pakistan	In force	1999	Uruguay	In force	2004	Armenia	In force	2008
Norway	In force	1995	Bahrain	In force	1999	India	In force	2005	Zambia	In force	2010
Sweden	In force	1995	Tanzania	Provisional	1999	Paraguay	In force	2005	Israel	In force	2010
Luxembourg	In force	1995	Portugal	In force	1999	Maldives	In force	2005	Trinidad & Tob. Tobago	In force	2010
Austria	In force	1995	Slovak Rep.	In force	2000	Ethiopia	In force	2005	Barbados	In force	2010
Iceland	In force	1995	Namibia	C&R[a]	2000	Thailand	In force	2005	Japan	In force	2010
Switzerland	In force	1995	Burkina Faso	In force	2000	Mali	In force	2005	Colombia	In force	2010
Czech Rep.	In force	1995	Turkey	In force	2000	Bosnia & Herz.	In force	2005	Brazil	N/A	2010
Germany	Provisional	1996	Gambia	In force	2000	Cameroon	Provisional	2006	Saudi Arabia	In force	2011
Jordan	In force	1996	Nigeria	Provisional	2000	Cook Islands	In force	2006	St. Kitts	In force	2011
Singapore	In force	1997	Morocco	In force	2000	Chad	Provisional	2006	Montenegro	In force	2011
Taiwan	In force	1997	Ghana	In force	2000	Kuwait	In force	2006	Suriname	In force	2012
Costa Rica	In force	1997	Rwanda	In force	2000	Liberia	In force	2007	Sierra Leone	In force	2012
El Salvador	In force	1997	Malta	In force	2000	Canada	In force	2007	Macedonia	In force	2012
Guatemala	In force	1997	Benin	N/A	2000	Bulgaria	Provisional	2007	Seychelles	In force	2012
Honduras	Provisional	1997	Senegal	In force	2000	Cyprus	Provisional	2007	Yemen	C&R3	2012
Nicaragua	In force	1997	Poland	In force	2001	Estonia	Provisional	2007	Guyana	In force	2013
Panama	In force	1997	Oman	In force	2001	Greece	Provisional	2007	Bangladesh	C&R3	2013
New Zealand	In force	1997	Qatar	Provisional	2001	Hungary	Provisional	2007	Botswana	In Force	2013
Brunei	In force	1997	France	In force	2001	Ireland	Provisional	2007	Equatorial Guinea	In force	2014
Malaysia	In force	1997	Sri Lanka	In force	2001	Latvia	Provisional	2007	Burundi	C&R3	2014

(Continued)

Table 4.1 US Open Skies Partners (2017) *Continued*

Partner	Status/Date		Partner	Status/Date		Partner	Status/Date		Partner	Status/Date	
Aruba	In force	1997	Uganda	In force	2002	Lithuania	Provisional	2007	Togo	In force	2015
Chile	In force	1997	Cape Verde	In force	2002	Slovenia	Provisional	2007	Serbia	In force	2015
Uzbekistan	In force	1998	Samoa	In force	2002	Spain	Provisional	2007	Ukraine	In force	2015
Korea	In force	1998	Jamaica	In force	2002	United Kingdom	Provisional	2007	Côte d'Ivoire	In force	2015
Peru	In force	1998	Tonga	In force	2003	Georgia	In force	2007	Azerbaijan	In force	2016
The Netherland Ant.	In force	1998	Albania	In force	2003	Australia	In force	2008	Curaçao[b]	N/A	2016

Complied using US Department of State, Full List of Open Skies Partners.
[a]*Comity and Reciprocity.*
[b]*The Netherlands.*

world.[26] IATA reports are viewed as standard across the industry, and the organization holds an annual summit to facilitate the discussion of policy issues and to share resources that promote education and transparency in aviation.

INTERNATIONAL SOCIETY OF TRANSPORT AIRCRAFT TRADING

International Society of Transport Aircraft Trading (ISTAT) began in 1983 and since been *dedicated to fostering and promoting interest and educational opportunities in commercial aviation while providing a forum for those involved in the aviation and supporting industries.*[27] ISTAT is the leading association for industry networking and education, and it currently represents over 4100 global members in manufacturing, sales, financing, and more. It also runs the International Appraiser Program, which consists of all training and certification on aircraft and supporting equipment. ISTAT educates through publications and conferences and continues to provide scholarships, grants, and internships to students and organizations all over the world.

CONCLUSION

As we have discussed, aviation is highly regulated in terms of how and where a plane can operate. From a financing standpoint, the primary factor is that airplanes move. But a mobile asset is even more complex when every problem can be a seven-figure or greater situation. The lessee's job is to operate legally and safely, carry insurance, and perform all obligations under the operative agreement. The lessor's job is to make sure the operator does so while protecting the value of the asset. Does the Cape Town Convention apply? What remedies fall under the US bankruptcy law? When it comes to cross-border transactions, financiers should have a thorough understanding of the legal environment of each jurisdiction and any available remedies. They must properly assess and identity location-based risk and always pre-confirm whether or not an aircraft can be deregistered. A key takeaway from this chapter is the importance of laying groundwork. A lessor who develops relationships with the operator and regulators before entering into a contract is less likely to experience a complicated legal battle.

APPENDIX 4A: THE ENGLISH BLUE SKY CASE

Blue Sky v. Mahan Air1 is a case involving an international dispute over the mortgage rights of six Boeing 747-422 airplanes. These aircraft were acquired under English law through special purpose vehicles. The owners leased the assets to a company in Armenia, but the planes were chartered and operated by Mahan Air, a private Iranian airline. The dispute surfaced as a result of the US sanctions against exporting certain aircraft assets to Iran, and in 2010, the English High Court addressed the validity of their existing mortgages. This case specifically addresses two of these aircraft. One

[26]www.IATA.org, *Fact Sheet: IATA Facts & Figures.*
[27]www.istat.org/aboutus.

plane held Armenian nationality and was allegedly located in Iran, while the other plane held English nationality and remained parked at Schiphol International Airport in The Netherlands.

The two aircraft were mortgaged to PK AirFinance, a financier in the United States. Moreover, the signatories had explicitly agreed to use the English law. When the debtor defaulted, PK AirFinance commenced foreclosure proceedings in England, and Mahan Air subsequently challenged the validity of the mortgages. Because the situation involved several countries with differing laws, the court had to decide which to apply. A further question was whether or not to use local choice of law rules (*renvoi* doctrine). In the end, the court agreed on *lex situs* and did not use *lex registrii* for either asset. However, for the Armenian-registered plane supposedly in Iran, the court felt that there was not substantial evidence as to the asset's location. Under English property law, this mortgage was considered invalid. As for the English-registered plane at Schiphol, the Dutch choice of law was the English law, or *lex registrii.* The court did not want to use *renvoi* doctrine and revert back to English law. Thus, the mortgage was unenforceable in England but ruled invalid under Dutch law. As a result, PK AirFinance was left with an unenforceable claim, thereby losing the entire value of $43.1 million.

PK AirFinance had sought justice under the Geneva Convention, arguing for the strict use of *lex registrii* based on the fact that aircraft move regularly "from situs to situs" (Honnebier, 2011, p. 4). The court's response simply emphasized its intent to use the most appropriate law given the situation. To solidify this decision, the judge referenced a prior case in which *lex situs* was applied to the transfer of aircraft ownership and in which *lex registrii* was dismissed as a general application to aviation. However, lawyers have since emphasized other English legal writings, which indicate a clear preference for *lex registrii* over *lex situs*. The consensus appears to view aircraft nationality as the key factor in determining ownership. Therefore, many argue that PK AirFinance should have encouraged the court to address these publications more closely.

Please prepare a memo (no more than 3 pages) on the Blue Sky Case in which you address the following:

- Summarize the case (feel free to research what really happened with the leases).
- State the problem described in the case.
- Discuss the consequences of the court decision.
- Provide an analysis on the applicability of Geneva Convention to the situation described in the case.
- Provide an analysis on the applicability of the Cape Town Convention to the situation described in the case.

REFERENCES

Boyle, R. P. (1973). The Guatemala Protocol. *Akron Law Review*, *6*(2). Article 2. Retrieved from: http://ideaexchange.uakron.edu/akronlawreview/vol6/iss2/2.

Gerber, D. N. (2012). Chapter 7 aircraft finance. In I. Shrank, & A. G. Gough (Eds.), Equipment leasing-leveraged leasing (5th ed.). Practicing Law Institute.

Gerber, D. N., & Walton, D. R. (2014). Deregistration and export remedies under the Cape Town Convention. *Cape Town Convention Journal.*

Honnebier, P. (2011). *The English blue sky case—Topical international aviation finance law issues*. Utrecht: Air and Space Books.

IATA. (2014). *Are governments crowding out the Chicago Convention?*. Regulations & Taxation/Global/August 20, 2014. <https://airlines.iata.org/analysis/are-governments-crowding-out-the-chicago-convention>.

ICAO. *The history of ICAO and the Chicago Convention*. (2017). Retrieved from <http://www.icao.int/about-icao/History/Pages/default.aspx>.

International Air Transport Association (IATA). (November 2016). *Montreal Convention 1999 (MC99)*. Fact Sheet. Retrieved from <https://www.iata.org/pressroom/facts_figures/fact_sheets/Documents/fact-sheet-mc99.pdf>.

International Civil Aviation Organization (ICAO). (2004). *Manual on the regulation of International Air Transport*. 2nd ed.

International Monetary Fund (IMF). *Special Drawing Rights*. (October 2016). IMF Factsheet. Retrieved from <http://www.imf.org/external/np/exr/facts/sdr.htm>.

InterVISTAS. (2015). *Economic impacts of air service liberalization*. Published on the U.S. Department of State website.

Narayanan, N. (2013). *Aircraft Repossession in India—Turbulence ahead, Buckle Up!. 8 Annals of Air and Space Law*. (pp. 445–460). McGill University.

Securities and Exchange Commission (SEC). (2012). Exhibit 10.44. *Amended and restated master aircraft dry lease agreement*. Retrieved from SEC Lease Archives February 03, 2017 <https://www.sec.gov/Archives/edgar/data/1393818/000119312512085636/d232355dex1044.htm>.

Shupe, J.D., & Buhler, G.W. (2004). *Liability of owners and lessors of aircraft*. Schnader Harrison Segal and Lewis LLP. Presented at AIA Annual Conference May 2004.

United States Postal Service (USPS). *Shipping Label, Item 11FGG1, GXG international Air Waybill*. (2017). Photo Retrieved February 13, 2017 from <http://about.usps.com/postal-bulletin/2009/pb22269/html/kit_002.htm>.

U.S. State Department, Bureau of Economic and Business Affairs. *Open Skies agreement Fact Sheet*. (2017). Retrieved on January 21, 2017 from <https://www.state.gov/e/eb/tra/ata/>.

Vedder Price. (2017). *Getting the deal through: Aviation finance and leasing*. London: Law Business Research LTD.

CHAPTER

AVIATION INSURANCE AND THE IMPACT ON RISK MANAGEMENT 5

CHAPTER OUTLINE

Insurance is a risk-management method that developed from the economic need for an insurance company (the insurer) to protect an individual or entity (the insured) against financial losses for certain liability and/or property damage or destruction resulting from the occurrence of an event covered by such insurance (an insurance event). Such insurance involves a contractual agreement (an insurance policy) between the insured and the insurer, whereby the insured pays the insurer an agreed amount (the premium) in exchange for such coverage by the insurer. When writing an insurance policy, the underwriter carefully evaluates each risk before determining the premium.

There is a certain degree of business risk in every industry; aviation is no exception. Aircraft accidents, fuel price volatility, terrorist attacks, natural disasters, and political instability are examples of risk-associated events that airlines, leasing companies, and aircraft owners face. As such, insurance is a critical aspect of aviation. It is important to understand the different types of coverage options, factors that affect the premium, and the legal regulations of the airline business, as these are all part of the process of drafting an effective insurance policy. The focus of this chapter is to expand upon the insurance terms briefly mentioned in Chapter 4. We begin with an overview of risk management and follow with a detailed discussion of the different types of aviation

Aircraft Leasing and Financing. DOI: https://doi.org/10.1016/B978-0-12-815285-0.00005-5

insurance coverages, the structure of a contract, and how premiums are calculated. Specific chapter topics include the following sections.

INTRODUCTION TO RISK MANAGEMENT

Every person in the world faces risk on a daily basis. Consider the food we eat, the cars we drive, or the investments we make. A driver faces the risk of physical injury when operating a vehicle, whereas an investor faces the risk of a low-financial return or losses when he/she chooses to invest in a volatile stock. What then is the true meaning of the word "risk" in business terms? While every individual and entity faces different risks and takes on risks in different ways, the fundamental idea is management. In other words, the driver may manage the risk of injury by driving slower or avoiding the use of a cell phone, whereas the investor can manage the risk of a poor return by creating a diversified portfolio. Broadly speaking, risk is characterized by

1. The probability of loss or uncertainty.
2. The probability that the outcome will be different from what is intended or expected.

In other words, risk exists when the outcome of a situation is uncertain or contingent on other factors, or if the magnitude of potential loss is unknown.

TYPES OF RISK

Risk classification is an important part of risk management because not all risk can be transferred to the insurance company. Similarly, some risks simply cannot be managed. While there are many different types of risk, we will discuss four classifications that are most common and relevant to industry today.

Static risk

Static risk is caused by irregular threats of nature or of human behavior. This type of risk involves either damage to the asset or a change in its possession. Static risks are not tied to the economy, meaning that some people will have a tendency toward theft and embezzlement, regardless of the current state of the economy. Likewise, earthquakes, tornadoes, and hurricanes can happen at any point in time. It is important to note that static risk occurs on a regular basis and therefore can be predicted and managed with insurance programs (Willett, 1951).

Dynamic risk

Dynamic risk is brought about by changes in what humans want and need. In other words, dynamic risk is directly tied to the economy. For example, technology typically makes processes cheaper and more efficient and often generates a demand shift from one product to another. Dynamic risk affects large groups of people, but unlike static risk, it does not occur on a regular basis. As the result, it cannot be transferred to an insurance company, because events and losses are difficult to predict (Willett, 1951).

Table 5.1 Risk Classification

Pure Risk	Speculative Risk
Insurable	Not insurable
Chance of loss or no change	Chance of loss, gain, or no change
e.g., Natural disaster	*e.g., Gambling*

Fundamental risk

Fundamental risk is a group risk that affects whole cities or countries. Associated losses are not tied to any one individual nor are they within the insured party's control. Wars, unemployment, inflation, interest rates, political instability, and natural disasters are all examples of fundamental risk. Because the loss tends to be relatively large and widespread, governments may establish social insurance programs to subsidize these losses.

Particular risk

Particular risk is a personal risk that affects an individual rather than a group or large population. Examples of particular risks include vandalism, death, and physical illness. Suppose a shopper walks out of a grocery store only to discover that someone has stolen his car from the parking lot. Neither the event itself nor the loss (cost to replace the car) directly affect the other shoppers who have parked their cars in the same lot. Instead, it is the individual's responsibility.

It is worth mentioning that many risk-related terms stem from traditional economic theory that suggests ways in which society can mitigate risk and either anticipate or deal with uncertainty in a reasonable manner. The most useful theory classifies all risk types as either pure or speculative (Table 5.1). *Pure risk* exists when there is a chance of loss but no chance of gain. This was the case with the shopper in the previous example; by purchasing the car, he faced the chance of it being stolen or not being stolen. Put another way, pure risk leads to one of two outcomes: loss or break even. *Speculative risk*, on the other hand, exists when there is a chance for loss but also a chance for gain. One of the best examples of this is gambling; players may win more than they paid in, lose more than they paid in, or simply come out even. Speculative risks are also very common in the business world, although there have been many instances in which society gains from a company's loss (e.g., a low-cost competing product).

RISK-MANAGEMENT TECHNIQUES

It is worth noting that risk is not inherently bad. Individuals and organizations may choose the types of risks they want to be exposed to, which does necessarily mean risk reduction (Culp, 2001). Nonetheless, it is a process. Once risk is identified and properly measured, it can then be managed. There are two techniques used to manage risk: risk control and risk finance.

Risk control

Risk control is a broad method of risk management used to lower a company's liability and reduce exposure to property or personal loss. In essence, controlling risk is attempting to make potential losses more predictable. This can be practiced in a number of ways:

- Avoidance
- Hedging
- Prevention
- Dissipation
- Diversification

Risk avoidance means rejecting untrusted programs or projects and dismissing unreliable contractors and partners. In other words, the first step in risk management is simply to not take the risk. An airline, for example, may practice risk avoidance by operating a young fleet, properly maintaining that fleet, not flying in dangerous regions, training pilots on an annual basis, and continually monitoring the health status of its flight crew.

Hedging is like insurance in which it involves the transfer of risk from a person or entity to another. The entity willing to hedge pays a premium to transfer the risk to what is essentially an insurer, thereby protecting itself from uncertainty in the future. However, the strategy involves using financial instruments, such as forwards, futures, and options, to offset the risk of negative price movements. Airlines exhibit the best example of this. Because fuel is such a large expense and because high jet fuel prices can impact cash flow and influence investors, airlines have a huge incentive to hedge fuel price risk. This allows firms to purchase discounted assets from struggling airlines during periods when fuel prices are high. It also allows them to honor existing purchase commitments. Hedging can help an airline protect its stock value, take advantage of value-added capital-investment decisions, streamline its budget, and stay profitable.

Risk prevention is not the same as simply avoiding risk altogether but rather is an attempt to prevent loss by minimizing danger. Consider how an airline handles some of the risks inherent to flying. Prevention methods include preflight safety checks, no smoking signs, concrete boarding procedures, oxygen masks, and seat belt guidelines. Similarly, moving aircraft to another airport before a pending tornado or windstorm prevents the airline from incurring unnecessary damage costs. For some risks, full prevention is not possible. In this case, the objective would be loss reduction, which aims to reduce the severity of a loss or damage once it has occurred. Safety inspections, fire protections, and claims management are all ways to reduce risk.

Diversification helps reduce total risk simply by spreading it among different investments. Insurance companies practice this strategy by offering different types of coverage options or selling policies in different geographical regions. We can also consider this concept from a lessor's perspective. Which scenario is riskier—leasing several aircrafts to many airlines or leasing an entire fleet to one airline? To answer this question, consider what would happen to the lessor if his/her only client went bankrupt. Spreading risk among different smaller parts is the main idea behind diversification.

Dissipation is the final technique of risk control. This method essentially transfers the overall risk to other parties interested in taking on risk exposure in exchange for premium. A company can reduce its own level of risk by "selling" a portion of it to a willing buyer.

To effectively manage risk, a company must implement some types of risk analysis along with a monitoring program that allows managers to better estimate the probability of a loss event.

Risk finance and insurance

We can now get into the concept of insurance by discussing the other form of risk management—risk finance. Once they accept risk, businesses and individuals must decide how to finance any negative impacts. The main way to do this is to purchase insurance from a third-party provider as a way to handle the uncertainty and avoid a huge financial loss. Recalling our earlier discussion about the types of risk, one key distinction between pure risk and speculative risk is that speculative risk cannot be transferred to an insurance company. On the contrary, most pure risks are predictable and therefore insurable. So, the idea behind the concept of insurance is to substitute uncertainty with certainty and to provide security for the insured party. Fundamentally, insurance involves

1. the transfer of risk from one person or entity to a group *and*
2. the sharing of losses when they occur.

An insurance company essentially takes on the burden of loss and agrees to cover all or a portion of the costs that result from damage to, or an accident involving, the insured object. This is known as an *insurance event*. Under a coverage policy, the individual or entity pays the provider a regular *premium*, which is generally a small amount relative to the cost of an event. Insurance is often referred to as intangible because the insured does not receive any type of physical product. But the social advantage is that the financial burden is spread among a group of individuals. Furthermore, an underwriter or provider may become licensed in different countries or states as a way to further spread the risk.

In addition to the premium is the insurance *deductible*. Although it does not apply to every policy, a deductible is simply a fixed amount of money that the insured must pay out of pocket before the insurer will pay for the claim. Therefore, the insured should fully understand the value of object that is being covered. For instance, a company might accept a $10,000 deductible on a $1,000,000 piece of equipment, because the cost to ensure the asset would only be a fraction of the cost to replace the asset in the event of a total loss. However, with multiple policies or multiple insured objects, the deductible may be higher than the insured is willing to handle. An airline, for example, may choose not to insure the hull value of an old aircraft or engine that is owned and not subject to financing with a short economic life remaining. On the other hand, operating a large fleet of brand new narrow body jets can become a financial disaster in the event of an accident. The key is to assess the possibility of all risk events in the context of one total deductible for an entire insured structure.

Chance of loss vs degree of risk

It is important to remember that insurance does not simply remove risk from an object. For example, driving a car with auto insurance does not directly decrease the chance of getting in a crash. Rather, in the event of a crash, insurance provides full or partial compensation for the insured object, which in this case would be the vehicle and/or the driver. Auto policy providers use variables such as driver age and vehicle model to determine the probability of having to pay out for a claim, but they can never know exactly the extent of the damage or exactly which customers will get into an accident. In many ways, insurance is about quantifying chance.

Chance of loss is expressed as a percentage. This shows the probability of an event occurring, an event which will ultimately lead to a financial loss. For example, suppose 1,000 aircraft are exposed to damage at a particular airport, but the service manager expects that 20 of these aircraft will actually be damaged. Thus, we can say that the chance of loss is 2% (20 out of 1,000 aircraft). Such an estimate may be based on an airport's track record of safety, historic weather patterns, or a combination of many factors. However, it is important to understand the difference between the chance of loss and the degree of risk. The chance of loss is the percentage of loss-occurring events (i.e., 1 out of 50 aircraft), whereas the degree of risk depends on the fluctuation of variables which is used to estimate the chance of loss. The more fluctuated and uncertain the event, the higher the degree of associated risk.

Many insurance companies find it useless to provide financial coverage for exposure that is likely to occur for the majority of cases. Consider auto collision and personal injury coverage; if 99 out of 100 drivers were involved in an accident, it would very difficult for insurers to stay in business. Thus, chance of loss and degree of risk attached are the two main determinants of insurance premiums.

Self-insurance

Self-insurance can also be an instrument of risk finance, whereby a company sets aside its own special account to guarantee a loss appearing from a given event. This is not the same as risk prevention. Moreover, the technique is called self-insurance because there is no transfer of risk from one entity to another. Self-ensuring essentially means carrying the risk. However, a company will typically only do so when the potential loss is expected to be lower than the cost of purchasing and maintaining an insurance policy. A business can self-insure for any type of event. Doing so can certainly have a positive impact on cash flow, but typically only when events are infrequent.

Setting a projected maximum loss at a specific level enables a company to better plan it's operating, investing, and financing activities. Moreover, paying a relatively small price for a premium gives the company more certainty about the future.

CHOOSING A STRATEGY

Risk managers are tasked with choosing the best way to minimize loss, and many believe that companies should implement elements of both risk control and risk finance. For example, a driver might prevent her car from being stolen by installing an antitheft alarm system and parking only in secured lots. In addition, she might opt for an insurance policy that covers theft, in the event that her prevention measures fail to deter a thief. These all are methods of risk control. In the business world, risk managers determine the appropriate methods based on the frequency and severity of an event (Fig. 5.1).

In the real world, the matrix above would be more complex, but the main idea is to allocate each operating activity into an exposure category. For events that are low in severity, a manager might implement active retention and prevention techniques. It is often cheaper to simply pay the costs of these risks than it is to maintain insurance. High-frequency events with a high severity of damage should generally be avoided if possible, as risk cannot be transferred to an insurance

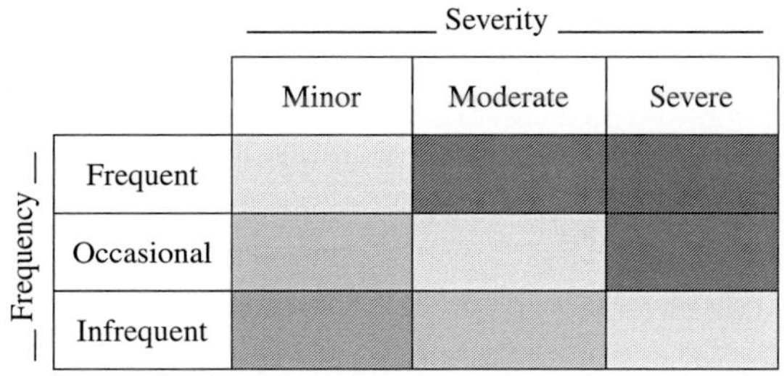

FIGURE 5.1

Sample risk matrix.

company. As we mentioned before, a large number of small claims can add up to a massive expense for a provider.

In general, risk transfer is most appropriate for events with low frequency and high severity. Aircraft hull coverage is a prime example. The remaining portion of this chapter focuses on insurance as it applies to aviation.

AVIATION INSURANCE

Insurance operates under the principle of many customers paying for few losses. But how does this work in an industry with a much smaller customer base? This, along with narrower premiums, is precisely how aviation insurance differs from the regular insurance market. On top of that, the potential exposure for a single airline is considerably large. That is why the risk is usually spread among several different providers, which offer coverage for airlines, airports, manufacturers, lessors, and other stakeholders. Today, there are many distinct categories of aircraft insurance coverage, all of which are based on the degree of risk.

BACKGROUND

Throughout history, different societies developed different methods of distributing and sharing risk, but the common idea was collective assistance provided by mutual obligation. Roman colleges, for example, developed as guild associations comprised of artisans who acted as both insureds and insurers. These organizations provided material assistance to members and their families in the case of accident, illness, or death. As we can see, the burden of loss and the amount of aid fell on a group of people rather than on one individual. It is worth noting that insurance evolved as a protection mechanism, not simply for personal enrichment. We even see evidence of this in the original Jewish Talmud, for example, which states that if a rider's donkey dies, the other riders are to give him another donkey as opposed to money.

The concept of personal insurance actually dates back to the imperial age when merchants began transporting their goods on multiple ships. The aim was to prevent a total loss if one ship happened to sink (Vaughan, 1997). As maritime laws evolved, merchants began paying extra amounts to ship their goods on the same vessel. These "premiums" were then used to compensate those customers whose goods were lost or damaged. By the 14th century, marine coverage providers began offering separate contracts and calculating premiums based on the estimated risk attached to the cargo. This marked a key turning point—the separation of insurance from investment.

By the late 17th century, London had become a central location for the insurance business, due in large part to the company, Lloyds of London. Originally a coffee house and informal news hub, Lloyds began creating coverage solutions for merchants and quickly grew into a global leader in shipping insurance. Today, the company is not an insurer, but rather a market within which specialty insurance is written. It comprises over 50 companies and over 200 brokers worldwide.[1] Lloyds also wrote the first aviation policy in 1911. After World War II, the aviation industry experienced a sharp increase in the number of commercial flights and began mass production of multi-passenger aircraft. This naturally led to growth in the insurance sector. Today, London remains the largest business hub for aviation insurance.

A recap on conventions

In Chapter 4, we learned how various aviation conventions have helped shape the way the industry operates today. Although we have already discussed these events in detail, it is useful to reiterate some of their main outcomes related to liability.

Remember that the Warsaw Convention, which took effect in 1929, was the first true attempt to address the mobile nature of aircraft from a liability standpoint. Specifically, Chapter 3 of the agreement states that the carrier is liable for any damages related to passenger safety, without the need for a passenger to prove the carrier's fault or negligence. Again, this is also meant to protect the operator from a large financial loss. Thus, the monetary cap on passenger claims was limited to 125,000 gold francs (roughly $8300).[2] The treaty also held the carrier responsible for any damage to cargo and passengers' baggage while in transit—up to $20/kg. Discussions concerning the limitation of liability continued until 1955 when The Hague Protocol raised the limit to 250,000 francs (roughly $16,600). Finally, after the Guadalajara Supplementary Convention of 1961 extended Warsaw's rules to code-share flights, the Guatemala City Protocol of 1971 created an unbreakable per passenger limit of liability of 100,000 special drawing rights (SDRs). This amendment established strict liability.

In 1999, the Montreal Convention essentially updated these liability limits and adjusted for inflation. The amount was initially set at 100,000 SDR, but this is subject to a review every 5 years. As of 2016, damages for passenger injury and death were set at 113,100 SDR (roughly $160,000).[3] Furthermore, liability is now strictly based on possession as opposed to negligence. As such, carriers are strictly liable for up to 19 SDR/kg for the destruction, loss, damage, or delay of passenger baggage, unless the consignor has made a special declaration of interest in delivery at destination and has paid for it.[4] As of June 2016, there are 120 parties to the Montreal Convention, which requires all carriers to hold an approved insurance policy.

---

[1] www.lloyds.com/lloyds/about-us.

[2] *Convention for the Unification of Certain Rules Relating to International Carriage by Air*, Oct 12, 1929, art. 22, Stat. 1.

[3] US Department of Transportation, *Inflation Adjustments to Liability Limits Governed by the Montreal Convention*, 74 FR 59017, Nov 16, 2009.

[4] *Montreal Convention*, 1999, Art 22, Stat 2.

Not surprisingly, the evolution of the insurance business paralleled the progression of aviation technology as well as major industry events throughout history (Fig. 5.2).

In addition to hull coverage and liability, other types of aviation-relation coverage plans also developed, such as aircraft crew insurance, liability insurance for airport operators, and aircraft manufacturer insurance. Today, the aviation business is constantly changing, and stakeholders all around the world continue to face new challenges related to mergers, consolidation, and other economic factors. On top of that, airlines continue to order new, more expensive, and more fuel-efficient aircraft. While the accident rate is slightly fluctuating, the amount of compensation for passenger health and safety as well as for property damage is steadily increasing.

INSURANCE PARTIES

In aviation, the insurance market is much like real estate. You have a buyer who is looking for a product, a seller who is offering a product, and an intermediary person who is connecting the buyer and seller (Fig. 5.3). Before getting into coverage types of policy structure, it is necessary to become familiar with the role of each participating party. These terms will appear regularly throughout the chapter.

Insured

The "insured" is the customer, or the party who has purchased an insurance policy on an object or operation. In aviation, the aircraft is the most commonly insured object. The insured party is also referred to as the "policyholder," or "subject." This may be an airline, lessor, service provider (SP),

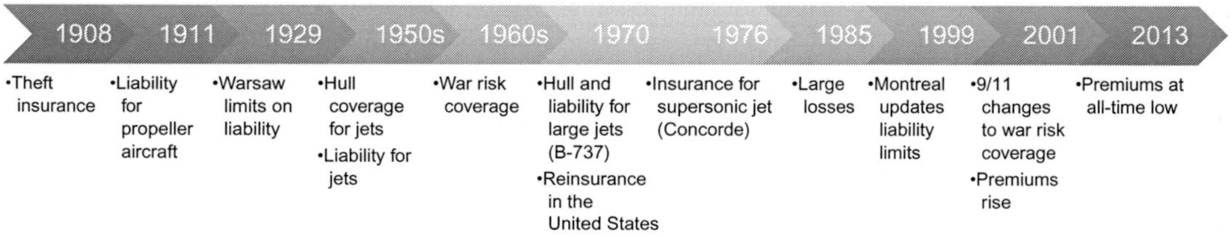

FIGURE 5.2

Aviation insurance timeline.

FIGURE 5.3

Insurance parties.

charter, private or corporate jet owner, or other industry stakeholder. Examples of SPs include hangar keepers, fuelers, airports, and parts suppliers.

Before becoming a policyholder, the person or corporation buying an aircraft is known as the "prospective insured," meaning that the entity is currently needing, or will be needing, some form of insurance coverage to protect the newly acquired asset.

Broker

The prospective insured first contacts an insurance broker or agent who will ask specific questions to better understand the buyer's needs. This role is a consultant of sorts and is hired by the buyer. The agent will want to know the company's name, aircraft type, where the aircraft flies, what the aircraft is used for, pilot's history and information, safety records, and what type of coverage the buyer is looking for. The broker will then use this information to create a marketing plan that he or she will present to an underwriter. A common misconception is that the broker actually writes the insurance policy and determines the premium. On the contrary, he or she is simply an intermediary whose goal is return from the underwriter with a favorable quote for the buyer.

Agent commission fees are usually written within the policy.

Underwriter

The seller of the insurance coverage is referred to as the underwriter, underwriting company, insurer, or insurance provider. An underwriter can be a business or an individual, and mostly specialize in a specific category of insurance, such as aviation, automotive, liability, or property. Also, most work for and independently from insurance companies, but for the purposes of this chapter, we use the terms "underwriter" and "insurer" interchangeably.

The job of an underwriter is to decide whether or not to take on a potential risk, and if so, at what rate. By writing or selling insurance, the insurance provider agrees to accept a risk for a premium. Because aviation risks are so relatively few in number, the underwriter should monitor the market on a daily, if not weekly basis. While there is large number of brokers and agents, there are only a few underwriting companies, and each specializes in certain types of risks, as discussed throughout this chapter.

TYPES OF INSURANCE

Underwriters today offer a wide range of insurance coverage options for various stakeholders in the aviation industry. Some offer policies for aircraft with a low hull value and limit of liability, while others write policies for high-value aircraft with high limits of liability. Likewise, some specialize only in helicopters, while others focus on engines. Some of these coverage options are standard, while others are less common and must be requested and negotiated specifically.

However, every aircraft insurance policy contains a clause that describes the proposed use of the aircraft (purpose of use) as well as a clause for pilot requirements (pilot warranty). This prevents the policyholder from submitting a claim for damages unrelated to the aircraft's main function, while also ensuring that the pilot is properly trained and has logged the necessary number of flight hours. Failure to comply with either clause effectively voids the coverage. Note that being an approved pilot and being an insured pilot are two different concepts. For instance, a pilot who works as an independent contractor may hold all necessary qualifications to fly the aircraft, but he/she might not be insured due to a specific exclusion to such pilots.

An insurance company can always modify a contract and make an amendment. This is especially true when it comes to high-value aircraft. Unlike other forms of insurance, aviation policies are highly individualized, and there is no standard. This is largely due to the limited number of aircraft, which prohibits underwriting companies from applying the law of large numbers as do most other insurers. Even though most insurers use published rates, premiums vary from company to company. On top of that is the high operational risk of flying; passengers on commercial jets are exposed to far greater risk than when they are participating in many other activities.

We return to the structure of contracts and premiums later in the chapter when we discuss how quotes can be vastly different, even on the same aircraft type. Similarly, some coverage might be offered by one underwriter but omitted by another. But first, let us expand on our brief summary of coverage types in Chapter 4. In the following sections, we discuss how each of these options is applied in the market today.

Hull insurance

An aircraft hull is derived from the marine term hull, which means the watertight body of a ship. Hull insurance refers to direct physical damage to the aircraft itself and covers all aircraft parts against physical damage that occurs on the ground or in flight. Before we address the scope of hull coverage, it is helpful to understand the meaning of several key terms:

- *In-flight:* The time period between when the aircraft begins its actual takeoff run to the point the aircraft has completed its landing roll (from touchdown to taxi speed). In the case of rotorcraft, in-flight begins when rotor starts moving and ends when it ceases to rotate.
- *In-motion:* Time during which the aircraft is moving under the power of its own engine or momentum. For rotorcraft, this is any time while rotors are rotating.
- *Taxi:* Movement of an aircraft on the ground under its own power. This does not include pushback or tow.

Hull coverage is designed to protect the entity who has a financial interest in the aircraft, including owners, operators, and other parties who may use an aircraft hull policy to cover the costs needed to replace the aircraft or recoup the financial loss when necessary. A hull policy is similar to collision coverage on a vehicle, but with a few key differences. First, an aircraft is more sensitive to damage than is a car; a car can still operate without a window or a bumper, whereas an aircraft that has sustained even minor damage is prohibited from operating in commercial service, unless such damage falls within certain "allowable limits." Second, the value of an aircraft is much higher. And finally, because of the high values, depreciation is much more critical for aircraft, especially considering the equity nature of the industry.

In general, there are two main types of hull policies. *All risks-ground and flight* is the broadest form of protection and provides coverage whether or not the aircraft is damaged in flight. All damages to aircraft are covered within the agreed value or stated value basis, which depends on the deductible. The other type is *all risks-not in motion* coverage, which applies to physical damage while the aircraft is on the ground and not moving under its own power. While this covers loss or damage while the aircraft is being pushed into a hangar or towed by a tractor, it does not cover damage incurred when the aircraft is taxiing. Such damage would however be covered under a separate policy type, known as *all risks-not in flight.*

Insured value

The insured value is the maximum amount of coverage the insurer agrees to repay in the case of an insurance event. Usually, this represents the purchase price of the aircraft if new, or the current market value if used. The insured value must represent actual cash value of the aircraft, because again, the basis of insurance is not to make a profit or to pay high premiums for undervalued aircraft. For every renewal cycle of the insurance coverage, the insured value is reassessed.

Deductible

When it comes to hull policies, there are two major types of deductibles. The straight deductible is defined as the fixed amount or percentage of loss for which the policyholder is responsible to pay. The rest of the loss is covered by the insurer. This is common practice in the insurance world for both business risks and leisure risks. The second type is called a franchise. Unlike a straight deductible that represents the portion that the insurer does not cover, a franchise represents the threshold at which the insurer becomes liable for the entire loss. This is usually expressed as a percentage of the insured value. For example, suppose the insured value of an aircraft is $100,000 with a 10% franchise attached. The policyholder would be responsible for paying the entire claim if it is below $10,000, whereas the insurer would be responsible for paying the entire claim if it is $10,000 or more.

Exclusions

Most aircraft hull policies also feature a limited number of exclusions. These may also be listed in an insurance contract under "What is not covered." Below are some of the most common exclusions:

1. *Wear and tear*—Damage or loss is not covered if it is due to freezing, deterioration, or mechanical or structural breakdown, unless the loss is the direct result of other physical damage covered by the policy. While the insurer will not pay for a cracked wing caused by freezing, it will cover a cracked wing caused by an accident, as stated in the policy.

   Ultimately, the wear and tear exclusion prevents operators from making claims for parts that are designed to wear out over time.
2. *Tires*—The insurer is not obliged to cover the cost of tires, unless the loss was caused by vandalism, theft, or physical damage to the aircraft, as stated in the policy.
3. *Conferment or requisition*—No coverage applies for the insured aircraft if the other party has a legal right to repossess the aircraft.
4. *War or confiscation*—Aircraft hull insurance excludes any damage or loss to the aircraft caused by war, invasion, hijacking, rebellion, or arrest by any government.
5. *Depreciation or loss of use*—Operators cannot make claims for depreciation.
6. *Other exclusions*—Some policies state additional exclusions that eliminate the insurer's responsibility for any damage or loss to the aircraft. Any changes to aircraft should be approved by the underwriting company and stated in the insurance policy. Otherwise, the contract will not cover the insured aircraft.

Total loss

Total airframe loss is considered total aircraft loss, but the insurer can offer to pay the agreed value for both the airframe and the engines in exchange for salvage rights on all equipment. In the event of a total loss, the insurer will pay the agreed value or the insured value regardless of the aircraft's current market value. Insured values are common in general aviation and require owners to actually prove the loss. Agreed value, on the other hand, does not require proof of loss and is common practice in commercial aviation.

There are two types of agreed value: Actual cash value basis or valued basis. Actual cash value is determined as the replacement cost for a new aircraft less accumulated depreciation. This value is difficult to estimate because depreciation policies vary and can be undervalued in order to maximize the value of repayment. If the insurance contract estimates the agreed value on a valued basis, the underwriter will check the present market value of the aircraft and pay the same amount for the insured. If the cost to repair damage is equal to 75% or more of the agreed value, the aircraft may be declared a constructive total loss with the insurer to pay as if a total loss had occurred.

Partial loss

In the case of partial loss, the primary issue becomes the repair. Repair work can be done by the policyholder or it can be transferred to a third party. If the policyholder performs the repair, then the amount is estimated as a sum of all materials, wages to employees, and any necessary transportation costs. However, supervisory wages cannot make up more than 50% of the labor expense. If a third-party performs the repairs, then the provider pays all costs, including transportation. In other words, the insurance company simply pays the bill sent from the repair facility. Again, any deductible stated in the aircraft hull insurance is carried by the policyholder. Note that in both cases of partial loss, there is no place for depreciation.

Oftentimes, the repair cost for partial loss can be quite high. This is common for old aircraft with parts that are priced at the same level as those for new aircraft. Because of this, insurance contracts will state that the total amount of partial loss cannot exceed the amount paid for a total loss. Policies also state that when transportation is needed, it must be the least expensive means, regardless of whether it involves moving the damaged aircraft or securing spare parts and materials. Damaged aircraft must be transported to the most practical repair facility, and materials should be secured from the nearest source. Transportation costs include the expense of taking the aircraft from the place of accident to the repair facility and the expense of returning it to the place of accident or to the insured's airport, whichever is closer or less expensive.

Detached parts and substitutes

Aircraft hull insurance does not automatically cover the loss or damage to a substitute aircraft that is being used when the insured aircraft is out of service due to maintenance or repair. However, if the policyholder reports the temporary aircraft within 30 days from delivery, it can be covered under the policy. Similarly, spare engines and parts that are temporarily detached from the aircraft are not automatically covered. In this case, the owner or operator should purchase supplementary hull insurance or ensure that such a provision is written into the initial policy. They may also purchase an extended policy that automatically factors in any change in value to these parts.

Appraisal provision

If insured and insurer fail to agree on the amount of loss, each shall select a disinterested appraiser upon written demand by the other party. Some companies require that the process of selecting the appraiser should be made within a specified time period. Once the appraiser is chosen, the appraisers then select a disinterested umpire whose job is to try to get the two appraisers to agree on a value (a court will select the umpire if the appraisers cannot agree on a candidate). The appraisers then estimate the parts or portions of the loss in question. If they cannot come to a mutual decision, the umpire will side with one of the appraisers to officially establish the value via the written appraisal. The insurer and insured each pay for their own appraiser and then share costs for the appraisal and the umpire.

Liability insurance

Aviation exposes operators and passengers to the innate risks of flying. An aircraft accident can significantly impact owners, operators, passengers, maintenance facilities, and airports. Without insurance, claims for damages would simply be transferred to a court to decide who is responsible for covering the loss. This is why organizers of the Warsaw and Montreal conventions were so concerned with safety liability.

Liability insurance covers physical injury to passengers as well as any damage to public (third party) persons or property resulting from an aircraft's operation. It also protects those with financial interest in the aircraft. However, this type of coverage is capped and limited to claims arising from a single occurrence. As such, an airline or operator may be left to handle additional losses that were caused by a particular event. There are many types of liability coverages offered in the market, but the three most common are as follows:

1. *Passenger bodily injury liability* protects the insured from liability imposed for damages for bodily injury, disease, sickness, mental distress, or death suffered only by passengers in the case of insurance event stated in the insurance contract. A passenger is defined as any person who is in, on, or boarding the aircraft for the purpose of flying therein or any person who alights (exits) the aircraft following a flight or attempted flight. Limits of liabilities are stated per person and per accident.
2. *Bodily injury excluding passengers* protects the insured from liability imposed for damages for bodily injury, disease, sickness, mental distress, or death suffered by any person or persons other than passengers in the case of an insurance event stated in the insurance contract.
   Again, separate per person and per accident limits apply.
3. *Property damage liability* covers any third-party property damage caused by the use of an aircraft. The limit for this type of insurance coverage is set as maximum value of loss per accident. The coverage in many cases is written on an occurrence basis. This means that the policyholder is protected from being liable for continuous damage as long as the cause or incident occurred within the coverage period. If so, it does not matter when the claim was filed.

Remember that the Montreal treaty holds the carrier liable, because an aircraft accident can create a financial catastrophe for both small and large operators. Limits vary by country. In the United States, for example, any passenger carrier is required to "maintain aircraft accident liability insurance coverage for bodily injury to or death of aircraft passengers, with minimum limits of

$300,000 for any one passenger, and a total per involved aircraft for each occurrence of $300,000 times 75 percent of the number of passenger seats installed in the aircraft."[5]

It is not uncommon to purchase additional layers of liability. Many major airlines carry total liability limits of up to $1 billion and, in some cases, make additional payments simply to avoid further costs in court. For example, right after the US Airways Flight 1549 crash landed in the Hudson River in 2009, the airline offered each passenger $5,000 to cover immediate needs.[6] This was aside from any legal liability limits.

Policyholders can add separate limits to their contract for each type of liability coverage. However, the region of operation is important when determining any additional limits. For instance, if the aircraft is flying to/from a hub airport, it faces a higher chance of an accident due to the higher amount of traffic. In general, most additional layers of liability are written on an occurrence basis.

Combined single limits

A Combined Single Limit (CSL) policy pays the insured party up to a certain dollar amount for each claim. This is unlike a Split-Limit (SL) policy that designates a maximum dollar amount for each component of a claim. For example, a CSL agreement might pay up to $100,000 per incident, whereas an SL agreement might pay up to $20,000 in bodily injuries per person and up to $100,000 per incident. Under the CSL policy, a person could claim $100,000 in bodily injuries, but only $20,000 under the SL policy. Therefore, an SL policy would only pay the maximum amount if five different people submitted a maximum-allowed claim. In aviation, most underwriters use CSL policies to provide airlines and operators with more flexibility when handling major losses.

Exclusions

Just as we saw with hull coverage, most liability insurance policies come with one or more exclusions, such as follows:

- Property owned, leased, or cared for by the policyholder
- Intentional damage or injury unless the intention is to prevent a hijacking or safety threat
- Any claim which is covered by any other employee agreement, such as unemployment or disability benefits
- Bodily injury or property damage caused by noise or pollutants
- Bodily injury or property damage caused by war, hijacking, and other perils

The events above are just some examples of what might not be covered in an insurance contract. Remember that each situation is different. For example, when insuring a crop-dusting aircraft, the insurer would likely write in a chemical exclusion clause stating that the operator is liable for any bodily injury related to use of fertilizers. To avoid a legal battle, both parties should mention all relevant information in the insurance contract.

[5]Code of Federal Regulations, Title XIV Chapter II (A)(205.5).
[6]New York Times, "A.I.G. Balks at Claims from Jet Ditching in Hudson" June 11, 2009.

Non-owned aircraft and add-ons

An operator may need to protect a temporary substitute aircraft while the scheduled aircraft is out of service due to repair or maintenance. Not all policies automatically include this provision, and it may or may not affect the premium. When it comes to non-owned aircraft, liability protection is very similar to aircraft hull protection in which it comes with separate provisions for in-flight, on ground, or both. Non-owned aircraft liability coverage usually requires a separate policy or add-on. While this may be obvious for an airline that leases its fleet, it is also critical for other operations. Consider an employee who uses a company plane for business, a pilot undergoing recurrent training on a borrowed aircraft, or a company that rents an aircraft from a charter company to make a large shipment. Aircraft type and maximum seat capacity are generally the two main considerations when underwriting non-owned aircraft liability coverage.

Just as insurers do with exclusions, operators can always negotiate additional coverage if necessary. For example, liability coverage for hangar keepers may cover property damage to non-owned aircraft that is in control of a policyholder and on insured premises. Goods, merchandise, and property of others that is carried on an insured aircraft can also be covered by a supplementary cargo liability policy. Protection against false arrest or defamation arising from the operation of a covered aircraft is called personal injury liability contract. Even if the passenger was injured as a result of serving alcoholic beverages, for example, that person is covered under the host liquor liability coverage.

War risk and allied peril insurance

There are two categories of war risk insurance, the first being hull war risk protection. As we saw from the exclusions above, war risks are explicitly omitted from regular hull policies and are insured under a separate type of contract in a separate market. This is a direct result of 9/11. The second category is passenger and third-party war risk, which are both add-ons to traditional liability policies. The Federal Aviation Administration (FAA) defines war risk as follows:

1. War, invasion, acts of foreign enemies, warlike hostilities, civil war, rebellion, revolution, insurrection, martial law, exercise of military or usurped power, or any attempt at usurpation of power.
2. Any hostile detonation of any weapon of war, including any employing atomic or nuclear fission and/or fusion or other like reaction of radioactive force or matter.
3. Strikes, riots, civil commotions, or labor disturbances.
4. Any act of one or more persons for political or terroristic purposes and whether the loss or damage resulting therefrom is accidental or intentional, except for ransom or extortion demands.
5. Any malicious act or act of sabotage, vandalism, or other act intended to cause loss or damage.
6. Confiscation, nationalization, seizure, restraint, detention, appropriation, requisition for title or use by or under the order of any foreign government or foreign public or local authority.
7. Hijacking or any unlawful seizure or wrongful exercise of control of the aircraft or crew made by any person or persons onboard the aircraft or otherwise, acting without the consent of the insured.
8. The discharge or detonation of any weapon or explosive device while on an aircraft covered by the insurance.[7]

[7] www.faa.gov.

Similar to liability insurance, war and peril coverage is limited to fixed amounts per occurrence or event.

Pre-9/11

Before the terrorist attacks on the United States on September 11, 2001, war risk coverage was an add-on to both hull and liability policies and came with very low premiums. In fact, some underwriters did not charge a premium at all. It was really only a concern for airlines flying to third-world countries in Central or South America and in the Middle East. However, claims for hull and liability had already exceeded premiums in the years leading up to 9/11. In addition, most existing war policies included a 7-day[8] review clause that, in the event of a war risk situation, allowed insurance providers to reevaluate the risk and amend or even cancel the coverage entirely. This is precisely what happened after the attacks, and it changed the insurance market dramatically.

Post 9/11

9/11 was an unprecedented event. Not only did the losses exceed those of all previous man-made and natural catastrophes, but providers were immediately faced with the possibility of a similar event. From an insurance standpoint, the impacts were unquantifiable. The potential exposure to this type of risk had not been estimated based on real risk because such an event was so uncommon. Previously collected war risk premiums were not sufficient to cover the amount of insurable loss, which estimates claim was nearly $40 billion (Freitas, 2006). As a result, all commercial war risk coverages were canceled on September 17, 2001, and all quotes were withdrawn (Gassen, 2012). This market essentially became a blank slate for underwriters, although hull and liability policies remained intact.

It is worth nothing that the cancelation of coverage was not issued until airlines had received an offer for a revised basis of coverage. The offer was full coverage for up to $50 million for all third-party claims for bodily injury and property damage that occurred within a 12-month period. After discussions with airlines and brokers, the insurance providers also introduced an additional per passenger premium charge of $1.25. This was mainly an attempt to restore the confidence of investors and to ensure the availability of capacity going forward (Gassen, 2012).

In response to the soaring rates in the commercial market, the US Congress passed the Air Transportation Safety and System Stabilization Act of 2001 to compensate airlines for the losses incurred on 9/11. This act allocated up $10 billion (aggregate) in federally backed credit for qualified applicants.[9] FAA-issued war risk programs had existed before 9/11, but these were available on a limited basis and did not extend to terrorism.[10] By 2002, insurers had lowered the per passenger charge, raised the third-party limit, and extended the $50 million to airports and SPs. However, the cost was still high and made it impossible for many airlines to obtain war and risk coverage through the private market, which prompted Congress to pass the Terrorism Risk Insurance Act of 2002. This extended the FAA's existing programs and provided *coverage for losses or injuries to aircraft hulls, passengers, and crew at the limits carried by air carriers for such losses and injuries as of such date of enactment and at an additional premium comparable to the premium charged for*

[8]48-hour notice prior to 1951.
[9]Air Transportation Safety and System Stabilization Act, PL 107-42, Title 1, 101(a).
[10]Issued through indemnification agreements with the Department of Transportation.

Table 5.2 Additional Coverage

Trip Interruption	Ferry Flights	Search and Rescue
Aviation property and automobile	Cargo legal liability	Political risk
Products/operations liability (OEM)	Geographic limits	Refueler's liability (SP)
Environmental impairment liability	Grounding liability	Personal injury extension
Chemical liability	Unearned premium coverage	Hangarkeeper's liability (SP)
Trespassers cost	Engine rental expense	Workers' compensation
Medical and related expense	Personal effects and baggage	Premises liability (SP)
Consequential damages	Hull and spares deductible	Incidental damages
Contractual liability	Non-owned aircraft liability	Broad form named insurance

OEM, *Original Equipment Manufacturer;* SP, *Service Provider.*

third-party casualty coverage under such policy.[11] In addition, this act requires all insurance companies to offer every policyholder the opportunity to purchase terrorism coverage.

Present

The most recent extension of federally backed insurance programs expired in 2014. Since then, there has been an industry shift back to the private sector. This is largely the result of increased capacity and traffic, which has restored competition and forced providers to lower their rates. Today, airlines can purchase full coverage for hull and passenger liability, and the $50 million third-party limit has increased to $1 billion for airports and SPs and to $2.25 billion for airlines.[12] In addition, providers offer more layers of protection, and the per passenger charge is now an object of negotiation, often going as low as $0.70. Airports and SPs are the main customers for these supplemental layers, as it allows them to protect their exposure to such risk. The most common sublimits for third-party war risk are $150 or $250 million (Gassen, 2012).

Additional coverage

For airlines, an aircraft is making money only when it is in the sky, and an operational disturbance can have a big impact on the company's bottom line. This is also true for general aviation. Table 5.2 lists some additional coverage options available in market, some of which have already been discussed or will be discussed later in the chapter. Note that SP refers to insurance policies for aviation service providers.

Insurance companies offer add-ons according to the nature of the operation, and as we learned from 9/11, premiums often increase as a result of an occurrence. For example, search and rescue coverage became a global question in 2014 when Malaysia Airlines Flight 370 disappeared while en route from Kuala Lumpur to Beijing. If an aircraft goes unreported and cannot be located for 60 days following takeoff, it is considered a loss under a typical hull policy. Normally, search and rescue procedures are managed and performed by the government where the aircraft is registered, but

[11]Homeland Security Act of 2002, Title XII, Sec 1202.

[12]The introduction of the Airbus A380 promoted a third-party limit increase for airlines from $2 to $2.25 billion.

some of the expense may be transferred to the airline. If insured, the airline could pass this onto the insurer.

Insurance for lessors

Although airlines assume the operational risk of the aircraft, lessors and owners are also entitled to insurance proceeds associated with a loss event. Moreover, there are coverage options designed specifically for financiers. The first category is financial contingencies, such as an operator's inability to meet liabilities, coverage gaps arising from cancellation or nonrenewal, and the operator's failure to notify the financier of a new interest.

The second category is political risk/repossession insurance, which protects a lessor against government action or inaction in the aircraft's registry state. This coverage includes state failure to deregister an aircraft, inability to obtain an export certificate, confiscation, requisition, or the inability to physically repossess an aircraft or obtain aircraft records. It also extends to tax risks, currency inconvertibility, trade issues, confiscation, and government refusal of deregistration (Gerber, 2012).

Insuring an aircraft is more involved than insuring a personal vehicle. First, terrorism has altered the way that premiums are calculated, and it highly possible that future events might prompt further changes both in the government and commercial sectors. For private insurers, war risk makes diversification even more critical, and a healthy portfolio consists of airlines, lessors, and SPs across a diverse geographic range.

MEASURING A LOSS

As we have already pointed out, there are two main risks in a loss situation: loss of aircraft and third-party liability. In the case of aircraft loss, different types of damages can be treated differently by the owner, the insurer, and the operator.

Direct physical damage

Direct physical damage to the aircraft or one of its components is typically covered by the hull policy, and if caused by a third party, an insurer may seek to recover the cost from the third party directly. Direct physical damage is measured as the total cost of repair or, in the case of total loss, by the aircraft's market value or depreciated value at the time of loss. All values are stated in the insurance policy.

Loss of use

Loss of use is indeed a financial loss, particularly for airlines that only earn revenue when an aircraft is in the air. Repairs take time, and that time is an opportunity cost to the operator. This type of damage is often called a consequential damage when it is the result of the aircraft being misused. The amount of loss is equal to the revenue that would have been earned during the days the aircraft was grounded.

Diminution of value

Aircraft value after an event is one of the most subjective losses and thus the most commonly debated. It is not considered damage and is therefore excluded from hull coverage. The question comes down to which aircraft a prospective buyer would choose among two identical models: one that has never been in an accident or one that has been in an accident but has been fully repaired. If there were any heavy structural repairs performed, the buyer would likely ask for a discount, which would lower the aircraft's value. Quantifying this value is the job of an appraiser, but it becomes particularly difficult during periods when demand is low for a particular aircraft type. Average loss values typically range between 10% and 15% of market value.

Liability loss

Liability loss refers to third-party property damage, bodily injury, or personal injury (damage to character or reputation). Bodily injury can be a sum of medical expenses incurred, but when it comes to pain, suffering, and personal injury, there is no standard measurement. Values are often settled in court and may account for severity, frequency of treatment, career impact, etc. Other examples of liability loss are errors and omissions and employee-related event, such as embezzlement.

Loss from incidental damage

Incidental damage refers to any other economic loss that reasonably results from the insurance event; for example, any travel expense incurred to reposition crew. It does not include things like attorney fees, unless otherwise negotiated. Coverage for incidental damage is typically purchased as an add-on or separate policy (see Table 5.2) and depends on the credit record of the insured.

THE INSURANCE CONTRACT

Ultimately, insurance policies vary from one underwriter to the next, based on the insurer's view of the market and the risk profile of policyholder. In the section, we outline the structure of an aviation insurance contract and learn what variables providers use when calculating the premium.

Policy components

The insurance agreement is a contract between two or more entities, which serves to establish, modify, or terminate legal relations between these parties. Each contract must contain

- Document title
- Insurer's name and address
- Insured's name and address
- Description of the insured object
- Sum of insurance
- List of insurance events
- Premium amount and terms of payment
- Contract terms, including exclusions
- Changes and termination orders
- Rights and responsibilities of signers, in the case of failure or improper performance of the contract
- Other conditions agreed to by participating parties
- Signatures of all parties

The insurance policy defines the rights and duties of each signer. While different types of risk are written in differently, every insurance contract will include declarations, insuring agreements, definitions, exclusions, and conditions.

Contract formation

There are two basic instruments used in the formation of insurance contract: the application and the binder. When a prospective policyholder applies for coverage, the application is treated as an inducement for an underwriting company to make an offer. There is no standard form, but a hull insurance application, for example, should contain the following information:

- Name and business of the applicant
- All information on the aircraft (i.e., certificates, equipment)
- Detailed pilot information
- Information on the lien holder (if any)
- Safety records and history of accidents
- Needed coverage and desired limits

The underwriter can also request additional information from the applicant if necessary. In some cases, the provider may offer coverage while the application is being processed. This is called a binder. It is a temporary contract, pending the issuance of the policy.

Before a contract is made valid, several conditions must be met. First, the insurance provider and the applicant must agree to the offer. This usually involves negotiation. The applicant first makes a written or verbal offer, which the insurance company either accepts, rejects, or returns with a counteroffer. Or, the insurance company can make the initial offer with the proposed premium. Second, all insurance contracts must be supported by legal consideration. This involves an exchange of value, meaning the offer (application) must include payment for the amount of the initial premium. Third, the purpose of the contract must be legal. A legal purpose can be to recover value of the aircraft in the case of accident, but it is important that the purpose is agreed upon and accepted. For example, an insured cargo aircraft will not be covered if it is found delivering drugs or contraband. Fourth is competence. The policy must be written by a licensed insurance company, and the applicant must be of sound mind and of legal age (varies by country). Finally, the structure of the contract must abide by the laws and regulations of the state in which it was created. Coverage is not valid until the contract is accepted and signed accordingly.

FACTORS THAT AFFECT THE PREMIUM

Why do insurance companies quote different rates for the same insured object? As we mentioned earlier, insurance pricing is a complex process. As an applicant, it is critical to supply the insurance agent with every piece of information about the aircraft and its operation, including all certificates and records. Even a minor detail omitted can have a big impact on the quote. In general, there are several common factors that underwriters use to calculate the premium.

Purpose of use

Every aircraft insurance policy has a section called "purpose of use" which describes what the aircraft flies for, who it flies, and where it flies. The purpose of use section is important because if a loss occurs when the aircraft is flying for a purpose other than that which is stated in the contract, the insurance company can simply deny the claim. As technology and society advance, the purpose of use section becomes more sophisticated, but the main operational difference is commercial vs noncommercial use.

Commercial

Commercial use means that the operator is attempting to profit from the flight. Examples include charter passenger transport, cargo transport, sightseeing, crop dusting, aerial photography, movie production, fire patrol, rental, banner towing, instruction, and of course, airline passenger transport. The FAA assigns a part number to each commercial flight, as defined in the Federal Aviation Regulations (FARs). Furthermore, each part has specific rules about the aircraft equipment and airworthiness, maintenance, pilot operations (instrument vs visual), record keeping, crew training, and safety procedures. Table 5.3 provides a summary of FAR designations. Charters, for example, typically operate under FAR Part 135. This designation applies to turbojet, turbofan, and turboprop aircraft capable of carrying between 1 and 30 passengers. Among other requirements, the operator must have exclusive use of at least one aircraft, and the pilot-in command must have logged a certain number of flight hours.[13]

Airlines normally operate under a FAR Part 121 or Part 135 certificate that allows them to transport passengers for a fee. Coverage for commercial air carriers is written in a special policy form and includes the unique exposures that we have already discussed. Again, due to the high value, seat capacity, and use frequency of commercial jets, Part 121 and 135 insurance risks are usually spread among multiple underwriters. Premiums for airlines are typically based on the average number of seats, and this is often adjusted at the end of the year based on the number of revenue passenger miles that were actually flown. In this case, the insurer will charge the airline any additional premium, or the airline will receive a refund.

Similar to the FAA, the regulatory authorities around the world establish rules and regulation for commercial air transport operations. For example, the European Aviation Safety Agency in its Commission Regulation (EU) No 965/2012 that lays down detailed rules for commercial air transport operations.

Noncommercial

Noncommercial means that the operator is not intending to profit from the flight as a service. This can be for business, pleasure, or industrial aid. If a flight does not fall under a commercial designation, then by default, it is noncommercial. General aviation accounts for a large portion of noncommercial flight operations, yet it is still very important to distinguish between the different uses of an aircraft for insurance purposes. Many private jet owners, for example, use their aircraft for both business and pleasure. If so, this should be explicitly stated in the contract. Industrial aid refers to business flights that are operated to transport employees and guests. This does not include charters or any other operation that collects a fee from the passengers. However, industrial aid does mean that the aircraft is operated by a professional pilot who is employed for that specific purpose.

Ultimately, there are many ways in which an aircraft can be used, and the riskier the operation, the higher the premium. In some cases, the underwriter will deny coverage altogether because the proposed

[13]Code of Federal Regulations, Title XIV, Chapter I (G).

Table 5.3 Main Federal Aviation Regulations (FARs) Applicable to Aircraft Operators

Part of 14 CFR[a]	Description
Part 23	Airworthiness standards: normal category airplanes
Part 25	Airworthiness standards: transport category airplanes
Part 26	Continued airworthiness and safety improvements for transport-category airplanes
Part 27	Airworthiness standards: normal category rotorcraft
Part 29	Airworthiness standards: transport category rotorcraft
Part 33	Airworthiness standards: aircraft engines
Part 35	Airworthiness standards: propellers
Part 39	Airworthiness directives
Part 43	Maintenance, preventive maintenance, rebuilding, and alteration
Part 45	Identification and registration marking
Part 47	Aircraft registration
Part 61	Certification: pilots, flight instructors, and ground instructors
Part 67	Medical standards and certification
Part 91	General operating and flight rules
Part 119	Certification: air carriers and commercial operators
Part 121	Operating requirements: domestic, flag, and supplemental operations
Part 125	Certification and operations: airplanes having a seating capacity of 20 or more passengers or a maximum payload capacity of 6000 lb or more, and rules governing persons on board such aircraft
Part 129	Operations: foreign air carriers and foreign operators of the US-registered aircraft engaged in common carriage
Part 135	Operating requirements: commuter and on demand operations and rules governing persons on board such aircraft
Part 136	Commercial air tours and national parks air tour management
Part 137	Agricultural aircraft operations
Part 141	Pilot schools
Part 198	Aviation insurance
Part 205	Aircraft accident liability insurance certification
Part 298	Exemptions for air taxi and commuter air carrier operations

[a]Title 14 of Code of Federal Regulations.
Federal Aviation Administration.

purpose of use is simply too hazardous. In other cases, the underwriter may be unfamiliar with the true exposure of a particular operation, in which case, any offered premium is likely to be high. This is why communication and updated information are so important in the contract formation process.

Hull value

Underwriters estimate hull rates based on the value of the aircraft, or for airlines, the average fleet value. Surprisingly, coverage for high-valued aircraft typically comes with a lower hull rate, while a low-valued aircraft is typically charged a higher hull rate. Why is this the case? The underlying assumption here is that the cost to cover the repair of less-expensive aircraft can go as high as the repair of higher priced model. For example, cathode ray tubes (CRTs) were introduced to cockpit displays in the 1980s and are found in many airframes that were manufactured through about 2005. When LCDs replaced CRTs, the technology became obsolete. As a result, replacing a CRT today would be relatively expensive due to a lack of parts. On the other hand, the Original Equipment Manufacturers (OEMs) have been mass producing new lines of narrow body jets. Parts availability for these aircraft will remain relatively high, at least over the next several years.

It is worth mentioning that technology can affect limits as well as premiums. If you remember from our war risk discussion, the introduction of the A380 jet airliner in 2005 prompted an across-the-board increase in third-party liability limits.

Pilot qualification

In the early days of aviation, pilots were thought of as bearing a low level of risk, but technology has since widened the gap between professional and nonprofessional. The introduction of GPS, in particular, has had a major impact on the industry. The modern-day cockpit reduces pilot workload, while fly-by-wire technology controls the aircraft during bad weather. Whereas pilot's salary usually increases with the number of flight hours logged, underwriters care more about which aircraft type those flights hours come from. To illustrate, let us compare the experience of two different pilots. Suppose Pilot A has accrued 3000 total flight hours, 2000 of which were in the A319 aircraft. Pilot B, on the other hand, has accrued 6000 total flight hours but has only recently begun flying the A319. The airline would likely face a higher premium on an A319 that was flown by Pilot B vs one that was flown by Pilot A. When it comes to insurance, specific experience is more a measure of competency than total time.

Experience goes hand in hand with training. In fact, statistics show that better pilot training is strongly tied to better safety records. New-generation aircraft with high-tech retrofits are much more complex than older models. Underwriters can even write in requirements for additional training (usually on an annual basis) to further decrease exposure to human-factor risk.

Finally, a pilot's age can also impact the premium. Life expectancy today is much higher than it was even in the 1950s. It is not uncommon to live beyond the age of 85, and, as a result, we are seeing more people waiting longer to retire. In fact, in 2009, the FAA officially increased the mandatory retirement age of pilots from 60 to 65.[14] The economic effect is that senior pilots are more expensive to maintain, while young pilots receive much lower pay scales. The insurance effect is that older pilots pose a higher risk as they become less likely to pass annual medical checks.

Geographic region

Aviation is inherently riskier in some parts of the world than in others. This is true in terms of both natural and state-induced threats. In Chapter 4, we discussed many of the jurisdiction-related risks that are relevant to financiers. Insurance companies usually charge higher premiums on assets that are operating in war zones or less-developed regions, such as Africa. Corruption and terrorism present unique threats not only to inbound and outbound traffic but also for carriers that pass through the city or country in question. This is also why we see political risk policies designed specifically

[14]Fair Treatment for Experienced Pilots Act, Public Law 110-135.

for lessors. Ultimately, every country has different prices, and airlines in countries with a good aviation infrastructure will typically be offered lower rates.

Insurers also consider natural geographic factors, such as wind storms, tsunamis, extreme temperature, or high altitude. High exposure to such factors usually results in a higher premium. Each type of aircraft has its own runway and visibility limits, and minimums are predicted based on the airfield being at sea level and its runway temperature being a constant 59°F. Thus any increase in altitude or temperature will increase these minimums. For example, a 1000-ft rise in elevation or a 15° rise in temperature can increase the minimum required runway length by 10%. Therefore, operating the aircraft in the cool coastal areas of New England is entirely different than flying into Mexico City International Airport where the elevation is 7343 ft. We will revisit this topic with different examples, when we discuss credit analysis in Chapter 7.

Safety record

The safety records of the airline play a crucial role in determining the risk premium charged by the underwriting company. The better the safety record, the lower the risk, which means the policyholder will pay a lower premium. One of the key factors in safety is maintenance history. If an aircraft misses a scheduled maintenance event, this could lead to a serious disaster, not only in terms of asset value but also passenger safety. Another factor is technology, which continually makes flying safer and therefore more profitable for underwriters. Consider the US sanctions against Iran that prohibit the cross-border transfer of the US products. Without access to new aircraft models, Iranian operators are forced to fly much older fleets. As a result, the country has one of the worst aviation safety records in the world. Similarly, insurers have seen a rash of losses in Nepal, which has driven up the coverage premiums.

Note that changing underwriters does not guarantee a lower risk premium, because the new company will verify all documents and safety records before providing a new quote. Furthermore, the premium charge is attached not only to a specific type of aircraft and pilot but also to the company's credit profile. Therefore, the way an airline operates its business also affects what it pays out for insurance coverage (see Chapter 7).

The market

Since 2010, air passenger traffic has increased year-over-year at an average growth rate of 6.2% (Boeing, 2016). In comparison, the number of underwriters is increasing at a much slower rate, so when a new entrant does enter the market, the impact can be significant. This is what happened in July 2006. The increased capacity from two new companies immediately impacted the renewal cycles of existing providers. One year later, buyers began to see a decrease in their premiums. Premiums also tend to go down when the market is in decline. Sudden changes like this cause the entire industry to lose money. Some providers tough it out, while others leave the market for good. The only way to capture increased market share is by decreasing premiums, as operators select providers largely based on price.

So, the question is—why would a hull policyholder not cancel an existing contract and repurchase at a lower rate? Common industry protocol says that no underwriter will cancel or rewrite insurance without good reason. Some airlines chase the underwriters who offer lower premiums for senior pilots, for example, but the cost of switching providers and establishing a new relationship may outweigh the immediate reduction in premiums. Plus, searching every year for a new provider can be counterproductive, especially since underwriters prefer inquires only from shoppers who are serious about switching. If the market is stable, it is better to request a quote from only one or two underwriters. This allows an operator to confirm that rates are stable and that it is not a good time to switch.

REINSURANCE

Now that we have addressed coverage types, policy structure, and premiums, we will end this chapter by revisiting the concept of risk sharing and discussing a final subset of the market—reinsurance. This is essentially insurance for insurance companies. In other words, reinsurance is a way for the provider to protect itself from extensive loss and better handle the volatility of the business. It also frees up capacity to take on more or larger risks.

In a reinsurance contract, Insurer A (cedent) passes on or cedes a portion of its risk to Reinsurer B (reinsurer). In exchange for accepting the risk, Reinsurer B receives a premium from Insurer A. Reinsurance is a huge global business because it provides another way to spread risk and access capital markets all over the world. In fact, nearly half of all premiums for property reinsurance policies in the United States are written by the non-US companies.[15]

There are two main categories of reinsurance: facultative or treaty. In a facultative contract, the reinsurer assumes a specific, individual, and often high-value risk. In a treaty, the reinsurer assumes a share of the risk associated with all policies that the cedent has issued within a broad category (i.e., automotive). Furthermore, there are two main ways that reinsurance premiums and losses are distributed: proportionally and nonproportionally.

Proportional reinsurance

In a proportional reinsurance agreement, the reinsurer and cedent share the premium and any losses, essentially on a pro rata basis. This can be arranged in one of two ways. In a quota share arrangement, the cedent transfers a fixed percentage of each policy, whereas in a surplus agreement, the cedent establishes a retention limit. For example, if the retention limit was set at $50,000, the cedent assumes the full risk up to $50,000. The remaining portion is reinsured. Surplus reinsurance may have many lines which are covered by more than one reinsurer.

Proportional reinsurance is more a tool for small insurers rather than large companies, because it allows them to boost their presence in a particular specialty. However, it does cut into their premiums. Therefore, it is usually only used when the insurer is skeptical about its ability to handle loss. As an example, regional jets and some types of narrow-body aircraft can be insured by one underwriter, but liability limits are almost always reinsured among several companies. Likewise, hull values of wide-body aircraft, such as the Boeing 777 or Airbus 380, require risk sharing among multiple underwriters.

Nonproportional reinsurance

In a nonproportional agreement, the cedent establishes a retention limit for the loss, and the reinsurer only pays out when the loss exceeds that amount. This is the excess-of-loss method. For example, if the cedent is willing to accept up to $2 million in losses, it might purchase a fixed

[15]Reinsurance Association of America (RAA), www.reinsurance.org/landing.

amount of reinsurance if there is a chance that a loss will exceed $2 million. Excess-of-loss agreements are written as per risk, per occurrence, or for an aggregate. However, per occurrence contracts in aviation disappeared after 9/11, and today, it is difficult to obtain limits less than $300 million. The other method is stop-loss, whereby the reinsurer agrees to cover a fixed amount of loss. The insurance event is determined when the annual loss burden exceeds the agreed deductible. This deductible is defined as either a fixed sum or a determined portion of premium income. Ultimately, a stop-loss arrangement gives the cedent protection from fluctuations in annual losses.

Nonproportional reinsurance allows the cedent to protect a certain grade of risk. It is not selling a portion of risk portfolio and sharing a premium. Like proportional agreements, nonproportional insurance may involve multiple parties at various layers.

It is worth mentioning that reinsurance companies can themselves purchase insurance. This type of risk transfer is sometimes referred as "retrocession." Such a contract can take a variety of forms based on a company's risk profile and business. Similarly, some risks can be reinsured through nontraditional methods, such as catastrophe bonds or privately financed arrangements (i.e., sidecars). Ultimately, reinsurance is another way to share risk and minimize financial loss.

CONCLUSION

As we have learned throughout this and other chapters, the aviation industry is highly capital intensive. Aircraft values range from millions to hundreds of millions of dollars, and a single loss can potentially bankrupt an operation. This is why owners and operators of aircraft purchase aviation insurance coverage—to protect their financial interests. There are many types of coverage options available in the market, but the universal concept is the exchange of risk for a premium to cover any damage or loss as the result of an accident. The amount of a premium depends on a variety of factors. Nonetheless, an insurance policy is like any other legal contract, and any breach in conditions will likely result in the policyholder being denied a claim.

Some insurance companies are only willing to write policies for both turboprop and turbofan aircraft, while others prefer to work only with jets. Just like in the leasing business, few insurers deal exclusively with one aircraft type. Similarly, if an operator is having trouble financing a less-common aircraft, he or she will likely face higher rates to insure that asset. Looking at the market and following trends is crucial to get low premiums. Today, rates are low, and there is over 200% capacity in North America alone. It is definitely a buyer's market, and underwriters are fighting for their positions. In fact, the global airline premium in 2015 was just over $1.1 billion, which is one of the lowest levels in 10 years. But, as we saw from 9/11, market pressure can have dramatic and sudden affects, and we will continue to see the insurance industry evolve alongside aircraft technology, increased traffic, and future events.

CASE STUDY

ABC Airways is a small charter airline in Eastern Europe. The carrier operates a fleet of 12 Bombardier CRJ 100 aircraft (50 seats) and one Boeing 737-500 aircraft (leased from another airline). ABC offers short-range scheduled passenger service between several cities in Europe and the Middle East as well as nonscheduled charter service to several islands in Mediterranean.

On January 10, one of ABC's CRJ aircraft veered off the runway during takeoff and skidded across the taxiway into a private cargo facility roughly 250 yd east of the runway. The crash resulted in one fatality; most surviving passengers sustained minor to severe injuries. Investigators of the crash found wheel marks on the ground, but eyewitnesses claim that the aircraft was briefly airborne. Crosswinds had been recorded at 31 kts. Following the investigation, it was confirmed that a wheel had locked up and caused the landing gear to malfunction.

The aircraft sustained unrepairable damage to its airframe and landing gear. Current market value of the aircraft before the crash was estimated at $11,500,000, and damage to the cargo facility was estimated to be $2,000,000. Finally, 13 passengers filed bodily injury claims, each for $10,000. This single fatality resulted in a combined claim of $450,000.

At the time of the incident, the CRJ was covered under an all risks–ground and flight hull policy through BWC Jet Services, with a $1,000,000 deductible on an insured value of $12,000,000. Exclusions include wear and tear, tire replacement, and war or confiscation. The airline also held minimum coverage on a SLs liability policy for passenger bodily injury, with a $1,000,000 limit on property damage. This policy was under the same provider. ABC's jurisdiction requires the same liability limits for bodily injury as does the United States.

1. Calculate the total amount that ABC Airways can expect to receive from BWC Jet Services.
2. What total amount would ABC have received under a combined-limits liability policy?
3. What total amount would ABC have received under an all risks-not in flight hull policy?
4. Assume it was discovered that the crash was caused by pilot error. Would the outcome change? If so how?
5. Referring to the original scenario, how would the outcome change had BWC discovered that pilot in command had failed her annual medical check the morning of the flight?
6. Would ABC Airways benefit from a nonownership liability add-on? Why or why not?
7. Explain the risks that BWC faces as ABC's sole insurance provider. Should BWC purchase a reinsurance policy? Explain.

REFERENCES

Boeing. *Current market outlook: 2017–2036.* (2016). From <https://www.boeing.com/commercial/market/commercial-market-outlook/> Retrieved December 12, 2017.

Culp, C. L. (2001). *The risk management process.* New York: John Wiley & Sons Inc.

Freitas, P. J. (2006). Aviation war risk insurance and its impact on US passenger aviation. *Journal of Transport Literature*, *7*(2).

Gassen, D. (2012). *A guide to aviation insurance.* International Union of Aerospace Insurers. From <https://www.oecd.org/daf/fin/insurance/4.DavidGasson-background.pdf> Retrieved December 1, 2017.

Gerber, D. N. (2012). Chapter 7 aircraft finance. In I. Shrank, & A. G. Gough (Eds.), Equipment leasing-leveraged leasing (5th ed.). Practicing Law Institute.

Vaughan, E. J. (1997). *Risk management.* New York: John Wiley & Sons.

Willett, A. H. (1951). *The economic theory of risk and insurance.* Homewood, IL: Richard D. Erwin Inc.

CHAPTER

6 AIRCRAFT FUNDING—DEBT, EQUITY, AND THE CAPITAL MARKETS

CHAPTER OUTLINE

Aircraft Leasing and Financing. DOI: https://doi.org/10.1016/B978-0-12-815285-0.00006-7

HOW AIRLINES AND LEASING COMPANIES RAISE CAPITAL FOR FLEET FINANCING

Airlines' and leasing companies' treasurers, CFOs, and CEOs are looking for the most attractive, least expensive long-term source of funding they can find on an aggregate basis to fund their business. They are looking for targets of opportunity: places where they can find capital available that is more attractively priced on a risk-adjusted basis relative to elsewhere. Capital markets are one place that they can potentially reach out, and within capital markets, there are different avenues to access the capital. Accordingly, the treasurer ultimately has many different levers that he or she can pull and a number of different avenues or opportunities to raise funds, but often it comes down to the lowest cost of capital, which is not just the lowest interest rate for the company. However, companies are not always moving from space to space to constantly get the cheapest source of finance and ignoring everything else. Diversification is another consideration: most thoughtful treasurers and CFOs would diversify staying in contact with all sorts of markets and capital sources. Thus, when one market becomes more expensive, or even potentially closes as it happened in 2008, treasurers and CFOs are known to and have experience with different institutions and forms of financing.

Leasing aircraft is one form of fleet financing for airlines that, as discussed in Chapter 1, becomes more and more popular among airlines every year. In general, airline and leasing companies can raise capital to finance the acquisition of aircraft through following traditional channels:

- Retained earnings
- Commercial banks
- Debt markets
- Equity markets
- Manufacturer financing
- Export credit agency (ECA) financing

There has been a rapid evolution with the development of new fleet financing capital sources over the recent 20–30 years, such as aircraft securitization, the use of private and public debt financing with warehouse facilities, bilateral and syndicated loans, corporate revolving credit facilities, term loans, and others. New and complicated instruments to finance aircraft are developed every year by institutional investors and fintech, and the innovation does not show signs of slowing down.

THE PECKING-ORDER THEORY

The pecking-order theory is generally attributed to S.C. Myers' article "The Capital Structure Puzzle" in the 1984 Journal of Finance (Myers, 1984; Lovell, 2017a,b,c). The basic ideas behind the pecking-order theory are asymmetric information (between firm managers and investors) and the necessity to consider taxes, financial distress, and agency costs when managers make financing decisions. One can see a rigorous model and extended discussion in Dr. Myers' paper, but the practical implications of the theory are that firms follow a hierarchy choosing sources of funding: (1) Internal financing (e.g., retained earnings), (2) debt financing, and (3) equity financing. The main reason for this hierarchy is that investors are uncertain about the fair value of securities and typically are skeptical when they price debt or equity issues. Hence, to avoid worrying about investor skepticism, managers finance projects using retained earnings without going to investors. However, when outside financing is required, debt should be issued before equity because investors perceive debt as a safer security, and they are less skeptical when pricing it. The pecking-order theory suggests that firms should issue the safest securities first. This rule works within security categories also. For example, since convertible debt is riskier than straight debt, the theory implies that firms should issue straight debt before issuing convertibles. With respect to fleet financing, secured debt [e.g., Enhanced Equipment Trust Certificate (EETC) discussed later in this chapter] is safer than senior unsecured debt, and senior unsecured debt is safer than mezzanine financing (also discussed later in this chapter). Hence, according to the pecking-order theory, airlines should issue secured debt before unsecured debt and unsecured debt before employing a mezzanine structure. However, in real life firms often issue unsecured debt before secured debt to have more flexibility with the assets that would be used to secure debt. While using aircraft to secure debt reduces the explicit cost of financing by making it safer for investors, it increases the implicit costs by restricting operations and potential transfer of ownership of these aircraft. The following sections of the chapter will discuss various sources of funds for fleet financing, not necessarily in the pecking order.

EQUITY FINANCING

Like any other commercial enterprise, airlines and leasing companies can satisfy their capital needs by issuing new equity when the forecasted future cash requirements cannot be financed entirely through debt without exceeding the desired debt/equity ratios. Equity financing is usually done by issuing common or preferred stock. There is nothing special about equity financing for airlines and leasing companies—it is structured similarly to any other industry where funds are raised to finance projects or capital assets.

Equity funds can be raised through private placements (issuing equity to private investors) or public offerings when the securities are registered with the US Securities and Exchange Commission and are traded on public stock exchanges. Public offerings can be initial (IPO) or seasoned when additional shares of currently traded stock are offered. Investment banking firms typically assist with public equity offerings through the process known as underwriting. Airlines and lessors may choose to remain private for reasons of disclosure and control and hence place minority equity stakes with financial institutions like commercial banks and insurance companies or with wealthy individual investors. Recently several airlines have privately placed minority equity stakes with other airlines in conjunction with alliance partnerships. For example, Qatar Airways has a 20% stake in IAG (the parent company of British Airways and Iberia), 10% stake in LATAM, and 10% stake in Cathay Pacific. Since we are trying to focus on asset financing specific to airlines and commercial aircraft lessors, an extended discussion on equity financing is outside the scope of this chapter.

Typical equity investors in aircraft-leasing companies are pension funds, private equity firms, and large Chinese and Japanese banks that are looking for higher yields than are available in the debt markets. Historically, private equity firms have been investing in fast-growing start-up lessors aiming to exit in about 5 years through selling their investments privately or via IPOs. Table 6.1 lists some of the private equity firms and aircraft lessors they invested.

Pension funds and other institutional investors typically take minority positions in aircraft lessor equity looking for steady cash flows. They provide capital to experienced and knowledgeable lessor-management teams through joint ventures, sidecars, or special purpose vehicles (SPVs). These types of investors are not typically looking for high returns, but for safe and steady cash flows. Table 6.2 presents several pension funds and institutional investors and their corresponding investments in aircraft lessors.

Chinese and Japanese banks and conglomerates have been targeting developed leasing companies with good track records and scalable platforms. Thus, among many examples, Jackson Square Aviation was acquired by Mitsubishi Corporation, Development Bank of Japan invested in TES Aviation, HNA Group in Avolon, and SMBC in RBS Aviation Capital.

DEBT FINANCING

Debt financing is one of the most readily available forms of financing for the airlines and lessors. Debt can help in meeting almost all of their financial needs, such as working capital requirements, aircraft purchases, and corporate acquisitions. Debt financing is also an integral part of leasing and manufacturer-financing alternatives.

Table 6.1 Private Equity Investments in Aircraft Lessors

Private Equity Firm	Investment in Lessors
Oaktree	Elix Aviation Capital
	Jackson Square Aviation
CVC Capital Partners	Avolon
Fortress	Aircastle
Onex	Fly Leasing
	BBAM
Centerbridge	Intrepid
Oakhill	Avolon
EQT	Nordic Aviation Capital
Napier	Air Lease Corporation
Carlyle Group	Landmark Aviation
Waterwood	Asia Pacific Aviation Leasing

Ishka Research (Lovell, 2017c).

Table 6.2 Pension Funds and Institutional Investors Investing in Aircraft Lessors

Pension Funds and Institutional Investors	Investment in Lessors
Ontario Teachers' Pension Plan	GE Aviation
	Aircastle
Canada Pension Plan	AWAS
PSP Investments	Sky Leasing
Pacific Life Investments	Aviation Capital Group
GIC	Avolon
Kuwait Finance House	ALAFCO

Ishka Research (Lovell, 2017c).

Unsecured debt represents the most senior class of an airline's capital structure because the money that is owed under debt is considered to have a higher priority than the others. In the event of a default, the senior class debt holders are paid first before other junior class creditors are paid. Due to this priority over other creditors, the cost of senior debt is much less compared to other forms of financing.

Commercial banks have been one of the most critical sources of debt financing for the airlines and lessors. This is almost certain to continue as banks have over the years gained an understanding of the complexities of lending in commercial aviation and the values of aircraft as assets. In addition to providing short-term financing solutions in terms of overdrafts and lines of credit, banks play an integral role in medium-term corporate loans and leveraged leases for aircraft purchase. Bank loans are typically floating rate debt, with the interest rate based on London Interbank Offer Rate (LIBOR) throughout the term of the loan. The interest rate is typically quoted in basis points over the LIBOR. A basis point is 1/100 of a percent. For example, if 6-month LIBOR is 4%, 50 basis points over 6 month-LIBOR means 4.5% interest rate.

A typical bank financing is between a 5 and 12-year mortgage loan that is used to finance a single aircraft or a group of aircraft and can be amortized over the term of the loan completely (to zero) or to some kind of a balloon that will be repaid at the end of the term.

Another form of debt financing available to the airlines and lessors is the bond market. The bond market offers the full range of maturities, the highest liquidity, and the capacity to absorb large issues. Typically, bonds are issued with long-term maturities (25−30 years). The interest rates on the bonds are usually fixed and paid in the form of semiannual or annual coupon payments. For a typical bond, the principal (also called face value or par value) does not need to be repaid before maturity. However, based on an issuer credit risk, the bond indenture may include sinking fund provisions that will require an airline or lessor to accumulate funds over the life of the bond to be able to pay creditors in full at the bond maturity. Alternative sinking fund provisions may include requirements to retire a predetermined percentage of the bond issue based on a particular schedule (e.g., 5% every year) to ensure that a company has enough funds available to repay the remaining principal when it is due. Many covenants may accompany bond issues, such as restrictions on additional debt and extraordinary dividends, as well as others. By including these covenants in the bond indentures, bond investors protect themselves and ensure that the interest rate paid by the company (and collected by the investors) corresponds to the risk of the investment.

The bank market tends to be very relationship-driven. If a bank makes a loan to an airline or leasing company, it typically means that a bank has spent a considerable amount of time getting to know the business of that airline or leasing company. That means developing a deep relationship with them by developing business outside of that particular loan, such as hedging, cash management, investment banking, or other business. Whereas in the capital markets a particular money manager, insurance company, or another financial institution that ends up buying a bond issued by an airline or leasing company may follow them from the research perspective but may not necessarily have a relationship that leads to other repeat business.

Another difference between the bank and bond markets is that for the most part when banks make loans, they intend to hold those loans to maturity—that is part of the relationship that banks try to maintain with their clients. However, in the bond market the debt securities are built to be traded and, thus, need to have ratings, which bank loans usually do not have. The third-party rating agencies, such as Standard & Poor's, Moody's, and others provide bond ratings that portfolio managers can use in their decisions to buy or sell bonds. Banks do sell or transfer some of their loans, but that happens a lot less frequently than it would in the capital markets.

Besides, the bond market deals are typically larger than the bank deals due to liquidity, covenants, long-term relationships (banks) versus trading (bonds), and simply access to capital for a lender. The difference in scale is substantial: a borrower can do a much more sizeable transaction in the capital markets than in the bank market. There are cases where several banks would come together in what is called "a club" and do a club deal or a big revolving credit facility. However, if an airline needs to finance a hundred aircraft over the next 3 years, typically this airline is going to do a couple of large bond deals. These bonds could be secured or unsecured and raise anywhere between four hundred million to a billion and a half dollars in a single transaction. There is a scale in the bond market which typically is not seen in the bank market.

Similar to equity financing, there is nothing special with unsecured debt financing in the airline and aircraft-leasing industry. Of course, to appropriately assess the risk, bond investors need to understand the airline and aircraft-leasing industry and the position of the issuer in that industry. Corporate bonds issued by airlines and lessors are backed by their corporate credit. Since the majority of the airlines typically have poorer credits than companies in other industries, bond financing is not available or prohibitively expensive for new airlines. Often the only feasible way for airline bond financing is when they use their largest assets—aircraft as collateral for those bonds by issuing EETC. As we will discuss later, EETC structures can be enhanced through overcollateralization and diversification and, thus, reduce the risk for investors and in turn reduce the cost of borrowing.

There is a variety of factors that are going to come into play when an airline or leasing company is making a decision on how to finance their primary revenue generator—aircraft. First of all, the current liquidity of the particular airline or aircraft lessor. How much equity do they want to use in purchasing aircraft? Second, access to various debt providers. How strong are their relationships with banks? How are they viewed in the banking community? What type of debt financing deals can they get? What is the access to the capital market? Depending on what country the company is, what jurisdiction it is in, an airline or lessor may have broad access to capital markets or limited access to capital markets. Another critical factor for both airlines and leasing companies is their desire and requirement for flexibility. For example, depending on how flexible an airline wants to be, it may finance the aircraft for 12 years and never have to think about selling it, which would require repaying the debt. Similarly, leasing companies can invest in the aircraft with a long-term mindset or can buy it as an asset that they are going to trade in 2 or 3 years depending on how the market for that particular aircraft type is developing. Consequently, depending on those factors, either an airline or a leasing company is going to choose the type of financing that will allow the requisite degree of flexibility. A bank financing, for example, is more flexible than a bond. Bank financing is done on a floating rate basis because banks are natural floating rate lenders. If a prepayment is something either an airline or a leasing company wants to have as an option, then they are more likely to finance aircraft in the bank market. If a prepayment is something that is not particularly important, then a bond market might be a better alternative.

Whether an airline or a leasing company raise funds from the bank or capital markets often depends on where this company is in its lifecycle. Typically, relatively new airlines or leasing companies have very sizeable financial needs. Their first stop in the financing journey is usually the bank market. Then once they become more comfortable with the bank market and the bank market becomes more comfortable with them, a natural next step is the bond market with usually secured bond deals such as EETC or aircraft asset-backed security (ABS). The following step is unsecured financing. As a company develops and becomes more sophisticated, it progresses from more vanilla type mortgage financing to corporate deals that could be secured or unsecured.

Another consideration is whether an airline or leasing company wants to borrow on a recourse or nonrecourse basis. This is especially important for a leasing company. Some leasing companies put their guarantee against the financings, whereas others do it based on just the value of the collateral itself. In both the bond and bank markets, the lender can either lend against a corporate obligation or promise to pay from a company that is secured by the collateral. Alternatively, they can do by just looking at the collateral itself and lending against that without recourse back to the borrower. Nonrecourse financing has security in a specific airplane, but it does not have recourse back to the owner of that airplane, that is, to the corporation. The creditor claim only goes as far as the specific asset against which the creditor is lending.

What about secured versus unsecured financing? Secured financing is secured by an asset. For airlines and aircraft lessors, that asset usually is an aircraft. However, airlines, in particular, have been successful in securing other assets from real estate to routes, landing slots, gates, spare parts, and engines. Unsecured financing by definition is not secured by any asset, but it is recourse to the corporation which means there is a guarantee from the issuing company to pay back the debt when it matures. In addition to having security, the big difference between secured and unsecured financing is amortization. Secured debt, for the most part, has some type of amortization built into it depending if it is a bank or capital market borrowing. Bank markets usually have a more aggressive amortization schedule where the borrower is paying back more of the loan during the term versus a secured bond which typically has somewhat less of an amortization profile. Since there is no asset attached to unsecured borrowing, it is non-amortizing. Different types of investors will participate in the different types of financings. In general, unsecured financing is going to be more expensive than secured financing because it does not have the security for creditors and is thus perceived to be riskier.

Consider the relationship between the term of financing and amortization. It is a pretty direct relationship: normally, the longer the term of the financing, the more of the loan amount gets amortized during that term and the less of the initial loan balance the borrower is going to have at the end. For example, for a $100-million loan over 10 years, with a full payout structure and equal principal payment, the borrower will repay $10 million of principal in each of the 10 years. The borrower will end up with zero at the end of the loan term. If the loan has the same 10-year amortization profile, but the term is only 5 years, then at the end the borrower will have a balloon of $50 million, which it might have an option to either refinance to avoid such a large cash-out or just repay outright. If the borrower needs to have the $100 million loan repaid entirely during 5 years, then apparently it has to amortize it more aggressively and instead of a $10 million make a $20 million principal payment every year. The longer the term, the more of the principal is going to be amortized during that term and the smaller balloon the borrower is going have at the end.

With this perspective of the basic relationship and the practical implications of this relationship, the investors or the bank lenders must have an opinion of a particular collateral (aircraft) type. The more comfortable they are with a particular type of aircraft, the more likely they are to lend longer term and have better risk tolerance for the residual value, which translates into the balloon at the end of the financing term. For example, if a new Boeing 737-800 is being financed for a decent credit over 10 years, it is entirely possible that a bank might be comfortable with a sizeable (e.g., 40%) balloon at the end of year 10. If it is a weaker credit or if the aircraft type is not favored by the bank or bond-investor community, then the lender may require a much steeper amortization schedule over the same number of years, and the balloon payment will be much smaller.

With respect to current debt markets, from 2013 to 2017, the borrowing costs for most lessors substantially decreased. For most companies, the average cost of borrowing is determined by the pricing of their most senior unsecured bonds. Many large publicly traded lessors have de-risked their portfolios and improved their credit ratings, which lead to competitive pricing of their bonds. As a result, lessors raised record levels of unsecured debt, which has become the major source of financing. In turn, this unsecured debt improved the credit rating metrics for lessors as unsecured borrowing leaves their main assets—aircraft unencumbered. Consequently, with better credit ratings, lessors will be able to raise even more unsecured debt assuming no significant macro events on the capital markets.

BILATERAL VERSUS SYNDICATED LOANS

When a borrower deals only with one lender, the loan the lender offers to the borrower is a bilateral loan. For example, if an airline or lessor finances an aircraft using a bank loan, this is a bilateral loan. Bilateral loans can be secured or unsecured. Syndicated loans, that can also be secured or unsecured, involve multiple lenders and a single borrower. Syndicated loans are larger financing deals and typically are headed by a managing bank that arranges financing and is compensated by a fee paid by the borrower. Also, syndicated loans typically are more complicated deals, international transactions involving different currencies. Consortium financing is similar to syndication and involves one borrower and several lenders. However, typically there is no one arranger in consortium financing: several banks organize and jointly supervise a single borrower with equal shares in the transaction. Consortium loans are not as complicated as syndicated loans and occur when the deal is too large or too risky for a single bank to handle. Because of the additional fee paid to the arranger of syndicated financing, syndicated loans are usually more expensive than bilateral or consortium loans.

SCHULDSCHEIN

According to Ishka Global, Corporate Schuldschein (CSD) is increasingly popular among aviation financiers in Europe and getting traction internationally (Lovell, 2017a). Corporate Schuldschein is the German equivalent of a private placement loan with lean documentation, low issuance costs, and diversified investor base (Lovell, 2017b). A CSD is a collection of bilateral loan contracts, which is much simpler than a bond or syndicated loan, which is an agreement among multiple parties. Typical CSDs have between 3 and 10 years of maturity and offer different maturities to different investors.

LESSOR WAREHOUSE FINANCING

Warehouse lending involves lessors borrowing funds to build portfolios of aircraft that later will be used to issue aircraft ABS or financed by syndicated loans or any other means. This is a type of short-term financing that is somewhat similar to accounts receivable financing for distributors or manufacturers. It can be presented as a revolving credit line with aircraft as collateral. When a lessor issues an aircraft ABS or refinances the aircraft that were purchased using warehouse lending, the warehouse lender will be paid back. Warehouse facilities as a financing tool are more important for smaller lessors with sub-investment grade credit ratings that do not have the same access to funds as larger lessors with investment-grade ratings. These lessors often rely on warehouse lending to build portfolios of aircraft. Warehouse financing typically provides lessors with extra flexibility, for example, some of the aircraft that are used as collateral can be replaced with similar value aircraft. Typical warehouse financing deals are between \$300 and \$700 million and used for portfolios of narrowbody aircraft.

BRIDGE LOANS

A bridge loan is a short-term loan used by a lessor until it secures permanent financing through a long-term bank loan or via capital markets, hence the name "bridge." Bridge loans are somewhat similar to warehouse financing, but typically it is not as flexible—swapping collateral aircraft are not allowed. However, bridge loans provide lessors with a low-cost short-term (up to 1 year) financing solution that is usually available almost immediately. For example, in June 2016, Turkish Airlines used a bridge loan provided by Standard Chartered Bank for the purchase of two B737-800 and one B777-300ER. The commercial funding was provided by Credit Agricole CIB. The bridge loan was used in anticipation of a US Ex–Im Bank guarantee for the commercial funding (Segal, 2016).

ROLE OF RATING AGENCIES

The stronger the airline or aircraft lessor financial conditions, the wider the range of debt markets it can access and better the terms it can negotiate. The bigger airlines with their stronger balance sheets and financials can typically raise unsecured debt, while new or smaller airlines have to rely on asset-based financing. The borrowing capacity of companies is reflected in their credit ratings.

The credit ratings are issued by credit rating agencies that assess the relative credit risk of airlines and leasing companies and specific debt securities or structured finance instruments issued by airlines and lessors. A higher credit rating means lower risk for investors and, consequently, lower cost of borrowing. The "Big Three" credit-rating agencies: Moody's Investors Service, Standard & Poor's, and Fitch Ratings all are based in the United States and control approximately 87% of the nongovernment security rating business (SEC, 2017). Kroll Bond Rating Agency (KBRA) has been very active in commercial aviation debt space providing aircraft ABS and lessor ratings. KBRA has rated every commercial aircraft ABS transaction since 2016.

Fig. 6.1 illustrates the breakdown among nongovernment securities ratings reported outstanding on December 31, 2016.

In addition to the US based credit agencies, there are a number of smaller rating agencies that primarily serve non-US markets. For example, China Lianhe Credit Rating Co. Ltd. and China Chengxin Credit Rating Group, Japan Credit Rating Agency, ICRA Limited (India), Universal Credit Rating Group (Hong Kong), and others.

While the investors and lenders conduct their own credit analyses, they at least partially make their decisions based on the credit ratings of airlines and leasing companies. A good credit rating has the potential to broaden the lender base for airlines or lessors that are raising money for fleet financing. The "Big Three" rating grades, as well as selected airline and lessor ratings, are presented in Table 6.1. Many aircraft lessors are divisions of larger financial or industrial corporations, and consequently, rating agencies do not rate them separately from their parent companies. For example, Boeing Capital is a division of Boeing, and GECAS is a division of General Electric. Out of the 50 largest lessors based on 2017 ranking by fleet size, Moody's has separated credit ratings for only nine lessors presented in Table 6.3. Overall, as a group, lessors have better credit ratings than airlines.

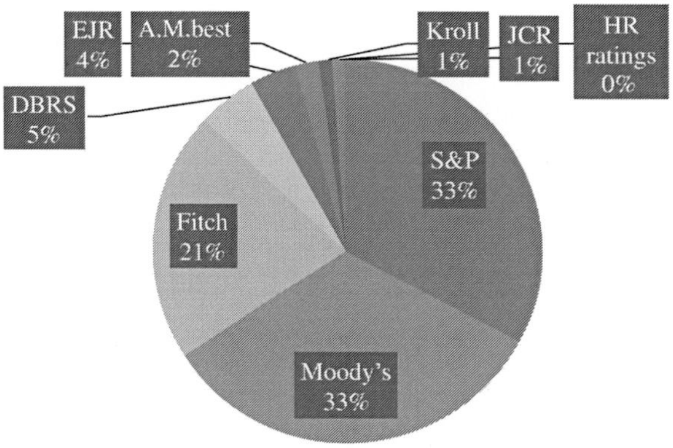

FIGURE 6.1

Breakdown of nongovernment security ratings reported outstanding on December 31, 2016.

SEC Report, December 2017 (SEC, 2017).

Table 6.3 Selected Airline and Lessor Credit Ratings (April 2018)

Rating Grade		S&P	Fitch	Moody's	Selected Airline Moody's Ratings	Selected Lessor Moody's Ratings
Investment Grade	Highest grade	AAA	AAA	Aaa		
	Very high grade	AA +	AA +	Aa1		
		AA	AA	Aa2		
		AA −	AA −	Aa3		
	High grade	A +	A +	A1		ICBC Leasing; CCB Financial Leasing
		A	A	A2		
		A −	A −	A3	Southwest Airlines	
	Good credit grade	BBB +	BBB +	Baa1	EasyJet; JetBlue	BoCom Leasing; CMB Financial Leasing
		BBB	BBB	Baa2	Air New Zealand; Qantas; WestJet Airlines	
		BBB −	BBB −	Baa3	British Airways; Delta Air Lines; LATAM; Wizz Air Holding	AerCap
Speculative Grade	Speculative grade	BB +	BB +	Ba1	American Airlines	Aircastle Limited; Embraer Netherlands Finance BV
		BB	BB	Ba2	United Continental Holding	Avolon
		BB −	BB −	Ba3	Air Canada; Allegiant; Azul	FLY Leasing Limited
	Very speculative grade	B +	B +	B1	Hawaiian Holding; SAS AB	
		B	B	B2	Virgin Australia	
		B −	B −	B3		
	Substantial risks	CCC +	CCC +	Caa1		
		CCC	CCC	Caa2		
		CCC −	CCC −	Caa3		
		CC	CC	Ca		
		C	C			
	In default	SD	DDD	C		
		D	DD			
			D			

MEZZANINE FINANCING

Mezzanine financing is a hybrid form of financing that has features of both debt and equity. In the firm's capital structure, mezzanine takes place between senior debt and equity. In the case of a default, the mezzanine investors have the right to convert to equity after senior debt holders are paid. Mezzanine is more expensive than senior debt but somewhat cheaper than equity financing. A company that is seeking to raise funds through mezzanine financing typically must demonstrate a track record, an established reputation, and positive cash flows to support contractually obligated interest payments. The advantage of mezzanine financing for borrowers is that the interest is still tax-deductible (same as with regular debt financing); however, if a borrower cannot make scheduled interest payments, some or all of the interest may be deferred (which is not the case with conventional debt financing). Also, mezzanine financing can easily be restructured into senior debt with a lower interest rate if a growing company's value can support it. The disadvantage of mezzanine financing is that the interest is higher than the interest on senior debt and the company shareholders sacrifice control and upside potential due to the dilution of their ownership. Mezzanine financing is similar to convertible debt and includes equity instruments, such as warrants, in addition to debt instruments. The most common components of mezzanine financings are subordinated notes and preferred stocks.

Typically, a mezzanine comes with cash interest, paid in kind (PIK) interest, and an equity component:

- Cash interest: A periodic payment of cash interest based on the outstanding balance of the principal amount. Interest rate can be fixed or floating based on LIBOR.
- PIK interest: PIK interest is a periodic form of payments in which the interest is not paid in cash but paid out at the end of the term in addition to the principal amount. For example, a $10 million bond with 8% PIK interest is worth $10.8 million at the end of the term.
- Equity component: Mezzanine financing has equity instruments associated with it in the form of stock warrants. These warrants allow the mezzanine investor to buy the stock at a predetermined (often nominal) price.

A typical mezzanine financing deal may look like this: $100,000,000 senior debt with 10% cash interest and 6% PIK interest and warrants representing 3% of the diluted ownership of the company.

EXPORT CREDIT AGENCIES

ECAs are public agencies that provide government-backed loans, guarantees, credit enhancement, and insurance to encourage exports of goods and services produced in their home country. Typically, ECA support is used by weaker credits in emerging markets where the demand for aircraft is high, but commercial banks are reluctant to lend without credit and political risk enhancements that ECAs offer. Most industrialized nations have at least one ECA that is usually organized as an official or quasi-official branch of their government. For example, Export–Import Bank of the United States (Ex–Im Bank) provides trade financing solutions to assist exporters of US goods and services. Similarly, UK Export Finance, Bpifrance Assurance Export, Export Development Canada, Brazilian Guarantees Agency, and others support exporters for goods and services from their home countries. According to Boeing Capital Corporation, about 30% of Boeing deliveries during financial crisis of 2009–12 were financed by Ex–Im Bank (Boeing Capital, 2018). When capital markets are healthy and multiple financing options are available, ECA financing is decreasing. Currently, in 2017 and 2018, ECA financing volume is at the historic low level and is expected to stay low assuming no major capital markets liquidity problems.

While types and forms of support vary among ECAs, typically they offer several forms of support to mitigate the credit risk of a foreign buyer. For example, Ex–Im Bank provides support in following forms:

- Direct loans to a buyer
- Loan guarantees to cover debt obligations to a commercial bank in the event of default
- Export credit insurances to exporters to protect them from default risk of a foreign buyer. This insurance makes it easier for an exporter to access bank financing
- Working capital loan guarantees for repayment of working capital loans made by commercial banks to exporters and secured by foreign receivables

Following are examples of ECA's fixed rate support in the form of zero premium interest option and floating rate support in the form of pure cover:

- Interest rate option with no premium to pay: ECA support offers a no-cost interest rate option. An airline receives an offer from the ECA to finance up to 85% of the aircraft purchase price at a fixed interest rate. This option is valid for 90 days before it expires. The airline will have to choose if it is going to accept the offer or not within the 90-day period. This option is valid for deliveries up to 3 years in advance. If the airline chooses not to exercise the option, then the offer lapses, but the airline may receive another offer in the future. If the airline chooses to exercise this option, then it is under obligation to use this interest rate for the aircraft financing. However, if at the time of delivery the airline is able to secure a cheaper alternative source of financing, it has the right to simply walk away. An advantage of such an option is that the airline can lock the low interest rate for financing and protecting itself against potentially higher interest rates at the time of aircraft delivery, but if the market interest rates decrease, there is no obligation for the airline to proceed with the higher interest rate financing.
- Pure cover: This is a floating rate option when an ECA provides insurance cover to a commercial bank. The commercial bank then lends to an airline at a floating rate. The loans are backed by the ECA for up to an 85% guarantee. With the pure cover ECA support, airlines could typically get inexpensive financing that is 40–60 basis points above 6 months LIBOR rate.

Even though ECAs support their domestic manufacturers, there are concerns that some of them would offer unreasonably favorable terms that would give an unfair advantage to a manufacturer located in economically stronger countries. To address these concerns, the Organization of Economic Cooperation and Development (OECD) established export credit rules for the civil aviation sector in 1986 with its Large Aircraft Sector Understanding (ASU) (LASU) that was part of a broader agreement—the Arrangement on Officially Supported Export Credits. The mission of the OECD is "to promote policies that will improve the economic and social well-being of people around the world" (OECD, 2018). It is an organization with, as of May 2018, 35 member countries, including the United States, Canada, France, United Kingdom, Germany, and other countries with advanced economies. The LASU was later replaced with the ASU that in addition to large commercial aircraft also includes regional turboprops and jets, as well as small aircraft such as helicopters and business aircraft. The first ASU went into effect in 2007, and the new ASU was signed in 2011. The ASU governs export financing rules for aircraft manufactured in all OECD countries and Brazil (which is not currently a member of the OECD). The ASU establishes the most favorable terms that can be extended by ECAs to eligible parties acquiring aircraft. The new ASU that was signed in 2011 and went into full effect after the 2-year transition period in 2013 also addressed the concerns of the United States and EU carriers that, being "home airlines," are barred from utilizing ECA financing. The "home country rule" prohibits ECAs from providing assistance for the purchase of Airbus and Boeing aircraft to airlines located in France, Germany, Spain, United Kingdom, and the United States. The issues that were raised by "home airlines" are that some highly profitable airlines around the world have benefited from using ECAs as a reliable and relatively less expensive source of financing, which may give them an unfair advantage.

Since the new ASU increased the minimum premium rates paid by borrowers and the capital markets are providing plenty of liquidity, the ECAs financed only 4% of aircraft deliveries in 2017 and are expected to finance about 8% in 2018 (Boeing Capital, 2018). As a result, the ECA financing controversies are not in the news in 2018. However, during the financial crisis, when the ECA support was critical for fleet financing, the "home airlines" were very vocal about these issues. Thus, the Air Transport Association of America representing several "home airlines" sued the Ex–Im Bank in 2012 for providing a financing solution to Air India for its Boeing 787 deliveries, creating an uneven playing field to a direct competitor.

Overall, the ASU has been an effective instrument in providing financing rules for fleet financing. Appendix III of the 2011 ASU and Appendix IV of the 2007 ASU stipulates the minimum interest rates that shall apply to official financing support for ECAs for civil aircraft. Table 6.4 presents ASU stipulated rates for April 15–June 14, 2018.

AVIATION FINANCE INSURANCE CONSORTIUM

Aviation Finance Insurance Consortium (AFIC) was launched by an insurance broker, Marsh, and Boeing Capital to provide a private alternative to Ex–Im Bank. AFIC offers AFIC Nonpayment Insurance (ANPI)—a product provided by a panel of insurers that support secured aircraft financing and gives insurance underwrites much more control of the structure of the deal and consequently better protection than traditional nonpayment credit insurance products. Since the insurance panel that underwrites AFIC deals is not part of the government, the interest rate margin on an AFIC-supported aircraft financing is higher than on Ex–Im Bank-backed financing. However, being a private organization, AFIC is not bound by the ASU and is not required to follow the minimum exposure fee set forth by the ASU and hence can provide cost-effective market-driven financing. In addition, the use of ANPI may result in capital regulatory relief for commercial banks as the regulatory authorities should consider AFIC-backed loans as lower risk transactions.

Table 6.4 Minimum Interest Rates for ECA Official Financing Support for Civil Aircraft

Currency	ASU	Repayment Terms (years)	May 15–June 14 2018 Rates	April 15–May 14 2018 Rates
JPY	ASU 2007	≤ 12	1.14	1.13
		≤ 10	0.90	0.89
		>10 ≤ 15	0.94	0.93
	ASU 2011	≤ 9	1.10	1.09
		>9 ≤ 12	1.14	1.13
		>12 ≤ 15	1.21	1.20
GBP	ASU 2007	≤ 12	2.49	2.48
		≤ 10	2.11	2.09
		>10 ≤ 15	2.29	2.48
	ASU 2011	≤ 9	2.31	2.29
		>9 ≤ 12	2.49	2.48
		>12 ≤ 15	2.64	2.64
USD	ASU 2007	≤ 12	4.02	3.97
		≤ 10	3.70	3.63
		>10 ≤ 15	3.82	3.77
	ASU 2011	≤ 9	3.90	3.83
		>9 ≤ 12	4.02	3.97
		>12 ≤ 15	4.05	4.02
EUR	ASU 2007	≤ 12	1.47	1.48
		≤ 10	0.95	0.96
		>10 ≤ 15	1.27	1.28
	ASU 2011	≤ 9	1.15	1.16
		>9 ≤ 12	1.47	1.48
		>12 ≤ 15	1.72	1.73

ASU, *Aircraft Sector Understanding;* JPY, *Japanese Yen;* GBP, *British pound sterling;* USD, *U.S. dollar;* EUR, *Euro*
www.oecd.org.

GENERAL AGREEMENT ON TRADE AND TARIFF/WORLD TRADE ORGANIZATION

The General Agreement on Tariffs and Trade (GATT) was signed by 23 nations in Geneva in 1947. The primary goal of GATT was to promote international trade by reducing or eliminating trade barriers. GATT included an integrated set of trade agreements aimed at the abolition of quotas and reduction of tariff duties among the nations. GATT incorporated an extended schedule of specific tariff concessions for each contracting nation, representing tariff rates that each country had agreed to extend to others. GATT remained in effect until 1994, when it was replaced by the World Trade Organization (WTO).

The WTO was established in 1995 as the successor to GATT, and the original GATT text is still in effect under the WTO framework. The WTO now is a single United Nations-sponsored institutional framework encompassing the GATT. The WTO presides over international trade, making sure that the trade between two countries is carried out according to the rules established by the WTO trade agreements. The WTO also serves as an international forum to settle disputes between countries concerning international trade. For example, the WTO was involved in the settling of the dispute between Embraer and Bombardier and their respective governments regarding the subsidies extended by these governments for the purchase of aircraft. Both countries accused each other of violating the Agreement on Subsidies and Countervailing Measures (ASCM) of the WTO trade agreements. The PROEX, Brazil's export financing agency, provides export credits to Brazilian exporters by direct financing or interest equalization payments. In 1998–99, Canada argued that the subsidies granted under PROEX to foreign purchases of Embraer aircraft violate the ASCM. The WTO panel agreed with this position and granted Canada authority to impose up to $1.4 billion in retaliation on Brazilian imports. Brazil challenged this decision stating that its financing program was similar to a $1.2 billion loan guaranteed by the Canadian Government to Northwest Airlines to purchase aircraft from Bombardier. There were several similar disputes between Canada and Brazil in 2003 and later. The most recent case was in January 2018 when Boeing submitted a petition that argued that its business was hurt by Bombardier receiving illegal government subsidies and selling the CSeries to Delta Airlines at very low prices.

ENHANCED EQUIPMENT TRUST CERTIFICATE

EETCs are investment grade–rated corporate bonds that airlines use to fund purchases of new aircraft. EETCs are essentially secured recourse debt instruments collateralized by the aircraft that are purchased from the proceeds. Also, in the event of a default, if a shortfall exists even after liquidating the collateral, EETCs allow for a claim on the airline itself. EETCs have considerable structural enhancements over traditional Equipment Trust Certificates and Pass-Through Trust Certificates. EETC bonds are issued by bankruptcy remote SPVs. These SPVs in turn own equipment notes that are backed by underlying financing on each aircraft under collateral. Usually, EETCs are given higher credit ratings than the underlying airline itself.

Main characteristics of EETCs:

- Bankruptcy remote structure
- Section 1110 protection
- Use of liquidity facilities
- Tranching
- Cross-default
- Collateral nature and diversification

BANKRUPTCY REMOTE STRUCTURE

Since EETCs are issued out of bankruptcy remote SPVs that typically are located with tax-friendly jurisdictions that emphasize and protect investor rights, they remain virtually unaffected by the bankruptcy filings of the issuing airlines. In most cases, EETCs are backed by high-value modern aircraft that form an essential part of the core fleets of issuing airlines. This means that even in the case of bankruptcy reorganization, airlines may choose to affirm the aircraft under that EETC after the bankruptcy filing and continue making all payments to EETC holders. By doing this, the airline prevents the aircraft under the EETC from being seized, and the EETC note holders remain unaffected. For example, during Delta and Northwest Airlines bankruptcies in early 2000s, the airlines remained current with EETC payments and EETC investors, and the corresponding aircraft remained unaffected through the bankruptcy process.

SECTION 1110 PROTECTION

Section 1110 of the US bankruptcy code places aircraft and aircraft equipment outside of the standard bankruptcy law for secured creditors. As a result, rather than being subject to the typical 210 days that other secure creditors in a Chapter 11 proceeding have to wait before seizing the assets, EETC holders can take possession of the aircraft after 60 days of the non-cured default. This rule provides EETC holders with significant negotiating leverage early in the process and helps them avoid lengthy stalemates that other secured lenders might go through.

USE OF LIQUIDITY FACILITIES

EETCs also come with liquidity facilities that provide regular payments on EETCs for up to 18 months in the event of a default. The liquidity facilities are typically funded by a highly rated bank and are intended to provide the EETC holders with a significant amount of time during which they may repossess the aircraft and arrange for recovery of debt while being kept current on the interest payments.

TRANCHING

Tranching is another critical feature of EETCs that allows for different leverage and seniority levels within an EETC issue. A typical EETC structure has three tranches with the following Loan-to-Value (LTV) ratios:

- A tranche with 45% LTV
- B tranche with 65% LTV
- C tranche with 80% LTV

The senior most bond in the EETC structure is the A tranche, followed by the B and C tranches. In a default scenario, the A tranche holders are the ones who will make decisions on behalf of the whole trust. Also, in a default situation, A tranche holders have the seniority with respect to the cash flows and will be paid first, ahead of the junior tranches. B tranche holders will be paid only after A tranche holders are repaid in full. The C tranche holders are the last in line to receive the cash flow after both senior tranche holders are paid in full. This is called cross-subordination and is an enhancement specific to the EETCs. This enables faster recovery of debt for the senior tranche holders in the event of a default. The rating agencies distinguish between the different classes of tranches in the EETC structure and issue investment grade ratings to the A tranche bonds and BB rating to B tranches. Highly rated EETCs are typically over-collateralized and benefit from strong asset coverage even during weak market conditions when the aircraft values are significantly lower.

CROSS-DEFAULT

Cross-default is another typical characteristic of the newer EETCs introduced after 2007. This enhancement of the EETCs stipulates that the airline must continue to make all payments on all aircraft in the EETC pool throughout bankruptcy or it will lose all of the aircraft in the EETC. The reason for this enhancement is to protect investors against selective defaults by an airline. For example, if there are several types of aircraft in the EETC pool, the airline cannot default on one type and continue to service debt on another type. When one aircraft in the EETC pool is subject to an uncured default, then all the aircraft are rendered in default by the cross-default clause. This allows the bondholders to seize any or all of the aircraft in the EETC pool as needed.

COLLATERAL NATURE AND DIVERSIFICATION

Typically, EETCs are backed by the most modern aircraft in the airline's fleet. This is important because during a default, the airline will choose to affirm these newer aircraft in the fleet. Also, from the investor's perspective, newer aircraft are easier to remarket and liquidate. In addition, often EETCs are backed by a large pool of aircraft with three or four different types in a single issue. Since different aircraft types depreciate differently, this provides a degree of diversification. Finally, as we already mentioned above, EETCs are typically over-collateralized and, thus, provide additional protections to the investors.

Due to a low spread between EETCs' coupons and the 10-year US Treasury notes, EETC financing continues to be popular among the US carriers. Thus, United Airlines issued $935 million worth of EETCs to fund 16 aircraft in 2018. Air Canada, American Airlines, and Spirit went to the EETC market in 2017 with the average coupon rate of 3.56% on A notes and 4.03% on B notes. However, with interest rates climbing, airlines may start looking at different sources of fleet financing. According to Bloomberg, total EETC issuances were $5.732 billion in 2015, $5.41 billion in 2016, and $3.14 billion in 2017.

Non-US airlines have been less enthusiastic about EETC because non-US issues would not be able to provide the creditor protection offered by Section 1110 of the US Bankruptcy Code. The provisions of the Cape Town Convention offers an equivalent method of creditor protection, but the robustness of such protection with respect to EETCs has yet to be tested. Nonetheless, as investors become more comfortable with the Cape Town Convention provisions, non-US carriers are also reaching to the EETC market especially in countries with creditor protection similar to Section 1110. Thus, British Airways issued EETCs in 2013 and 2018. Air Canada issued a Canadian dollar denominated EETC in February 2018. Norwegian Air Shuttle issued an EETC worth approximately $350 million in 2016 to purchase 10 new B737-800 aircraft.

Table 6.5 UAL 2014 EETC Structural Summary

	Class A	Class B
Face amount	$736,647,000	$212,812,000
Expected ratings (S&P/Fitch)	A − /A	BB + /BB +
Initial LTV	55.1%	71%
Interest rate	Fixed, semiannual, 30/360 days count	
Initial average life (in years)	8.8	5.9
Regular distribution dates	April 11 and October 11	
Expected principal distribution window (in years)	1.5–12.0	1.5–8.0
Final expected distribution date	April 11, 2026	April 11, 2022
Final maturity date	October 11, 2027	October 11, 2023
Section 1110 protection	Yes	
Liquidity facility	3 semiannual interest payments	
Depositary	Funds raised will be held in escrow with the depositary and withdrawn from time to time to purchase equipment notes as the aircraft are financed	

LTV, *Loan-to-Value.*

Exhibit 6.1: United Airlines Series-1 2014 EETC (United Airlines, 2014)

Early in 2014 United Airlines issued an EETC worth $949 million that was used to finance the purchase of 25 aircraft:

- 13 new Boeing 737-924ER aircraft scheduled for delivery between June 2014 and March 2015
- 2 new Boeing 787-8 aircraft scheduled for delivery between May and October 2014
- 1 new Boeing 787-9 aircraft scheduled for delivery between September 2014 and March 2015
- 9 new Embraer ERJ 175 LR aircraft scheduled for delivery between March 2014 and 2015

Lead bookrunners for the EETC were Morgan Stanley and Credit Suisse. Liquidity facility provider, Credit Agricole Corporate and Investment Bank, was acting via its New York branch. The EETCs were offered in two tranches: Class A certificates worth $736.6 million with an interest rate of 4% and Class B certificates worth $212.8 million with an interest rate of 4.75%. The Class A and B certificates were initially over-collateralized by 44.9% and 29%, respectively. Table 6.5 presents the structural summary of the EETC.

Key structural elements

- Buyout rights: Class B certificate holders have the right to purchase all (but not less than all) of then outstanding Class A certificates at par plus accrued and unpaid interest upon certain events during a United bankruptcy.
- Cross-default: Yes, from day 1.
- Cross-collateralization: Yes, from day 1.

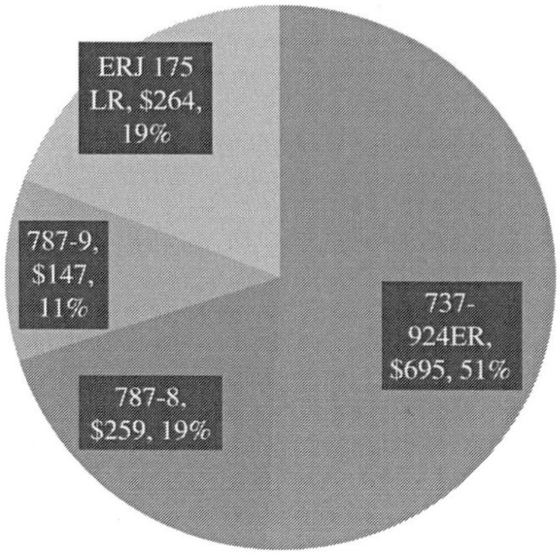

FIGURE 6.2

UAL 2014-1 EETC Collateral Mix.

- Collateral: Strategically core aircraft types to United's fleet operations, all of which are expected to be delivered new in 2014 or 2015. United expects to finance 13 of 22 eligible Boeing 737-924ER aircraft, 2 Boeing 787-8 aircraft, 1 of 4 eligible Boeing 787-9 aircraft, and 9 of 21 eligible Embraer ERJ 175 LR aircraft with the proceeds of this transaction.

Collateral information

The collateral pool benefits from diversification of three strategically core aircraft types: 51% narrowbody, 30% widebody, and 19% regional jets. All of the aircraft are new. United has obtained Base Value Desktop Appraisals from three appraisers (AISI, BK, and mba). The aggregate aircraft appraised value is approximately $1,362 million. Fig. 6.2 presents the EETC collateral mix with aircraft values as of March 2014 using the lower of the mean and median of three base value appraisals for the aircraft.

Transaction structure

The certificates were issued out of bankruptcy remote trusts that were created specifically for each class. The proceeds from the sale of certificates are initially held in escrow, and interest on the escrowed funds will be payable semiannually on April 11 and October 11, commencing October 11, 2014. The trusts use the escrowed funds to acquire equipment notes. The equipment notes are issued by United Airlines, Inc. and secured by 16 new Boeing aircraft and 9 new Embraer aircraft scheduled for delivery from March 2014 to 2015. Payments on the equipment notes held in each trust are passed through to the holders of certificates of such trust.

Distributions on the certificates are made in the following order:

- First, to the holders of the Class A certificates to pay interest on the Class A certificates.
- Second, to the holders of Class B certificates to pay interest on the Preferred B Pool Balance.
- Third, to the holders of the Class A certificates to make distributions in respect of the Pool Balance of the Class A certificates.

- Fourth, to the holders of the Class B certificates to pay interest on the Pool Balance of the Class B certificates not previously distributed under clause "Second" above.
- Fifth, to the holders of the Class B certificates to make distributions in respect of the Pool Balance of the Class B certificates.

Liquidity facility: Liquidity facilities are made available for each class of debt holders, and it provides for interest payment for up to three semiannual periods.

Cross-collateralization: The equipment notes held in the trusts will be cross-collateralized. This means that any proceeds from the exercise of remedies with respect to an aircraft will be available to cover shortfalls then due under equipment notes issued with respect to the other aircraft. In the absence of any such shortfall, the relevant loan trustee as additional collateral will hold excess proceeds for such other equipment notes.

Cross-default: There are cross-default provisions in the indentures. This means that if the equipment notes issued with respect to one aircraft are in default and remedies are exercisable with respect to such aircraft, the equipment notes issued with respect to the remaining Aircraft will also be in default, and remedies will be exercisable with respect to all aircraft.

Section 1110 protection: United's outside counsel will provide its opinion to the trustees that the benefits of Section 1110 of the US Bankruptcy Code will be available with respect to the equipment notes.

AIRCRAFT ABS

Aircraft ABSs are security instruments that are used by aircraft lessors to raise funds for fleet financing. In many ways, Aircraft ABS are very similar to EETCs, but there are distinct differences between these two securities. Similar to EETCs, Aircraft ABS are issued out of a bankruptcy remote SPV. Aircraft ABS also come with liquidity facilities, cross-subordination, tranching, and over-collateralization. The differences come from the fact that Aircraft ABS are issued by leasing companies rather than airlines, and the securities are collateralized by a pool of aircraft that are under operating lease to different airlines around the world. The Aircraft ABS holders are primarily paid from the lease receivables of the aircraft in the ABS pool.

The risk profile of Aircraft ABS is different from EETC in terms of the following:

- Diversification risks
- Re-leasing risks
- Risk of aircraft valuations

DIVERSIFICATION RISKS

The aircraft under operating lease in an Aircraft ABS are diversified by geography, lessor, and aircraft types. However, not all types of diversification may reduce risks. For example, aircraft that airlines use as collateral for EETCs are typically the newest and best ("core") aircraft in the airline's fleet. Hence, when an Aircraft ABS pool is diversified with older and less liquid aircraft, this diversification may not improve collateral and may not reduce the risk for the investors on their own. As such, other areas of diversification must be recognized to provide comfort to the investor. For this reason, diversifying ABS pools with multiple lessees operating in different geographic regions would reduce risks for the investors since the probability of multiple lessees defaulting is very small. In addition, in the case of a default by one of the lessees, its aircraft can be remarketed and re-leased. On the contrary, when EETCs are under default, all the aircraft are seized and sold. Therefore, an appropriately designed Aircraft ABS would provide investors with lower risks due to better credit diversification.

RE-LEASING RISK

The aircraft under operating leases have to be typically remarketed and leased out again about every 5–7 years. Consequently, aircraft ABS are exposed to re-leasing risk. For this reason, the experience and capabilities of the ABS servicer are carefully evaluated to ensure the investor can take comfort that the asset will continue to generate the necessary revenue after the initial lease. EETCs are exposed to no such risk as they are generally fully amortized corporate obligations over the life of the security. EETCs are however exposed to the credit risk of the issuing airline, and in the event of a default, the aircraft will have to be remarketed and liquidated in what could be a distressed market due to the large supply of aircraft on the market at the same time.

RISK OF AIRCRAFT VALUATIONS

Both EETCs and an Aircraft ABS are protected by over-collateralization. Yet, fluctuations in the values of the underlying aircraft change LTV ratios and may increase risks for investors in these securities. Aircraft ABS have annual review requirements to update the base values of the underlying aircraft. If the base values drop by more than 5%, the scheduled amortization of the senior classes is generally accelerated at the expense of junior classes to bring LTVs in the deal back to balance. EETCs do not have such annual appraisal requirements. Hence, Aircraft ABS are more exposed to aircraft value risk. EETCs, on the other hand, are exposed to market value risk, as the aircraft under EETCs will have to be sold in the case of the airline default. Typically, EETCs have lower LTV ratios than Aircraft ABS. The reason is that EETCs are dependent on the realizable value of the underlying aircraft in the case of a default, while Aircraft ABS values are more sensitive to the cash flows that lessors generate by leasing the aircraft under ABS than to the liquidation values of these aircraft.

While Aircraft ABS financing is not as widespread as auto loans, student loans, and credit card ABS, they are getting more traction every year. There were approximately $20 billion in Aircraft ABS issued between 2013 and 2018. However, the secondary markets for Aircraft ABS have not been as active as for non-aviation ABS. One potential reason for that is the lack of transparent aircraft portfolio data after issuance (Ishka Global, April 9, 2018 "Lack of transparency holds back aircraft ABS secondary market."). Without such data, secondary investors are uncertain about how each Aircraft ABS has performed after issuance. Another reason that secondary trading for Aircraft ABS has been relatively slow is the small size of the market compared to non-aviation ABS.

Recently, several Aircraft ABS issuers are coming back to the market with the refinancing of earlier issuances, and the industry anticipates more such deals in 2018 (Ishka Global, February

19, 2018. Update: Issuer contemplate more aircraft ABS refinancing.). The motivation for refinancing deals is to improve the terms of the ABS, such as the coupon rate and flexibility on disposing of aircraft.

Exhibit 6.2: Avolon Aerospace Leasing Limited ABS issues

Emerald Aviation Finance Limited Aircraft ABS (EAFL 2013-1) (KBRA, 2013)

In 2013, Avolon announced the issue of an aircraft lease-backed ABS, through Emerald Aviation Finance Limited, the SPV that was created for this purpose. The issued notes by Emerald are supported by a portfolio of 20 aircraft initially leased to 15 airlines around the world in 14 different countries. The notes were issued in two tranches: Class A notes worth $546 million issued at the interest rate of 4.65% and Class B notes worth $90.2 million issued at the rate of 6.35%. The notes amortize on a 16-year straight-line schedule.

EAFL 2013-1 ABS issue is benefited from sufficient credit enhancements and liquidity along with a dynamic transaction structure that accelerates payments to the senior tranches upon weakening cash flows or asset performance. Some of the salient credit enhancement features of this transaction are listed below:

- The Class A notes are over-collateralized by 34%, and the junior Class B notes are over-collateralized by approximately 23%.
- A liquidity facility with a maximum amount equal to the sum of 9 months current interest payable on both note classes throughout the life of the transaction.
- Maintenance reserve account equal to the sum of $3 million plus the projected next 18-month maintenance expenses.
- Provision for cash entrapment in a sub-reserve account when the Debt-Service Coverage Ratio (DSCR) is less than 120%. Upon recovery and DSCR maintaining above the minimum recovery for at least 3 consecutive months, the funds will be released. Otherwise, the funds will be used to reduce outstanding senior note debt. Provisions are also made for rapid amortization in the case of risky circumstances.

The aircraft in the portfolio are manufactured by three different manufacturers: Boeing, Airbus, and Embraer. The average age of the aircraft at the beginning of the transaction is relatively young—3 years. Approximately 72.9% of aircraft by value are narrowbody, while the remaining are widebody and regional jets. The credit quality of the lessees of the aircraft in the portfolio is a non-investment grade, which is typical for securitization in the airline industry. The average remaining term of the operating leases of the aircraft in the portfolio is 7.2 years, with the first expiry occurring in 3 years.

Sapphire Aviation Finance I Aircraft ABS (SAPA 2018-1) (KBRA, 2018)

In 2018, Avolon announced the issue of an aircraft lease-backed ABS, through Sapphire Aviation Finance Limited, the SPV that was created for this purpose. The issued notes by Sapphire were supported by a portfolio of 41 aircraft initially leased to 30 airlines around the world in 19 different countries. The notes were issued in three tranches: Class A notes worth $633 million issued at the interest rate of 4.25%, Class B notes worth $97 million issued at the rate of 5.926%, and Class C notes worth $38.38 million issued at the rate of 7.385%. The Class A and Class B notes amortize on a 12-year straight-line schedule for the first 4 years and an 11-year straight-line schedule thereafter. Class C notes amortize on a 7-year straight-line schedule.

Similar to EAFL 2013-1, SAPA 2018-1 ABS issue is benefited from sufficient credit enhancements and liquidity along with a dynamic transaction structure that accelerates payments to the senior tranches upon weakening cash flow or asset performance. Some of the salient credit-enhancement features of this transaction are listed below:

- The Class A notes are over-collateralized by 36%, Class B notes are over-collateralized by 24%, and Class C notes are over-collateralized by approximately 20%.
- A liquidity facility sized to 9 months of interest due on the Class A and Class B notes. The initial liquidity facility provider is BNP Paribas.
- Maintenance reserve account is funded on the closing date with approximately $25 million with subsequent required amounts to be greater of $14 million and a specified 12 months look forward of projected maintenance costs.
- DSCR Cash Trap Event triggered by the DSCR is less than 120% and greater than 115%. Cash is held in an account to be used upon the cure of the DSCR Cash Trap Event or can be used to amortize the notes in sequential order with majority approval from equity holders. If the DSCR is less than 115% in one payment date ("DSCR Amortization Event"), it will cause a Rapid Amortization Event. In the following payment date if the DSCR is above 115% the transaction will no longer be in a Rapid Amortization Event; however, the transaction would still be in a DSCR Cash Trap Event for at least the next two payment dates. The difference between a Rapid Amortization Event and a DSCR Cash Trap Event is that a Rapid Amortization Event directs excess cash to pay down the Series A notes and then the Series B notes, sequentially, while a DSCR Cash Trap Event directs excess cash to be held in an account until such event is cured.

The aircraft in the portfolio are manufactured by two manufacturers: Airbus (63.2%) and Boeing (36.8%). An average age of the aircraft at the beginning of the transaction is 12 years. There are 38 mid-life aircraft (6–18 years of age), one relatively new aircraft (2.1 years of age) and two end-of-life aircraft (25 + years of age). Approximately 61.5% of aircraft by value are narrowbody, while the remaining aircraft are widebody. The average remaining term of the operating leases of the aircraft in the portfolio is 4.4 years, with the first lease expiration occurring in 1 year and the last expiration in 10 years.

Table 6.6 presents summary for SAPA 2018-1 and EAFL 2013-1 structure and collateral pool.

PREDELIVERY PAYMENTS FINANCING

Predelivery Payments (PDPs) represent the progress payments that the purchaser makes to the manufacturer, while a new aircraft is still in production. PDPs mean significant cash outflows without any corresponding revenues generated by aircraft that are being built. PDPs represent as much as 30% or more of the price of the aircraft. Purchasers often borrow to finance their obligations under PDPs. Typically, the interest is payable throughout the term of financing, while the principle is payable at the end of the term. The collateral in the PDP loan is a lien on the purchaser's rights in the aircraft purchase agreement. When PDP financing is used, the manufacturer is a party in the agreement through a manufacturer's consent. The manufacturer's consent

Table 6.6 Summary SAPA 2018-1 and EAFL 2013-1 Structure and Collateral Pool

	SAPA 2018-1	EAFL 2013-1
Servicer	**Avolon Aerospace Leasing Limited**	**Avolon Aerospace Leasing Limited**
	Collateral Information	
Maintenance adjusted base value ($)	962,400,401	824,022,085
No. of aircraft	41	20
No. of lessees	30	15
No. of countries	19	15
Weighted average aircraft age (years)	12.0	3.2
Weighted average lease term (years)	4.4	7.2
Narrowbody	61.5% (33)	72.9% (18)
Widebody	38.5% (8)	20.9% (2)
Regional jets	N/A	6.2% (2)
	Lessee Information	
Largest lessee	Quantas: 12.3%	Virgin Atlantic: 12.0%
Second largest lessee	Sri Lankan: 10.3%	American Airlines: 9.8%
Third largest lessee	Sun Country Airlines: 7.4%	Frontier: 9.4%
Total top three lessees	30.0%	31.2%
	Geographic Concentration	
Largest country	Australia: 12.3%	United States: 19.2%
Second largest country	United States: 10.7%	United Kingdom: 12.0%
Third largest country	Brazil: 10.5%	Russia: 8.9%
Total top three countries	33.5%	40.1%
	Face Amount	
Series/Class A ($)	633,000,000	546,000,000
Series/Class B ($)	97,000,000	90,210,000
Series/Class C ($)	38,380,000	N/A
Total ($)	768,380,000	636,210,000
	Amortization Profile (years)	
Series/Class A	12 for first 4 years, then 11	16
Series/Class B	12 for first 4 years, then 11	16
Series/Class C	7	N/A
	Initial LTV	
Series/Class A (%)	65.8	66.2
Series/Class B (%)	75.9	77.1
Series/Class C (%)	79.8	N/A

(*Continued*)

Table 6.6 Summary SAPA 2018-1 and EAFL 2013-1 Structure and Collateral Pool *Continued*

	SAPA 2018-1	EAFL 2013-1
Servicer	**Avolon Aerospace Leasing Limited**	**Avolon Aerospace Leasing Limited**
	Maintenance Reserve	
Look forward (months)	Up to 12	Up to 18
Minimum floor (million)	$14	$3
	KBRA Ratings	
Series/Class A	A	A
Series/Class B	BBB	BBB
Series/Class C	BB	N/A

LTV, *Loan-to-Value.*
Kroll Bond Rating Agency.

is the document that establishes the agreement of the manufacturer to the PDP financing by the lender for the purchaser of the aircraft. The manufacturer's consent also establishes the rights of the lender in the case of a default by the purchaser. Negotiations on the manufacturer's consent often require compromise from both the manufacturer and lender. While the manufacturer seeks to achieve what is equivalent to a bilateral purchase agreement with no PDP financing, the lender needs to establish the rights of a secured asset-based financing. The critical elements of the manufacturer's consent negotiations are discussed in the sections below.

PURCHASE PRICE AND AIRCRAFT VALUE

The most significant aspect that the manufacturer's consent sets forth is the price for which the manufacturer agrees that the lender can purchase the aircraft in the case of a purchaser default when the lender assumes the position of the purchaser. The purchaser's final aircraft price is confidential information, and it is not disclosed to the lender. Typically, the purchaser's final price is excluded from the portion of the purchase agreement that is made available to the lender (Gee, 2009). Therefore, the initial step for the lender in determining the value of its collateral is the price agreed upon in the manufacturer's consent.

Since manufacturers do not use a fixed price in the aircraft purchase agreements. The price in the manufacturer's consent is determined by reference to the time when the initial purchase agreement was executed. Then, the price includes the escalation by an agreed formula that continues until delivery of the aircraft.

The purchase price of the aircraft is also affected by configuration and specification changes by the purchaser. These changes can increase the price of the aircraft, but not necessarily increase the value of the aircraft as collateral. Typically, as part of the PDP financing agreement, the purchaser has to notify the lender in the event of increase in the cost of the aircraft and also to compensate the lender by prepaying the loan in the amount of the increased costs, placing deposits with the lender, or prepaying increased costs directly to the manufacturer.

The lender also has to pay attention to future market conditions as it may affect the market value of the aircraft and in turn affect its security position, as in a default the lender will remarket the aircraft or the right to purchase the aircraft to realize the collateral. Since defaults are more likely in difficult market conditions, the aircraft values could be lower than the lender expects.

The purchaser and the lenders also need to decide what percentage of the PDPs they finance. PDPs funded by the purchaser is an important part of the lender's collateral and also affects the purchase price of the aircraft that the lender will pay in the event of a default. The lenders typically ask for the manufacturer's consent that the portion of PDP payments made by the purchaser can be applied toward the final purchase price of the aircraft if the lender has to step in. Usually, the purchaser's portion of PDPs can be paid by one of two ways: the buyer pays its portion of the PDPs first and then the lender comes in and pays the remaining PDPs; alternatively, the purchaser and the lender share each PDP payment according to an agreed percentage. The first method provides more protection to the lender since the lender can apply the full portion of the purchaser's PDP toward the final price of the aircraft regardless of the timing of the default. In addition, lenders typically ask for the manufacturer's consent that the PDP payments made in the PDP financing transaction cannot be applied toward any of the other obligations that the purchaser might have to the manufacturer.

PURCHASE RIGHTS

Another key element of the manufacturer's consent for the lender is to ensure that it has the right to purchase the aircraft in the case of a default by the buyer. Typically, manufacturer's consent is structured such that in the event of a buyer's default the lender has the right but not the obligation to replace the buyer in the aircraft purchase agreement. When the lender intends to replace the buyer, it gives the manufacturer a notice within 20–30 days of the default. If such a notice is not received by the manufacturer, the PDP financing lender faces the following consequences: The lender loses its rights to its already funded PDPs and also the rights to the collateral (strong form consequence); or the lender loses all rights to the collateral, but the already funded PDPs can be recovered after remarketing and sale of the aircraft by the manufacturer (weak form consequence).

When the lender makes a decision to step in the place of the buyer, the lender should consider potential outcomes of such a decision. If the lender steps in and makes payments to take delivery of the aircraft, additional payments can be significantly higher than the PDPs it had agreed to fund. If the lender walks away, it may lose all or a significant portion of its collateral. The lenders make decisions after determining if they can sell the aircraft for a price higher than the purchase price agreed upon with the manufacturer. If there is an upside in the aircraft market and the lender decides to step in, the manufacturer usually buys the aircraft out from the lender. If there is no significant upside, the lenders would have to do valuations of their own before deciding to step in or walk away. If the lender has accurately projected the value of the aircraft and determined that the buyer has made significant PDP contributions, stepping in would prove to be economically viable.

ASSIGNMENT

If the lender steps in and is ready to purchase the aircraft, the ability to immediately dispose of the collateral is essential. The lender assigning its right to purchase the aircraft from the manufacturer would help to achieve it. The benefit of the right of assignment is that the lender would not have to wait until the aircraft delivery and making all remaining payments before it has the collateral that is remarketable. Typically, the manufacturer's consent restricts the assignment right in order to protect specific interests of the manufacturer. The manufacturer needs the assignee to be creditworthy to honor the complete purchase and the lender to be unable to challenge the manufacturer's marketing efforts by competing with the manufacturer's own sales program.

MANUFACTURER'S PURCHASE OPTION

The manufacturer's purchase option gives the manufacturer the right, but not the obligation, to step in and buy out the lender's rights during a specific period that either commences following the default by the purchaser or enforcement by the lender of its lien on the purchase agreement. It gives the manufacturer the right to prevent the lender from assuming the purchaser's right to buy aircraft and then to compete in the market with the manufacturer.

BASEL III ISSUES

"Basel III" is a comprehensive set of reform measures, developed by the Basel Committee on Banking Supervision, to strengthen the regulation, supervision, and risk management of the banking sector. These measures aim to improve the banking sector's ability to absorb shocks arising from financial and economic stress, risk management, and governance. Developed as a response to the events of the economic collapse of 2008, Basel III aims to strengthen banks at the individual level to prevent a system-wide shock. Banks will implement the new regulations between 2019 and 2023 and Basel III will affect the banks in terms of four key areas:

- Core capital ratio
- Leverage ratio
- Funding structure
- Liquidity coverage ratio

One significant change with Basel III is that aviation lending is included in the same specialized lending bracket as shipping, real estate, and project financing. This will likely affect aircraft financing agreements and increase the costs for two specific reasons. The Basel III leverage ratios do not take into account the risk associated with a particular loan. Capital requirements are standard and have to be set aside based on the amount of the loan, irrespective of the credit risk involved. Basel II leverage ratios allowed for lower capital requirement since the aircraft loans are considered to be good quality assets with low risk. Basel III will result in the increase of capital requirement that in turn will increase the cost of lending for aircraft. Second, the long-term nature of aircraft loans is likely to make them more expensive due to the new liquidity coverage ratio requirements.

REFERENCES

Boeing Capital. (2018). Current aircraft financing market outlook 2018. Boeing Capital Corporation. Retrieved from: <http://www.boeing.com/company/key-orgs/boeing-capital/current-aircraft-financing-market.page>.

Gee, C. A. (2009). Aircraft pre-delivery payment financing transactions. *The Journal of Structured Finance*, *15*(3), 11–21.

KBRA. (2013). Emerald aviation finance limited, series 2013–1 ABS New issue report. Kroll Bond Rating Agency.

KBRA. (2018). *Sapphire aviation finance I limited sapphire aviation finance I (US) LLC ABS new issue report*. Kroll Bond Rating Agency.

Lovell, C. (2017a, November 20). Aviation Schuldschein gathers momentum. Ishka Insights by Ishka Global. Retrieved from: <https://www.ishkaglobal.com/News/Article/5715/Aviation-Schuldschein-gathers-momentum>.

Lovell, C. (2017b, April 26). Investor's guide: What is Schuldschein? Ishka Insights by Ishka Global. Retrieved from: <https://www.ishkaglobal.com/News/Article/5607/Investors-guide-What-is-Schuldschein>.

Lovell, C. (2017c, March 8). Snapshot: Aviation equity investors. Ishka Insights by Ishka Global. Retrieved from: <https://www.ishkaglobal.com/News/Article/5588/Snapshot-Aviation-Equity-Investors>.

Myers, S. C. (1984). The capital structure puzzle. *Journal of Finance*, *39*(3), 575–592.

OECD. (2018). About the OECD. The Organization for Economic Co-operation and Development. Retrieved from: <http://www.oecd.org/about/>.

SEC. (2017). *Annual report on nationally recognized statistical rating organizations*. The U.S. Securities and Exchange Commission.

Segal, S. (2016, June 13). Turkish gets bridge loans for expected Ex–Im-guarantees. Flight Global. Retrieved from: <https://dashboard.flightglobal.com/app/#/articles/426300?context = newssearch>.

United Airlines. (2014). *2014-1 EETC investment presentation*. Securities and Exchange Commission. Retrieved from: <https://www.sec.gov/Archives/edgar/data/319687/000119312514111469/d696366dfwp.htm>.

CHAPTER

AIRLINE CREDIT ANALYSIS

7

CHAPTER OUTLINE

The goal of every airline is to fill seats, but with so much competition and volatility, carriers cannot always push back at full capacity. Aircraft lessors must consider separately the airline's historic operating performance, jurisdiction, the risk–reward profile, the asset type in question, and the airline's credit quality. Only then can the lessor determine the proper lease terms and whether or not to enter into the agreement at all. As a lessor's principle security, an aircraft is a mobile, high-value asset that may potentially be operating in geographically or politically volatile markets. In the case of default, repossession can be a difficult process that may involve extensive costs for legal proceedings, overdue repairs, and asset remarketing. Therefore, the primary concern for any potential lease is the airline's ability to perform under current and future lease terms. Leasing risk is essentially a function of asset risk and repossession risk, which in turn equates to the airline's credit risk. The most basic way for assessing credit is simply looking at the airline's track record of making payments to creditors. However, this does not tell the full story.

In this chapter, we discuss the process of airline credit analysis, which is a full evaluation of financial and operational performance factors. In other words, we look at both business and financial risk as a way to determine an airline's credit. Essentially, lessors want a higher return from weak-credit airlines as a way to compensate for taking on a higher level of risk. This also means

Aircraft Leasing and Financing. DOI: https://doi.org/10.1016/B978-0-12-815285-0.00007-9

lower rates for long-term leases and higher rates for short-term leases. As we will see in Chapter 9, lessors also use an airline's credit profile to structure maintenance reserves, which are generally paid in cash for weaker credit airlines.

Leasing companies often rely in part upon the corporate ratings published by major credit rating agencies (CRAs), namely, Moody's, Standard & Poor's (S&P), and Fitch. While each agency follows its own methodology, public company ratings serve as a great foundation for analyzing lessee credit. Again, the objective is to score each factor individually and then come to a final holistic evaluation. For some metrics, we can compare an airline's performance against that of other carriers based on a particular category or region, whereas other measures are used only to make internal comparisons. However, most airlines are not publically traded and do not raise public debt and therefore are not rated by the big three ratings agencies.

We begin our discussion by introducing credit, risk, ratings, and airline business models. We then move into quantitative factors, including airline revenue structure, cost structure, and financial profile. Keep in mind that financial ratios provide the most value when we are looking at both current and historical data. Finally, the chapter discusses how to put the numbers in context by evaluating the carrier's operating region, market strategy, and ownership structure.

INTRODUCTION TO CREDIT ANALYSIS

Credit is synonymous with debt. If party A borrows money or resources from party B with the intention of making repayments over time or at a later date, then party A is taking on debt. Likewise, party B is extending credit and will require extra compensation (interest) in return. This form of reciprocity is the basis for a wide variety of transactions between companies, consumers, investors, governments, and foreign entities. It is no surprise that banks account for the majority of these transactions, as credit is the fundamental premise behind modern banking.

Borrowing typically falls into one of two categories. *Secured credit* is backed by some form of collateral and is a common method for obtaining large, high-value assets, such as a home or aircraft. If a borrower defaults on a loan, the creditor can simply assume ownership of the asset. *Unsecured credit*, on the other hand, requires no collateral and is therefore riskier. This is a common method for credit cards and student loans, and lenders will typically require higher interest rates to account for the added degree of risk.

THE BUSINESS CYCLE

Credit is the driving force behind modern trade because it allows companies and individuals to immediately acquire assets and products. This promotes spending and puts more money into the economy, which in turn increases income levels, raises the GDP, fuels innovation, and speeds up productivity. Of course, this is a cyclical process (Fig. 7.1). As an investment increases in value over time, the associated credit risk of financing that investment decreases. This gives banks more incentive to lend with lower interest rates, and companies and individuals are thereby more willing to make purchases and borrow money. But peaks are always followed by periods of contraction, during which interest rates rise, funds tighten, and fewer people want to purchase products and/or borrow money.

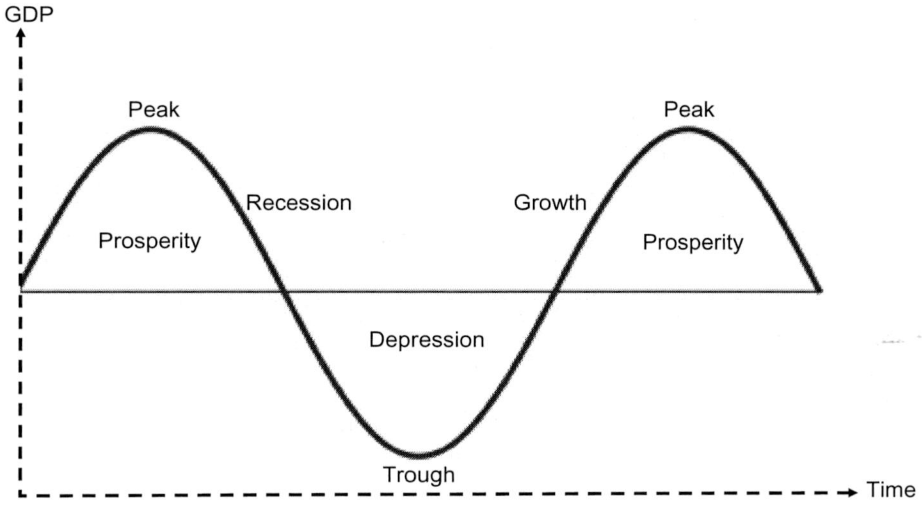

FIGURE 7.1

The business cycle.

The state of the economy affects some industry sectors more than others. Cyclical industries are characterized by high betas and high fixed costs and are therefore more sensitive to the business cycle; profits increase during peak periods and decrease during contraction periods. This is the case for airlines, automobile manufacturers, and other producers of discretionary goods or services. Defensive industries, on the other hand, are characterized by low betas and a lower proportion of fixed costs. Thus, they are much less sensitive to the business cycle. Examples include utility companies, pharmaceutical companies, food suppliers, and other producers of nondiscretionary goods. In other words, there is still a demand for these products during recessions.

High-value assets typically depreciate during economic troughs when it becomes more difficult for indebted individuals and businesses to pay back loans, which means more risk for those who extend credit. To cope with the increasingly volatile bond markets and record default rates over the last few decades, financiers have developed structured methods for assessing the risk of lending.

BUSINESS RISK VS FINANCIAL RISK

The ultimate goal of investors and lenders is to earn a return on the money or resources they extend. Ideally, this return should be commensurate with the associated risk, so the purpose of credit analysis to estimate the probability that a borrower will or will not default on a short-term or long-term debt obligation. Broadly speaking, this involves three general assessments:

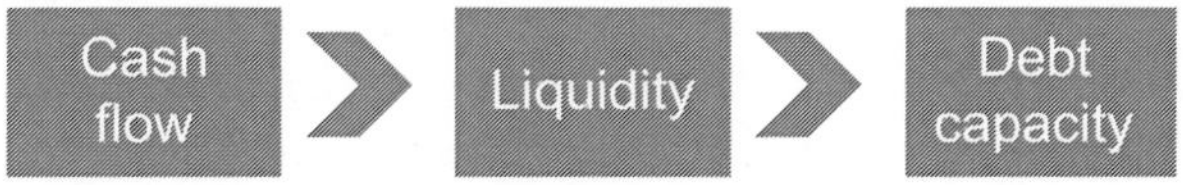

These three factors go hand in hand. To fully understand a company's cash flow and revenue potential, we need to think in terms of capital return and whether or not the business can maintain leverage. A full risk assessment also looks at management structure, competitive strategy, market share, and historic and present liquidity. The aim is not simply to make a yes or no decision, but rather to determine the level of risk involved with the specific borrower and the specific debt instrument. Most firms operate with some degree of debt, but ideally, a company should compose its capital structure according to specific uncertainties, or in other words, the nature of its business.

Risk generally falls into one of two categories. First, *business risk* reflects the volatility of expenses, revenue, and cash flow. Analyzing this type of uncertainty involves looking at a firm's operational performance, operational decisions, and how it responds to ups and downs in the business cycle. Business risk is measured by beta and refers to uncertainty in the market demand, product sales price, product liability, input costs, company reputation, industry competition, and the firm's operating leverage (fixed vs variable costs). Essentially, these are the factors that affect the operating section of the income statement, so a firm with high business risk is more likely to fall short of profit expectations. Another form of business risk is compliance or regulatory risk. Consider a winery, an airline, or a petroleum producer. How might a change in government policy affect the way these firms generate profit?

The second category is *financial risk*, which arises from the decision to finance operations with debt. When measuring this type of risk, analysts want to know how well the firm is managing debt and financial leverage—the extent to which fixed-income securities are used to purchase assets. Put another way, this is a shift of business risk from the debt holders to the stockholders; more debt in the capital structure usually results in higher interest payments and lower earnings per share. In many cases, high leverage reflects an inability to cover debt, but it can also equate to power. An airline, for instance, can use financial leverage as a bargaining tool before signing an aircraft lease agreement. It all comes down to balance.

To better understand the concept of financial risk, consider the basic home mortgage example. If John pays $200,000 in cash for a house that cost $200,000, then he is not leveraged. On the other hand, if Maria pays $200,000 in cash for a house that cost $400,000, she is in control of a $400,000 property, even though she fronted the same amount of cash. Now suppose that both properties are sold after a 10% increase in value; John will realize a gain of $20,000, whereas Maria will realize a gain of $40,000. As you can see, leverage is an advantage when an asset holds value and the borrower continues to make payments. However, the opposite is also true. If instead, the two properties decreased in value, Maria would incur the greater loss from the sale. Thus, leverage increases shareholder risk and, to compensate for this risk, provides the potential for a higher return.

Ultimately, the amount of debt that a company can sustain is a function of cash flow. High volatility resulting from business risk tells a lender that the firm's cash flow may be insufficient to completely cover its operating expenses. Poor cash flow in turn limits the degree of leverage or debt a company can successfully maintain. So, a firm that is unable to generate enough cash to satisfy its debt obligations after covering all of its operating costs will eventually go bankrupt. While companies generally can minimize business risk by making better operational decisions, reducing financial risk requires the firm to make adjustments to its capital structure and sources of funding.

METHODOLOGIES

A credit assessment typically begins with financial analysis. Analysts use ratios to assess operating performance, liquidity, cash flow, and capital structure. In other words, is the company profitable? Does it have enough cash to cover financial obligations? How does it fund its assets? This is a holistic process that requires a considerable degree of judgment. Moreover, the process is similar to that of an equities analyst, but from a different perspective. Equity analysts focus on growth potential, whereas credit analysts focus on risk and obligation. While the process is more or less the same for both valuations, the objective is different in that debt should hold the same value from the issue date through to the maturity date.

Traditional credit analysis takes a subjective, or fundamental approach, whereby the analyst looks at five distinct borrower characteristics. These are commonly referred to in the industry as the five Cs:

1. *Character:* Who is running the firm and how? Lenders look at leadership profiles and current strategy, as well as how these variables impact the public opinion and reputation of the firm.
2. *Capital:* What is the company worth? Analysts look carefully at a firm's capital structure—the number of bonds and notes payable vs retained earnings and the number of outstanding shares.
3. *Capacity:* Cash flow is a key performance indicator. Ideally, a firm should generate enough cash to comfortably cover both expenses and debt obligations.
4. *Collateral:* The question here is what is the value of the firm's current assets? Lenders want to know about every alternate source of debt repayment.
5. *Conditions:* It is important to look at numbers in the right context. Thus, lenders need to understand the underlying purpose of the loan, the dynamics of the firm's niche and industry, and how the business fits into the economy and its competitive environment.

We will detail specific accounting ratios and metrics later on in this chapter, but the general idea is to look at a firm's performance record, industry profile, and current strategy to make a reasonable judgment about its future position.

The fundamental approach is much like traditional bank portfolio management. However, it is not conducive to large-scale needs because the process tends to be expensive, slow, and labor intensive. This is why agencies and banks eventually directed more attention toward technology. The first computerized models took a univariate approach, pumping out accounting ratios that analysts could then benchmark against those of other companies. Today's models are highly cost effective and much more statistically advanced, but the downside is their failure to capture certain qualitative elements.

CREDIT RATINGS AND AGENCIES

When using a more fundamental approach, an analyst will typically apply his/her subjective judgment against some type of scale or system. A CRA is a company that provides investor risk assessments in the form of a rating. These ratings are based on public financial statements, information from the potential debtor, and information from other nonpublic sources. The obligor (issuer) can be a corporation, financial intuition, or municipality. Note that a rating is different from a consumer credit score, which is a separate process handled by credit bureaus and is beyond the scope of this chapter.

Credit agencies provide ratings of entities, but they also rate the actual debt instruments, such as corporate bonds, government bonds, municipal bonds, collateralized bonds, and other debt securities. However, CRAs do not rate common stock. Credit ratings are commonly expressed alphabetically or alphanumerically, as shown in Table 7.1. Some agencies also use symbols (− or +) to further distinguish high grade from low grade.

In the United States, the Securities and Exchange Commission closely monitors the activities of the credit rating industry and allows qualifying companies to register as Nationally Recognized Statistical Rating Organizations (NRSRO). As of December 2015, there were 10 registered NRSROs:

- S&P Global Ratings
- Moody's Investors Service, Inc.

Table 7.1 Major Credit Ratings

S&P	Moody's	Fitch	Grade		Risk Level
AAA	Aaa	AAA	Investment	Prime	Minimal
AA +	Aa1	AA +		High	Very low
AA	Aa2	AA			
AA −	Aa3	AA −			
A +	A1	A +		Upper medium	Low
A	A2	A			
A −	A3	A −			
BBB +	Baa1	BBB +		Lower medium	Moderate
BBB	Baa2	BBB			
BBB −	Baa3	BBB −			
BB +	Ba1	BB +	Non-investment	Speculative	Considerable
BB	Ba2	BB			
BB −	Ba3	BB −			
B +	B1	B +		Highly speculative	High
B	B2	B			
B −	B3	B −			
CCC +	Caa1	CCC +		Substantial risk	Very high
CCC	Caa2	CCC			
CCC −	Caa3	CCC −			
CC	Ca	CC		Near default	
C		C			
SD	C	DDD		In default	
D		DD			
		D			

S&P, *Standard & Poor's.*
Compiled by the authors using agency rating scales.

- Fitch Ratings, Inc.
- A.M. Best Rating Services, Inc.
- DBRS, Inc.
- Egan-Jones Ratings Company
- HR Ratings de México, S.A. de C.V.
- Japan Credit Rating Agency, Ltd.
- Kroll Bond Rating Agency, Inc.
- Morningstar Credit Ratings, LLC

Most of these agencies are qualified to rate a full range of entities and debt instruments. However, the industry is heavily concentrated among three main players: S&P, Moody's, and Fitch. Together, these "Big Three" account for approximately 87.6% of all nongovernment outstanding securities ratings [Securities and Exchange Commission (SEC), 2016].

Overall, credit rating methodology remains a debate, and CRAs have faced a lot of criticism in recent years, particularly in the wake of the financial crisis of 2008. This period generated widespread skepticism toward purely quantitative models that had forecasted minimal losses on mortgage-backed securities. Of course, we eventually saw that actual losses were much larger in the end. As a result, many industry leaders began stressing the need to analyze character and not just money and assets.

The bottom line is that credit analysis should help investors and financiers minimize risk and make smarter decisions. Technology is a powerful tool, but as former S&P director Edward Zimmer stated, it is an art, not a science (Ganguin & Bilardello, 2004, ix). This is especially true when it comes to the airlines. For better or for worse, airlines serve as a model for both business and financial risk. Not only is the industry highly regulated, but these commercial carriers are also highly leveraged. As such, aircraft lessors can mitigate uncertainty by thoroughly assessing each potential lease partnership.

AIRLINE CREDIT ANALYSIS

Commercial air transportation is a particularly interesting platform for credit. In fact, some analysts would go so far as to label the airlines credit agnostic. As we mentioned in Chapter 4, the average financial and operational issue at any airline company is usually a seven-figure problem. On top of that, we are dealing with high-value assets that are being flown all over the world. Even still, aircraft values can be incredibly volatile, and it is the aircraft itself which is the primary security for lessors.

Aircraft financiers are mainly concerned with operational jurisdiction, asset value, risk–reward profile, and credit quality. Due to high fixed costs and extreme volatility in fuel price and overall demand, most airlines receive speculative ratings from the agencies. An airline's credit profile matters a great deal when it comes to leasing, because not all carriers have access to the unsecured market. Cash flow, liquidity, and debt capacity are paramount, but there are also several industry-related factors that come into play, including geography, degree of regulation, competitive position, and so on. Clearly, high leverage itself does not tell the whole story, because it cannot indicate either success or imminent failure. So, some of the more important questions are:

- How is the carrier managing its leverage?
- Why have the financial ratios changed, and how did the company respond?
- What is the carrier's business model and route structure?
- What does the competitive landscape look like?
- How politically and geographically volatile is the operating environment?
- To what degree does the airline receive government support?

Again, this is an international business that requires a holistic approach. If there is one universal rule to apply, it is to always assess historical performance. At the very least, we should include the past 3 years of operation, and no lessor should limit his/her credit analysis to 1 years' worth of data. For brand new airlines, this may involve a deeper look into the structure and performance of similar competitors.

The end goal is to forecast the airline's ability and willingness make payments and to determine what a lessor would lose if the carrier were to default. The rest of this chapter focuses on airline credit analysis, specifically in the context of aircraft leasing. While we discuss ways in which lessors can utilize the various CRA ratings mentioned above, it is important to consider the unique nature of the industry. Therefore, the process presented in the following sections draws heavily from the practices of industry professionals with extensive global experience in aircraft leasing. We begin by looking at industry risk and current airline business models before moving into a quantitative discussion of revenue, cost, and financial risk analysis. Finally, we cover additional qualitative factors that lessors consider when assessing business risk. In the end, the results of the analysis should be compared to the airline's peers and against its own historical performance, while keeping a close eye on trends, changes, and outlying metrics.

INDUSTRY RISK

The airline industry operates in cycles. Moreover, these are high-risk, capital-intensive businesses. As previously mentioned, the demand for air travel tends to parallel the economic cycle and GDP growth; low demand is strongly correlated with high unemployment and vice versa. Demand also fluctuates daily, weekly, and by season. Another factor is the industry's general fixed-cost structure. Whether the plane takes off at capacity or with 100 empty seats, the cost to the airline is essentially the same. In addition, carriers must deal with ever changing fuel prices and heavy government regulation. The open skies movement has certainly lowered some of these barriers, but as a result, the industry is now facing systemic overcapacity and high competition.

Commercial air transportation is also vulnerable to external shocks. Case in point: the credit of most global carriers fell to speculative ratings after 9/11. Delta Airlines was the first US legacy carrier to restore its credit rating, but that was after 16 years, a Chapter 11 bankruptcy, and a 60% cut in its overall debt burden. Natural disaster is another exogenous factor. In 2010, European airspace shut down for several days following the eruption of Iceland's Eyjafijallajökull volcano, an event that cost the industry roughly \$1.7 billion in revenue.[1] Hurricanes, tsunamis, and even health epidemics (H1N1, SARS, Zika) all play a role in reducing demand.

[1] International Air Transport Association (IATA) (2010).

So, what does this mean for lessors? Inherently, this is a speculative-grade market, but it is not all doom and gloom. Capacity, as measured by available seat miles (ASMs) has increased considerably in nearly every global region over the last decade, and overall, airlines are getting better at matching demand with capacity to sustain higher load factors (LFs) in both peak and off seasons. Commercial air transportation can be a profitable business, but investors should first understand the dynamics of the industry and then proceed to assess how individual carriers manage these elements of business risk.

Broadly speaking, firms that operate in low-risk sectors are more likely to receive a higher credit rating. Nonetheless, industry risk does not automatically dictate a minimum or maximum company rating. As we will see later in the chapter, a lessor's decision also depends heavily on airline's financial strategy.

AIRLINE BUSINESS MODELS

Before we get into numbers, let us introduce the two main business models of commercial air carriers. Note that the focus of this chapter is on passenger service rather than cargo-only service (i.e., UPS, FedEx), but we will also discuss cargo as a revenue source for airlines. The specific business model is a major focus for lessors because not all carriers operate under the same revenue or cost structure; the fundamental difference lies in the way the company segments its passengers.

Full-service, passenger

Prior to US deregulation in 1978, airlines essentially offered the same services for the same prices. Today's carriers, however, incorporate a wide range of routes, aircraft models, destinations, and service offerings. Full-service airlines are often referred to as the majors, the network carriers, or the legacy airlines, the latter of which usually indicates some degree of prior or current government ownership. We will discuss ownership later in the chapter. Examples of full-service carriers include

- American Airlines, *United States*
- British Airways, *United Kingdom*
- Lufthansa, *Germany*
- Air Canada, *Canada*
- Emirates, *United Arab Emirates*
- Singapore Airlines, *Singapore*
- Korean Air, *South Korea*
- Qantas, *Australia*
- Turkish Airlines, *Turkey*

A key strategy for most major carriers is revenue management, which serves to separate passengers according to price sensitivity. Business travelers, for example, are less sensitive to ticket price than are leisure passengers. Therefore, full-service carriers typically offer multiple fare classes, different levels of cabin services (i.e., business, first, economy), and a wide range a wide range of in-flight and airport-level amenities. In addition, most of these airlines offer both domestic and international service, with complex hub-and-spoke route networks, codeshare/alliance agreements, and mixed fleets of both regional and long-haul aircraft.

Low-cost, passenger

Low-cost carriers (LCCs), on the other hand, market heavily to price-sensitive consumers, thereby offering simple fare structures and fewer amenities. This "no-frills" business model was essentially a product of deregulation (liberalization in Europe), which gave airlines the freedom to set their own prices and choose their own routes. While network carriers offer "bundled" service, many LCCs charge fees for basic on-board amenities, and they often configure their aircraft with a higher seat density. The LCC trend quickly picked up steam outside of the United States and has become particularly successful in Europe and Southeast Asia. Some of the most notable budget carriers include

- Southwest Airlines, *United States*
- Ryanair, *Ireland*
- easyJet, *United Kingdom*
- Indigo Airlines, *India*
- Spirit Airlines, *United States*
- Air Asia, *Malaysia*
- Frontier Airlines, *United States*
- Cebu Pacific, *Philippines*
- Lion Air, *Indonesia*

Most LCCs operate mainly domestic point-to-point service, which is perhaps the most important factor from a credit perspective, because it involves fewer aircraft types and shorter routes. In a later section, we discuss how route strategy plays a major role in an airline's cost structure and competitive strategy.

While most airlines fall under one of these two business models, we are also seeing many LCCs attempt to rebrand themselves as "ultra-LCCs." In addition, a lessor may deal with cargo carriers, charter operations, or regional carriers. Regional airlines are not always standalone carriers. Rather, many times they are contracted to fly the short-haul routes of larger airlines, either as subsidiaries or independent companies. BA CityFlyer, for example, is a standalone UK-based budget carrier that is fully owned by British Airways. However, this diversification strategy is rarely successful, as we have seen many failed attempts in both Europe and the United States.

Each business model requires a different approach to segmentation and costs, but again, it all depends on how effective the airline is at managing business and financial risk. In the next section, we introduce the key quantitative tools used for measuring operational and financial efficiency.

QUANTITATIVE FACTORS

The "numbers" are arguably the most critical component of airline credit analysis, and because financial statements really serve as the basis for this part of the process, it is necessary to have a background in or knowledge of basic accounting principles. In this section, we discuss revenue structure, cost structure, and how to use financial ratios to measure a carrier's profitability, liquidity, cash flow, and leverage. Furthermore, we introduce several industry-specific metrics that lessors can use to gauge the operational performance of airlines.

Revenue structure

Commercial air carriers generate revenue through three primary sources: Passenger transport, freight transport, and ancillary products. However, because passenger service is an airline's core business, this tends to be the main focus when looking at revenue.

Passenger

As previously mentioned, most airlines try to maximize profit through strategic pricing and market segmentation, but to fully understand revenue generation, lessors must understand several key metrics. First, ASMs/available seat kilometers are the standard airline measure of capacity, or supply. It refers to the total number of seats available for sale on each flight multiplied by the distance flown. For example, an aircraft with 200 seats (occupied or unoccupied) that flies a 700-mi route from New York to Chicago generates 140,000 ASMs.

Similarly, revenue passenger miles (RPMs)/revenue passenger kilometers are a measure of demand, or actual passenger traffic. In other words, it is the number of available seats filled by paid passengers. So, if the same 200-seat airplane flies only 150 passengers on the same 700-mi route, that flight has generated 105,000 RPMs. RPM is calculated by multiplying the number of paid passengers by the number of miles flown. The reason we use miles is because this best reflects the company's product—to fly × number of passengers × number miles. In general, a rising RPM is a good sign for creditors, as it indicates that more passengers are buying tickets.

Load factor (LF), expressed as a percentage, is another measure of consumed capacity. Airlines measure LF systemically and for each individual flight. Specifically, LF is calculated by dividing RPMs by ASMs. From a lessor's perspective, a high LF is generally favorable, as it shows how successful the airline is at selling its "inventory." Moreover, carriers that are able to maintain consistently high numbers are usually given higher ratings by agencies. Historically, the average LF among US carriers has hovered between 70% and 85%.

For per-unit revenue, we look at passenger revenue per ASM (PRASM), which is computed by dividing the airline's total revenue from passengers by its total ASMs. This is usually expressed in cents per mile. In addition, passenger yield represents an airline's average fare per mile and is the standard measure for airline pricing. Yield is calculated by dividing total passenger revenue by total RPMs. It typically ranges between 10% and 20% for US carriers and slightly higher for non-US carriers.[2] Like PRASM, yield is a useful for assessing changes over time, but it is not useful for comparing different fare classes, flights, markets, or airlines. For example, passenger yield on a long-haul network flight with a high proportion of business travelers will likely be higher than that on a short-haul destination flight with a high proportion of price-sensitive passengers who all paid lower fares. Nonetheless, credit agencies generally consider yield as the most complete measure of revenue, and higher numbers typically earn higher ratings.

When analyzing revenue, the general rule is to assess each measure holistically. Revenue from ticket sales is essentially a function of pricing and capacity utilization, where capacity utilization is measured by LF. However, selling all available seats at a huge discount is not always profitable. Again, what matters is how the airline manages its yield.

[2]Standard & Poor's (2010).

Nonpassenger

In terms of passenger revenue, analysts tend to look favorably upon airlines with a high proportion of business travelers who are less price sensitive than their leisure counterparts. However, the fare gap is narrowing as more LCCs enter the market, and ancillary sales are becoming a more important source of revenue. Low-cost airlines generate a lot of non-ticket revenue by charging fees for in-flight beverages, checked baggage fees, carry-on baggage fees, in-flight entertainment, and even seat assignments; collectively known as ancillary revenue. Likewise, additional revenue streams for network carriers may include priority boarding, premium seating, access to airport lounges, and partner commissions; most major airlines have one or more cross-selling agreements with various hotels, car rental companies, and insurance providers. Another small but increasingly important source of profit is air freight. This refers to transported cargo that is not passenger luggage. Finally, some airlines even choose to operate their own maintenance, repair, and overhaul (MRO) services for third-party carriers.

Credit agencies tend to view some income streams, namely cargo, as more volatile and cyclical than others. Nonetheless, revenue diversity is generally seen as a positive sign and can be a differentiating factor when it comes to lease rates and credit ratings. Bag fees, for example, naturally come with very high profit margins.

One way that we can make comparisons between different airlines is by calculating RASM. This refers to the airline's total revenue divided by its total ASMs. Although it is similar to PRASM, RASM provides a clearer picture of overall profitability because it captures all streams of revenue. Credit analysts will often benchmark an airline's overall growth against the traffic growth in the various markets it serves. In other words, airlines that are more focused on sustaining profit rather than constantly entering new markets are often determined to be more financially stable. Again, revenue diversification (cargo, hotel commissions, maintenance, ancillary, etc.) is generally considered a positive factor, but the primary focus should be how effectively the airline is generating profit from its core operation—transporting passengers.

Cost structure

Moving from revenue, we can now start looking at the airline's cost structure, which is more a management concept than an accounting concept. It refers to the amount and proportion of both fixed and variable costs. For a general measure, we can compute the cost per ASM (CASM), which is calculated by dividing total operating expenses by total ASMs. CASM is reported as cents per ASM and often excludes fuel costs (CASM Ex-Fuel) or transportation-related expenses (CASM Ex-Transport). These are useful metrics for assessing a carrier's cost strategy because they isolate operating expenses and factor in only those costs for which the airline can control. Transportation-related expenses include insurance premiums, airport landing fees, MRO facility costs, in-flight menu costs, and other expenses associated with ancillary or incidental service revenue.

> Cost efficiency is critical for an airline's ability to compete and survive. Yet, this does not mean that every airline should seek to be the lowest cost operator. Instead, it is important that the costs appropriate for the standard of service provided to the customer are achieved in the most efficient manner.—International Air Transport Association (IATA) (2016)

CASM, however, is not always the best way to make comparisons across different airlines. One reason is that the number usually decreases as flight length increases, so long-haul carriers tend to have a lower CASM than do short-haul carriers. In addition, budget carriers tend to have lower overall costs than do full-service carriers or those with more revenue diversification.

Nonetheless, fuel, labor, and ownership are the largest expense categories for most airlines. As such, we can get a better picture by separately looking at three cost components: fleet strategy, labor efficiency, fuel hedging.

Fleet strategy

Even though aircraft production is highly concentrated between two main manufacturers, there are many ways in which carriers can structure their fleets. Since few airlines actually disclose information about specific maintenance outlays, we can use average fleet age as a proxy for measuring efficiency. Not surprisingly, younger fleets receive higher ratings due to the fact that newer engines are more fuel efficient and require fewer repairs in the short run. In addition, manufacturer warranties can help reduce maintenance expenses. An airline may also upgrade its aircraft in order to realign or revamp its strategy, in which case a newer fleet may be better suited to the company's desired business model and consumer base. Ultimately, airlines that operate older fleets will inevitably face higher capital expenditures in the short term and end up with limited financial flexibility. An average age of 3 years or younger is considered favorable, while an average of 15 years or more is considered poor in terms of credit. Keep in mind, however, that salvage value on an older aircraft is much lower than the cost to upgrade to a newer model. Therefore, a lessor must evaluate how the airline is balancing debt with efficiency.

Fleet size is another factor, but only in the context of route structure. LCCs, for instance, typically only fly domestic or short-haul routes using narrow-body aircraft, whereas international carriers operate a mix of narrow- and wide-body jets. The main benefit of a homogenous fleet is that it requires a simpler maintenance operation, which can drastically lower costs for training, inventory, and labor. This is one of the ways that Southwest Airlines maintains its investment-grade rating. On the other hand, larger carriers with diversified fleets are better able to integrate new models into their systems and expand their networks using both short- and long-haul routes. For most international carriers, this usually yields a higher RASM. But it can also come at a higher CASM. Thus, another key factor is how the airline finances its fleet. This will make more sense when we get into financial ratios.

It is worth noting that some credit agencies weigh fleet strategy more heavily than others do. Moody's, for example, uses a 9% factor weight and assigns the highest ratings to new fleets with more than one aircraft type.

Ownership costs

Ownership costs also claim a substantial proportion of an airline's total expenses, often upwards of 20%. This includes operating accounts, such as leases as well as nonoperating accounts, such as depreciation and interest. It is interesting to note that airlines that lease rather than own the majority of their aircraft usually have a higher CASM. However, they also pay more in interest. This is why lease-adjusted debt tends to be higher for airlines with longer lease agreements.

While airlines have typically recorded aircraft rentals as an operating expense, analysts and lessors tend to view them as capital expenses. In fact, as we discussed in Chapter 3, recent changes to the International Financial Reporting Standards (IFRS) will require airlines to report most operating leases on the balance sheet rather than on the income statement. This is good news for credit analysts because it provides transparency into an airline's true indebtedness. It also makes it easier to make comparisons between carriers that lease and carriers that borrow to own.

With that said, a lessor must consider how this new accounting treatment affects the lessee's financial statements. Delta Air Lines, for example, had roughly $13 billion in operating lease obligations in 2016.[3] Shifting this dollar amount to assets and liabilities will have a noticeable impact on some key financial metrics discussed below.

Airlines have also been successful in securing debt with other assets, such as real estate, routes, gates, spare parts, and engines. Recalling our introduction to credit, an unsecured loan is going to be more expensive than a secured loan because it does not provide a security backing to creditors. Another key difference is amortization. Secured debt, for the most part, has some type of amortization built into it, depending on the specific market. Bank markets usually have more aggressive amortization schedules than do secured bonds, and unsecured borrowing is non-amortizing. From an airline perspective, unsecured borrowing is much more flexible, because it does not amortize or tie up assets. From an operational standpoint, it is also much easier to move the aircraft around. Nonetheless, a good mix of unsecured and secured debt is arguably the most prudent strategy because, as we will discuss in a later section, it opens up an airline to different sources of funding.

Labor efficiency

Another differentiating cost factor is how efficient the company is with labor, which, for many airlines, accounts for roughly one-third of all operating expenses. For the most part, these are fixed costs, at least in the short run. This is mainly due to the industry trend toward organized labor; many airline employees in North America are members of the Airline Pilots Association, the International Association of Machinists and Aerospace Workers, or the Association for Flight Attendants. These types of union groups often dictate a company's benefits, pay scale, job flexibility, work rules, and in some cases, its fleet mix and airport contracts. Unions also pose the threat of strikes and operational downtime.

Furthermore, commercial airlines have traditionally favored seniority when it comes to pay and benefits, which can become a major barrier when two companies try to merge. From a credit perspective, a seasoned workforce usually correlates with higher labor costs. Moreover, inefficiency is very common among carriers with highly regulated work practices.

One way to measure labor efficiency is by comparing full-time staff to the number of revenue-generating passengers. Specifically,

$$\frac{\text{Revenue Passenger Miles (RPM) in Millions}}{\text{Full-Time Equivalent (FTE) Personnel}}$$

Ideally, this ratio should be greater than 4.5, whereas anything under 2 is considered poor.[4] However, it is important to note that FTE refers to an airline's entire staff, whereas RPM refers only to passenger revenue. This means that this relative cost metric is less useful when assessing an airline with a large cargo sector or a large proportion of ancillary revenue. Note that many budget

[3]Delta Air Lines, 2016 Form 10-K.
[4]Moody's Investor Services (2009).

carriers operate short-haul networks that require more ground personnel. Thus, when assessing the labor efficiency of an LCC, it is important to do so in the context of other factors like yield, which will generally be higher.

Jurisdiction is another factor. While labor efficiency varies with each airline, lessors should always determine which labor laws the company is subject to.

Fuel hedging

Fuel is another major expense category for any commercial air carrier and, given the historic volatility of crude oil prices, a critical component of cost structure. During the 1990s, the fuel proportion of overall operating costs trended around 20%. Today, that figure is usually 30% or higher. All airlines are subject to essentially the same oil prices, but they can manage the volatility of these prices through *fuel hedging*. This is precisely why credit agencies care so much about fuel strategy.

If you recall from your previous finance courses, hedging is a strategy that involves purchasing one investment to reduce or offset the loss or risk of another investment. A stock trader, for example, may purchase an out-of-the-money put option to protect against a potential price decline on a stock he/she already owns. Likewise, people who purchase auto insurance are essentially hedging themselves against the risk of an accident. Airlines apply the same concept to fuel through financial derivatives (options, swaps, and futures) based on the price of a specific petroleum product. Today, crude oil is the common proxy, as there is not a substantial market for jet fuel derivatives (Turner & Lim, 2015).[5] Carriers know that they cannot always pass oil price increases on to their passengers' tickets. As an alternative, fuel hedging allows the airline to buy or sell a specified amount of fuel at a specified price and time in the future, thereby protecting itself from rising oil prices. This also helps the company more effectively budget this expense.

> We actively manage our fuel price risk through a hedging program intended to reduce the financial impact from changes in the price of jet fuel. We utilize different contract and commodity types in this program and frequently test their economic effectiveness against our financial targets. We closely monitor the hedge portfolio and rebalance the portfolio based on market conditions, which may result in locking in gains or losses on hedge contracts prior to their settlement dates.—Delta Air Lines, 2015 Form 10-K

Fuel contracts are based on estimated future oil prices, but most airlines only hedge a certain portion of their future fuel needs up to 12 months. Therefore, the common practice in credit analysis is to look at the percentage of fuel hedged over the next year. This information is usually found on a company's annual statement (10-K). Higher percentages earn higher ratings. Likewise, long-term hedging is considered a better strategy than short-term hedging. Southwest Airlines, for example, has historically maintained a high percentage of hedged fuel, a strategy that has played a large role in the company's positive track record of profitability. In fact, Southwest had increased its hedge maturities to 3 years and was paying well below the market price for fuel; that is, until the

[5]Per the Dodd-Frank Wall Street Reform and Consumer Protection Act of 2010, most OTC derivatives must be traded on exchange.

airline was forced to dramatically reduce its percentage following the financial crisis of 2008 (Liu & Jones, 2016).

Airlines are constantly changing their fuel hedging strategies, but not all will be effective. When they get it wrong, that is where it becomes a risk for lessors. While a contract can safeguard against future price increases, a high position can hurt the company's profits when fuel prices fall. Delta Airlines, for example, recorded a $2 billion fuel hedge loss for the year 2015.[6] Nevertheless, a higher percentage of hedged fuel is generally a positive sign, as it shows lessors that the company is prepared to handle a fuel price increase should it occur. More importantly, however, is how effectively the airline is monitoring the risk and adjusting its fuel program accordingly.

And then there are some carriers that refuse to hedge at all, as they have no interest in locking in a cost that they do not like to begin with. Among those that do play the game, most have been "burned by fuel hedging" at one point or another. Furthermore, while Southwest remained profitable during the financial crisis, many creditors view fuel hedging for revenue generation as an unnecessary financial risk. In general, fuel hedging for cost certainty is more conservative and therefore more favorable from a lending standpoint. Airlines may also choose to impose a fuel surcharge on passenger tickets. However, unlike hedging, this is rarely disclosed in the income statement and is thus difficult to assess.

Overall, the way an airline manages its costs is a major consideration for lessors. Again, historic performance is the key. Consider, for example, an airline that is successful at managing costs during an economic downturn or when fuel prices rise. This is generally considered to be a primary distinguishing factor from a credit perspective.

Financial profile

Financial ratios are essentially the foundation for credit analysis, from both a fundamental and model-based approach. But, remember that it is not just about plugging in the numbers. Consider, for example, the well-known case of Swissair in 2001. What we saw was a reputable international carrier and an iconic symbol for its country, Europe, and the industry as a whole. In fact, it was even coined the "Flying Bank" due its long track record of profitable stability. However, the airline had an aggressive acquisition strategy through the 1990s and up to 2001. This evolved into a major cash flow problem that eventually resulted in a massive shutdown of its entire global operation shortly after 9/11. Unable to weather this shock, the company could not make its massive debt payments, failed to get a credit increase, and ultimately collapsed.

The Swissair grounding is a good example of how numbers can lie. Therefore, the key to ratio analysis is to continually ask "why" and "how." Specifically, why did a particular ratio change from 1 year to the next? Trends and patterns reveal a lot of information, so again, we always strive for at least 3 years of data. This is the only way to bring true relevance to the numbers. In this section, we begin with profitability measures using information from the income statement. We then move on to look at equity, leverage, cash flow, liquidity, and funding.

Profitability

When looking at an airline's profitability, lessors pay close attention to the top section of the income statement. But is this more important than balance sheet metrics? The answer is unclear

[6]Delta Air Lines, *2015 SEC Form 10-K.*

without considering both components together. Simplistically, the income statement has to be more important because cash is king and cash comes from profit and loss. However, if the income statement does not coincide with the balance sheet, then there is something wrong. For example, suppose an airline is making $200 million a year and has a net equity of $300 million. Where is the profit going? Is something being pulled out or is something out of balance? What if you have an airline that has a billion dollars in equity and is making a million dollars a year of profit? This sounds like an airline in decline, but without context, you cannot properly weigh the two figures together. It is possible for a growing LCC or a recovery legacy carrier to be generating strong cash without a strong balance, but again, there has to be a story.

If you recall from your accounting courses, operating income [earnings before interest and taxes (EBIT)] equals revenue minus expenses. So, the simple method of determining profitability is to calculate the airline's operating margin to determine the percentage of revenue that remains after deducting operating expenses.

$$\text{Operating Margin} = \frac{\text{Operating Income}}{\text{Total Revenue}}$$

Operating margin using EBIT provides a basic indicator of an airline's ability to sustain its business model and reinvest its profits. Because operations are so volatile, a high ratio for an airline (over 15%) would be considered median range for similarly rated companies in most other sectors. So, by adding back paper expenses, such as depreciation and amortization [earnings before interest, taxes, depreciation, and amortization (EBITDA)], investors can get a better idea of the airline's profitability. Although it is a non-generally accepted accounting principals (GAAP) metric, EBITDA margin is the typical way to measure the profitability of most industrial companies. Obviously, companies want to have a high EBITDA. It is particularly useful for airlines because aircraft assets involve large amounts of depreciation, which can deceptively disguise the profits of a company that owns the majority of its fleet. Put another way, it is possible to have very high operating revenue but a very low net income after taxes.

EBITDA margin is also a measure of cost efficiency, as it reflects the relationship between the airline's cost strategy and its ability to generate revenue from both passenger and nonpassenger sources. It provides a better way to compare, for example, the profitability of a large network carrier with the profitability of a smaller LCC. The higher the EBITDA margin, the more financially stable the airline is. For most US carriers, margins fell below 10% during 2008, but we have been seeing steady increases upwards of 20%, which generally falls in the high range for the transportation sector. On the low end, a ratio below 5% is typical of a weak-credit airline. Across all industries, an EBITDA margin in excess of 40% generally receives the highest rating, whereas anything below 10% is considered very poor. Keep in mind, however, that EBITDA ignores the cost of capital.

A more comprehensive measure that is particularly relevant to airlines is EBITDAR (earnings before interest, taxes, depreciation, amortization, and rent). This is another non-GAAP measure, but it is widely viewed as more accurate than EBITDA, because it excludes the full dollar amount of aircraft lease expense. EBITDAR is sometimes referred to as operating cash flow and can be easily calculated using the airline's income statement. To illustrate, suppose that GoFly Airways generated $5 billion in passenger revenue and incurred $4 billion in operating expenses, of which $500 million went toward aircraft lease expenses and $200 million toward the rental of an airport hangar.

Annual depreciation was \$300 million, and annual operating income was \$1,000 million. To calculate GoFly's EBITDAR, we first locate the line item for EBIT (\$1000) and then add back depreciation (\$300) and rent (\$500 + \$200) to get an EBITDAR of \$2 billion. Hence, with \$7 billion in revenue, the EBITDAR margin sits at 28%. Because we add back lease expense, the standard here is slightly higher—above 25% on the high end and below 10% on the low end.

$$\text{EBITDAR Margin} = \frac{\text{EBITDAR}}{\text{Total Airline Revenue}}$$

EBITDAR is useful for making comparisons between airlines, while minimizing factors or costs that are unique to each carrier. Furthermore, since airlines differ significantly in terms of how they finance their fleets (lease vs purchase), EBITDAR margin is arguably a more accurate way to compare profits and gauge long-term financial health. While EBITDA is a common tool in the transportation sector, many practitioners consider EBITDAR to be the standard metric for commercial airlines.[7]

Cash flow

Credit analysts and lessors look at cash flow relative to how successful the airline is at meeting debt obligations and funding its operation. Because passengers purchase flight tickets in advance, airlines generate high cash flow without relying too heavily on working capital. Furthermore, the typical airline balance sheet is relatively simple in terms of assets and liabilities, so there is not usually a major gap between the two accounts. Nonetheless, airlines do have high fixed costs and take on large amounts of debt to fund high-value aircraft through loans or leases. Thus, cash flow is a key indicator of overall sustainability. Specifically, cash from operating activities indicates the carrier's ability to finance investments, pay off its debts, and pay out dividends, without seeking alternative sources of financing. Keep in mind, however, that cash is not the same as accounting profit.

Fixed-charge coverage ratios show the relationship between debt and cash from operations. Specifically, we can use the income statement to calculate the EBITDA interest coverage ratio as follows:

$$\text{EBITDA Interest Coverage} = \frac{\text{EBITDA}}{\text{Interest Payments}}$$

This measure tells us simply whether or not the airline is generating enough revenue to cover its fixed interest obligations to creditors. A ratio of at least one indicates minimum coverage ability, but it still raises questions. In general, agencies assign A-grade ratings to ratios of four and above, while anything below one is rated speculative. To earn a triple-A rating with credit agencies, the EBITDA interest coverage ratio must be at least six. Similarly, a lessor may instead use EBITDAR and therefore add lease payments to the denominator.

A second coverage ratio is cash flow to debt. Similar to interest coverage, this ratio tells lessors if the airline is generating enough cash flow from operations to fulfill its existing debt obligations.

$$\text{Cash Flow to Debt} = \frac{\text{Operating Cash Flow}}{\text{Total Debt}}$$

[7]Kroll Bond Rating Agency (KBRA) (2016).

We can find the above numerator from the statement of cash flows or by taking revenue minus operating expenses, interest, and taxes. Total debt includes short-term and long-term debt, as well as the current portion of long-term debt, all of which are balance sheet items. Ratios above 30% are indicative of high-credit airlines, whereas anything below 10% is usually a sign of a cash flow problem.

Another approach is to take the measure of net debt rather than total debt. This metric, commonly referred to as retained cash flow (RCF), measures the difference between incoming cash and outgoing cash during a particular financial period. RCF is what the airline has left after paying debt and expenses. It provides insight into the company's upcoming budget and is a good way to gauge how much cash it will be able to reinvest into operations during the following period.

The extent of debt service ability is important because cash is not reserved exclusively for paying off creditors. Recall the Swissair case and some of the industry risks discussed at the beginning of the chapter. Whether it is a hurricane, a terrorist attack, or an epidemic, cash flow is a fair indicator of whether or not an airline will be able to handle external shocks as they arise.

One major caveat to coverage ratios is debt maturity. Cash flow to debt, for example, does not factor in a maturity date. If an obligation is nearing its maturity date, then it is possible that the airline will be unable to pay off the debt, even though it boasts a favorable cash flow to debt ratio. This was precisely the problem that occurred during the 2008–09 financial crisis when many airlines were faced with the risk of not being able to roll over their debt.

Capital structure and leverage

Recall our discussion of leverage at the beginning of the chapter. We have already emphasized the level of volatility inherent in the airline industry and the fact that most airlines are highly leveraged. One way to measure this leverage is by calculating debt as a percentage of revenue. This measures the size of the company's debt burden while also capturing the size of the airline. Lessors often consider this measure when assessing US airlines, particularly those carriers that have recently emerged from bankruptcy.

Another way to measure leverage is by calculating the airline's debt-to-capital ratio as follows:

$$\text{Debt to Capital Ratio} = \frac{\text{Total Debt (Short-Term Debt + Long-Term Debt)}}{\text{Total Capital (Debt + Equity)}}$$

We cannot fully assess a company's capital structure simply by looking at the total amount of liabilities. Hence, the debt-to-capital ratio measures the proportion of debt in the capital structure. All things being equal, the more leveraged the airline is, the higher the risk. Put another way, a higher percentage of debt puts the carrier closer to the tipping point if there is a cyclical swing in the performance of the industry, or of the airline itself. That is why lower levered airlines, or airlines that lease more aircraft, have more flexibility, because they do not have such significant debt on their balance sheets. From a lessor's perspective, the ideal ratio for a prospective lessee would be below 30%.

Compared to firms in other industries, most airlines have a relatively high average debt-to-capital ratio. However, this ratio can be misleading considering how much volatility exists in the industry. For instance, consider a European airline that owns multiple high-value landing slots at a high-volume airport like London Heathrow. Assets are always recorded at historical value, but the equity value of assets can erode during periods of economic downturn when fewer people are traveling by air.

Another relevant leverage ratio is debt to EBITDA, which essentially tells lessors how many years it would take the airline to pay off its debt, all numbers being held constant. Thus, a low ratio (one or below) is ideal, whereas anything above four or five should raise concern. However, in the case of airlines, we often look instead at debt to EBITDAR.

$$\text{Debt}/\text{EBITDAR} = \frac{\text{Debt}}{\text{EBITDAR}}$$

Again, this is a more accurate measure of debt levels for air carriers, because it adds back the full dollar amount of aircraft lease expense. To illustrate, recall our previous example of GoFly Airways. Using the same EBITDAR of $2 billion and assuming $6 billion in debt from the balance sheet, we can calculate a debt/EBITDAR ratio of 3.0. While this is considered poor in low-capital industries such as software and data processing, it is more reasonable for capital-intensive businesses such as those in mining and transportation. Now, suppose that over the next 3 years, GoFly managed to pay off 50% of its debt and increase its EBITDAR to $3 billion. This would result in a highly favorable ratio of 1.0.

Assessing leverage also means looking at an airline's debt relative to the maturity dates of any current aircraft leases. Most rentals, including aircraft leases, are classified as operating leases. As such, credit agencies have often used adjusted debt in the above calculation, which essentially capitalizes the operating lease by adding to the balance sheet the net present value of the future stream of rental payments. Typically, in this case, a lessor would choose a discount rate based on the implicit lease rate or the lessee's incremental borrowing rate.[8] The alternative, and perhaps the simpler method, is to multiply the airline's total annual rental expense by a sector multiple. This number ranges from 4× to 10× depending on the industry, but analysts have traditionally used a multiple between 6× and 8× when capitalizing aircraft leases. Essentially, this method is meant to simulate an asset purchase and thereby capture the full life of the aircraft rather than simply account for the present value of its lease payments.[9] Like most ratios, adjusted debt/EBITDAR should not be considered exclusively, but rather, in addition to other leverage metrics.

Finally, given the recent IFRS changes detailed in Chapter 3, it is important to assess EBITDA in the correct context. In fact, among airlines, analysts expect a median increase in debt of 47% and a median increase in EBITDA of 33% (PWC, 2016). Because these companies will be required to capitalize their operating leases, credit analysts will be less likely to use adjusted debt when assessing leverage.

Liquidity

Some of the most important quantitative ratios for lessors involve liquidity and short-term factors. This is particularly true in the case of high-risk airlines. Recall the sharp decrease in passenger traffic following the 9/11 terrorist attacks or the SARS outbreak in Asia in 2003. Ideally, even investment-grade airlines want to operate with a sizeable balance of cash in order to protect

[8]IFRS/FASB meeting March 21, 2011 Agenda paper 11H/FASB Memo 152, "Determination of the Discount Rate in a Lease".

[9]Moody's Investor Services (2010).

themselves from disastrous weather, labor strikes, epidemics, and other industry risk factors that would reduce demand or ground their fleets. Therefore, aircraft lessors pay close attention to near-term cash potential, not only to gauge a carrier's ability to support day-to-day operations, but also to determine its level of protection and how quickly its assets can be sold at market price. Fortunately, the nature of the business requires upfront cash payments from passengers, which in turn allows airlines to maintain a relatively high balance of cash.

The current ratio is the basic way to measure liquidity. This is the proportion of current assets (cash, marketable securities, stock, accounts receivable) to total current liabilities (short-term notes, overdrafts, sales in advance of carriage, accounts payable), where 1 is generally considered stable and any number below 1 means that current liability exceeds current assets. For example, if GoFly Airways has $2 billion in current assets and $2.5 billion in current liabilities, its current ratio is 0.80. Put another way, the company has negative working capital (2.0 minus 2.5) and may have trouble meeting its short-term obligations.

A more informative liquidity ratio is unrestricted cash as a percentage of revenue. This accounts for the size of each carrier. Unrestricted cash is not tied to any particular business use and is part of the airline's liquid fund, which also includes cash, cash equivalents, and short-term investments. The typical range for US airlines is 10%–30%, where 20% is generally viewed as a minimum acceptable standard and is equivalent to having 2.4 months' worth of liquidity on hand. The alternative approach is to divide cash and cash equivalents by gross unadjusted debt. For this measure, any ratio above 200% receives a very high rating, whereas any ratio below 25% is rated poor.

$$\frac{\text{Unrestricted Cash}}{\text{Total Revenue}}$$

Lessors may also want to consider the booking curve and year-over-year changes to the airline's unearned revenue account (using the same quarter to account for seasonality). Airlines have been known to offer deep discounts in order to maintain liquidity, which often leaves them unable to adjust their prices when the cost of fuel increases. Consider what happens in the US retail sector on the day after Thanksgiving, Black Friday simply brings forward sales that would have been made at Christmas. Similarly, with less inventory with which to manage revenue, airlines will have less cash on hand as they enter the low season.

Finally, the operating expense ratio is less common among credit agencies and more common among aircraft lessors. Given the loss-making nature of airlines and the constant pressure to maintain high yields, seeing revenue as a percentage of operating costs can put those costs into perspective.

$$\text{Operating Expense Ratio} = \frac{\text{Total Operating Expense}}{\text{Total Operating Revenue}}$$

Obviously, airlines want to lower their operating costs, but by looking at changes in the operating expense ratio, we can relate changes in cost with changes in yield. European airlines, for example, often fail to cut costs fast enough to meet declines in passenger yield.

Funding and flexibility

As previously mentioned, airlines face a lot of pressure to remain liquid and maintain adequate near-term cash flow. For a struggling carrier, this may require various internal funding strategies, such as selling off aircraft or facilities, subleasing aircraft (subject to lease terms), reducing capital expenditures, or selling off contingent assets such as routes or landing slots. Doing so, however, may inhibit future growth.

An airline's financial flexibility and ability to raise funds internally is often measured by its degree of unencumbered assets. An unencumbered asset is any tangible, unsecured asset that is available for sale, be it an aircraft, facility, spare part, etc. Recalling our earlier discussion of credit, secured debt is backed by assets, and a company with a high amount of secured debt usually has limited flexibility in terms of future financing. Thus, the degree of unencumbered assets measures the proportion of assets not tied to any creditor claims or listed as collateral on any liens. This ratio is calculated by dividing total secured debt by total tangible assets. Ideally, this number should be as close to 0% as possible.

$$\text{Degree of Unencumbered Assets} = \frac{\text{Total Secured Debt}}{\text{Tangible Assets}}$$

When it comes to external funding, cost of debt is a major indicator of financial flexibility for commercial air carriers. Unfortunately, high capital requirements and the extreme volatility of airline stock prices make it difficult to rely on equity financing. US carriers have immediate access to capital markets and also issue more enhanced equipment trust certificates (EETC), although we are starting to see more EETCs issued by companies in other parts of the world. While few airlines have the luxury of borrowing with low rates against unencumbered assets, most still rely on bank debt. Asian carriers, in particular, are rapidly using bank funds to finance hundreds of newly delivered aircraft. However, they tend to have a higher percentage of short-term debt that gets rolled over, which means their EBITDAR can be quite low.

Governments may also serve as an external support. For US carriers, this means the option to restructure under Section 1110 of the federal bankruptcy code. Other carriers, including Japan Airlines and All Nippon, have enjoyed substantial support from government-backed funds or export-credit agency funding. Ultimately, access to meaningful funding is a positive sign, and it is strongly tied to the qualitative components that we discuss in the following section.

QUALITATIVE FACTORS

While operational and financial metrics provide valuable statistical evidence, numbers alone can never tell the whole story. In this section, we discuss some of the more qualitative elements of airline credit analysis, namely, regional factors, competitive strategy, reputation, service quality, and management. Again, this is a holistic process, and qualitative factors essentially provide the context or color behind the numbers we looked at above. More specifically, lessors look to qualitative factors to explain the changes in quantitative factors. What are the key trends? What caused EBITDA margin to increase? You cannot properly assess the financial statements without knowing where those figures came from.

Ultimately, the two main questions are why and how. Why did the numbers change and how is the airline going to proceed? A lessor could have one income statement showing $200 million in annual revenue and another income statement showing $100 million in annual revenue. Which airline is better? You simply cannot know without more information. It is certainly possible that the low-earning carrier may have recently merged with a competitor or decided to launch 20 new routes in highly lucrative markets. Or, perhaps it is in fact losing money. Similarly, you may find that the high-earning carrier was actually making double the profit 3 years earlier, thereby indicating that it is in a steady decline. While banks and credit analysis tend to be very quantitatively focused, lessors are continuing to direct more attention toward theses qualitative components. In this section, we learn that context is every bit as important as the actual number.

Operating region

As we learned from the regulatory chapter, lessors must be mindful of an airline's state of registry and the jurisdiction in which it primarily operates. The nature of commercial aviation is such that new carriers usually face high barriers to entry, which is due in large part to the industry risks mentioned earlier. In addition, carriers in developing nations often face chronic problems with air traffic control and poor infrastructure at hub airports. Overall, we need to consider both natural and state-induced factors.

Political volatility

Some airlines face considerable risk as a result of political instability. As illustrated in Fig. 7.2, this is less common in the United States and Europe and more relevant to carriers in war zones or less-developed regions such as Africa and the Southeast. Corruption and terrorism present unique risks not only for inbound and outbound traffic but also for carriers that pass through the city or country in question. Furthermore, as we saw from the global effect of 9/11, the negative impact is not always direct.

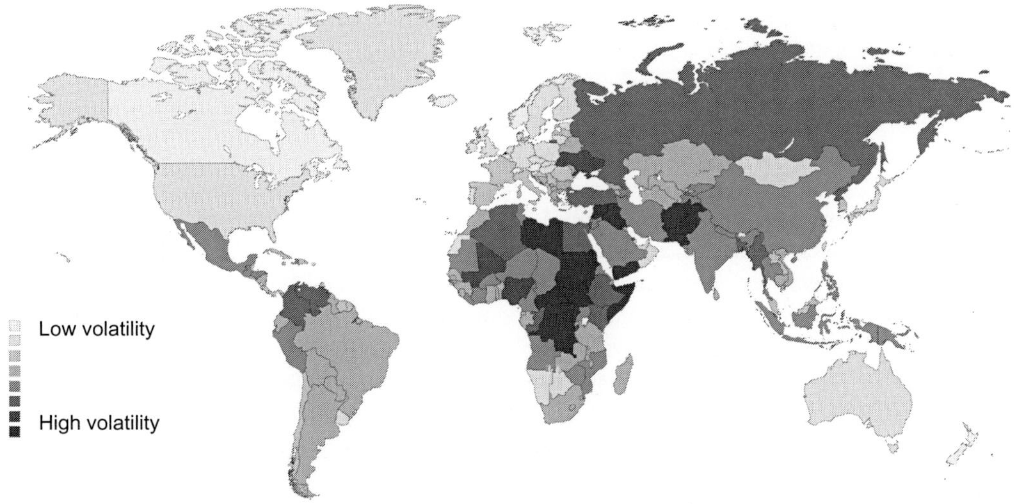

FIGURE 7.2

Political volatility by country, 2015.

Adapted by the authors using data from The World Bank Political Instability Index, 2015.

Government influence

In terms of credit risk, government intervention can be either positive or negative, particularly when it comes to recent changes in a state's regulatory policy or open skies position. On the one hand, regulation can come with a heavy tax burden for both domestic and foreign airlines. In addition, a state that grants unrestricted air rights to foreign carriers can create severe overcapacity and greatly reduce the profitability of its local carriers. On the other hand, sovereign support may come in the form of bankruptcy protection measures, state-back subsidies, or simply the freedom to fully engage in the market. In states where the government is more restrictive with air rights for foreign carriers, the indirect benefit of reduced competition can be a major advantage for the local airlines.

Regulation also goes hand in hand with safety. Although aviation is largely privatized throughout much of the world, government agencies in developed nations still play a large role in maintaining rigid safety standards, at least domestically. According to Boeing, the US airlines were responsible for only 3 out of the 28 commercial jet accidents that occurred globally during 2015. The vast majority of the remaining incidents were concentrated in Indonesia, India, Africa, and the Middle East.[10]

FX exposure

Finally, most airlines around the world are making fuel, lease, and debt payments in US dollars. Therefore, a weakening currency can deflate a carrier's net profit while inflating other costs that it pays for with local currency. If an airline is not generating enough dollar income to cover its capital expenditures, which is primarily buying new planes, the impact can be costly. The value of the Russian Ruble, for example, dropped 50% between 2013 and 2015. Likewise, the Euro has devalued against the dollar much like nearly every other currency. While 5% or 6% may not sound significant, keep in mind that an aircraft becomes more expensive by the same percentage. So, for an A380 that cost over $300 million, a 5% increase equals $15 million plus the additional interest rate cost if the asset was financed. Ultimately, FX exposure is not as much a single cost but rather a combination of several factors that can create a huge financial burden for airlines.

Geographic threats

Finally, it may also be useful to consider natural threats, such as winter storms, volcanoes, or tsunamis. For example, pilots often cite Tenzing–Hillary Airport in Nepal as having one of the most dangerous landing strips in the world, due to chronic high winds and limited visibility. A prospective lessor may want to investigate the crash accident history of an airline that chooses to fly into this airport.

Stage of development

We have already stressed the importance of historical analysis. On a similar note, the developmental stage of an airline can shed a lot of light on recent changes in profitability and on the carrier's future prospects. To start, it helps to generate a historical timeline of the company. When did it launch operations? Who were the initial founders? For startup airlines, it may be necessary to conduct an additional assessment of similar carriers in similar markets.

[10] Boeing Statistical Summary of Commercial Jet Airplane Accidents, Worldwide Operations, 1959–2015.

Mergers are another factor to consider, particularly when dealing with airlines in Europe and the United States. The 2008 merger of Delta Air Lines and Northwest Airlines sparked a wave of consolidation that actually strengthened the market in America. Mergers can result in better cost efficiency because they allow carriers the chance to eliminate duplicate routes, expand their networks, better utilize aircraft, and achieve higher LFs. When assessing an airline that has recently merged, there are several key factors that indicate a well-chosen strategy:

- Network expansion as opposed to network overlap
- Cooperation between labor unions
- Financial resources for merging fleets, systems, and facilities
- Solid forecasts of all potential integration costs

In general, lessors should be cautious of new carriers, especially those that attempt to grow too quickly or aggressively enter saturated markets. All too often, this tactic results in eventual loss. Alternatively, a steady and well-timed growth strategy is much less risky.

Competitive strategy

To receive an investment-grade rating from the credit agencies, an airline must exhibit a solid competitive position in addition to a strong financial profile. S&P, for example, rewards carriers that focus on attractive markets and are either regionally or globally diversified.[11] Likewise, a lessee that maintains a defensible, competitive advantage is less likely to default on its lease agreement. Let us discuss several factors that play into an airline's competitive strategy.

Geographic diversity

Most airlines publish detailed network maps that list exactly which countries and cities they service. Ideally, an airline should operate a diversified network with no more than 20% of its revenue coming from any one market. Why? Because diversification is as much a financial buffer as it is a growth strategy. Recall the earlier scenario involving a winter storm along the Northeast Coast of the United States. If a domestic carrier operates exclusively in this region, there is a high probability that it will be forced to ground its entire network due to weather at least once during the year. On the other hand, most full-service and/or flag carriers operate both domestic and international services, so a problem in one region does not necessarily affect flights in other parts of the network. In fact, the Gulf airlines have enjoyed immense success by focusing almost exclusively on international service; their geographical position gives them easy access to nearly every major market in the world.

However, regional diversification can be an equally effective strategy, particularly for LCCs. Southwest Airlines, for example, operates only in North and Central America and flies most of its routes within the contiguous United States. Likewise, Alaska Airlines, has been consistently profitable with a Northwest-focused market. Both airlines maintain investment-grade ratings (as of the time of this writing).

---

[11]Standard & Poor's (2010).

Route structure

A second competitive factor is how the airline structures its network. Most carriers around the world operate the traditional hub-and-spoke system, whereby each route branches off one or more hub cities. By using transfer points, hub carriers can improve utilization, increase LFs, fly the same route multiple times each day, and concentrate business operations in one central location. The major drawback, and caveat to the weather scenario above, is that a problem occurring on a spoke or at the hub can potentially affect the entire system.

A common alternative to the hub strategy is point-to-point service, which is a popular tactic among LCCs, namely, Southwest in the United States and Ryanair in Europe. By eliminating hub cities, these carriers can offer shorter flight times and more easily avoid losing passengers' luggage. The downside is a lower flight frequency and fewer city-pair options for travelers.

The question then is how effectively does the airline employ its chosen route strategy and what is the company doing to maximize the trade-offs? Either structure can be successful, but lessors want to see airlines flying profitable routes to major markets or to markets with high-growth potential. In addition, the high-performing airlines are usually those that offer convenient departure/arrival times and a high frequency of daily flights.

Passenger mix

As we mentioned earlier, passengers on business are typically willing to pay higher fares for premium services. Therefore, flying a high proportion of business travelers is considered a positive indicator. This is more characteristic of network carriers that fly to major business markets while offering catered products to this group of consumers. Conversely, LCCs tend to focus their cost advantage toward capturing a higher proportion of the price-sensitive leisure segment. It is worth noting, however, that profit from corporate travel is often more volatile than profit from leisure travel.

Market position

It is not enough simply to look at how and where an airline flies; equally important is the company's relative position within those markets. One way to measure market share is by the number of enplaned passengers at each airport. We can also look at flight share on the carrier's major routes as well as the amount of revenue that each segment generates. Another consideration is the number of landing slots at major airports, particularly those in Europe. British Airways, for example, maintains a large number of slots at Heathrow in London. This particular airport has only two runways, and slot dominance gives carriers the ability to reallocate short-haul and long-haul routes as needed. Put another way, it is an indicator of market dominance and the carrier's ability to grow and expand.

It is highly advantageous to have a large presence in high-traffic markets with high barriers to entry, mainly because air traffic in and out of major cities tends to coincide with the level of business travel. In many cases, the dominant carrier is the preferred carrier by default. Such is the case with Delta Air Lines in Atlanta, and KLM at Schiphol in Amsterdam. Business travelers are heavy users of frequent flier programs, but again, even dominant carriers must defend their territory. This means maintaining attractive schedules, high flight frequencies, and quality service on the ground and in the air. For LCCs, price leadership tends to be the main measure of competitive strength.

For feeder airlines, the analysis is slightly different. Regional carriers such as Skywest Airlines and Republic Airways operate a different business model and therefore face a unique set of risks. Ultimately, their competitive strategy involves being the lowest bidder to the major carriers.

Partnerships

Codeshares, alliances, and open skies agreements all give carriers a great opportunity to diversify and offer more destinations to passengers. Therefore, another positive factor is if the airline is a member of a global alliance (Table 7.2). If not, a credit agency will typically want to see at least some level of code sharing with one or more airlines.

Reputation and service quality

An airline's reputation says a lot about its revenue potential, but mostly in terms of its ability to draw in more of the business segment. Broadly speaking, business travelers tend to care more about in-flight service quality, streamlined boarding, airport lounge access, and frequent flier rewards, whereas budget seekers are primarily interested in cost. Premium services are generally positive credit factors. A robust rewards program can actually be a big advantage in terms of flexibility and credit. In fact, some airlines use frequent flier programs as another source for financing, either by selling miles to third-party entities like credit card companies or by creating a separate entity. This is what Air Canada did with Aeroplan, a global rewards program that was sold through an initial public offering (IPO) in 2005.

Operational performance is another measure of service quality. This includes aircraft delays, cancellations, and mishandled baggage, all of which are potential response variables when looking at overall cost structure. Some would argue that LLCs have a larger margin of error because the

Table 7.2 Global Airline Alliances, 2017

Star Alliance		OneWorld	SkyTeam	
Adria	Ethiopian	Air Berlin	Aeroflot	Korean Air
Aegean	EVA Air	American Airlines	AeroMexico	MEA
Air Canada	LOT Polish Airlines	British Airways	Aerolineas Argentinas	Saudi
Air China	Lufthansa	Cathay Pacific	Air Europa	TAROM
Air India	Scandinavian Airlines	Finnair	Air France	Vietnam Airlines
Air New Zealand	Shenzhen Airlines	Iberia	Alitalia	XiamenAir
ANA	Singapore Airlines	Japan Airlines	China Airlines	
Asiana Airlines	South African Airways	LATAM	China Eastern	
Austrian	Swiss	Qatar Airways	China Southern	
Avianca	TAP Portugal	Malaysia Airlines	Czech Airlines	
Brussels Airlines	Thai Airways	Qantas	Delta Air Lines	
Copa Airlines	Turkish Airlines	SriLankan Airlines	Garuda Indonesia	
Croatia Airlines	United Airlines	Royal Jordanian	Kenya Airways	
EgyptAir		S7 Airlines	KLM	

Alliance websites.

service expectation is relatively low. Perhaps this is true to some extent, but a chronically late LCC can still easily lose thousands of customers to a timelier competitor with the exact same ticket price.

An airline's reputation often coincides with its historical performance and represents much of that color behind the numbers. Carriers that are committed to serving their customers are usually rewarded with loyalty and therefore higher credit ratings. Another question is how important is the carrier to its immediate community and to its country's transportation infrastructure as a whole? Playing a large role locally and nationally is a positive sign, as this signifies a certain degree of consumer loyalty, industry respect, and long-term sustainability. This may also lead to a level of implied support by the national or local government. As an example, if the economy of an island nation depends on tourism, it is in the country's best interest to maintain frequent and reliable air service to the island, even if the local carrier is having financial difficulty.

Ownership

Some airlines operate as publicly traded companies, while others are private. Outside the United States, we still see many international flag carriers that are wholly state-owned entities. This is particularly common among airlines in Africa and the Middle East. More common, however, is a quasistate status, whereby ownership is a public–private partnership. Kenya Airways, for example, was privatized in 1996, and while the government is still the primary shareholder, over two-thirds of the company's shares are held by corporate or individual owners.[12] Similarly, Lufthansa was a sovereign-owned flag carrier until 1994. As of April 2017, the airline's largest single investor held only 9.95% of its stock; over half of the all shares were held by institutional investors, while private individuals accounted for roughly 45.5%.[13]

The benefit of sovereign status is that these airlines often receive substantial government support, which again may be in the form of solvency measures, financial subsidies, or market protection against new entrants. Most US legacy carriers, for example, used Chapter 11 bankruptcy provisions to restructure their fleets and renegotiate with labor unions. For wholly state-owned flag carriers, it can be assumed that the government will not allow the airline to fail. However, this is less so the case today. A recent example is Malaysia Airlines, which was allowed to go bankrupt but immediately recapitalized as a new airline. Creditors and lessors took big losses, and many had no choice financially but to transition aircraft to the new carrier at reduced rates, or face the prospect of repossessing the aircraft back in its current condition with no further compensation. This was also the case for Italy-based Alitalia. Nonetheless, when making such assumption, a lessor should write a special ownership maintenance clause into the lease agreement.

It is important to note that government funding or ownership can also have a negative impact on credit if such support comes with excessive control. State ownership often means that company decisions are driven by politics rather than by the needs of the business. Lessors must also understand the nuances of a particular state or policy. EU airlines, for example, are subject to the "one-time, last time" principle, which restricts repetitive government aid to companies that have already received such assistance within the past 10 years. This is meant to avoid wasting public money on subsequent interventions for companies that are clearly unable to effectively compete in the market.

---

[12]Kenya Airways *Annual Report & Financial Statements, 2016.*
[13]Lufthansa Group *Annual Report, 2016.*

In the case of Hungarian flag carrier, Malev, the European Commission actually called back previous state funds. The airline had received government assistance between 2007 and 2010 without having presented a viable restructuring plan. Unable to make recovery payments, Malev eventually ceased operations.

Financiers should always investigate the degree to which a sovereign state regulates the industry. The same goes for private and public airlines. EVA, Korean, and Asiana are all publicly traded companies in Asia, yet their free float is actually quite small because they are still dominated by their founders or owners. Ideally, lessors should seek out airlines that operate under strong governments that facilitate industry safety measures and promote the activities of leasing and financing. For privately owned carriers, shareholders should be focused more on profits than on dividends. For public companies, the goal should be a large market cap.

Management

Our final qualitative factor involves the airline's organizational structure and approach to management. How does the company treat its employees? What is the turnover rate in both the upper and lower ranks? An airline that is constantly changing out its leadership team is likely experiencing internal problems. Referring back to ownership, many flag carriers are run by retired politicians or retired military officers with limited business experience. One of the main reasons that the Gulf carriers have achieved such success is that they are government-owned but professionally managed.

A further question is where the management team is directing its free cash flow. As we learned earlier, this has a big impact on the credit profile. For public companies, a commitment to stockholders is generally a good sign. However, if the airline is paying out dividends or buying back shares at the expense of paying down debt, this can have negative impact on its credit rating. For private companies, the effect is often that shareholders and managers have different agendas. Ideally, the management team should have a clear goal for debt reduction and credit quality. A lessor can then assess progress to determine whether or not the company is successfully on target.

CREDIT SCORECARD

Now that we have covered the main components of an airline's credit profile, the next step is to create a weighted scorecard. Again, each credit agency and lessor uses a different methodology and weighting scheme. Moody's, for example, assigns a 31% weight to the airline's cost structure, with disaggregate percentages for each subfactor (i.e., fuel, labor).[14] Financial ratios generally account for roughly 50% of the total rating under most agency methodologies, but again, this tends to be more subjective in the leasing world.

Regardless of the specific weighting scheme, every strategy circles back to the two different types of risk discussed at the beginning of this chapter. So, a common approach is to compile the final results under either business factors or financial factors, as shown in Tables 7.3 and 7.4. The ratings columns provide summary conditions (or value ranges) that constitute a high, average, or weak rating for each factor. For a credit agency, these categories would equate to alpha-numeric

[14]Moody's Investor Services (2009).

Table 7.3 Summary of Business Factors

	High	Average	Low
Revenue structure	High-quality, highly diversified revenue streams	Some revenue diversity	Passenger-only revenue
	High RPM, LF, and yield	Average RPM, LF, and yield	Low RPM, LF (<70%), and yield
Cost structure	Fuel efficient fleet with an average age of <3 years	Average fleet age of 3–15 years	Average fleet age: >15 years
	Homogenous fleet with high utilization	Multiple aircraft types with average utilization	Multiple aircraft types with low utilization
	RPM/FTE: >4.5	RPM/FTE: 2–4.5	RPM/FTE: <2
	Strong labor relations/cooperative unions	Average labor relations/ strikes may cause some disruption	Poor labor relations/high disruption from unions
	Well-balanced fuel program, hedging 90%–100% forward 12 months	Reasonably balanced fuel program, hedging 10%–90% forward 12 months	Reasonably balanced fuel program, hedging <10% forward 12 months
Operating region	Mild climate and low chance of extreme weather or disaster	Some harsh terrain and/or chance of extreme weather/ disaster	Harsh terrain and/or high chance of extreme weather/disaster
	Very politically stable	Some political volatility	High political volatility, war zone, corruption, or terrorism
	Strong, supportive government	Some government support	No state support/weak government
	Strong currency	Some FX exposure	Weak currency
	Superior safety record	Average safety record	Poor safety record
Competitive strategy	Good mix of domestic and international flights; no more than 20% of revenue from one region	Some international service, but the carrier may have one or two dominant regions	Regional-only service
	Strong presence in major and high-growth markets	Some presence in major and high-growth markets	No focus on relevant markets
	High proportion of business travelers	Moderate proportion of business travelers	No attempt to attract the business segment
	High flight frequency and attractive schedules	Moderate flight frequency; some convenient schedules	Limited or weekly service with inconvenient schedules
	Majority share of landing slots at major/high-growth airports	Adequate share of landing slots at major/high-growth airports	Limited growth capacity at major airports
	Alliance member with considerable codesharing	Some codesharing; carrier may be an alliance member	No alliances, and limited codesharing

Table 7.3 Summary of Business Factors *Continued*

	High	Average	Low
Reputation/ Service	Strong brand, community presence, and service quality	Moderate brand recognition; slightly more focus on costs than service	Cost-focused brand with poor/inconsistent service quality
	Robust, popular loyalty program	Some form of rewards	Weak/nonexistent rewards
Ownership/ Management	Country with high activity of lessors and financiers	Lessors and financier are present, but may require government guarantees	Country has no leasing or financing activity
	No state management	Some state influence in operations	Strong state influence in operations
	Strong focus on profit (private)	Some focus on profit (private)	Only focused on dividends
	High market cap (public)	Adequate market cap (public)	Very low market cap (public)
Funding/ Flexibility	Unlimited access to secured debt, EETCs, and/or ECA	Some access to secured debt, EETCs, and/or ECA	No access secured debt, EETCs, and/or ECA

RPM, *Revenue Passenger Mile;* LF, *load factor;* FTE, *full-time equivalent;* EETC, *enhanced equipment trust certificates;* ECA, *export-credit agency.*

Table 7.4 Summary of Financial Factors

	High	Average	Below Average	Low
EBITDAR margin	>25%	10%–25%	0%–10%	<0%
EBITDA/Interest	>6×	4–6×	1–3×	<1×
Cash flow/debt	>30%	20%–30%	10%–20%	<10%
Debt/Capital	<30%	30%–50%	50%–75%	>75%
Debt/EBITDAR	<2×	2–4×	4–6×	>6×
Unrestricted cash/ revenue	High ancillary revenue	Some ancillary revenue	Low ancillary revenue	No/poor ancillary revenue
Degree of unencumbered assets	0%/majority of aircraft are owned	<10%	<30%	>30%/no aircraft are owned

EBITDAR, *Earnings Before Interest, Taxes, Depreciation, Amortization, and Rent.*

ratings, such as BBB, BB, and B. Remember that we are conducting primarily an intra-industry assessment; airlines carry considerable risk relative to many other industries, and it is very rare to see an A-grade carrier. Finally, Table 7.5 displays a sample scorecard. Each applicable factor is assigned a subscore based on the lessors chosen weighting strategy. The weighted scores are then added together for a final overall rating.

Table 7.5 Sample Credit Scorecard

	Score	Weight	Weighted Score
Business			
Revenue structure Cost structure Operating region Competitive strategy Reputation and service Ownership and management Funding and flexibility			
Financial Ratio			
EBITDAR margin EBITDA/Interest Cash flow/debt Debt/Capital Debt/EBITDAR Unrestricted cash/revenue Degree of unencumbered assets		*Total* =	

EBITDAR, *Earnings Before Interest, Taxes, Depreciation, Amortization, and Rent.*

CONCLUSION

As we have learned throughout this chapter, a full credit analysis means breaking down the complex airline business model into individual components. Only then can a lessor set the appropriate lease terms and reserve rates for each prospective airline. We looked at cost structure, revenue structure, and key financial ratios before moving into the qualitative elements of an airline's operating region and strategic position. Again, the primary goal is to determine the most accurate degree of both business and financial risk. While credit agencies provide an excellent groundwork, we cannot rely on mere ratings alone. Fortunately, most of the fundamental data used in airline credit analysis is easily accessible through company filings and annual statements, and most airlines are very public about their networks and scope. In addition, lessors can access operational performance statistics through government agencies, such as the US Department of Transportation and the European Commission.

The key takeaway from this chapter is that numbers are only useful in context. Ratios alone do not tell us if an aggressive network expansion is a good idea or whether a carrier's renewed focus on customer service will in fact boost near-term profits. By putting color to the ratios that we generate, we can determine the reason behind specific changes, trends, and behaviors of the airline in question.

APPENDIX 7A CASE STUDY: ALASKA AIRLINES GETS A DOWNGRADE

Alaska Airlines was founded in 1932 and currently operates as part of Alaska Air Group Inc. Regional service is handled by Horizon Air, but all flights are sold and marketed under the Alaska Airlines brand. Due to its historic ties to America's "last frontier," the company and its employees remain actively involved in the Pacific Northwest community. Although the carrier has a large share of routes to and from Alaska, Oregon, and Washington, it operates a variety of medium-haul flights across the United States via hubs in Seattle, Portland, Los Angeles, San Francisco, and Anchorage. The airline also provides international service to Canada, Mexico, and Costa Rica. Passengers can take advantage of a robust frequent flier program, and while the airline has never been part of a global alliance, it does codeshare with 16 domestic and international carriers. In 2016, Alaska Airlines ranked number one by J.D. Power and Associates for customer satisfaction, for the ninth consecutive year.

Since inception, the airline has enjoyed relatively stable profits and is one of the few US carriers that did not declare bankruptcy after 9/11. While its service level is widely considered in line with its legacy rivals, its fares and cost strategy are more indicative of an LCC; the company operates a homogenous mainline fleet and outsources a large portion of its airport ground services. This strategy, paired with a sharp focus on service and employee engagement, is a key reason behind the airline's investment-grade rating. Below are Alaska's main operating statistics for the prior 3 years (Tables 7A.1–7A.4).

At December 2015, Alaska's mainline fleet of B737s had an average age of 9.7 years. Of these aircraft, 120 were owned and 27 were leased. In addition, the company owned 39 of its 65 regional jets operated by Horizon; the average age of the regional fleet was 8.9 years.

Despite a solid track record, the company was facing increasing competition, particularly out of its Seattle hub, which accounts for over 60% of its daily flights. In an effort to remain large enough to compete in the consolidated domestic market, Alaska Air Group Inc. acquired fellow West Coast carrier, Virgin America. The deal closed on December 14, 2016 with plans to integrate all operations under one certificate by 2018. This merger positioned Alaska as the fifth largest airline in the United States, and aside from minor criticism, the announcement was generally well-received by consumers. However, investors were skeptical of the $1.4 billion in debt and leases that Virgin America brought to the table. Analysts also anticipated high integration costs, largely due to the addition of Virgin's 63 Airbus aircraft. By the end of 2016, S&P had downgraded Alaska's credit rating to BBB—on account of the increased debt risk.

Table 7A.1 Operating Statistics, Alaska Air Group Inc.

	2016	2015	2014
Revenue passengers (000)	34,289,000	31,883,000	29,278,000
RPMs (000)	37,209,000	33,578,000	30,718,000
ASMs (000)	44,135,000	39,914,000	36,078,000
Load factor	84%	84%	85%
Fuel gallons	554,000,000	508,000,000	469,000,000
Average FTEs	14,760	13,858	12,739

RPM, *Revenue Passenger Mile;* ASM, *available seat mile;* FTE, *full-time equivalent.*
Alaska Air Group, Form 10-K, 2016

Table 7A.2 Statement of Operations, Alaska Air Group Inc. (in millions)

	2016	2015	2014
Operating revenue			
Passenger			
Mainline	$4098	$3939	$3774
Regional	908	854	805
Total passenger	5006	4793	4579
Cargo	108	108	114
Other	817	697	675
Total operating revenue	5931	5598	5368
Operating expenses			
Wages and Benefits	1509	1374	1252
Aircraft fuel and hedge loss/gain	831	954	1418
Aircraft maintenance	270	253	229
Aircraft rent	114	105	110
Landing fees and other rent	320	296	279
Contracted services	247	214	196
Selling and administrative	225	211	199
Depreciation and amortization	363	320	294
Food and beverage service	126	113	93
Other	577	460	336
Total operating expenses	4582	4300	4406
Operating income	1349	1298	962
Nonoperating income (expense)			
Interest income	27	21	21
Interest expense	(55)	(42)	(48)
Interest capitalized	25	34	20
Other	(1)	1	20
Income before tax	1345	1312	975
Income tax expense	531	464	370
Net income	*$814*	*$848*	*$605*

Alaska Air Group Inc, Form 10-K, 2016

Based on this information and the accounting statements described in this chapter, assess Alaska Air Group's financial profile as of December 31, 2016.

1. How does Alaska's credit ratios align with the industry norms? Which ratios have changed and how do changes affect the airline's outlook?
2. As a lessor, how would you weigh the company's post-merger business factors?
3. Do you agree with S&P's decision to downgrade the airline's credit rating? Why or why not?

Table 7A.3 Balance Sheet, Alaska Air Group Inc. (in millions)			
ASSETS	**2016**	**2015**	**2014**
Current assets			
Cash and cash equivalents	$328	$73	$107
Marketable securities	1252	1255	1110
Accounts receivable	302	212	259
Inventory, net	47	51	58
Prepaid expenses and other	121	72	105
Total current assets	2050	1663	1639
Property and equipment			
Aircraft and other flight equipment	7492	6461	5720
Other property and equipment	1103	955	896
(Less accumulated depreciation)	(2929)	(2614)	(2317)
Total property, plant and equipment	5666	4802	4299
Other Assets			
Goodwill	1934	–	–
Intangible assets	143	–	–
Other noncurrent assets	169	65	126
Total other assets	2246	65	126
Total Assets	*9962*	*6530*	*6064*
Liabilities and stockholders' equity			
Current liabilities			
Accounts payable	92	63	62
Accrued salaries and wages	397	298	276
Air traffic liability	849	669	631
Other accrued liabilities	878	661	585
Current portion of long-term debt	319	114	117
Deferred income tax	463	682	633
Unearned revenue	640	431	374
Total current liabilities	3638	2918	2678
Long-term liabilities			
Long-term debt	2645	569	686
Pension and postretirement benefits	331	270	246
Other liabilities	417	362	327
Total long-term liabilities	3393	1201	1259
Owner's equity			
Common stock	1	1	1
Paid in capital in excess of par	110	73	296
Treasury stock	(443)	(250)	(4)
Accumulated other comprehensive loss	(305)	(303)	(310)
Retained earnings	3568	2890	2144
Total owner's equity	2931	2411	2127
Total liabilities and owner's equity	*$9962*	*$6530*	*$6064*

Alaska Air Group Inc., Form 10-K, 2016

Table 7A.4 Statement of Cash Flows, Alaska Air Group Inc. ***(in millions)***

	2016	2015	2014
Cash flows from operating activities:			
Net income	$814	$848	$605
Adjustments to reconcile net income to net cash provided by operating activities:			
Depreciation and amortization	363	320	294
Stock-based compensation and other	26	25	6
Changes in certain assets and liabilities:			
Changes in deferred tax provision	94	56	114
Increase (decrease) in accounts receivable	(46)	47	(110)
Increase (decrease) in air traffic liability	9	38	67
Increase (decrease) in deferred revenue	83	57	40
Changes in pension and other postretirement	23	36	(18)
Other	20	157	32
Net cash provided by operating activities	1386	1584	1030
Cash flows from investing activities:			
Property and equipment additions:			
Aircraft and aircraft purchase deposits	(528)	(681)	(498)
Other flight equipment	(53)	(79)	(131)
Other property and equipment	(97)	(71)	(65)
Total property and equipment additions	(678)	(831)	(694)
Acquisition of Virgin America, net of cash	(1951)	–	–
Purchases of marketable securities	(960)	(1327)	(949)
Sales and maturities of marketable securities	962	1175	1092
Proceeds from disposition of assets	5	53	10
Net cash used in investing activities	(2622)	(930)	(541)
Cash flows from financing activities:			
Proceeds from issuance of long-term debt	2044	–	51
Long-term debt payments	(249)	(116)	(119)
Common stock repurchases	(193)	(505)	(348)
Cash dividend paid	(136)	(102)	(68)
Other financing activities	25	35	22
Net cash from financing activities	1491	(688)	(462)
Net increase (decrease) in cash and cash equivalents	255	(34)	27
Cash and cash equivalents at beginning of year	73	107	80
Cash and cash equivalents at end of year	*$328*	*$73*	*$107*

Alaska Air Group Inc, Form 10-K, 2016

REFERENCES

Ganguin, B., & Bilardello, J. (2004). *Fundamentals of corporate credit analysis. Standard & poor's series.* New York: McGraw Hill.

International Air Transport Association (IATA). *Volcano crisis costs airlines $1.7 billion in revenue—IATA urges measures to mitigate impact.* Press Release. (2010). From <https://iata.org/pressroom> Retrieved February 14, 2017.

International Air Transport Association (IATA). (June 2, 2016). Economic performance of the airline industry. *IATA economics report.*

Liu, C. A., & Jones, K. J. (2016). Integrated risk management on fuel hedging program: A case study on southwest and china eastern airlines. *Academy of Business Research Journal*, *2*, 74–85.

Kroll Bond Rating Agency (KBRA). (August 10, 2016). Global passenger airline rating methodology. *Corporates: Aviation rating methodology.*

Moody's Investor Services. (2009). *Rating methodology: Global passenger airlines.* Moody's Global Corporate Finance.

Moody's Investor Services. (December 21, 2010). *Moody's approach to global standard adjustments in the analysis of financial statements for non-financial corporations.* Global Corporate Finance, Rating Implementation Guidance.

PWC. (September 2016). *IFRS 16: The lease standard is changing Are you ready?*. From <https://www.pwc.com/gx/en/services/audit-assurance/assets/ifrs-16-new-leases.pdf> Retrieved December 10, 2016.

Securities and Exchange Commission (SEC). (December, 2016) *Annual report on nationally recognized statistical ratings organizations.*

Standard & Poor's. (October 22, 2010). *Key credit factors: Criteria for the rating the airline industry.* Global Credit Portal Ratings Direct.

Turner, P. A., & Lim, S. H. (2015). Hedging jet fuel price risk: The case of U.S. passenger airlines. *Journal of Air Transport Management*, *44–45*, 54–64.

CHAPTER

LEASING PORTFOLIO MANAGEMENT AND RISK MANAGEMENT

8

CHAPTER OUTLINE

Aircraft Leasing and Financing. DOI: https://doi.org/10.1016/B978-0-12-815285-0.00008-0

IMPORTANCE OF RISK AND PORTFOLIO MANAGEMENT FOR AIRCRAFT LESSORS

Aircraft lessors are highly leveraged companies that operate in a very capital-intensive industry that caters to the other highly leveraged and capital-intensive airline industry. While aircraft lessors as a group historically have been performing better financially than airlines, there has been lease rate factor pressure in recent years, particularly in the sale–leaseback market with reported lease rate factors of lower than 0.6 (KPMG, 2018). Low lease rate factors translate into thin margins for lessors that pursue such deals. Any risk or portfolio mismanaging would destroy these margins and threaten the survival of these lessors. The low lease rate factors also need to match with low-cost of funds, good credit profiles of the lessees, appropriate lease terms, and return conditions. To be successful in a very competitive aircraft-leasing industry, lessors should have a thorough understanding of potential risks, their mitigation techniques, and how lessors' portfolio management can reduce risks and maximize investment returns.

Purchasing the right aircraft at the right price, managing them well, and selling (or disposing) them at the right price and time are essential for a leasing company's success. A small mistake at any stage (purchasing, managing, or disposing of aircraft) may reduce a leasing transaction return to an unsustainable level. In this chapter, we start with a brief overview of aircraft acquisition channels and risks inherent with the business of leasing aircraft. While risk and portfolio management are overlapping concepts, we present them in two different subsections: understanding and mitigating risks on asset and liability sides and managing lessors' portfolios by diversifying their exposure to large individual risks. We describe major risks faced by aircraft-leasing companies and the techniques used to mitigate them. Interest rate risk management is discussed in detail as it is critical for lessors that manage the spreads between the cost of funds and returns on assets. Two appendixes at the end of the chapter contain an example of interest rate swap pricing and a short case study on lessor's portfolio management.

AIRCRAFT PORTFOLIO ACQUISITION CHANNELS

There are three primary portfolio acquisition channels for aircraft-leasing companies: new aircraft orders directly from manufacturers; sale and leaseback transactions with airlines; and secondary markets acquisitions from airlines or other lessors. Leasing companies are looking for new business by responding to airlines' request for proposals, establishing their own channels to track leasing opportunities through engagement with airlines, and using industry databases that track airline fleets, such as Flight Global, Airline Monitor, OAG, and others. Fig. 8.1 depicts primary aircraft portfolio-acquisition channels.

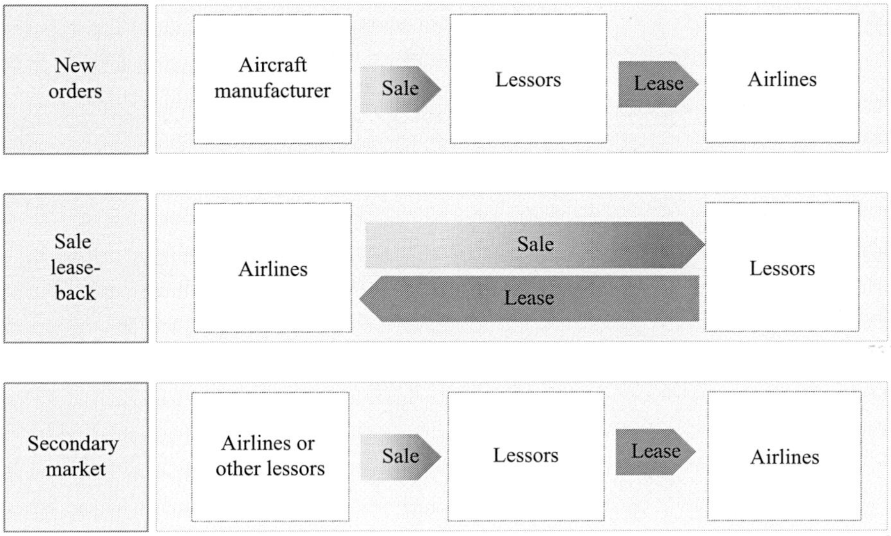

FIGURE 8.1

Aircraft portfolios acquisition channels.

RISKS INHERENT WITH THE BUSINESS OF LEASING AIRCRAFT

There are two sides to the business of leasing aircraft: the asset side, which are the aircraft, the leases themselves, and the lessees that lease the aircraft; and the liability side, which is the debt and equity capital that lessors use to support the investment decision they make on the asset side. The risks that lessors take are also related to these two sides. On the asset side, the risks are related to leases, lessees, and asset types and include jurisdictional, political, currency, individual credit, environmental and shocks to the industry risks. On the liability side, the risks are related to funding the assets and include the capital structure of the company, types of debt instruments that are used, the degree of leverage, and the interest rate risks. A lease is a stream of cash flows. The funding side also has a stream of cash flows. The cash inflows from the lease and the cash outflows from the funding side should be managed to meet company obligations. In the financial institution world, this is called asset liability management that addresses the risk taken by a lessor due to a mismatch between assets and liabilities because of liquidity or changes in interest rates. If a lessor takes risks on the asset side, these risks can be mitigated either through derivative instruments or a funding structure. For example, typically fixed-rate aircraft leases are funded with fixed-rate debt instruments or floating debt instruments that are hedged. On the asset side, lessors want to make sure they are investing in aircraft that they can trade out of and have the greatest potential for creating stable cash flows for the longest possible period of time.

Fig. 8.2 presents the components of the return on equity for a leasing company. Each of the components is a subject to different risks that we will discuss below.

Table 8.1 lists aircraft-leasing risk factors that can influence asset side, liability side, or both sides of the business.

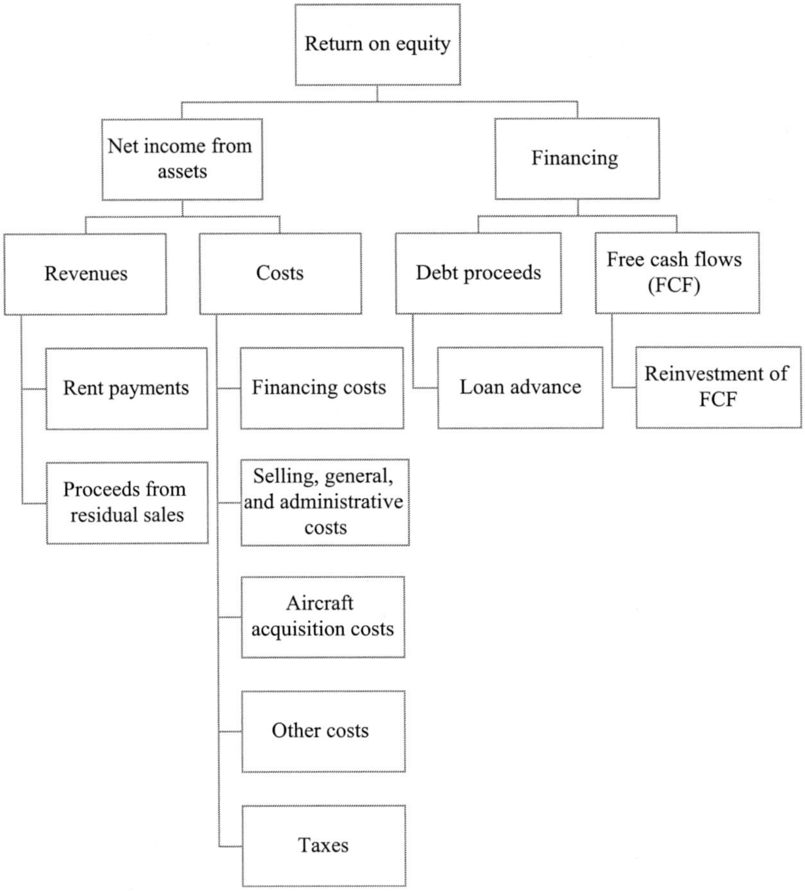

FIGURE 8.2

Components of lessor's ROE. *ROE*, Return on equity.

UNDERSTANDING AND MANAGING ASSET SIDE RISKS

Lessors invest in aircraft that can be purchased at a reasonable price, are not expensive to finance and manage, generate acceptable rent payments, and can be sold or disposed of with cash inflows that support the economics of the transaction. The approach to aircraft selection is different for different lessors and depends on their niche and business model. However, a typical lessor is looking at three basic criteria: user base, production run, and ease of financing.

If the aircraft has a very broad user base, it means that there are multiple potential customers and whenever it comes off lease, the lessor will have a new customer to lease that airplane to. It provides the lessor with higher confidence in a continued stream of lease cash flow, whether it is with a current customer or not.

Table 8.1 Aircraft-Leasing Risk Factors		
Asset side risk factors		
Financial strength of lessees	Periods of oversupply in the aircraft industry	Increases in fuel costs
Values of acquired aircraft and market rates for leases	Changes in the appraised value for aircraft	Aircraft limited economic useful lives and increased cost of operation with age
Lessees' defaults and costs of aircraft repossessions	Competition from other lessors	Potential maintenance issues, improper maintenance of aircraft
Ability to sell aircraft on favorable terms	Failure of aircraft and engine manufacturers to meet their obligations	Potential aircraft liens that lessee fails to discharge
Ability to re-lease aircraft on favorable economic terms	Airline bankruptcies/lease restructurings	Lessee's failure to maintain required insurance
Technology obsolescence	Lessees' failure to obtain required licenses and approvals	Terrorist attacks or fear of such attacks
Decrease in demand of the aircraft in lessor's portfolio	Early termination options of leases	Natural disasters that affect airline industry
Epidemic diseases or fear of such diseases	Lessees' failure to comply with aircraft registration requirements	Cyber attacks
Significant regional political and economic risks due to the location of lessees	The effects of various environmental laws and regulations	Significant rise in fuel price
Liability side risk factors		
Availability of capital on acceptable terms	Adverse changes in interest rates	Downgrades of lessor credit ratings
Risk factors and affect both asset and liability sides		
General economic and financial conditions	Loss of key personnel	Complexity of transacting business in multiple countries
Provisions of the Dodd-Frank Wall Street Reform and Consumer Protection Act	EU credit risk retention New EU credit rating agency regulations	New standards for lease accounting
LIBOR, *London Interbank Offered Rate.*		

A large production run, which means that many units of a particular airplane type were produced, makes this aircraft type ubiquitous and creates a stable, more predictable market environment for lease rates and residual values. Even though aircraft leasing is a cyclical business and is subject to economic cycles globally, investing in aircraft that have very large production runs and broad user bases mitigates the impact of those cycles on the lease cash flows and residual values.

The ease of aircraft financing and trading is related to two criteria discussed above. Large production runs and a broad user base make it easier to finance and trade aircraft. In turn, the ease of financing and tradability of an aircraft reduces the transition costs for this aircraft. If a lessor invests in an aircraft that has moderate transition costs in terms of time and money, has a broad user base and a large production run, this lessor will manage its risks on the asset side. The aircraft that tend to fit that mold the best are single-aisle aircraft: in particular, the Boeing 737 and Airbus A320 families. There are several widebody aircrafts that would fit also: they have a large user base, large production run, and relatively low transition costs (for a widebody), but they are still not as liquid as narrowbody aircraft. The risk profile for widebody and specialty aircraft is different and requires specialized expertise to manage. We will discuss it at length later in this chapter.

GENERAL ECONOMIC AND FINANCIAL CONDITIONS

Deteriorating global or regional economic conditions have an adverse effect on lessees' business and consequently their ability to meet their financial obligation. If the slowing economy is accompanied by high fuel prices, the risks of lessees' defaults are even higher. When lessees default or renegotiate the terms of their leases, lessor's cash flow and results of operations are affected.

General economic and financial conditions that directly or indirectly affect aircraft leasing:

- Global economic growth and strength of local economies
- Inflation
- Interest rate fluctuations
- Investor and consumer confidence
- Unemployment levels
- Volatility of fuel prices
- Volatility in capital markets
- Availability and cost of credit (for lessees)
- Demand for airline passengers and cargo
- Restructuring and mergers in the airline industry

COMPETITION

Aircraft leasing is a highly competitive industry with more than 50 significant participants that are regularly active in the leasing and aircraft-trading markets, and almost 300 lessors who own one or more aircraft. Leasing companies compete in the acquisition of new aircraft from airlines, aircraft manufacturers, financial institutions, aircraft brokers, and other aircraft lessors. They also compete for leasing transactions based on lease rates, delivery dates, lease terms, reputation, management expertise, aircraft condition, specifications, configurations, and the availability of certain types of aircraft. Finally, they compete in the purchase and sale of used aircraft based on the availability, price, the terms of the lease to which an aircraft is subject, and the creditworthiness of the lessee.

LIMITED NUMBER OF AIRCRAFT AND ENGINE MANUFACTURERS

The supply of large commercial jets is dominated by two airframe manufacturers (Boeing and Airbus) and three engine manufacturers (GE, Rolls Royce, and Pratt & Whitney). Such a small number of suppliers are a source of risks for leasing companies. Lessors are dependent on these manufacturers staying financially stable and producing aircraft for lessors' portfolios. Missed or late delivery of aircraft and engines could result in an inability to meet a lessor's contractual obligations to its customers. Lessors may have the right to terminate a purchase agreement in the event of substantial manufacturing delays; however, it will affect the lessors' customers and impact the lessor's revenue stream and profitability. An inability to acquire aircraft and engines and related components on terms which will allow a lessor to lease those aircraft and engines to customers at acceptable lease rates will result in lower growth rates or a contraction in the lessor's aircraft portfolio. Poor customer support from the manufacturers of aircraft, engines, and components is another potential source of risk. Manufacturer reputational damage, resulting in reduced demand for a particular manufacturer's product, would create pressure on demand for those aircraft and engines in a lessor's fleet which translates to lower market lease rates and sale prices for those aircraft and engines.

A reduction in a lessor's competitiveness due to deep discounting by the manufacturers may lead to reduced market lease rates and sale prices and may affect lessor's ability to release or sell some of the aircraft in its portfolio.

FINITE ECONOMIC USEFUL LIVES OF AIRCRAFT

Assets that aircraft-leasing companies are dealing with are long-lived assets with long lead times to develop and manufacture. Some aircraft types and models become obsolete due to a variety of reasons, including economic and functional obsolescence, changes in airline preferences, and government regulations. The demand for such types and models decreases or even disappears, and the life cycle becomes shorter. The obsolescence also negatively impacts lease rates, triggers impairment charges, and increases depreciation expense. With age, aircraft depreciate and typically generate lower revenues and cash flows. Older aircraft require more expensive maintenance; they are less fuel efficient and may need investment in modifications required by new regulations imposed by regulatory authorities and related airworthiness directives. Higher operating costs of older aircraft may result in increased lessee defaults, renegotiation of lease terms, and may impact a lessor's ability to re-lease them. Also, some countries restrict or prohibit the import of aircraft older than a certain age, leading to a reduction in the potential leasing market for these aircraft.

DEFAULTS AND COST OF REPOSSESSIONS

In the event of a default, lessors face substantial costs associated with taking possession of the aircraft, preparing them for different lessees, and remarketing and re-leasing them. The following are major costs and considerations that arise when lessees default:

- Legal and other expenses of court or other governmental proceedings (especially if the lessee is contesting the proceedings or is in bankruptcy) can be substantial.
- In the time preceding defaults, lessees may disregard proper aircraft maintenance and care. Even with maintenance reserves and security deposits, lessors may incur large maintenance, refurbishment, or repair costs.
- In most cases, immediate re-lease of the aircraft will not be possible, making lessors responsible for storage, maintenance and insurance costs while the aircraft is remarketed.
- In order to take possession of the aircraft, lessors may be responsible for paying off liens, taxes, and other governmental charges (sometimes even liens that the lessee have incurred in

connection with the operation of its other aircraft) in addition to amounts owed by the lessee to maintenance facilities for prior services and especially where such maintenance facilities may have seized the aircraft or engines and won't release them until paid for their services.
- If the lessee is owned, in whole or in part, by government-related entities in third world or more corrupt countries, the costs of repossession of aircraft in that lessee's domicile can be much higher, and repossession may be more difficult. Also, deregistration can be a problem.
- Termination of the lease as a result of default may trigger a mandatory prepayment of the debt used to finance the aircraft after certain standstill and remarketing periods.

LESSEES' FAILURE TO DISCHARGE AIRCRAFT LIENS

During normal operations, lessees are likely to incur aircraft liens that secure payments of airport fees, taxes, customs duties, air navigation charges, landing charges, and others. Aircraft may also be subject to mechanics' liens. If a lessee fails to pay the aircraft liens, the liens may attach to lessor's aircraft and, in some jurisdictions, liens may give the holder the right to detain or sell the aircraft. In such an event the lessor may have to pay the claims secured by aircraft liens in order to repossess the aircraft.

SECURITY DEPOSITS AND MAINTENANCE RESERVES AS RISK-MANAGEMENT TECHNIQUES

During the lease term, the lessee is responsible for all maintenance of the aircraft unless the lessor agrees to share the cost of certain maintenance. The failure of a lessee to maintain the aircraft in compliance with lease requirements, in addition to regulatory requirements, can have an adverse impact on the value of the aircraft and could even destroy the economics of a lease transaction. In order to ensure the value of the aircraft is being maintained, most lessors inspect their aircraft, including documentation of maintenance, usage, and other records on an annual basis and more frequently if deemed necessary. Improper maintenance will reduce market values of aircraft and result in lower revenues from their lease or sale.

Security deposits and maintenance reserves are ways to mitigate lessee's credit risks by ensuring that the lessee can meet the immediate obligations on that lease. The two most significant obligations on the lease are the stream of lease and maintenance reserve payments. The security deposits mitigate the loss of lease payments by covering lost rent, hence allowing the lessor time to repossess the aircraft and place it back in revenue service. The maintenance reserve that will be discussed in depth in Chapter 9 is a payment by the lessee based upon the actual utilization of the aircraft and its respective engines which is in addition to the rental payment. The maintenance reserve is held by the lessor to ensure funds are available to pay for high cost maintenance such as overhauls of the engines and landing gear. Upon lease termination, if a lessee is not in default and has complied with its obligations under the lease, the security deposits will be returned to the lessee. Likewise, assuming there is no event of default, the cost of maintenance covered by the maintenance reserve is reimbursed from the maintenance reserve fund held by the lessor upon completion of such maintenance by the lessee.

JURISDICTIONAL AND POLITICAL RISK

Aircraft leasing is a global industry and lessors often structure cross-border transactions when lessors are based in one country, their lessees are in the second country, and banks or investors that fund the deal are based in the third country. Such international exposure means understanding jurisdictional and political risks are vital to lessors' business. Jurisdictional risks come from lessees operating aircraft in different countries and regions with different laws and regulations, various degrees of protection for investors, as well as potential subjects for embargos, sanctions, and restrictions. For example, in July 2014, the European Union placed sanctions on Russian individuals and entities, including Russian low-cost airline Dobrolet. In response to the sanctions, Dobrolet's lessor, SMBC Aviation Capital had to cancel leasing agreements for their B737-800 aircraft. Soon after the sanctions were placed, Dobrolet ceased its operations. SMBC Aviation Capital had to remarket and re-lease the aircraft that unexpectedly came out of the lease.

Similar to jurisdictional risks, political risks increase when lessors and lessees are based in different countries. Political risks come from political and economic instability in the country of aircraft operators. In addition, war conflicts and corruption increase political risks for lessors.

CURRENCY RISKS

Currency risks are more pronounced for lessees than lessors. However, if currency risks are increasing the probability of lessees' insolvency, they are also transferred to lessors. Lessors manage currency risks by matching currency for costs, revenues, and financing. Traditionally, this currency is US dollars. Sometimes, the costs of funds are lower in particular countries, and the lessor may take advantage of it by structuring cross-border lease transactions and borrowing in a currency other than US dollars. In this case, lessors would hedge their currency risk exposure with currency swaps, futures or forward contracts, or with currency options. Lessees that operate domestically in countries with declining currencies have the highest exposure to currency exchange risk. Since their lease payments and fuel expenses are paid in US dollars, but revenues are collected in a local currency, declines in the currency exchange rates would adversely impact their financials. Recent significant declines in values of the Brazilian Real, Russian Ruble, and Argentinian Peso put signification pressure on domestic airlines operating in these countries. International airlines have more opportunities for a natural hedge when they match currencies of their revenues and expenses as much as possible. For example, the US international airlines have most of their expenses in US dollars, but large portions of revenues are collected in Euros, British Pounds, and other foreign currencies. By paying for catering and aircraft maintenance in local currencies, they will use natural hedging—matching currencies for at least a portion of their expenses and revenues. Any additional currency risk exposure can be reduced by hedging with financial derivatives or hedging contracts.

UNFORESEEN SHOCKS IN THE INDUSTRY

The airline industry is very sensitive to unexpected shocks that may significantly affect the global demand for commercial air travel. The risks of these shocks faced by lessors and airlines are significant, and the only mitigation technique is their ability to manage and react quickly to such events. Airlines would respond to the industry shocks by redeploying capacity, parking older aircraft, and modifying schedules. Lessors would closely monitor their lessees for early signs of trouble so they can reduce potential costs of lessee defaults. There are multiple examples of unexpected events that affected airline industry: disease outbreaks and epidemics (e.g., bird flu in 2003; SARS and MERS in 2013 and 2015; Ebola and Zika viruses in 2014 and 2016), natural disasters (e.g., Eyjafjallajokull volcano eruption in Iceland in 2010), acts of terror (e.g., September 2001 terrorist attack in New York City). For instance, the US airlines lost $5 billion in only three and a half months following the September 2001 attack (Guzhva, 2008).

UNDERSTANDING AND MANAGING INTEREST RATE RISK

While most of the leases are structured as fixed rate transactions, some of them use floating rates. Most of the financing for lessors, however, is floating rate. Ideally, lessees would prefer floating rate leases matching floating rate financing with some predictable spreads. Sophisticated lessors should be agnostic to a fixed rate or a floating rate lease because at the end of the day they care about the spread. To run a successful aircraft-leasing business, lessors should be good in managing that spread, managing the credit risk against the put option on the aircraft that lessees have, and price the interest rate risk and credit risk properly. If rates go up, a lessee with floating rate lease might ask to renegotiate the lease to a fixed rate lease for the remaining term or extend the term out. If the lessor can pass along any breakage costs in their financing and/or any future hedge costs, the lessor should be agnostic about that because it will set its spread based on the swap curve. However, there is a difference in risk profile in a rising interest rate environment. If the short rate spikes, the likelihood that the lessee will be able to meet that much higher obligation very quickly is decreasing. Hence, the interest rate risk and credit risk interact with each other. Nonetheless, the primary concern of a lessor is to make sure that spread between its assets and its liabilities is maintained irrespective of what interest rates do.

Another important consideration is the duration of the asset and liability sides. The aircraft leases as any fixed stream of cash flows have durations that depend on the cash flows, its timing, maturity, and lessors' discount rates. Since different leases have different cash flows and maturities, they would have different durations. On a funding side, lessors have liabilities with different durations. Duration immunization is a common technique to manage interest rates risk. Lessors would make sure that their duration of liabilities matches the duration of the assets. The fact that an aircraft is a depreciating asset also affects the duration characteristics. What lessors want to do is make sure the cash flow characteristics of the assets, which are the leases, are offset by the cash flow characteristics of the liabilities. Lessor pool of aircraft may have floating rate leases and fixed rate leases that have maturities that are staggered over time. Lessor's exposure to the market comes from the change in potential borrowing cost differences to the spread that the lessor is earning from effectively lending that asset to the customer at whatever specified lease rate. If lessors borrow at a floating rate basis and use the funds to finance assets that have fixed rate leases with different maturities, it is important to balance out the duration of both assets and liabilities such that the duration mismatch is minimized. Typically, lessors are looking to have a duration mismatch of under a year.

There are several other considerations with managing assets and liabilities. A lessor may have a perfectly managed book on the asset side, and the liabilities side with the cash flows totally even, so changes in the interest rate environment do not change the spread. However, we need to consider the roll-over risk on the funding side. If a lessor funded with short-term loans to make the spread better, the risk is that when the funding matures and the lessor has to refinance that asset, the market rate may move higher.

Another consideration is the interest rate hedge rebalancing. A lessor might be perfectly hedged today, but every day that passes by may create a mismatch between its assets and liabilities. Proper risk management is to continually rebalance hedging positions to make sure that the durations of the assets and liabilities match.

One more consideration in optionality. Every lessee, effectively, has a put option—the right to return that airplane to the lessor even though that right is not in the lease contract. A lessee can default, which creates a put option. Hence, even if a lessor has a perfectly matched book, in case of a lessee, default assets and liabilities are unmatched again. There are two basic areas of that optionality. One is that the default put that every lessee has. The second is the lessor's option to sell that asset. From the interest rate risk perspective, a sale is the same as the lessee's put option. If the lessor sells that asset, there is no stream of cash flow generated by the lease of that aircraft. Until the lessor replaces it with another aircraft, it will have a mismatched book. There is, however, several ways to manage the liability side to give the lessor the flexibility on the asset side. One way is to buy the optionality back. The lessor can use cancellable swaps, for instance. The lessor is buying the optionality back because it can always cancel the swap, pay off the debt at par and get rid of the mismatch. However, this option is expensive. The second way is to use interest rate caps rather than interest rate swaps. The cap will protect from the spikes in interest rates but will not penalize the lessor if the interest rates decline. The problem with interest caps is that they are expensive. The third way is to recognize that there will always be a certain percentage of the lessor's portfolio that will default, that some aircraft will be sold and under hedge a portion of the portfolio to retain the flexibility and maintain the duration gap with a slight positive bias. This option is not expensive but may have implicit costs if the market moves to an unfavorable direction. The constant rebalancing is the key for this option.

Typically, for new aircraft that are placed with lessees, the leases have a float-to-fix adjustment. The lease is written with a base lease rate and an adjustment factor for changes in the long-term swap rate up until aircraft delivery. This adjustment protects both sides: a lessor and lessee. If the interest rates go up, then the lease rates go up. If the interest rates go down, then the lease rates go down. The spread stays consistent.

EXAMPLE OF INTEREST RATE SPREAD

For example, for a narrowbody aircraft that is priced at approximately $50 million, a 1% change in the interest rate would mean an interest payment difference of about $48,000. If the lease of this aircraft comes with $400,000 rent payment, a 1% change in funding interest rate means that to be spread neutral, the lessor could have effectively a $350,000 lease payment. Assuming the typical long-term rates between 4% and 5%, current rates of 1.5% imply an interest rate change of over 3%. Therefore, $140,000–$150,000 decrease in lease payment would keep the lessor spread neutral. If the lessor does not hedge its interest rate exposure, such a change in interest rates can have an enormous impact on profitability because the spread will go up by $140,000–$150,000. However, if rates go the other way, the lessor may go out of business. Interest rate hedging helps to manage the interest rate risk exposure and manage the spread making it consistent regardless of changes in interest rates.

HEDGING INTEREST RATE RISK

As discussed above, lessors are exposed to the interest rate risk because they primarily use floating rate debt to finance leases with fixed lease payments. There are several financial instruments that assist with hedging interest rate risk: interest rate caps, floors, and collars; and interest rate swaps.

Interest rate caps, floors, and collars

Interest rate caps are agreements that provide a leasing company an interest rate ceiling on interest payments on floating rate debt. A cap requires an insurance-style premium to be paid to the bank, similar to the premium payable by the buyer of a currency option. A cap provides the buyer the right, but not the obligation, to exercise the cap. The borrower will only do this when LIBOR (London Interbank Offered Rate), a commonly used benchmark interest rate, is higher than the strike rate of the cap. The notional principal amount is used to calculate the premium that the lessor will pay to the bank and the bank payments to the lessor if LIBOR exceeds the strike rate.

For example, Table 8.2 presents the cost for a borrower with and without the interest rate cap with following characteristics:

- The premium of 1% of the notional amount for the agreed number of days and for each of the borrowing periods is payable in advance to the bank.
- The cap strike rate is 2.75%.
- Floating rate is LIBOR + 2.5% margin.

The borrower pays 1% premium to the bank, effectively increasing the interest rate by 1% when LIBOR plus margin rate is below the strike rate. However, when LIBOR plus margin is above the strike rate, the borrower saves money. The borrower caps the cost of borrowing at 6.25%.

Interest rate floors provide the buyers with the lowest rate, below which the bank will compensate the buyer, effectively creating the "floor." For example, if a lessor that has a floating rate lease (unusual, but technically possible) is concerned about declining interest rates because the lease

Table 8.2 Example of the Interest Rate Cap

LIBOR (%)	Margin (%)	Total Cost Without Cap (%)	Cap Strike Rate (%)	Premium Payable by Cap Buyer (%)	Total Cost for Borrower With Cap (%)	Cap Used?	Saving to Borrower by Using Cap (%)
0.50	2.50	3.00	2.75	1.00	4.00	No	− 1.00
1.00	2.50	3.50	2.75	1.00	4.50	No	− 1.00
2.00	2.50	4.50	2.75	1.00	5.50	No	− 1.00
3.00	2.50	5.50	2.75	1.00	6.25	Yes	− 0.75
4.00	2.50	6.50	2.75	1.00	6.25	Yes	0.25
5.00	2.50	7.50	2.75	1.00	6.25	Yes	1.25

LIBOR, *London Interbank Offered Rate.*

revenues will also decline. The lessor can enter into the interest rate floor agreement with a bank that will compensate the lessor if the interest rates decline below the floor strike rate based on the agreed notional principal amount.

For both interest rate caps and floors, the terms of the agreements include

- The reference rate
- The strike rate (cap rate of floor rate) that sets the ceiling or the floor
- The length of the agreement
- The frequency of settlement
- The notional principal

For example, the cap reference rate is 3-month LIBOR, the strike rate is 6%, the agreement is for 4 years, settlement is monthly, the notional principal is $20 million. Under this agreement, every month for the next 4 years, a bank will pay a lessor whenever 3-month LIBOR exceeds 6% at settlement date. The payment will equal the dollar value of the difference between 3-month LIBOR and 6% times the notional principal divided by 12. If 3-month LIBOR on a settlement date is 8%, then the bank will pay the lessor 2% times $20 million divided by 12, or $33,333.33.

Table 8.3 presents an example of cap and floor payments. Suppose that a 4-year cap has a cap rate of 7%, and a 4-year floor has a floor rate of 5%. Both have a notional amount of $100 million. The frequency of settlement is monthly, and the reference rate is 3-month LIBOR. Assume that 3-month LIBOR for the next 12 months is as shown in Table 8.3. The payoff for each month is calculated as follows:

$$Cap\ Payment = (LIBOR - 7\%) * \$100\ million\ /\ 12$$

$$Floor\ Payment = (5\% - LIBOR) * \$100\ million\ /\ 12$$

A combination of an interest rate cap and a floor is an interest rate collar. A collar is created when a lessor is buying an interest rate cap and selling an interest rate floor. The premium from

Table 8.3 Example of Interest Rate Cap and Floor Payments

Period	3-m LIBOR (%)	Cap Payment	Floor Payment
1	6.7	$0	$0
2	7	$0	$0
3	7.5	$41,666	$0
4	8	$83,333	$0
5	8.6	$133,333	$0
6	6	$0	$0
7	5.5	$0	$0
8	5	$0	$0
9	4.4	$0	$50,000
10	4	$0	$83,333
11	3.9	$0	$91,666
12	3.8	$0	$100,000

LIBOR, *London Interbank Offered Rate.*

selling the floor can reduce the cost of buying the cap. Since a cap sets a maximum interest rate that a borrower would have to pay if the reference rate rises and a floor sets a minimum interest rate that a borrower can benefit from if the reference rate declines, a collar will establish a range for the interest rate that the borrower will be paying if the reference rate changes (between the floor and the cap). Collar net premium is the difference between the premium paid for the cap and the premium received from the floor. For example, for a collar from Table 8.3, if LIBOR exceeds 7%, the lessor receives a payment; if LIBOR is less than 5%, the lessor makes a payment. So, the lessor's borrowing cost is in the range between 5% and 7%. The lessor's effective interest rate should be adjusted by the net premium of the collar.

Interest rate swaps

An interest rate swap is a contract between two parties to exchange periodic interest payments based on a specified notional principal amount. The interest payments on the notional principal amount are calculated by multiplying the specified interest rate times the notional principal amount. These interest payments are the only amounts exchanged; the notional principal amount is only a reference value. The traditional swap has one party (fixed-rate payer) obligated to make periodic payments at a fixed rate in return for the counterparty (floating-rate payer) agreeing to make periodic payments based on a reference floating rate. The reference interest rates used for the floating rate in an interest rate swap are those on various money market instruments: treasury bills, LIBOR, commercial paper, bankers' acceptances, certificates of deposit, the federal funds rate, and the prime rate. However, LIBOR rates are the most often used reference rates.

For example, if a lessor is borrowing at LIBOR plus 2.5% to finance aircraft and wants to hedge the interest rate risk, the lessor can enter a swap agreement with a swap bank at a current market rate for a swap of 2.75%. Fig. 8.3 illustrates this swap example.

As presented in Table 8.4, the lessor effectively fixes its borrowing rate at 5.25% regardless of LIBOR rate. If LIBOR rate is below 2.75%, the lessor would be better off without the swap. However, if LIBOR goes up, the lessor's borrowing rate without the swap would also go up, potentially reducing or even eliminating the spread between financing and lease rates.

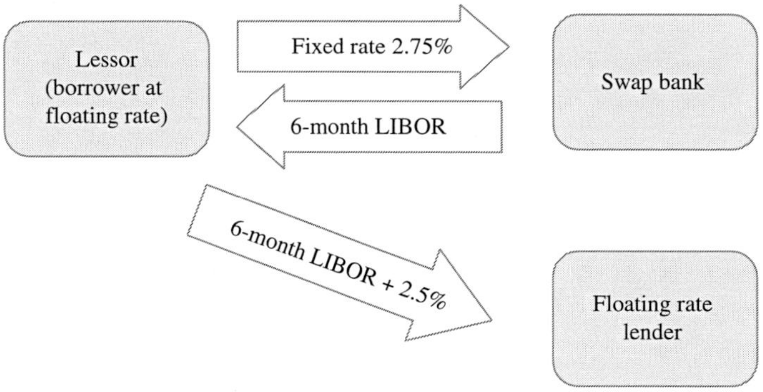

FIGURE 8.3

Example of interest rate swap.

Table 8.4 Example of Interest Rate Swap

LIBOR (%)	Margin (%)	Total Cost Without Swap (%)	Swap Fixed Rate (%)	Lessor Pays to Swap Bank (%)	Swap Bank Pays to Lessor (%)	Total Cost Using Swap (%)	Saving to Borrower by Using Swap (%)
0.50	2.50	3.00	2.75	2.25	0	5.25	− 2.25
1.00	2.50	3.50	2.75	1.75	0	5.25	− 1.75
2.00	2.50	4.50	2.75	0.75	0	5.25	− 0.75
3.00	2.50	5.50	2.75	0	0.25	5.25	0.25
4.00	2.50	6.50	2.75	0	1.25	5.25	1.25
5.00	2.50	7.50	2.75	0	2.25	5.25	2.25

LIBOR, *London Interbank Offered Rate.*

INTEREST RATE SWAP EXAMPLE

Suppose, on December 15 Lessor XYZ borrows money for 5 years from Bank ABC. The loan is \$50 million and specifies that XYZ will make monthly interest payments on the 15th of each month at the rate of LIBOR plus 25 basis points. At the end of the 5th year, XYZ will pay back the principal as a balloon payment. XYZ believes that it has a good rate, but fearing a rise in interest rates. XYZ receives fixed lease payments and would prefer a fixed-rate loan. XYZ approaches Bank DEF and requests a quote on a swap to pay a fixed rate and receive LIBOR, with payments on the dates of its loan payments. DEF prices the swap and quotes a fixed rate of 6.2%. The fixed payments will be made based on a day count of 30/365, and the floating payments will be made based on 30/360. Current LIBOR is 5.9%. Therefore, the first fixed payment, which XYZ makes to DEF, is \$50 million × 0.062 × 30/365 = \$254,795. The first floating payment, which DEF makes to XYZ, is \$50 million × 0.059 × 30/360 = \$245,833. They settle and XYZ pays DEF \$8962. If in the following month LIBOR goes up to 6.7%, XYZ's payment will be the same as \$254,795, but DEF's payment would be \$279,167. DEF will pay XYZ \$24,372 to settle.

Problem: Determine the upcoming payment in a plain vanilla interest rate swap in which the notional principal is €70 million. The end user makes semiannual fixed payments at the rate of 7%, and the dealer makes semiannual floating payments at Euribor, which was 6.25% at last settlement period. The floating payments are made on the basis of 180 days in the settlement period and 360 days in a year. The fixed payments are made on the basis of 180 days in the settlement period and 365 days in a year. Payments are netted, so determine what party has to pay to settle and what amount.

It should be noted that even with interest rate risk hedging, the risk would remain if the derivative financial instruments are not correlated with lessor's financial liabilities. Also, credit risk of counterparties should also be considered. For example, if a financial institution that sold the lessor an interest rate cap becomes insolvent, this cap will not help to hedge the interest rate risk.

PORTFOLIO MANAGEMENT

Leasing portfolio management is not unlike any other investment portfolio management when investors are trying to maximize their return while managing (minimizing) their risks. The risks can be managed by investing in safe assets, diversification, and hedging. In the aircraft-leasing business, as with any other investment field, safe investments do not generate high returns, and in order to increase returns, lessors need to accept higher risks. Diversification and hedging can reduce risks more than they reduce returns, and, thus, they are commonly employed by portfolio managers. A safe asset from a lessor perspective is the one that is easily financeable and can be cost-effectively transferred from one lessee to another in an active and liquid market. The asset that fits this description is a new generation narrowbody aircraft (B737 or A320) leased to an airline with excellent credit. Lease rates for such an aircraft would be low leading to low albeit safe returns for the lessor.

DIVERSIFYING AMONG LESSEES

Most lessors manage their risks by diversification across lessees. While credit analysis is important, diversification is equally important. This is because not all of the risks are evident through an analysis of financial statements, and misjudgments of lessees' credit risks are possible. When a lessor, let us say, has 300 airplanes and 100 customers, on average it has three airplanes per customer. If something goes wrong with a customer, only three airplanes will be affected. Whereas if a lessor takes concentrated positions even with the safest airline in the world, it can still go bankrupt, and a large portion of the lessor's portfolio will be affected. There are certain advantages of having concentrated positions with few customers: better customer relationships, economies of scale with lease origination and monitoring, lower aircraft transition costs, etc. However, the importance of credit analysis and monitoring for this customer is magnified by the degree of portfolio concentration. For example, Swissair was the solid, successful, premier airline in the early 1990s. No one would predict, but it went bankrupt in 2001. Another example is Air Berlin that ceased operations in October 2017 following its bankruptcy in August 2017. Most of the aircraft from Air Berlin went to Lufthansa and EasyJet. However, as of December 2017, 54 aircraft that were leased by Air Berlin still needed to be remarketed (Lovell, 2017). While most lessors that were still looking for customers for their Air Berlin aircraft had between 1 and 4 aircraft in this position, GECAS needed to place 14 A320-200 aircraft and AerCap was looking for a home for 10 A330-200 aircraft (Lovell, 2017). While it may not be considered a concentrated position for the two largest lessors (in 2017 GECAS and AerCap had fleets of 1324 and 1076 aircraft, respectively), placement of these aircraft come with substantial costs and efforts.

DIVERSIFYING ACROSS ASSET TYPES

In addition to diversifying their portfolios across lessees, lessors diversify across aircraft types. As was discussed above, modern narrowbody aircraft are the most liquid and safe investment, but widebody aircraft generally come with better credit airlines, longer leases, and higher return per dollar invested. However, to make a higher profit per dollar invested, lease transactions for widebody aircraft should be structured properly. Widebody aircraft come with benefits and with additional risks. One of the risks is that they are not as easy to be redeployed as narrowbody aircraft in a market downturn. In many cases, these aircraft are the flagships of the given airlines, and the flagship of Emirates is very different from the flagship of Delta Air Lines, even though they are both world class carriers and both offer great customer service. When lessors need to redeploy them, they will spend millions of dollars taking out the seats, taking out the lessee furnished equipment, changing the colors, moving the monuments around, upgrading the inflight entertainment system, and moving the galleys around. It is very destructive to the value of the investment when lessors have such a large redeployment cost at some point during their ownership. During the widebody aircraft transition lessors need to find someone, who is willing to work with the lessor to change that configuration. Often the second lease for widebody aircraft is with carriers that are more in the low-cost end of the business and are just interested in putting more seats in the airplane. They are less dependent on having every feature standardized. It is always a much more challenging proposition to standardize a widebody airplane than a narrowbody airplane.

Even though as assets widebody aircraft are riskier for a lessor, usually airlines that operate them have better credit. Airlines that fly long haul, widebody aircraft are good customers, and typically lessors have all sorts of financing options (e.g., export credit financing, banks, insurance companies) when they have long-term stable leases of a widebody aircraft.

While narrowbody aircraft dominate lessors' portfolios, an average leasing company has about 20% of its portfolio in widebody assets. For example, if a lessor wants to increase its portfolio from $9 billion or 250 aircraft to $18 billion. This new $18 billion portfolio can include 500 narrowbody aircraft or 350 aircraft that is a mixture of narrowbody and widebody airplanes. Therefore, at some point, the scale that a lessor wants to reach leads it into adding widebody aircraft in the portfolio. If a lessor has a long-standing relationship with customers and they ask for a proposal on a particular airplane that is not part of the lessor's fleet, the decision comes to whether the lessor is going to risk losing that relationship or the portfolio needs to grow with certain types of aircraft. It seems that when lessors' portfolios grow, they add widebody aircraft to their fleets of narrowbody planes. However, there are niche players who lease only widebody aircraft or only regional jets.

Moreover, not all widebody aircraft are created equal. It seems that current route network and traffic developments favor the twin-engine widebody aircraft (Narkhede, 2016). This presents challenges for A380 as there are not many airlines that can fit this aircraft in their networks. In addition, since it is very expensive to reconfigure, there is no secondary market for A380s. Airlines that operate A380s use them as flagship aircraft with very customized configurations. Low-cost operators cannot afford $150–$200 million aircraft, and they do not have long-haul routes for them. Recognizing that the demand has not yet materialized, Airbus reduced the production rate from about 30 per year in 2014–15 to 12 in 2018 (Narkhede, 2016). The difficulties with placing the A380 for the second lease may lead to extreme discounts with lease rates or sales of a used A380 at much lower prices than forecasted residual values, reducing returns for lessors and investors.

LESSOR STRATEGIES FOR ASSET TYPES

There are many different leasing companies with different strategies and sizes. As discussed above, large leasing companies typically have a mix of narrowbody and widebody aircraft, and some even have regional jets and turboprops. They cater to airlines around the world with extensive marketing strategies. Many large carriers have affiliations with smaller airlines, and large lessors can provide value to them by offering multiple solutions. However, not every leasing company can do this. Some lessors focus on newer aircraft, while others may focus on mid-life aircraft. Typically, smaller leasing companies concentrate on acquiring narrowbody aircraft for several reasons, such as how easily they are moved, the continuous interest in smaller aircraft, and their relatively low-cost modifications to move them from one airline to another. Other leasing companies may focus on areas where they feel that they can compete. For small lessors, it is difficult to compete with large leasing companies that have very low-cost of capital using the same business model. Therefore, some smaller lessors employ the strategy of focusing on portions of the market that the big contenders do not focus heavily on. Eventually, the company with the lowest cost of capital is going to beat the company with higher cost of capital if they compete in the same market. For a smaller lessor, it is essential to find the right market niche and competitive advantage, which will not be the cost of capital.

STAGGERING LEASE MATURITIES

Another way to diversify lessors' portfolios is staggering lease maturities that allow lessors to diversify across time. There are pros and cons to staggering lease maturities. It is a question of how much you stagger them. Obviously, a lessor does not want to get a large number of aircraft back off lease at the same time. There could be a downturn in the market when all of those aircraft are coming back at the same time, and the lessor will need to find a way to lease them out, probably at lower lease rates.

Aircraft lessors operate in a cyclical business environment. As with any investment portfolio, dollar cost averaging helps with navigating cyclical and unpredictable markets. A lessor would want to take aircraft back at the top of the market when it can get top lease rates, but it is difficult to predict the state of the market at the end of the lease when it is several years out. Even if a lessor has a perfect foresight of the future market, it may get their aircraft back unexpectedly due to a default. Some aircraft are going to come back to the lessor at the bottom of the market. Dollar cost averaging will help lessors to have acceptable returns by averaging high and low-market lease rates. With staggered lease maturities, lessors can ride through market cycles and do fine, on average.

On the other hand, sometimes lessors want to get several aircraft back at approximately the same time, especially if those aircraft are sister ships. For example, if a lessor leased 10 aircraft to a particular airline, and all of the leases expire next year (e.g., one every month), the lessor has a marketing advantage. The lessor can offer 10 identical aircraft with identical sets of records and build specifications to an airline, and these aircraft can be supplied one per month. Such an offer would be attractive to larger airlines. Another advantage here is the economies of scale: the cost of redelivery, remarketing, and re-leasing of several aircraft at the same time will be lower on per transaction basis.

Another reason to stagger lease maturities is that a lessor would be adding risks if it gets the aircraft back, and it has financing with balloon payments due at the end of the lease. If the financial and leasing markets are in trouble, it will be difficult to place those aircraft and refinance them to repay the balloon payments. Staggering lease maturities will allow spreading the risk of refinancing also.

SELECTING LEASE TERMS

Another important consideration is the lease term. In general, lessors prefer longer leases for their long, predictable stream of cash flows and fewer costly transitions. However, lessors would also consider the state of the market. For example, if the market is low, a lessor would not want to sign a 10-year lease at a low lease rate reflecting the current market. The lessor may want to go for a short lease in this case. An airline, on the other hand, would prefer a long lease in this situation.

In addition, with narrowbody aircraft, lessors can afford to do a relatively short lease term because they can take that aircraft and move it to several other airlines with minor changes, such as paint and other minor modifications. With widebody aircraft, the cost of modification is so high that lessors need a long-term lease to amortize the specific configuration that they put in that aircraft. Banks that are lending on widebody aircraft also want to see a long-term lease with a good credit. It tends to be that widebody aircraft have longer lease terms than narrowbody aircraft.

Finally, it is important to try and align the lease term with major maintenance events. An aircraft that is fresh from a major airframe maintenance visit or engine performance restoration shop visits is much easier to remarket. It also removes risk to the lessor that there are significant maintenance findings discovered after redelivery which the lessor would then be liable to rectify.

RESIDUAL VALUE MANAGEMENT

Aircraft residual value is a key component of an overall investor return. If the residual value is lower than projected, the net present value of the transaction and the investors' return will be lower. While the streams of lease cash flow can be estimated with a high degree of confidence (assuming good credit and low probability of default), residual values are subject to variability and uncertainty.

There are multiple market, economic, and aircraft/technical factors that influence residual value retention. Market factors include market liquidity, production run and cycles, storage and surplus, and the development of the secondary market. Market liquidity probably supports the aircraft value retention the most. The liquidity comes from the aircraft order book and market penetration. The order book reflects the number of firm orders (backlog and deliveries) for that aircraft and demonstrates its market share, while market penetration comes with the number and geographic distribution of customers using that aircraft. Obviously, the more liquid the market is, the more value the aircraft retains, resulting in its higher residual value. For example, the market liquidity for B737 and A320 aircraft is very high with a large number of firm orders and hundreds of operators around the world. According to Flight Global, there are 6277 B737NG and 7208 A319/320/321 aircraft currently in service (Flight Global, 2018). They also have a combined backlog of 11,549 aircraft (Flight Global, 2018).

In addition, aircraft with longer production runs have greater value retention than aircraft with shorter product life cycles. Again, B737 and A320 family aircraft have almost 30 years of production runs that lead to better residual values. Aircraft position in the production cycle also influences its value retention. For example, aircraft that are produced early in the production cycle can experience value volatility because they tend to be heavier, have lower operating weights, and cost more to operate. Manufacturers, however, often offer very competitive prices for such aircraft. Aircraft that are produced in the middle of the production cycle (stable production period) have production issues resolved, and their values tend to decline on a more stable and predictable basis. Aircraft that are produced in the late stage of the production cycle typically experience a faster rate of decline in value because they compete against newer technology aircraft that offer better performance and lower operating costs. Then again, manufacturers typically offer heavy discounts on late production units.

Aircraft production rates may also provide additional insights for residual value forecasting. While high production rates indicate a high demand for the aircraft that lead to capacity growth and better market penetration, it may also create concerns for oversupply that precedes volatility in lease rates and aircraft values. Also, the number of stored aircraft is often used as an indicator of surpluses that may push aircraft values down. The reason for the aircraft storage is important though. If the aircraft are stored due to economic or functional obsolescence, the impact on the residual values will be large and permanent. If the aircraft are stored due to the cyclical nature of the business, the residual values will not be impacted as much.

There are several potential secondary markets for an aircraft coming out of the first lease: lease to second or third tier operators; sale to another lessor or operator; passenger to freighter conversion; and part out for engines and other valuable components. Active secondary markets obviously help the aircraft to retain values.

The economic factors that influence aircraft residual values are inflation and fuel prices. For the same "real" residual value, higher inflation means higher residual value in the current (contemporary) currency. "Real" values mean values in real (not inflated) currency. For example, if an aircraft was purchased in 2010 for $40 million, its projected 2030 residual value in 2010 dollars will be $12 million. However, if the average inflation over the 20 years is 3%, the "real" residual value of $12 million will be $21.67 million in 2030. If the inflation over the same period is 4% on an average, the residual value in 2030 will be $26.29 million. Fuel prices also add complexity to aircraft residual value forecasting. If fuel prices stay low for some sustained period of time, it will support demand for older aircraft and thus will improve their residual values. Alternatively, if fuel prices are high, the demand for older aircraft will be depressed, shifting operators' preferences toward newer, more efficient aircraft.

Finally, aircraft/technical factors, such us optional features and if the aircraft is part of the family, affect residual values. In simple terms, "generic is good, but unique is bad" for aircraft values. Standard configuration aircraft are easier to place, and, thus, they have higher resale values. However, some optional features, such as engine and thrust options, optional operating weights, winglets, and crew rest areas, typically help aircraft to retain values. For example, higher maximum takeoff weight enhances aircraft's utility and marketability and consequently their residual values. Also, the fact that the aircraft is part of a family (e.g., A319/320/321 or B737-700/800/900) helps the aircraft to retain values as the operators benefit from lower investment in parts, equipment, and training.

Fig. 8.4 illustrates that different aircraft retain values differently by presenting projected market values for A320-200 and A330-300 as a percentage of the value of new aircraft. The aircraft current and projected market values are provided by the ISTAT certified appraisal firm Collateral Verifications, LLC in their Turbine Aircraft Guide "Values—Lease Rates—Maintenance Costs" as of January 2018. While the economic factors should influence values for both aircraft very similarly, the market and aircraft/technical factors make A320-200 residual values higher than A330-300 residual values (in relative terms). As projected by Collateral Verifications, LLC, the A320-200 will retain 31% of its original value in 2038, whereas the A330-300 will retain only 25% of its original value (Fig. 8.4).

PLANNING FOR CONTINGENCIES

Contingency planning is a part of risk management. Preparing for actions is always easier when you have time to think them through—before an unfavorable event occurs and even a short delay

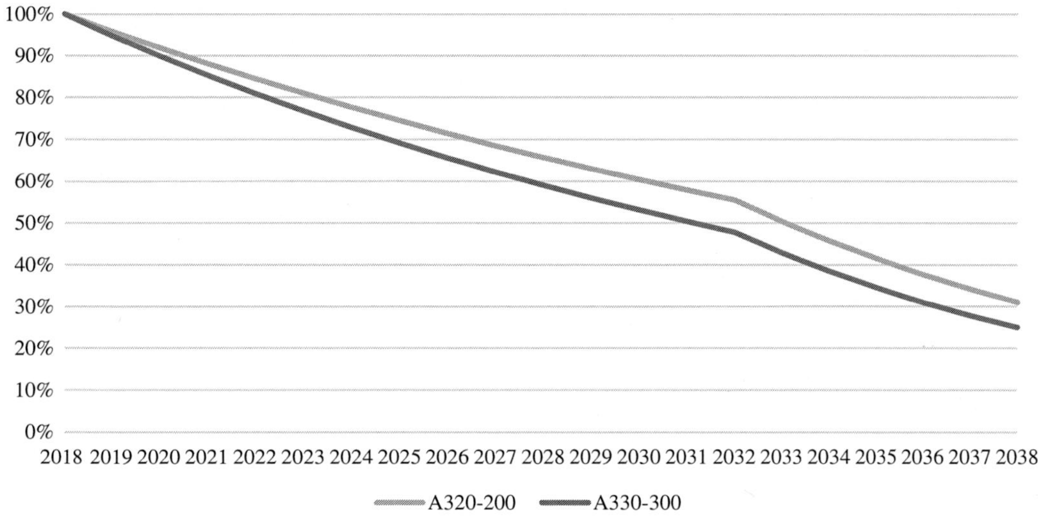

FIGURE 8.4

Projected market values for A320-200 and A330-300 of 2017 production year. (Percent of 2018 values).

Compiled by authors using Collateral Verifications, LLC. Turbine Aircraft Guide "Values-Lease Rates-Maintenance Costs." January 2018.

may cost your company large sums of money. For a lessor, planning for contingencies starts with having a good platform. In the highly competitive airline industry, there will always be airlines that default. Airlines have to rely on selling seats when they have to respond to each other strategies, discounts, regulations, entering new markets, dealing with new competitors, fuel price spikes, terrorism, earthquakes, volcanoes, and other things that nobody can predict. Lessors may not predict those things, but based upon the assumption that something like this could happen, lessors should prepare and manage their portfolios accordingly.

In order to be ready for contingencies, a lessor should know:

- Everything about its customers.
- Current and future markets for all of its products.
- Where it would place its aircraft if it gets them back on an unscheduled basis.
- If it will have adequate maintenance records for all of its aircraft if some of the lessees go bankrupt or liquidate.
- If the aircraft are in the right maintenance condition and configuration.
- If the aircraft can be transitioned easily and efficiently.
- If it has relationships with maintenance facilities.
- If it has the right team to handle the technical issues.
- How it will handle a repossession and deregistration.
- If it has relationships with local law firms in various jurisdictions.

Planning for contingencies should be embedded in every stage of the transaction.

MANAGING THE TRANSITION OF AIRCRAFT COMING OFF LEASE

The efficient transition process from the current lessee to the next is critical in preserving the integrity and value of the asset, good customer relations, and Return on Investment (ROI) for a lessor. If a lessor does not have established procedures and the parties who originally negotiated the redelivery conditions in a lease contract do not work for the lessor or airline any longer, nobody will understand the context around any contractual ambiguities at lease end.

During lease negotiations, a clear, appropriate, and enforceable set of return conditions and timescales should be documented. In the months leading up to a redelivery, compliance status with the lease return conditions should be monitored, and the ability of the lessee to redeliver the aircraft on time should be assessed. Both lessors and lessees should accurately estimate the magnitude of a redelivery project and be prepared to dedicate substantial resources to it.

Good practice is to have a meeting with the lessee 6–8 months ahead of the redelivery date and discuss the scope of work, allocation of costs, and responsibilities of the parties.

A carefully prepared work scope will allow a lessor to assess what major component changes may be required, order any desired modification kits, make arrangements for aircraft parking, insurance, and short or long term storage maintenance during any gaps between leases.

A lessor will need to balance the need to keep the aircraft in revenue-generating service for as long as possible against the economic consequences of failure to return a compliant aircraft at the pre-agreed time.

CONCLUSION

As we discussed in this chapter, aircraft lessors are exposed to numerous risks on the asset and liability sides of the business. Only deep understanding of the risks, their mitigation, and portfolio-management techniques will ensure lessors' success and sustainability. Aircraft leasing is a very capital-intensive business that usually involves a high degree of financial leverage that magnifies both: positive and negative returns. Every day aircraft lessors face hundreds of decisions with aircraft financing, purchasing, managing, and disposition. Even a small error with one of those decisions can destroy the leasing transaction returns and threaten the existence of the lessor. A properly designed risk and portfolio-management strategy may reduce the consequences of errors with contingency planning, managing, and mitigating risks, and diversifying leasing portfolios among lessees, asset types, and lease maturities.

REFERENCES

Flight Global. (2018, May 17). *Fleets*. Retrieved from Snapshots: Orders, deliveries, and fleet <https://dashboard.flightglobal.com/app/#/reports/search/>.

Guzhva, V. S. (2008). Applying intervention analysis to financial performance data: The case of US airlines and September 11th. *Journal of Economics and Finance*, *32*, 243–259.

KPMG. (2018, January 19). *The aviation industry leaders report 2018: Navigating the cycle*. Retrieved from KPMG Insights <https://home.kpmg.com/ie/en/home/insights/2018/01/lessors.html>.

Lovell, C. (2017, December 5). *What next for airberlin's leased fleet?* Retrieved from Ishka Insights by Ishka Global <https://www.ishkaglobal.com/News/Article/5724/What-next-for-airberlins-leased-fleet>.

Narkhede, S. (2016, September 5). *The Airbus A380 is here to stay despite current challenges*. Retrieved from Ishka Insights by Ishka Global <https://www.ishkaglobal.com/News/Article/5503/The-Airbus-A380-is-here-to-stay-despite-current-challenges>.

APPENDIX A: PRICING INTEREST RATE SWAPS

Pricing an interest rate swap means finding the fixed rate that equates the present value of the fixed payments to the present value of the floating payments. Hence, the market value of the swap is zero at the start of the swap agreement.

For example, consider a 1-year swap with quarterly payments on days 90, 180, 270, and 360. The reference rate is 90-day LIBOR. The annualized LIBOR spot rates today are 0.0345, 0.0358, 0.0370, and 0.0375 correspondingly.

Present value factors are calculated as follows:

$$PVF(90) = \frac{1}{1 + 0.0345(\frac{90}{360})} = 0.9914$$

$$PVF(180) = \frac{1}{1 + 0.0358(\frac{180}{360})} = 0.9824$$

$$PVF(270) = \frac{1}{1 + 0.0370(\frac{270}{360})} = 0.9730$$

$$PVF(360) = \frac{1}{1 + 0.0375(\frac{360}{360})} = 0.9639$$

The fixed payment is found as $FP = \frac{1 - 0.9639}{0.9914 + 0.9824 + 0.9730 + 0.9639} = 0.0092$

The quarterly fixed payment will be 0.0092 for each \$1 of notional principal. Annual fixed rate is $0.0092 \times 360/90 = 0.0368$ or 3.68%

Assuming in 60 days LIBOR rates change: 30, 130, 210, and 300 days; annualized LIBOR spot rates are 0.0425, 0.0432, 0.0437, and 0.0444 correspondingly.

The new present value factors are

$$PVF(30) = \frac{1}{1 + 0.0425(\frac{30}{360})} = 0.9965$$

$$PVF(120) = \frac{1}{1 + 0.0432(\frac{120}{360})} = 0.9858$$

$$PVF(210) = \frac{1}{1 + 0.0437(\frac{210}{360})} = 0.9751$$

$$PVF(300) = \frac{1}{1 + 0.0444(\frac{300}{360})} = 0.9643$$

From the party paying fixed and receiving floating, the value of the swap:

PV of remaining fixed payments and the hypothetical notional principal $= 0.0092$ $(0.9965 + 0.9858 + 0.9751 + 0.9643) + 1.0(0.9643) = 1.0004$

PV of the floating payment: on day 0, the 90-day LIBOR was 3.45%, making first floating payment 0.0345(90/360) = 0.0086. We know that the market value of the remaining floating payments on day 90, including the hypothetical notional principal, is 1.0. We should discount the payment and hypothetical notional principal back 30 days. So, (1.0 + 0.0086)(0.9965) = 1.0051

The value of the swap is 1.0051 − 1.0004 = 0.0047 per $1 notional principal. Assuming $30 million notional principal, the market value of the swap would be $141,000.

APPENDIX B: CASE STUDY

You have just been promoted to the role of Chief Investment Officer for Global Aircraft Leasing (GAL), a small upstart lessor that was formed to take advantage of market opportunities in the mid-life aircraft-leasing space. As part of your role, you must continuously assess the portfolio from a risk and portfolio-management perspective. Not only do you need to focus on the status of the current portfolio, but you also need to be mindful of the impact of future portfolio acquisitions. Given the small size, upstart nature of the company, and reliance on the commercial bank market for debt, this is an extremely important task. GAL's Head of Sales has just presented a unique opportunity to purchase a 25 aircraft portfolio from a lessor that is looking to reduce their exposure to older aircraft. This purchase would almost double the size of GAL's owned fleet. On the surface, the fact that this portfolio comprises mostly mid-to-late-life aircraft is not problematic, since the aircraft align with the company's strategy. Table 8.5 includes a snapshot of GAL's current portfolio and Table 8.6 is the portfolio of aircraft that your head of sales has proposed that the company

Table 8.5 GAL Current Portfolio

YOB	Type	Current Operator	Country	Lease Expiry	Security Deposit	Maintenance Reserves
2001	A319-100	Spirit Airlines	United States	March 22	Cash	Cash
2006	A319-100	Sky Airlines	Chile	May 19	Cash	Cash
2002	A321-200	Asiana Airlines	South Korea	April 21	Letter of credit	Letter of credit
2007	A319-100	EasyJet	United Kingdom	July 19	None	None
2005	A320-200	IndiGo	India	June 21	Letter of credit	Letter of credit
1999	B737-800	Korean Airlines	South Korea	November 20	None	None
2007	A330-200	Aeroflot	Russia	December 19	Letter of credit	Letter of credit
2011	A320-200	Iberia	Spain	May 23	None	None
2002	B737-700	GOL	Brazil	October 22	Cash	Cash
1998	B737-800	Jeju Air	South Korea	May 20	Cash	Cash
2008	B737-800	Travel Service	Czech Republic	May 22	Cash	Cash
2000	B737-800	Southwest Airlines	United States	September 25	None	None
2005	B737-700	Jet Lite	India	October 19	Cash	Cash
2000	A330-300	Aer Lingus	Ireland	April 19	Cash	Letter of credit
2005	A321-200	Volaris	Mexico	August 21	Cash	Cash

Table 8.5 GAL Current Portfolio *Continued*

YOB	Type	Current Operator	Country	Lease Expiry	Security Deposit	Maintenance Reserves
2005	A321-200	Volaris	Mexico	September 21	Cash	Cash
2002	B737-700	United Airlines	United States	April 23	None	None
2000	B737-800	TUI	United Kingdom	April 20	Cash	Letter of credit
2001	B767-300ER	Air Canada	Canada	December 21	Cash	Letter of credit
2006	A330-200	Wow	Iceland	April 24	Cash	Cash
2008	A320-200	Vistara	India	December 19	Cash	Cash
2008	A330-200	Air Europa	Spain	December 20	Cash	Cash
2006	B737-700	Aeromexico	Mexico	May 20	Letter of credit	Letter of credit
2005	A320-200	Air Canada	Canada	October 20	Cash	Letter of credit
2006	A319-100	Air India	India	June 21	Letter of credit	Letter of credit
2012	A320-200	Qantas	Australia	November 24	None	None
2009	A321-200	Interjet	Mexico	January 19	Cash	Cash
2003	B737-700	Southwest Airlines	United States	March 20	None	None
2010	B737-800	Virgin Australia	Australia	December 22	Letter of credit	Letter of credit

GAL, *Global Aircraft Leasing.*

Table 8.6 GAL Proposed Acquisitions

YOB	Type	Current Operator	Country	Lease Expiry	Security Deposit	Maintenance Reserves
2010	A330-200	Qantas	Australia	February 24	None	None
2012	A319-100	Spirit	United States	December 24	Cash	Cash
2002	A321-200	Asiana Airlines	South Korea	March 20	Letter of credit	Letter of credit
2003	A319-100	Avianca	Columbia	May 20	Cash	Cash
2004	A320-200	IndiGo	India	February 21	Letter of credit	Letter of credit
2004	A321-200	Asiana Airlines	South Korea	May 20	Cash	Cash
2005	A320-200	Red Wing Airlines	Russia	September 21	Cash	Letter of credit
2013	A320-200	Vueling Airlines	Spain	January 25	Letter of credit	Letter of credit

(*Continued*)

Table 8.6 GAL Proposed Acquisitions *Continued*

YOB	Type	Current Operator	Country	Lease Expiry	Security Deposit	Maintenance Reserves
2002	B737-700	GOL	Brazil	August 21	Cash	Cash
2002	B737-800	Jeju Air	South Korea	June 22	Cash	Cash
2004	B737-800	Enter Air	Poland	May 22	Cash	Cash
2004	B737-800	Sun Country Airlines	United States	May 24	Cash	Cash
2005	B737-700	Jet Airways	India	March 20	Cash	Cash
2006	B737-800	KLM	The Netherlands	May 20	Letter of credit	None
2001	A330-200	Air Transat	Canada	December 21	Letter of credit	Cash
2005	A330-300	Evelop	Spain	April 23	Cash	Cash
1998	A320-200	Small Planet Airlines	Lithuania	October 19	Letter of credit	Letter of credit
2008	A330-200	Air Europa	Spain	May 20	Cash	Cash
2014	B777-300ER	Emirates	UAE	January 26	Letter of credit	Letter of credit
2005	A319-100	Bulgaria Air	Bulgaria	October 21	Cash	Cash
2005	A319-100	Air India	India	March 20	Letter of credit	Letter of credit
2007	A320-200	Qantas	Australia	March 21	Letter of credit	None
2006	A320-200	Interjet	Mexico	June 22	Cash	Cash
2001	B737-700	Sun Country Airlines	United States	June 19	Cash	Cash
1999	B737-800	Eastar Jet	South Korea	June 21	Cash	Cash

GAL, *Global Aircraft Leasing*.

purchases. Your CEO has asked you to review the new portfolio from a risk and portfolio-management standpoint and provide an analysis of your findings.

Consider the following factors in your analysis:

- Discuss the impact to the current aircraft portfolio that this acquisition would have by aircraft type and variant, by lease expiration, and by geographic location of a customer.
- Provide your assessment of the risks inherent in the combined portfolio of your company. Try to address all possible risks (e.g., fleet composition, customer credit profile, etc.).
- Provide your recommendation as to whether GAL should proceed to acquire this portfolio of aircraft from a risk and portfolio-management perspective.
- Regardless of your recommendation, if the CEO does not agree to purchase the portfolio, provide your suggestions on how GAL could rebalance its existing portfolio to reduce risks.

CHAPTER

PRINCIPLES OF MAINTENANCE RESERVE DEVELOPMENT AND MANAGEMENT

9

CHAPTER OUTLINE

Aircraft Leasing and Financing. DOI: https://doi.org/10.1016/B978-0-12-815285-0.00009-2

NEW AIRCRAFT ORDERS

The "technical" life cycle of an aircraft starts when it is ordered from a manufacturer. For a lessor, this requires multiple considerations. First and foremost is the configuration of the aircraft. Typically, a lessor would be required to submit a configuration by a deadline imposed by the manufacturer. This way, the manufacturer will have been provided all of the configuration requirements beforehand, thereby minimizing modification costs at the time of the delivery to the airline.

If a lessee's configuration had not yet been provided by the deadline, the lessor would have the option to place an order for a generic aircraft with basic features that can be modified later. This is usually more expensive because airlines rarely lease generic aircraft, and postdelivery customization or modifications are generally costlier than modifications during production. Thus, lessors start marketing potential aircraft as soon as an order is placed and prior to configuration deadlines with the aircraft manufacturer.

A further alternative is a sale-and-leaseback transaction with an airline that has already purchased an aircraft from a manufacturer. This is most cost effective as there are no modification costs associated with leasing the aircraft back to the same airline.

AIRCRAFT PREPURCHASE/PREDELIVERY

A thorough technical analysis of the aircraft is required prior to any purchase or lease. For a new aircraft, the lessor or the lessee will normally have a representative on site during the manufacturing process to oversee the process and work with the manufacturer to resolve any problems that may arise. In the case of a used aircraft, the purchaser or lessee should conduct a thorough technical inspection of the aircraft and its associated records to ensure that the aircraft complies with all delivery conditions outlined in the purchase or lease agreement. In many cases, the initial delivery terms will serve as the basis for the redelivery or return conditions (see Appendix 9D for a sample purchase agreement).

The analysis involves a detailed inspection of the airframe structure for physical damage, corrosion, cracks and existing structural repairs. The inspection will also include an operational check of all systems and an internal inspection of the engines using a video borescope, as well as a complete review of all relevant technical documents including records of compliance with airworthiness directives. The purpose of these inspections is to verify compliance with the delivery conditions of the purchase or lease agreement. They do not serve as a required inspection of the aviation authority, nor are they intended to and in many cases they exceed any airworthiness inspections that may then be due.

The aviation authority of the country of manufacture, as well as the country of registration of the aircraft, may issue *airworthiness directives* (ADs) to aircraft owners or operators when it discovers an unsafe condition. An AD may require a special inspection or modification, and repairs as necessary based upon the inspection results.

A service bulletin (SB), on the other hand, is issued by the manufacturer to notify owners of any product improvements and compliance with a service bulletin is optional, unless the compliance is a contractual obligation of the lease agreement. An alert SB refers to a condition that the manufacturer feels is safety-related rather than product enhancing. This type of SB may result in the issuance of an AD, which may reference the alert SB as a method of compliance with the AD.

DELIVERY CONDITIONS

Delivery conditions refer to the physical and technical state of the aircraft once it is ready to be delivered. The predelivery inspection references these conditions and is an important safety step that may also involve price concessions or commitments on the part of the manufacturer. Once the delivery conditions are met or the parties agree otherwise, the predelivery inspection report is finalized and the aircraft is ready for delivery. At this point, maintenance becomes the responsibility of the lessee. The following sections discuss maintenance program approval, reserves, and proper tracking methods for aircraft systems.

AIRCRAFT MAINTENANCE

Aircraft maintenance is heavily regulated, and the FAA works with the US industry players to develop guidelines for minimum scheduled task requirements for new aircraft as outlined in FAA Advisory Circular (AC) 121-22C (FAA, 2012). It is then up to the airlines to use these guidelines in order to develop their own maintenance program for subsequent approval by the FAA.

Today's maintenance programs stem from maintenance steering group 3 (MSG-3), an industry task force consisting of industry groups such as Airlines for America (A4A) formerly known as the Air Transport Association and, including specialists who are responsible for developing standard protocol for a specific system, structure, or engine. Following the approval of a Maintenance Review Board (MRB), all proposals move onto the Industry Steering Committee, which consists of airline representatives, regulators, and the original equipment manufacturer (OEM)/type-certificate holder. Final approval comes from the FAA in the form of a MRB Report (MRBR). This defines the minimum requirements and becomes the framework that individual airlines and operators use to develop their own maintenance programs.

Once at the operator level, maintenance is typically classified into five categories based on the major components of an aircraft:

- Airframe
- Engine
- Engine life limited parts (LLPs)
- Auxiliary power unit (APU)
- Landing gears

Understanding how to predict maintenance events is critical to understanding how they are calculated. Two key terms are *aircraft utilization* and *utilization measures*. Utilization, which is different for each component, refers to the amount of time that an aircraft or component has been operating over a fixed interval. It can be quantified in various ways, namely, flight hours (FHs), flight cycles (FCs), engine FHs, APU Hours, and calendar months. These quantifications are the *utilization measures*.

FHs refer to the actual number of hours flown by an aircraft over a specified time period from the moment the aircraft leaves the ground on takeoff until the moment the wheels touch the ground on landing. An FC consists of a takeoff and a landing.

The utilization measure for engine components is engine FHs, and engine FCs. If an aircraft operates on very short flight segments, the number of engine FCs can exceed the number of engine

FHs and could result in an increased number of engine maintenance intervals due to the increased stress placed on the engines during takeoff.

Similarly, aircraft operators use APU Hours to track maintenance utility for APUs. Most commercial aircraft APUs are only used for engine starting and to supply electric power, air-conditioning, and hydraulic pressure on the ground. In other words, they are not used in flight. APU Hours are essentially APU operating hours.

AIRCRAFT MAINTENANCE PLANNING DOCUMENT (MPD)

All maintenance events are combined to form a program specific to each component and aircraft. This process is recorded using a maintenance planning document (MPD), which contains all MRBR minimum standards as well as any additional mandates for scheduled events. For example, a program for the B737-800 might state a C-Check interval of 20 months. This means that operators must perform a C-Check every 20 months, regardless of whether it is operated or not. Likewise, other components have specially mandated maintenance intervals.

MAINTENANCE RESERVES

Naturally, airlines want to maximize cash flow and therefore prefer to pay for maintenance at the time it is performed. However, lessors need a way to ensure the lessee will have the money to pay for very expensive maintenance when it comes due. Maintenance reserves are usually paid monthly in arrears by the lessee to the lessor and are based upon each calendar month elapsed during the lease with respect to the airframe structural heavy maintenance visit and landing gear overhaul; FH operated by each engine; FC consumed by the engine LLPs; and APU Hours operated by the APU. Maintenance reserves collected by a lessor usually amount to millions of dollars and serve several purposes for a lessor. When a covered maintenance event is accomplished by a lessee, the lessor will disburse funds collected for that event, ensuring that the money is available to pay for the maintenance. It also serves to protect the lessor for time consumed on the aircraft in the event of a default and also for when the aircraft is redelivered at the end of a lease. This concept is key to understanding the risk and return of aircraft leasing. Moreover, it is often one of the most contentious topics during lease negotiation (Ackert, 2011a).

$$\text{Maintenance Reserves} = \text{Payment for Time Consumed}$$

or

$$\text{Maintenance Reserves} = \text{Full-Life Maintenance Value} - \text{Maintenance Utility Remaining}$$

Lessors propose reserve amounts based upon the lessor's own experience with the cost of the maintenance on other aircraft owned by the lessor and the maintenance intervals (FHs, FCs, APU Hours and calendar time) per the MPD.

All reserve funds are retained by the lessor upon termination of the lease. However, the lessor will reimburse the lessee from the reserve account once the required maintenance has been completed in accordance with the terms specified in the lease. The maintenance reserves are normally commingled with the lessor's other funds, but are accounted for separately and repayment only occurs if the lessee is not in default under the lease. Reserve funds cannot be transferred from one component account to another to cover any shortfall incurred during a maintenance event, even if the accounts are for the same aircraft. Therefore, if the cost of a particular event exceeds the associated reserve balance, the remaining cost is the responsibility of the lessee during the lease period or the lessor if the maintenance is performed while the aircraft is off lease.

WHY MAINTENANCE RESERVES?

A conventional operating lease states that the lessee is liable for the ongoing maintenance costs required to keep the aircraft airworthy in accordance with the manufacturer's MPD. However, what happens when an airline has an event of default under the lease and the lessor invokes a forcible repossession of the aircraft just before a major maintenance event? Reserve funds protect the lessor from this large financial exposure, so the aircraft can have the necessary maintenance performed before it is re-leased or sold.

In general, maintenance reserves help mitigate the risk of leasing to airlines that have poor credit and to those that operate within volatile jurisdictions. Not only that, but implementing the provision gives the lessor exposure to the scope and quality of airline maintenance activities, thereby allowing a certain degree of control over the minimum level of how the asset is maintained.

WHAT IS COVERED?

Maintenance reserves typically cover five major maintenance events: airframe heavy structural inspection (a heavy maintenance visit or "HMV"), APU restoration, landing gear overhaul, engine performance restoration (PR), and engine LLPs replacement, and if a turboprop, propellers.

Airframe heavy maintenance visit (structural inspection)

The airframe is the largest component of an aircraft. Depending on the type of aircraft, the first HMV is performed after either 6 or 8 years of service. The second check is, in most cases, done after 12 years in service.

Auxiliary power unit restoration

The APU is a component that provides pnuematics for starting the engines, electrical power, hydraulic pressure, and air-conditioning when the main aircraft engines are not running. It is a small jet engine that does not provide propulsion but does have the same major components as the main engines. APU restoration involves a major refurbishment of the compressor, combustion section and power section (turbine).

Landing gear overhaul

Landing gear consists of the complete strut assembly of each landing gear installed on the Airframe and includes the inner and outer cylinders of the main landing gear and the nose landing gear, including the truck assembly and axles of the landing gear. Landing gear overhaul means the complete refurbishment or major restoration of the Landing Gear in accordance with the overhaul or restoration procedures in the manufacturer's repair manual, the extent of which refurbishes or restores such Landing Gear to a "zero time since overhaul" condition in accordance with the manufacturer's repair manual.

Engine performance restoration

The major focus of this maintenance event is to restore performance levels of an engine. The engine is the most critical and costly component of the aircraft. While in operation, the engine core deteriorates due to heat, fatigue, and erosion, and the exhaust gas temperature (EGT) increases with the number of hours the engine operates. Increased EGT causes accelerated wear as well as micro cracks in the airfoils, which lead to decreased performance. An OEM will specify a maximum EGT that an engine cannot safely exceed and if an engine cannot reach full takeoff power without exceeding that limit, the engine is considered EGT limited and the aircraft will not be able to take-off without sacrificing some of its payload or carrying less fuel in order to use less power on take-off, which can cause the aircraft to make an unscheduled technical stop in order to refuel. Engine performance restoration means any engine shop visit having a workscope that, at a minimum, includes a complete refurbishment or full overhaul of the high pressure compressor, high pressure turbine and combustion section of the relevant engine, accomplished in accordance with the engine manufacturer's shop manuals and recommended procedures (Workscope Planning Guide in the case of GE and CFM engines).

Engine life limited parts replacement

FAA Advisory Circular 33.70-1 defines engine life limited parts as "engine rotor and major static structural parts whose primary failure is likely to result in a hazardous engine effect". Typically, these are rotating compressors, turbine hubs, shafts, and disks. At the end of their operating life, LLPs must be replaced and cannot be used again. The engine life limited parts reserve typically reimburses an amount per the lease agreement for the purchase of a life limited part, but does not reimburse for labor to install the part.

Each of the maintenance events and their associated reserve rates are discussed in detail in the following sections.

COVERAGE STRUCTURES

Again, maintenance reserves are lease provisions that usually involve extensive negotiation. Even if an airline that is considered a strong credit airline negotiates away the requirement to make regular payments, the lessor will still require a payment at the end of the lease, for time consumed on the components that normally make up the maintenance reserves. In general, most agreements fall under one of three coverage structures:

1. *Payments in arrears*

   This is the most common coverage structure and requires the lessee to pay the reserve payments at the end of each month. All payments are specified in the lease agreement and are based on aircraft utilization.
2. *End-of-lease financial adjustment*

   Typically, end-of-lease financial adjustments are utilized by airlines with good credit. Under this method, the lessee does not make any reserve payments during the lease term. The aircraft maintenance status examination and appropriate financial adjustments are all made at the end of the lease. If the maintenance status of the aircraft is less than at delivery (as specified in the lease agreement), the lessee is required to make an end-of-lease payment to the lessor. On the other hand, if the maintenance status of the aircraft is better than at delivery, the lessor may be required to pay the lessee. Two methods are used for end-of-lease financial adjustments:

a. Mirror-in/mirror-out: A one-way mirror adjustment requires only the lessee to make an end-of-lease payment, and only if the aircraft is returned with less time remaining for a certain maintenance event than at delivery. With a two-way mirror adjustment, the lessor may also have to pay the lessee, but only if the aircraft is returned with a better maintenance status than at delivery.
b. Zero-time or full-life: With this method of adjustment, the lessee has to pay for all aircraft time used since the last overhaul or since the aircraft's original delivery date when delivered new from the manufacturer if an overhaul had not previously been accomplished.

3. *Letter of credit*

Financial institutions issue letters of credit (LOC) to guarantee payment. In this case, an LOC is a bank-backed promise that the lessee will return the asset in the condition specified in the lease agreement. These amounts are usually reconciled annually or semiannually to reflect maintenance utility consumed and maintenance performed by the lessee. See Appendix 9A for a sample LOC.

MAINTENANCE RESERVE ECONOMICS AND RATE DETERMINATION

Lessors typically calculate estimates or baseline rates when determining how much to charge for maintenance reserves. Internal reserve claims are a common source for data, as these reflect the actual cost of maintenance events. The more claims a lessor accumulates, the easier it is to create a baseline metric that more closely reflects the true or airline-specific cost of a particular event. For example, an engine restoration claim will provide a plethora of detailed maintenance data, such as removal cause, restoration costs, flight leg, and cost per FH. Lessors can also use industry publications to analyze various aircraft and engines used by multiple carriers. This makes it easier to develop industry-standard costs and performance intervals. Key publications include *Aircraft Commerce*, International Bureau of Aviation's *Maintenance Cost Journal*, and *Aircraft Technology Engineering & Maintenance*.

OEMs are the third source for data. Most aircraft and engine manufacturers publish product and maintenance cost handbooks that can be used for developing maintenance reserves. Boeing, for example, provides an annual guide that includes the calculations used to determine the direct maintenance cost (DMC) of specific engine, airframe, APU, and landing gear components. Furthermore, maintenance cost is a common topic at industry conferences where OEMs may disclose data that is not yet published.

After gathering sufficient data, the lessor can then benchmark the estimate against what was actually reported. This way, the cost metric is more consistent. Reserve rates vary for each aircraft and component and are often adjusted for engine age, flight length, operating environment, etc. Table 9.1 presents rate formulas for the five major maintenance categories.

Some costs above are more variable than others. For example, it is difficult to predict the HMV cost on older equipment, while PR costs are also difficult to quantify. With catalog costs, there is

Table 9.1 Rate Determination Formulation

Application	General Equation	Specific Equation
Engine LLP replacement	$\frac{\text{Fixedcost}}{\text{Fixedinterval}}$	$\frac{\text{Catalogcosts}}{\text{Cycliclimit}}$
Airframe HMV	$\frac{\text{Variablecost}}{\text{Fixedinterval}}$	$\frac{\text{HSIcosts}}{\text{FixedMointerval}}$
Landing gear overhaul		$\frac{\text{Overhaulcosts}}{\text{Overhaulinterval}}$
Engine PR	$\frac{\text{Variablecost}}{\text{Variableinterval}}$	$\frac{\text{PRcosts}}{\text{MTBR}}$
APU PR		$\frac{\text{PRcosts}}{\text{MTBR}}$

LLP, *life limited parts;* HMV, *heavy maintenance visit (structural inspection);* PR, *performance restoration;* APU, *auxiliary power unit;* MTBR, *mean time before removal.*
From Ackert, S. (2012). Basics of aircraft maintenance reserve development and management. *Aircraft Monitor.*

very little uncertainty. Engine manufacturers define LLP costs and life limits, so the reserve rates are fairly predictable. Conversely, notice the variability in both the numerator and denominator of the rates for the last two applications. The cost of PRs are much more uncertain and require further analysis when determining reserve rates.

For aircraft models that have been in production for a number of years, historical cost data (e.g., A320, A330, B737) and patterns for engine or APU removals are generally used for reserve rate calculations. For newer aircraft (e.g., B787, A350), OEMs provide guidance about the estimated maintenance event costs. While such guidance is not as reliable as historical data, it can be used to develop reserve rates until appropriate data are collected. An alternate technique for newer aircraft is a *proxy approach* that compares a new aircraft to an existing aircraft that is being replaced. For example, the B787 has similar landing weights to the A330 and B767. Thus, the cost of landing gear overhaul for the B787 is expected to be similar to the overhaul of landing gear for the A330 or B767. This assumption helps in developing the reserve rates for B787 landing gear overhauls.

The biggest challenge with calculating a rate for the 787 and A350 airframe HMVs is that their airframes are constructed primarily from composites, and no historical data or appropriate proxy exists. In such cases, HMV rates will rely heavily on OEM guidance, and the leases will typically carry a clause to reevaluate the rates when data is available from work performed on aircraft of the same type.

These five maintenance events are discussed further in the following sections.

AIRFRAME HEAVY MAINTENANCE VISIT (STRUCTURAL INSPECTION)

Airframe reserve rates are typically estimated using the MPD. Generally, heavy maintenance visit structural inspections are scheduled every 6–12 years, depending on the aircraft type. An HMV requires the aircraft to be out of service for a few weeks, on average. The first step during this check involves stripping exterior paint and removing the large outer panels. This exposes the underlying airframe for zonal and structural inspections. Scheduled maintenance tasks for the airframe are categorized into three programs (Ackert, 2012):

1. *Systems and power plant*—Operational and functional checks on pneumatics, flight controls, hydraulics, electrical systems, etc.
2. *Zonal inspection*—Assessment of the general condition of system and structure attachments. Visual checks cover wiring, plumbing, fittings, pneumatic duct work, and hydraulic tubing.
3. *Structural inspection*—Visual inspection for detection of structural damages–corrosion, fatigue cracking, and stress corrosion. This inspection may also involve nondestructive-testing procedures to uncover internal defects without causing damage to the component.

As we saw in the rate formula table, HMV costs are based on several key factors, namely, the *age of the aircraft*. Inspection requirements become more costly and/or complex with each year of operation. Specifically, more nonroutine maintenance is required for subsequent heavy airframe checks. This refers to work that is in addition to the scheduled inspection tasks, such as repairs and additional work requested. Nonroutine maintenance is measured using the nonroutine ratio, otherwise known as the defect ratio:

Nonroutine man hours/routine man hours

This measures the incremental time required estimated to correct routine defects. For example, if an HMV of an aircraft requires 6000 routine man-hours in addition to 3000 nonroutine man-hours, the nonroutine ratio for this inspection is 50%. Nonroutine ratios can even exceed 100% as the age of the aircraft increases. Fig. 9.1 displays the three distinct HMV phases and the proportion of nonroutine maintenance required.

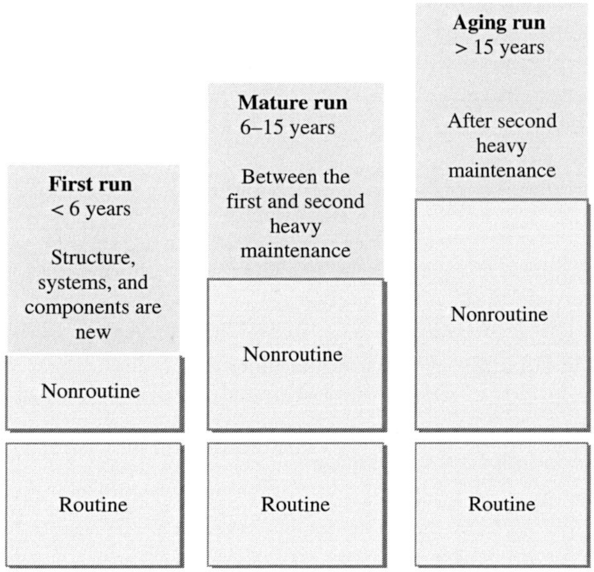

FIGURE 9.1

Routine and nonrouting maintenance for aging aircraft.

From Ackert, S. (2012). Basics of aircraft maintenance reserve development and management. Aircraft Monitor.

Table 9.2 Heavy Maintenance Visit Structural Inspection Sample Rates

Aircraft	Check	Phase	Interval (Months)	Costs—2010 ($)	Rates ($/Month)
A320-200	4C/6Y HMV	First run	72	750k−850k	10,400−11,800
A320-200	8C/12Y HMV	First run	144	850k−900k	5500−5900
A330-300	4C/6Y HMV	First run	72	1.4M−1.6M	19,500−22,200
A330-300	8C/12Y HMV	First run	144	1.5M−1.7M	10,400−11,800
B737-800	C6-C8 equivalent	First run	120/144	1.3M−1.5M	9000−12,500
B747-400	C4/D-Check	Aging run	72	4.0M−4.5M	55,500−62,500
B757-200	S4C	Aging run	72	1.5M−1.7M	22,200−23,600
B767-300ER	S4C	Aging run	72	2.0M−2.3M	27,800−31,900
B777-300ER	C4/HMV	First run	96	2.5M−2.8M	26,000−29,100
E190	C4/HMV	First run	96	475k−575k	4900−5900
CRJ-700	HMV	First run	96	425k−525k	4400−5400

HMV, *heavy maintenance visit (structural inspection).*
From Ackert, S. (2012). Basics of aircraft maintenance reserve development and management. *Aircraft Monitor.*

Additional cost drivers

Even for relatively new aircraft, there can be an increase in airframe maintenance costs as a result of flight operations with a high number of *FCs*.

Scope of work is another factor and, in most cases, is established by using one of two structures. Under *Structure A*, the work includes reimbursement, subject to certain exclusions specified in the lease agreement, for material, routine and nonroutine labor for systems, and structural and zonal tasks. *Structure B* covers reimbursement for material and routine and nonroutine labor for structural and zonal tasks. Work under structure A is more comprehensive since it includes work on the electronic systems and the power plant program. Table 9.2 presents sample HMV costs for various aircraft types.

Reserve rates can also vary by *calendar interval factors*. The two main types of interval structures are as follows:

Structure A: Calendar intervals based on the OEM generic and/or sample block program. For example:

Generic block: A320/A330 family; 6-year and 8-year intervals

Sample block: 737NG family; at 8-year intervals

Structure B: Calendar intervals based on the timing of the majority of zonal/structural tasks that are reflective of a customized maintenance program. For example:

737NG family; 8, 10, and 12-year intervals

747-8 8-year intervals

Eligible for Reserve Reimbursement	Not Eligible for Reserve Reimbursement
• Hours and nonroutine hours associated with MPD routine tasks • Material costs associated with routine and nonroutine tasks • Standard cabin refurbishment • Notable overhaul for time-controlled components	• Man-hours associated with SBs, ADs, and service letters • Airline-specific tasks • Vendor specific task • Local regulatory tasks • Cabin reconfigurations • Repairs for accidental damages • Packaging/shipping fees

MPD, *Maintenance Planning Document;* HMV, *heavy maintenance visit;* SB, *service bulletin;* AD, *airworthiness directive.*

LANDING GEAR OVERHAUL

An aircraft's landing gear comprises nose gear and two to four main gear assemblies. Each gear assembly includes the strut assembly (inner and outer cylinders), drag braces/side struts, and hydraulic actuators to extend and retract the gears. Depending on the aircraft model, overhauls typically occur every 8 to 12 years, but the exact interval is based on the need to inspect and/or treat corrosion. This is a particularly lengthy maintenance event. Thus, most overhaul facilities loan out replacement landing gear or offer to exchange the current set. Under an exchange agreement, upon completion of the overhaul the landing gear becomes part of the exchange pool for future customers of the maintenance facility. The cost of either the loan or an exchange fee is added to the maintenance cost. According to Ackert (2012), the primary cost drivers are as follows:

- Size and complexity
- Number of modifications to incorporate
- Operational environment and maintenance practices
- Market penetration (number of Maintenance, Repair, and Overhaul (MRO) facilities supporting the gear)
- Cost of exchange fee

The timing of the overhaul is based on the performance interval that is more limiting, either calendar time or FCs. For example, if a landing gear overhaul interval is 10 years or 20,000 FCs, and an aircraft is operating 1800 FCs per year, then the landing gear overhaul would be conducted at the end of the 10th year. If an aircraft is operating for over 2000 FCs per year, then the overhaul would take place upon completion of 20,000 FCs. Once the limiter has been determined, the maintenance reserve rates can be estimated by dividing the total estimated cost by the time period determined (Table 9.3).

Table 9.3 A320 Landing Gear Reserve Sample Rates

Operator	Annual Utilization (Flight Hours/Flight Cycles)	Cyclic Limiter (Months)	Calendar Limiter (Months)	Overhaul Limiter (Months)	Rates ($/Months)
A	3500 FH/1500 FCs	160	120	120	3500
B	3000 FH/3000 FCs	80	120	80	5250

Overhaul intervals: 120 months or 20,000 flight cycles. Overhaul cost: $420,000. FC, *Flight Cycle;* FC, *flight cycle.*
From Ackert, S. (2012). Basics of aircraft maintenance reserve development and management. *Aircraft Monitor.*

Eligible for Reserve Reimbursement	Not Eligible for Reserve Reimbursement
• Assembly and overhaul work that restores landing gear to a "zero-time since overhaul" condition in accordance with the OEM's repair manual and event specifications • Loan or exchange fees (most lessors)	• Man-hours associated with SBs, ADs, and service letters • Packaging/handling/shipping charges

OEM, *Original Equipment Manufacturer;* SB, *service bulletin;* AD, *airworthiness directive.*

ENGINE PERFORMANCE RESTORATION

Core engine deterioration is the primary contributor of performance reduction. This is usually caused by heat damage, erosion, and fatigue. Over time, EGT increases and leads to cracking in the airfoil. During a PR, the core module is dismantled and, as a minimum, a complete refurbishment or full overhaul of the high pressure compressor, high pressure turbine and combustion section the engine is accomplished in accordance with the engine manufacturer's shop manuals and recommended procedures (Workscope Planning Guide in the case of GE and CFM engines).

The goal of engine PR is to restore the engine to a condition where it can be expected to operate without limitation for a predetermined amount of time and without any requirement for a shop visit during such time period. Primary cost drivers include engine build goals, time accumulated since last overhaul, and operational factors.

Engine build goals

There are two ways an engine restoration shop visit can be carried out, depending on the requirements of the customer (Ackert, 2011b):

- Maximizing usage of LLP hardware (no LLP replacement; this results in lower shop visit costs but higher DMC)
- Minimizing number of shop visits (with LLP replacement; this results in higher shop visit costs but lower DMC)

For example, consider an operator flying 3000 FHs per year at 2 hours per leg, who would like to compare two alternatives to assess the restoration DMC and shop DMC.

Option 1—No LLP Replacement	**Option 2—With LLP Replacement**
Build goal: 7000 FCs	Build goal: 10,000 FCs
Expected TOW: 14,000 FH	Expected TOW: 20,000 FH
Restoration cost: $1,650,000	Restoration cost: $1,800,000
Restoration DMC: $117.85/FH	Restoration DMC: $90.00/FH
LLP cost: $0	LLP cost: $1,000,000
Total shop visit cost: $1,650,000	Total shop visit cost: $2,800,000
Shop visit cost per FH: $117.85	Shop visit cost per FH: $140.00
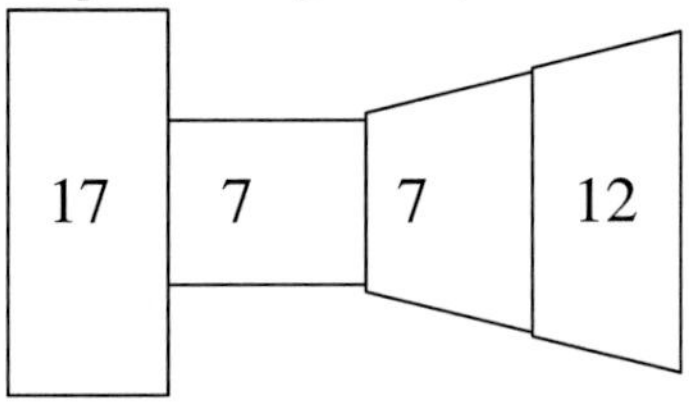	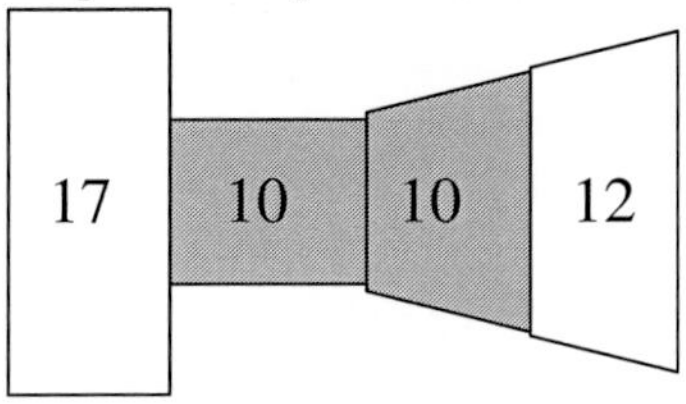

TOW, *Time On-Wing;* FH, *flight hour;* DMC, *direct maintenance cost;* LLP, *life limited parts;* FC, *flight cycle.*

Option 2 minimizes the number of shop visits, thus resulting in lower DMCs, but a higher total cost for the shop visit.

Age of the engine

Engine hardware deteriorates more rapidly as the engine ages. Thus, older or aging-run engines are typically more expensive to maintain, fly fewer hours, and require more frequent shop visits (Fig. 9.2).

Operational factors

1. *Engine thrust rating:* A considerable thrust increase leads to deterioration of EGT, which results in a lower time on-wing for the engine. In other words, the engine would be in the shop earlier than normal.

   For a high-thrust rating engine, the EGT limit is lower, implying that the engine would reach the limit faster at, say, 8000 FCs. Conversely, an engine with a low thrust rating would have a higher EGT limit and last at least 10,000 FCs before needing a shop visit (Fig. 9.3).
2. *Flight length:* Aircraft that fly short segments build up FCs faster than long-haul airplanes. Furthermore, smaller flight legs force engines to spend a larger percentage of total flight time using takeoff and ascending power settings. This results in increased performance deterioration and higher DMC ($/FH) (Figs. 9.4 and 9.5).

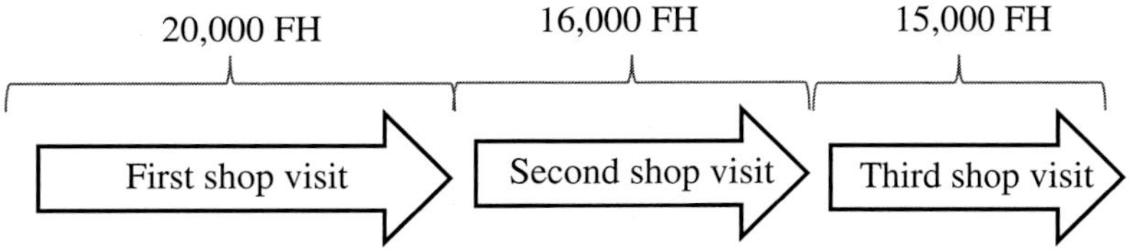

FIGURE 9.2

Engine age and time on-wing.

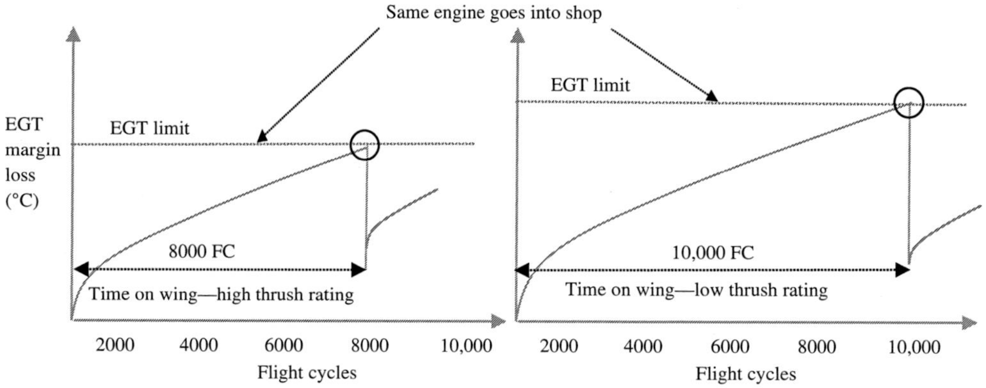

FIGURE 9.3

Impact of thrust rating on EGT limit. *EGT*, Exhaust Gas Temperature.

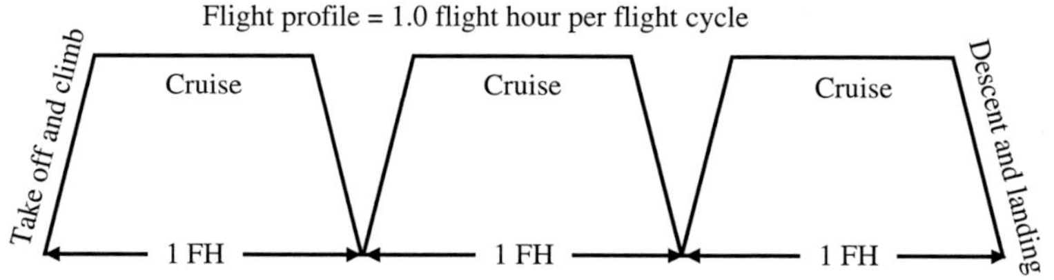

FIGURE 9.4

Smaller flight legs [higher DMC ($/FH)]. *DMC*, Direct Maintenance Cost.

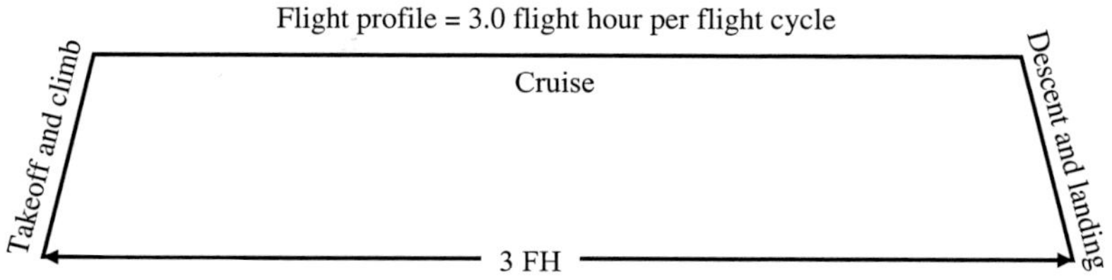

FIGURE 9.5

Longer flight leg [lower DMC ($/FH)]. *DMC*, Direct Maintenance Cost.

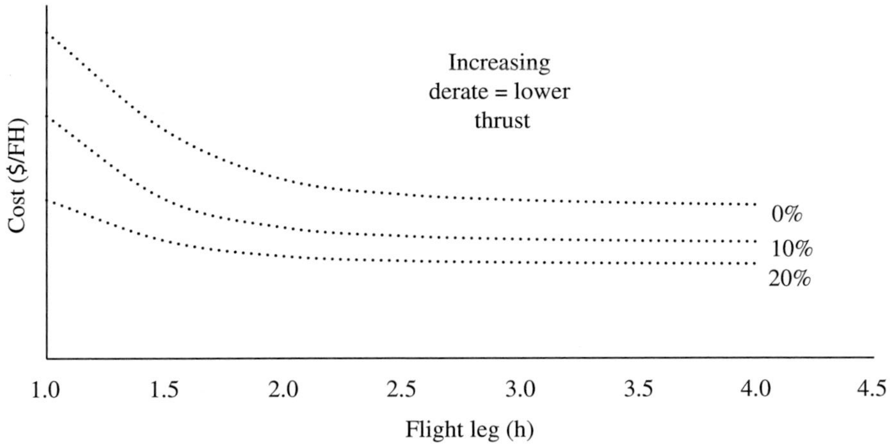

FIGURE 9.6

Larger engine derate lowers DMC ($/FH). *DMC*, Direct Maintenance Cost.

3. *Engine derate:* Derating reduces the engine takeoff and climb thrust to below the rated maximum capability. Engines are approved for specific takeoff thrust ratings, and operating a higher derate essentially means utilizing less power. Ultimately, this lowers the EGT, which slows deterioration and reduces maintenance costs (Fig. 9.6).
4. *Environment:* Recall that maintenance reserves mitigate the risks associated with region of operation. This includes natural threats, such as sand, dust, excessive heat, pollution, and other corrosive factors that increase engine blade distress and speed up deterioration.

$$\text{Temperature factor} = 1.00$$
$$\text{Hot/dry factor} = 1.10$$
$$\text{Erosive factor} = 1.2$$

Oxidation takes a particular toll on engine life, which is why lessors adjust their rates according to region. Fig. 9.7 displays Ackert's (2012) heat map of severity and rate of occurrence. Notice that the dark dots are highly concentrated in areas with excessive heat, moisture, or pollution.

Another important calculation used to determine the reserve rates for engine PR is the severity factor (Fig. 9.8). Severity factor is developed based on the flight leg and derate level to correspondingly alter the base reserve rate to match the degree of operation for a given engine.

The base maintenance reserve rate is assumed to be $80/FH, and the base points of operation are 2.0 FHs, 10% derate, and a temperate environment. Consider the example of an aircraft operating at 3.5 FHs with a 5% derate in a hot/dry environment. The severity factor observed from the table is 0.800. Since it is a hot/dry environment, the environment factor is 1.10. This results in an overall adjustment factor of 0.88 (0.800 × 1.10). Hence, the adjusted maintenance reserve rate for the aircraft considered would be $70.4/FH (0.88 × 80).

ENGINE LIFE LIMITED PARTS (LLP) REPLACEMENT

The rotating compressor, turbine hubs, shafts, and disks within the engine have a specifically defined operating life, at the end of which the parts must be replaced and cannot be used again. As

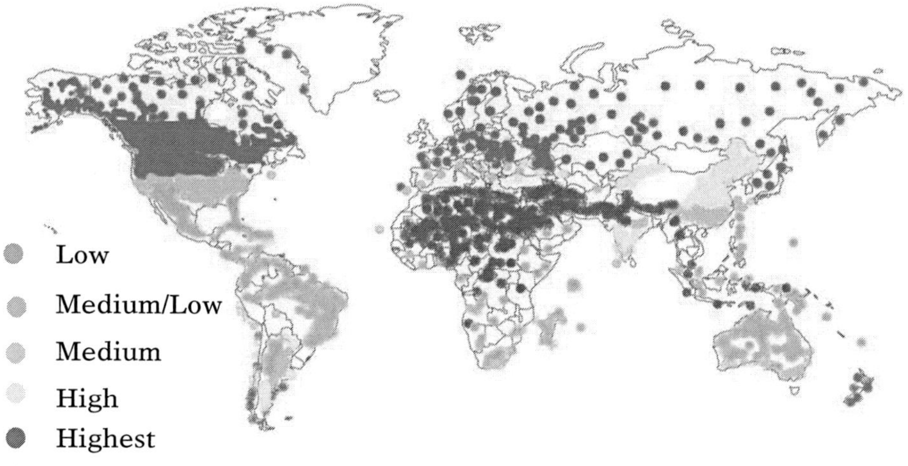

FIGURE 9.7

Environmental distress chart.

From Ackert, S. (2012). Basics of aircraft maintenance reserve development and management. *Aircraft Monitor.*

we mentioned earlier, the OEM determines the life of LLPs, which typically range from 15,000 to 30,000 FCs, with some LLPs having a considerably lower life limit. This is another reason why short-haul aircraft with more FCs require more frequent maintenance. In fact, some engines operating on long-range networks never even hit the FC count and therefore never need LLP replacement.

Lessors may use a stub factor that in order to compensate for LLPs that are replaced before reaching their life limit to avoid the necessity for the engine to require the next shop visit prematurely due to expiration of a low time remaining LLP that was not replaced: 10% for narrowbody engines and 5% for widebody engines. *Stub life* refers to the engine's shortest remaining LLP life among all LLPs installed on a specific engine. For example, if we impose a stub factor of 10% on the LLP of a narrowbody engine (and assume the certified life is 20,000 FCs), then the life of the LLP becomes 18,000 FCs (90% of 20,000).

The primary cost driver for engine LLP replacement is OEM part price escalation, which averages between 4% and 6% annually (Ackert, 2012). Static LLPs represent the secondary cost factor. Although these parts are not classified as critical, their failure could create a hazard to the aircraft.

To observe a sample calculation of reserve rates, consider an LLP costing $180,000 and with a FC limit of 30,000. The actual reserve rate would be $6.00 per FC ($180,000/30,000). If the LLP has a stub factor of 10%, the rate is calculated as follows:

$$\text{Reserve rate} = \frac{\text{Cost}(\$)}{90\% \times \text{FC Limit}}$$

$$\text{Reserve rate} = \frac{\$180,000}{90\% \times 30,000} = \$6.67\text{per FC}$$

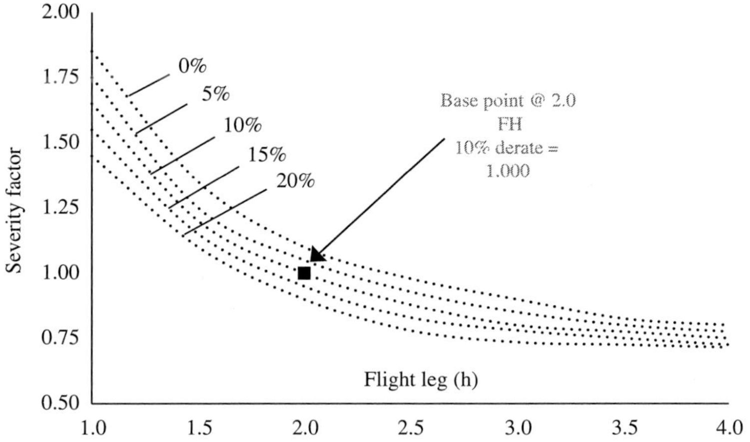

FL	0%	5%	10%	15%	20%
1.0	1.850	1.750	1.650	1.550	1.450
1.5	1.350	1.250	1.200	1.150	1.100
2.0	1.100	1.050	1.000	0.950	0.900
2.5	0.980	0.930	0.880	0.830	0.780
3.0	0.900	0.850	0.800	0.780	0.735
3.5	0.825	0.800	0.775	0.750	0.725
4.0	0.800	0.775	0.750	0.725	0.715

FL	0%	5%	10%	15%	20%
1.0	148.00	140.00	132.00	124.00	116.00
1.5	108.00	100.00	96.00	92.00	88.00
2.0	88.00	84.00	80.00	76.00	68.00
2.5	78.40	74.40	70.40	66.40	62.40
3.0	72.00	68.00	64.00	62.40	58.80
3.5	66.00	64.00	62.00	60.00	58.00
4.0	64.00	62.00	60.00	58.00	57.20

FIGURE 9.8

Severity curve.

AUXILIARY POWER UNIT RESTORATION

The APU consists of three major modules: load compressor, power section, and the gearbox. The reason behind modular construction of current technology APU engines is to allow for easier maintenance. Recall MTBR, or mean time before removal, from the earlier rate calculations. When it comes to maintenance reserves, this is the most important parameter for measuring APU reliability. It represents the average time between all causes—unscheduled removals, confirmed removals, foreign object debris inspection, and no fault found (Ackert, 2012). MTBR varies by manufacturer and model but typically ranges between 5000 and 7000 APU Hours.

APU maintenance cost drivers are very similar to those listed for the engine restoration. The environment in which the APU is operated has a significant impact on MTBR and cost. A higher cycle operation will lead to shorter removal intervals and incur lower shop visit costs, whereas a lower cycle operation will result in the APU remaining longer on-wing and thus incur greater hardware deterioration and higher shop visit costs. Moreover, similar to engines, material accounts for roughly 70%–80% of the total APU restoration cost, while labor accounts for only 20%–30% (Ackert, 2012).

If the MTBR for an engine is 6500 APU Hours and the overall cost of APU restoration is $260,000, then the reserve rate will be $40 per APU Hour ($260,000/6500). Refer to Appendix 9B to see the structure of a "form of status" report for all the components.

MAINTENANCE RESERVE CONTRACT MANAGEMENT

Lease contracts involve a lot of legal and technical jargon, much of which is directly correlated with maintenance reserves. Because ambiguity leads to misinterpretation, it is important that lessors define each term explicitly and clearly. The following definitions are drawn from Ackert's (2012) report on reserve development and management. These examples are in reference to A320-200 aircraft and CFM56-5B4 engines:

"4C/6 Year Check" means the intermediate airframe structural, CPCP, and zonal inspection of the Aircraft (and resulting repairs), including a C Check, all MPD tasks having an interval of 6 years, and performed concurDQrently therewith such additional Flight Hour or Cycle controlled MPD structural and zonal inspections and including all lower level checks then falling due.

"8C/12 Year Check" means the heavy airframe structural and zonal inspection of the Aircraft (and resulting repairs) including a C Check, all MPD tasks having an interval of twelve years, and performed concurrently therewith such additional Flight Hour or Cycle controlled MPD structural and zonal inspections and including all lower level checks then falling due.

"Engine Performance Restoration" means, at a minimum, the accomplishment of a performance level workscope on the High Pressure Compressor (HPC), Combustor, and High Pressure Turbine (HPT) pursuant to the then current engine manufacturer's (CFM International or CFM) Workscope Planning Guide and minimum performance level workscopes required on the Fan/Booster, Low Pressure Turbine (LPT) and Gearbox pursuant to the CFM Workscope Planning Guide.

"Engine Life Limited Parts" means, those Parts, defined in the Engine Manufacturer's maintenance manual, or by the FAA or EASA or the Aviation Authority through Airworthiness Directives (which may require an earlier removal of an LLP than the life listed in the manufacturer's manual), that require replacement on a mandatory basis prior to or upon the expiration of the Engine Manufacturer's certified life for that Part.

"APU Performance Restoration" means, with respect to the APU, disassembly and rework of the power section, load impeller and gearbox modules according to the Manufacturer's then current performance restoration and full gas path overhaul criteria.

"Landing Gear Overhaul" means an overhaul of a Landing Gear assembly in accordance with the Manufacturer's repair manual that restores such Landing Gear to a "zero time since overhaul.

RESERVE ESCALATION

Maintenance reserve escalation is sometimes referred to as maintenance reserve inflation. Unlike inflation, however, escalation refers to a price or cost change over time in a specific class, product, or economic category. It is also driven by specific industry practices. Major individual economy-driven factors affecting maintenance cost are labor and material repair & replacement. Thus, maintenance cost can be split primarily into two components: labor and material.

In most cases for young aircraft, the labor component during an HMV is 65%–75%, while the material component is only 25%–35%. Whereas, for engine restoration, the material component is 65%–75%, while the labor component is only 25%–35%. Inflation in aerospace labor has been averaging about 2.5%–3.5% in the last 5 years. Inflation in materials has been roughly 5%–7% during the same time period. Hence, it can be inferred that HMV costs will have a lower overall inflation relative to engine restoration, APU restoration, or landing gear overhaul, all of which are highly material oriented. This complication of varied inflations arises if actual inflation rates are considered for each maintenance event. However, lessors focus on simplifying the process and determining a universal inflation rate for all the maintenance events.

To measure and forecast changes to these cost inputs, lessors may factor in the price escalations of key economic indices that correlate to them. These key indices mainly consist of

- The employment cost index (ECI) for aircraft-manufacturing wages and salaries. The ECI tracks the changes in cost of labor. Labor-related outlays on wages, salaries and the gamut of fringe benefits account for 60% of the cost of manufacturing in the aerospace industry. Fig. 9.9 is an account of the ECI for the past 5 years in the aircraft-manufacturing industry.
- The producer price index (PPI) for industrial commodities. The PPI measures changes in prices that manufacturers and wholesalers pay for goods during various stages of production. Fig. 9.10 gives an account of the PPI for the previous 5 years.

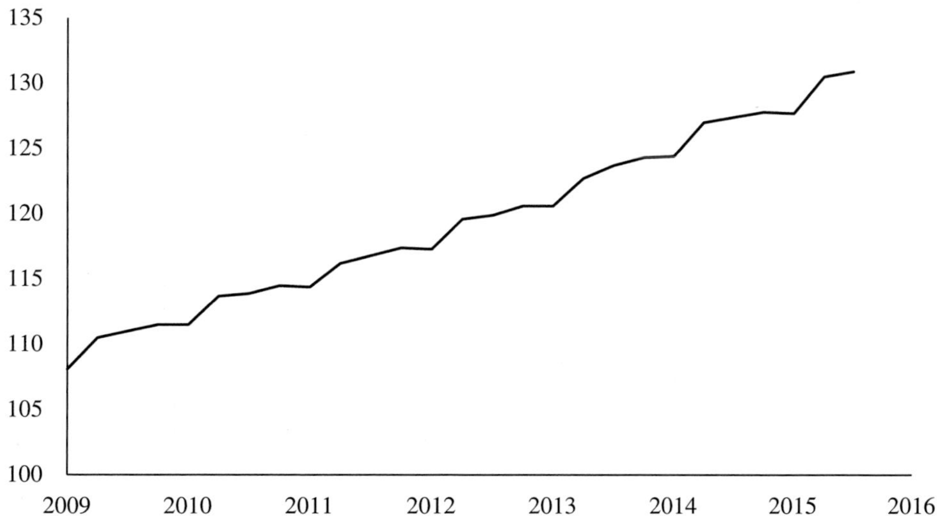

FIGURE 9.9

Employment Cost Index (ECI).

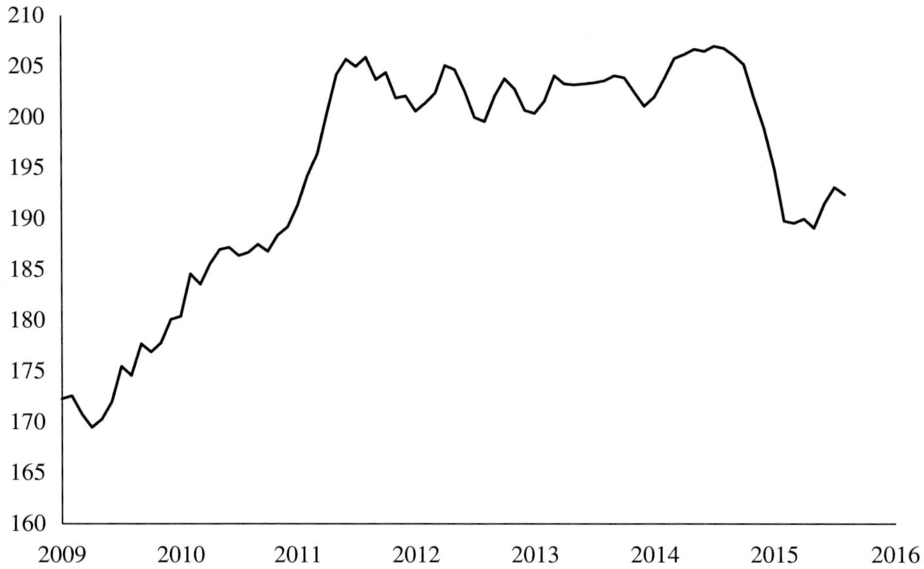

FIGURE 9.10

Producer Price Index (PPI).

A reasonable balance of 70% labor and 30% material is assumed in order to come up with an overall escalation rate averaging between 3% and 4% per year—a range that is generally consistent with many lease contracts, (although it should be noted that maintenance reserve rates and escalation are heavily negotiated during lease negotiations). The escalation rates are not applicable to engine LLPs since they escalate in correspondence with the manufacturer's published escalation rates.

EXPOSURE ANALYSIS

The effectiveness of maintenance reserve management can be quantified and analyzed via numerous performance indicators, the most common of which are *maintenance coverage* and *maintenance exposure*. To an extent, it can be stated that the major goal of collecting maintenance reserves is to protect the lessor from the potentially high levels of maintenance exposure.

Ideally, the lessor wants to "remain whole" and have the lessee cover all maintenance costs, including the residual condition of the aircraft (Ackert, 2012). Maintenance coverage measures how much of the actual maintenance cost is covered by the reserve rate. For example, suppose the maintenance coverage for a Boeing 737-800 was 93.8%. This would mean that the lessor is covered for only 93.8% of the total maintenance expenditure. In other words, the lessor has 93.8% in maintenance reserves for every maintenance dollar consumed by the lessee.

Maintenance coverage can be applied in four major forms:

- Cash reserves
- LOCs
- Maintenance service agreements
- Redelivery payments

If a lessee provides an LOC in place of cash reserves, this is considered equal to cash because LOCs are highly liquid. In the case of redelivery payments, even though they occur at the end of the lease term, they must be considered a form of maintenance coverage.

Maintenance exposure is the value of consumed utility minus the value of collected reserves. It can be construed as the opposite of maintenance coverage, since it shows the level of maintenance that is forced on the lessor due to the lessee's inability to make proper payments.

The main difference between maintenance coverage and maintenance exposure is that maintenance coverage is a measure of how effectively the lessor managed to achieve his/her target maintenance reserve payments, whereas maintenance exposure is the actual excess cost which the lessor would incur after consuming all the collected maintenance reserves.

A lessor can also recover maintenance exposure from subsequent leases. The negotiation skills of a lessor prove vital in such situations in order to convince the subsequent lessee of the desired maintenance reserve rates.

PRE-PAID MAINTENANCE PROGRAMS

Customers and suppliers of critical aerospace components (i.e., jet engines) are recognizing that the acquisition of world-class products is not sufficient, but rather, it is necessary to provide superior, cost-effective maintenance and support services throughout the after-sales phase of the customer–supplier relationship. A major focus of these efforts is redesigning the contractual and implicit relationships between customers and suppliers in the service support supply chain. An important step in this direction was the introduction of the Power by the Hour (PBH) program by Rolls Royce. Since its inception, other manufacturers have been developing their own versions of the program.

Pre-paid maintenance programs, such as PBH eliminate the uncertainty associated with the timing and cost of an engine shop or maintenance event. The expected costs for maintenance are collected on a "by the hour" basis, depending on the number of FHs incurred. This eliminates any uncertainty regarding possible coverage of expenses during a sudden requirement for maintenance. Engine manufacturers also provide ancillary benefits, such as a pool of standby engines, as an incentive to take the PBH agreement, thus eliminating the need for airlines to have an inventory of spare engines. Also, all the hardware is constantly updated, thereby enhancing the life of the engines or the APUs.

From the lessor's perspective, pre-paid maintenance programs have a downside since the lessors no longer hold the payments for maintenance reserves of those components. A direct payment is made by the lessee to the service provider—in most cases, the manufacturer. This raises the issue of what happens to the money for maintenance reserves that is no longer being paid to the lessor. At the end of a lease, the PBH provider will have collected money for a future maintenance event that has not yet occurred. The same applies in a default situation where the PBH contract is terminated by the PBH provider. That provider will typically want to retain the money paid to them, even though they may not have performed the maintenance yet. As a result, it is imperative that the lessor negotiate an agreement with the PBH provider regarding how such money will be returned or credited back to the lessor prior to agreeing to waive reserve payments by the lessee.

On the contrary, a positive element from the lessor's point of view is that *technology risk* is shifted entirely to the manufacturer. Technology risk involves any possible advancement in technology which could mean a further increase in maintenance costs. In addition, pre-paid mainenance contracts typically improve the residual value of an aircraft. Since lessors bear the residual value risks, this fact also offsets the downside of not holding maintenance reserves.

As part of its 787 introduction, Boeing also introduced a new "Gold Care" scheme, which provides coverage for almost all the components on an aircraft (including the airframe) in a type of huge pre-paid maintenance contract. Boeing is now expanding the Gold Care scheme to some of its Next-Gen aircraft as well (Boeing, 2012). This could potentially abolish the idea of maintenance reserve payments to the lessor, which would disrupt the industry but reduce the ambiguity faced by lessees in regard to the lease agreement.

PERIODIC TECHNICAL RECORDS AUDITS

Apart from collecting maintenance reserves, the lessor also has a duty to carry out aircraft due diligence on a periodic basis. This due diligence is referred to as a "Technical records audit."

An audit of all the technical records and the maintenance status of all the main components is carried out by lessors as stipulated in the lease agreement. The frequency of such audits could be annual or in some cases mid-lease. During such an audit, the lessor has representatives rigorously examine all the aircraft documents and records for the period which is being audited. They ensure that operational characteristics, such as weights, are within limits specified in the agreement and that technical characteristics, such as utilizations on all components, are within stipulated levels. These audits are similar to the prepurchase inspection carried out by the lessee prior to the lease. However, the technical records audit focuses more on documentation and the overall maintenance status of the aircraft and its parts.

AIRCRAFT REDELIVERY

Redelivery conditions are specified in lease agreements to help ease the asset transfer to subsequent leases. In most cases, an aircraft at redelivery is expected to fly without major maintenance for a period equal to a normal C-Check interval. The physical condition of the aircraft typically has the most financial significance for both parties, and this can be categorized into four main redelivery requirements (Ackert, 2014):

1. *Physical:* A physical condition assessment of the airframe units, components, systems, and cabin interior. Requirements also include a visual inspection of certified repairs and modifications and a video borescope examination of the engine and APU.
2. *Records:* Lease and regulatory compliance audit of all records—manuals, certificates, statements, repair and modification records, and status reports (ADs, SBs, airframe, engine, APU, landing gear, and components).
3. *Performance:* Verification that the aircraft is operating according to the terms in the lease agreement. For example, the lessor may require an engine power assurance run or trend monitoring report, as well as a demonstration test flight of the aircraft with the lessor's representative on board to verify all systems are functioning properly.

4. *Certification:* Verification of compliance with local regulations—certificate of airworthiness (CoA), export airworthiness approval, supplemental type certificate, and EASA Form 1/FAA Form 8130-3.

Recall from the beginning of the chapter that delivery conditions often dictate return conditions. According to Ackert (2014), redelivery considerations can be split into two main categories: preredelivery and return conditions.

PRE-REDELIVERY CONSIDERATIONS

Returning a leased aircraft is a comprehensive process involving preredelivery meetings, an aircraft records review, and a physical inspection of the asset. Fig. 9.11 displays a typical timeline.

During the preredelivery meetings, the lessor should discuss airworthiness, delivery and redelivery condition gaps, the current status of high-cost components, and any factors that might delay the final transfer. Ultimately, both parties should review all lease terms prior to redelivery. Furthermore, lessors should consider obtaining full technical report including the scope of upcoming maintenance events, up-to-date interior configuration, recent shop visit history, engine disk sheets, trend monitoring results, and a copy of the lessee's current maintenance program.

Following the initial meeting, the lessor should review all records to ensure that they are accurate, complete, compliant, and easy to understand. Because this is such a time-consuming process, the lessee is expected to provide all documents in an organized and timely manner.

The last step is the physical inspection. This typically takes place between 1 and 2 weeks prior to the scheduled redelivery. The inspection addresses the technical requirements mentioned above and culminates into an overall condition assessment of the aircraft's structure, components, systems, and interior.

RETURN CONDITION CONSIDERATIONS

Because proper maintenance is so critical to the residual value of an aircraft, return condition is a high priority for lessors. We covered some of these conditions (i.e., mirror-in/mirror-out and zero

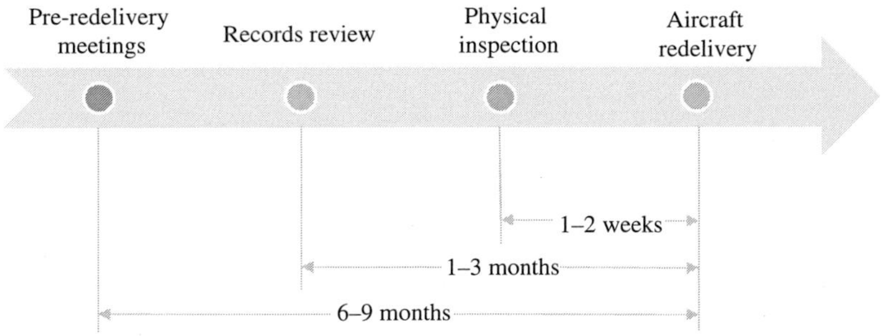

FIGURE 9.11

Timeline for preredelivery considerations.

From Ackert, S. (2012). Basics of aircraft maintenance reserve development and management. *Aircraft Monitor.*

life/full life) earlier in the chapter. General return considerations include aircraft condition at return, airworthiness certification, redelivery checks and part lives, and aircraft documentation and standards.

Again, the condition of aircraft at return is generally expected to be in line with the delivery conditions. No components should have abnormal levels of deterioration. Once these return conditions have been complied with, the lease may be terminated and the applicable regulatory body will remove the aircraft from the lessee's operating certificate and, in the case of a foreign registration, deregister the aircraft. Moreover, if the new lessee intends to operate the aircraft in an outside jurisdiction, the lessor must obtain an export CoA. Without this certificate, the aircraft cannot be re-registered to operate under the new lessee.

Lessors must also ensure that redelivery checks have been completed and that part lives are in line with the approved maintenance program. This involves thorough checks of each component to verify the amount of life remaining. The final consideration is to ensure that all aircraft documents are accurate and up to standard. Any discrepancy will make delivery of the aircraft to the next lessee much more difficult.

Once all considerations are satisfied, the aircraft is redelivered to the lessor who can then re-lease the asset to a new lessee, sell to a buyer, or part it out. Ideally, if a lessor wishes to re-lease or sell the aircraft, he/she would begin remarketing the aircraft well in advance of its redelivery. This minimizes downtime and maximizes the revenue on the overall investment.

APPENDIX 9A: LETTER OF CREDIT

LETTER OF CREDIT

_________ [__]

Letter of Credit No. ____________

Beneficiary: Lessor XXXX Aircraft Leasing No. Three Ltd (the "**Beneficiary**")

Attention:	[•]
Applicant:	Operator YYYYY Limited
Amount:	[$-----------------------]
Expiry:	[------------------------]
Place:	-------------------------
Payable:	at the counters of ----------------

Sir:

We hereby establish in your favor, at the request and for the account of Operator XYZ Limited, our irrevocable, unconditional and transferable standby letter of credit in the amount of $[-------------] ([------------------------------------] United States Dollars) (the "**Stated Amount**") towards deposit for aircraft bearing manufacturer serial number------. This Letter of Credit is available against presentation of a certificate in the form of **Exhibit A** hereto (signed by an authorized representative of the Beneficiary or another individual being or purporting to be your authorized representative, if not submitted by SWIFT).

Such presentation must be made on a Business Day to our Letter of Credit Department [in New York] at [Bank's address] (Facsimile Number: [____]; Confirmation Number: [___________]) on or before [---------------------] ("**Expiry Date**") or if such date is not a Business Day, then on or before the following Business Day. Any such presentation may be made by means of Authenticated SWIFT to ______________, marked clearly for the attention of --------------------. In addition, any certificate hereunder may be presented by mail, express courier (e.g., DHL) or in person.

A certificate presented hereunder may be in an amount of up to the Stated Amount. You shall be entitled to present an unlimited number of certificates hereunder, subject to the aggregate amount of such certificates not exceeding the Stated Amount.

All sums payable to you pursuant to this Letter of Credit shall be unconditionally and irrevocably paid in United States Dollars, in immediately available funds, in full, without any set-off or counterclaim whatsoever and free & clear of all deductions or withholdings whatsoever.

We hereby agree with you that each certificate presented hereunder in compliance with the terms hereof will be duly honored by our payment to you (or in accordance with your instruction) of the amount of such certificate in immediately available funds.

The amount available for drawing under this Letter of Credit will be automatically reduced by the amount specified in each certificate, which is paid in accordance with the terms hereof. Except as otherwise provided herein, this Letter of Credit shall be governed by and construed in accordance with the Uniform Customs and Practice for Documentary Credits (1993 Revision), ICC Publication No. 500 (the "**UCP**").

This Letter of Credit may be transferred and assigned by you in its entirety more than once provided we receive notice of each transfer in entirety pursuant in the form of **Exhibit B** (Transfer Form).

This Letter of Credit sets forth in full the terms of our undertaking and shall not in any way be modified, amended or amplified by reference to any documents, instruments or agreements referred to herein, or in which this Letter of Credit is referred to, or to which this Letter of Credit relates and any such reference shall not be deemed to incorporate herein by reference any such documents, instruments and agreements.

All banking charges, including any advising and negotiating bank charges, are for the account of Applicant.

This Letter of Credit is effective from the date hereof.

All communications under this Letter of Credit by the beneficiary shall be addressed to:

Bank Name:	[------------------------------]
Bank Address:	[•]
Contact Name:	[•]
Tel: -	[•]
Fax: -	[•]

With copy to:

[Operator XYZ Ltd]

Attn: [----------------------]

Address: [---]

Telephone: [----------------------]

Fax: [----------------------]

In this Letter of Credit:

"**Business Day**" means a day other than a Saturday, a Sunday or a holiday scheduled by law on which banks are open for business in New York City, London, and --------------------.

Yours faithfully

[•]

By ____________________

Name:

Title:

APPENDIX 9B: FORM OF STATUS REPORT

FORM OF STATUS REPORT

To: Lessor ABC Aircraft Leasing No. Three Limited

From: Operator XYZ Limited

Aircraft: One Airbus ------- AC TYPE -------- 200 Aircraft Manufacturer's Serial Number -------- MSN ---------

Month of: _________

Aircraft Total Time (Flight Hours) Since New:	
Aircraft Total Cycles Since New:	
Airframe Flight Hours Flown During Month:	
Airframe Cycles/Landing During Month:	
Time Remaining to ** Check:	

Engine Serial Number:		Engine Serial Number:	
Original Position:		Original Position:	
Actual Location:		Actual Location:	
Total Time Since New:		Total Time Since New:	
Total Cycles Since New:		Total Cycles Since New:	
Running Hours During Month:		Running Hours During Month:	
Cycles During Month:		Cycles During Month:	

APU Serial Number:	
Original Position:	
Actual Location:	
Total Time Since New:	
Total Cycles Since New:	
APU Hours During Month:	

Cycles During Month:				
Landing Gear:	Time Since Overhaul:	Time Since New:	Cycles Since Overhaul:	Cycles Since New:
RH Main:				
Central Main:				
LH Main:				
Nose:				

Note: If an Engine is removed or installed on another Aircraft (subject to the provisions of the Agreement) it must be reported monthly on this form.

Any engineering modifications or changes:

……………………………………………………………………………………………

……………………………………………………………………………………………

[Any service bulletins and Airworthiness Directives accomplished for/during [the previous year/since Delivery:

……………………………………………………………………………………………]

	Flight Hours Running Hours Cycles During Month	x	US$ Per Flight Hour/Running Hour/Month	=	Reserve payment
Airframe:	Flight Hours:	x		=	
Original Engine Serial Number:	Running Hours:	x		=	
Original Engine Serial Number:	Running Hours:	x		=	
Total Engines:	Running Hours:	x		=	
LLP:	Cycles:	x		=	
Landing Gear:	Running Hours:	x		=	
APU:	APU Hours:	x		=	
Total					

APPENDIX 9C: REDELIVERY RECEIPT

REDELIVERY RECEIPT

This Redelivery Receipt is delivered, on the date set out below, by Lessor ABC Aircraft Leasing No. Three Limited (the "Lessor") and Operator XYZ Limited (the "Lessee") pursuant to the Aircraft Lease Agreement dated [•] 2008 between the Lessor and the Lessee (the "Agreement").

Capitalized terms used in this Receipt shall have the meanings given to such terms in the Agreement.

1 Details of acceptance

The Lessor hereby confirms to the Lessee that the Lessor has at ______ o'clock [am/pm] (London time) on this ______ day of ______, at ______ accepted redelivery of the following under the Agreement:

(a) Airframe

Airbus

_______AC TYPE_______200

Reg.: S/N:

(b) Engines

_______Engine Type______ S/N No.1: S/N No. 2:

(c) APU

Type: __________ S/N:

(d) Equipment Check List: as per list signed by the Lessor and the Lessee and attached hereto;

(e) Manuals and Technical Documents: as per list signed by the Lessor and the Lessee and attached hereto at Annex 1; and

(f) Place of acceptance:

2 Fuel at Redelivery

Fuel on board at Redelivery: ______ kilos (______ gallons).

3 Flight Hours / Running Hours / Cycles

The Airframe and Engines had the following Flight Hours/Running Hours/Cycles at the date hereof:

(a) Airframe:

Total hours Total landings since last "12 years" Check

______ Flight Hours

______ Cycles

(b) Engines:

Position	Serial No.	Total Running Hours	Total Cycles	Since last shop visit	Since last Engine Performance Restoration Visit
1				______ Flight Hours ______ Cycles	______ Flight Hours ______ Cycles
2				______ Flight Hours ______ Cycles	______ Flight Hours ______ Cycles

(c) APU:

Part No. / Serial No. Total APU Hours since last shop visit / new

______ APU Hours

(d) Landing Gear:

Landing Gear	Serial No.	Time Since Overhaul	Time Since New	Cycles Since Overhaul	Cycles Since New
RH Main:					
Central Main:					
LH Main:					
Nose:					

(e) **Brakes** (information to be provided on attached sheet)

Serial No. Pin Length

4 The leasing of the Aircraft by the Lessor to the Lessee pursuant to the Agreement is hereby terminated without prejudice to the Lessee's continuing obligations under the Agreement.

5 The Lessor confirms to the Lessee that at the time indicated above the Aircraft, Manuals and Technical Documents listed in Annex 1 attached hereto are in accordance with the specifications of the Agreement and satisfactory in all respects, subject to the discrepancies noted on Annex 3. The acceptance of the Aircraft is subject to the Lessee fulfilling its obligation to remedy each of the items listed in Annex 3 hereto.

In witness whereof, the Lessor and the Lessee have, by their duly authorized representatives, executed this Receipt on the date specified in paragraph 1 above.

Lessor ABC Aircraft Leasing No. Three Limited

____

By:

Title:

Operator XYZ Limited

____

By:

Title:

Annex 1 Manuals and Technical Documents

Annex 2 Aircraft Equipment List

Annex 3 Discrepancy List

Annex 4 List of Engine LLPs showing number of Engine Cycles since new

Annex 5 Brakes Pin length

APPENDIX 9D: PREDELIVERY INSPECTION

PRE DELIVERY INSPECTION

Excerpt from a purchase agreement:

Section 4: Pre Delivery Inspection

Purchaser, at its cost and expense, shall be entitled to inspect the Aircraft on or before the Delivery Date in order to satisfy itself that the Aircraft meets the Delivery Condition Requirements. Unless otherwise specified in Part I, point 14 of the Purchase Agreement, such inspection (the "Inspection") shall be made at a time and place to be notified by Seller, but in any event within 10 days after the date of this Agreement. The Inspection shall include:

i. A physical inspection of the relevant Aircraft Documents;
ii. A physical inspection of the Aircraft and Parts; and
iii. Unless otherwise specified in Part I, point 14 of the Purchase Agreement:
  a. Completion of a full video borescope inspection of (A) the low pressure and high pressure compressors and (B) the turbine area of the Engines and a full video bore scope of the APU, with the Party selecting the inspector and bearing the cost of the inspection being as specified in Part I, point 14 of the Purchase Agreement;
  b. Completion of engine condition runs in accordance with the applicable maintenance manual;
  c. Inspecting the Aircraft for existence of structural repairs and the conformity of those repairs to the Manufacturer's Structural Repair Manual or Manufacturer's Recommendations, as applicable; and
  d. Completion of a demonstration flight in accordance with the procedure agreed between Seller and Purchaser (with the Party bearing the cost of the flight, the maximum duration of the flight, the procedure agreed to by Purchaser and Seller for the flight and number of Purchaser's representatives permitted as on board observers being as specified in Part I, point 14 of the Purchase Agreement).

If on completion of the Inspection, Purchaser is not satisfied that the Aircraft meets the Delivery Condition Requirements, Purchaser shall provide prompt notice to Seller in writing thereof, specifying in reasonable detail the items which do not conform to the Delivery Condition Requirements.

APPENDIX 9E: MINI CASE STUDY

MINI CASE STUDY

Syndicate Leasing is an aircraft leasing company headquartered in Los Angeles, California. Syndicate has a well-diversified fleet of aircraft that includes both widebody and narrowbody models. Syndicate's fleet mix is slightly more weighted towards Airbus but also possesses a wide range of Boeing models. The current fleet is composed of 140 aircraft, 90 of which are Airbus and 50 of which are Boeing. As is the case with any growing leasing company, Syndicate is more invested in the narrowbody aircraft due to their liquid nature. Sixty five out of the 90 Airbus aircraft are A320s and 40 out of the 50 Boeing aircraft are B737s.

In the next few months, one of the A320s, which is currently leased to Direct Jet Airlines, is coming off lease. Direct Jet, having used the aircraft for its first six years, has maintained the aircraft extremely well, and as of today, all the return conditions of the aircraft are expected to be successfully met. Syndicate would now like to re-lease the aircraft to Star Airways, who approached them with a request to lease an A320 for 10 years. The timing of the release of aircraft from Direct Jet is in line with the required delivery date proposed by Star Airways. Currently, Syndicate and Star are in the process of negotiating the final lease agreement.

Upon a detailed credit analysis by Syndicate, it was found that Star Airways is a start-up low cost carrier and does not have a good enough credit rating to bypass payment of maintenance reserves. Star Airways has agreed to make cash maintenance reserve payments. Thus, Syndicate must now provide Star Airways with the reserve rates for the various maintenance events.

As an analyst working for Syndicate, it is your responsibility to thoroughly analyze all the available data and present the appropriate reserve rates for the five major maintenance events covered by the maintenance reserves. Combining the data obtained from the previous operator Direct Jet and the expected operation criteria provided by Star Airways, the following information has been compiled:

Direct Jet operated the aircraft for an average of 4,000 FH per year, over the six years. Also, the APU on average was operated for 3,000 APU FH per year. Star Airways expects that its average utilization will be 3,750 FH for the aircraft and 2,800 FH for the APU. Both Direct Jet and Star Airways consider the engine flight hours to be in line with the overall flight hours for the aircraft. Also, Star Airways, being headquartered in Norway, is expected to fly short haul, with an average of 3 Flight Hours for every 2 Flight cycles. This will be the average utilization used to predict the appropriate reserve rates for Star Airways. Star Airways has agreed to pay all payments in US currency, so the rates need to be provided in USD. Direct Jet followed a certain Maintenance Planning Document (MPD) laid out by Airbus, and Star Airways has agreed to follow the same Maintenance Program. The intervals laid out in the Maintenance program are as follows:

Maintenance Equipment	Maintenance Event	Maintenance Interval		
		Flight Hours	Flight Cycles	Calendar Months
Airframe	4C/ 6 Yr SI	18,000	12,000	72 months
	8C/ 12 Yr SI	36,000	24,000	144 months
Landing Gear	Overhaul	-	20,000	120 months
APU	Restoration	6,500	-	-
Engine	Restoration	25,000	-	-

The Engine LLPs life limits and cost of replacement for each of the LLPs is provided by the OEM, and is shown below:

LLP	FC Limit	Maintenance Cost
1	25,000	$150,000
2	20,000	$30,000
3	30,000	$100,000
4	27,600	$120,000
5	20,000	$240,000
6	25,000	$80,000
7	30,000	$180,000

Syndicate would like to assume a stub life of 10% for all the LLPs.

In order to determine the correct reserve rate for the engine, the severity factor and the environment adjustment factor must be appropriately applied to the base rate.

The severity factor, based on various levels of flight legs and derates for the engine, is provided below. The assumed base operation for the engine can be seen from the table, but the expected average flight leg for Star Airways must be applied to the base rate. The engine is expected to be operated at a 10% derate.

FL	Engine Derate				
	0%	5%	10%	15%	20%
1.0	1.850	1.750	1.650	1.550	1.450
1.5	1.350	1.250	1.200	1.150	1.100
2.0	1.100	1.050	1.000	0.950	0.900
2.5	0.980	0.930	0.880	0.830	0.780
3.0	0.900	0.850	0.800	0.780	0.735
3.5	0.825	0.800	0.775	0.750	0.725
4.0	0.800	0.775	0.750	0.725	0.715

The environment adjustment factors for different regions of operation are as follows:

Region of Operation	Environment factor
Temperate Region	1.00
Cold Region	1.05
Hot/Dry Region	1.10
Erosive Region	1.20

Finally, the expected cost of maintenance for each of the major maintenance events are provided below:

Maintenance Equipment	Maintenance Event	Maintenance Cost
Airframe	4C/ 6 Yr SI	$1,550,000
	8C/ 12 Yr SI	$1,700,000
Landing Gear	Overhaul	$890,000
APU	Restoration	$360,000
Engine	Restoration	$1,900,000 (Base Cost)

Using all the above information, provide Syndicate Leasing with the most accurate and appropriate reserve rates to be charged for the five main maintenance events. An annual escalation of 3% is applied to all the maintenance reserve rates.

Assuming the first lease with Direct Jet started on Jan 1st 2011 and the lease with Star Airways will start on Jan 1st 2017, estimate the possible event dates (prior and next) for all major maintenance events. Also, model the maintenance reserve cash flow for Syndicate from the Star Airways lease.

ACKNOWLEDGMENT

We would like to thank Shannon Ackert of Jackson Square Aviation for providing guidance and significant portions of information that is presented in this chapter.

REFERENCES

Ackert, S. (2011a). Aircraft Monitor. *The relationship between an aircraft's value and its maintenance status.* Aircraft Monitor.

Ackert, S. (2011b). *Engine maintenance concepts for financiers.* Aircraft Monitor.

Ackert, S. (2012). *Basics of aircraft maintenance reserve development and management.* Aircraft Monitor.

Ackert, S. (2014). *Redelivery considerations in aircraft operating leases.* Aircraft Monitor.

Boeing. (2012). *The advantages of lifecycle solution from the airplane OEM.* Boeing Edge, Integrated Services.

Federal Aviation Administration (FAA). (2012). *Advisory circular 121-22C, subject: Maintenance Review Boards, Maintenance Type Boards, and OEM/TCH Recommended Maintenance Procedures.*

CHAPTER

TRANSACTION COST MODELING 10

CHAPTER OUTLINE

INTRODUCTION

Currently 40% of the world's fleet is on operating leases, and forecasts predict that this percentage will continue to grow (Boeing, 2018). With estimated annual growth of about 6%, the aircraft leasing industry reports that its top 50 lessors alone manage 7500 aircraft valued at $200 billion.

Aircraft Leasing and Financing. DOI: https://doi.org/10.1016/B978-0-12-815285-0.00010-9

Mergers and acquisitions have led to consolidation, and countries like Ireland are becoming leasing hubs. Recently China Construction Bank has elected to locate the global headquarters of its growing aircraft leasing business in Dublin—the fourth to do so directly in recent years (Raghavan, 2017). Some of today's top leasing companies are GE Capital Aviation Services, AerCap, Airlease, and Avolon. According to Boeing's *Current Aircraft Finance Market Outlook (2018)*, lessors accounted for 70% of the volume in the capital markets as they accessed the capital markets for unsecured debts and Asset Backed Securities to finance their portfolios (Boeing Capital Corporation, 2018). New funding sources, such as the Aircraft Finance Insurance Consortium (AFIC), have emerged to bring insurance risk capital to aircraft finance. Because of the growing popularity of aircraft leasing, it is important to understand the variables that impact a lease transaction and how to model cash flows for a lessor.

In Chapter 3 we outlined the lease versus buy decision for the lessee and discussed some important variables (such as lease payment, depreciation, and residual value) that affected the lessor's return calculations and then examined the range of lease payments that would be acceptable to both the lessee and lessor. In Chapter 9 we discussed maintenance reserves (MRs) and how it impacts the lessor's returns. In this chapter we integrate and extend these ideas discussed in Chapters 3 and 9 and examine in detail the factors that drive the lessor's return. Our focus throughout this chapter is on the lessor as the lessee's decision to lease versus buy was discussed in detail in Chapter 3.

Transaction modeling is a multifaceted process in aircraft leasing. For a lessor, the evolving method of aircraft acquisition over the past several decades has led to two main types of leases—sale and leaseback (incremental acquisitions)—and used or order book leases (placement of aircraft a lessor already owns or has committed to purchase from a manufacturer). The important factors that drive a lessor's return in these two types of lease structure will be very different. For example, in a new aircraft order book transaction, the lessor needs to take into account the availability of the aircraft from the manufacturer, the extent of customization required for not only the first lessee, but subsequent lessees as well. For used aircraft, from the lessor's existing portfolio, the lessor has to analyze the proper lease rental to charge, residual value, and target return for this aircraft at the time of release. In a sale and leaseback transaction, on the other hand, the lease rental charged would be a function of the purchase price. If the lessor pays a high purchase price upfront, then the lessor would seek to recover this over time by charging a higher lease payment in order to get an adequate rate of return and vice versa.

In effect, for the lessor, the cash flows from a lease are inputs into a capital-budgeting process. The cash flow model will include factors such as aircraft purchase price, lease payments, interest payments, inflows and outflows of MRs or end of lease adjustment, sales proceeds, and residual value at the end of the lease term. All these factors will have an impact on return calculations. Using financial models, the above cash flows from the lease are used to determine the estimated return and conduct sensitivity analysis. Net present value (NPV) and internal rate of return (IRR) tools are used to make decisions about whether the lease will add value or not. At the backend, the lessor finances the cost of the acquisition of the aircraft with either commercial bank debt, accessing the capital markets, or by paying cash. The lease is profitable only if the cash flows of the lease result in the desired rate of return on investment (IRR) greater than cost of capital to finance the aircraft and a positive NPV for the project. It is important therefore to understand the key cash flows in transaction modeling. In the next section we examine each of these cash flow variables in detail.

FACTORS AFFECTING CASH FLOWS FOR A LESSOR

We discuss below the important cash flows for a lessor and the factors that influence these cash flows.

PURCHASE PRICE

Purchase price can be thought of as the current market value of an aircraft. Purchase prices are not often disclosed, and it is often difficult to get a sense of what the true transaction price is. Apart from the confidential nature of the transaction, an important reason for lack of transparency in prices is because every aircraft order is unique. For example, the price for an airline that orders 100 aircraft of the same type and configuration, requiring one type of training package for pilots, mechanics, and instructors, would be lower than a lessor who wants each aircraft to be customized to meet the specific needs of each of its lessee. The need for customization increases the cost to the manufacturer and therefore the price of the delivered aircraft. This is the primary reason that lessors may pay more than airlines for a new aircraft. Further, the industry standard is to think of current market value as the value of an aircraft in half-life condition (halfway between significant overhauls of major parts and components). From a modeling perspective, one should think of current market value as a price the lessor should pay for an aircraft and expect to make a fair return on the investment in the medium term. The factors that affect purchase price can be grouped into four important factors, namely, aircraft determinants, manufacturer determinants, market determinants, and regulatory factors.

Aircraft determinants

The important aircraft determinants that affect the value of the aircraft are the aircraft's age, aircraft specifications, aircraft operating history, aircraft family and technology, aircraft operating economics, aircraft production, and aircraft geographic and customer dispersion. We discuss each of these factors below.

Aircraft age

Though an older aircraft can be operational as long as it is properly maintained, as an aircraft ages, its residual value tends to decline and becomes less stable as newer technology aircraft become available. For example, the A320ceo's value declined once Airbus introduced the A320neo because the A320neo incorporated new technology. Further, as the aircraft ages, future maintenance checks would involve greater amount of nonroutine airframe and engine maintenance tasks which increases the cost of maintenance of the older aircraft, leading to greater costs and less time in service (lower productivity).

Aircraft specifications

Aircraft are usually offered with optional features such as engine and thrust options, operating weights, avionics, winglets (sharklets), and interior configurations (cabin and Buyer Furnished Equipment). Of these factors, operating weights, engine and thrust options, and flight deck configuration have the most impact on value (Ackert, 2012b). For example, an aircraft having a higher maximum certified weight increases an aircraft's utility, and airframe manufacturers routinely charge premiums for higher design weights. The 737-800, for example, has maximum takeoff weight (MTOW) options ranging from 155,000 lb up to 174,000 lb, making it a popular aircraft. For a new aircraft, the value differential between the lower and higher MTOW alternatives is approximately $1.75 million.

Aircraft are also offered with engines from different manufacturers and at different thrust levels. For example, the A320neo has a choice of two new-generation engines (the Pure Power PW1100G-JM from Pratt and Whitney and the LEAP-1A from CFM International) while the 737 Max comes with one engine option (the LEAP-1B from CFM International). However, when it comes to engine options, fragmentation among multiple manufacturers tends to make remarketing more difficult.

In addition to engine options from manufacturers, engine types are offered with a range of thrust ratings to choose from. Engines with a higher thrust level option command a premium compared to aircraft equipped with the standard thrust level. For example, the value difference between a 737NG equipped with a CFM56-7B26 engine rated at 26,300 lb compared to a CFM56-7B24 rated at 24,200 lb can be on the order of $1.4–$1.6 million. Finally, with regard to an aircraft flight deck configuration, a good rule of thumb is that uniqueness is bad and generic is good. This is one of the reasons why avionics and airframe manufacturers are designing aircraft today with cockpits that can be reconfigured with software changes (e.g., converting from metric to imperial). A more generic or adaptable flight deck will increase an aircraft's market value because of its ability to be transitioned at a lower cost into a follow-on airline's fleet.

Aircraft operating history

An aircraft that is operated in normal conditions with average utilization and stage length will retain its value better than another aircraft that is operated under extreme climate and has been operated on frequent smaller flight legs.

Aircraft family and technology

Aircraft family is attractive for an airline because they provide fleet and capacity planning flexibility. There are economic and logistic benefits of operating within a family of aircraft such as the A320 and B737 families. Aircraft in these families share common parts, training requirements, and other characteristics. For example, the A320 family that includes the A318, A319, A320, and A321 all feature fly-by-wire flight control systems and seat passengers ranging from 110 for the A318 to 240 for the A321neo, providing for fleet commonality, common parts and common training for the pilots. This allows an airline more flexibility in how and where they deploy aircraft, matching capacity to demand seasonally, or even on a day-by-day or hour-by-hour basis.

Technological improvements in engines and airframe have improved economic performance and have extended the economic life of the aircraft. For example, the engine manufacturers have constantly strived to introduce new technology such as the geared turban fan and have been able to increase fuel efficiency and reduce engine noise and emissions. The airframers have introduced new lightweight composite material and introduced winglets (sharklets) to improve fuel efficiency and performance. Composite material is also more resistant to fatigue (cracks) and corrosion that reduce the number and frequency of maintenance inspections, and thereby lowering the associated maintenance cost.

Aircraft operating economics

Aircraft operating economics will depend on payload characteristics (number of seats available and cargo space), range capability, and speed characteristics. The key expense drivers for an aircraft are maintenance, fuel, and ownership costs. As mentioned above, new engine and airframe technology have improved fuel efficiency and reduced maintenance cost, contributing directly to an airline's bottom line.

Manufacturer determinants

The actions of the original equipment manufacturer (OEM) will also have an effect on aircraft value or price. The important factors that drive the value of an aircraft from the manufacturer side are as follows: pricing strategy of the manufacturer, manufacturer demise, and production run decisions. We briefly examine each of these factors and its effect on aircraft value.

Pricing strategy of the manufacturer

It is well known that manufacturers usually give deep discounts from their list prices when they sell their aircraft. The discounts offered by manufacturers to customers influence the value of the aircraft because aircraft sold for a higher price and therefore lower discounts tend to maintain their value better than aircraft sold at deep discounts. For aircraft that are not popular, the manufacturer is forced to continue discounting the prices of these aircraft. If deep discounts persist then it can have an adverse impact on value over time, and in particular, the residual value. The control exercised by the OEMs also influences the price. For example, some engine manufacturers such as Rolls Royce control the network of repair shops to owned facilities, which can limit competition for the repair work as well as limit the ability to utilize used parts (Rolls, in this case, is incentivized to sell new parts for their engine overhauls) which in turn can drive up operating costs for aircraft that use the Rolls Royce engines. This is often offset through additional discounting at the time of purchase or through hourly maintenance agreements.

Manufacturer demise

The demise of either the airframe and engine manufacturer will have a negative impact on values as there is no certainty that a manufacturer will be around to support through its life cycle, such as issuing service bulletins, product improvements, updates to the maintenance planning document, etc.

Production run

Aircraft that are still in production tend to retain their values and lease rates better than aircraft that have ceased production. If an OEM has an aircraft with a large production run, the aircraft residual values tend to be higher than industry average. For example, the Boeing 737 is a very popular aircraft because it has been in production since 1965 and has variants flying today.

Further, the stage in the production run for the aircraft is also an important determinant of value. For example, aircraft early in their production run tend to be heavier, have lower gross weights and thrusts, and have higher direct operating cost compared to mid and later production run aircraft. In contrast, aircraft manufactured at the end of a production run tend to have steeper declines in future value as they are competing with newer technology aircraft (Ackert, 2012b).

For example, the B787s will have a higher price than an aircraft in its last leg of the production cycle such as A330ceos. It is however possible that a couple of years after production has ceased for an aircraft, the aircraft demand and supply dynamics may change which may make these aircraft a better investment down the line. For example, Boeing discontinued the production of the B757 in 2004 as sales waned. Now about 14 years later, airlines feel there is still a need for an aircraft of this type as it fills a crucial gap in the middle of the market between the B737 and B787. Unfortunately, there are not a lot of these aircraft currently available, and therefore, anyone having access to this aircraft can negotiate a favorable sale price or lease rate for the aircraft relative to the net investment. Thus, though investing in the B757 in 2004 may not have been optimal investment, for an investor purchasing the B757 a decade later, it was a very profitable investment as supply dwindles and the last of the line aircraft are the highest quality aircraft available.

Aircraft supply and demand

Manufacturers influence the aircraft's price by their level of production. If they produce more than the prevailing demand, it creates excess supply and therefore drives the price lower. Table 10.1 illustrates the increasing demand for newer aircraft as reflected by increasing prices. As demand for air travel increases worldwide, the backlogs of Boeing and Airbus (for certain aircraft) continue to result in 5 + years of order delays. This will impact the supply of these aircraft and hence the purchase price.

Further, as manufacturers incorporate the latest airframe and engine technology in their production, older less efficient aircraft are retired or taken out of service, which leads to decline in the current market value of these aircraft. For example, most of the first generation pre-1995 A320s with CFM56-5A or V2500-A1 engines were retired, because they had a performance disadvantage, compared to the more recent engine variants. Another example was the increase in the retirement rates for the A340, because airlines considered it to be an inefficient aircraft (four engines versus two for the B777 and A330) and replaced with the B777 and later the A330. This led Airbus to discontinue the production of A340 in 2011. Thus, when an aircraft is inefficient, airlines take it out of service, and because there is less demand and more supply, values tend to fall, which then leads to relatively high retirement rate and manufacturers discontinuing production.

Table 10.1 New Average Aircraft List Prices in 2018 (in $ Millions)

	Aircraft Type	Price		Aircraft Type	Price
Widebody	787-9	281.6	*Narrowbody*	737-700	85.8
	777-300ER	361.5		737-900ER	108.4
	747-8	402.9		737 MAX 8	117.1
	A330-300	264.2		A319	92.3
	A350-900	317.4		A320	101.0
	A380-800	445.6		A320neo	110.6

Boeing and Airbus.

Manufacturer reliability and support

Aircraft production is a combination of product strategy, engineering, large-scale manufacturing, ability to support and ability to attract asset-based financing at reasonably attractive terms. It is very important for a manufacturer to assure their customers that the aircraft they purchase are reliable and the manufacture will support their product. There are a lot of new aircraft manufacturers that have entered the market in recent years such as the Commercial Aircraft Corporation of China, and the Russian Manufacturer, JSC Sukhoi Company. These new entrants, however, will have to establish themselves and convince their buyers that their aircraft will have the same reliability, support, and financing available as that of currently established manufacturers such as Boeing, Airbus, Bombardier, and Embraer. To help offset this concern, they maybe forced, at least until they have established a positive reputation, to offer a competitive price or demonstrate that they have the necessary infrastructure to support their aircraft after it is sold to the customer.

A recent example of how important manufacturer support is for maintenance and other work on the aircraft is the issue facing Interjet, a Mexican low-cost carrier, which purchased the Sukhoi Super jet 100 (SSJ100). The airline was very pleased initially with its purchase, as it was able to get very favorable pricing with JSC Sukhoi for the SSJ100. However, shortly after delivery, they ran into issues with delays in engine maintenance, which grounded the jets. Part of the issue comes from the fact that JSC Sukhoi does not have a single maintenance facility in the Americas, whereas Airbus SE, which supports the rest of Interjet's fleet of A320 and A321 aircraft, has multiple maintenance facilities in the Americas. In order to solve the issue, Interjet has had to resort to the extreme measure of cannibalizing parts of some of the fleet in order to keep the rest of the fleet running. This example shows that reliability and support from the manufacturer is a crucial determinant of price of an aircraft. In retrospect, the reputational damage from thousands of canceled flights, and the lost revenue from those canceled flights, was likely to be well in excess of the initial discounts received on the purchase price of the aircraft.

Market determinants

Market determinants that have an important effect on value retention can be grouped as aircraft's order book, market penetration, surplus/shortages, secondary market and liquidity, economic determinants, and regulation. The following sections discuss each of the market-driven factors further.

Order book

An aircraft's order book shows details about the number of firm orders outstanding, which is subdivided into number of deliveries (in service and storage) and number on firm backlog. The order book is an indication of the market share of an aircraft and has a large impact on value retention. Aircraft with large order book are more liquid, and have lower risk, as they are easier to purchase and finance and can be easily remarketed. Currently the most liquid aircraft tend to be narrowbody aircraft such as the A320 family from Airbus and the 737NG family from Boeing. Table 10.2 shows the order book for some popular narrow- and widebody aircraft. When reviewing an aircraft order book, it is important to look not only at the quantity of backlog in the order book but also for the quality of the order book. While a healthy backlog is important to ensure long production run, an excessive backlog may show problems with production and supple bottlenecks. Further, it is important to analyze the order book to see that they are predominantly from airlines rather than

Table 10.2 Airbus and Boeing Aircraft Orders and Backlog (as of April 30, 2018)

Aircraft Type	Orders	Deliveries	Backlog
A320neo	4098	267	3831
A330-300	787	741	46
A350–900	664	166	498
A380	331	226	115
B737 MAX	4504	120	4384
B777-X	326	0	326
B787-9	753	326	457

Airbus and Boeing.

from lessors as the lessor orders tend to be more speculative than based on future need. Finally, it is important to discern how the aircraft is being deployed and the user base (low cost, network, and regional). In general, wider deployment and broader carrier usage would tend to support higher residual values.

Market penetration

Market penetration has a significant influence on an aircraft's value retention. Aircraft with significant market penetration implies that the aircraft has a wide customer and geographical base. If multiple airlines operate the aircraft in different parts of the world, the market will be much more liquid and the residual higher than if there are only a few operators. Currently the most liquid new generation aircraft, the A320neo and B737 MAX, have a wide customer base spread out over a wide geographical base. For example, B737 MAX (all variants) has over 4504 firm orders spread over 97 customers (Boeing, 2018). Table 10.3 shows that on the other hand, the A380 has not retained its value, partly because it has only 331 orders and 13 customers and its geographical base is restricted to Europe, Asia-Pacific, and the Middle East (Airbus, 2018).

Surplus/Shortages

Surplus aircraft, as indicated by higher numbers in storage, may indicate that there is oversupply of aircraft that may result in current market values being depressed. On the other hand, a shortage of aircraft implies strong demand leading to an increase in current market value. However, it is important to distinguish whether aircraft are stored due to technological obsolescence or for economic factors (Forsberg, 2015). The important difference is that an aircraft that is stored for technological obsolescence may not return to service as compared to aircraft stored for economic reasons (Ackert, 2012b). Usually during an economic recession or period of elevated fuel prices, older aircraft are the first to be placed into storage, compared to younger or newer aircraft. Often the values of these older aircraft never recover following a recession (Ackert, 2012b).

Secondary market considerations

The liquidity of the secondary market for an aircraft will also influence its value. There are different options available to deploy older aircraft in the secondary market. First, these aircraft can be

Table 10.3 Airline Operators of Different Aircraft Types

Aircraft Type	Number of Operators
737-800	178
737 MAX 8	54
A320	240
A320neo	68
A330	124
A350	17
A380	13

Mason (2017) and Airbus.

sold or leased to second/third tier operators. Second, if it is feasible, these aircraft can be converted into freighters. Third, the aircraft can be parted out for engines and other usable components (Ackert, 2012b). For example, with a limited operator base, the 777 and A380 market values have suffered due to the lack of secondary market prospects. There are a very limited number of airlines which can operate an aircraft of this size, and hence a limited market to lease the aircraft. At present there is not a cargo conversion available to create an alternative market either.

Economic determinants

An aircraft, just like any other manufactured good, is affected by market factors. If there is a recession, aircraft prices tend to be depressed compared to when the economy is healthy. If interest rates are high, then cost of borrowing is higher and demand for older aircraft maybe higher, as customers would prefer that over more expensive newer aircraft. Market availability will also influence price. The higher the number of available aircraft, the lower the value and lease rates.

The price of oil also plays a significant role in aircraft values as well. As fuel prices began to rise in 2000, aircraft manufacturers made it a priority to invest and build fuel efficient aircraft. Airlines also began to place orders for these fuel efficient aircraft such as the 787, A350, A320neo, and the 737MAX. In 2015, the price of fuel began to decline rapidly. At that time, it made greater economic sense for airlines to continue using older and less fuel efficient aircraft instead of purchasing the newer models. The decrease in fuel prices through 2017, therefore, increased demand for older aircraft and decreased demand for newer and more fuel efficient aircraft, thus affecting current market values of both types. Currently fuel prices are on the rise again, which may lead to increased demand for newer and more fuel efficient aircraft and less demand for the older, less efficient aircraft, depending on the impact of interest rates as discussed further down. The aircraft financing environment is another economic determinant that will influence aircraft prices. If there are alternative sources of financing the aircraft, then the market values will hold up better. For example, during the financial crisis of 2008–09 when credit markets were frozen, the OEMs were able to use the Ex–Im Bank to finance the purchase of the aircraft which helped to support aircraft values (Ackert, 2012b). Boeing has been recently working with insurance companies to create the AFIC to find alternative sources to finance aircraft, which will help support aircraft values in the future.

As aircraft price is denominated in the US dollar, one of the less thought of economic determinants influencing the price of the aircraft is a foreign investor investing in an aircraft, to hedge against declining values in their domestic currency or strengthening of the dollar. Domestic capital flow restrictions may also make it easier to justify investing in an aircraft as opposed to other cash or marketable securities. This is one reason why aircraft as investments become attractive tools at periods of time and for certain countries. Currently the Chinese banks and investors see aircraft as attractive investments for this very reason. For example, the HNA group in China has invested in aircraft and other assets in the United States possibly as a hedge against declining value of the yuan and to circumvent restrictions by the government on capital outflows from the country.

Regulation

The last factor influencing the price of the aircraft is regulation related to aircraft noise, emissions, and age of an aircraft. In the United States, the Federal Aviation Administration (FAA) has developed noise requirements for aircraft landing in US airports. The FAA regulates aircraft noise through standards. The standard requires that aircraft meet or fall below the designated noise levels. For civil jet aircraft, there are four stages that are identified, with Stage 1 being the loudest and Stage 4 being the quietest. Current regulation requires, for all civil jet aircraft, to meet Stage 3 or Stage 4 to fly within the contiguous United States (Federal Aviation Administration, 2018). These regulations force the airlines to seek quieter aircraft in countries with restrictions and limit the options available to deploy louder aircraft. Aircraft developed today have decreased noise output by as much as 80% than aircraft built in the 1950s and was one reason for the elimination of older aircraft from service in the 1990s, even during a period of very low fuel prices

Further, certain countries (e.g., China, Indonesia, and some Middle Eastern countries) impose age restrictions on aircraft and ban import of an aircraft over certain age, usually ranging between 10 and 20 years of age, because those jurisdictions consider the aircraft unsafe. This is a debatable point, as the safety of an aircraft has nothing to do with its age but is related more to its maintenance status. Normally, these regulations are put in place for political reasons, and typically after a notable air disaster where the ruling government at the time wants to appear to be addressing a high-profile topic like air safety. Nevertheless, age restrictions do have an impact on the price. Finally, government policies regarding the state of the Export Credit Agencies impact an OEM's ability to sell to foreign carriers and can indirectly affect aircraft prices.

LEASE RATES

The above factors, namely, aircraft determinants, manufacturer determinants, market determinants, and regulation that influence purchase price will also influence lease rates. In addition to these factors, one can think of six additional factors, namely, purchase price, credit risk, current market interest rates and financing mix, lease terms, political risk, and residual value risk that will impact lease rates. Rent will ultimately be determined by multiplying a lease rate factor by the purchase price of the aircraft. The lease factor is highly confidential because it is the key to the lessor's perceived value of the asset.

Purchase price

The purchase price of a new aircraft or current market value of a used aircraft will factor heavily into the lease rate. This is true especially in a sale and leaseback transaction where an airline sells an aircraft it owns to a leasing company and turns around and leases it back. If an airline sells for a higher price to the lessor, then the lessor will demand a higher lease rental compared to if the airline had sold for a lower price. This is referred to in the industry as high–high or low–low. In general, aircraft with higher market value will demand higher lease rates and lease rates will tend to fall as market values decline.

Credit risk

An airlines' credit risk is considered to be their ability to pay off debts to creditors. The higher the credit risk of an airline, the higher the lease rentals the lessor would charge to cover the risk of the lessee defaulting. An airline with better credit is therefore in a better position to negotiate not only lower lease rentals but also get other favorable concessions such as not paying MRs during the term of the lease, having higher insurance deductible, etc.

Current market interest rates and capital structure

Interest rates can also impact the demand, and hence values of aircraft. As previously discussed in this text, the vast majority of commercial aircraft are either financed or leased.

If the current market rate of interest is higher, lease rates will tend to increase as the lessor has to cover the cost of financing the aircraft. Further, if the lessor is financed more with equity than debt, then lease rates would increase as well, because equity financing is more expensive than debt financing.

This increase in capital cost can offset the benefits gained from rising fuel costs. Used aircraft are by their nature lower in value as they have had the benefit of depreciation. As such, the interest cost for a loan on a used aircraft will be less (lower principle to lend against) and the impact of a higher interest rate is therefore less on used aircraft. This corresponds to an increased demand for used aircraft and a lower demand for newer aircraft in a high interest rate environment, all other factors being equal (which they rarely are).

However, one has to realize that in a competitive market place, the lessor may not be able to increase the lease rates in tune with increasing market interest rates or increase in their cost of capital. Recently competition and new sources of financing in the leasing market has been driving down the IRR for lessors. The research of Harris (2018) shows that for a new narrowbody aircraft (0–5 years), unlevered equity returns range from 4% to 6%, 5% to 8% for midrange narrowbodies (8–12 years) and less than 10% for end of life narrowbodies (15–25 years). Also according to Harris (2018), average lease rates in the last 12 months have declined below 0.6% in select cases, especially for sale and leaseback transactions. Widebody lease rates in general are about 0.5%–1% higher than narrowbody lease rates, but like the narrowbody aircraft, have also declined in the past 12 months (Harris, 2018).

Term of the lease

In general, short-term leases of 3–6 years are more expensive than long-term leases of 6–15 years as the lessor has a longer period to recoup the purchase price and amortize any customization in the aircraft for the lessee. Also, residual values at the end of the long-term lease have less of an impact on return calculations as lease payments over a longer period would cover the cost (principal and interest payments) of the initial investment for the lessor.

Political risk factors

Political risks play an important role in determining the lease rates. For example, in certain countries it is difficult for a lessor to repossess their aircraft. Some countries have ratified the Cape Town Convention, which makes repossession easier and thereby reducing the political risk to the lessor. In general, higher political risks will result in higher lease rates as well as required MR schedule.

Environmental factors

Lease rates will depend on the environmental conditions in which the aircraft is operated. For example, an aircraft flying over hot Middle Eastern deserts or in a corrosive environment (salty or heavily polluted air) will have more wear and tear than an aircraft operated in a normal environment. Flying in such harsh conditions will increase maintenance costs as well as lower the aircrafts' residual value as the parts, in particular the engines, have a higher scrap rate. A lessor, therefore, has to charge a higher lease rate for a lessee intending to operate under such harsh environmental conditions in order to achieve their desired rate of return on their investment in the aircraft.

Residual value risk

Finally, residual value risk, which is the expected value of the aircraft at the end of the lease, plays a sizeable role in determining lease rates. A lessor will input the expected residual value as a final cash flow item in their transaction model to determine the NPV of the lease and determine the lease rates that will achieve the lessor's target rate of return.

MAINTENANCE RESERVES

We discussed MRs in detail in Chapter 9. In this chapter we want to examine MRs from a cash flow perspective. We review and briefly summarize the ideas on MR from the previous chapter and examine the cash flow implications of MR in this chapter.

MRs use fees, or supplemental rent, are primarily used for

- Short-term leases
- Long-term lease when the credit is not top tier

MRs serve as a mechanism to mitigate credit risk, and therefore, are generally imposed on weaker credit airlines. However, in the event a lessee is able to negotiate to not pay MRs, they may still be required to provide collateral security in the form of an end of lease financial adjustment or through a Letter of Credit.

As discussed in Chapter 9, typical maintenance on an aircraft consists of engine performance restoration, engine life-limited parts (LLP), auxiliary power unit, landing gear overhaul, and airframe checks. These checks are performed either based on calendar time, flight hours, flight cycles or, in some cases, whichever limit is reached first. These costs can vary based on engine thrust outputs, engine derate, operating environments, and other factors that will affect the wear and tear on the engine and are, in turn, based on the industry norm for that aircraft type, or in the case of a new aircraft, based on manufacturers' recommendations. If an airline is required to pay MRs to a lessor, there is typically a set rate for each calendar month elapsed, or flight hour or cycle operated of each maintenance reserve covered event. MR payments are usually paid monthly in arrears and have a built in escalation to account for inflation, labor, and materials cost that increases normally on a yearly basis.

MRs can be expressed as follows:

$$M\times\ reserves = M\times\ utility\ consumed$$
$$Or$$
$$M\times\ reserves = Full\ life\ M\times\ value - M\times\ utility\ remaining$$

MR can be thought of as reimbursable or nonreimbursable. Usually, most short-term engine leases will tend to have nonreimbursable MRs with the engine lease terminating and the engine returned to the lessor if the engine requires a shop visit. In a reimbursable MR scenario, the lessee will pay MRs to the lessor and submit claims for reimbursement by the lessor when maintenance covered by the maintenance reserves is performed on the aircraft.

From a financing perspective, some lenders allow the MRs to be applied against the debt—allowing them to amortize the loan amount and interest payments. During a maintenance event, the lessor would either have to use their own equity to pay for the maintenance or if the bank/financier would allow—to reapply debt against the maintenance amount. However, lenders would not allow MRs to be used to pay down the debt.

An MR cash flow is an inflow to the lessor when the lessee makes periodic MR payments to the lessor to cover the cost of major maintenance events. In addition, there is an outflow when the lessee incurs maintenance expenditure and the lessor reimburses the lessee for those expenses from the MRs collected.

From a cash flow perspective, a lessor can usually take one of two approaches to MRs payments. Under the first approach, the lessor can recognize the maintenance cash inflows as income and use cash outflows to pay for maintenance as expenses. If a lessor recognizes cash flows as income, they can use this money to reinvest in the firm's operations, thus receiving more gains than if it remained in the MR account. This method however increases the risk for the lessor if the lessee defaults or if they do not have sufficient funds available to cover regular maintenance events.

Conversely, a lessor can choose not to recognize MR payments as income and let it remain in MR accounts. This is a conservative approach, because the funds for a maintenance event will be readily available and not affect a firm's finances unless there is a top-up exposure. However, this approach means that the MR payments cannot be employed elsewhere to improve the profitability of the lessor.

Maintenance reserve exposure

In case MR payments are either not collected or underfunded, the lessor will be subject to a top-up exposure. The value of this exposure would be the difference between the maintenance utility consumed by the lessee less any MRs, collected by the lessee (Ackert, 2012a, 2017). The example below shows the maintenance exposure for a lessor for an A320 aircraft following an event of default at year 4 since entry into service; the unfunded maintenance exposure of the aircraft would

Table 10.4 Maintenance Reserve Exposure

Maintenance Event	Full Life Cost ($)	Residual ($)	(A) Maintenance Consumed ($)	(B) Reserves ($)	(C = B − A) Exposure
4C/6 Year-HSI	810,000	270,000	540,000	0	(540,000)
8C/12 Year-HSI	875,520	583,680	291,840	0	(291,840)
Landing gear overhaul	435,000	261,000	174,000	0	(174,000)
Engine 1 performance restoration	2,300,000	972,160	1,327,840	0	(1,327,840)
Engine 2 performance restoration	2,300,000	972,160	1,327,840	0	(1,327,840)
Engine 1 LLP replacement	2,440,000	1,894,453	545,547	0	(545,547)
Engine 2 LLP replacement	2,440,000	1,894,453	545,547	0	(545,547)
APU performance rest	250,000	55,456	194,544	0	(194,544)
Total	11,850,520	6,903,362	4,947,158	0	(4,947,158)

LLP, *Life-Limited Parts;* HSI, *Heavy Structural Inspection.*
Ackert (2017).

total approximately $4.9 million, which the lessor would have to bear in a subsequent lease and would be a drain on the lessor's cash flow (Table 10.4).

RESIDUAL VALUE

Residual value has a huge impact on cash flow and is therefore a crucial input into the financial model. As we mentioned above, the residual value is a very important aspect of a lease because it weighs heavily on the calculated lease rate. All other things remaining equal, lease rates will decrease as the residual value increases. In general, the lessor will try to maximize the residual value at the end of every stage in the lease by weighing the following options:

- Extending with the current lessee
- Taking the aircraft back and remarketing the aircraft to a new lessee
- Sell the aircraft
- Part out the aircraft or a consignment sale of its parts

The residual value is, however, very difficult to predict and model and is one of the most challenging variables in a transaction modeling process. For this reason, investors often rely on appraisal firms that employ certified aircraft appraisers who have developed complex models to provide a view on future values.

TRANSACTION COSTS AND SECURITY DEPOSIT

Transaction costs include all the cash flows associated with the transaction. These costs can include legal fees, administrative costs, and other costs required to complete the transaction. Security deposits for aircraft leases typically amount to 2–3 months of lease payments. This security deposit is returned at the end of the lease if prior agreements regarding the lease are met.

LIFE CYCLE OF A LEASE

One can think of three different lease stages that an aircraft would typically go through in its life. The first lease usually is from new to up to 12 years, the second lease lasts anywhere from 4 to 6 years, and the third and final lease lasts from 3 to 5 years. At the end of the third lease, usually the lessor would consider whether or not to part out the aircraft. It should be noted that defaults and other events may lead to more than three leases in an aircraft's history.

FIRST LEASE

The first lease is typically for a period ranging from 0 to 12 years and usually coincides with a major airframe heavy maintenance check. The crucial return drivers during this first stage includes the purchase price paid for the aircraft, the lease rental, residual value of the aircraft, MR payments (or end of lease adjustment (EOLA)), and transaction and financing cost to finance the lease for the lessor. At the end of the first lease, the lessor has to make a decision whether it is better to re-lease the aircraft or sell the aircraft.

If a lease has to be transitioned to a different lessee, the lessor has to take into consideration any reconfiguration and transition costs incurred. The reconfiguration cost of a narrowbody is generally around $500,000 but can range as high as $1–$2 million. A widebody, on the other hand, has a much higher level of customization and is typically around $2–$3 million but can range as high as $10–$20 million, and for a very large aircraft, such as the A380, run as high as $25–$30 million. The lessor would also assume, for the purpose of modeling the life of an asset, that they would forego rents of 2 months (downtime with no rent), between operators for a narrowbody, and forego 3 months' rent for a widebody.

Finally, the lessor has to make sure that the aircraft is returned in a proper condition and all the maintenance has been performed on the aircraft. It is generally during this period when a first tier lessor will consider whether it is best to sell the aircraft with its lease attached to another lessor, in order to avoid the cost and expense of the transition, or to hold the aircraft and remarket it for the next lessee.

SECOND LEASE

The second lease usually lasts from 4 to 6 years. If there was a default from the previous lessee, the lessor may have a top-up exposure to ensure that there are adequate MRs to defray the cost of maintenance events in the future. At this stage in its life cycle, the aircraft is aging and may require more nonroutine maintenance as well. If the airline does not have good credit, the lessor has to make sure that it collects adequate MRs. The crucial return drivers at this stage are therefore the lease rentals and MRs collected. At the end of the second lease, an important consideration for a passenger aircraft is conversion to a freighter.

THIRD LEASE AND END OF LEASE SOLUTIONS

The third and final lease typically lasts about 3–5 years. At this stage in the life of the aircraft, the crucial drivers are the part out value or value of green time remaining in the engines. In general, as the aircraft ages, there is more value in the engines than in the airframe. A part out residual value usually consists of green time (engine life remaining before next maintenance event) on the engine. If the engine or aircraft has maintenance life remaining, the lessor can use a short-term lease which could stipulate that the engines and airframe can be redeployed together or separately. If there is no maintenance life remaining, residual value usually consists of metal value or value of an airframe, engines, auxiliary power unit (APU), landing gear less any disassembly cost, scrap cost, warehouse costs, repair costs, and sales costs. Selling parts is a process that usually takes anywhere from 12 to 36 months. During this time, the lessor needs to consider the interest costs on the loan for the aircraft as well.

Fig. 10.1 details a typical life of a leased aircraft. The first lease is typically the longest and will most likely be with a stable airline. The lessor will be concerned with the residual value of the aircraft at the expiry of the lease, because that amount will most likely be the main driver of the profitability of the lease, and a function of the next lease rate needed for a profitable deal. At the expiry of the first lease, the lessor is then likely to move the aircraft to a lesser credit quality airline or cargo operator because the aircraft value and technology is now much lower than what the market can offer. The residual value at the end of the lease is still important but not as much as the first lease, because the value is expected to be much lower, and one is on the flatter portion of the residual value curve. Once the aircraft reaches 15 + years, it is in the final stage of its life. Cargo conversion or part out will most likely be the end of life scenario for the aircraft.

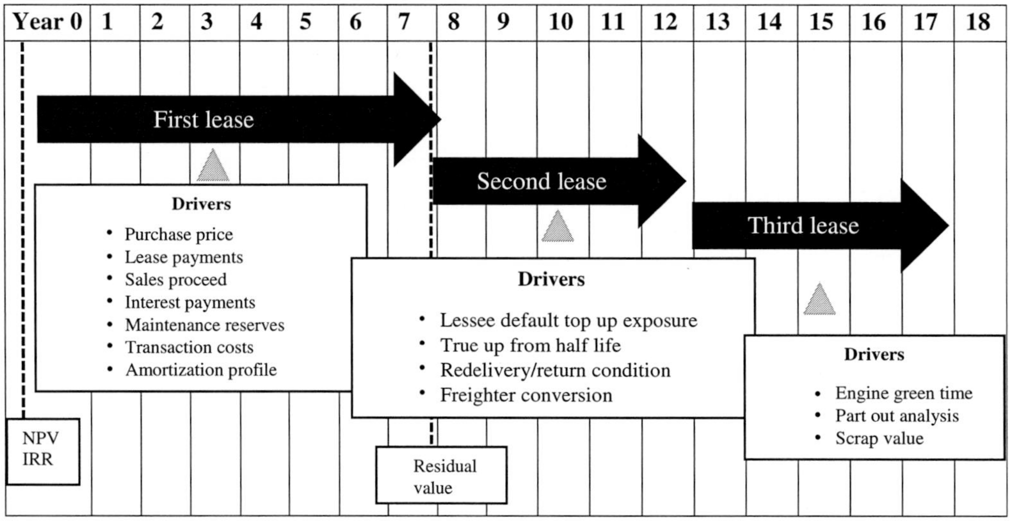

FIGURE 10.1

Life of a leased aircraft.

MODELING A LEASE TRANSACTION

In the previous section we discussed the important cash flows and factors that affect these cash flows in a lease transaction. In this section we discuss several scenarios where a lessor would have to model these cash flows from a lease in order to make a seasoned decision. We illustrate these scenarios with numerical examples, wherever necessary, to bring out the essential details in the underlying decision-making process. We discuss the following scenarios:

- Calculating the NPV and IRR of a lease
- Solving for minimum lease payments
- Amortizing the loan and financing the transaction
- Sale versus re-lease scenario
- Aircraft sale with lease attached
- Advanced modeling considerations

CALCULATING THE NPV AND IRR OF A LEASE

A lessor is primarily interested in getting an adequate return on its investment. In order to analyze whether the lease generates an adequate return on investment, the lessor needs to calculate the rate of return on the lease or the NPV of the lease to examine if the lease is profitable. The lessor may also need to know what lease payments and residual value of the aircraft will help it reach its target rate of return.

The important cash flow inputs into this decision process are the purchase price, the lease rental, the MR inflow (collection of MRs from the lessee) and outflow (when the lessor pays for maintenance events incurred by the lessee), end of lease adjustments (in the event MRs are not collected), and the final residual value of the aircraft. The residual value of the aircraft can be calculated as the sum of its component parts (airframe and engines) at the end of an aircraft's useful economic life.

We use a simple example below to show the essential cash flows in a lease and how to calculate the IRR and NPV of the lease.

EXAMPLE CASE STUDY FOR CALCULATING NPV AND IRR

You are a senior analyst at SkyHigh leasing and are analyzing a lease transaction for a 2005 A320-200 for a period of 5 years (60 months).

- Lease start date: 5/1/2018; lease expiry date: 5/1/2023.
- Purchase price: $14,000,000.
- Lease rate factor: 0.90%.
- Transaction cost: $500,000.
- MRs are maintained in a separate account and recognized only if the maintenance event cost exceeds reserves (reserve outflow). The balance in MRs is recognized at the end of the lease (month 61).
- MRs are initially assumed to be $130,000 per month and increasing at 3% every year thereafter.

- There is a maintenance event in the 22nd month of $1,320,000 and Engine restoration and LLP replacement of $2,500,000 and $2,632,823 in month 40.
- Residual value for Airframe is $2,000,000, Engine 1 is $3,134,634 and Engine 2 is $4,833,381 and is recognized in month 61 along with MR balance remaining.
- Discount Rate per year is 5%.
- There is a bullet residual value at the end of the lease.

In order to calculate the NPV and IRR of the above transaction, you need to set up this problem on an excel spreadsheet. Your monthly rent would be $126,000 ($14,000,000 × 0.90%). The initial investment cost in month zero would be $14,500,000 (the cost of the aircraft of $14,000,000 plus the transaction cost of $500,000). MRs collection would be $130,000 for the first month and would increase at 3% from January 1st of each year. The bullet residual value in the 61st month would be $9,968,025 (consisting of Airframe residual of $2,000,000, Engine 1 value of $3,134,644 and Engine 2 value of $4,833,381). There are two maintenance events—in month 22 of $1,320,000 and in month 40 of $5,132,823 (consisting of engine restoration cost of $2,500,000 and LLP replacement cost of $2,632,823).

This yields an IRR of 7.16% and an NPV of $1,310,033. Since the IRR is greater than the discount rate of 5% and the NPV is positive, this lease transaction would be profitable for the lessor.

CONDUCTING SENSITIVITY AND SCENARIO ANALYSIS

Once you complete the base-case analysis, you can stress test the above model for different ranges of inputs such as the lease rate factors, residual value for the airframe and engines as well as the discount rate and look at the impact on the final output metrics such as IRR and NPV.

For example, in the above example, you can stress test by varying the following assumptions:

- Lease rate factors can vary from 0.5% to 2% with a median value of 1.5%.
- Transaction cost can vary from $300,000 to $700,000 with a median value of $500,000.
- Residual value for Airframe can vary from $1,000,000 to $3,000,000 with a median value of $2,000,000.
- Residual value for Engine 1 can vary from $2,000,000 to $6,000,000 with a median value of $4,000,000.
- Residual value for Engine 2 can vary from $3,000,000 to $7,000,000 with a median value of $5,000,000.
- Discount rate can vary from 5% to 10% with a median value of 8%.

Financial modeling software is available to help you identify the key drivers that affect your model.

FINDING MINIMUM LEASE PAYMENTS

Once you have set up your base case and have computed the NPV and IRR and conducted sensitivity analysis on the model, you should understand how to calculate the minimum lease payments that would be acceptable to a lessor in order to generate a certain rate of return or ensure that the lease is profitable. Tools such as "Goal Seek" and "Solver" are available in popular spreadsheet packages to find the minimum lease payments that will be needed to achieve a certain rate of return or achieve breakeven point for a lease. We discuss an example below to show how one can compute the minimum lease payments on a lease.

EXAMPLE: FINDING MINIMUM LEASE PAYMENT

SkyHigh is negotiating a sale and leaseback transaction for a 2005 A320-200 with LatinAir. They are interested in knowing what they should charge as a lease payment in order to have a profitable lease. SkyHigh, in a high–high or low–low deal, offers a purchase price of either $16,000,000 or $14,000,000 to LatinAir. Details of the lease are given below:

- Purchase price: $14,000,000 or $16,000,000.
- Transaction cost of $500,000.
- Security deposit of $2,000,000 at the beginning of the lease which is returned at the end of the lease (49th month).
- Term of the lease: 48 months.
- MR collections: $130,000 per month, maintenance event requiring a payment of $2.5 million at the end of year 2 (24 months).
- SkyHigh recognizes MR as income when it is received and as an outflow during a maintenance payment.
- Residual value at the end of the lease term (49th month): $4,000,000.
- Discount rate: 6% per year.

In this example, you need to set up this problem on a spreadsheet and find the minimum lease payment by setting the NPV = 0 and solving for the minimum lease payment. Some important factors to consider are the following:

The initial investment for the low–low scenario would be the purchase price ($14,000,000), transaction cost ($500,000), and the security deposit of $2,000,000 received by the lessor. This would add up to a total cash flow of − $12,500,000 as your initial cash flow.

Next make sure you take into account the inflow of the MR payments each month as well as the maintenance event in month 24 requiring an outflow of $2,500,000 as payment to the lessee. In the final month (49th month), the lessor has to return the security deposit, but the aircraft would have a residual value of $4,000,000, giving you a net positive amount of $2,000,000.

You can input a fictitious lease payment to start your computation and then set up the NPV formula to calculate the NPV of the lease. After that, set your NPV = 0 and use "Goal Seek" or "Solver" to find the minimum lease payment. Be careful to discount the cash flows at the monthly discount rate rather than the annual interest rate given to you in the example. (In other words, divide the 6% annual rate by 12 to get the monthly discount rate.) If your model was correctly formulated, the minimum lease payment you calculated would be $178,866.

Try the exercise again to find the minimum lease payment for the high–high scenario. In some cases, the lessor is more interested in knowing the minimum lease payment that would achieve a certain rate of return. Think about how you can set up the problem in order to find the minimum lease payment that will achieve a certain rate of return.

FINANCING AND AMORTIZATION

The lessor would look for financing from a commercial bank or the capital market, at the backend, to finance the cost of the aircraft. The bank would normally charge an interest on the loan based on LIBOR (London interbank offered rate) plus a premium to cover the additional risk of the loan. The lessor would service the debt by making periodic payment of interest and principal balance on the loan. This process is referred to as amortizing the loan. The period of loan payments is often longer than the length of the lease for the lessor and therefore the lessor would be left with a balloon payment at the end of the lease. The balloon payment is the remaining principal outstanding on the loan for the lessor at the end of the lease. In the example below, we show how to calculate the principal and interest on the loan and find the balloon payment.

Example: Amortization and finding the balloon payment

You are planning to finance the purchase of a $17,500,000 aircraft with 75% debt.

- The period of the lease is 10 years (120 months).
- The loan period is 15 years (180 months).
- The interest on the loan is LIBOR of 4.0% plus premium of 0.75% per year.
- Compute the payment for the loan and show the split between interest and principal.
- Compute the balloon payment at the end of the lease period (121st month).

In this example, the lessor is financing 75% of the loan that gives you a loan amount of $13,125,000. The annual interest rate is 4.75% (LIBOR of 4.0% plus premium of 0.75%). The monthly interest rate is 0.40%. We can then use the payment (PMT) function in excel to calculate the payment. The annuity payment in this case works out to be $102,090. For the first month of this total payment of $102,090, the interest amount would be $51,953 and the principal amount would be $50,137. This leaves an outstanding loan balance of $13,074,863 at the end of the first month. The payment will remain the same until month 180 when the loan is paid off but the split between interest and principal will change as more of the outstanding principal balance is being paid off.

At the end of the lease (120th month) the loan amount outstanding or the balloon payment would be $5,442,817.

Levered and unlevered return

Leverage is the amount of debt assumed by the lessor. In the previous example, the lessor contributed $4,375,000 (25% of the purchase price of the aircraft of $17,500,000) and financed the rest ($13,125,000) of the aircraft purchase price through a loan. The lessor then leases the aircraft out and collects lease payments and MRs. One can therefore calculate a levered and unlevered rate of return for the lessor. The unlevered return reflects the return the lessor would earn from the lease rentals and final resale value of the aircraft if the lessor did not finance the transaction with a loan and used their own funds. The levered return, on the other hand, assumes that at least part of the loan is debt-financed. The lessor's goal is to increase the spread between the rate of return on their investment and the cost of financing the amount borrowed.

SALE VERSUS RELEASE DECISION

A lessor is often faced with a situation, typically at the end of the first or second lease, whether to extend or re-lease the aircraft or sell the aircraft at the end of the lease term. The decision to lease or sell will depend on calculating the NPV of the sale and comparing it to the NPV of re-leasing the aircraft. We use a simple example below to illustrate the decision-making process. Table 10.5 provides the relevant information necessary for you to make the sale or re-lease decision. We make the assumption that the lease ends 5 months from now, at which point the lessor would face a decision whether to sell or re-lease the aircraft. You can set up your analysis on a spreadsheet so that it is easier to conduct sensitivity and scenario analysis by changing the key inputs in the model.

Sale scenario

The important factor to consider if the lessor decides to sell the aircraft is the profit or loss from the transaction. The lessor has invested $15,000,000 in the aircraft at the beginning of the lease and has an MR balance of $8,000,000. Five months from now the aircraft would have depreciated to a value of $14,375,000 (assuming a monthly depreciation of $125,000). If the lessor decides to sell this aircraft at the end of the lease, then the forecast Current Market Value (CMV) is $21,000,000 (to be realistic and conservative, one can assume that the lessor would receive less than this value based on future market conditions). One can then add the part-out bonus of $3,000,000 with the rental income for the 5 months to arrive at the final profit from the sale of the aircraft.

Table 10.5 Data for Sale Versus Release Decision

Maintenance Event Time Before Next Event & Cost of Repair/Overhaul		
6Y/12Y HSI	At redelivery	$2,500,000
Engine 1 performance restoration	3 Years	$4,000,000
Engine 2 performance restoration	3 Years	$4,000,000
Landing gear overhaul	3 Years	$ 500,000
Monthly depreciation	$125,000	
Monthly maintenance reserve collection	$130,000	
Months until end of lease	5 Months	
Re-lease term	4 Years/48 Months	
Current rent	$230,000	
Future re-lease rent	$207,000	
Annual discount rate	5%	
Half-life current market value (2018)	$21,000,000	
Half-life current market value (2022)	$13,000,000	
2018 Part-out value "bonus" due to increased demand	$3,000,000	
Net investment today	$15,000,000	
Current maintenance reserves collected	$8,000,000	

HSI, *Heavy Structural Inspection.*

Re-lease scenario

If the lessor decides to re-lease the aircraft, the lessor would continue to receive rental income of $207,000 for the next 48 months. At the end of the 48 months the CMV of the aircraft would be $13,000,000 (to be realistic and conservative, one can assume that the lessor would receive less than this value based on future market conditions). If the lessor decides to re-lease the aircraft, then the lessor has to reimburse the lessee from the MRs collected, for the cost of the 6Y/12Y maintenance event of $2,500,000, which is incurred immediately, and in 3 years' time, another $8,500,000 cost for the engine(s) and landing-gear maintenance. The aircraft is also assumed to depreciate at $125,000 per month and would be worth $8,375,000 at the end of the 4-year lease term. One can discount the above values using the discount rate of 5% (be careful to convert this yearly rate to a monthly rate) to get at the present value of re-lease.

Comparing the sale and re-lease scenario

The profit from sale plus the rent collection for the sale scenario works out to be $15,206,498 compared to the re-lease scenario where the total profit plus rent collection is $14,772,891. You can check these calculations by setting up the above information on a spreadsheet. In this particular example, therefore, it turns out that the lessor is better off selling the aircraft. One important consideration missing from the above analysis is any cost associated with the reconfiguration and transition of the lease to the new lessee, and often this can be substantial.

AIRCRAFT SALE WITH LEASE ATTACHED

A lessor sometimes may want to sell an aircraft, currently on lease to an airline, to another lessor, with the lease attached. The reason for this sale may be to reorient their portfolio due to risk of overexposure to the current lessee, or a need to transition from one type of aircraft to another (widebody aircraft to a narrowbody aircraft) in their portfolio.

For example, let us assume that a major lessor such as AerCap has an A320neo on lease to Delta Airlines for 7 years. Four years into the lease, let us assume that AerCap decides to sell the aircraft leased to Delta Airlines with the lease attached. AerCap may solicit bids from other lessors for the aircraft and choose the one that offers the best sale price for the aircraft. Let us assume that there are three lessors competing to buy the aircraft from AerCap. Each of these lessors will have a different offer price based on their target return and residual value calculations, and AerCap will choose the best offer from the competing offers from the lessors. AerCap will then execute a *Novation* contract to transfer the lease to the new lessee. From Delta's standpoint there will be no change in their lease terms or conditions other than the fact that they now have to send their lease payments to the new lessor.

If the lease was to an airline with lower credit rating, and AerCap was collecting MRs, then the airline may want to ensure that the current lessor can be relied upon to reimburse, in a timely manner, to the airline, for any maintenance undertaken on the aircraft and honor the return conditions previously negotiated with AerCap.

Table 10.6 outlines the relevant details for the example in the above scenario and calculations for the purchase price paid by different lessors.

Table 10.6 Assumptions and Calculation of Offer Price for Different Lessors

	Remaining Lease Term (Months)	Lease Rental Per month ($)	Expected Target Return (%)	Expected Residual Value ($)	Sale/Purchase Price Offered ($)
Lessor A	36	350,000	5	31,000,000	38,368,259
Lessor B	36	350,000	7	31,000,000	36,478,710
Lessor C	36	350,000	10	34,500,000	36,436,952

As you can see, even though Lessors A and B have the same residual value assumption, the lower expected target return requirement means that lessor A can pay the highest price. Lessor C has a higher residual value assumption, but the higher return hurdle means that the price they can pay is still not as high as Lessor A. In this case, all things being equal, AerCap would want to sell the aircraft to Lessor A to maximize their gain on the sale.

ADVANCED MODELING CONSIDERATIONS

In our above discussions we kept our analysis very simple and did not include dynamic factors that can influence the return calculations. There are three important considerations that need to be incorporated in the above model to make it dynamic and more realistic. The first is that the model should include the probability of default by the airline as that will affect the return calculations for the lessor. Second important consideration to understand is that the aircraft residual values are not static but can change over time from the initial assumptions of the lessor. This can occur if the aircraft becomes less popular (e.g., the A380 was popular when it was first introduced but its value has since dropped), or a lessee default, forces the lessor, to sell the aircraft at below market value as part of a distressed sale. Finally, interest rates can change over time, affecting the lessor's borrowing cost and hence their profitability. The above uncertainties of default risk, aircraft residual value risk, and interest rate risk mean that NPV and IRR values should be thought of, not as static numbers, but as probability distributions of possible outcomes (Hallerstorm, 2010). Monte Carlo simulations can be used to incorporate these uncertainties into the model and achieve better accuracy in forecasting the default rates, residual values, and interest rates.

CONCLUSION

There are various decisions the lessor faces, ranging from finding a minimum lease payment, to whether to sell or re-lease an aircraft at the end of a lease, or to sell an aircraft to another lessor with a lease attached. For a lessor, leasing is a capital-budgeting decision and the important cash flows are purchase price, lease rentals, lease term, MRs, and residual value. At the backend of the lease, the lessor finances the lease through a loan. In order for the lease to add value, the NPV of the lease must be positive (or the IRR should be greater than the cost of capital).

Financial models can help the lessor make these decisions by modeling the relevant cash flows, identifying the key drivers, and stress testing the model for different scenarios.

CASE STUDY: TRANSACTION COST MODELING

You are planning to finance the purchase of a $20,000,000 aircraft with 75% debt. You are provided with the following information:

- Lease rate factor is 0.58%.
- The period of the lease is 10 years (120 months).
- The period of the loan is 15 years (180 months).
- The interest on the loan the bank will charge you is LIBOR of 3.0% plus a borrowing spread of 0.75% per year.
- MRs are $62,625 and are recognized as income. There is a maintenance outflow in the 62nd month requiring a payment of $3,757,500.
- Insurance payment is $26,000 per year (hint you need to convert this to monthly).
- Asset management fee is 1% of the monthly lease payment.
- Residual value (121st month) is $7,320,000

Based on the above information, compute the following:

1. Lease rental per month.
2. The payment for the loan and the split between interest and principal for the period of the lease. What would be the balloon payment at the end of the lease period (121st month)?
3. Compute your levered and unlevered rate of return and show if the lease would add value to the lessor.

ACKNOWLEDGMENT

We would like to thank Eddo Weijer and Joel Hussey for providing guidance and significant portions of information that is presented in this chapter.

REFERENCES

Ackert, S. (2012a). *Basics of aircraft maintenance reserve development and management*. Retrieved from Aircraft Monitor <http://www.iata.org/whatwedo/workgroups/Documents/Paperless%20Supply%20Chain/Basics-AC-MR.pdf>.

Ackert, S. (2012b). *Basics of aircraft marker analysis*. San Francisco, CA: Aircraft Monitor, March.

Ackert, S. (2017). *Maintenance reserve guidance and general practices*. San Francisco, CA: Airline Monitor, Jackson Square Aviation.

Airbus. (2018, January 15). *Airbus 2018 price list press release*. Retrieved from Airbus Web site <http://www.airbus.com/newsroom/press-releases/en/2018/01/airbus-2018-price-list-press-release.html>.

Boeing. (2018). *About Boeing Commercial Airplanes*. Retrieved from Boeing Corporation Website <http://www.boeing.com/company/about-bca/#/prices>.

Boeing Capital Corporation. (2018). *Current aircraft finance market outlook*. Retrieved from Boeing <https://www.boeing.com/company/key-orgs/boeing-capital/current-aircraft-financing-market.page>.

Federal Aviation Administration. (2018, January 9). *Aircraft noise issues*. Retrieved from Federal Aviation Administration Website <https://www.faa.gov/about/office_org/headquarters_offices/apl/noise_emissions/airport_aircraft_noise_issues/>.

Forsberg, D. (2015, March). *Aircraft Retirement and Storage Trends*. Retrieved from Avolon <http://avolon.aero/wp/wp-content/uploads/2015/03/Avolon-White-Paper-FInal-30-March-2015.pdf>.

Hallerstorm, N. (2010, March). *Modeling aircraft loans and leases*. Retrieved from PK Airfinance <www.pkair.com/common/docs/modeling-aircraft-loan-and-lease-portfolios.pdf>.

Harris, D. (2018, May 17). *Equity returns squeezed for leased aircraft*. Retrieved from Ishka Global <https://www.ishkaglobal.com/News/Article/5806/Equity-returns-squeezed-for-leased-aircraft>.

Mason, S. (2017, August). *737 Max-taking flight: A product assessment*. Retrieved from Avolon <http://avolon.aero/wp/wp-content/uploads/2017/08/737Max_Thought_Leadership_Paper_CA7_web.pdf>.

Raghavan, S. (2017). Modeling an aircraft lease transaction for a lessor. *Journal of International Finance and Economics*, *17*(2), 15–21.

CHAPTER

LEASE AGREEMENT AND NEGOTIATION

11

CHAPTER OUTLINE

Aircraft Leasing and Financing. DOI: https://doi.org/10.1016/B978-0-12-815285-0.00011-0

An aircraft lease agreement needs to be very comprehensive, covering important details with respect to the aircraft being leased and the obligations and responsibilities of the lessor and lessee. The lease document identifies the aircraft being leased and technical specifications of the aircraft and its major components such as engines, landing gear and the auxiliary power unit (APU). Unlike a lease for a car or an apartment which can be done on just a few pages, a commercial aircraft lease can total well in excess of 100 pages and contains sections that cover lease rentals, lease term (length of the lease and any renewal options), acquisition price (in a sale and leaseback transaction), delivery conditions (for a used aircraft), maintenance during the lease term and return conditions. Other important sections of the lease include legal, taxes, insurance, maintenance reserves, security deposits, subleasing and more. Lease negotiation is both an art as well as a science. While factors such as acquisition price and lease rentals are market driven and could be considered a science, negotiation around collection of maintenance reserves, security deposits as well as return conditions are more of an art and requires both the lessor and lessee to compromise in order to complete a lease. If not part of the negotiating team, experts in technical, legal, taxes and insurance should review and advise with respect to proposed language prior to agreeing to the terms.

INTRODUCTION TO THE LEASE NEGOTIATION PROCESS

This chapter will introduce you to the lease negotiation process and delve into the specifics of what is contained in a lease document. A lease document for a commercial aircraft can usually be in excess of 100 pages and is a legal document that spells out the terms and conditions of a lease agreement between the lessee and the lessor. In the event of disagreement between the lessor and lessee, the terms specified in the lease document will be reviewed and, if an agreement cannot be reached between the disputing parties, the dispute will be resolved by a judge or arbitrator based upon their interpretation of the language in the lease. Therefore, it is important to understand the lease negotiation process as well as the different components of the lease document very clearly. We discussed the different types of leases in Chapter 3. You might want to familiarize yourself with this material to understand this chapter better.

A lease is a contractual obligation between a lessee and a lessor which provides the lessee the right to use the aircraft for a specified period of time in return for periodic payment of rent to the lessor, the owner of the asset. The lessor therefore does not operate the aircraft and views the aircraft as an investment. Within the aircraft leasing industry, the lessee is responsible for the maintenance of the aircraft. The lease contract also specifies whether the lease is cancellable and if the lessee has the right to purchase the aircraft at the end of the lease. It also spells out the condition and technical status the aircraft is required to be in at the end of the lease term (the return condition).

STAGES IN THE LEASE NEGOTIATION

One can identify three distinct stages in the lease negotiation process. These are prospecting stage, memorandum of understanding (MoU) or the letter of intent (LoI) stage, and the definitive documentation stage. We discuss below these three different stages.

PROSPECTING STAGE

This is a preliminary stage in the process where the lessor and lessee are trying to understand what the needs of the lessee are, and what available aircraft the lessor has in their portfolio to rent, that might suit the needs of the lessee. The lessor may have a portfolio of used or new aircraft and may also be able to help the lessee with their financing needs. At this stage, the discussions are usually preliminary and mostly verbal as both the lessee and lessor are trying to position themselves in order to get a favorable deal. Once the needs of the lessee are properly understood the lessor may provide the lessee with a high-level detail about the type of aircraft that might suit the needs of the lessee. This might include details of the aircraft such as interior configuration, engine type, takeoff weights, engine thrust and the maintenance status of the aircraft, and high dollar value avionics in the aircraft (Fig. 11.2).

MOU OR LOI STAGE

At this stage in the lease negotiation process, there is usually a written document which can range from 2 to 16 pages depending on whether the lessor has a prior relationship with the lessee or if this is a new MoU possibly in a challenging jurisdiction with complex tax issues. Some lessors would opt for a shorter MoU in order to clinch a deal before their competitors while other lessors may want a more detailed document which clearly lays out all the details. There is often an advantage to clinching a deal for a lessor, especially in a competitive market, but there is often a tradeoff between speed and detail and a lessor who is able to sign with a lessee quickly with a shorter MoU might find down the road that there is room for misunderstanding between the parties which may impose additional cost on the lessee and lessor. In general, the MoU spells out details about the lessor and lessee, the type of aircraft and engine (Fig. 11.2), lease term, lease rentals, security deposit, maintenance payments (if required), maintenance of the aircraft, aircraft documentation, registration, insurance, redelivery conditions, and if subleasing is permitted or not. It should be noted that for the purpose of leasing an aircraft either of the terms, Memorandum of Understanding (MOU) or Letter of Intent (LOI) can be used as they both outline the main points of the proposed deal. Neither of the two documents are binding and the terms may still be subject to further negotiation.

DEFINITIVE DOCUMENTATION STAGE

Difference between an MoU vs lease

The final stage in the lease negotiation process is the execution of the lease agreement. While the MoU is nonbinding and requires corporate approval, the lease is a binding legal document and does not require corporate approval and spells out in detail all document terms and conditions (Fig. 11.1). It typically takes between 60 and 75 days to transition from an MoU to final lease. During this process corporate, board and risk committee approvals are obtained, the lease goes through different draft stages, and back and forth negotiation on terms and conditions between the two parties. The final stage in the process is the signature stage where the parties agree to the contents of the lease document, and at this point, the lease becomes binding.

Parties in a lease transaction

The important personnel involved in a lease transaction from a lessor's side is the marketing vice president, and for a lessee, it is either the chief executive officer (CEO), chief financial officer

MoU Term Sheet—Summary Document	Lease Agreement—Expanded Document
1. Lessor	1. Lessor
2. Lessee	2. Lessee
3. Aircraft description	3. Aircraft description
4. Term	4. Term
5. Rental—fixed/floating 6. (*Base year dollars and indexing*)	5. Rental—fixed/floating 6. (*Base year dollars and indexing*)
7. Spec budgets	7. Spec budgets
8. Security deposit and form	8. Security deposit and form
9. Insurance	9. Insurance
10. Delivery and registration	10. Delivery and registration
11. Limitations on use	11. Limitations on use
12. Maintenance	12. Maintenance
13. Warranties and support	13. Warranties and support
14. Assignment of costs	14. Assignment of costs
15. Confidentiality	15. Confidentiality
16. Conditions precedent	16. Conditions precedent
17. Board approvals and timing	17. Board approvals and timing
18. Spec/delivery conditions	18. Spec/delivery conditions
19. Redelivery conditions	19. Redelivery conditions
	20. Obligation to perform unconditional
	21. Payment
	22. Interest
	23. Retention of payments
	24. General operation of the aircraft
	25. Maintenance, modification, and alteration of aircraft
	26. Subleasing and wet leasing rights
	27. Reporting and inspection
	28. General indemnity
	29. Loss and damage to the aircraft and equipment
	30. Taxes
	31. Return of aircraft
	32. Law and jurisdiction
	33. Events of default
	34. Lessor rights
	35. Remedies following default
	36. Amendments
	37. Supplements

FIGURE 11.1

MoU and lease format content.

(CFO), fleet director, or manager. If it is a new aircraft, there is a configuration manager who is familiar with the purchase agreement with the manufacturer and understands what is possible to configure in the aircraft to suit the airline's specifications. If it is a used aircraft, there is usually a technical manager from the lessor's side and a director of maintenance for the lessee's side. Further there is a corporate credit committee representing the lessor which will examine the credit and risk profile of the airline while the airline board will do the same for the airline. Finally, there will be a legal or a contract team involved for both the lessor and lessee. It is also possible there would be

Aircraft Specifications			
Aircraft Data			
Type:	Airbus/A319-100	Line number:	
Placarded engine model:	International Aero Engines/V2524-A5	Registration number:	N510SG
Date of manufacture:	April 29 1999	Current passenger accommodation:	144Y
Serial number:	1010	Max certified passenger accommodation:	145 (FAA/EASA)
Airframe hours:	38,425 h	Current operator:	No Operator-AOG
Airframe cycles:	40,399 h		
As of	Apr 30 2013		
Marketing Highlights			
MAX thrust upgradable to:		24,408 LBS.	
Last shop visit:		ESN V10535–Aug 11, 2011	
		ESN V10536–Aug 31, 2012	
Weight and Fuel Data			
Max taxi weight		167,329 lb	75,900 kg
Max takeoff weight		166,447 lb	75,500 kg
Max landing weight		137,788 lb	62,500 kg
Max zero fuel weight		128,969 lb	58,500 kg
Basic empty weight		89,254 lb	40,485 kg
Total fuel capacity	6303 gallons	42,079 lb	19,087 kg
Note: (gallons*6.67600 = lb) (gallons*6.67600/2.2046 = kg)			
Maintenance Status	**Date**	**Time Since**	**Cycles Since**
10Y tasks	Sep 9 2008	11,810 h	11,552 cycles
5Y tasks	Sep 9 2008	11,810 h	11,552 cycles
12Y check	Mar 25 2010	7588 h	7224 cycles
6Y check	Mar 25 2010	7588 h	7224 cycles
C1	Oct 5 2011	3044 h	2892 cycles
Landing Gear Overhaul Status	**O/H Date**	**Time Since**	**Cycles Since**
Nose gear	Apr 27 2012	1299 h	1289 cycles
Left main	Apr 25 2012	1299 h	1289 cycles
Right main	Apr 27 2012	1299 h	1289 cycles

Engine Serial Number V10535					
Total cycles:	31,828	Total Hours:	38,486	As of Date:	Apr 30 2013
Last shop visit:	Aug 11 2012	Hours Since:	2409	Cycles Since:	1611
Limiter:	Multiple LLPs			Cyc to limiter:	7586
Engine Serial Number V10536					
Total cycles:	35,049	Total hours:	36,619	As of date:	Apr 30 2013
Last shop visit:	Aug 31 2012	Hours since:	14	Cycles since:	4

FIGURE 11.2

Sample aircraft specification: A319.

Limiter:	Multiple LLPs			Cyc to limiter:	3819

Avionics Equipment	Qty Manufacturer/Model No	Part Number
Navigation		
Adf receiver	2 Collins/	822-0299-020
Air data internal reference unit	3 Honeywell Intl/	HG2030AD11
ATC transponder	2 Collins/	822-0336-020
DME interrogator	2 Collins/	822-0329-020
Enhanced ground proximity warning system	1 Allied Signal/	965-0976-003-206-206
Multimode receiver	2 Rockwell/	822-1152-121
Radio altimeter transceiver	2 Collins/	822-0334-020
TCASS II processor	1 ACCSS-AN L3 Communicat/	7517900-10003
VOR receiver	2 Collins/	822-0297-020
Weather radar control unit	1 Rockwell Collins/	622-5129-021
Weather radar transceiver	1 Collins/	622-5132-622
Communications		
Cabin intercommunication data system director	2 KID-Systeme GMBH/	Z010H0005119
Cockpit voice recorder	1 Substandard/	980-6022-001
HF transceiver	1 Collins/	822-0330-020
LH 8.4 LCD retractable monitor	7 Rockwell Collins/	1303 153-101
LH 8.4 LCD retractable monitor	7 Rockwell Collins/	1303 153-100
Seat electronic box	48 Rockwell Collins/	1142400-130
VHF transceiver	3 Rockwell/	822-1047-030
Video control center	1 Rockwell Collins/	1303 194-002
Video system control unit	1 Rockwell Collins/	610860-0001
Indicating and Recording System		
Flight warning computer	2 Aerospatiale/	350E053021010
Solid state flight data recorder	1 Allied Signal/	980-4700-003
System data acquisition concentrator	2 Aerospatiale/	350E5151331

FIGURE 11.2

(Continued).

other tax experts or special legal counsel who may be brought in. The lessor would normally go to meet with an airline's team, and the lessor's team would typically involve a team of five. The airline might have a constant team or might bring in experts in different areas such as legal, technical, credit, and so on during the lease negotiation process (Fig. 11.3).

Lessor	Lessee
1. Marketing VP	1. CEO/CFO/fleet director/manager
2. New aircraft configurations team—spec and budgets (new a/c only)	2. Director of maintenance
3. Technical	
4. Corporate credit committee	3. Board
5. Legal/contracts	4. Legal/contracts

FIGURE 11.3

Parties in a lease negotiation.

OVERVIEW OF AN AIRCRAFT LEASE DOCUMENT

As was mentioned before, a lease is a contractual and a binding agreement between the lessee and the lessor, whereby the lessor lends the asset for use by the lessee for a specified period of time in return for periodic payments of rent. The lease document therefore spells out in detail the key lease terms and conditions of the agreement which we will discuss below.

RENTAL RATE

For a new aircraft, the delivery date can be around 18–36 months from the time the agreement is reached between the lessor and lessee. Hence, the lease contract is a long-dated transaction, and due to this the rents are often indexed and quoted in a base month or year and are often adjusted upward or downward immediately prior to delivery by a formula based on fluctuations in a US-indexed reference rate. This is done in order to take into account the uncertainty surrounding where the future market rates and borrowing costs would be, in order to ensure that the lessor earns a reasonable rate of return and the lessee pays a reasonable rent, commensurate with future market conditions, when the aircraft is actually delivered.

Rent can also be adjusted upward or downward based on changes to the build specification of the aircraft. The rent that the lessor would charge would be based on the initial specification for the aircraft. If before the aircraft delivery date, the airline wants to either upgrade or downgrade these initial specifications, the lessor has to adjust the rental either upward or downward based on the cost of the new specification required by the airline. The lessor would generally look to amortize the cost of the specification over the period of the first lease, though options such as increase in takeoff weight (maximum takeoff weight, MTOW) or engine thrust may provide value to a subsequent lessor.

Rent is also quoted in base year dollars and is escalated until actual delivery date in accordance with the manufacturer's price revision formula in order to provide for increases in labor and material cost over time. It is possible that manufacturers can cap the increase in the escalation cost to the lessor, and in this case, the lessor may pass on that benefit to the lessee by capping the escalation in the rent. Lessors however are cautious, in agreeing to a rental cap, and may do so only if the manufacturer is willing to cap the increase in the escalation price of the aircraft, as otherwise they can lose money from the transaction.

EXAMPLE 11.1 LEASE RENTAL ADJUSTMENT

The base rent of US$500,000 (in delivery dollars) per month is based on an assumed 12-year swap rate of 2% (the "assumed swap rate").

The base rent shall be adjusted upwards or downwards by US$324 for every 100th of 1% (0.01%) difference between the assumed swap rate and the actual 12-year swap rate prevailing on the date falling 2 business days before the delivery date, in accordance with the following formula:

Formula:	Base Rent + (Actual Rate − Assumed Rate) × N × 100
Base Rent:	US$500,000 (in delivery dollars)
Actual Rate	the US$ 12 year ask swap rate (as shown on Bloomberg IRSB 18, rounded to two decimal places and expressed as a number rather than a percentage) on the date falling two (2) Business Days before the Delivery Date
Assumed Rate	2%
N	US$324

Rent for a used aircraft is typically a fixed amount, and there is often no indexing to this rental as the time until delivery is short term and ranges from 6 to 12 months from the date of the transaction. Reconfiguration cost for a used aircraft is usually amortized over the lease term. Example 11.1 shows a sample lease rental adjustment formula for a new aircraft.

LEASE TERM

A typical lease term for a new aircraft is between 120 and 144 months (10−12 years). This is an optimal period for a lessor to amortize the cost of the airline's specification and to obtain a reasonable rate of return on their investment. In general, a lessor would prefer a longer term and airline would push for a shorter term, but 120−144 months is a typical length for the first lease.

For a used aircraft, the lessor would set the lease term based on the maintenance status of the aircraft. For example, for an A320 which has just completed its 6/12-year structural maintenance check, it is better to lease it for 6 years rather than 5 years in order to prevent the next lessee from the operational impact of taking the aircraft out of service to complete the next due structural maintenance check on it. It is often therefore preferable to align the lease term with when the expected heavy airframe maintenance events are due. Lease terms will also vary based on the specific aircraft and engine type; if there is a large supply of a particular aircraft and engine type relative to demand in the market, it may depress the lease rates, and therefore, it is better to have a lease term that ends before they come on the market. The operator's utilization profile (whether the airline operates over a shorter leg or a longer leg) is another factor that may affect the optimal lease length. The operator environment (whether the aircraft is operated in a normal climate or in a harsh and corrosive environment) may also dictate the lease term. For example, if you lease to an airline which is an island-based carrier, which operates the aircraft in a salty and corrosive environment, a longer lease term would cause more wear and tear on the airframe and engines requiring more frequent and expensive maintenance and reducing the residual value of the aircraft. It is therefore preferably in this case to have a shorter lease term.

Both the lessor and the lessee are trying to optimize the lease term which will increase their bottom line, and therefore, the lease term often needs to be negotiated and often involves compromises on both sides. Where the aircraft stands in its life cycle is also an important consideration that the lessor has to take into account when deciding the appropriate lease term. For example, if the aircraft is at its end of its life, and the lessor has used up the maintenance reserve collected on the aircraft on the maintenance of the aircraft during the lease, and the aircraft has to be scrapped immediately after it comes off its lease, the lessor could lose a lot of money from their investment, as there is very little value in parting out the aircraft. Therefore, it is very important to think about when to get the aircraft back from a cash flow and optimization point for the lessor.

SECURITY DEPOSIT

Security deposit can be a fixed amount or can be a multiple of agreed monthly rental. If it is a multiple of monthly rental, typically the security deposit is about 2–3 months of the lease rental. The lessor and lessee agree on a schedule of payment, and the first tranche is usually due shortly after the MoU execution for the lessor to remove the aircraft from the market for exclusive lease to the lessee, while the other tranches would be based on a negotiated schedule. Security deposits are based upon jurisdictional and airline credit risk assumed by the lessor.

Jurisdictional risk

The security deposit collected will reflect the risk of the jurisdiction of the country to which the aircraft is leased. This would involve considerations such as legal and political remedies available for the lessor to repossess the aircraft in case of default or bankruptcy of the airline. For example, strong labor laws in some countries may make it difficult to repossess the aircraft if the local court feels that it may cause job loses if the airline loses the use of its aircraft. In these instances, security deposits would normally be higher for leasing to airlines in these jurisdictions.

Airline credit risk

Airlines are assigned credit ratings based on their management team, business plans, company financial statements, market outlook, extent of competition, and the region in which they operate. Security deposits collected will reflect the airline credit risk that the lessor is exposed to.

Security deposits are intended to offset the lessor's risk from rental payments, reserve payments, maintenance obligations, liens against the aircraft, misuse of the aircraft, insurance deductibles, and loss of use of the aircraft. Security deposits can be either cash or letter of credit issued by a local bank. Letter of credit is more popular, especially for an airline with a better credit profile. The letter of credit must be in a form and substance acceptable to the lessor and should be extremely precise, otherwise the banks may be reluctant to pay in the event an airline default as the onus then falls on them to collect from the airline. Further for a lessor, it is better to have a letter of credit drawn against a local bank rather than a foreign bank, as the risk to the lessor is less if it can transact directly with their local bank as opposed to dealing with a foreign bank. If the airline insists that they want to issue a letter of credit from a foreign bank, the lessor may require that it be confirmed by a local bank to reduce their risk. In the event of a default, the letter of credit effectively transfers the risk to the local bank, who then would transact with the foreign bank to get the funds. In some jurisdictions it is better to have a letter of credit as opposed to cash, as in a bankruptcy, letter of credit is often considered as a payment before the bankruptcy and is therefore protected, while cash payment maybe considered payment from the future earnings of the company, which may not be permitted in a bankruptcy. Therefore, a letter of credit may be more bankruptcy proof than a cash payment in some jurisdictions. If there is no difference in how cash payment or letter of credit is treated, then the lessor would usually be indifferent between the two methods of payment of the security deposit by the lessee.

The security deposit is returned by the lessor to the lessee at the end of the lease term, provided no event of default has occurred and is continuing and upon redelivery of the aircraft in compliance with the redelivery conditions set forth in the lease.

INSURANCE

In addition to liability insurance, two other major forms of insurance are hull and war risk insurance (Scheinberg, 2014). For a new aircraft, a lessor would insist that the lessee insure the aircraft for 110%–115% of its book value. The extra insurance is normally used to cover the loss of future earnings and to provide liquidity in the aircraft, so that the aircraft could be sold to another lessor for a higher price without requiring the lessor to increase the insurance limits on the aircraft. Liability insurance is usually about 3 and 4 million USD for a passenger seat. Deductible limits are based on the airlines credit ratings. While airlines with a strong credit rating can insist on high deductibles, airlines that are weaker credits may have lower deductibles. Self-insurance by the airline is also based on the credit worthiness of the airline today and in the future. Finally, the lessor may insist on a nondiscriminatory clause which would insist that the airlines not insure the aircraft from the lessor for a lower amount than what they insure other aircraft in their fleet.

QUIET ENJOYMENT

Quiet enjoyment clause allows the lessee to operate the aircraft without interference from the lessor as long as they are meeting their obligations in terms of payment of rent, maintenance reserves, and other conditions set forth in the lease. The lessor may require the right to periodically inspect the aircraft and its associated records, but as long as the lessee is meeting their obligations, the lessor usually has to take a hands-off approach to the lease and cannot insist on where and how the airlines operate the aircraft. The lessee may be able to sublease the aircraft if it is provided for in the lease contract (Fig. 11.4).

HELL OR HIGH WATER CLAUSE

This clause says that the lessee (airline) has to make rental and other payments no matter what their condition is including being subject to natural calamities. This is important because it affects the lessor's ability to finance the cost of the purchase of the aircraft as the lessor has to rely on the cash flow to make payments to their bank. It also affects the liquidity of the aircraft to the lessor if the airline does not make periodic payments. Finally, the clause helps to prevent ambiguity in a

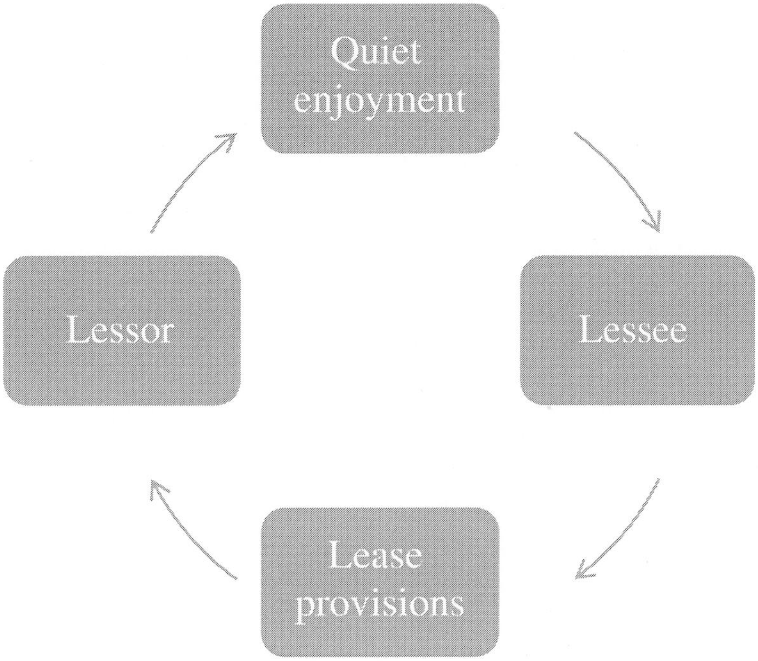

FIGURE 11.4

Lease concept: quiet enjoyment.

bankruptcy situation, as the clause allows the lessee to still make payments when the airlines are going through bankruptcy (Littlejohns & McGairl, 1998).

AIRCRAFT DELIVERY CONDITIONS

With a new aircraft delivery, there is a contractual relationship between the aircraft manufacturer and the leasing company. With that relationship, the leasing company may order certain aircraft based on the specification requirement of the airline. Seasonality affects when the airline would want to take delivery of the aircraft. Usually in the Northern Hemisphere, the busy season for an airline is late spring to summer. In the Southern Hemisphere, the busy season is reversed. Further the lessor has to also decide the right time to take delivery of the aircraft based on the demand for that particular type of aircraft. It is also important that the lessor be aware of the product life cycle of the aircraft. It is not very lucrative for the lessor to take delivery of an aircraft whose production run is set to end. The lessor in these instances should negotiate a lower price for the aircraft which is nearing the end of its life cycle. For example, though Airbus is still selling the A320ceo even after the introduction of the A320neo, the price of A320ceo has dropped significantly, as airlines have opted for the more technologically advanced and fuel efficient A320neos.

New aircraft specification and condition

The aircraft specifications that the lessee might require with respect to the new aircraft include the engine model (where there is a choice) and the thrust rating, interior modifications to include the layout of passenger accommodations (LOPA), buyer-furnished equipment (BFE), in-flight entertainment (IFE), and so on. It should also specifically address how changes in these specifications from the lessee will be addressed in the future. These changes are often incorporated into the specific change notice agreement. The lessor needs to think about the future usefulness of any equipment installed in the aircraft and not just for the first lease but for the second and third lease. For example, if a lessee needs Direct TV as part of the IFE system, will a subsequent lessee want this as well? Will the equipment become outdated over time? It is possible that the first lessee might want the equipment but the subsequent lessee's may not require it, and the lessor therefore has to do a cost−benefit analysis to determine if this is something they need to negotiate with the lessee.

Finally, the lessor needs to be cognizant about the requirements of different regulating bodies such as Federal Aviation Administration (FAA) or European Aviation Safety Agency (EASA). It is possible the first lessee may be based in the United States and may be concerned only about the FAA regulations, but subsequently, if the aircraft is leased to a European carrier then the airline might want the aircraft to be EASA compliant. The lessor might therefore decide to make the

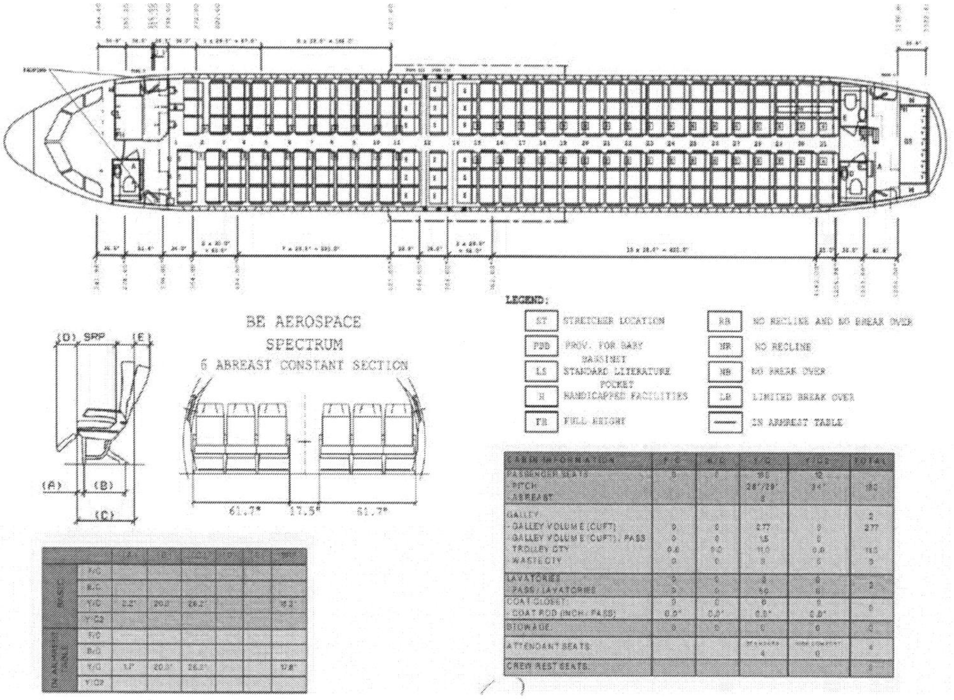

FIGURE 11.5

Sample LOPA A320−200. *LOPA*, Layout of passenger accommodations.

aircraft dual complaint with the FAA and EASA regulations, but the first lessee may not want to pay the additional cost of the EASA regulation. In this case, the lessor has to make a decision on whether the additional cost of dual compliant aircraft is worth the subsequent benefit from a future lease (Fig. 11.5).

New aircraft configuration time frame

Usually a new technology widebody such as Boeing 787 or Airbus 350 has the longest lead time ranging from 34 to 36 months, because they are early in the production cycle, and it takes longer for Boeing and Airbus to take the specifications, design, build, and deliver the aircraft. This means the lessor needs to get the specifications far in advance from the airline or the lessee which gives the airline an edge in the negotiating process. If it is a current technology widebody such as Airbus 330 or Boeing 777, the configuration time can range from 14 to 16 months before delivery. The narrow-body aircraft configuration time frame is usually 12 months before delivery and does not vary significantly between new technology and current technology aircraft. If prior to delivery the lessee goes into a financial distress or bankruptcy, the lessor needs to go back to the manufacturer to see what can be changed in the configuration. If it is a new technology aircraft, unfortunately, not a lot can be changed and the lessor has to take delivery of the aircraft with the existing specifications (Fig. 11.6).

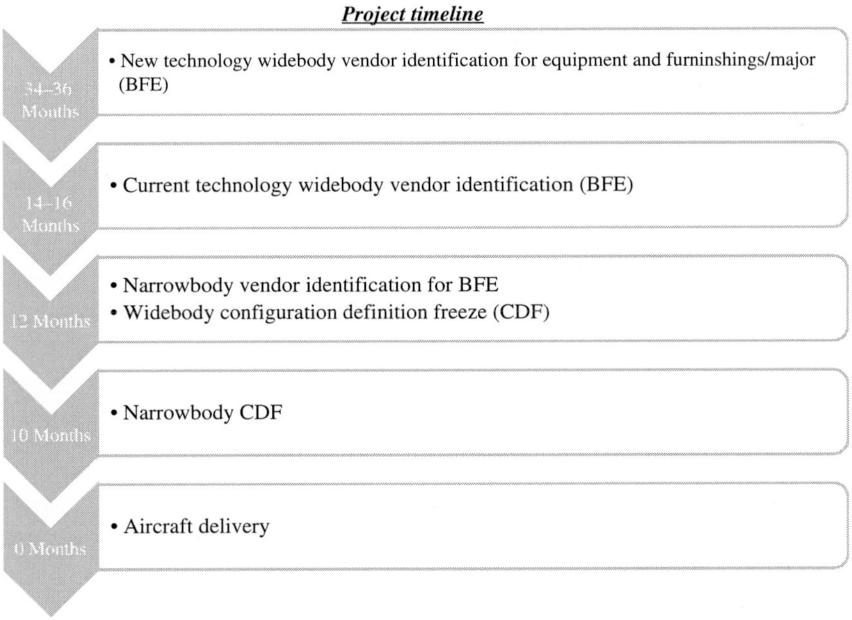

FIGURE 11.6

New aircraft configuration framework.

Used aircraft: Specification and condition

The lessor would often refer to the estimated cost of configuring and transitioning an aircraft from one lessee to the other as a rough order of magnitude (ROM) based on the new configuration. These costs include the cost of the interior, IFE cost, regulatory compliance cost, and other costs mentioned above. Once the cost is determined then the lessor and lessee need to negotiate how the cost is going to be shared between the two parties. In general, the lessor needs to have a transition plan in place 18 months before the first lease ends for a widebody and about 12 months before the lease ends for a narrow-body aircraft. Usually an increase in MTOW or upgrades to the engine thrust can take longer to complete than the time allotted for the transition process. The lessor also has to consider any new maintenance conditions that would be required from the new lessee and how it will matchup with the redelivery condition from the existing lessee, as well as take into account the current maintenance condition of the major maintenance components of the aircraft such as flight hours accrued since the most recent performance restoration of each engine, life remaining of the life-limited parts (LLPs) of each engine, and time remaining to the next due airframe heavy maintenance visit, landing gear overhaul, and auxiliary power unit (APU) refurbishment. If an aircraft is close to any of the maintenance checks, the lessor may decide to incur the cost of the maintenance in order to improve the marketability of the aircraft to the second lessee. The lessor also has to ensure the aircraft is compliant with all applicable regulations, airworthiness directives (ADs) and service bulletins.

Aircraft redelivery conditions

The focus here is from a documentation and lease negotiation perspective. It is important that the lease document clearly spells out where the aircraft is redelivered, who is going to cover the cost of the redelivery, and so on. The document should allow for some flexibility for both the lessor and lessee. The lessor would probably want the aircraft redelivered close to the where their next lessee is or where there are maintenance facilities to enable them to do transition work on the aircraft. It is therefore important to have a degree of flexibility built into the lease. For example, if the lease specifies that the aircraft would be delivered in Reykjavik, Iceland, but the lessor prefers that the aircraft be delivered in Shannon, Ireland, and is willing to bear the additional cost of ferrying the aircraft from Reykjavik, Iceland, to Shannon, Ireland, there should be such a ferry provision in the document. It is also very important to thoroughly inspect the aircraft records during the redelivery process as without proper records the aircraft will not be able to be placed on the next airline's operating certificate and therefore the value will be significantly diminished. A significant portion of the lease document is therefore devoted to the records the lessor has provided to the lessee and detailed guidelines for the lessee to maintain those records during the lease and how they have to be returned to the lessor at the end of the lease. Lessors often expect the original records to be updated and returned at the end of the lease and often expect to see the "dirty fingerprints" of the mechanics on the documents to make sure they are the original records and the records have been kept diligently by the airline. Having said that, electronic record keeping is gaining popularity and original paper records might soon become a thing of the past.

The redelivery process generally includes a test flight to ensure the aircraft operates within the manufacturer's parameters. If there are any anomalies recognized, they are reported and then corrected. The lessor and lessee's representatives would be present during the test flight to identify and confirm any discrepancies noted during the test flight.

Care should also be taken to ensure that modifications performed on the aircraft are properly performed, and documented, and the work meets regulatory approval. If due care is not exercised in this area, it may cost the lessor a significant amount of money to reengineer the modification, and the additional time on the ground may result in lost lease rental revenue stream.

Maintenance covenants and reserves

We covered maintenance reserve in detail in Chapter 9, and here our goal is to focus on the lease documentation and negotiation aspect of maintenance reserves.

From a lessor's perspective, it is important to understand the relationship between the maintenance condition of the aircraft when it is delivered with the expectations of the maintenance condition of the aircraft when it is redelivered back from the lessee. Lessors often set the maintenance redelivery condition based on remarketability of the aircraft and the anticipated requirements of the next lessee. If there were accidents or incidents with the aircraft during the lease, the lessor will require documentation that the issue has been properly addressed or need a no accident or incident statement.

Purpose of maintenance covenants

The principal purpose of the maintenance covenants

- is to ensure that the aircraft is in an acceptable condition as mutually agreed between lessee and lessor, prior to delivery to the lessee;
- states lessee's obligation regarding qualifying maintenance events, along with specific minimums on the condition and certification of the airframe, engines, and various components during the lease term;
- includes lessee's obligation regarding the treatment of maintenance reserves for the aircraft during the lease term; and
- outlines the required maintenance of the aircraft upon return to the lessor.

Maintenance reserves

To review, there are five major components that require expensive maintenance and where the lessor seeks to cover the cost of the maintenance for these components through the collections of maintenance reserves. The unit of maintenance consumption is measured in flight hours (FHs), APU hours, flight cycles (FCs), or calendar interval. The five major maintenance components are

airframe heavy structural inspection,
engine performance restoration,
engine LLPs,
landing gear overhaul, and
APU restoration.

The lessor seeks to collect maintenance reserves from the lessee due to the following reasons:

- To cover the usage of different components of the aircraft listed above.
- Provide resources for the next technical restoration.
- Protect the lessor in the event of the lessee's default.

In general, the cash collected, as part of the maintenance reserves, stays with the aircraft as it transitions to the next lessee.

END OF LEASE OPTIONS

At the end of the lease, the lease may also provide options to the lessor such as an early termination option, extension option, or purchase option.

Early termination option

A lessor usually may provide an early termination option in order to create a follow on deal with the lessee. This option may specify that the lessor would agree to an early termination of the lease if the lessee is willing to agree to a new lease or if certain conditions are met such as agreeing to lease a newer version of the aircraft that will be available from the lessor at a later date. Such an arrangement might enable the lessor to convince a lessee to an initial longer lease term with an option for early termination than if the lessee did not have the early termination option. An early termination option also gives an airline fleet rationality and flexibility to adjust their aircraft requirements based on current market demand for travel. For a lessor, an early termination may provide a situation where current market lease rates may be better at the time of the termination, if the airline decides to take the option, then when the original lease was executed.

The downside of the option to the lessor is that an aircraft with a lease attached with an early termination option may not be very liquid. For example, if the lease term is for 8 years with an early termination option at 5 years then the buyer of the aircraft has to price it as if the lease rental stream is for 5 years and not 8 years, as they do not know if the lessee will exercise their option for early termination. Further even if the lessee does not want to exercise the option, they may use it as a negotiating tool to reduce the rent they are paying on the lease.

Extension option

This option would allow the lessee to extend the lease subject to an agreement on a new rental rate for the extension term. This situation has benefits for both the lessor and lessee. For the lessee, it gives some stability in their fleet, and for the lessor, it cuts down on the cost of transitioning the aircraft to a new lessee. The one issue that the lessor may face if they have agreed to a lease rental for the extension in advance would be that the airlines will be unwilling to renegotiate if the lease rentals are higher but may want to extend the lease if the lease rentals are lower. Therefore, the lessor in effect has limited their upside from the extension while being exposed to the downside. Further, the lessor also needs to reset the redelivery condition and maintenance condition requirements for the extension as well.

Purchase option

A purchase option is usually very rare in an operating lease agreement and if they do exist the purchase price is usually set to the market price at the time of the expiration of the lease. If a lessor has granted a purchase option to the lessee, a lessor needs to prepare in advance and not remarket the aircraft as the lessee might exercise the purchase option.

EXAMPLE 11.2 CALCULATING AD COST SHARING BETWEEN LESSEE AND LESSOR

If the cost to the lessee of incorporating an AD issued on a terminating action basis exceeds $75,000, the lessor will reimburse the lessee for the permitted lessee's share of such cost in an amount equal to "X" determined in accordance with the following formula within 30 days of receipt of a satisfactory detailed invoice specifying the direct costs incurred by the lessee in incorporating such AD, provided that the lessor shall have no obligation to reimburse any such amounts for so long as any default has occurred and is continuing:

$$X = \frac{(Z - Y) \times (C - T)}{Z}$$

where X is the amount to be reimbursed to the lessee. Y is the number of months between (1) the earlier of (a) the date of completion of the incorporation of such AD and (b) the date on which the AD was originally required to be incorporated and (2) the date of expiry or earlier termination of the Lease. Where the date specified in (b) above is after the end of the lease term or the earlier termination of the lease for such aircraft, Y shall equal 0. C is the reasonable cost to the lessee of completing the AD, excluding any costs associated with inability to operate the aircraft whilst incorporation of the AD was being carried out and including all subsidies and discounts provided to the lessee. T is the threshold amount in dollars, equal to $[ ]. Z is lease term in months.

OTHER TECHNICAL PROVISIONS IN A LEASE

AD cost sharing

ADs are mandatory orders issued by the regulating authority of the type certificate holder or the state of registration for the aircraft. The ADs issued by the regulatory authority of the type certificate holder are normally the ones that lessors are interested in, and they usually require inspections or modifications of the applicable aircraft or engines within a defined period. The terms of the lease will require the lessee to ensure compliance with all applicable ADs. Some leases also have cost sharing arrangements, which mean that the lessor may share the cost of an AD with the lessee in the event that the cost exceeds an agreed threshold. To protect future lessees, the compliance requirement often extends beyond the end date of the lease to ensure that ADs issued later, but effective retrospectively, are also covered. The example below shows how AD cost sharing arrangement would be covered in the lease (see Appendix 2, Section 9) (Example 11.2).

Parts manufacturer approval (PMA)

PMA parts are a misnomer for non-original equipment manufacturer (OEM) parts. Lessors will preclude the installation of parts on an aircraft that are not approved for use by the OEM. PMA is an FAA abbreviation for Parts Manufacturer Approval, which is an FAA approved system for approval to manufacture parts that is given to third parties. It can be used to provide parts as a cheaper alternative to those specified by the equipment OEM, which to all intents and purposes meet the technical standards of the original part but have not been approved for use by the OEM.

It's the non-OEM approved PMA part that lessors seek to prevent the use of. The use of PMA parts is not illegal per se, but lessors will generally want to prevent their installation on their assets (Karesh & Burns, 2009). The reason for that is best illustrated in the example of a PMA part installed into an engine. If that engine subsequently goes into an OEM overhaul shop, the part will be discarded, no matter the condition of that part. More recently, engine OEMs have made it clear that they will not vouch for the serviceability of LLPs if they have been installed in an unapproved configuration, meaning an engine that contains any non-OEM approved parts or parts that have been repaired in a manner not approved by the OEM. The costly consequence of this is that the entire LLP stack may need to be replaced before reaching its limits, even though the majority of parts installed in the engine may not be PMA parts. Another problem the lessor may face is that a PMA part approved by the regulatory authority and installed in an aircraft or engine may not be acceptable to a subsequent regulatory authority when the aircraft is re-leased. This could result in the lessor being required to replace all such PMA parts that were installed by the prior lessee.

Subleasing and pooling of engines

The lease may permit the lessee to sublease the aircraft to another lessee as well as transfer engines and other parts to a different aircraft within the fleet of aircraft operated by Lessee (Karesh & Burns, 2009). This arrangement, though not preferred by the lessor because it may make the redelivery of aircraft more complicated, is nevertheless offered to the lessee in the lease. Engine pooling arrangements with other airlines or maintenance providers, while desirable for an airline, is detrimental for a lessor. In such a pooling arrangement, the pooled engine may be installed on a different airline's aircraft and in a default situation the lessor may have difficulty getting its engine returned as the lessor will not have a contractual relationship with the airline utilizing the pooled engine.

SALE/PURCHASE AGREEMENT

One can distinguish two major types of operating lease transactions, namely, an owned used or new order book lease transaction and a sale and leaseback transaction. In a sale and leaseback transaction, the lessor will purchase the aircraft from the lessee and immediately lease it back to the lessee. Appendix 1 shows an LoI for a sale and leaseback transaction. In an order book transaction for a new aircraft, the lessor will agree to lease an aircraft to a lessee which it has on order with the OEM such as Boeing or Airbus. The lessor would obtain the aircraft specifications from the lessee and request the aircraft manufacturer to build the aircraft to the lessee's specification. Appendix 2 shows an LoI for an order book transaction.

The important difference between an order book transaction and a sale and leaseback transaction is that the sale and leaseback transaction will also have a purchase agreement between the seller (lessee) and buyer (lessor) in addition to the lease agreement. Further if it is a new aircraft, there is also a tripartite agreement with the OEM to cover off on what happens to any PDPs if the buyer (lessor) assumes the obligation, but the seller defaults (lessee) on the lease. We discuss PDPs in detail below.

In a sale and leaseback transaction, there is an often a tradeoff for the lessee between obtaining a higher acquisition price or a lower lease rental. This tradeoff is referred to as the high–high or low–low deals, where if the lessor pays a high acquisition price, they are likely to charge a higher rental, and if they pay a lower acquisition price, they may charge a lower rental, in order to achieve their target return.

From a lessor's perspective, the two types of lease transactions, namely, the order book and sale and leaseback transaction represent two alternative growth channels, which open additional business opportunities with their customers. The two transactions also provide cyclical risk balancing as the two channels will have different and often opposing financial characteristics at different points in the industry cycle. In a strong market, airlines will pay a premium for additional lift from a lessor's order book, compared to weaker points in the cycle. But at the same time, competition for sale and leaseback campaigns is higher as more lessors have an appetite for growth which drives up acquisition prices, dilutes some of the key terms, and thereby lowers returns. As the lessor's business model is built on actively trading assets, lowering the economic returns that facilitate future sales of aircraft from the portfolio will result in fewer viable sale and lease back opportunities in a strong market relative to a weaker one, but better placement transactions can be secured. The dynamics would be reversed in a weak market as then lessees are willing to trade the aircraft for a lower price in order to increase their cash inflow and reduce the lease rentals. In these weaker economic conditions, therefore, sale and leaseback transactions would be more profitable for the lessor compared to an order book transaction.

PARTIES TO THE TRANSACTION

The major parties to a lease transaction would be the lessee (airline), the lessor, and a lender which finances the lease transaction. If it is a new aircraft transaction and PDP financing is involved, then the manufacturer may also be a party to the transaction.

Tax considerations

The lease will specify that all payments by lessee to lessor shall be made free and clear of all taxes and duties, including but not limited to withholding tax, income tax, sales, use and excise taxes, and value-added tax (VAT).

Assignment of rights and obligations (PDPs etc.)

PDPs are progress payments that a purchaser makes to the manufacturer while a new aircraft is being built. PDP payments represent a significant cash expense for the purchaser amounting to up to 30% of the final aircraft price. Purchaser's often finance this obligation using PDP financing.

In a sale and leaseback transaction, the lessee (airline) would purchase an aircraft from a manufacturer and finance a percentage of their PDPs through a secured loan from a bank or a third party. Interest is payable throughout the term of the loan, and principal is payable upon delivery of each aircraft that is the subject of the loan. As collateral, the purchaser (lessee) will grant a lien in favor of the lender over its rights in the aircraft purchase agreement. The purchaser will also arrange a tripartite agreement with the manufacturer. This will include the manufacturer's acknowledgment of the lender's lien and contractual agreements as to how the parties' rights to the aircraft and the PDPs may be dealt with following a default by the purchaser. Such an arrangement would protect a lessor by allowing them to step into the shoes of the buyer (lessee) in the event the lessee ends up defaulting on their interest payments or falls into a financial distress situation (Gee, 2009).

This protection will include an agreed upon purchase price and other commercial terms between the manufacturer and the lessor, which may or may not be the same price as the lessee has with the manufacturer. It may be different, because in many cases, the purchase price is an item held confidential between the buyer (lessee) and the seller (manufacturer). The lessor then has the option to step into the shoes of the lessee in the event of a default, purchase the aircraft, and sell or lease the aircraft to another airline, without concern for loss of the PDPs paid on behalf of the defaulting lessee. In this instance, however, the lessor must carefully consider the specification of the aircraft they are stepping in the shoes to purchase. The defaulting lessee may have had a very bespoke configuration which could be costly to modify and make the aircraft marketable to other airlines. As such, it is generally the case that PDP financing is targeted toward airlines of better credit standing, or for weaker credits, those airlines with a more generic or marketable specification.

It should be noted that the agreement may contain claw back provisions which may enable the purchaser to retrieve its PDP if they can prove to the court that these payments are indeed security deposits made to the manufacturer rather than compensation for the cost of the construction of the aircraft. In order to prevent this under most purchase agreements, the PDPs are described as absolute and unconditional payments to the manufacturer and as such only the manufacturer has interest in the PDPs and not the purchaser. In general, if the manufacturer interest is upheld, the claw back of the PDPs should not occur.

THE ART AND SCIENCE OF LEASE NEGOTIATION

The key to any successful negotiation is reaching acceptable compromises on both sides. A lease negotiation where either party sets out to win every contestable point is unlikely to be successful. Or if it does get done, the subsequent business relationship is not going to be harmonious. Before starting out, each side will need to have determined what “the must have”, items are, what non-essential issues can be traded for other more important ones, and what the bottom line position is for negotiable items.

As outlined before, from a lessor’s perspective, a lease will serve two main purposes. First, to structure an economic return and second, to manage asset and credit risk. A lease transaction will be defined, first and foremost, by the economic returns required by the business. Hard-wired elements of the deal will include a maximum acquisition price for the asset, in the case of a sale and lease back, the details around aircraft specification and return conditions, and deal economics that can be heavily influenced by the lessors cost of funds to finance the acquisition. Further the financeability of the lessee as well as the asset will be a subject for separate due diligence and consideration. Around these key items, the lease will be structured to include mitigants to the key risks identified. These mitigants include security deposits, the lease rental rate, maintenance reserves, and perhaps some financial covenants, that might for example trigger a change from letters of credit to cash in the event that the airlines liquidity position falls below an agreed threshold.

THE SCIENCE OF THE LEASE NEGOTIATION PROCESS

Is lease negotiation a science or an art? The answer is that it is both a science and an art. There are certain elements of the lease which can be considered a science. For a lessor, the areas where a firm stance is usually required, which are also typically science rather than art driven are the financial ones, principally the acquisition price of the asset and the lease rate. This is because the acquisition price and lease rentals are market driven and are closely linked to financing costs and the return requirements for the business. It is hard for the lessor to compromise on these factors as the lessor's spread between lease rental and financing cost may be adversely affected if they do so. While the drafting of the lease can be left to the lawyers it is important to ensure that the commercial and technical content have the required input and sign off from the relevant experts. The lease must be water tight: no ambiguities, undefined terms, or confusing wording. This is important because often those who draft and negotiate the lease are not the same parties looking at it later or at lease return 8–12 years later. Experience and a second, or even third, pair of eyes are invaluable.

The art of lease negotiation process

Lease negotiation is an art because a lease involves a compromise between the lessee and the lessor. A lease negotiation is not usually a race. Speed is not the main objective, while excessively slow progress can also be counterproductive. Getting the terms of the lease right is an essential precursor to a good business relationship and avoiding ambiguity later. The outcome must be one that leaves both parties happy. While the art aspects of a lease negotiation generally will depend on the individual lessor, lessee, and transaction, one can think of the negotiation around the risk mitigants, namely, maintenance reserves and security deposits, as areas requiring compromise and negotiation. The extent of the compromise from a lessor's perspective will depend on factors such as lessee's track record of performance under previous leases, additional protection that the lessee can provide, or if the lessee is located in a country which is signatory to the Cape Town Convention.

For the lessee, the first requirement if they are sourcing additional aircraft from lessor order books is availability, both in time and the right model and specification. Beyond that, it becomes a matter of negotiating down from the lessors opening position on lease rate, terms, and risk mitigants and preserving as much flexibility as possible and minimizing restrictions and obligations. The outcome or success in the lessee's pursuit of a more attractive deal will be largely dependent on supply and demand dynamics at the moment in time. In the case of a sale and leaseback, the airline will often have a figure in mind for an acquisition price and for the associated lease rate. This will largely be dependent on the number of potential financiers in the market, and the availability and prevalence of capital. From there, an airline should focus on their objective to maximize their sale price or reduce the amount of monthly lease rate burden. For an airline, there is always a trade-off between up front trading gains on the aircraft's sale versus the running cost of the lease rental for the duration of the lease.

From a lessor perspective, the important factors, starting at the top and working down, are essentially selecting the right assets, paying the right prices for them, placing them on appropriate leases that generate acceptable returns for the business, managing the risk associated with the leases and assets throughout the period of the lease and then having a process in place that ensures that your redelivery activity and you're remarketing the asset to the next lessee works in a seamless manner and reflects the same level of diligence that the lessor would have gone through in that initial lease.

Lease negotiation therefore is a recurrent process, it's a cyclical process, and in terms of managing risk, it is absolutely an ongoing process.

SUMMARY AND CONCLUSION

This chapter focused on the key elements of a lease contract and the lease negotiations process. The key elements contained in a lease include acquisition price in the case of a sale and lease back, lease terms, lease rental, technical specification of the aircraft being delivered, technical return conditions and details on how deviations from these conditions will be compensated, security deposits, maintenance reserves, other risk mitigants and covenants, restrictions on quiet enjoyment, which may include limitations on subleasing or operation in restricted jurisdictions, provisions for AD compliance and cost sharing, both during and after the end of the lease and restrictions on changes to aircraft specification and, to the extent applicable, the use of PMA parts. The appendix to this chapter contains a sample LoI of an order book lease and a sale and leaseback transaction.

The lease negotiation process is both an art as well as a science. For a lessor, one can think of the acquisition price of the asset and the lease rate as more science rather than art as both these factors are linked to financing costs and the return requirements for the business. While the art aspects of a lease negotiation generally will depend on the individual lessor, lessee, and transaction, one can think of the negotiation around the risk mitigants, namely, maintenance reserves and security deposits, as areas requiring compromise and negotiation. The extent of the compromise from a lessor's perspective will depend on factors such as lessee's track record of performance under previous leases, additional protection that the lessee can provide or if the lessee is located in a country which is a signatory to the Cape Town Convention. Case study at the end of the chapter simulates a lease negotiation process and lets you practice your skills in negotiating a lease from a lessor and lessee perspective.

CASE STUDY: LEASE NEGOTIATION

SECTION 1: LESSOR DETAILS

Global Mega Aircraft Leasing, Inc.

- New York–based lessor
- Offices in Dublin, New York, and Hong Kong
- Owns and manages a fleet of 1224 aircraft valued at $45bb
- Current order book of 185 Boeing and 212 Airbus aircraft
- Customers include over 120 airlines in 62 different countries

Industry background

It is the spring of 2018 and the aviation industry is by all accounts doing well. Oil price is low and labor rates are stable. Airlines and leasing companies are enjoying a period of sustained profitability. However, storm clouds are on the horizon. Revenue per available seat mile (RASM) is falling due to increased competition from ultra low-cost carrier (ULCC) airlines which enjoy the benefits of a young (and cheap) labor force and relatively new aircraft; financed and leased while interest rates were very low. Interest rates are forecast to rise by at least 150 basis points over the next 24 months and geopolitical instability is rising around the world. Over the past 9 months, four airlines have declared bankruptcy: three in Europe and one in Russia. Three of those airlines have shut down, leaving large fleets of aircraft that need to be re-leased. Despite these potential warning signs, Airbus and Boeing both enjoy historically large and long-dated order books.

Company specific background

Outwardly, Global Mega Aircraft Leasing (GMAL) is doing well. The stock price is at an all-time high on the back of continuously improving profits. However, privately, GMAL's CEO Hans Hoffmeister has been fretting in internal meetings that six used A320s, two 787s, three 737s, and four A330s are sitting on the ground, in need of a new lessee after the recent bankruptcies. This number of aircraft on the ground will have a significant impact on the stock price, especially if GMAL has to report on the earnings call next month that a majority of the aircraft remain available and are not committed via an MoU. In addition, one of the airlines that shut down, Air Sofia, the flag carrier of Bulgaria, committed to lease four new A320neo aircraft to deliver in the first quarter of 2019. Time is very short to change the configuration of these aircraft before Airbus begins production in mid-2018. Changes made after production commences can cost over 50% more than pre-production. This additional cost can turn a profitable lease into a deal that loses money for the entire lease term. Hans recently said on the internal global marketing call for his staff that placing these new and used aircraft was the company's number one priority. If he needs to report these facts on the earnings call, the CFO estimates the stock could decline by as much as 30%. As employees, everyone's compensation comprised a reasonable salary, but the bonus is paid in shares of company stock. Therefore, this news could prove to be disastrous for everyone. On the other hand, rushing to place the aircraft at terms that aren't economically viable could be equally as bad as the aircraft would drag down earnings for the foreseeable future. Luckily, the Hong Kong–based marketing team is very close to securing a deal to lease the used 737 and A330 aircraft.

Market background

Past transactions on used aircraft leased by GMAL for aircraft similar to those that became available in the bankruptcies were leasing for $225,000 per month for A320ceos. You have heard in the market that used 787s lease for around $800,000. The typical deal calls for 2–3 months cash security deposit and either cash maintenance reserves or a letter of credit. Used narrowbodies generally lease for a term of 6 years and used widebodies for 8 years. For new aircraft, rents on the A320neo were leasing around $400,000 late last year, but more recently have fallen to around $380,000 based on a lease term of 12 years.

GMAL's breakeven analysis shows that you can decrease the rent by roughly $15,000 per month for a used narrowbody, $30,000 per month for a new narrowbody, and $70,000 per month for a widebody based on the average terms above before the deals start to lose money. The impact of shortening the lease duration by 1 year equals roughly $5000 less in rent on a narrowbody and $15,000 less on a widebody.

Objective

As the marketing deal team for GMAL, your objective is to place as many of the aircraft as possible at the best possible terms and conditions. You know that your credit committee will likely focus on lease components outside of the rent and the term, so it is important to focus on the deal holistically. You have recently observed that your CEO is becoming agitated with the lack of progress in placing aircraft, quite possibly because he has the majority of his compensation tied to the performance of the company stock.

SECTION 2: LESSEE INFORMATION

Fly4Less Air, Ltd

- Stansted-based ULCC
- Service to over 100 airports in Europe, Africa, North America, and Asia
- Operates a fleet of 30 Boeing 787 and 110 Airbus 320ceo aircraft
- Current order book of 20 Boeing 787s and 220 Airbus 320neo aircraft

Industry background

It is the spring of 2018 and the aviation industry is by all accounts doing well. Oil price is low and labor rates are stable. Airlines and leasing companies are enjoying a period of sustained profitability. However, storm clouds are on the horizon. RASM is falling due to increased competition from ULCC airlines which enjoy the benefits of a young (and cheap) labor force and relatively new aircraft: financed and leased while interest rates were very low. Interest rates are forecast to rise by at least 150 basis points over the next 24 months, and geopolitical instability is rising around the world. Over the past 9 months, four airlines have declared bankruptcy, three in Europe and one in Russia. Three of those airlines have shut down, leaving large fleets of aircraft that need to be re-leased. Despite these potential warning signs, Airbus and Boeing both enjoy historically large and long-dated order books.

Company specific background

Outwardly, Fly4Less Air (FLA) is doing well. The airline has been in business for 8 years and is already one of the largest ULCC airlines in the world. Two years ago, FLA listed on the London stock exchange, and the response from investors has been good. However, analysts have started to question the airline's ability to increase profits as the fleet is ageing. To rectify this, FLA placed a large order for new aircraft earlier this year from both Airbus and Boeing. Pricing was excellent, but the aircraft won't start to deliver until 2021 and finish delivering in 2025. The analysts are also starting to make noise that the PDPs for the order book are putting a strain on the airline's cash position. FLA's fiery CEO Jane Whiteside committed to stock analyst's last quarter that they would accelerate their fleet growth by picking up aircraft from lessors to fill the gap until their own orders start to deliver—and at terms that will preserve cash flow wherever possible. The analysts are skeptical that FLA can continue its growth in the medium term given the tight supply of aircraft in the market. Jane has until the earnings call late next month to prove them wrong. If she is correct, the stock will surely takeoff. If she is wrong, the price will plummet–and heads will roll within the airline.

Earlier this week, Jane called the fleet team into her office to explain the growth dilemma the airline is facing. She made it clear that they need to source as many aircraft as possible, but at terms that are extremely favorable to the airline. FLA is known to command the best pricing from suppliers to keep fares low, and aircraft are no exception. Rumor has it that the previous fleet team was fired because the discount they secured on the last leased aircraft was only 3% less than their competitor was reportedly able to achieve. She stated that the bankruptcies of the other airlines were a gift to FLA and the team should secure deals that are amazing, not just in terms of rent but also the other associated lease terms. From a recent industry conference, the team learned that a large chunk of the aircraft from those bankruptcies has already been secured by other airlines, but Jane wants to hear no part of that. As she motioned the team out of the office, the last words they heard were her spattering on about pushing the envelope for a deal with no maintenance reserves and the shortest possible lease term to dovetail with the existing order book deliveries.

Market background

While at a conference, after a few drinks, you learned from your counterpart Jim Morrison at London-based Highfly Air that they recently leased used aircraft prior to the summer season. Lease rates for A320ceo aircraft similar to those that became available in the bankruptcies were $225,000 per month for A320ceos and $800,000 for a few used 787s. You know from experience that used narrowbodies generally lease for a term of 6 years and used widebodies for 8 years. For new aircraft, it was said that rents on the 320neo were leasing around $400,000 late last year, but more recently you have heard that they have fallen to around $380,000 based on a lease term of 12 years.

Objective

As the fleet procurement team for FLA, your objective is to lease as many of the aircraft as possible at the best possible terms and conditions. Even a few aircraft are better than none, depending on the conditions you can achieve from lessors. You have recently observed that Jane has had Jim Morrison coming to visit her at the office, quite possibly to interview for the head of fleet procurement, in the event your team isn't successful. On the flip side, she promoted the team that purchased the Boeing and Airbus aircraft and awarded them with handsome bonuses for their extraordinary efforts.

APPENDIX 1: SAMPLE LETTER OF INTENT (SALE AND LEASEBACK TRANSACTION)

September 15, 2017

SuperJet Limited
Aviation House
Megagrad, Mesopotamia
Attention: Vice President, Leasing

Dear Sir,

- This Letter of Intent ("**LoI**") records the understanding reached between SuperJet Limited ("**SuperJet**") and Aircraft Aerospace Leasing Limited in respect of one (1) A320-200 aircraft as more fully described below.

1. **Purchaser/Lessor**

   Aircraft Aerospace Leasing Limited, and/or its affiliate, owner trust, assignee or nominee. (Lessor will be registered and domiciled in a jurisdiction acceptable to Lessee and will have a minimum tangible net worth of US$25,000,000.)

2. **Seller/Lessee**

   SuperJet (or any affiliate or subsidiary of the foregoing).

3. **Aircraft and Delivery Dates**

Airframe	Engines	MSN	Scheduled Delivery Month
A320-200	CFM56-5B4/3 PIP	1234	November 2019

   The Aircraft shall be new ex-factory as described in more detail in Appendix 1.

   Seller shall notify Purchaser of the Scheduled Delivery Date no later than 1 month before the start of the Scheduled Delivery Month.

   The actual delivery date shall be the date of delivery of the Aircraft from Airbus (the "**Manufacturer**") at its facilities in Toulouse (the "**Delivery Date**"). Seller and Purchaser may agree an extension to the Scheduled Delivery Date if delivery of the Aircraft is delayed by the Manufacturer, but Purchaser shall have no obligation to purchase the Aircraft if the Delivery Date has not occurred by (6) months after end of the Scheduled Delivery Month.

4. **Purchase Price**

   US$42,000,000 per Aircraft in delivery Dollars.

5. **Purchase of Aircraft**

   The Aircraft is subject to a purchase agreement (the "**SuperJet PA**") between Seller and the Manufacturer. Seller will assign to Purchaser (with the consent of the Manufacturer) its right to take title to the Aircraft (including all BFE installed on the Aircraft) under the SuperJet PA (but Seller shall remain responsible for payment of all pre-delivery payments for the Aircraft and all of its other obligations under the SuperJet PA). Seller will sell the Aircraft to the Purchaser on the Delivery Date.

6. **Lease Term**

   72 months.

7. **Rent**

   Lessee shall pay Rent monthly in advance commencing on the Delivery Date.

   Fixed Rent

   The Base Rent of US$355,000 (in delivery dollars) per month is based on an assumed 12 year swap rate of 2% (the "**Assumed Swap Rate**").

   The Base Rent shall be adjusted upwards or downwards by US$174 for every 100th of 1% (0.01%) difference between the Assumed Swap Rate and the actual 5 year swap rate prevailing on the date falling two (2) Business Days before the Delivery Date, in accordance with the following formula:

SWAP Rate Formula:	Base Rent + (Actual Rate − Assumed Rate) × N × 100
Base Rent:	US$355,000 (in delivery dollars)
Actual Rate	the US$ 5 year swap rate (as shown on Bloomberg IRSB 18, rounded to two decimal places and expressed as a number rather than a percentage) on the date falling two (2) Business Days before the Delivery Date
Assumed Rate	2%
N	US$174

8. Security Deposit

US$710,000 in cash payable by Lessee to Lessor as follows:

- US$355,000 within two (2) Business Days following signature of this LoI (the "**LOI Deposit**");
- US$250,000 upon signature of the Lease Agreement; and
- the balance payable no later than two (2) Business Days prior to the Delivery Date.

Interest at 2% will accrue on the Security Deposit and is payable to Lessee at the lease expiration date. The Security Deposit may not be comingled with Lessor's general funds and/or assigned or charged in connection with Lessor's financing of the Aircraft without the express written consent of Lessee. Provided no event of default has occurred and is continuing, the Security Deposit will be repaid to Lessee immediately upon expiry or earlier termination of the Lease, at the lease expiration date.

(Lessee shall have the option, to be exercised either prior to Delivery or at any time during the Lease Period, to substitute the cash Security Deposit with an irrevocable letter of credit issued by a bank satisfactory to Lessor. Lessee will have the right to, at any time during the Lease Period, substitute such letter of credit for cash.)

9. Maintenance Payments

Lessee shall make Maintenance Payments to Lessor in accordance with Appendix 2.

10. Maintenance

Lessee shall be responsible for all maintenance, inspections, repairs, and modifications required for the Aircraft during the Lease Term and at redelivery.

The Aircraft shall be maintained in accordance with Lessee's maintenance program, which shall be in accordance with the maintenance program specified in the Manufacturer's Maintenance Planning Document, as approved by the Aviation Authority and Lessor. The Maintenance Performer for the Aircraft, Engines and Parts shall be approved by Lessor and shall hold the appropriate FAA and/or EASA Part 145 approvals to carry out the required work.

All repairs to the Aircraft, Engines, and Parts, and materials associated with such repairs, must meet the applicable OEM standards and specifications. All Parts that are installed on the Aircraft or Engines during the Lease Term must meet the applicable OEM standards and specifications.

11. Aircraft Documents

Lessee shall maintain all technical records and documents associated with the Aircraft, Engines, and Parts in accordance with the requirements of the Aviation Authority, the

Maintenance Program, and the FAA or EASA and Air Ops, as applicable. All technical records and documentation shall be maintained in English.

12. Redelivery Conditions

Lessee shall redeliver the Aircraft to Lessor on the expiry or earlier termination of the Lease ("**Lease Expiry**") in conformity with the conditions outlined in Appendix 3. The Lease Agreement will include the complete redelivery procedures and conditions.

13. Redelivery Location

Megagrad, Mesopotamia, or other such location agreed between Lessee and Lessor.

14. Registration

Throughout the Lease Term, the Aircraft will be registered with Mesopotamian Civil Aviation Authority (the "**Aviation Authority**") at Lessee's expense on terms satisfactory to Lessor. Lessee shall be responsible for all costs associated with perfecting and recording Lessor's interests in the Aircraft and/or the Lease in the state of registration of the Aircraft. Lessee may change the state of registration of the aircraft without Lessor's consent.

If the Cape Town Convention becomes effective in Mesopotamia or any other relevant jurisdiction, Lessee shall, at no cost to Lessee, take all steps possible to establish and register under such convention all international interests of Lessor in the Aircraft, the Lease and shall provide Lessor with an IDERA authorizing Lessor to deregister the Aircraft on Lease Expiry.

15. Subleasing and Pooling of Parts and Engines

Lessee shall, without the prior written consent of Lessor and subject to usual terms and conditions to be set out in the Lease, have the right to sublease the Aircraft to any airline that is in the SuperJet group of airlines. Lessee shall have the ability to change the state of registration and habitual base of the Aircraft while it is subject to such sublease. Any other sublease shall require Lessor's prior written consent, such consent not to be unreasonably withheld. Any costs incurred by Lessor in connection with any proposed subleasing shall be for the account of Lessee.

- The Lessee may subject engines and parts to normal interchange or pooling agreements within its A320 fleet and with other air carriers or other lessors customary in the airline industry and entered into by Lessee in the ordinary course of its business.

16. Insurance

Lessee shall maintain, at its expense, hull all risks, hull war risks, and liability insurances (including war liability) with insurers acceptable to Lessor and on terms and in amounts acceptable to Lessor with the following limits and/or deductibles:

Insurance	
Hull Value:	US$110% of Purchase Price
Maximum Deductible:	US$250,000
Minimum Liability Coverage:	US$750,000,000

17. Taxes

Purchaser shall be responsible for all taxes relating to the sale and purchase of the Aircraft.

All payments by Lessee to Lessor shall be made free and clear of all taxes and duties, withholding tax, income tax, sales, use and excise taxes, and VAT in Mesopotamia. All taxes other than those on the overall net income of Lessor in its jurisdiction of incorporation and any taxes arising as a result of any lease of the aircraft through Aruba required for Mesopotamian withholding tax purposes, shall be the responsibility of Lessee.

18. Net Lease

The Lease shall be a "net" lease. Lessee's obligation to pay Rent and to perform all of its other obligations under the Lease shall be absolute and unconditional other than where Lessor has breached the terms of the Lease.

Lessee shall be responsible for all costs and expenses associated with the delivery, possession, use, operation, return, maintenance, insurance, import/export of the Aircraft, and compliance with applicable regulations and airworthiness directives.

19. Assignment/Financing

The Aircraft ownership interest and Lessor's interest in the Lease and the Aircraft shall be freely transferable and assignable, and Lessor and/or Owner reserves the right to leverage its interest or to put in place such other financing or other arrangements as Lessor or Owner may consider necessary; provided that (1) such transfer, assignment, financing, or other arrangement does not affect Lessee's quiet enjoyment of the Aircraft; (2) Lessee shall not at any time incur any greater obligations or reduction of its rights under the Lease as a result of such sale, assignment, transfer, novation, disposal, or other arrangement; and (3) any assignee or transferee of Lessor's rights shall not be a competitor of Lessee and shall be otherwise acceptable to Lessee in its sole discretion.

Lessee shall cooperate fully with Lessor in connection with any such transfer, assignment, financing or other arrangement, and if such transfer, assignment, financing, or other arrangement is implemented after the Delivery Date, all legal expenses incurred by Lessee in connection therewith shall be reimbursed by Lessor.

20. Transaction Expenses

Each of Lessee and Lessor shall be responsible for its own costs and expenses associated with the negotiation and completion of this transaction for the sale and lease of the Aircraft, including their respective legal fees.

21. Confidentiality

This LoI is personal to Lessee and Lessee must keep the terms of this LoI strictly confidential and not reveal them to any person other than those employees, directors, officers, and professional advisers of Lessee who are responsible for analyzing, negotiating, and approving the transaction and who are made aware of the confidential nature of it.

22. Documentation

Lessor shall draft a lease agreement and other documentation incorporating the terms of this LoI and other terms normal to sale and leaseback transactions (including, but not limited to, representations and warranties, conditions precedent, payment, maintenance, operational and other covenants, indemnities, and events of default).

It is the intent of Lessor and Lessee that such documentation be agreed as soon as reasonably possible and executed no later than October 15, 2014 by both parties hereto or such other date as Lessor and Lessee may agree (the ***Documentation Date***). Lessor and Lessee agree to negotiate in good faith toward the prompt execution of documentation on or before the Documentation Date.

This LoI is not intended to be and does not constitute a binding or enforceable agreement. A binding commitment with respect to the matters contemplated in this LoI will result only upon execution of the Lease, save that the provisions of the sections relating to the LoI Deposit, Confidentiality and Purchase Documents Withdrawal from Market shall be legally binding as from signature of this LoI.

23. Payments

All payments to Lessor under this LoI and the Lease shall be made in immediately available US Dollars to an account notified by Lessor to Lessee.

24. Withdrawal from Market

By signing this LoI, Seller/Lessee agrees to withdraw the Aircraft from the market.

25. Conditions Precedent

The obligation of Purchaser/Lessor to enter into the Lease and associated transaction documentation is expressly conditional upon:

a. receipt by Lessor of all requisite corporate approvals as well as necessary third party consents;
b. completion of satisfactory transaction documentation on or before the Documentation Date;
c. receipt by Lessor of the LoI Deposit;
d. satisfactory review by Lessor of the technical specification of the Aircraft; and
e. receipt of tax and legal opinions satisfactory to Lessor, at the cost of the Lessor.

26. Validity of Terms

This LoI supersedes all previous proposals and offers and is valid for acceptance until the close of business on [ ] (Irish time).

27. Governing Law

This LoI, the Lease, all other transaction documents and any noncontractual obligations arising out of or in connection with any of them, shall be governed by, and construed in accordance with, the laws of Mesopotamia.

28. No Brokers

Neither Lessor nor Lessee has engaged the services of a broker or similar representative agent for the purposes of this transaction. Each party shall represent to the other the absence of such brokers and representative agents and indemnify the other with respect to any breach of such representation.

Please confirm your acceptance of this LoI by executing a counterpart of this LoI in the space provided below and returning a signed copy to Lessor before the expiry of its validity.

Very truly yours,

AIRCRAFT AEROSPACE LEASING LIMITED

By:

Name:

Title:

Date:

SUPERJET LIMITED
By:
Name:
Title:
Date:

APPENDIX 2: SAMPLE LETTER OF INTENT (ORDER BOOK TRANSACTION)

[Date]

SuperJet Limited
Aviation House
Megagrad, Mesopotamia
Attention: Vice President, Leasing

Dear Sir,

This Letter of Intent ("**LOI**") records the understanding reached between [Airline name] and [Leasing Company] in respect of the leasing of two B737-800 aircraft (the "**Aircraft**") as more fully described below.

1. **Lessor**

   [Leasing Company], and/or its subsidiary, affiliate, owner trust, assignee, or nominee.

2. **Lessee, Initial Lessee, and Guarantor**

   Lessee: [Airline Name]

   Initial Lessee: [Subsidiary of Airline]

   Guarantor: [Parent Company of Airline Group] shall fully guarantee all the obligations of Lessee

3. **Aircraft and Delivery Dates**

Airframe	Engines	MTOW	MSN	Scheduled Delivery Month
B737-800 x 2	CFM56-7B26E	174,163	TBA	TBA

   The Aircraft shall be new ex-factory as described in more detail in Appendix 1.

   Lessor shall notify Lessee of the Scheduled Delivery Date no later than 1 month before the start of the Schedule Delivery Month.

   The actual delivery date shall be the date of delivery of the Aircraft from Boeing (the "**Manufacturer**") at its facilities in Seattle (the "**Delivery Date**").

4. **Lease Term**

   120 months.

5. **Rent**

   Lessee shall pay Rent monthly in advance commencing on the Delivery Date.

   Fixed Rent

   The Base Rent of US$[ ] per month is based on an assumed [ ] year swap rate of [ ]% (the "**Assumed Swap Rate**").

The Base Rent shall be adjusted upwards or downwards by US$[ ] for every 100th of 1% (0.01%) difference between the Assumed Swap Rate and the actual [ ] year swap rate prevailing on the date falling two (2) Business Days before the Delivery Date, in accordance with the following formula:

Formula:	Base Rent + (Actual Rate − Assumed Rate) × *N* × 100
Base Rent:	US$ [386,000] (in [Jan 2017] dollars)
Actual Rate	The US$ [10] year swap rate (as shown on Bloomberg IRSB 18, rounded to two decimal places and expressed as a number rather than a percentage) on the date falling two (2) Business Days before the Delivery Date
Assumed Rate	[2]
N	US$[189]

6. Security Deposit

Two months' actual rent, US$[772,000] per aircraft in cash payable by Lessee to Lessor on the earlier of (1) two (a) Business Days prior to the date of any forward fixing or (2) two (b) Business Days prior to the Delivery Date.

No interest is payable on the Security Deposit and it may be comingled with Lessor's general funds and/or assigned or charged in connection with Lessor's financing of the Aircraft. The Security Deposit will be repaid to Lessee within 30 days of the end of the Lease Term, subject to Lessee having complied with all of its obligations under the Lease Agreement.

Lessee shall have the option at any time to substitute the cash Security Deposit with an irrevocable letter of credit issued by a bank satisfactory to Lessor and with a minimum credit rating of A − with S&P and A3 with Moody's and otherwise in form and substance satisfactory to Lessor (acting reasonably) and following receipt by Lessor of such letter of credit, any cash Security Deposit shall promptly be returned to Lessee.

7. Maintenance Payments

Lessee shall make Maintenance Payments to Lessor in accordance with Appendix 2.

8. Maintenance

Lessee shall be responsible for all maintenance, inspections, repair, and modification required for the Aircraft during the Lease Term and at redelivery.

The Aircraft shall be maintained in accordance with Lessee's maintenance program, which shall be in accordance with the maintenance program specified in the Manufacturer's Maintenance Planning Data document, as approved by the Aviation Authority and Lessor. The Maintenance Performer for the Aircraft, Engines, and Parts shall be EASA approved.

9. AD Cost Sharing

If the cost to the Lessee of incorporating an Airworthiness Directive issued on a terminating action basis exceeds seventy five thousand Dollars ($75,000) the Lessor will reimburse the Lessee for the Lessee's Share of such cost in an amount equal to "X" determined in accordance with the following formula within thirty (30) days of receipt of a satisfactory detailed invoice specifying the direct costs incurred by the Lessee in incorporating such Airworthiness Directive, provided that the Lessor shall have no obligation to reimburse any such amounts for so long as any Default has occurred and is continuing:

$$X = \frac{(Z - Y) \times (C - T)}{Z}$$

where

X = amount to be reimbursed to the Lessee

Y = the number of months between (1) the earlier of (a) the date of completion of the incorporation of such Airworthiness Directive and (b) the date on which the Airworthiness Directive was originally required to be incorporated and (2) the date of expiry or earlier termination of the Lease. Where the date specified in (b) above is after the end of the Lease Term or the earlier termination of the Lease for such Aircraft, Y shall equal 0.

C = the reasonable cost to the Lessee of completing the Airworthiness Directive, excluding any costs associated with inability to operate the Aircraft whilst incorporation of the Airworthiness Directive was being carried out and including all subsidies and discounts provided to the Lessee.

T = the threshold amount in Dollars, equal to $[75,000].

Z = Lease Term in months

10. Pooling of Engines

Lessee may install any Engine on an aircraft operated by such Lessee provided that

a. the terms of such lease or other agreement to which such aircraft is subject does not prohibit such installation;

b. the terms of any lease or other agreement or applicable law do not contemplate a transfer of title to such Engine by reason of such Engine being installed on the aircraft;

c. Lessee as owner or any other lessor or secured party of such airframe provides a written acknowledgment also for the benefit of Lessor and finance parties that it will not acquire any right to such Engine by reason of such Engine being installed on such airframe (this acknowledgment may be contained in the lease agreement or other agreement covering such airframe, if such acknowledgment is provided for the express benefit of other lessors, owners, and financing parties);

d. Lessee shall not discriminate between the Engines and any other similar engines owned or leased by Lessee,

e. the interests of Lessor and finance parties, in the case of the hull and war risks insurance, and the Indemnities, in the case of liability insurances are protected in the same manner as if the Engine was installed upon the Airframe; and

f. as soon as reasonably practicable, but in any event no later than the end of the Lease Period, the Engine is removed from the airframe and reinstalled on the Airframe.

11. Modifications

Lessee will not require prior consent for modifications below the aggregate value of $[54,000] that do not affect the value, utility or useful life of the Aircraft, or impair the condition or airworthiness thereof or invalidate any warranty associated with or attached to the Aircraft, and for modifications, alterations, or additions required to maintain airworthiness of the aircraft.

All other modifications may only be made by Lessee with the written consent of Lessor not to be unreasonably withheld.

12. **Aircraft Documents**

Lessee shall maintain all technical records and documents associated with the Aircraft, Engines, and Parts in accordance with the requirements of the Aviation Authority, the Maintenance Program, EASA Part M, and Air Ops. All technical records and documentation shall be maintained in English.

13. **Redelivery Conditions**

Lessee must redeliver the Aircraft to Lessor at the expiry or earlier termination of the Lease ("**Lease Expiry**") in conformity with the conditions outlined in Appendix 3. The Lease Agreement will include the complete redelivery procedures and conditions.

14. **Redelivery Location**

A main operating base of a [Airline Group] or other such location agreed between Lessee and Lessor.

15. **Registration**

Throughout the Lease Term, the Aircraft will be registered with the Aviation Authority of the state of registration of Lessee or any Approved Sublessee (the "**Aviation Authority**") at Lessee's or Approved Sublessee's expense (as applicable) on terms satisfactory to Lessor. Lessee shall be responsible for all costs associated with perfecting and recording Lessor's interests in the Aircraft and/or the Lease and/or any reinstate in the state of registration and habitual base of the Aircraft, including the pre-agreed, capped cost of legal opinions from counsel in those jurisdictions acceptable to Lessor acting reasonably.

If the Cape Town Convention becomes effective in any relevant jurisdiction, the Lessee shall, at no cost to the Lessor, take all reasonable steps to establish and register under such convention all "international interests" of Lessor, Lessee in the Aircraft and shall provide Lessor with an IDERA from the Lessee or Approved Sublessee authorizing Lessor or its nominee to deregister the Aircraft on the expiry or early termination of the Lease Agreement. Notwithstanding this paragraph neither the Lessee, nor any Approved Sublessee, shall not be required to terminate or re-execute any document to which it is a party.

16. **Subleasing**

Subleasing of the Aircraft to (1) any airline subsidiary or affiliate company of the Guarantor, including the Initial Lessee, (subject to the Guarantor's direct or indirect shareholding in such entity of at least [51]%) and (2) to any airline listed as an Approved Sublessee in the lease shall be permitted (together, "**Lessees**").

Subleasing of the Aircraft shall be on a subject and subordinate basis and for a term not expiring beyond the term of the Lease.

Any costs incurred by Lessor in connection with any proposed subleasing shall be for the account of Lessee.

17. **Insurance**

During the Lease Term, the Lessee and/or Approved Sublessee, as the case may be, shall maintain hull, hull war risk, spares, comprehensive airline liability, and war risk airline liability insurance in accordance with AVN67B or in another form that is standard and customary in the airline industry for international air carriers operating this type of aircraft. The Insurances shall be effected on a direct basis with Insurers of recognized standing in the leading primary international insurance markets who normally participate in aviation insurances. All Insurances shall be in accordance with normal industry practice of operators of aircraft similar to the Aircraft in similar circumstances. Lessee's (and/or Approved Sublessee's, as the case may be) hull and hull war risk insurance will insure the aircraft for the stipulated loss value with a deductible not to exceed the maximum deductible, as detailed below. Lessee's (and/or Approved Sublessee's, as the case may be) minimum comprehensive airline liability coverage will be at least US$750 million. Lessor and its financing parties will be named as additional insured and loss payees as their interest appear on the respective lessee's required insurance policies.

Insurance	
Hull Value:	US$[55,000,000]
Maximum Deductible:	US$[250,000]
Minimum Liability Coverage:	US$750,000,000

18. Taxes

All payments by Lessee to Lessor shall be made free and clear of all taxes and duties, including but not limited to, withholding tax, income tax, sales, use and excise taxes, and VAT. All taxes in connection with Lessee and the operation of the Aircraft shall be the responsibility of Lessee, subject to such exceptions as are normal to leasing transactions including but not limited to any taxes (1) on the overall net income of Lessor in its jurisdiction of incorporation or any other jurisdiction where Lessor has a place of business or is resident for tax purposes (other than any taxes which are imposed by reason of the presence, registration, use or operation of the Aircraft in such jurisdiction); (2) arising as a result of any financing arrangements in respect of the Aircraft (3) arising in connection with the delivery of the Aircraft to Lessor by the manufacturer under the relevant purchase agreement or (4) arising as a result of any gross negligence or willful misconduct of Lessor)

19. Net Lease

The Lease shall be a "net" lease. Lessee's obligation to pay Rent and to perform all of its other obligations under the Lease shall be absolute and unconditional.

Lessee shall be responsible for all costs and expenses associated with the delivery, possession, use, operation, ownership, return, maintenance, insurance, import/export of the Aircraft, and compliance with applicable laws, regulations, and airworthiness directives.

20. Assignment/Financing

The Aircraft ownership interest and Lessor's interest in the Lease and the Aircraft shall be freely transferable and assignable and Lessor and/or owner reserves the right to leverage its interest or to put in place such other funding or other arrangements as Lessor or owner may consider necessary, provided that

a. such transfer, assignment, leveraging, funding, or other arrangement does not affect Lessee's quiet enjoyment of the Aircraft (and Lessor shall procure that any person holding an interest in the Aircraft or the Lease in connection with such transfer, assignment, leveraging, funding, or other arrangement gives an undertaking of quiet enjoyment in favor of Lessee and the Approved Sublessee).

b. The transferee shall be an experienced asset manager and lessor and shall have a minimum net worth of US$[25,000,000] prior to transfer, or be guaranteed or supported by an entity with a minimum net worth of US$[25,000,000].

c. The transferee shall not be a competitor of Guarantor, Lessee, or any Approved Sublessee.
d. The transfer will not result in any increase of the obligations (including financial obligations) or diminution of any rights or interests of Lessee, Approved Sublessee, or Guarantor, according to application law at the time of transfer.

Lessee shall cooperate fully with Lessor in connection with any such transfer, assignment, leveraging, or funding or other arrangement, and if such transfer, assignment, leveraging or funding, or other arrangement is implemented after the Delivery Date, all reasonable legal expenses incurred by Lessee in connection therewith shall be reimbursed by Lessor.

21. **Transaction Expenses**

1. Each of Lessee and Lessor shall be responsible for its own costs and expenses associated with the negotiation and completion of this transaction for the leasing of the Aircraft, including their respective legal fees.

22. **Confidentiality**

This LOI is personal to Lessee and the Guarantor and Lessee and Guarantor must keep the terms of this LOI strictly confidential and not reveal them to any person other than those employees, directors, officers, and professional advisers of Lessee who are responsible for analyzing, negotiating, and approving the transaction and who are made aware of the confidential nature of it.

23. **Documentation**

Lessor's counsel shall draft a lease agreement and other documentation incorporating the terms of this LOI and other terms normal to leasing transactions (including, but not limited to, representations and warranties, conditions precedent, payment, maintenance, operational and other covenants, indemnities, and events of default which shall include but not be limited to

- Failure to make rental payment within 3 business days of due date
- Failure to make payment of any other amount within 5 business days of due date
- An agreed breach by Lessee unremedied 15 business days after notification by Lessor of such breach
- Failure to insure in accordance with the Lease

Cross default provisions will apply between all operating leases between any Lessor group entity and Lessee group entity, provided that in respect of any lease to a Lessee group entity that a Lessor group entity may acquire in the future (an "**Acquired Lease**"), an event of default under an Acquired Lease will only trigger a cross default under the Leases in respect of the Aircraft if that event of default under an Acquired Lease would also constitute an event of default if it occurred under the Leases in respect of the Aircraft.

It is the intent of Lessor and Lessee that such documentation be agreed as soon as reasonably possible and executed no later than (60 days from the execution of this LOI) or such other date as Lessor and Lessee may agree (the "**Documentation Date**"). Lessor and Lessee agree to negotiate in good faith toward the prompt execution of documentation on or before the Documentation Date.

This LOI is not intended to be and does not constitute a binding or enforceable agreement. A binding commitment with respect to the matters contemplated in this LOI will result only upon execution of the Lease, save that the provisions of 22 [*Confidentiality*] and 27 [Governing Law] shall be legally binding as from signature of this LOI.

Payments

All payments to Lessor under the Lease shall be made in immediately available US Dollars to an account notified by Lessor to Lessee.

24. **Conditions Precedent**

The obligation of Lessor to enter into the Lease and associated transaction documentation is expressly conditional upon

receipt by Lessor and Lessee/Guarantor of all requisite corporate approvals as well as necessary third party consents;

Lessor being satisfied (acting reasonably) with the financial and commercial condition of Guarantor;

completion of transaction documentation satisfactory to Lessor and Lessee (each acting reasonably) on or before the Documentation Date;

receipt of tax and legal opinions satisfactory to Lessor.

The obligations of Lessee to enter into the Lease and associated transaction documentation is expressly conditional upon

a. receipt by Lessee of all required corporate approvals as well as necessary third-party consents;
b. completion of transaction documentation satisfactory to Lessor and Lessee (each acting reasonably) on or before the Documentation Date;
c. receipt of tax and legal opinions satisfactory to Lessor and Lessee (each acting reasonably)

25. **Validity of Terms**

This LOI supersedes all previous proposals and offers and is valid for acceptance until the close of business on [ ].

26. **Governing Law**

This LOI and the Lease and all other transaction documents shall be governed by, and construed in accordance with, the laws of England.

27. **No Brokers**

Neither Lessor nor Lessee has engaged the services of a broker or similar representative agent for the purposes of this transaction. Each party shall represent to the other the absence of such brokers and representative agents and indemnify the other with respect to any breach of such representation.

Please confirm your acceptance of this LOI by executing a counterpart of this LOI in the space provided below and returning a signed copy to Lessor before the expiry of its validity.

Very truly yours,

[LESSOR]

By:

Name:

Title:

[AIRLINE]

By:

Name:

Title:

APPENDIX 3: MAINTENANCE PAYMENTS

At Lease Expiry, Lessee shall pay Lessor end of lease maintenance compensation payments ("Maintenance Payments") for utility consumed since new or since last Maintenance Event as appropriate based on actual utility consumed during the Lease Term.

Maintenance Payment Rates	
Airframe:	
8 Year structural check	US$[ ] per calendar month, or part of
10 Year structural check	US$[ ] per calendar month, or part of
12 Year structural check	US$[ ] per calendar month, or part of
Engine Performance Restoration Shop Visit:	US$[ ] per FH per Engine
The rate is based on a 10% derate and shall be split into the following modules;	
Fan and Booster 13%	
HPC 23%	
HPT 47%	
LPT 17%	
Engine LLPs	Compensation for each LLP shall be calculated as 100% of the Manufacturer's catalogue price at Lease Expiry multiplied by actual FC since new for such LLP [ ] of the Manufacturer's total approved life in cycles.
APU	US$[ ] per APU operating hour
Landing Gear	US$[ ] per month, or part of

FH, *Flight hour;* LLP, *Life-limited part;* APU, *Auxiliary power unit;* HPC, *High-pressure compressor;* HPT, *High-pressure turbine;* LPT, *Low-pressure turbine.*

The Maintenance Payment Rates in the table below are based on an assumed FH to FC ratio of [ ]8:1 ("Assumed Ratio") and an annual utilization of [ ] FH ("Assumed Utilization"). Maintenance Payment Rates will be adjusted accordingly where Lessee operates on a different FH-to-FC ratio from the Assumed Ratio or a different annual utilization from the Assumed Utilization.

The Maintenance Payment Rates for Airframe, Engine Performance Restoration, APU and Landing Gear are based on January [2017] costs, with Airframe, APU, and Landing Gear rates subject to escalation of [3]% annually on 1 January of each year. The Engine Performance Restoration rate shall be escalated at in accordance with the engine manufacturer's catalogue list price.

Below is a description of the Qualifying Maintenance Event for each component:

- "Airframe 8 Year Structural Check"—the airframe 8-year check which shall include the completion of the 8-year structural tasks, system and zonal tasks, and all scheduled lower level tasks in accordance with the latest revision of the maintenance planning data document (MPD).
- "Airframe 10 Year Structural Check"—the airframe 10-year check which shall include the completion of the 10 year structural tasks, system and zonal tasks, and all scheduled lower level tasks in accordance with the latest revision MPD.

- “Airframe 12 Year Structural Check”—the airframe 12-year check which shall include the completion of the 12-year structural tasks, system and zonal tasks, and all scheduled lower level tasks in accordance with the latest revision MPD.
- “Engine Performance Restoration”—an engine shop visit which shall include a performance restoration of the major modules (at a minimum HPC and HPT modules) in accordance with the then current Workscope Planning Guide, with a scheduled On-Condition, LLP, and AD Release of no less than [ ] FCs.
- “Landing Gear Overhaul”—the off-the-wing restoration of the Landing Gear involving complete disassembly of the Landing Gear to satisfy the system and structural requirements of the latest revision MPD.
- “APU Gas Path Refurbishment”—the APU shop visit which shall include a gas path refurbishment in accordance with the then current overhaul manual, with a scheduled On-Condition, LLP and AD Release of no less than [ ] APU Cycles and [ ] APU Hours.

Excluded maintenance for which no reimbursement shall be made (including costs otherwise covered by warranty or insurance, or arising from operational or maintenance mishandling, foreign object damage or Quick Engine Change kit maintenance or line replaceable unit component maintenance) will be set out in the Lease Agreement.

APPENDIX 4: REDELIVERY CONDITIONS

This is intended to be a summary of the principal redelivery conditions. Detailed redelivery conditions shall be contained in the Lease.

Redelivery location	A main operating base of (Airline) or location to be agreed between Lessor and Lessee
Aircraft inspection	Prior to redelivery, Lessee and Lessor will agree a timetable for a Lessor physical inspection of the aircraft, engines, aircraft records, and uninstalled parts Immediately prior to the Redelivery Date, Lessee will make the Aircraft and Aircraft Documents available to Lessor for inspection. The final inspection will include (1) an inspection of the Aircraft manuals and Technical Records, (2) a complete video borescope inspection of all engine modules, and (3) an acceptance flight of at least 2 h duration (following Operator’s acceptance procedures) at Lessee’s cost including takeoff performance test and engine ground runs, to demonstrate that each Engine performance including EGT margin is consistent with the Engine FH and FC operated since the previous Engine Performance Restoration, but in any event no less than (20) degrees Celsius at maximum rated take off power 26,000 lb Thrust at sea level, standard ambient pressure conditions and an outside air temperature of (30) degrees Celsius
Interior condition	The Aircraft interior will be clean and substantially free from dirt, stains, grime, nicks, cracks, and damage consistent with commercial airline standards and shall be cosmetically acceptable to Lessor acting reasonably, fair wear and tear accepted. The Aircraft shall be in the same configuration as at delivery or as agreed by Lessor and Lessee acting in good faith

General condition	The Aircraft shall have installed the full complement of systems, equipment, parts, accessories, furnishings, and loose equipment as installed in the Aircraft at Delivery and shall be in good working order for its intended use and shall be acceptable to Lessor acting reasonably
Weight at redelivery	The MTOW at redelivery will be no less than 174,163 lb as at delivery
Engine thrust at redelivery	The operating thrust at redelivery will be no less than 26,000 lb operating thrust as at delivery
Airworthiness matters	The Aircraft shall have a current CofA, a valid Airworthiness Review Certificate (if applicable) with a minimum of 180 days remaining and shall be compliant with all mandatory operational requirements pursuant to Air OPS to permit immediate operation by a commercial air carrier in an EASA member state without additional work being required If requested by Lessor a Certificate of Export from the Aviation Authority will be provided
Airworthiness directives	On the redelivery date, all Airworthiness Directives issued by the Aviation Authority, the FAA and EASA will be accomplished on a terminating action basis where compliance is required (1) prior to the Redelivery Date, (2) within 180 days after the Redelivery Date, and (3) prior to the next C Check falling due after the Redelivery Date, if C Check level access is required for such compliance. Airworthiness Directives having no terminating action shall be cleared to the highest level of accomplishment as applicable
Airframe check at redelivery	Immediately prior to redelivery the aircraft will have completed a maintenance input sufficient to clear the aircraft, structures, system, zonal, and CPCP tasks for (4500) flight hours, (3000) cycles, and (18) months or the then current C check interval in accordance with Lessees approved maintenance program
Paint	The Aircraft including fuselage, wings, and tail shall be stripped and painted in a livery to be advised by Lessor, such livery to be supplied no later than 21 days prior to paint input. Any cost in excess of the cost of Lessee's livery shall be to Lessors account, In the event that no livery drawings are provided prior to paint input then the Aircraft will be painted white
Hard time and life limited components	All Hard Time Components installed on the aircraft will have an FAA Form 8130-3 or EASA Form One and all Life Limited Components will have documentation evidencing complete back to birth traceability No Part/Components of the Aircraft or Engine (excluding Life Limited Parts on the Engine) will have total FHs and total FCs since new greater than (125)% of the Airframe total time since new and with respect to all Parts/Components as a group shall average a total time since new and total cycles since new no greater than (115)% of the Airframe total FHs and total FCs Hard-time Components will have no less than 6000 flight hours, 4000 cycles, and 24 months remaining to its next due maintenance event or 40% of hard time life if the maintenance interval is lower as applicable in accordance with Lessee's maintenance program
On condition and condition monitored components	On condition and condition monitored components changed during the lease term will be serviceable and will have an FAA Form 8130-3 or EASA Form One as applicable

Engines	Each Engine shall have no less than 4500 FH and 3000 FC on condition life remaining to the next anticipated Engine Performance Restoration and 4500 FH, 3000 FC, and 18 months clearance to any applicable Airworthiness Directives and shall have no defect with an in-service limitation No Engine Life Limited Part shall have less than [ ] cycles scheduled life remaining. Each Engine LLP installed shall be supported by full back to birth traceability
Engine borescopes	Immediately prior to redelivery and after satisfactory completion of the Demonstration Flight and any subsequent engine run, both engines will be subject to a complete gas path Video Borescope inspection of all Engine modules in accordance with the Aircraft Maintenance Manual. Any defects exceeding the Aircraft Maintenance Manual limits will be rectified at Lessee's expense prior to the return of the Aircraft. For the avoidance of doubt, any defect subject to any AMM continue in service limitation shall be rectified by the Lessee prior to the return of the Aircraft
APU	The APU will be serviceable and shall have no more than 1500 APU operating hours since last APU Gas Path Refurbishment and no less than 1000 APU operating cycles to the first life limited part restriction
Landing gear	The original Landing Gear shall be fitted to the Aircraft at redelivery. Each Landing Gear will have no less than 4000 cycles and 24 months remaining to the next Landing Gear Overhaul and no Life Limited Component shall have more than 125% of the Airframe total cycles since new. Each Landing Gear LLP shall have full back to birth traceability
Tires and brakes	Tires and Brakes will on average have no less than 50% of their useful life remaining and each unit individually will have no less than 40% of its useful life remaining
Repairs	All repairs to the Aircraft, Engines, and parts shall be permanent and accomplished in accordance with instructions from the original equipment manufacturer, structural repairs to the Airframe shall be certified in accordance with Manufacturer's Structural Repair Manual, or to the extent the repair is outside the scope of Structural Repair Manual then such repair shall be supported by Manufacturer's repair instructions and shall be supported by FAA approval

FH, *Flight hours;* FC, *Flight cycles;* MTOW, *Maximum takeoff weight;* CofA, *Certificate of airworthiness;* EASA, *European Aviation Safety Agency;* FAA, *Federal Aviation Administration;* LLP, *Life-limited part;* APU, *Auxiliary power unit.*

ACKNOWLEDGMENTS

We would like to thank Dick Forsberg of Avolon Corporation for providing guidance and background information in the development of this chapter.

REFERENCES

Gee, C. A. (2009). Aircraft pre-delivery payment financing transaction. *Journal of Structured Finance*, *15*, 11–21.

Karesh, J., & Berns, A. V. (2009). *Strategic issues in operating leases. World Leasing Yearbook*. London: Euromoney Institutional Investor PLC.

Littlejohns, A., & McGairl, S. (Eds.), (1998). *Aircraft financing* (3rd ed.). London: Euromoney Publications, PLC.

Scheinberg, R. (2014). *The commercial aircraft finance handbook*. London, United Kingdom: Euromoney Institutional Investor PLC.

CHAPTER

AIRCRAFT VALUATION AND APPRAISAL

12

CHAPTER OUTLINE

Aircraft Leasing and Financing. DOI: https://doi.org/10.1016/B978-0-12-815285-0.00012-2

INTRODUCTION TO AIRCRAFT APPRAISAL

DEFINITION OF AN APPRAISAL

Value is estimating monetary worth of an asset, goods, or service. An appraisal is a process of determining an unbiased opinion of value of an asset. An appraisal needs to be numerically expressed as a single value or as a range of values.

Valuing an aircraft is an intricate process yet critical for all the members of the aviation industry, given that the major asset within the industry is the aircraft itself. Different stakeholders such as airlines, lessors, and financial institutions are interested in obtaining an accurate value for the aircraft. Major factors that affect the value of an aircraft are age, seating configuration/capacity, engine thrust, maximum takeoff weight (MTOW), size, and fuel efficiency. For example, as an aircraft ages, value declines due to deterioration/wear and tear on the aircraft, introduction of newer technology aircraft as well as end of the production run for the particular aircraft type. Aircraft value is also affected by the availability of maintenance documents, maintenance status, future revenue, and its cost of operation. External environmental factors like interest rates, demand, fuel cost, production cycle, new safety regulations, and environmental regulations also affect the valuation.

For any valuation, the evaluator/appraiser needs to collect information pertaining to the aircraft in question. Historical data often provides the appraiser with a good starting point in this process. In a typical aircraft appraisal, therefore, the appraiser gathers information on the aircraft history, previously recorded operating costs, future economic prospects, and maintenance records. These metadata are then examined and analyzed to develop a value for the aircraft. Depending on the needs of the client, there are different types of appraisals. We discuss below some of the common types of appraisals.

DIFFERENT TYPES OF APPRAISAL

The below definitions on different types of appraisal are based on the ISTAT (International Society of Transport Aircraft Trading, 2013) appraiser's handbook.

Desktop appraisal

Desktop appraisal does not include an inspection of the aircraft and review of the aircraft maintenance records. In a desktop appraisal, the appraiser would ascertain the aircraft condition and maintenance status from the appraiser's own database or from the information that the client provides. These are usually used when a client may not want to expend the resources necessary to support a physical inspection of the aircraft. For example, an Airbus A320 may be located in Asia, and the client may not want to pay an appraiser to travel to Asia to do a physical inspection of the aircraft. The important factor for an appraiser in a desktop appraisal, in arriving at a good estimate of value, is the availability of detailed information from the client or other secondary sources. Desktop appraisals assume midlife or mid-time condition of the aircraft.

Extended desktop appraisal

Like the desktop appraisal, an extended appraisal excludes an on-site inspection of the aircraft or its maintenance records, but it does include maintenance status information of the airframe, engines, landing gear, and auxiliary power unit (APU), which is provided by the client, or the aircraft operator, or ascertained by the appraiser from another appraiser's report. An extended desktop appraisal therefore would provide an opinion of a value that includes adjustments for aircraft's actual maintenance status. The adjustments are made from a mid-time midlife basis.

Full appraisal

Full appraisal would include an on-site inspection of the aircraft and its maintenance records. This inspection is focused on determining the overall condition of the aircraft and its maintenance records to support the appraiser's opinion. This appraisal is a high-level inspection of the aircraft and records and does not include a detailed examination of the aircraft or the maintenance records (e.g., opening of inspection panels of the aircraft or a detailed review of maintenance records). An appraiser may walk around the aircraft to inspect the aircraft and verify the general condition of the aircraft and might take pictures to support valuation conclusions. A full appraisal would provide an opinion of a value that includes adjustments for an aircraft's actual maintenance status and other adjustments from midlife/mid-time to factor in the findings of the inspection of the aircraft and its maintenance records.

Comprehensive appraisal

This appraisal also includes on-site inspection of the aircraft and its maintenance records. However, a more in-depth detailed appraisal is required to insure that the records are complete and accurate to determine whether the aircraft is in full compliance with regulatory requirement and is airworthy. This appraisal is usually performed when an aircraft is deregistered in one jurisdiction and reregistered in a different jurisdiction.

Financial appraisal

A financial appraisal is performed when an investor is interested in the value of the aircraft based upon aircraft's future cash flow potential from its lease payments and residual value at the end of the lease. This appraisal is usually performed in conjunction with either full or desktop appraisals.

DEFINITIONS OF VALUES AND APPRAISING TERMINOLOGY

Value can be thought of as "value in use" or value in exchange. Value in use refers to the utility of a particular object, and value in exchange refers to the power of the object in purchasing other goods, which the possession of that object conveys (Svoboda, 2006). When appraisers refer to value, they usually mean value in exchange or current market value (CMV). However, different professional societies have different definitions of value. In this chapter, we will focus on ISTAT and American Society of Appraisers (ASA) definitions of value.

ASA definition of value

ASA is a nonprofit international organization of professional appraisers representing different appraisal disciplines such as Appraisal Review and Management, Business Valuation, Gems and Jewelry, Machinery and Technical Specialties, Personal Property, and Real Property. ASA addresses the value of machinery and equipment (including aircraft) in its book, Valuing Machinery and Equipment (Machinery and Technical Specialties Committee of the American Society of Appraisers, 2011). Given the mobile nature of machinery and equipment such as an aircraft, ASA groups its definition of value into three broad categories, namely,

1. Sale for removal for a similar or alternate use;
2. Continued (or as installed) use of the asset for the purpose for which it was designed and acquired; and
3. Liquidation.

Fair current market value

According to ASA, "Fair Current Market Value is an opinion expressed in terms of money, at which the property would change hands between a willing buyer and a willing seller, neither being under any compulsion to buy or to sell and both having reasonable knowledge of relevant facts, as of a specific date."

Fair current market value—removed

Also as per ASA, "Fair Current Market Value—Removed is an opinion, expressed in terms of money, at which the property would change hands between a willing buyer and a willing seller, neither being under any compulsion to buy or to sell and both having reasonable knowledge of relevant facts, considering removal of the property to another location, as of a specific date."

Fair current market value in continued use with assumed earnings

ASA defines *Fair Current Market Value in Continued Use with Assumed Earnings* as "an opinion, expressed in terms of money, at which the property would change hands between a willing buyer and a willing seller, neither being under any compulsion to buy or to sell and both having reasonable knowledge of relevant facts, as of a specific date and assuming that the business earnings support the value reported, without verification."

Fair current market value in continued use with an earnings analysis

As per ASA, *Fair Current Market Value in Continued Use with an Earnings Analysis* "is on opinion, expressed in terms of money, at which the property would change hands between a willing buyer and a willing seller, neither being under any compulsion to buy or to sell and both having reasonable knowledge of relevant facts, as of a specific date and supported by the earnings of the business."

Fair current market value—installed

The final definition of fair CMV, namely, "Fair Current Market Value—installed is an opinion, expressed in terms of money, at which the property would change hands between a willing buyer and a willing seller, neither being under any compulsion to buy or to sell and both having reasonable knowledge of relevant facts, considering market conditions for the asset being valued, independent of earnings generated by the business in which the property is or will be installed, as of a specific date."

All the definitions assume that the property is able to be used in its current location and therefore includes direct and indirect cost to make it fully operational. The fair CMV concepts above though appear similar have subtle differences. According to ASA, the continued use ideas consider the property as a part of a business enterprise, while the *installed* concept considers the property separate from the business enterprise and does not take into account whether the property is being used or not. Further, since continued use concepts assume the use of the property, it is important to justify the determined value. While under the assumed earnings concept, the appraiser assumes earnings exist, under the earnings analysis concept, the appraiser has to provide justification for the reported value.

Liquidation value

Liquidation value is the price of the subject aircraft when there is insufficient time allowed to sell it in a fair and open market. Liquidation value is usually lower than the fair CMV.

Orderly liquidation value

ASA defines *Orderly Liquidation Value as* "an opinion of the gross amount, expressed in terms of money, that typically could be realized from a liquidation sale, given a reasonable period of time to find a purchaser (or purchasers), with the seller being compelled to sell on an as-is, where-is basis, as of a specific date."

Forced liquidation value

Forced liquidation value according to ASA "is an opinion of the gross amount, expressed in terms of money, that typically could be realized from a properly advertised and conducted public auction with the seller being compelled to sell with a sense of immediacy on an as-is, where-is basis, as of a specific date."

Liquidation value in place

ASA defines Liquidation Value in Place as "an opinion of the gross amount, expressed in terms of money, that typically could be realized from a properly advertised transaction, with the seller being compelled to sell, as of a specific date, for a failed, non-operating facility, assuming that the entire facility is sold intact."

The important distinction between the liquidation values and fair CMVs definitions is that all the liquidation values presume a compulsion to sell, while under fair CMVs, the seller is willing and is under no compulsion to sell. Further, while orderly liquidation provides for a reasonable amount of time, forced liquidation implies a sense of urgency or immediacy. Finally, while liquidation in place assumes that the entire facility would be sold intact, orderly and forced liquidation assume the property can be sold piecemeal.

ISTAT value definitions

The ISTAT appraiser's handbook has its own definition of value which is adhered to by the ISTAT appraisal community (International Society of Transport Aircraft Trading, 2013). We outline some of these definitions and concepts below which are important to understand the ISTAT appraisal process (Ackert, 2012).

Base value

ISTAT defines *Base Value (BV) as* "Appraiser's opinion of the underlying economic value of an aircraft in an open, unrestricted, stable market environment with a reasonable balance of supply and demand, and assumes full consideration of its 'highest and best use.' An aircraft's BV is founded in the historical trend of values and in the projection of value trends and presumes an arm's-length, cash transaction between willing, able and knowledgeable parties, acting prudently, with an absence of duress and with a reasonable period of time available for marketing. In most cases, the BV of an aircraft assumes its physical condition is average for an aircraft of its type and age, and its maintenance time status is at mid-life, mid-time (or benefiting from an above-average maintenance status if it is new or nearly new, as the case may be)."

Based on the above definition one can see that BV assumes a balanced market, where both supply and demand are equal, and neither supply nor demand is influenced by short-term events.

Examples of short-term events can be fluctuations in jet fuel price, recessions, political unrest, or the original equipment manufacturer (OEM) offering deep discounts. BV is therefore a theoretical value, as the market would never be unaffected by short-term events and would never be perfectly balanced between supply and demand. The BV definition is often used to analyze historical values and project future residual values as they are based on long-term market trends.

Market value or current market value

According to ISTAT market value or CMV is the "Appraiser's opinion of the most likely trading price that may be generated for an aircraft under the market circumstances that are perceived to exist at the time in question. CMV assumes that the aircraft is valued for its highest, best use, that the parties to the hypothetical sale transaction are willing, able, prudent and knowledgeable, and under no unusual pressure for a prompt sale, and that the transaction would be negotiated in an open and unrestricted market on an arm's-length basis, for cash or equivalent consideration, and given an adequate amount of time for effective exposure to prospective buyers."

A CMV represents an appraiser's judgment of the most probable trading price of the aircraft under current market conditions. The CMV assumes that the transaction is an open single aircraft sale with no lease attached, and there is a willing buyer and seller. In order to arrive at the CMV, the appraiser would factor in perceived demand for the particular aircraft type, its availability in the market, and different analysis from reliable industry resources. Like BV, CMV assumes that the aircraft's maintenance cycle is at half-life, and the appraiser would arrive at an average value based on a normalizing process based on aircraft's maintenance condition and other relevant factors.

- If BV = CMV then market is in an equilibrium condition
- If BV > CMV then market is supporting lower prices
- If BV < CMV then market is supporting higher prices

The BV of an aircraft will tend to be consistent with the CMV in a stable market environment. In conditions where there is no reasonable equilibrium between supply and demand, a divergence between BV and CMV indicates an imbalance in the market. In theory, CMV should oscillate around BV, but in reality, values move in relation to macroeconomic events and shocks to the system such as recessions, financial crisis, fuel price spikes, liquidity crisis, dotcom bubble, and terrorist attacks. Opinions on BV and CMV of aircraft can often vary to a wide extent amongst aircraft appraisers. This discrepancy is due to the differences in methodology and an appraiser's opinion about the market (optimistic or pessimistic). On the other hand, the following three philosophies are consistent across all aircraft appraisers:

- There exists a systematic relationship in the values of a given type of aircraft from year to year of build, assuming all else equal.
- There exists a systematic relationship between values of a competitive aircraft type, assuming all else equal.
- Values of an aircraft type under consideration should be in context of all the values of an aircraft.

Future base value

Future BV represents an appraiser's projection of future aircraft values from an initial starting point, which usually is an aircraft's BV. A curve is then generated using normalized data points resulting from a BV, and an extension of this curve forecasts the future BV of the aircraft type. Future BVs are estimated in current dollars and as such take into account inflation. Appraisers usually project future BVs assuming a current inflation rate. An appraiser does not attempt to forecast future market value, as they are not in a position to determine the aircraft's utilization or future maintenance requirements as well as its future value.

Adjusted current market value

Adjusted CMV reflects that the BV or the CMV of the aircraft has been adjusted from presumed half-life condition to account for actual maintenance status. An aircraft that has recently had a major engine performance restoration, airframe and landing gear work completed would have a positive impact on an aircraft's value. Because there exists a strong relationship between cost of performing maintenance and value, it is important to quantify in monetary terms the maintenance status of the subject aircraft.

Soft value

Soft value reflects values of aircraft in a recession scenario in the bottom market. It is usually calculated as a percentage of the BV. The soft value curve is usually a proportional shift, downward from the BV curve.

Difference between current market value and soft value

- CMV is based on historical transactions, whereas soft value is determined as a percent of BV.
- CMV is used for transactions and to value assessment, whereas soft value is used for loan proposals and worst case-scenario or downside projections.
- CMV can be either half-life, full-life, or adjusted values, whereas soft value is usually half-life or full-life.

Distress value, forced sale value, and liquidation value

ISTAT defines these values as "Appraiser's opinion of the price at which an aircraft (or other assets such as an engine or spare parts) could be sold in a cash transaction under abnormal conditions—typically an artificially limited marketing time period, the perception of the seller being under duress to sell, an auction, a liquidation, commercial restrictions, legal complications, or other such factors that materially reduce the bargaining leverage of the seller and give prospective buyers a significant advantage that can translate into heavily discounted actual trading prices." ISTAT further requires that depending on the nature of the assignment, the appraiser qualify his opinion in terms of disposition within a specified time period such as 60 days, 90 days, or 6 months as appropriate. ISTAT further adds, "Apart from the fact that the seller is uncommonly motivated, the parties to the transaction are otherwise assumed to be willing, able, prudent and knowledgeable, and negotiating at arm's-length, normally under the market conditions that are perceived to exist at the time, not an idealized balanced market."

Lease-encumbered value

Lease-encumbered value usually refers to the value of an aircraft with lease attached. Lease-encumbered valuation is also so referred to as securitized valuation or financial valuation. ISTAT defines lease-encumbered value as "the appraiser's opinion of the value of an aircraft, under lease, given specified lease payment stream (rents and term), and estimated future residual value at lease termination and an appropriate discount rate."

Lease-encumbered value therefore is the present value of a subject aircraft, which is under lease, and generates a net cash inflow stream (rent and maintenance reserve inflow and reimbursement, any lessor top-off) and includes a forecasted residual value using an appropriate discount rate. It may be similar to the appraiser's opinion of CMV; however, the appraiser might not be fully aware of all factors relevant to the lease such as security deposits, end of the lease purchase options, sub-lease rights, term extensions, return conditions, reserve payments, and credit risks of all the parties involved (Forsberg, 2016). The appraiser has to therefore look to the client to provide additional information and guidance in order to arrive at an appropriate value. If possible, the appraiser should seek to obtain a copy of the lease agreement from the client when tasked with estimating lease-encumbered values, but often times the client may not be willing to share sensitive information about the lease, which makes the task of the appraiser challenging.

Apart from the above important value definitions used by ASA and ISTAT, there are other definitions used by the two organizations as well.

Salvage value

For ASA, *Salvage Value* "is an opinion of the amount, expressed in terms of money, that may be expected for the whole property or a component of the whole property that is retired from service for possible use elsewhere, as of a specific date. Salvage value is an opinion of the value that maybe expected for the subject aircraft, which is nearing the end of its economic life and closer to be retired from service."

For ISTAT, *Salvage Value* "is the actual or estimated selling price of an aircraft, engine or major assembly based on the value of marketable parts and components that could be salvaged for re-use on other aircraft or engines."

ISTAT further recommends that the salvage value clearly addresses whether it includes any adjustment for removal costs.

In general, as an aircraft ages, engines on the aircraft may worth more than the airframe and parting-out the aircraft may be better option.

From an accounting, perspective salvage value refers to value of an asset when it has been fully depreciated over its book depreciation period. In the accounting context, therefore, salvage value may not be the same as CMV.

For the purpose of this chapter, we will use salvage value as defined by ISTAT or ASA.

Scrap value

Since the definitions by ISTAT and ASA are similar in the case of scrap value, we look at the ISTAT definition here. ISTAT defines *Scrap Value* as "the actual or estimated Current Market Value of an aircraft, engine or major assembly based solely on its metal or other recyclable material content with no saleable reusable parts or components remaining."

The scrap value is usually net of removal costs and in some cases the scrap value maybe zero if the dismantling and disposal costs are high (such as in the case of hazardous or composite assemblies which are difficult to recycle) and outweigh the metal value. Aircraft aluminum alloys are usually used as automobile wheels, beer cans, and bodies for trucks.

Residual value

This refers to the value of an aircraft, engine, or other item at a future date, such as the end of a lease term.

The concepts of residual value, salvage value, and scrap value are often misused as well as erroneously used interchangeably. It is important therefore to understand the crucial and subtle differences between these concepts. Residual values are the estimates of a value of the aircraft at some future date (end of the lease and end of period of ownership), salvage value refers to value that comes from reusing part of the aircraft such as engines, landing gear, and APU, and finally scrap value refers to the pure metal value of the aircraft.

Apart from the value definitions outlined above the below concepts and definitions are important for understanding the ASA and ISTAT appraisal process.

Reproduction cost new

Reproduction cost new is the current cost of reproducing an exact replica of the subject aircraft with exact or close to similar characteristics.

Replacement cost new

Replacement cost new is the current cost of replacing the subject aircraft with a new aircraft with exact or similar characteristics of the subject aircraft. This concept is important to understand in order to arrive at fair CMV under the cost approach, which is one of the three approaches to value, recommended by ASA.

Half-life vs full-life

The concept of half-life and full-life is very important for an ISTAT appraiser as he/she often starts with the half-life status of the aircraft as the starting point and adjusts the value upward or downward based on its current maintenance status.

A half-life assumes that the landing gear, engines, airframe, life-limited parts (LLPs), and other components are half-way between their next major maintenance event. For instance, the aircraft would be half-way between its next HMV check, LLPs would have used 50% of the total life established by the OEMs, all the engines and the APU are half-way between their next anticipated performance restorations and the landing gear are half-way between their next overhaul.

A full-life status indicates that all the major maintenance events have been completed, and that all the major components are overhauled to zero-time condition or fully restored, the landing gear has been overhauled with zero hours and cycles on it, pertinent HMV checks have been performed on airframe, all LLPs have been replaced, and performance restoration have been performed on all the engines and the APU (Example 12.1).

EXAMPLE 12.1 CALCULATING MAINTENANCE ADJUSTMENT FROM HALF-LIFE TO FULL-LIFE

Maintenance Status Adjustment From Half-Life

2017 US Dollars in Millions

Component		Cost in $m	Life Remaining (%)	$m Adjustment
C-check		0.25	100	0.12
HMV 1		0.95	100	0.47
HMV 2		0.73	100	0.36
Landing gear		0.46	100	0.23
Engine 1	Restoration	2.59	100	1.29
	LLP	2.86	100	1.43
Engine 2	Restoration	2.59	100	1.29
	LLP	2.86	100	1.43
APU	Restoration	0.24	100	0.14
Total adjustment from half-life				6.79

LLP, *Life-Limited Part;* APU, *auxiliary power unit;* HMV, *Heavy Maintenance Visit.*

PURPOSE OF AN APPRAISAL

There are numerous motivations for appraising an aircraft. This includes among others, allocation of purchase price, bankruptcy, condemnation, financing, insurance, transfer of ownership, and various types of taxation and tax planning (Machinery and Technical Specialties Committee of the American Society of Appraisers, 2011). Aircraft appraisers first and foremost need to understand the intended use of their appraisal (Ackert, 2012). If for example, an aircraft is appraised for a future sale or financing, then a suitable appraisal of its airworthiness needs to be conducted. Similarly, if an aircraft needs an appraisal for an insurance claim purpose, it may indicate that the aircraft is not airworthy or may be damaged. Once the intended use and the users of the appraisal are determined, the appraiser can look toward the purpose of the appraisal. Appraisers are often asked to give an opinion of CMV. This value may be wholesale, inventory, or retail value. The appraiser's job is to help the client identify the correct definition of value to be used based on the client's use of the appraisal. Once the appraiser has identified the intended use and users of the appraisal and arrived at the appropriate definition of value, the appraisal process begins. Below we elaborate on some of the reasons for an appraisal and outline the appraisal process.

ALLOCATING PURCHASE PRICE

When lessors and airlines are interested in purchasing multiple aircraft, the owner of these aircraft would like to know what the values of each single aircraft are in order to set up a depreciation schedule, forecast maintenance reserves, and build appropriate asset and other pertinent records. In such a circumstance, the owner might want to know the purchase price of each individual aircraft. An appraisal may therefore be required to allocate the purchase price amongst individual aircraft.

BANKRUPTCY

In the event of a bankruptcy, creditors may prefer to be paid back in cash, rather than equipment. In this case, a liquidation value appraisal may be required. Depending on the degree of urgency with which the asset needs to be liquidated, the relevant value may be either an orderly liquidation value or a forced liquidation value. The appraiser would review previous court proceedings and rulings and may even seek guidance from legal counsel before making the final decision on assigning a value.

FINANCING

When a financial institution or a bank is involved in an asset-backed loan, the collateral (which usually is the subject aircraft) needs to be appraised. There are strict rules which govern what the borrower can borrow. In general, the amount of borrowing cannot exceed the value appraised by the appraiser. To protect the financial institution or the bank from default and to warrant full recovery of the loan, the appraised value is usually close to, or based on, liquidation value. If the borrower has excellent credit, the financial institution may certify an appraisal on CMV definitions.

INSURANCE

Insurance appraisals are one of the most common appraisals that are required. These are performed to determine a value for insurance coverage to insure against loss. Owners, lessors, lessees, insurance agencies, and brokers are concerned about the insurable value. Insurance value is close to replacement cost new because the insurance coverage is usually provided as a replacement policy.

TAXATION

Taxes and income are usually a primary motivation for appraisals for accounting firms. Aircraft owners may also donate aircraft which are beyond their economic life to aircraft museums or educational institutions. In this instance, an appraiser needs to seek council from client's legal team, accountants, and tax managers before making the final decision on the value.

APPRAISAL PROCESS

AIRCRAFT IDENTIFICATION

The aircraft that needs to be appraised must be evidently identified and verified to confirm that the correct items and components are being appraised. (Machinery and Technical Specialties Committee of the American Society of Appraisers, 2011) For engines and LLPs, the manufacturer serial number makes identification of the appropriate asset straightforward. This enables the appraiser to collect aircraft manufacturer name, model, type, year of manufacture (YOM), and other pertinent details that needs to be cross-referenced, identified, and accounted for. Once this step is completed, the aircraft can be correctly assessed in accordance with appraisal regulations. Special attention needs to be given to identifying aircraft engine parts and LLPs. In the course of operating an aircraft, engines and other components are routinely swapped out to allow for uninterrupted operation of the aircraft. If an appraiser values an aircraft with a particular engine and post-appraisal, the appraiser discovers that the engine was loaned while the actual subject engine was not installed on the aircraft, this would result in an incorrect value for the aircraft. Similarly, avionics and other pertinent flight instruments should be inventoried to ensure they are accurately accounted for.

PHYSICAL ASSESSMENT

A physical inspection might not always be required for some appraisals (Vasigh, 2012). Nonetheless, examining the aircraft and records relevant to it may be helpful in carrying out the appraisal. Conducting a physical inspection requires extensive planning, as aircraft records are not kept with the aircraft and may be at more than one location. However, the records may also be stored electronically, which would allow them to be much easier to obtain. During the planning process, any security concerns relevant to conducting the inspection should be carefully addressed, including release forms, approval to take photos of the aircraft, and access to the aircraft. Table 12.1 highlights key components that should be included in physical inspection.

Table 12.1 Physical Inspection Checklist

Components	Description
MSN	This is located on a mandatory data plate installed on the exterior of the aircraft so that it is legible from the ground
Aircraft registration number	Should be painted on the exterior of the aircraft, however, decals may be used instead of paint
Airworthiness certificate	Required to be present inside the aircraft and visible to passengers or crew
Weight and balance	
Operation handbook	
Wings	Overall damage check
Empennage	Overall damage check
Fuselage	Overall damage check
Engines	Authenticate serial number and make sure it's not swapped
Interior	Overall damage check, seat configuration, etc.
Exterior	Overall damage check

MSN, *Manufacturer's Serial Number.*
Valuing Machinery and Equipment: The Fundamentals of Appraising Machinery and Technical Assets, Third Edition, American Society of Appraisers.

REVIEWING RECORDS

Depending on the type of appraisal requested (desktop, extended desktop, full, comprehensive), different levels of inspection of the records may be needed (Machinery and Technical Specialties Committee of the American Society of Appraisers, 2011). A general rule of thumb is the older the aircraft and the greater its utilization is, the larger are the number of accompanying records (Vasigh, 2012). Inspecting aircraft records should be done in a methodical manner to identify crucial components. Records usually include the following:

- Engine maintenance schedules
- Airframe maintenance records
- Computer generated maintenance records
- Propeller (if any) maintenance records
- Federal Aviation Administration (FAA) or European Aviation Safety Agency (EASA) forms
- Records of any accidents or incidents.

Aircraft appraisers need to meticulously inspect all the pertinent records for damage history, airworthiness directives, and maintenance history. The reason of inspecting each record is outlined in Table 12.2.

MAINTENANCE LOGS

All operators are required to maintain and keep proper maintenance records for engine, airframe, equipment, and propellers (Vasigh, 2012). The records are required to contain detailed reports on type of maintenance performed, dates of maintenance performed, mechanic's authorization, FAA certificate, and certificate of the mechanic authorizing aircraft's approval to return to service. The records should also contain the inspections that would be required at a future date, complying with Code of Federal Regulations (CFR) required by regulatory bodies such as the FAA and EASA.

There are incidents when maintenance records and logbooks go missing or left incomplete intentionally or by accident (Machinery and Technical Specialties Committee of the American Society of Appraisers, 2011). Irrespective of the intent, a missing maintenance record or a logbook would mean that a part of aircraft's history is not available for appraiser's review and scrutiny, which would

Table 12.2 Review of Records

Components	Description
Serial numbers	To make sure all the components belong to the subject aircraft
Continuousness	If the records are uninterrupted since the date of production
Impairment history	Any previous accident or damage
Linguistic	What language are the records in? They are preferred to be in English
Replacement history	When was the last interior replacement and paint job done?
Equipment	When were the equipment installed and approved?
Inspection history	Dates of minor and major inspection

Valuing Machinery and Equipment: The Fundamentals of Appraising Machinery and Technical Assets, Third Edition, American Society of Appraisers.

negatively affect an aircraft's final value. Updates on the following components can be found from the maintenance records or logbooks, which would directly influence the value of the aircraft.

- Aircraft age
- Limitations on the aircraft
- Previous maintenance inspection methods used and current status
- Paint and interior conditions
- Airworthiness directives status
- Corrosion updates
- Noise classifications and possible airport restrictions
- Engine overhauls and LLPs status
- Projected operating costs—routine maintenance, fuel

DEPRECIATION

An aircraft depreciates in value overtime, and it is important for an appraiser to understand the extent of depreciation in order to arrive at the value of an aircraft and to aid in the projection of future values. Depreciation is the decrease in the value of an asset with the passage of time, due to physical, functional, and economic obsolescence. Depreciation can be both curable and incurable. Curable depreciation is any form of depreciation that is economically reasonable to repair while incurable depreciation is any form of depreciation that is not economically reasonable to repair, because the resulting increases in value is less than the cost to repair.

PHYSICAL DEPRECIATION

Physical depreciation is decrease or loss in value or utility of the aircraft due to expiration of the subject aircraft's economic age caused by wear and tear, exposure to harsh environmental conditions, deterioration, and physical stress. During physical inspection of the subject aircraft, major components need to be assessed to find the extent of physical depreciation of the aircraft.

Physical depreciation is caused by the following:

- Wear and tear from utilization
- Deterioration caused from age
- Exposure to harsh environmental conditions
- Lack of maintenance
- Stress and fatigue

The physical condition due to wear and tear is usually caused more by the actual utilization and the environment the subject aircraft is flying in than by its age. The external appearance does not necessarily reflect an aircraft's physical condition. For instance, an aircraft that is greasy, dirty, and dusty may not reflect the physical depreciation or useful life remaining on the aircraft or the amount of life consumed. An appraiser also needs to make sure that only physical wear and tear is measured and not factor in functional loss of utility. It is often easier to determine depreciation of some components than others. For example, LLP expiration is set by the OEMs, and it is relatively easy for the appraiser to measure the deterioration on them. Maintenance records and logbooks should enable the appraiser to establish physical depreciation for the LLPs. Other major parts that are not life-limited need to be analyzed differently, as appropriate for each. Further, the depreciation of other components of an aircraft would affect the total value of the aircraft. There may be instances where there is another 10 years remaining on the airframe, but the remaining components do not have enough life remaining to support the airframe. In this case, the value of the aircraft would be significantly lower than if the life remaining on the other components matched that of the airframe.

FUNCTIONAL OBSOLESCENCE

Functional obsolescence is the decrease or loss in usefulness or value due to the inadequacies or inefficiencies of the subject aircraft compared to a more efficient or less expensive replacement aircraft. Functional obsolescence is the functional efficiency or capacity impairment brought upon by factors such as inadequacies, overcapacity, and advanced technological replacements available in the market. In simple terms, it is the inability of the subject aircraft to economically perform the function for which it was originally designed. For instance, newer aircraft tend to make the older aircraft functionally obsolete because of the new generation instrumentation, advanced engines, lightweight materials, and avionics available in it compared to the subject aircraft.

Functional obsolescence is caused by the following:

- Surplus capacity
- Lack of utility
- Technological advancement
- Inefficiency
- Change of design
- Change in needs

Appraisers can sometimes measure functional obsolescence and some forms of economic obsolescence as the difference between replacement cost new and reproduction cost new. However, once the replacement cost new is determined, a deduction for physical deterioration is still in order.

ECONOMIC OBSOLESCENCE

Economic obsolescence, also known as external obsolescence, is the decrease or loss in usefulness or value of the aircraft due to external factors. External factors such as increased competition, high interest rates, environmental or other regulations, reduced demand for the product, or other similar factors can lead to economic obsolescence.

Economic obsolescence can be caused by the following:

- Availability of raw materials
- Management ability
- Government regulations
- Competition
- Earning power
- Availability of labor supply
- Market's accessibility
- Market's acceptability

For example, government regulation requiring Stage 3 noise criteria made Stage 2 aircraft lose value due to the new regulation. Similarly, FAA requirements for an aircraft to have a three-person crew instead of a two-person crew can also lead to economic obsolescence for the aircraft requiring a three-person crew.

AGE/LIFE ANALYSIS

When appraising an aircraft, an appraiser has to estimate the extent of depreciation of the aircraft in order to determine its current value. Age/life analysis is often the method used by the appraiser to measure physical deterioration of an aircraft (Machinery and Technical Specialties Committee of the American Society of Appraisers, 2011). In this process, the appraiser uses an estimate of the normal useful life (NUL) and remaining useful life (RUL) of the aircraft to arrive at the effective age (EA) of the aircraft. Depreciation is then computed as a ratio of EA over NUL (Example 12.2).

Age/life analysis study usually involves the following:

- Examining client's records
- Inspecting subject aircraft and its conditions
- Determining subject aircraft's NUL
- Determining subject aircraft's EA
- Determining physical depreciation

The below definitions are important to understand age/life analysis.

ECONOMIC USEFUL LIFE

According to ASA, "the estimated period of time over which it is anticipated an asset may be profitably used for the purpose for which it was intended (The time span may be limited by changing factors of obsolescence and physical age.)."

EFFECTIVE AGE

According to ASA, "The estimated age of an asset in comparison with a new asset of like kind and often calculated by deducting the remaining useful life of an asset from the normal useful life (In other words, it is the age indicated by the actual condition of the asset.)."

ESTIMATED REMAINING (PHYSICAL) USEFUL LIFE (RUL)

According to ASA, "The period over which an asset will remain in use before deteriorating to an unusable condition."

NORMAL USEFUL (PHYSICAL) LIFE

According to ASA, "The life, usually in terms of years, that an asset will be used before it deteriorates to an unusable condition or is retired from service (It is derived from mortality data and the study of specific assets under actual operating conditions)."

CHRONOLOGICAL AGE

According to ASA, "The number of years elapsed since an item of property was originally built."

TOTAL LIFE

According to ASA, "Total life can be an extension of normal useful life for various reason."

Age/life = Percentage depreciated

AGE/LIFE FORMULA AND RATIO

Effective age/total life = effective age/(effective age + remaining useful life) = percentage of depreciation

$$NUL = EA + RUL$$

Or by transposition

$$NUL - RUL = EA$$

Or by transposition

$$RUL = NUL - EA$$

Note that the NUL of the aircraft is established when it is put into service. Hence, over time, the EA increases and RUL decreases.

EXAMPLE 12.2 AGE/LIFE ANALYSIS

Below is information for an MD80:

- NUL is 35 years
- Replacement cost new today is $40 million
- The subject aircraft is 7 years old
- Maintenance has been up-to-date and records are in order
- Aircraft's utilization has been normal

Find the amount of physical depreciation using age/life analysis.

Solution

Chronological age = 7 years (given)

Finding RUL:

NUL = 35 years

EA (under normal maintenance) = 7 years

RUL = 35 − 7 = 28 years

Finding physical depreciation:

Depreciation (in %) = EA/NUL = 20%

Dollar amount of physical depreciation = 20% of $40,000,000 = *$8,000,000*

CURABLE AND INCURABLE DEPRECIATION

Curable depreciation is any form of depreciation that is economically reasonable to repair and the resulting increase in value is equal to or greater than the cost to cure. Incurable depreciation is any form for depreciation that is not economically reasonable to repair because the resulting increase in value is less than the cost. The major cause of curable and incurable depreciation is due to physical deterioration, functional obsolescence, or economic obsolescence described before.

ACCOUNTING DEPRECIATION VS APPRAISING DEPRECIATION

It is important for appraisers to understand the difference between accounting depreciation and depreciation relevant for appraising purposes. Accounting depreciation is a systematic allocation of costs over time and may not be relevant to determining the actual value of the subject aircraft. In contrast, appraising depreciation identifies and establishes depreciation to determine a value of the subject aircraft. Appraisers would therefore adjust the value of an aircraft due to depreciation from physical wear and tear, functional obsolescence, or economic obsolescence.

AIRCRAFT VALUATION METHODOLOGY

In the U.S. aircraft appraising industry, two major organizations are recognized for aircraft appraisal. They are the following:

- ISTAT
- ASA

The ISTAT was founded in 1983 and has more than 4000 members worldwide. ISTAT members consist of aircraft manufacturers, maintenance repair organizations (MROs), operators (airlines), lessors, financing institutions, and aircraft appraisers. ISTAT is governed by its bylaws and a volunteer ISTAT Board of Directors, which is composed of and elected by current members. ISTAT has its own group of professional aircraft appraisers who work compliantly for the advancement of the appraisal professional within the aviation community. ISTAT has four stages of appraiser categories.

- Appraiser
- Senior appraiser
- Appraiser fellow
- Appraiser emeritus

The ASA was founded in 1936. It is a multidiscipline organization of appraisers. ASA is the oldest and the only organization that represents all disciplines of appraisal specialists. ASA members perform appraisal on businesses ranging from machinery, gems and jewelry, technical specialties, real estate, aircraft, and personal property. Aircraft appraisers are listed under Machinery and Technical Specialty. They are required to complete four principles of valuation courses as well complete the *Uniform Standards of Professional Appraisal Practice* (USPAP) and ASA code of ethics exam and submit an appraisal report to get accreditation. USPAP is the generally recognized ethical and performance standards for the appraisal profession in the United States. USPAP was adopted by Congress in 1989 and contains standards for all types of appraisal services, including real estate, personal property, business, and mass appraisal. USPAP is updated every 2 years, so that appraisers have the information they need to deliver unbiased and thoughtful opinions of value. Based on appraisal experience, ASA awards the Accredited Member designation, which requires 2 years of full-time appraisal experience, or the Accredited Senior Appraisers designation, which requires 5 years of full-time appraisal experience.

APPROACH TO VALUATION

These are three methods to appraise an aircraft, namely,

- Cost approach
- Income approach
- Sales comparison approach

Cost approach

The cost approach is based on the concept that a well-versed buyer would not want to pay more for the aircraft than the cost of buying a substitute or comparable aircraft with the same features as that of the subject aircraft (Remsha, 2014). In other words, in this approach, the utmost value of the subject aircraft to a well-informed buyer is the cost currently required to reproduce a new aircraft with same or identical characteristics. This concept is also known as the principle of substitution. In this approach, the costs are adjusted for all forms of depreciation to arrive at the value of the subject aircraft. The cost approach can be stated as follows:

Cost New − Deprecation = Value

The first step in the cost approach is to determine an appropriate level of current cost, either *replacement cost new or reproduction cost new*. There is an important distinction between replacement cost new and reproduction cost new that the appraiser should be aware of. Replacement cost refers to the current cost of a similar property having the same utility as the subject aircraft, whereas reproduction cost is current cost of reproducing a new replica of the property. For most appraisal purposes, finding replacement cost of a substitute aircraft would be more economical than reproducing an identical asset. One usefulness of having an estimate of reproduction cost for an appraiser is to be able to quantify functional obsolescence due to excess capital costs. If one assumes that the reproduction cost is more than replacement cost of an asset, functional obsolescence due to excess capital cost, can be measured as the difference between reproduction cost and replacement cost. The excess capital cost exists, because it is often less expensive to obtain a newer aircraft with the same functionality as an older aircraft. Reproduction cost can also be useful when an appraisal has to be compared to other indicators computed based on an index or trending.

Once the current cost is established, physical deterioration, functional obsolescence, and economic obsolescence are subtracted to arrive at the value of the aircraft. Below we look at an example (Example 12.3) to compute physical depreciation and compute the value of an aircraft given the replacement cost new.

EXAMPLE 12.3 CALCULATING DEPRECIATION AND FAIR MARKET VALUE

Below is the information for a B737 in continued use and with no functional or economic obsolesce.

- NUL is 25 years.
- Replacement cost for new today for B737 is $81,000,000.
- Subject aircraft is 32 years old.
- Maintenance has been up-to-date and records are in order.
- Aircraft's utilization has been normal.
- Subject aircraft was completely rebuilt 5 years ago. It is estimated that this rebuilding exercise brought the aircraft up to 80% of its useful life.
    - Compute the EA of the aircraft.
    - Compute the physical depreciation using age/life analysis.
    - Compute the fair market value.

Finding EA
NUL = 25 years
Restored life 5 years ago = 80% of 25 years = 20 years
RUL today = 20 − 5 years = 15 years
EA (NUL − RUL) = *10 years*
Finding physical deprecation
Depreciation (in %) = EA/NUL = 40%
Physical depreciation = 40% of $81,000,000 = *$32,400,000*
Fair market value = 60% of $81,000,000 = *$48,600,000*

Approaches to determine current cost new

There are many ways to determine current cost new of the subject aircraft. The keys methods are detail method and trending (Machinery and Technical Specialty Committee of the American Society of Appraisers, 2011).

Detail method

In the detail method, all the components of the aircraft are itemized and documented, so that the sum of all these components reflects the current cost new of the whole aircraft.

In this method, all direct and indirect costs need to be included. The summation of all indirect costs, direct costs, and direct material costs are known as assemblage costs. Direct costs are labor, material, and other pertinent expenses usually incurred during purchase and installation of any asset, or a group of assets into operations.

Examples of direct costs for any machinery or equipment including an aircraft can be

- Direct labor costs for installation
- Direct material costs or purchase price
- Rigging and moving
- Freight and handling
- Piping
- Electrical
- Foundations

Indirect costs are those expenses that are usually necessary to purchase and install an asset or a group of assets but typically are not usually included on the purchase invoice.

Examples of indirect costs:

- Administrative costs
- Legal fees
- Engineering fees
- Licenses and permits fees
- Insurance

Under the detail method, typical direct and indirect costs are included, but atypical costs are excluded. For example, a large project might need overtime labor to complete which is considered normal but using overtime labor to complete a project in a shorter period of time may be considered atypical and should be excluded.

While the detail method should result in greater accuracy than less detailed methods, it may not always be practical or possible to create a complete list of all the components or their respective costs. The detail method is also time consuming, and it is easy for the appraiser to overlook or omit important components, which will have a bearing on the final value. Often detailed specifications and documentation for the aircraft may not be available making the task of the appraiser using the detailed method difficult. Ultimately the choice of whether to use the detail method or not will depend on the extent of detail required by the client. If the detail method is used, the appraiser should be diligent and compare the results with other methods to check for consistency before arriving at the final opinion of value.

Trending method

In trending method, the appraiser estimates reproduction cost new of the subject aircraft in which a trend factor or an index is applied to the subject aircraft's historical cost to convert the historical known costs to an estimate of current cost new. Under this method, historical cost refers to the cost of an aircraft when it was first placed in service by the first owner.

Trending method exercise

An index is a valuable tool in determining aircraft's reproduction cost new from its historical cost. We look at an example below (Example 12.4) which details how to compute this cost.

EXAMPLE 12.4 USE OF INDEX NUMBERS TO FIND TREND FACTOR

Let us assume that the cost of a Boeing 777 manufactured in 1995 is $100 million. Determine the reproduction cost of the aircraft in 2002 assuming the base year is 1990.

Year	Index
1990	100
1995	116
1996	121
1997	127
1998	132
1999	138
2000	143
2001	149
2002	154

Trend factor = Current index (2002)/historic index (1995)
154/116 = 1.3276
Current cost new = Trend factor × historical cost
= 1.3276 × $100,000,000
= *$132,760,000*

Index numbers are useful for computing reproduction cost new but do not indicate replacement cost new, as they do not reflect improvements in technology, which may over time reduce current cost. Further cost indexes are based on average value, but the subject aircraft may differ from the average. The appraiser should also make sure that trending is applied to historical cost and not costs resulting from allocation of purchase price and when the historical cost used does not exclude indirect or other costs.

Income approach

The income approach is based on the premise that the value of an aircraft is based on the current or present value of the income generating potential of the aircraft in the future (Example 12.5 & Example 12.6). The income approach is not widely used by an appraiser of general or corporate aviation aircraft, as it is often difficult to determine income that can be directly attributed to a specific aircraft. Further, the valuation methodology involves making projections of future income and use of a valid discount rate in the process, which often imposes additional constraint on the resources available to an appraiser and may delay the process of arriving at an opinion of value. However, USPAP requires the ASA appraiser to consider all three approaches to value, and hence, it is important for an ASA appraiser to understand how to use this method of valuation.

One area where the income approach is useful is in determining lease-encumbered value where the appraiser needs to compute the value of an aircraft based on present value of the future lease income stream and a residual value for the aircraft.

In this section, we will therefore introduce the basic terminology and inputs necessary to apply the income approach and discuss examples of the application of the income approach.

An aircraft lessor views the aircraft as an investment. As an investor, the lessor needs to understand the expected return to be generated by the aircraft, the period of time over which the return will be earned, and the risk of the investment. In an aircraft lease, the future lease payments and the final residual value of the aircraft are typically what accrues to the investor, the lessor, over time. Since these benefits accrue to the investor in the future, the investor needs to know the current value of the all the future benefits from the investment. In order to know the present value of the future benefits, the future benefits have to discounted to present value using an appropriate discount rate for the investor to understand if it worthwhile to make the investment today. The essence of the income approach therefore is that present value today is based on an aircraft's discounted future benefits.

The income approach is also sometimes referred to as the discounted cash flow (DCF) method. In a DCF or income method, the discount rate is applied to a series of future cash flows (e.g., lease payments) of an aircraft over time and the final residual value at the end of the lease. The cash flows over time can remain constant, grow, or even decline over time as in a floating lease or remain constant as in a fixed lease. A series of equal payments over an equal time period (a month, quarter, or year) is called an *annuity*. An annuity that lasts forever is called a *perpetuity*. For a perpetual income stream, one can state the income approach as follows:

$$\text{Value} = \text{Income}/\text{Capitalization rate}$$

where a *capitalization rate* = discount rate minus projected growth of the earnings to be capitalized, where the projected growth can be stable (or zero growth), declining (negative), or increasing (positive).

EXAMPLE 12.5 USING *CAPITALIZATION* RATE (INCOME APPROACH) TO DETERMINE VALUE

Determine the value of an A320 using income approach, if its expected income is $200,000 per year and lasts forever and the discount rate is 20%.

$$\text{Value} = \$200,000/20\% = \$1,000,000$$

EXAMPLE 12.6 USING DISCOUNT RATE (INCOME APPROACH) TO DETERMINE VALUE

- A B747 has a net operating income of $250,000 a year
- Interest rate is 7.5%
- Operator can sell it for $100,000 at the end of its economic life
- The aircraft has 15 years of economic life remaining

This can be solved by hand, financial calculator, or the present value (PV) function in Excel.

$$\text{PV} = \$250,000/(1+0.07) + \$250,000/(1+0.07)^2 + \cdots + \$250,000/(1+0.07)^{15}$$
$$+ \$100,000/(1+0.07)^{15}$$
$$\text{Or PV} = \$1764,539.63$$

Sales comparison approach

Sales comparison approach arrives at the value of the subject aircraft by comparing recent sales of aircraft that are similar to the subject aircraft. If the comparable aircraft is not exactly the same as the subject aircraft the selling price of the comparables is adjusted up or down to match the characteristics of the subject aircraft. Like the cost approach and the income approach, the sales comparison approach assumes that a knowledgeable and informed buyer would not pay more for an aircraft than the cost of acquiring a similar aircraft with the same utility.

METHODS OF COMPARISON

Direct match

This method establishes a value for the subject aircraft based on a direct match to an identical aircraft. For example, cost and revenue data for a King Air 250 of exact age, time, make, and condition could be used as a proxy to arrive at the value of the subject aircraft. However, recent sales of aircraft that are identical to the subject aircraft may not be found in that case one has to look to a comparable match or sale.

Comparable match

This method establishes a value for the subject aircraft based on analysis of a comparable but not identical aircraft using some measure of utility (size, configuration, costs, etc.) as a foundation of comparison. For example, if an appraiser is appraising a Beechjet and cannot find any sales but finds sales of a same size and condition CitationJet then the sales of CitationJet could be used; however, the appraiser must adjust these values for any differences. Usual adjustments to the comparable aircraft may include adjustments for the following:

- Age and condition
- Avionics and instrumentation condition
- Interior and exterior condition
- Alterations and damage history
- Time on airframe, engine, and LLPs
- Time remaining between two major maintenance checks
- Location of the aircraft
- Manufacturer and quality
- Motivation of parties
- Quantity sold

The following equation represents sales comparison approach in its simplest form:

$$\text{Comparable Sale} \pm \text{Adjustments} = \text{Value}$$

Age and condition

One of the important adjustments to the comparable the appraiser has to make is adjusting the age and condition of the aircraft to match the subject aircraft. For example, if appraising the Beechjet, the subject aircraft's age is 10 years, while the CitationJet's age is 15 years then the CitationJet value would be adjusted upward from its actual selling price, so that the appraiser can get a realistic estimate of the value of the CitationJet if it was 10 years old rather than 15 years old.

Better avionics and instrumentation as well as interior and exterior conditions have a bearing on value. However, adjustments for condition of the aircraft often are challenging. While the condition of the subject aircraft may be known, the appraiser may not be aware of the condition of the comparable. It is important therefore to investigate the condition of the comparable.

Usage and maintenance

The time used on airframe, engine, landing gear and LLPs will need to be adjusted on the comparable to resemble the subject aircraft.

Location of the aircraft

The location of the comparable sale aircraft may affect the selling price. If the aircraft is located in a foreign country, it may add additional cost in relocating the aircraft to local country.

Manufacturer and quality

The appraiser should as far as possible to compare the subject to a comparable manufactured by the same manufacturer. For example, a Boeing aircraft being appraised should be compared to another Boeing aircraft with same or similar features. Actual or perceived quality differences in the manufacturer of an aircraft will affect value, and the appraiser should be cognizant of such impacts on the value of the aircraft.

Motivation of parties

The motivation of buyers and sellers would also affect the value of the subject aircraft. An aircraft purchased by a dealer for resale will have a very different value compared to the purchase price paid by customer for his/her personal use.

Quantity sold

Actual price of a single aircraft differs considerably on the number of aircraft sold. Airlines when they order 200 of the same aircraft type from an OEM always get deep discounts compared to a lessor trying to order a customized aircraft to suit the needs of a particular client.

Percent of cost

This method simply establishes ratio between selling price and current cost of the aircraft at the time of sale. With adequate data, appraiser may be able to statistically examine and establish relationships in the used market developed among selling price, new costs, and age. Under this approach, suppose the appraiser has collected enough data to conclude that aircraft of size, age, and condition similar to the subject aircraft are in the 50%–60% range of current cost new; it would be prudent to conclude that the value of the subject aircraft is in the 50%–60% range of the current cost new.

Having discussed the three approaches to value, namely, the cost approach, income approach, and sale comparison approach we look at a simple example of a Gulfstream IV (G-IV) using all three approaches to value (Example 12.7). Case studies at the end of the chapter take a detailed look at the sales comparison and ISTAT approach to value.

EXAMPLE 12.7 USING COST, MARKET, AND INCOME APPROACH

Finding a value of a G-IV using all three approaches.

You are an appraiser and have been tasked with appraising a G-IV with YOM of 1990 at a cost of $18 million. Current replacement cost for a new Gulfstream 450 is $40 million. You have estimated all forms for depreciation to be 70%. The capitalization rate is 15%. Brokers indicate that similar G-IVs are readily available on the market with selling prices ranging from $10 to $16 million. Operators indicate that gross operating income is $2 million per year, less 15% operating expenses. Calculate fair market value by all three approaches to value discussed above.

Cost approach

Replacement cost = $40,000,000

Depreciation (less) = 70%

Fair market value = $12,000,000

Sales comparison approach

Average market selling price ($10–$16 million) = $13,000,000

Fair market value = $13,000,000

Income approach

Gross operating income = $2,000,000

Operating expenses (less) = $300,000

Net operating income = $1,700,000

Capitalization rate = 15%

Fair market value = $11,333,333

When an appraiser evaluates an aircraft, the typical terms of values used are BV and CMV of an average aircraft of similar type. Apart from BV and CMV, a client may also be interested in adjusted values, encumbered values, distressed value, part-out (salvage) value, scrap value, or a diminution value report (usually for a damaged aircraft). As discussed above, BV is a theoretical value that assumes that the supply and demand is in equilibrium, whereas the CMV is the actual value of recent transactions in the market. Both BV and CMV assume a hypothetical average aircraft condition of aircraft similar or identical to the subject aircraft. An average aircraft is defined as an operational airworthy aircraft with a standard unrestricted certificate of airworthiness and clear title, no damage history and configuration and level of add-ons which is typical for its use and age, and is in average physical age, condition, and average utilized flight cycles and hours. An average aircraft should not be one that is stored. Appraisers also assume that the airframe, engine and its components, and LLPs are from the OEMs and that aircraft's engines have not been swapped.

Half-life condition assumes that all the components of the aircraft and its maintenance are halfway between next major maintenances/performance restorations/overhaul events. The appraiser would then make a positive or negative "adjustment" from half-life assumption to reflect the actual condition of the subject aircraft, flight hours and cycle utilization, life remaining on the airframe, and engine utilization. It should be noted that when an appraiser gives his/her opinion regarding a subject aircraft, it only applies to a transaction involving a single aircraft, as a transaction involving more than one aircraft is often discounted based on buyer's purchasing power and number of aircraft purchased.

Traditional approach

Base value estimation

BV is an appraiser's opinion of the underlying economic value with a reasonable balance of supply and demand. As the definition discussed indicates BV assumes an open and unrestricted market, absence of duress, and a reasonable time for marketing the aircraft. It also assumes that it is a single-unit transaction and half-life condition unless the aircraft is new or nearly new. An aircraft's BV is based on historical trends and future expectations when the aircraft first enters the market. There is usually a statistical relationship between aircraft values and independent variables such as age, range, seats, operators, and so on. Aircraft values tend to decline overtime due to depreciation, obsolescence due to the introduction of new technology, and increase in nonroutine maintenance activities as the engines and other parts age as shown in the figure below.

Future base value estimation

Future BV is based on historical data and forward-looking parameters. Historical value trends adjusted for current inflation rates would be used to generate a generic depreciation curve and then forward-looking parameters such as fleet size and distribution, secondary market prospects, production cycle, and technological factors. This BV curve is further adjusted for long-term macroeconomic trends such as gross domestic product (GDP) and oil forecast. GDP growth is believed to be a good measure of airline passenger traffic growth, which affects demand for new and used aircraft and therefore has a direct effect on its value. Appraisers also track interest rate trends, as the cost of borrowing affects the demand for aircraft. The US Federal Reserve has kept the interest rates low since the 2008 financial crisis to stimulate demand. The low interest rate environment helps improve lessor's spread over their cost of borrowing and therefore goes to support aircraft values. Finally, appraisers track crude oil prices and jet fuel price trends, as they have a bearing on the operator's cost. Jet fuel prices plummeted in late 2014 and have remained relatively low over last 3 years as compared to early 2010. These low fuel prices can be both a boon and a curse for aircraft demand. On the one hand, when jet fuel prices are low, operators tend to extend the use of older fuel inefficient aircraft, which dampens the demand for expensive fuel-efficient aircraft. On the other hand, low fuel prices, improves an airline/operator's balance sheet, and their financial ratios leading to higher demand for aircraft. On balance however both lessors and operators favor low fuel prices, as it lowers cost to an airline thereby improving its financial strength and leading to more robust demand for aircraft which supports higher values.

Finally, aircraft-specific qualitative factors are applied to further customize the curve. The appraiser will analyze each aircraft model to determine its historic, current, and projected competitive position with respect to similar aircraft types in terms of mission capability, economic profile, and market penetration. The key aircraft-specific factors that appraisers may consider are aircraft size/range, speed, engine type, number in service, number of operators, concentration of operators, geographic distribution, total production, and number of aircraft parked and in storage. Based on these characteristics, an appraiser would use market-strength band curves to characterize where the aircraft falls on a baseline curve (Fig.12.4). Based on these factors, a numerical strength factor is assigned to each aircraft and ranges from a value 10 (strongest) to 1 (weakest). Using a proprietary model, the appraiser will then translate these strength factors into the aircraft's base and future values based on its actual replacement cost. These values are then continually monitored and recalibrated based on current market information.

Fig. 12.1 shows a cluster of transaction data points based on the appraiser's proprietary database and a trend line fitted through this cluster. An R^2 of 0.56 indicates that age (independent) variable explains about 56% of value (dependent) variable in this case (Kelly, 2008). BV trends can however change based on new information which comes to the market after the aircraft is placed into service. For example, when the Airbus A380 was first introduced, there was a high expectation that it would hold its value well over time but that has not been the case due to lack of a secondary market for the aircraft and operational constraints such as weight of the aircraft and length and width of the runway. Further, the size and therefore the reconfiguration cost of the Airbus A380 has made it challenging for a lessor to place the aircraft on an economically viable second lease. In such circumstances, the appraiser has to rethink the BV curve and allow for a steeper decline in value overtime (as shown in Fig. 12.1).

In theory, the CMV of the aircraft at a point in time can either be above or below the BV and should oscillate around the BV. Fig. 12.2 shows how the CMV of the aircraft tends to fluctuate around the BV overtime. In reality, however, CMVs tend to move with macroeconomic events such as fuel price hikes, wars, and recessions (Fig. 12.3 & Fig. 12.5).

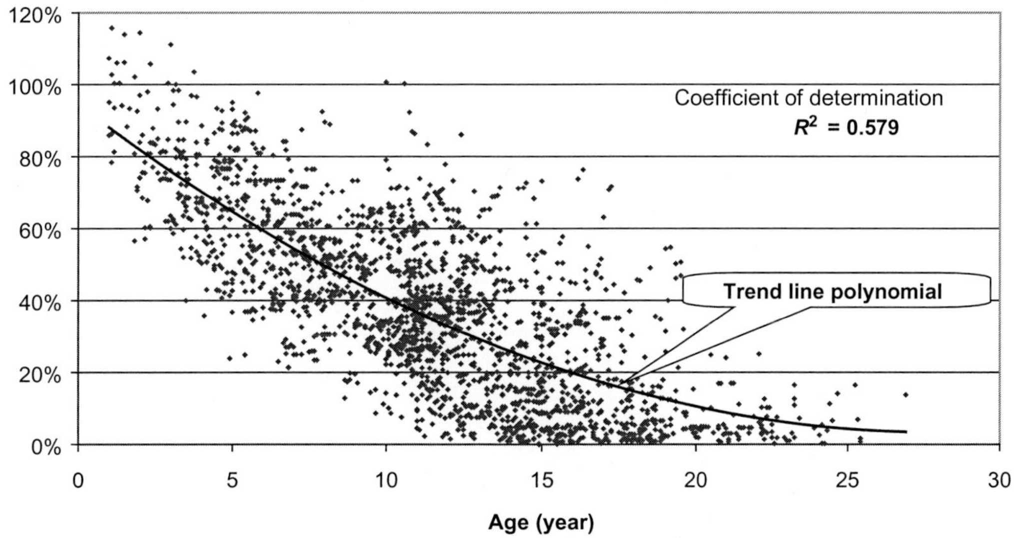

FIGURE 12.1

Real value as percentage of real original value for all jets.

AVITAS.

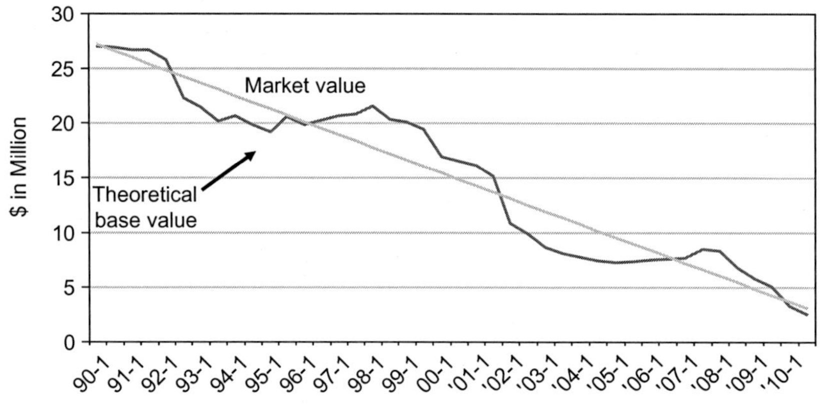

FIGURE 12.2

Historical 737-300 BlueBook values 1990 to present.

AVITAS.

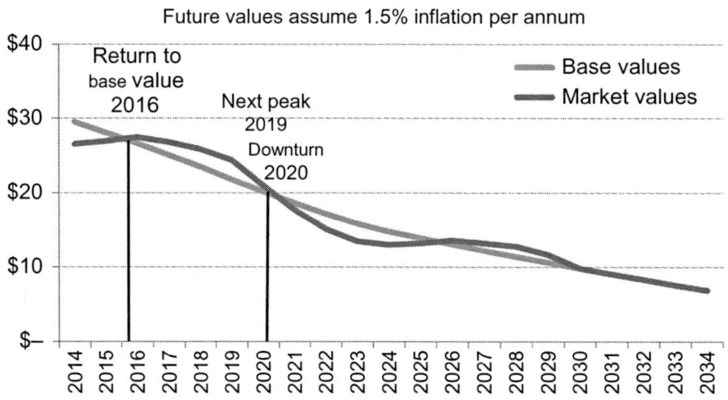

FIGURE 12.3

A320-200 (2008 vintage) current market and future values.

AVITAS.

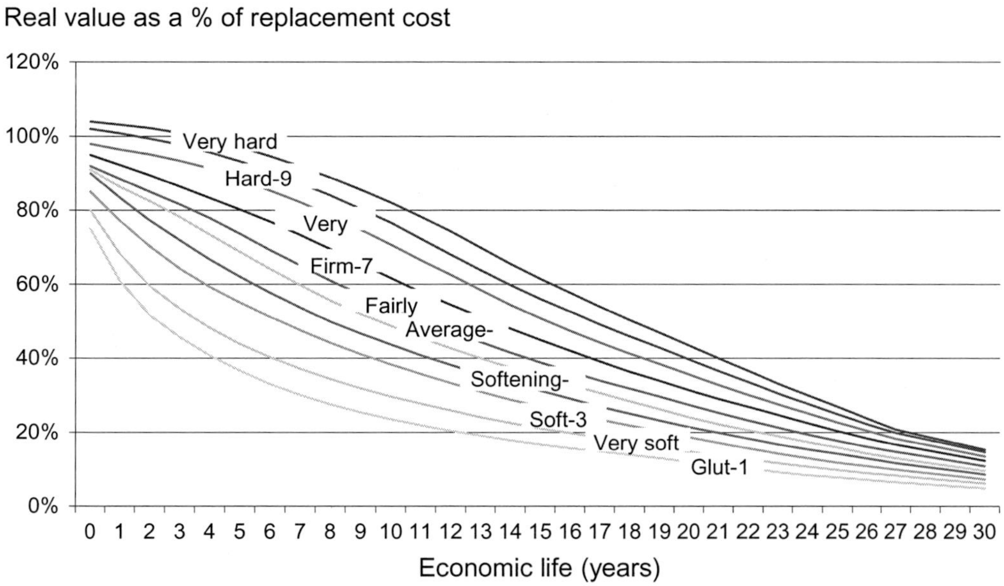

FIGURE 12.4

Baseline forecast curves: market-strength band curves.

AVITAS.

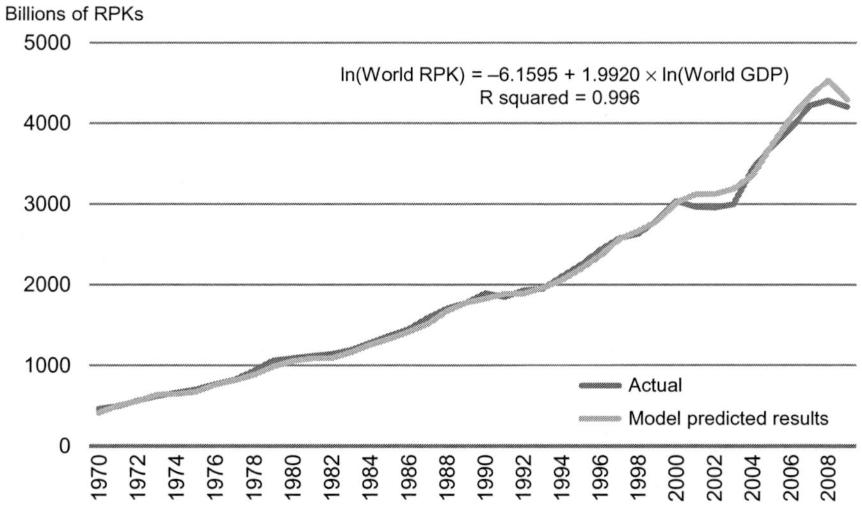

FIGURE 12.5

Correlation between world traffic and economy 1970–2009.

AVITAS.

Econometric approach

The traditional approach outlined above, while useful in forecasting future BVs, cannot help with forecasting future market values. In order to forecast future market values, appraisers may use an econometric approach which allows them to introduce additional independent variables in their model and also incorporate the effect of business cycles and rare events such as 9/11 terrorist attacks (Kelly, 2008). For example, an appraiser may consider additional independent variables which are aircraft characteristics such as size, range, speed, or consumer-related variables such as number in service, number of operators, concentration, and commonality. Econometric modeling is also helpful in conducting scenario and sensitivity analysis, which makes the analysis more robust. However, the traditional and econometric approach should not be thought of as competing but as complementary approaches to value. Thus, while age, inflation, and original cost which are considered in the traditional approach all matter, the introduction of additional explanatory variables in the econometric approach helps improve the predictability of the model and is useful for conducting scenario and volatility analysis.

ADJUSTED VALUE APPRAISAL PROCESS

In a typical ISTAT adjusted value appraisal process, the appraiser begins with half-life CMV or half-life BV. These values are then adjusted for different aircraft specifications such as MTOW, airframe modifications (doors, cargo, crew, and rest areas), avionics, certifications, interior, and if the aircraft is on power by the hour or similar engine programs. Then the value is adjusted for current maintenance status of the aircraft for engines, LLPs, landing gears, and APUs. Depending on the type of the appraisal (desktop vs full appraisal), the appraiser may make adjustments based on physical inspection of the aircraft. After these adjustments, the appraiser arrives at the adjusted CMV of the aircraft. The example below (Example 12.8) shows adjustment for the maintenance status of the aircraft from half-life condition.

EXAMPLE 12.8 ADJUSTED VALUE APPRAISAL

Calculating adjustments from half-time.

Time remaining for an HMV-check on an aircraft is 100 months. Interval between two MHV-checks is 120 months and it costs \$5.0 million. Calculate adjustments from half-time.

Life remaining to HMV-check—100/120 = 83%

Time remaining above half-time = 83% − 50% = 33%

Adjustment from half-time = \$5 million × 33% = *\$1,650,000*

LEASE-ENCUMBERED VALUE ESTIMATION PROCESS

A lease-encumbered value or securitized value is the appraiser's opinion of value of an aircraft, which has a lease attached to it. The process involves calculating the present value of the lease rentals plus the residual value at the end of the lease expiration as well as any compensation or adjustments to contractually agreed upon maintenance status at the end of the lease (Example 12.9). Lease-encumbered value therefore can be expressed as follows:

Encumbered Value = Present value of lease rental from remaining term + Present value of residual value at the end of the lease + Present value of maintenance status/compensation adjustment at the end of the lease.

Lease rentals can be monthly or quarterly and fixed as well as variable. The discount rate used to discount these rentals should reflect the risk of the lessee. In general, the higher the risk, the higher the discount rate that should be used to discount these values.

Residual value would depend on factors such as age of the aircraft at the end of the lease, engine choice and other specifications, fleet size and distribution, stage in production cycle, and OEM support. Often different discount rates can be used to arrive at the present value of the residual value than what is used to discount the lease rental payments.

Maintenance status compensation or adjustment would depend on the contractually agreed upon maintenance status at the end of the lease and the agreed compensation. For example, the lease contract may specify that the aircraft should be returned in full-life condition by the lessee, and, in this case, adjustments should be made to the aircraft value to get it to full-life condition.

EXAMPLE 12.9 LEASE-ENCUMBERED VALUE OF A 2012 A320-200

Calculate lease-encumbered value of a 2012 A320-200.

Type	A320-200
Year of build	2012
Lease expiry date	2022
Monthly lease rate	\$0.30
Remaining lease	50 months
Payments	In advance
Return conditions	Full-life
Discount rate for rents and residual	5.0%
Residual value factor for conservatism	90.0%
Future base value at 1.0% inflation	\$24.5 million
Future base value at 0.0% inflation	\$22.5 million

Assume it takes \$9 million at a 2% inflation rate to bring the aircraft back to full-life conditions

- Residual value 90% future BV at 0% inflation = \$22.5 million × 90% = \$20.25 million
- Assumed residual value for lease-end value (LEV) = \$20.25 million + \$9 million = \$29.25 million
- PV of rents = PV of \$0.3 using a 5% discount rate = \$13.52 million
- PV of residual = PV of \$29.25 using a 5% discount rate = \$23.77 million
- Total lease-encumbered value = *\$37.29 million*

APPRAISAL REPORT FORMAT AND REQUIREMENTS

The purpose and objective of an appraisal report is to communicate to the client the appraiser's opinion of value and outline the methodology and information used to arrive at that conclusion. While the fundamental elements of an appraisal report are similar for both ISTAT and ASA appraisers, however, ASA appraisers are required to adhere to the USPAP requirements in North America and to the International Valuation Standards outside the United States. Further, both ASA and ISTAT have their own ethical requirements.

Here we discuss the basic requirement of an ISTAT appraisal report.

DATE OF REPORT

An appraisal is an opinion of value as of a certain date. It is therefore important that the appraisal should contain the date of the appraisal.

IDENTIFICATION

Appraisal report has to identify the client and users of the report by name and by type.

DESCRIPTION OF PROPERTY

The report should contain a description of the property or aircraft that is being appraised. For an aircraft, this should include registration, serial number, year of build, passenger configuration, MTOW, engine type, current, and previous operator.

OBJECTIVE OF THE APPRAISAL

The report should contain the main objective of the report. For example, the report should specify whether it is a desktop, extended desktop, full or comprehensive appraisal.

ASSUMPTIONS

The appraisal report should detail the assumptions used in arriving at the final conclusion of value. For example, an appraiser could make the following assumptions about an aircraft that is being appraised.

- Aircraft is in good overall condition, unless otherwise noted in this report;
- The overhaul status of the airframe, engines, and other major components are in half-life or midlife condition, unless otherwise stated;
- Aircraft is free of any significant damage resulting from a major incident or accident;
- Historical maintenance records have been maintained to acceptable industry standards;
- The specifications of the aircraft are common for an aircraft of this type and vintage;
- The aircraft is in standard airline configuration;
- The aircraft is current on all airworthiness directives and service bulletins, unless otherwise stated;
- The aircraft modification status is considered common for an aircraft of this type and vintage;
- Its utilization is considered close to average for its type and vintage; and
- It is not encumbered by any financial or lease transactions, unless otherwise stated.

DEFINITIONS

The report should contain the different definitions used in the report. These definitions can include the different definitions of values used such as BV, CMV, lease-encumbered value, adjusted value, and so on.

APPRAISAL METHOD

The appraisal should explain the method used to arrive at the conclusion of value. Though ISTAT does not prescribe a methodology and an ISTAT appraiser is free to use any method, it is important to show the specific method used and the logical value conclusions arrived at based on the method employed.

STATEMENT OF CONTINGENCIES AND LIMITING CONDITIONS

The report should mention any contingencies or limiting conditions on which the appraisal report is based. For example, the appraiser for a desktop appraisal may state that she/he did not physically inspect the aircraft and based their conclusions solely on data provided by the client.

STATEMENT OF DISINTERESTEDNESS

An appraisal is an unbiased opinion of value, and therefore, it is important for the appraisers to state that the appraiser has no personal interest in the property being appraised.

SIGNATURE OF THE APPRAISER

The report needs to be signed by the appraiser attesting to the value conclusions arrived at in the report.

APPRAISAL FIRMS

There are numerous independent companies and sources that offer appraisal services for every aircraft type. These companies have access to their own valuation databases of values for different aircraft types and provide aviation consultancy services. These reports and values are used by financial institutions, aircraft brokers, airlines/operators, law companies, manufacturers, and MROs to put a price tag on an aircraft. All of these companies have data on major jet aircraft, including passenger and cargo. Some also provide valuation for general aviation aircraft and have both ISTAT and ASA-certified appraisers in their organizations. We discuss below the largest companies that offer appraisal services.

- AVITAS
- Flight Ascend Consultancy
- Morten Beyer & Agnew (mba)
- International Bureau of Aviation (IBA)

AVITAS

AVITAS is a full-service aviation-consulting firm founded in 1985. AVITAS provides aircraft related expert advice to airlines, financial institutions, maintenance facilities, manufacturers, government agencies, and law firms. They have offices located in Washington, DC, New York, and London. AVITAS provides technical and maintenance consulting, valuations and business planning, and forecasting. Their clients include financial institutions, airlines/operators, legal firms, manufacturers, and MROs. AVITAS appraises over 5000 aircraft and engines every year. They also publish the *BlueBooks* for jet aircraft, turboprop, and jet engine values and offer an online aircraft and engine value system.

FLIGHT ASCEND CONSULTANCY

Flight Ascend Consultancy is part of FlightGlobal, Reed Business Information, and the RELX group. Ascend and their predecessors have been delivering aviation data appraisals for close to 50 years. They appraise commercial jets, turboprops, business jets and general aviation aircraft, helicopters, engines, and simulators. The Flight Ascend Consultancy team includes both ISTAT and ASA certified appraisers, experts in accidents, and economists. They use their own unique modeling based upon their views of the market to support their opinion on aircraft valuations, fleet growth forecast, and asset ratings. Flight Ascend provides BV, CMV, future BV, soft CMV, aircraft ratings, lease-encumbered value, immediate sale (distressed) value, part-out (salvage) value, scrap value, and diminution of value for damaged aircraft as well as ASA-certified USPAP compliant appraisals.

MORTEN BEYER AND AGNEW

mba Is a global consulting firm with offices in the United States, Europe, and Asia, providing a broad spectrum of services to airlines, governments, and investors since 1992. Their consulting services include tangible valuation (such as aircraft, engines, and spare parts), intangible valuations (routes, slots, airlines, and nonpublic stock), financing and maintenance reserve modeling, market analysis and evaluation, due diligence, asset management, and technical and audit services. Their team includes ISTAT certified appraisers, airline executives, A&P mechanics, pilots, engineers, certified public accountants and Juris Doctors. Their clients range from private equity and hedge funds, investment banks, airlines, aircraft and engine lessors, government agencies, insurance companies, aircraft storage facilities, and parts distributors.

mba Publishes the *Redbook* which provides BV, CMV, and future value for aircraft at half-life, full-life, and in a soft market for more than 120 aircraft models, as well as lease rates.

INTERNATIONAL BUREAU OF AVIATION

IBA is an independent leading aviation consultancy established in 1988, which advises broad mix of lessors, operators, financiers, and investors. They provide a range of services from market analysis and competitive intelligence, due diligence, valuations, benchmarking, deal negotiations, risk management, asset management, risk monitoring, litigation, dispute support, sell-side advisory, end-of-lease options, and remarketing.

A full list of appraisal companies can be found in the ISTAT directory or on the website at www.istat.org.

In addition to the above major firms providing full-service appraisal consulting services, there are other companies, especially in the corporate and general aviation space, which provide aircraft value guides. The popular guides are the Aircraft BlueBook Price Digest, Airliner Price Guide, Aircraft Value Reference, and International BlueBook. As we discussed previously, one of the most popular and feasible approaches to appraising corporate and general aviation values is the sale comparison approach. Unfortunately, due to lack of standardized transaction data, it becomes important to often start with baseline values provided by these aircraft value guides.

CONCLUSION

In this chapter, we looked at how appraisers arrive at aircraft values. An appraisal is, in essence, an opinion of value derived based on a systematic process. Aircraft values come in a number forms, each of which can be provided at varying levels of detail, depending on the purpose for which they are used. Determining the value of an aircraft is important for different stakeholders such as leasing companies, financial institutions, aircraft brokers, airlines/operators, legal companies, manufacturers, and MROs. The fundamental approaches to value followed by appraisers are Cost Approach, Sale Comparison, or Market Approach and Income Approach.

There are two major organizations that conduct aircraft appraisals, namely, ASA and ISTAT. While ASA has predominantly focused on appraising business and general aviation aircraft, ISTAT has focused on commercial aircraft appraisals. Further, both ASA and ISTAT have their own definitions of value, which are similar but have subtle differences. There are many appraisal firms that provide aircraft values for different types of aircraft ranging from turboprops to very large commercial jets.

CASE STUDY 1: APPRAISING A BUSINESS AIRCRAFT FALCON 900B

You have been requested to provide an appraisal of the Fair CMV of the subject aircraft identified as 1992 Falcon 900B S/N 150 N578L. The scope of this case study is to include the following:

- Determining whether the sales comparison, income approach, or the cost approach would be relevant for this aircraft;
- Determining the fair CMV of the subject aircraft;
- Intended users are Bank of America and Chris Smith (owner);
- Intended use is for the purpose of analysis of a potential loan for Mr. Chris Smith;
- Location of the aircraft is Wichita, Kansas.

There have been no physical inspections performed on the subject aircraft, maintenance records, and its logbooks. However, thorough research was conducted on the pertinent data on the subject aircraft from a variety of sources, such as the information provided by the owner, FAA registry, aircraft advertised for sale, use of proprietary databases, and published value information.

Dassault produced the Falcon 900B from 1984 to 1998. A total of 158 aircraft were manufactured with a current active fleet of 155 aircraft, 105 of which are based in North America and 50 in other regions of the world. At present, 22 aircraft were listed for sale that represents 14.17% of the total active fleet. Asking price of aircraft for sale varies from $4.1 to $8 million with a mean of $5.5 million and median of $5.6 million. Current number of days on the market (DOM) for aircraft for sale is between 13 and 1624, with mean and median of 302 and 423 days, respectively. Total time on aircraft for listed aircraft is between 3606 and 14,712 hours with a mean of 8793 and median of 9439 hours. The mean value of DOM sold was 427 days in 2014 and 310 in 2013. The median value of DOM sold was 337 days in 2014 and 157 days in 2013. The aircraft flies 470 hours per year on average. You have estimated that the aircraft has 5 years of life remaining with no residual value.

The percent of total active fleet for sale (14.19%) is above 12.81%, which is the percent of total active fleet for sale for all large business jets. It seems that due to more modern options available among large business jets the Falcon 900B market is a bit softer than the market for the rest of large business jets. This fact may depress CMVs of Falcon 900B aircraft. Current replacement cost new for Falcon 900B is $8,500,000. You have estimated that all forms of depreciation to be 70%. You also believe that the subject aircraft would generate $250,000 in annual operating income, complimented with $150,000 in operating expenses. The capitalization rate (discount rate) is 10%

OVERALL CONDITION OF THE SUBJECT AIRCRAFT

Based on the data provided by the owner and other proprietary databases, the subject aircraft is in a good condition. The exterior was repainted in 2015. All the three engines and APU are enrolled in Honeywell Maintenance Service Plan (MSP). All service bulletins are complied with.

Asset Identification	
Make	Dassault-Breguet
Model	Mystere Falcon 900B
Year of build	1991
Type of aircraft	Fixed-wing multi-engine Jet
Airframe total time	4658 h
Number of landing	3759
Time life limited systems	No
Cycle life limited systems	No
Airframe condition	Good
Logbooks in aircraft	Original
Date of registration	3/24/2013
Registration expiration date	03/24/2019
Airworthiness certificate date	1/25/2013

Airframe Maintenance Status	
Make inspected by	WestStar Aviation/Dassault Falcon Jet
Maintenance notes	2C/4C/3B/7.1/GoGo Wi-Fi Scheduled 9/2015 @WestStar
Known airframe maintenance issues	None
Time life limited systems	No
Cycle life limited systems	No
Service bulletin status	All service bulletins are complied with at this time
AD's complied with	Yes
Tires condition	Good
Airframe modifications	None listed
Damage history	None listed
Cabin configuration	14 Passenger
Panel layout	Good
Window condition	Good

Engines (All Three)	
Engine manufacturer	Honeywell
Model	TFE731-5BR-1C
Engine type	Turbofan
Thrust reversers	Yes (Engine #2)
Logbook inventory and comments	N/A
Engine total time (TSN)	4498 h
Time since major overhaul	298 h
Engine overhauled by	Honeywell
Recommended TBO	4200 h
Engines comments	Enrolled in Honeywell Engine Maintenance Plan (MSP)
Engine modification	None

APU	
APU manufacturer	Honeywell
Model	GTCP36-150F
APU total time	2203 h
Recommended TTO	4000 h
APU overhauled by	Honeywell
APU comments	Enrolled in Honeywell APU Maintenance Plan (MSP)

APU, *Auxiliary Power Unit;* ADs, *Airworthiness Directives;* TBO, *Time between overhaul;* TSN, *Time since new;* TTO, *Time to overhaul.*

AVIONICS

Comments: the avionics are fairly standard for Falcon 900B manufactured in 1991–1994. One exception is two inertial reference systems (some comparable aircraft have three of them).

DATA FOR SALE COMPARISON APPROACH

	Aircraft 1	Aircraft 2	Aircraft 3	Aircraft 4	Aircraft 5
Model	Falcon 900B	Falcon 900B	Falcon 900B	Falcon 900B	Falcon 900B
Year	1991	1994	1988	1994	1988
Serial number	XX	XX	XX	XX	XX
Asking price	$4,750,000	$6,290,000	$5,950,000	$6,950,000	$4,590,000
DOM	349	299	573	1065	58
TTAF	12,289	5071	12,535	7242	13,071
Landings	6444	2426	5716	4327	6752
Engine 1 TSN	11,229	5011	10,273	7128	12,359
Engine 1 time SMOH	7029	811	3606	2928	3959
Engine 2 TSN	11,023	5011	9619	7071	12,393
Engine 2 time SMOH	6823	811	3606	2871	3993
Engine 3 TSN	11,349	5011	10,682	7004	12,608
Engine 3 time SMOH	7149	811	3576	2804	4208
Engines on MSP (Y/N)	Y	Y	Y	Y	Y
APU on MSP (Y/N)	Y	Y	Y	Y	Y
Fractional (Y/N)	N	N	N	N	N
Avionics: other	Standard	Standard	Standard	Standard	Standard
Avionics: navigation (LASREF)	2	3	N/A	3	3
Damage	N	N	N	N	N
Interior refurbishment	2009	2011	2009	N/A	2007
Exterior paint	2009	2006	2007 (touch-up)	2012 (touch-up)	2013

DOM, *Days on the Market;* APU, *auxiliary power units;* TTAF, *Total time airframe;* SMOH, *Since major overhaul;* TSN, *Time since new;* LASREF, *navigation option provider.*

CASE STUDY 2: COMMERCIAL AIRCRAFT APPRAISAL AIRBUS A320-200

OVERVIEW

The Airbus A320-200 first entered into service in 1988, and since then, it grown its market share in the active 150 seat single aisle aircraft to just over 50% market share. As of 2018, there are 4289 A320ceo aircraft in service with more than 325 operators and 4768 aircraft on order. The A320neo entered service in 2015, and its sales have been robust with aircraft on order of 4071 at the end of February 2018.

You have been asked to determine the CMV of an A320-200 with the following specifications.

A320-200 Specifications	
Build year	2007
Length	37.6 m
Wingspan	34.1–35.8 m
Height	11.8 m
Max takeoff weight	78,000 kg (highest)
Max landing weight	66,000 kg (highest)
Operating empty weight	42,100 kg
Max zero fuel weight	62,500 kg (highest)
Max payload	16,600 kg
Standard fuel capacity	27,200 L (highest)
Range with max payload	6100 km
Cruise speed	840 km/h
Max speed	890 km/h
Max operating altitude	11,900 m
Takeoff field length	2090 m
Landing field length	1530 m
Engines	IAE V2500-A5
	2 × 26,500 lb (highest)
Fuel efficiency	19.1 g/pass km
Fuel flow rate	2600 kg/h
Passengers	150 (2-class)
Cabin length	27.5 m
Cabin width	3.7 m

Your proprietary valuation model has generated the following values for a generic A320-200.

Values of a Generic A320-200									
Build year	CMV	CMB	2016	2017	2018	2019	2020	2021	2022
2001	14.1	15.2	14.3	13.4	12.5	11.7	10.9	10.1	9.3
2002	15.2	16.5	15.5	14.6	13.7	12.8	11.9	11.1	10.3
2003	16.5	17.9	16.9	15.9	14.9	13.9	13.1	12.2	11.3
2004	18.0	19.4	18.3	17.2	16.2	15.2	14.2	13.3	12.4
2005	19.7	20.9	19.7	18.6	17.6	16.5	15.5	14.5	13.6
2006	21.7	22.5	21.3	20.1	19.0	17.9	16.8	15.8	14.8
2007	23.5	24.3	23.0	21.7	20.5	19.4	18.3	17.2	16.1
2008	25.5	26.1	24.8	23.4	22.2	21.0	19.8	18.6	17.5
2009	27.4	28.1	26.6	25.3	23.9	22.6	21.4	20.2	19.0
2010	29.4	30.1	28.6	27.2	25.8	24.4	23.1	21.8	20.6

(Continued)

Continued

Values of a Generic A320-200

2011	31.6	32.3	30.7	29.2	27.7	26.3	24.9	23.5	22.2
2012	33.9	34.6	32.9	31.3	29.8	28.3	36.8	25.4	24.0
2013	36.3	37.0	35.3	33.6	32.0	30.4	28.8	27.3	25.9
2014	39.2	39.5	37.3	36.0	34.3	32.6	31.0	29.4	27.9
2015	43.5	43.5	41.6	39.8	37.9	36.2	34.4	32.7	31.1

CMV, *Current Market Value;* CMB, *Current Market Base.*

Please create a desktop appraisal report with following information.

- Methodology and definitions
- Macro analysis
- A320 market analysis
- Comparable aircraft
- Competitive outlook
- Adjustments made
- Valuation

REFERENCES

Ackert, S. (2012, March). *Basics of aircraft marker analysis*. San Francisco, CA: Aircraft Monitor.

AVITAS, Inc. (2018, October 14). *Appraisal Services*. Retrieved from https://www.avitas.com/:online.avitas.com/value_definitions.jsp.

AVITAS. (2017 2nd Half, 2017–2037). *Bluebook of Jet Aircraft Values*. Chantilly, VA: AVITAS.

Forsberg, D. (2016, Februrary 18). *Values and valuers: An assessment of the aircraft valuation business*. Ballsbridge, Dublin, Ireland: Avolon.

International Society of Transportation Aircraft Trading. ISTAT Appraisers program, International Board of Governors. (2013, January 30). Retrieved from: <http://www.istat.org/appraisers>.

Kelly, D. B. (2008). Forecasting aircraft values: An appraiser's perspective. *Airfinance Annual*, 24–30.

Machinery and Technical Specialty Committee of the American Society of Appraisers. (2011). *Valuing machinery and equipment: The fundamentals of appraising machinery and technical assets*. Reston, VA: American Society of Appraisers.

Remsha, M. J. (2014). The cost approach and its relationship to the sales comparison and income approaches. *The Journal of International Machinery and Technical Specialities Committee of the American Society of Appraisers*, *30*(1), 6–31.

Svoboda, R. S. (2006, January/February). Value in use vs. value in exchange. *Valuation Strategies*, 27–48.

Vasigh, B., Taleghani, R., & Jenkins, D. (2012). *Aircraft finance*. Fort Lauderdale, Florida, USA: J. Ross Publishing.

CHAPTER

TAXATION AND CONSIDERATIONS FOR CROSS-BORDER TRANSACTIONS 13

CHAPTER OUTLINE

Aircraft Leasing and Financing. DOI: https://doi.org/10.1016/B978-0-12-815285-0.00013-4

TAXATION AND LEASING

KEY TAXATION ISSUES

We discuss cross-border lease transactions later in the chapter but start our discussion with important tax consideration in this section, as cross-border lease transactions involve several tax-related issues which are important to understand at the outset. All transactions involve an element of structural tax risk that could be at least partially managed by taking advantage of relatively tax-friendly jurisdictions for transactions. The lessee will also provide indemnities to the lessor against loss or disallowance of tax benefits on which the transaction's economics are based. Tax considerations can potentially occur at multiple points of the transaction process, including origination of the lease, transfer of the aircraft, and commencement of the lease. As taxes are present in every aspect of the transaction, they are a very important consideration for all parties involved, when constructing the lease agreement.

TAX ISSUES ON ORIGINATION OF AIRCRAFT LEASES

Key taxes to consider upon the construction and origination of an aircraft lease include potential stamp duties, import taxes, and registration taxes. These taxes are levied when the lease is agreed upon and the aircraft is registered in its new jurisdiction.

Stamp duties

Once a lease agreement has been negotiated and drawn up between a lessee and lessor, various administrative taxes can be applicable, potentially in both the jurisdiction where the aircraft is located at the time where the lease is originated and in the jurisdiction where the lease was enacted. A stamp duty is one such administrative document tax historically levied on most contracts between parties, including bills of sale, mortgages, bonds, promissory notes, and lease agreements (Ajayi, 2018). The purpose of the stamp tax is a sort of notary to ensure the legality of the document in a specific jurisdiction. Often a stamp duty does not need to be paid unless the documents are physically brought into a jurisdiction that requires stamp duties to be paid, or if the parties would like the documents to be considered enforceable in a court of law. If stamp duties are not paid prior to pursuing legal action involving repossession of the aircraft, the lessor will have to pay stamp duties on the documents before presenting them in litigation. Each jurisdiction has its own rules for stamp duties on lease agreements, but most documents are not legally enforceable unless a stamp tax has been paid and the documents are stamped.

Import taxes

Cross-border aircraft leases involve moving an aircraft from the jurisdiction of the lessor to the jurisdiction of the lessee. When an asset changes hands and nationalities, an import tax, customs duties, and/or value added tax (VAT) might be applicable to the transaction [National Business Aviation Association (NBAA), 2018]. Local tax authorities should be consulted in each cross-border transaction to make sure the parties involved understand the necessary taxes and duties that must be paid, as well as take advantage of any treaties or temporary tax reliefs that might be applicable, in order to reduce tax liabilities.

VATs are levied when an asset is imported into a country and is measured by consumption as opposed to income. VAT for an imported aircraft can either be a fixed percentage of value or can be determined by the conditions of the lease. Several countries, especially in the European Union (EU), have a VAT of 0% for imported aircraft to be operated by a qualified international commercial operator. Not all EU member states apply the 0% VAT rate in the same way, however, so it is important for lessees importing an aircraft into the EU to know how the relevant state applies the tax. VAT can either be applied directly to the qualifying airline or it can be applied to transactions between two lessors where the eventual end user is a qualified airline.

It is important with any aircraft transaction to establish the proper EU VAT position of the aircraft. A qualifying aircraft is considered an aircraft "used by an airline operating for reward on international routes." Some states interpret the term "international" differently, either meaning an airline that does not primarily operate domestically in that particular member state or the airline can qualify via proportions of air miles flown in the jurisdiction or a turnover ratio from the proportion of international flights relative to domestic flights. The aircraft must also be on a civil registry and the lessee for the aircraft must be established, meaning the lessee is typically listed as the importer of record, having the primary obligation to discharge taxes. Some jurisdictions will not release the aircraft until all tax obligations have been paid, while others allow VAT to be deferred, usually with bank guarantees to account for potential risk of default with a non-EU lessor. Because of the complication and risk surrounding VAT, most lease transactions with a party in a VAT jurisdiction include terms requiring the lessee to prove that proper taxes have been paid.

Registration taxes

Once the lease agreement has been negotiated and all stamp and import taxes have been paid, the local aviation authority in each jurisdiction will charge a registration tax to register the aircraft. It is important to determine whether the owner/lessor or the lessee is responsible for registering the aircraft and paying the appropriate fees and taxes. Some local aviation registries are owner-based, while others are operator-based. For example, the Federal Aviation Authority in the United States is an owner-based registry, meaning the owner of all US registered aircraft must be a US citizen. Most other registries in the world are operator-based, where the operator assumes the tax liability for the aircraft. Prior to choosing a jurisdiction for registration of the aircraft, the lessor and lessee should evaluate the best option for tax purposes.

TAX ISSUES DURING AIRCRAFT LEASES

Tax obligations and concerns also occur during the course of the lease, including withholding taxes, sales taxes, stamp duties, and security deposits and maintenance reserves.

Withholding tax

Withholding tax is a portion of the lease payment taken immediately upon receipt by the government to be put toward the lessor's income tax for the year. Because of this, withholding taxes should be a consideration for the lessor during the lease negotiation, as they will be liable for them during the course of the lease. Several jurisdictions require the lessor to also file income taxes in the tax jurisdiction of the lessee, which can lead to a double taxation. Foreign tax credits are also typically available for corporations to take a deduction on foreign-earned income in the case of a cross-border lease transaction.

Double taxation

Double taxation occurs when the lessor and lessee operate in different tax jurisdictions which require the lessor to file and pay income taxes in both their jurisdiction of tax residence as well as the tax residence of the lessee. This means that the lessor is paying taxes twice on the same income. This then becomes a major consideration for the lessor when entering into a lease agreement with a lessee in a different tax jurisdiction. Some countries have entered into Double Taxation Avoidance Agreements (DTAA) in order to keep lessors from having to pay taxes twice on the same earned income. Lessees are not necessarily concerned with double taxation in lease agreements, as they are not typically responsible for those tax liabilities. It is possible, though, that sharing of the double taxation liability between the lessor and lessee could be negotiated into the lease contract.

There are multiple ways double taxation treaties between countries can take shape. One option is that the lessor would pay a reduced rate of income tax in the lessee's jurisdiction instead of the full income tax in both jurisdictions. Another option is to pay the residual tax on the difference in tax rates in the lessor's jurisdiction via a foreign tax credit. For example, if the income tax is 15% in the foreign jurisdiction and 20% in the lessor's home jurisdiction, the lessor would pay 15% to the foreign jurisdiction and the remaining 5% to the home jurisdiction. The last option for double taxation treaties between countries would be where the lessor is exempt from paying income taxes in the foreign jurisdiction altogether. Since double taxation treaties are different between different combinations of jurisdictions, it is important for lessors to take these treaties into consideration, as they will be paying these taxes during the lease. It is also important prior to entering a lease to ensure that the lease qualifies as the same kind of lease in both jurisdictions to ensure the same tax treatment from both sides. For example, in some jurisdictions, what might qualify as a capital/financial lease is in fact considered an operating lease in another jurisdiction.

Generally, it is an accepted idea that the lessee bears the risk of tax changes in their jurisdiction. This means that the lessee will indemnify the lessor of any additional or local taxes it incurs due to changes in local tax law. It should be negotiated in the lease contract, what taxes specifically each party is responsible for, and in what situation and administrative procedures should be set in place, to ensure all available deductions and tax credits are being utilized in terms of withholding taxes and double income taxation.

Sales and consumption taxes

As discussed previously in this chapter, VAT is a sales and consumption tax applicable in cross-border lease transactions. The lessee is generally responsible for sales and consumption taxes associated with the transaction. The lessee should be aware of any VAT agreements or special rates available when operating in certain jurisdictions. For example, the EU allows for 0% VAT rate on transactions with qualifying airlines, making VAT a major consideration for aircraft lessees. VAT can be administered in two different ways: either paid in full at the beginning of the lease based on the cash value of the asset or in installments, with the periodic lease payments. The first option, if applicable in the lessee's jurisdiction, could place an undue burden on the lessee at the initial stage of the lease, so VAT should be considered, if applicable in the lessee's jurisdiction.

Stamp duties

Stamp duties during the course of the lease include any local taxes the lessee might incur, including local sales taxes, withholding taxes, income taxes, asset taxes, use taxes, or document taxes on documentation and lease payments. The lessee is responsible for any local taxes applicable to the cross-border lease transaction.

Security deposits and maintenance reserves

Security deposits are not taxable when received by the lessor but are treated as taxable income if retained at the end of the lease, and not returned to the lessee. Maintenance reserves are funds paid to the lessor on a periodic basis, usually along with the lease payments, in order to cover large maintenance event costs on the airframe, engines, landing gear, and auxiliary power unit (APU). Since these payments are collected along with lease rental payments, they are often subject to withholding tax for the lessor. These are generally the way security deposits and maintenance reserves are treated, but specific treatment for each transaction and jurisdiction must be determined prior to the lease, as these taxes will need to be paid during the course of the lease.

TAX ISSUES ON TRANSFER OF AIRCRAFT

Sales taxes

Sales taxes apply to all transfers of assets, though how those asset sales are taxed depends on several considerations including the jurisdiction of sale, type of sale, whether the asset is for private or business use, or if any special rates or regimes apply. In fact, in most cases, if the transaction is planned properly, no sales tax need to be paid on the asset, though use taxes often cannot be exempted.

In terms of the jurisdiction of the sale, it is important to make sure the aircraft is physically located in a "tax friendly" jurisdiction at the time of sale to reduce potentially excessive sales taxes or even to eliminate them altogether. Most often, sales taxes are levied by the jurisdiction where the aircraft is physically located, so planning for the asset to be in the best possible location for tax purposes at the time of sale is crucial. Additional investigation should be undertaken to ensure all rules are followed properly at the same time taking advantage of all available tax benefits during the transaction. Typically, the purchaser of the aircraft is responsible for the sales and use taxes placed on the aircraft at time of transfer. In the case of transferring an aircraft for a lease, the lessee is responsible for any transfer or use taxes placed on the transaction.

The type and classification of a transaction can affect the sales tax on the transfer of aircraft. For example, it is important to determine whether a capital lease with bargain purchase option is considered a lease, or is it considered a conditional sale for tax purposes. Some jurisdictions might consider a financial lease with bargain purchase option to be a lease with future sale of the asset. These different types of transactions all come with their own tax treatments that differ by jurisdiction, especially since the same transaction can be classified differently depending on the jurisdictions involved. Many jurisdictions determine whether the transaction is taxable or not by examining whether there was legal transfer of title or transfer of beneficial ownership.

In some jurisdictions, tax imposed varies based on whether the aircraft is used for business or private purposes. Business assets are often treated differently for tax purposes than privately used assets. A commercial aircraft used by an airline will be taxed differently when sold than the same aircraft when it is being used for noncommercial purposes, such as for public emergency services. Because of this difference in tax treatment, it is important to understand that taxation will differ based on the use of the aircraft at the time of sale.

It is critical when drafting the lease agreement to determine who will be responsible for paying the tax liabilities and costs of the sale upon the sale or transfer of the aircraft. This is especially important if the aircraft needs to be moved to a different jurisdiction for the purpose of the transfer, as it can get very expensive due to fuel and crew cost to move the aircraft. In some cases, sales tax charged by the seller can be recovered after the transaction. Recovering sales tax is often a long and tedious process, so usually it is contracted in the sales agreement that the seller must assist the purchaser in the process of recovering sales tax.

Stamp duties

As discussed previously, stamp duties are relevant in every aspect of the lease, sale, and asset transfer processes. Stamp duties range by jurisdiction and often are owed in the country of transfer or sale. They often do not need to be paid until the documents have been physically brought into the jurisdiction or until the relevant party needs to present them in a court of law as binding legal documents.

Income and capital gains taxes

Leases and sales of aircraft are often subject to income taxes on the part of the lessor/seller. For the seller of an aircraft, income taxes and/or capital gains taxes would be due on the capital gain from the sale of the aircraft. For the lessor, income taxes are due on receipt of the security deposit, lease payments, and maintenance reserve payments. It is important to note that for lessors, tax liability might arise in multiple jurisdictions on the transfer of the asset due to having taxable presence in multiple jurisdictions, regardless of the specific jurisdiction where the aircraft is located. This double taxation is subject to different tax treaties between countries and should be analyzed prior to the transaction taking place to ensure the involved parties take advantage of optimal tax treatment for the specific transaction.

Typically, the seller bears the income tax risk in a transaction, but it should be negotiated between the parties and included in the agreement, as to who should bear any additional income or capital gains taxes from the buyer's jurisdiction.

Registration taxes

When an aircraft is transferred, it also requires transfer of ownership, which comes with its own associated fees and taxes. First the aircraft must be deregistered from its current jurisdiction's registry. Then it must be reregistered in its new jurisdiction's registry. This process takes time and money and must be agreed upon in advance as to which parties will bear which aspects of the risk and cost of the registration process. Local jurisdictions might have their own local levies on the registration process that one must be aware of as well.

TAXES AND CONTRACTS

As has been discussed throughout the chapter thus far, it is important that all tax considerations involved in a transaction are thoroughly understood and agreed upon by the involved parties to ensure that all taxes are appropriately handled, resulting in a successful transaction. Typically, one party will bear a majority of the tax risk in the transaction while the other party bears the credit risk. For example, if the party responsible for the tax liabilities goes bankrupt and cannot pay the taxes, the indemnified party will then be responsible for the tax liability. Ensuring that one party bears the tax risk is done through tax gross up or tax indemnity clauses written into the agreement. Local tax issues tend not to be included in tax gross up or tax indemnity clauses, so it is essential that both parties are aware of any additional local taxes applicable to the transaction. If all taxes are not properly paid for the transaction, this could result in significant fines and penalties, which will be borne by the non-indemnified party. However, if the non-indemnified party must bear penalties or fines due to negligence on the part of the indemnified party in filing their tax returns, these fines may not be covered by the indemnity clause.

CURRENT TAX CONSIDERATIONS

The following section discusses the current accounting measurements and recognition for operating leases, financial leases, and sale and leasebacks on the financial statements. We also look at financial ratios credit agencies use to rate airlines and how they are affected by leasing. We then discuss the proposed new accounting standard to recognize operating leases on the firm's balance sheet and its impact on these financial ratios. Throughout this section on taxation and leasing, we will take a look at two US carriers: Delta Airlines, which is a legacy carrier, and Spirit Airlines, which is an ultra-low cost carrier (ULCC) to better understand the differing impact of the lease accounting's standards on their financial statements and credit ratings as airlines transition from the old accounting standard, where operating leases were shown as footnotes to the financial statement, to the new accounting standard to recognize them on the balance sheet. Tables 13.1 and 13.2 show the current fleets for Spirit and Delta, respectively.

Spirit Airlines leases approximately 52% of its fleet of 112 aircraft and is highly dependent on leasing in its fleet structure. Spirit Airlines' strategy of leasing a large percentage of its aircraft is typical of a ULCC. These carriers tend to lease most of their aircraft due to capital constraints and the need to maintain a young fleet in order to minimize its operating costs and improve its efficiency. In contrast, Delta, a legacy carrier, leases only about 22% of its 856 aircraft and is less

Table 13.1 Spirit Airlines Current Fleet

Spirit Airlines Fleet as of December 31, 2017				
Current Fleet				Commitments
Aircraft Type	*Owned*	*Leased*	*Average Age*	*Purchase*
A319	8	23	10.9	0
A320ceo	21	30	3.9	6
A320neo	0	5	1.1	48
A321	25	0	1.2	5
Total	54	58	5.1	59

Spirit Airlines, 10K Report.

Table 13.2 Delta Airlines Current Fleet

Delta Airlines Fleet as of December 31, 2017								
Current Fleet						Commitments		
Aircraft Type	*Owned*	*Capital Lease*	*Operating Lease*	*Total*	*Average Age*	*Purchase*	*Lease*	*Options*
B717-200	3	13	75	91	16.3			
B737-700	10			10	8.9			
B737-800	73	4		77	16.3			
B737-900ER	52		37	89	2.3	41		
B757-200	88	9	3	100	20.4			
B757-300	16			16	14.9			
B767-300	2			2	24.5			
B767-300ER	55	2		57	21.7			
B767-400ER	21			21	17			
B777-200ER	8			8	18.1			
B777-200LR	10			10	8.8			
A319-100	55		2	57	15.8			
A320-200	55	3	4	62	22.4			
A321-200	14		20	34	0.8	93		
A321-200neo						100		100
A330-200	11			11	12.8			
A330-900neo	28		3	31	9	25		
A350-900	6			6	0.2	19		
A220						75		50
MD-88	92	17		109	27.5			
MD-90	65			65	20.9			
Total	*664*	*48*	*144*	*856*	*16.7*	*353*	*0*	*150*

Delta Airlines, 10K Report.

dependent on leasing as a component of the airline's fleet financing composition. In addition, 75% of Delta's leased aircraft are on operating lease versus capital lease. The low percentage of leased aircraft is because major carriers such as Delta are often able to negotiate favorable aircraft prices with the manufacturers and find it optimal to own and finance most of their core fleet over the long term.

OPERATING LEASES

Operating leases are not currently held on the airline's balance sheet but are required to be disclosed in the footnotes of the financial statements for publicly traded companies. Operating leases are typically for a short time (less than 90% of the useful life of the aircraft) and do not often feature a purchase option. Operating leases are currently disclosed as the present value of future lease payments in aggregate for the leased portfolio of an airline's fleet. On the income statement (or profit and loss statement), payments toward operating leases are shown as an operating expense, usually titled rent expense. Tables 13.3 and 13.4 show sections of Spirit's and Delta's notes to the financial statements disclosing their operating leases for the financial year 2017.

As can be seen, the two airlines choose to disclose their operating leases a little differently. Spirit includes capital leases along with operating leases on aircraft and spare engine leases, and property facilities leases. Delta shows operating lease payments for Delta mainline as well as Delta's contract carriers.

Table 13.3 Spirit Airlines Operating Lease Disclosure

		Operating Leases		
	Capital Leases	Aircraft and Spare Engine Leases	Property Facility Leases	Total Operating and Capital Lease Obligations
	(in thousands)			
2018	$537	$204,292	$45,737	$250,566
2019	504	189,106	36,852	226,462
2020	188	180,842	25,870	206,900
2021	28	170,643	12,740	183,411
2022	–	150,212	11,931	162,143
2023 and thereafter	–	419,908	61,211	481,119
Total minimum lease payments	$1,257	$1,315,003	$194,341	$1,510,601
Less amount representing interest	94			
Present value of minimum lease payments	$1,163			
Less current portion	476			
Long-term portion	$687			

From United States Security and Exchange Commission (2017b).

Table 13.4 Delta Airlines Operating Lease Disclosure

(in millions)	Delta Lease Payments (1)	Contract Carrier Aircraft-Lease Payments (2)	Total
2018	$1,469	$266	$1,735
2019	1,322	267	1,589
2020	1,189	241	1,430
2021	983	173	1,156
2022	883	153	1,036
Thereafter	8,819	471	9,290
Total minimum lease payments	$14,665	$1,571	$16,236

(1) Includes payments accounted for as construction obligations. (2) Represents the minimum lease obligations under our contract agreements with Compass Airlines; LLC; ExpressJet Airlines, Inc.; GoJet Airlines; LLC; Republic Airline, Inc.; and SkyWest Airlines, Inc.
From United States Security and Exchange Commission (2017a).

Table 13.5 Delta Airlines Capital Lease Disclosure

Capital Leases (in millions)	Total
2018	$116
2019	92
2020	65
2021	41
2022	24
Thereafter	126
Total minimum lease payments	$464
Less: amount of lease payments representing interest	(70)
Present value of future minimum capital lease payments	394
Less: current obligations under capital leases	(97)
Long-term capital lease obligations	$297

From United States Security and Exchange Commission (2017a).

Financial leases

Financial leases are held on the airline's balance sheet as an asset and associated liability. The value of the financial lease is amortized over the term of the lease, thus reducing the liability and asset by the amount of depreciation and interest (rental payment). On the income statement (or profit and loss statement), payments toward financial leases are split into asset depreciation expense and interest expense. Table 13.5 shows how Delta explains and discloses their capital leases in their financial statements.

Sale and leasebacks

Sale and leaseback transactions allow the airline to purchase an aircraft outright for a discounted price from the manufacturer, sell it to a lessor at a low price (or a high price), then lease it back

Table 13.6 Selected Financial Ratios for Delta and Spirit Airlines

	Delta	Spirit
Cash flow to debt	89%	53%
Debt to EBITDA	0.76	1.85
EBITDA to interest	21.93	17.26
Debt to capital	47%	78%

From Raghavan, S., & Zarb, B. (2018). Implications of the new accounting changes for aircraft leasing. Journal of International Finance and Economics, 18*(2), 49–58..*

from the lessor at a lower lease rate (high lease rate). This allows the airline to get cash inflow from the sale of the aircraft, while keeping the aircraft off the balance sheet. On the financial statements, a sale and leaseback appears as an operating lease with rental expenses shown on the income statement.

Financial ratios

Calculated in Table 13.6 are select financial ratios typically used in airline credit analysis by DBRS (2018) based on current accounting standards.

These ratios are used to assess the creditworthiness of airlines. Different rating agencies use different ranges of values for these ratios to determine a rating, which determines whether the airline is of investor-grade quality or below. These ratios are also used to assess an airline's performance in terms of maintaining debt and other covenants in financing arrangements. These ratios will change as the new accounting standards come into effect in January 2019, which will have negative impact for airlines as we detail in the next section of the chapter.

TAX LAW CHANGES

Recently, the US Financial Accounting Standards Board (FASB) and the International Financial Reporting Standards Board (IFRS) have been attempting to converge many of their financial accounting standards. Accordingly, FASB has passed ASC 842, and IFRS has passed IFRS 16, both effective January 2019. These rules attempt to increase transparency of an airline's true debt obligations by transferring all leases, operating or financial, with a term of 12 months or greater on to the company's balance sheet. Previous standards regarding leasing were passed in the 1980s and do not reflect the fact that operating leases are similar to debt and therefore should be reflected in the current debt obligations of companies.

Airlines would be particularly impacted by these new accounting changes as operating leases are widely used within the airline industry. The previous lease laws allowed airlines to keep operating leases off their balance sheets, thus creating a distorted view of the airline's debt obligations. According to a report by Price Waterhouse (PwC) (2016), the new change will mean that the median increase in on-balance sheet debt for airlines around the world would be about 47% and about 50% of the airlines will see their debts increase by 25%. Price Waterhouse (PwC) (2016) also concluded that airlines will be the second most affected industry (behind retail) when the accounting changes come into effect in January 2019. It is therefore imperative that airlines clearly communicate the financial effects of the accounting changes to stakeholders prior to the changes taking effect to prevent any reactionary market event.

ACCOUNTING CHANGES

The new rules, ASC 842 and IFRS 16, bring changes to the financial statements in terms of recognition and recording of the lease asset and its associated liability. It is important to note that the criteria to classify leases as operating versus finance leases have not changed. The change primarily is that most operating leases must now be held on the balance sheet and not shown as a footnote. This affects the assets and liabilities portions of the balance sheet, as well as the depreciation and interest expense portions on the income statement.

Fig. 13.1 shows the balance sheet and income statement impact of the new tax change. In the top portion of the figure, we show that with the new accounting standard, operating leases must be shown on the asset and liability side of the balance sheet. Previous rental expense on the operating leases must now be split into interest expenses and depreciation expenses on the profit and loss statements (or income statement). The resultant impact of the new law on the income statement would be to increase earnings before interest, depreciation and amortization (EBITDA), interest expense, and earnings before interest and taxes (EBIT). On the balance sheet, debt due to leasing and liabilities would increase and equity would fall. On the statement of cash flow, cash flow from operating activities would increase while cash flow from financing activity would decrease.

EFFECT ON LESSORS

Most experts agree that the changes in accounting rules will have minimal effect on lessors, as the lease classification test, to classify lease as an operating or financial lease, will remain the same. Further, lessors already show all their assets on leases (both operating and financial) on their balance sheet Price Waterhouse (PwC) (2016), Lovell (2016) and Deloitte (2016). Leasing companies, however, would be affected more by the impact of these new changes on their customers, the airlines. Lessors need to keep in mind how leasing will affect their lessee's balance sheets as they attempt to renegotiate current leases and structure new leases so as to appeal to airlines. Instead of competing amongst themselves for lessees, lessors will now have to also compete with manufacturers for airlines' business as the option to purchase aircraft outright may become more appealing for some airlines compared to leasing. Lessors need to be especially concerned about losing lessees who were paying a premium in rental payments to keep assets off their balance sheet, as these airlines might look to purchase aircraft now that all leases must be shown on the balance sheet regardless. The new tax law could potentially lead to further competition amongst lessors which could reduce returns and could lead to increased consolidation within the aircraft-leasing industry, as some lessors, weather the new rules more successfully than others.

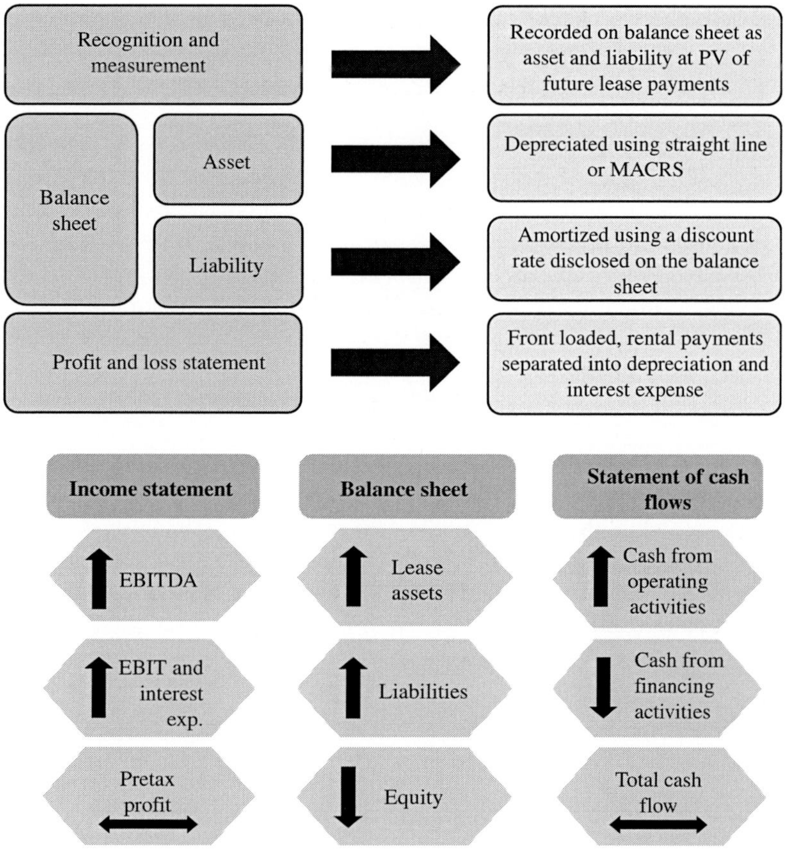

FIGURE 13.1

Balance sheet and income statement impact of new tax changes.

EFFECT ON AIRLINES (LESSEES)

Fleet planning and lease versus buy decisions

Generally, the types of aircraft airlines need will not change, and thus general fleet planning decisions will not be affected. When the new law takes effect in January 2019, leasing and purchasing strategies may change for some airlines, especially for legacy carriers, such as Delta Airlines, which might look more to purchasing aircraft instead of leasing. For ULCC carriers like Spirit and Frontier Airlines, however, leasing may continue to provide the needed operational flexibility and access to current technology aircraft that has made these airlines successful. For these carriers, the new accounting standard may not have an operational impact but is expected to impact their financial ratios as operating leases are transferred on to their balance sheet.

Sale and leasebacks

The purpose for many airlines to engage in a sale and leaseback transaction is to take advantage of lower lease rates while getting the asset off of their balance sheet. Since all leases must be held on the balance sheet, sale and leasebacks may fall as a result of the new accounting change (Lovell, 2016).

Lease contracts and restructuring

It is anticipated that airlines will request some existing lease contracts to be renegotiated to reflect the changes in accounting rules. Leases will need to feature new kinds of terms not currently included in lease contracts, as well as changes to existing terms. The overall structure of the lease contract should seek to minimize the effect on the airline's financial statements. The length of lease contracts is also expected to be reduced, as airlines aim to minimize the impact of the new changes on their liabilities and leverage ratios (Deloitte, 2016). All else being equal, lease rates may also have to change, most likely reduce, in order for leasing to remain competitive to the alternative of purchasing an aircraft and utilizing debt financing.

Financing decisions

There is little consensus on whether the accounting change will affect airline financing decisions. According to a survey conducted by Deloitte (2016), some respondents believe the cost of funding for airlines will increase, while the cost of funding for lessors will remain the same. If airlines' cost of funding increases, this could potentially push airlines to seek new and innovative sources of funding, including public and private equity, as well as financial instruments such as enhanced equipment trust certificates (EETCs).

Financial ratios

It is expected that the airline's reported equity values will drop, affecting leverage ratios such as debt to equity and debt to asset ratios. This reduction in the reported equity value will result from the fact that the lease asset will depreciate faster than the decrease in lease payments over time, though the value of asset and liability will remain the same at the beginning and end of the term (Lovell, 2016). The decline in equity might in turn affect the airline's share price.

The changes in accounting rules will not affect airline credit ratings, so long as the rating agencies are currently considering off-balance sheet financing when making credit rating decisions. However, as financial ratios change, and values for these ratios no longer fall within the credit agency's ranges, credit ratings may change regardless. An additional consideration for credit agencies beyond changes in financial ratios is changes in pricing risk in the capital markets, as additional risk could bring ratings down.

Raghavan and Zarb (2018) look at the implications of the new accounting changes on financial ratios for airlines in the United States if the present value of the operating leases from the footnote is transferred on to their balance sheet. Table 13.7 shows their calculated changes in financial ratios for Delta and Spirit Airlines should they add their off-balance sheet operating leases to their balance sheet.

For both airlines, coverage ratios (such as cash flow to debt and EBITDA to interest) are expected to drop significantly after the change, while leverage ratios (debt to EBITDA ratio and debt to capital) are expected to increase significantly. For example, for Spirit Airlines, cash flow to debt ratio and EBITDA to interest is expected to fall by 44% and 49%, respectively, and debt to EBITDA and debt to capital is expected to increase by 84%. While for Delta Airlines, cash flow to debt ratio and EBITDA to interest is expected to fall by 64% and 63%, respectively, and

Table 13.7 Financial Ratios for Delta and Spirit after Accounting Change

	Delta	(%) Change	Spirit	(%) Change
Cash flow to debt	33%	−64	29%	−44
Debt to EBITDA	2.08	175	3.4	84
EBITDA to interest	8.13	−63	8.81	−49
Debt to capital	137%	190	144%	84

From Raghavan, S., & Zarb, B. (2018). Implications of the new accounting changes for aircraft leasing. Journal of International Finance and Economics, 18*(2), 49–58.*

debt to EBITDA and debt to capital is expected to increase by 175% and 190%, respectively. The analysis by Raghavan and Zarb (2018), therefore, shows that the new accounting standard is expected to significantly and negatively impact financial ratios used by credit rating agencies.

Earnings

Earnings overall are expected to increase due to the accounting changes, as depreciation and interest expense will increase and the account titled rent expense on the income statement will be eliminated. Generally, EBIT and EBITDA are forecasted to increase upward of 33%, according to Lovell (2016). Some airlines will be affected more than others as the increase in earnings will be dependent on the size of the airline's leased portfolio.

With the change from expensing operating leases on the income statement to carrying these leases on the balance sheet, the rental payment for operating leases will be split into depreciation and interest expense on the income statement. Under current accounting rules, lease expense is typically a uniform amount over the course of the lease. The new accounting rules, however, will front-load the lease payments, which means that earnings can actually reduce initially, then increase as the lease continues and the interest expense portion of the rental payment decreases. Simply put, at the beginning of the lease, interest expense will be relatively large and decrease over time as the rental payments are amortized; thus, ceteris paribus, earnings will increase as the lessee gets further into the lease.

Discount rates

The major change considering discount rates with ASC 842 and IFRS 16 is that now relevant discount rates used to calculate the present value of future loan payments must be disclosed on the balance sheet. The discount rate is used to determine interest expense as well as the value of the lease for the balance sheet. The airline may use either their cost of borrowing or the discount rate implicit in the lease. It is assumed airlines will use their cost of borrowing, as lessors do not divulge the discount rate used in the lease to prevent airlines from knowing how much the lessor paid to purchase the aircraft initially. Theoretically, airlines' cost of borrowing should not change, as nothing has fundamentally changed with the airlines, and the change is merely an accounting change. However, credit ratings of the airlines might be affected due to changes in financial ratios and other soft factors, which might in turn change the cost of borrowing for airlines, and thus the discount rate.

Debt covenants

Leasing is considered equivalent to debt, and as airlines add operating leases on to their balance sheets, their lenders might feel the need to change their debt covenants to reflect their updated views on the airlines' creditworthiness.

Generally, debt covenants should remain mostly unaffected by the change in accounting rules, but that depends on the individual airlines. Some airlines are currently operating well below their required debt levels and have some cushion for changes, while others are operating closer to the maximum allowed. It is possible, therefore, that for some airlines, debt covenants can be breached with the changes in accounting standards, but usually credit agreements have clauses built-in to the covenants that protects companies from changes in accounting rules midterm. This means that if a company were to breach a debt covenant via a change in accounting rules, they cannot be penalized by the lender. In addition, most lenders already consider off-balance sheet leases, when they are deemed financially significant, when determining debt covenants.

Currency volatility

The new lease laws will further expose airlines to currency volatility as they attempt to properly hedge their foreign exchange risk associated with US dollar (USD)–denominated lease rental payments. All aircraft prices are listed in USDs; thus lessors issue leases in USDs to mitigate their foreign exchange risk. It is the lessee's responsibility to make lease payments in USD and mitigate their own risk via foreign exchange contracts. It is anticipated that currency volatility will most likely affect small and regional airlines, where leasing is not a fleet structure choice, but a necessity to acquire aircraft for operations. For international airlines, each reporting period's lease liabilities are translated into local domestic currency from USDs on their financial statements, exposing these airlines to additional currency volatility due to translating from their accounts from USD to local currency.

Complications arise when IFRS 16 and IFRS 9 combine, as airlines had previously hedged their currency exchange risk for leases past the January 1, 2018 effective date for IFRS 9. This has rendered hedging strategies for these leases ineffective. As lease expense will be reclassified as depreciation and interest expense, airlines must develop new strategies to hedge against currency exchange risk. This could potentially lead to lessees pushing lessors to issue leases in other currencies, like Euros, to help ease the burden of currency exchange risk. However, some airlines believe even if lessors price leases in other currencies, it might still be cheaper for the airline to do the currency swap themselves, as lessors will probably charge a premium for leases in other currencies. Lessor's resistance to issuing leases in multiple currencies could push airlines to choose to purchase aircraft instead of entering into operating leases, as purchases are unaffected by the rule changes and airlines could directly take depreciation and interest expense benefits. This will put more pressure on export credit agencies (ECAs) to support more cross-border transactions with the increase in cross-border purchases. The market could also see an increase in EETC and Japanese Operating Lease (JOL) with Call Option (JOLCO) transactions as airlines look for creative ways to structure their transactions (Lovell, 2018).

IT CONSIDERATIONS

In order to move operating leases on to the balance sheet, airlines may require to upgrade to specialized software and other infrastructure in the airline's information technology department, which may pose a challenge, especially for airlines with a large leased aircraft fleet (O'Callaghan, 2017). Airlines are exploring options for new software which are designed to manage the new accounting change. These changes to software and infrastructure are expected to increase the cost for airlines, especially for airlines, with a large lease aircraft portfolio.

CROSS-BORDER LEASE TRANSACTIONS

A cross-border lease involves parties from different jurisdictions engaging in a lease transaction. A lessor purchases an aircraft from a manufacturer or other seller and proceeds to lease the aircraft to a lessee in a different country for a specific term in exchange for predetermined rental payments. A third-party financier can also get involved, further complicating the transaction by potentially introducing a third jurisdiction's laws. Each jurisdiction involved in the transaction has its own set of regulations and laws concerning securement of an international party's ownership interest in the aircraft as well as different tax treatment for the transaction. This section focuses on the tax treatment and other considerations for cross-border lease transactions in various countries and provides a brief overview of major leasing markets.

UNITED STATES—LEASING MARKET OVERVIEW

The aircraft-leasing industry was born in the United States when McDonnell Douglas introduced a vendor aircraft finance business in 1968 to support its aircraft sales. One of the first US-based aircraft-leasing companies, International Lease Finance Corporation (ILFC), was founded in 1973—2 years before the first Irish leasing company, Guinness Peat Aviation (GPA), that was established in 1975. GPA was eventually acquired by GECAS, while ILFC was taken over by AerCap. As of 2018, 12 out of 50 largest aircraft lessors are headquartered in the United States. Moreover, of the 10 largest global aircraft-leasing companies, four are the US lessors, three are the Irish lessors, and China, Singapore, and United Arab Emirates each has one lessor in the top 10. Most of the international aviation contracts for the purchase or lease of aircraft use New York or the UK governing laws, as these jurisdictions have sophisticated and well-developed bodies of commercial and business laws that are applicable to aircraft transactions.

Historically, the United States has been a major center for aircraft leasing, though it has recently been overtaken by Ireland. Similar to other markets, the economics for lease transactions in the United States is driven by the tax benefits, cost of capital, lease rentals, and residual values of aircraft. While the cost of capital and lease rentals are market and credit driven, and tax benefits depend on the tax laws that periodically are changing. The leasing structures allow the US lessees to indirectly use the tax benefits associated with lessors' aircraft ownership and by locking the rental rates for the duration of the lease. A lessor prices a lease based on its assumptions of depreciation and interest deduction tax benefits and thus transfer some of these benefits to a lessee through lower rental payments. Typically, the lessee is assured of receiving the tax benefits in full, as it is not required to indemnify the lessor for inability to obtain the tax benefits priced in the transaction due to tax rate changes. However, in case of favorable tax rate changes, the lessor may retain tax benefits that were not priced into the lease transaction. Thus, the Federal Corporate Tax rates in the United States were reduced from 35% maximum rate to 21% beginning January 1, 2018. Consequently, lease transactions that were structured and priced before this tax reduction will improve the after-tax rates of return for the US-based lessors.

The Tax Cuts and Jobs Act introduced at the end of 2017 has changed the tax landscape for aircraft-leasing industry in the United States. In addition to the reduction of the Federal Corporate Tax rate from 35% to 21%, the tax reform enacted 100% bonus depreciation for new and used equipment placed in service before January 1, 2023. For property placed in service on or after that date, the deduction declines 20% each year until reaching zero (in 2027). This expensing is not available for property leased to government entities, nonprofit entities, or foreign individual or entities. There are no restrictions on a lessor in a sale—leaseback claiming expensing of used equipment where the lessee of the equipment remains the same. For example, an airline could have purchased an aircraft and, after depreciating and using the aircraft, the airline would enter a sale—leaseback agreement with a lessor. The lessor could claim expensing on the purchase price of the aircraft if the aircraft is used on US routes, even though the user of the aircraft (lessee) does not change.

IRELAND—LEASING MARKET OVERVIEW

Similar to the United States, Ireland was a home for aircraft-leasing pioneers in the early 1970s. The first Irish lessor, GPA became the leading European aircraft-leasing company in the 1980s. Since then, Ireland has emerged as a world hub for the aircraft-leasing industry. Most of the global commercial aircraft-leasing companies are based or have a presence in Ireland. About 55% of the world's leased commercial aircraft are managed from Ireland. In addition to being a home country for aviation industry visionaries, such as Mr. Tony Ryan, Ireland offers aircraft lessors many economic advantages that are a result of conscious efforts by the Irish government. The Irish government supports the aviation industry and maintains a friendly climate for the industry by quickly addressing any concerns. The following is the list of economic considerations that make Ireland an attractive domicile for global aircraft lessors:

- Ireland has a comprehensive network of double taxation treaties with about 70 countries that reduce or eliminate withholding tax on inbound lease rental (Osborne-Kinch, Coates, & Nolan, 2017).
- Low corporate tax rate of 12.5% on trading profits for companies incorporated in Ireland.
- A depreciation write-off period of 8 years (Osborne-Kinch et al., 2017).
- Flexibility in the adoption of recognized accounting standards (IFRS, US GAAP, or Irish GAAP) (Osborne-Kinch et al., 2017).
- No minimum capital requirements for Irish companies (Sivaramakrishnan, 2017).
- No stamp duty payable at the time of sale of aircraft (Sivaramakrishnan, 2017).
- No VAT on cross-border lease payments.
- Ease of forming bankruptcy remote special purpose vehicles (SPVs) (Sivaramakrishnan, 2017).

JAPAN—LEASING MARKET OVERVIEW

Japan has a well-established aircraft-leasing market dating back to the early 1960s mostly due to its history of successful and mutually beneficial financing strategies. Japan has helped finance most aircraft transactions in Asia as well as many around the world. Japanese aviation is dominated by two groups, the JAL Group and the ANA Group, with their subsidiary low-cost airlines coming to prevalence in the 2010s, leading to higher demand for leased aircraft in the country. Japan is currently still a major player in the aircraft-leasing industry with the JOLCO.

Since the 1970s, Japanese leasing companies have developed several forms of leases that made Japan a significant player in the cross-border leasing market (Stokes and Runagall, 2011). The leasing industry first developed the Samurai lease in the early 1970s, which was a lease from a Japanese lessor to a foreign company of equipment built outside of Japan. Samurai leases were typically long-term and held on Japanese companies' balance sheets as an import to help reduce Japan's trade surplus. The Ministry of Finance changed the laws associated with Samurai leases in the early 1980s and made them an obsolete form of financing.

Next came the Shogun lease, which was a long-term lease from a Japanese lessor to an international lessee. Shogun leases offered inexpensive long-term aircraft financing for foreign lessees. Another form of lease was the Kagonuke lease, which was merely a loan in the form of a lease that allowed corporations to raise billions of dollars in financing from nonfinancial institutions in Japan. This was done through third-party SPV's, and Japanese borrowers were hedged against risk via the interest rate differential. However, this method of leasing became unpopular in the late 1980s as interest rates for the yen began to soar. The 1980s gave way to the Japanese Leveraged Lease (JLL), followed by the JOL in the 1990s due to changes in government regulations.

JAPANESE LEVERAGED LEASE

The JLL was developed in the mid-1980s and was a hugely popular form of leasing for all depreciable equipment through the late 1990s until the Japanese government passed a regulation that reduced the tax benefits for lessors using JLLs and thus ended the use of the JLL altogether. Widebody aircraft were leased for 12 years and depreciated for 10 on a declining-balance basis, while narrowbody aircraft were leased for 10 and depreciated for 8 years on a declining-balance basis. The depreciation expense during the first half of the lease exceeded taxable income for the investors, allowing the investors in the lease to defer tax liability for several years. The JLL was not held on the balance sheet, thus helping the investors (usually small or midsized private companies) to improve their profitability ratios. Additional features that drew investors to the JLL were that the identity of the investors involved in the lease arrangement were unknown to all parties involved in the lease, including each other, and that investors took no residual value risk.

For a JLL, about 20%–30% of the purchase price of the aircraft is funded by private equity investors in Japan using yen as the denominated currency in what is known as a Tokumei Kumiai arrangement. A Tokumei Kumiai arrangement is essentially a silent partnership in which passive investors provide funds to the partnership, which is then run by an operator who acts as the owner and lessor in the lease arrangement. The remainder of the funding for the aircraft is provided by a loan in the airline's chosen currency, typically one in which the airline makes a majority of its cash flows to reduce foreign exchange risk. The Tokumei Kumiai purchases the aircraft and leases it to a foreign airline. In order for the lessee to make the yen portion of the lease payments, they either make a yen deposit that will mature at the time of payment, or enter into a FOREX contract. Floating interest rates for the bank loan are typically swapped by the airline for fixed rate interest, which is then paid to the lending bank. The airline then pays two lease payments to the lessor: one for the return on equity to the investors in yen and another in their chosen currency to the lessor matching the lessor's debt obligation on the loan.

In October 1998, the Japanese government enacted tax reforms that changed the rules that dictated the structure of the JLL. The new laws drastically reduced the tax benefits associated with the JLL, making it no more attractive than a plain vanilla loan, resulting in the end of the JLL popularity.

JAPANESE OPERATING LEASE

The JOL originated after the Japanese tax reform of 1998, with the first JOL transaction occurring in 1999. However, continued tax reform through the early 2000s left investors wary of using anything but a straight vanilla lease or finance lease transactions through 2003 due to the complicated requirements for a lease to be appropriately qualified as a JOL. The most important qualification for a JOL was known as the "90% test," which stated that the present value of the lease payments could not exceed 90% of the lessor's aircraft acquisition cost.

JOLs are based on their predecessor, the JLL, with some changes to comply with the stricter tax laws. Investors were no longer anonymous in the transaction and were now required to take on residual value risk as active investors. The requirement for active investment pushed several investors out of the JOL market as they did not have the knowledge to be in the leasing industry. The investors into the SPV that acted as the lessor could now be in any currency the lessee airline preferred to reduce currency exchange risk. In addition, it must be proven that the transaction was a true lease, as the tax benefits for the JOL did not apply for a sale disguised as a lease or a finance lease. A JOL with a purchase option at the end of the lease was referred to as a JOLCO. The purchase option in a JOLCO must be exercisable at or toward the end of the lease term and must be for a fixed price at the fair market value of the aircraft to ensure investors hold residual value risk of the aircraft. Investors also held residual value risk through changes in the laws around depreciation deductions. Now for any international lessees, depreciation could only be taken on a straight-line basis, reducing possible tax loss carryforwards, while domestic lessees could continue taking depreciation deductions on a declining-balance basis. Similar to the JLL, lease rentals are consistent over the lease term, so the lessee and bank/lender enter into an interest rate swap so that the bank pays the lessee a fixed coupon in exchange for a floating rate of interest from the lessee.

In the early 2000s, European airlines, especially Lufthansa, were the major users of the JOL, and JAL was the most significant domestic user of the JOL. In 2009 with the global economic downturn, use of JOLs depressed, as financing became more expensive, reducing the margins afforded by the JOL structure. However, more airlines began using the structure from 2009 to 2011, including KLM, SAS, British Airways, Malaysia Airlines, Air China, China Eastern Airlines, EasyJet, Ryanair, and TAM. Although not a common form of cross-border leasing currently due to the strict tax restrictions, JOLCO transactions are still used by certain European and domestic Japanese airlines.

GERMANY—LEASING MARKET OVERVIEW

The German aircraft–leasing market gained global prevalence in the 1980s with the development of the German-Leveraged Lease (GLL), which was made obsolete in 1999 after German tax overhauls eliminated depreciation tax benefits for investors. The GLL was replaced with the German Operating Lease (GOL), which is still a relevant form of structuring aircraft leases in Germany (Schott, 2011). Leases are managed by limited partnerships, and partnership shares are sold to investors, as we describe below.

Germany has no laws explicitly governing leases, so lease transactions are classified either as a rental agreement or an installment purchase agreement depending on the lease term amongst other determinants. The equity portion of German-structured lease transactions, unlike their Japanese counterparts, are funded by individual investors versus corporate investors. The reason is that at the time the lease structures were developed, the individual tax rate was significantly higher than the corporate tax rate in Germany. Concerning cross-border transactions, as Germany is located in the EU, if the equipment is being leased to an airline which services predominantly international routes, then the transaction qualifies for the EU 0% VAT. In addition, withholding taxes on rental or interest payments are not applicable for nonresidents in Germany. Germany is also involved in several tax treaties that reduce or eliminate withholding taxes in other nations as well.

German leases tend to be predominantly domestic with relatively few cross-border transactions occurring due to a predisposition for lease transactions to be conducted for German or European-manufactured equipment, that is, Airbus aircraft, though there is no law stating this must be the case.

FINANCE LEASE AND SPV LICENSE REQUIREMENT

An important aspect to note of German-structured leases is the finance lease and SPV-management licenses required to conduct lease transactions in Germany. In the German Annual Tax Law of 2009, under the German Banking Act, Germany enacted a license requirement for any corporation offering finance lease services and any corporation managing special purpose vehicles to conduct and manage lease transactions and property. A party to a transaction qualifies as "rendering finance leasing services" if they are a lessor organizing a finance lease and manage an SPV for the purpose of a lease transaction. An exception can be made for an SPV if all of the below conditions are met:

- It was set up to manage a single object.
- It provides no other services that require a license.
- It does not make its own business decisions.
- It is managed by a company located in a European Economic Area state, as long as they hold a finance lease license in their own country.

Under this exception, the SPV might not need a license to conduct finance leases in Germany, but the parent company still needs a license to manage the SPV. This licensing requirement provides additional limitations for the companies that are allowed to conduct lease agreements in Germany and must be kept in mind when deciding whether or not to get involved in a German-structured lease.

GERMAN-LEVERAGED LEASE

The GLL became popular in the early 1980s until its demise in 1999 due to significant German tax overhauls that negated the tax benefits for investors. The GLL was structured not unlike the JLL, which was popular at relatively the same time as the GLL. The GLL was used to finance narrowbody, widebody, and cargo aircraft, with narrowbodies falling out of favor with investors toward the end of the GLL.

In the GLL, German investors provide 20%–50% of the initial purchase price of the aircraft, with the rest funded by bank loans. The investors were grouped in a limited partnership, called a Kommanditgesellschaft (KG), managed by one or more active partners, typically fund/asset managers who conducted the business of the KG. The KG investors were typically high-income individual German investors, so the KG was made of thousands of individual investors to fund the aircraft purchase. The aircraft was then leased to an airline, which made regular rental payments to the lessor.

The benefit of the GLL to the investors was that they could take depreciation deductions for tax purposes proportionate to their initial investment in the KG, allowing investors to defer their tax liability. Depreciation could be taken on a straight-line or declining-balance basis, and if depreciation started on a declining-balance basis, it could later be switched to straight-line to continue to benefit the investors. In addition, while investors were taking advantage of the benefits of ownership of the aircraft, they did not have to carry the aircraft on their balance sheets. Airlines using the GLL benefitted from relatively inexpensive aircraft financing.

An important feature of Germany's depreciation tax law was that depreciation deductions could be taken not by the party with legal ownership of the aircraft, but by the party with economic ownership of the aircraft. It was essential to the success of the GLL that the KG maintained economic ownership of the aircraft during the lease term. This was accomplished by ensuring that the lease term was between 40% and 90% of the useful tax life of the asset, which is usually 12–14 years. However, the investors of the KG could not take depreciation deductions at all unless the KG could prove that it was profitable pre-tax to show that it is not set up as a "tax deferral scheme," or a structure that is set up to generate tax losses. The German Income Tax Act states that losses arising from tax deferral schemes can only be used in the future to offset income from the same source and not from any other source.

Germany's strict tax rules at the onset of the GLL required investors, KG's, and lessees to be cautious of the various tax laws associated with German-structured leases to gain any benefits. However, German tax overhaul in 1999 led to the demise of the GLL, as it virtually eliminated benefits from the GLL and resulted in the development of the similarly structured GOL.

GERMAN OPERATING LEASE

The GOL was developed around 2000 after the GLL lost its tax benefits. The GOL is similar to the GLL, though it is more structured in the way that it is set up and sold.

Like in the GLL, the equity portion of the GOL is funded by individual investors with the remaining aircraft purchase price funded by bank loans. The KG is run by one or more active partners who are typically asset managers experienced in the field. KG managers offering shares in a GOL arrangement must prepare a prospectus, similar to that written for exchange-traded securities, which must be submitted to and approved by the German Financial Services Supervisory Agency.

Once approved, shares to the KG can be purchased by individual investors through the arranger's sale program, independent distributors, or through banks and financial institutions. Shares for GOL's are not publicly traded securities. The KG then purchases an aircraft, new or used, and leases it to an airline for a fixed lease payment. GOL's can have purchase options at the end of the lease term, but it is not a necessary feature of the lease structure.

The GOL was popular until late 2001 when the 9/11 attacks have shaken the industry. The GOL raised in popularity again in 2007 when Singapore Airlines decided to fund its first two A380s using the GOL structure. Fast forward to 2018, both aircraft were returned to their German financiers in early 2018 after their leases expired. Dr. Peters Group, a German owner of the aircraft, was unable to negotiate a lease with another lessee and decided to part out the aircraft and sell their components. Dr. Peters Group said that the deal is expected to generate a positive return for investors, though one has to expect that the final return realized by the investors will fall short of their initial expectations (Hepher, 2018). Partially, this decision was based on the cost of A380 reconfiguration, which is $40 million or more per plane and the fact that early aircraft which are the first of the type to be parted out generally command the highest part out value realization.

After a brief decline during the global economic crisis of 2008, the GOL market came back, focusing primarily on widebody and cargo aircraft. Even though the narrowbody GOL market is improving, widebodies are still the most popular GOL investment. Current developments in the GOL structure include a move toward investing in a portfolio of aircraft as opposed to a single aircraft to help diversify investors over multiple aircraft types as well as global markets.

UNITED KINGDOM—LEASING MARKET OVERVIEW

The idea of leasing aircraft came to the United Kingdom in the early 1960s from the United States, where leasing started a few years earlier in the 1950s. American manufacturers Boeing and McDonnell Douglas were using leasing as a form of product financing and support. A UK manufacturer, British Aircraft Corporation (BAC) started doing it to help finance aircraft for regional and charter airlines in the United Kingdom. Initially, leasing was not popular amongst the UK financial institutions because they were highly concerned about liability risk involved in leasing aircraft.

However, the 1970s showed massive growth in the aircraft-leasing industry in the United Kingdom due to capital allowance laws that allowed aircraft owners to depreciate 100% of the aircraft purchase price in the first year, as long as they had the taxable income to offset it. Most UK airlines at the time did not have enough taxable income to take advantage of the 100% capital allowance and thus used leasing to receive deferral benefits indirectly. Lessors would purchase the aircraft and take the 100% capital allowance deduction; then the lessors would pass on the savings to the lessees in the form of reduced rental payments. This would effectively reduce the interest rate associated with financing below that of traditional bank financing, making leasing a more attractive option. In 1984, the first year 100% capital allowance law was phased out in exchange for a yearly write-down of the book value of the aircraft. However, by this time, the leasing market in the United Kingdom had been well-established, so the changes in the depreciation law did not affect the lease market. Since then, lease arrangements have become incredibly more sophisticated to both circumvent and take advantage of the tax laws in all jurisdictions involved.

Due to the early 1990s UK economic recession, the aviation industry overall and the aircraft-leasing industry, in particular, experienced a significant decline. During this time, almost no activity occurred in lease financing. However, by 1995, the UK economy was improving, and the leasing industry slowly got back on its feet. In 1997, two Finance Acts were passed that affected the industry. The first was an act that changed the nature of long-life assets as well as write-down percentages, and the second act changed rules surrounding sale–leaseback arrangements.

The Finance Act of 2006 was the start of the "long funding lease," which made tax deferral leases irrelevant and pushed UK companies, both lessors and lessees, to look at cross-border leasing, such as JOLCO, for possible tax deferral benefits. In 2011, there was a reduction in the UK corporate tax rate and a reduction in UK capital allowances in 2012, which aided in continuing the expansion of the UK cross-border lease industry.

CROSS-BORDER LEASING

Historically, inbound cross-border lease transactions are much more common in the United Kingdom than outbound cross-border leases due to relatively unfavorable domestic tax environment. UK airlines have historically taken advantage of JLLs, JOLs, and US leases to benefit most from domestic tax allowances. However, UK lessors could not use JLL or JOL lease structures when doing outbound lease transactions as they did not mix well with UK tax lease laws. While the amount of cross-border transactions has increased significantly in the United Kingdom in the last two decades, there are still considerable issues remaining, including withholding tax, transfer pricing issues, permanent establishment (PE) issues, and others. As a result, lease transactions involving the United Kingdom are only attractive to jurisdictions where lessees are not capable of taking advantage of tax benefits of ownership themselves. For example, when an airline does not have the requisite taxable income to take full depreciation deductions.

Traditionally, the United Kingdom and the United States have a long-standing relationship involving cross-border lease transactions. Initially, the lease structures between the United States and United Kingdom have been quite simple, but as tax laws surrounding leases in both jurisdictions have become more stringent, the lease structures have grown more sophisticated to maximize the tax benefit for both sides. Historically, the US and UK parties have been able to organize double-dip lease transactions, which has bolstered the lease relationship between the two nations. Double-dip transactions mean that through the combination of the United States lease structure and the UK lease structure, parties in both jurisdictions can take advantage of tax benefits of ownership. The US lessee can claim depreciation benefits on aircraft finance lease arrangements so long as the agreement contains a purchase option. UK lessors could then take capital allowances (depreciation expense) on assets that they do not have a title to but can prove they will have the title to in the future. A careful balance of legal versus economic ownership may allow both parties in the US and UK lease structures to claim ownership benefits on the same asset.

UK TAX ENVIRONMENT

The most relevant tax laws to cross-border leasing in the United Kingdom revolved around capital allowances, write-down allowances, and anti-avoidance laws. It is important to note that certain lease transactions may disqualify lessors from receiving capital allowances due to anti-avoidance laws. These anti-avoidance laws are an attempt to reduce the number of non-UK resident companies from taking advantage of UK capital allowance deductions via lease transactions with UK lessors. Careful examination of these laws is essential for participating parties to appropriate structure the transaction and not disqualify the lessor from taking capital allowance deductions.

Two Finance Acts in 1997 changed the landscape of the UK leasing tax environment. Before the first Finance Act of 1997, capital allowance write-downs could be taken at 25% in the first year and at a decreasing rate in following years. The Finance Act reduced the write-down rate to 6% for all depreciable assets. In January 2011, a new Finance Act increased the write-down rate to 8% in the first year. The second Finance Act in 1997 prescribed that write-down allowances can only be taken for the portion of the year that the company actually owned the asset. To be able to take the entire 6% write-down allowance for an asset, the company would have had to purchase the asset on the first day of the tax year. To combat this new law, lessors built their portfolio, so aircraft acquisitions happened throughout the year to maximize the amount of annual write-down deduction for the portfolio of aircraft. Lessors would pool their portfolios of aircraft and calculate capital allowances on the value of the portfolio, not on a single aircraft. The portfolio values are adjusted yearly for new aircraft acquisitions and old aircraft disposals. The second Finance Act also imposed new restrictions on sale and leaseback agreements, which virtually ended the sale and leaseback structures domestically. These two Finance Acts forced existing lease structures to be reorganized to account for and move around these new, more stringent regulations.

The last significant tax regulation that has shaped the UK tax leasing industry is the Finance Act of 2006, which introduced the concept of the long-funding lease. A long-funding lease is essentially a finance lease on capital equipment, machinery, and plant assets that are on lease for a majority of their depreciable lives, and the lease is used as a form of asset financing. In this situation, it is technically the lessee that is qualified to take the capital allowance deductions, while the lessor is liable for tax on interest expense and the lessee takes interest expense as a deduction for tax purposes. The purpose of the long-funding lease laws is to eliminate the lease arrangements that make financing using a capital lease cheaper than debt financing. Primarily, the law was an attempt to end the tax leases in the United Kingdom. This law, as well as the 1997 Finance Acts, were hugely influential in shaping the future of the aircraft-leasing and financing industry in the United Kingdom and should be kept in mind when negotiating UK lease agreements.

FRANCE—LEASING MARKET OVERVIEW

Historically, the French cross-border aircraft-leasing market has been quite small and limited. Since the 2010s, however, the market has been increasing due to the growth in Asia and expanded activity of Asian investors and airlines with purchasing and leasing aircraft produced in France and the greater EU. Transactions typically include Airbus and ATR aircraft, Safran Aircraft Engines, and aircraft with CFM engines, as the French banks conducting these transactions tend to favor French products. Overall, France is not necessarily a preferred jurisdiction for cross-border leases due to strict lease classification laws that can disqualify either party in the lease from claiming depreciation benefits on the aircraft altogether. French tax authorities have the right to reclassify the nature of the lease transaction according to the *abus de droit*, or abuse of rights concept, to prevent lessors from structuring lease transactions for the sheer purpose of avoiding taxes or taking more tax benefits than are deemed fair (Valentin and Perus, 2011).

There are significant double-dipping opportunities available with French cross-border lease transactions due to differences in ownership tax benefits with various jurisdictions, notably Germany and the United States. Essentially, the French lessor can hold the title to the aircraft in France and claim depreciation benefits as the legal owner, while a lessee in a different jurisdiction can claim economic ownership of the same asset and also claim depreciation benefits in their home country. Aircraft are depreciated in France over 12–15 years on a straight-line basis, though accelerated declining-balance depreciation is available for new aircraft sales. Once the level of the declining-balance depreciation deductions falls below that of what straight-line depreciation would be, the lessor can then switch to the straight-line method for the remainder of the aircraft's economic life. It is important to note that depreciation deductions are capped over the first 36 months of the lease depending on the location of use of the aircraft to limit the amount of depreciation benefits lessors can claim against their taxable income.

EXPORT CREDIT TRANSACTIONS

Export credit has become a significant aircraft financing tool since the late 2000s and early 2010s. Major ECAs that provide guarantees for French cross-border aircraft-lease transactions include COFACE, Euler Hermes, and ECGD. The banks that are typically used to finance these transactions include Crédit Agricole CIB, Société Générale, and BNP Paribas.

Export credit is not given directly to the airlines or lessors attempting to finance these transactions. A sort of partnership company is created among the financing banks in the transaction, called a Groupement d'intérêt économique (GIE) to facilitate the transaction. A GIE is a separate entity from the partner companies, though the profits and losses are distributed directly to the partners. Once the GIE is established, it purchases the aircraft from the manufacturer and leases it to the airline. The ECA guaranteed loans from the French, German, or English banks cover up to 85% of the purchase cost of the aircraft, while the remaining 15% of the value is financed via a direct loan without an ECA guarantee.

More recent lease transactions have utilized SPVs located in the Cayman Islands as opposed to the French GIE, though with virtually the same structure. Other developments have included combinations of export credit transactions with JLL's and Chinese tax leases to maximize tax benefits from the lease structures.

CROSS-BORDER LEASING

The classification of the lease by French tax authorities limits the benefits of lease structures for French lessors leasing aircraft to lessees in different jurisdictions. For a lessor to claim depreciation benefits, the lease must be structured as a *crédit-bail*. A *crédit-bail* is essentially a lease with purchase option, though the conditions surrounding the lease with purchase option are what determine whether tax authorities will accept it. For example, if there is a reasonable expectation that the purchase option will be exercised or the legal title changes hands during or at the end of the lease, the tax authority can reclassify the transaction as a conditional or installment sale, thus eliminating any tax benefits to the lessor. Therefore, if the lessor cannot claim depreciation benefits, the lessee cannot receive the capital allowance, as the depreciation benefits are not accounted for. Nevertheless, a *crédit-bail* is often considered an installment purchase in many other jurisdictions, which allows for double-dip transactions to occur where the French lessor maintains legal ownership of the asset, while the foreign lessee becomes the economic owner.

The only way for a French lessee to claim depreciation benefits is to hold the legal title to the aircraft at the initiation of the transaction. The transaction should not be considered a lease at all, but a conditional or installment sale from the French tax authorities point of view. Taxes applicable to lessees bringing foreign aircraft into France include withholding tax, VAT, and other France-specific taxes. Withholding taxes apply to any lease or rental payments by a French lessee to a foreign lessor at a rate of 33.33%. This withholding tax can be reduced or eliminated due to any double taxation agreements between France and the foreign jurisdictions, as well as if the aircraft are utilized 80% or more on international routes. There is also a 0% VAT rate applied to aircraft operated predominantly on international routes; however, if this requirement is not met, France charges 19.6% VAT on rental payments paid to a foreign lessor for aircraft domiciled in France. Other France-specific taxes, such as French TVA and turnover tax, may be applicable depending on the specifications of the transaction, so the local council should be advised when structuring transactions.

CHINA—LEASING MARKET OVERVIEW

While western leasing companies have traditionally dominated the global aircraft-leasing market, the Chinese market has been controlled almost entirely by local players. The economic environment in China has been very strictly regulated, and historically both aircraft lessors and lessees were owned by the government. However, a growing Chinese middle class that fuels the consistent air traffic growth has opened new opportunities for private capital as Chinese leasing companies, banks, and investors expand their presence in the aircraft-leasing market. This push for expansion has created a surge in demand for low-cost carriers as well as new aircraft in the region.

Since 2007, Chinese financial institutions have been actively developing their aviation leasing activities reaching approximately 75%–80% of the local market share in 2017 (Aviationpros, n.d.).

The Chinese capital is expected to claim more than a third of the $261 billion aircraft-leasing market by 2022. As demand for domestic air travel accelerates, China is expected to be the single fastest-growing market for aircraft sales in the next 20 years. The International Air Transport Association believes China is on track to displace the United States as the world's biggest aviation market by 2022.

To facilitate the development of the financial leasing industry in China, in 2011 the Ministry of Commerce circulated the "Guidance on Promoting the Development of Financial Leasing Industry during the 12th Five-Year Period." The guidance encourages the formation of leasing industry development centers to enhance the function of finance leasing in the nation's critical economic development zones. As of 2018, China has formed three such centers, including Tianjin Dongjiang Free Trade Port Zone, Shanghai Waigaoqiao Free Trade Zone, and Beijing Tianzhu Free Trade Zone.

Leases of aircraft to China may incur different taxes depending on the lessor's locations and whether the double taxation agreements between the lessor's jurisdictions and China are in place

(Ling, 2011). In China, the profits from leasing businesses are subject to Corporate Income Tax at a rate of 25%. There are however special free trade zones and available local financial incentives designed to attract leasing companies to establish their operations in these areas. The tax withholding rules in China could be complicated. For example, a Chinese aircraft lessor with a foreign parent will be a subject to withholding tax when it distributes income to the parent company. The VAT rules are complex and depend on aircraft type and whether it is purchased into a Free Trade Zone. Stamp Duty tax rates also depend on the type of the contracts (operating or finance lease).

Another important consideration is that any agreement between a Chinese lessor and a Chinese airline is required to be governed by Chinese law rather than English law, which is commonly used in aircraft leasing.

HONG KONG TAX REGIME

Given Hong Kong's unique position in China and its role as a business hub in Asia, international aircraft lessors that are expanding into China naturally consider setting up bases in Hong Kong. Many Chinese aircraft-leasing companies use Hong Kong as an international platform to raise funds for their businesses. Hong Kong Government had recognized its role in the aircraft-leasing space in Asia and ensured the competitive tax policy for aircraft lessors. For example, Hong Kong does not impose a sales tax on aircraft-leasing payments, resulting in the overall simpler tax system. Also, any capital gain from the sale of an aircraft that was used in qualifying leasing activities for a continuous period of not less than 3 years immediately prior the sale, are tax exempt. In addition, Hong Kong and Mainland China have the double taxation agreement, which offers a more favorable withholding tax rate of 5% to lessors leasing aircraft to Chinese lessees.

On March 10, 2017, Hong Kong's government introduced new legislation to offer competitive tax advantages to the aircraft-leasing business, including the following:

- A concessionary tax rate of 8.25%, which is 50% lower than the current income tax rate of 16.5%, for both qualifying aircraft lessors and qualifying aircraft-leasing managers;
- As compensation for the loss of depreciation allowances, the estimated taxable amount for income derived from the leasing of aircraft to a non-Hong Kong aircraft operator by a qualifying aircraft lessor will be equal to 20% of the tax base of the lessor concerned, i.e., their gross rentals less deductible expenses, but excluding tax depreciation (Hong Kong Inland Revenue, 2017).

INDIA—LEASING MARKET OVERVIEW

With its geographical location between the eastern and western hemispheres and growing middle-class population, India is well positioned for growth and is expected to become the third-largest civil aviation market after the United States and China by 2022. However, the Indian aviation industry is still young and requires massive investments in infrastructure, which along with mature judiciary and tax systems make an excellent case for cross-border leases (Bilawala, 2011).

Cross-border leasing of aircraft in India was eligible for a special exemption under Section 10 (15A) of the Income Tax Act of 1961 until the Finance Act of 2005 introduced a sunset clause stating that the exemption shall not be available for leases originated after April 1, 2007. After the withdrawal of the exemption, a direct tax is largely governed by the Income Tax Act of 1961 or bilateral tax treaties between India and various countries. The extent to which a direct tax liability arises depends on the nature of the lease agreement. The primary consideration is whether a nonresident lessor has a taxable presence in India by way of a PE, and the profits that are attributable to such PE are taxable in India.

Movement of goods from one state to another in India is subject to states' sales tax. However, the right to use goods is taxable only under the Central Sales Tax Act of 1956, which is a federal tax law. Therefore, aircraft lease payments from one state to another are considered interstate transactions and are not subject to states' sale tax. Also, cross-border lease transactions are characterized as import/export that is not subject to Central Sales Tax. It seems that lease payments made within India or cross-border do not lead to states' or central sales tax liabilities.

Currently in India, a service tax is leviable on service transactions if the place of provision of services is in India. This means that lessees located in India would be subject to service tax on their lease transactions. The Goods and Services Tax (GST) is another consideration for Indian lessees. The GST is paid on lease rentals and import of aircraft on lease. Recently, the Indian government provided exemption from the GST on the import of aircraft, engines, and aircraft parts on lease basis, thus eliminating double taxation issue when lessees had to pay taxes on import of aircraft on lease and then the GST on lease rentals.

Another consideration should be given to stamp duty implications on the various agreements executed in connection with a lease or a financing transaction. Stamp duty can be different in different states in India. Some states have enacted their own stamp laws, while other states have adopted the Indian Stamp Act of 1899 with state-specific amendments.

As mentioned above, import of aircraft is subject to customs duties, but some exemptions are issued by the Central Board of Excise and Customs. The exemptions that are relevant to cross-border transactions are

- where the aircraft is imported by an operator or on behalf of an operator, for operating scheduled air transport service or scheduled air cargo service or
- where the aircraft is imported by an operator, who has been approved by the competent authority in the Ministry of Civil Aviation to import aircraft for providing nonscheduled passenger or nonscheduled air cargo services.

Hence, it is advisable for an importer to consult with the Ministry of Civil Aviation regarding required approvals that will assist with customs clearance.

Supporting the growth of the civil aviation market, the Indian Government has recently proposed reforms in National Civil Aviation and Foreign Direct Investment (FDI) policies. Thus, National Civil Aviation Policy 2016 (NCAP 2016) stated partial abolition of the so-called 5/20 rule that required Indian carriers to fly on domestic routes for 5 years and have a fleet of 20 aircraft before they are allowed to start international operations. The NCAP 2016 removed the 5 years of domestic flying requirement but retained the 20 aircraft rule. Concerning the FDI policy, Consolidated FDI Policy Circular of 2016 announced a radical liberalization of FDI allowance up to 100% (from 49%) making it more attractive for foreign investors in the airline industry.

BRAZIL—LEASING MARKET OVERVIEW

Brazil continues to be the largest aviation market in Latin America, showing consistent growth through the 2000s and early 2010s. This growth has created significant demand from airlines for aircraft to fulfill their fleet requirements, making Brazil an important market for lessors abroad.

In 2014 Brazil fell into a severe economic recession. The Brazilian Real significantly depreciated, applying pressure on Brazilian airlines, as rental payments on leased aircraft must be made in USDs. This created a surge in aircraft sales and returns of leased aircraft from Brazilian airlines, and the lease market reduced significantly during the mid to late 2010s. Currently, Brazil's economy and the air transport industry is on a slow but steady climb back to their historical levels.

In October 2016, Brazil added Ireland, Austria, Curacao, and St. Martin to its list of tax havens making any transaction between these countries and Brazil (as well as countries that were already on that list) prohibitively expensive. Transactions between Brazil and these countries now require a 25% withholding tax, as opposed to the 15% before they were included in the list of tax havens. Brazilian airlines incurred approximately an additional charge of 1 billion Brazilian Reals (USD $316 million) per year in withholding tax only from transactions with Ireland, excluding the transactions with the remaining tax haven countries. Ireland is in the process of appealing to the Brazilian government to have Ireland removed from this list to make transacting with Brazilian companies possible again. As many aircraft lessors are based in Ireland, this tax increase is slowing down airlines' recovery from the political and economic crisis.

The cross-border lease market in Brazil is primarily restricted to Brazilian lessees leasing aircraft from foreign lessors. No market exists currently for cross-border leases with Brazilian lessors due to the associated tax burdens and regulations.

Lease transactions are heavily regulated by the Brazilian Central Bank (BACEN) and the Brazilian National Monetary Council, as all lease transactions must be submitted to and approved by both organizations (Sheard and Falkenburger, 2011). Types of lease transactions include finance leases, commercial leases, operating leases, and cross-border leases.

Finance leases and commercial leases are essentially the same with only the purchase option as the differentiator. In the case of finance leases, the purchase option is determined through negotiation between the lessee and lessor and does not have to be set at market value. However, in commercial leases, the purchase option must be set at market value to qualify as a commercial lease for tax purposes.

Cross-border operating leases are the most common form of leasing in Brazil because of the tax benefits to structuring a lease this way. Cross-border finance leases are uncommon due to typically prohibitive tax implications of importing aircraft in Brazil. Cross-border operating leases are not subject to import taxes due to Brazil's Special Regime of Temporary Admission, which is discussed further in the following section. The main considerations surrounding cross-border operating leases are the term of the lease and the purchase option. The term of the lease must be less than the useful life of the aircraft, and there can be no purchase option attached to the lease. Otherwise, there are very few laws governing cross-border leases specifically, so they are commonly held to the standard of domestic lease law.

As we already mentioned, depending on the type of transaction and the parties in the transaction, taxes associated with leasing can be high in Brazil. Major tax considerations include the Special Regime of Temporary Admission, withholding taxes, import taxes, and double taxation treaties. The Special Regime of Temporary Admission is the reason why cross-border operating leases are the most common form of aircraft leasing in Brazil. This regime makes it so that import taxes are suspended on aircraft (or other assets) brought into Brazil as long as the aircraft are not permanently domiciled in Brazil. Import taxes are paid based on the amount of time the aircraft is based in Brazil. Also, there are no taxes on lease payments except in the case of a capital gain. By suspending the full import tax on the leased aircraft, Brazil has made operating leases much more attractive. In addition to aircraft, any spare parts and engines also leased to a Brazilian lessee by a foreign lessor are not subject to any taxation.

Import taxes in Brazil can be a prohibitive factor when structuring a cross-border lease. They are mostly applicable to purchases and inbound finance leases, though not to operating leases, as we have previously discussed. At customs, taxes paid include import duty, tax on manufactured products, and tax on the distribution of goods and services. However, aircraft, especially those purchased by airlines for use on approved routes, can be made exempt from many of these taxes, but not the import duty itself.

Double taxation treaties are also an essential consideration for structuring a lease transaction. Brazil has entered into double taxation treaties with several European countries, Mexico, and Japan.

In addition, a lessor that considers leasing aircraft to a lessee in Brazil should study foreign exchange controls and insolvency risk. Foreign exchange controls in Brazil have been extremely strict in the past but currently is getting a bit less severe. Now, the major controls are that accounts can only be kept in local currency, forcing Brazilian lessees to enter into FOREX contracts with the BACEN-approved banks to make USD payments on aircraft. All cross-border transactions must be registered with and approved by the BACEN and the Registry of Financial Operations. A lessee must submit the lease agreement for approval. Once the lease agreement is approved, the lessee must submit a schedule of payments with the amount and dates of payments to be made to the foreign lessor for approval to purchase the appropriate FOREX contracts and move the funds outside of Brazil.

The other consideration for lessors is insolvency risk and the lessor's ability to repossess its aircraft in the case of lessee default. Brazil ratified the Cape Town Convention and Aircraft Protocol in 2011, improving international rights for lessors and lenders to access their aircraft in the case of insolvency. In February 2005, Brazil amended its bankruptcy law to better align with Chapter 11 reorganization bankruptcy in the United States. This bankruptcy law gave lessees the right to reorganize with a 180-day stay period, making it impossible for lessors to access their aircraft until this stay period is over. Lessors could not reclaim assets during this period if they were essential to the functioning of business operations. In November 2005, this law was further amended to exclude aircraft leases in the 180-day stay period, meaning that the lessee still needs to pay rental payments and follow the lease agreement to keep the aircraft. Current bankruptcy laws are favorable to lessors, as they have improved access to their assets via the Cape Town Convention and Brazil's bankruptcy laws.

UAE—LEASING MARKET OVERVIEW

The history of the UAE aviation industry started in 1985 with the launch of Emirates Airlines with $10 million in start-up capital and two aircraft on wet-lease from Pakistan International Airlines (Emirates Airlines, n.d.). Since then, the UAE have acquired extensive aviation credentials: Home to two global network carriers (Etihad and Emirates) and two low-cost carriers (Fly Dubai and Air Arabia); globally renowned airports; and a broad range of ancillary aviation sectors, such as aircraft component manufacturing and aircraft leasing.

The UAE is an attractive jurisdiction for the aircraft-leasing and finance industries due to the following main reasons:

- The UAE has established an extensive network of double taxation treaties, with 81 of them in force and 32 more in negotiations (ADGM, 2017).
- Zero percent corporate income tax
- No withholding tax
- Zero VAT on cross-border aircraft-leasing transactions
- Stamp duty is not applicable
- Full English common law environment
- No foreign ownership restrictions
- No limits on repatriation of profits
- Independent courts and a financial services regulator

Major aircraft financing and leasing companies that are based in the UAE:

- Waha Capital is an Abu Dhabi investment company that manages assets in several sectors, including aircraft leasing. It was established in 1997 and acquired 20% stake in AerCap in 2010.
- Dubai Aerospace Enterprise (DAE)—One of the top 10 global leasing companies. DAE was launched in 2006 and acquired AWAS in 2017.
- Sanad is an aircraft engine and component lessor based in Abu Dhabi. Sanad was established by Mubadala Investment Company in 2010.
- GE Capital entered into a joint venture with Mubadala Investment Company in 2013.

SINGAPORE—LEASING MARKET OVERVIEW

With the increasing demand for commercial aircraft in Asia and with the growing significance of Chinese financial institutions, this region will continue to be the focus of the aircraft-leasing industry. Being one of the largest financial hubs in Asia, Singapore offers an attractive base for lessors that want to expand their presence in Asia. Singapore has been competing with Hong Kong to draw aircraft-leasing business. On February 20, 2017, the Singapore government announced an updated Aircraft Leasing Scheme (ALS), extending it for 5 more years to December 31, 2022. The original ALS was set to expire in 2017. Any approved aircraft-leasing company can benefit from the following incentives:

- A concessionary tax rate of 8% on income derived from the leasing of aircraft or aircraft engines and qualifying ancillary activities (down from the headline rate of 17%).
- A withholding tax exemption on interest and qualifying related payments on loans obtained for the purchase of aircraft or aircraft engines.
- The incentive period is limited to 5 years. Extension of the incentive may be considered, subject to the company's commitment to undertake further expansion plans on its aircraft-leasing activities (Singapore Economic Development Board, 2017).

Singapore has double tax treaties with more than 80 countries. Also, the Singapore government has been renegotiating treaties with key countries to remove or reduce the effect of withholding tax on aircraft and aircraft engine payments. Since April 2011, Singapore and Ireland have a comprehensive DTAA that provides Irish lessors with full protection from Singapore withholding tax. The DTAA allows Singapore and Ireland to cooperate in developing cross-border aircraft-leasing solutions and provides greater flexibility for aircraft lessors to operate at these two aircraft-leasing centers.

Out of the top 10 global aircraft lessors, 8 have a business presence in Singapore (Lovell, 2017). Also, Singapore is the home for BOC Aviation Limited, a top tier global aircraft lessor. The company was founded in 1993 and acquired by Bank of China in 2006.

CONCLUSION

This chapter presented the important tax considerations in a cross-border lease transaction, a brief overview of regional aircraft-leasing markets, and highlighted the difference and similarities among them. It also discussed the recent change in the accounting standards to show operating leases on the airline's balance sheet, and the impact of these changes on aircraft leasing.

Taxes can occur at multiple points of the transaction process, including origination of the lease, transfer of the aircraft, and commencement of the lease. As taxes are present in every aspect of the transaction, they are a very important consideration for all parties involved, when constructing the lease agreement.

Cross-border aircraft-leasing transactions may involve two or more jurisdictions and diverse tax and regulatory regimes. While the United States and Ireland remain the world's largest centers for cross-border aircraft-leasing, new major aircraft-leasing centers are emerging in Asia and the Middle East due to favorable tax laws, which has led to the growing popularity of operating leases.

Though there is some concern as to how the new accounting standard, to show operating leases on an airline's balance sheet, would affect the aircraft-leasing industry, most believe that it would have minimal impact on the industry.

REFERENCES

ADGM. (2017). *UAE double tax treaty network*. Abu Dhabi: Abu Dhabi Global Market. Retrieved from https://www.adgm.com/media/189469/aviation-booklet-web-version.pdf.

Ajayi, D. (2018, June 8). *Detail*. Detail Solicitors. Retrieved from: <http://www.detailsolicitors.com/media/archive1/articles/article15.pdf>.

Aviationpros. *The Chinese march on the aircraft finance market*. Aviationpros. (n.d.). Retrieved from: <http://www.aviationpros.com/press_release/11670109/the-chinese-march-on-the-aircraft-finance-market>.

Bilawala, M. (2011). India. In R. Murphy, & N. Desai (Eds.), *Aircraft financing* (pp. 151–157). London: Euromoney Institutional Investor PLC.

DBRS. *Rating companies in the airline industry*. DBRS Website. (2018, January). Retrieved from: <https://www.dbrs.com/research/322323/rating-companies-in-the-airline-industry>.

Deloitte. *Aircraft leasing sector—Implication of the new leasing standard*. Deloitte. (2016). Retrieved from: <https://www2.deloitte.com/ie/en/pages/tax/articles/aircraft-leasing-new-leasing-standard.html>.

Emirates Airlines. *Emirates, our story.* (n.d.). Retrieved from: <https://www.emirates.com/us/english/about-us/>.

Hepher, T. (2018, June 5). *A decade after debut, first A380 jumbos to be broken up*. Reuters. Retrieved from: <https://www.reuters.com/article/us-airbus-a380/a-decade-after-debut-first-a380-jumbos-to-be-broken-up-idUSKCN1J10R2>.

Hong Kong Inland Revenue. (2017). *The Inland Revenue (Amendment) (No. 2) Ordinance 2017*. Hong Kong: Hong Kong Inland Revenue. Retrieved from https://www.gld.gov.hk/egazette/pdf/20172110/es3201721106.pdf.

Ling, W. (2011). China. In R. Murphy, & N. Desai (Eds.), *Aircraft financing* (pp. 157–162). London: Euromoney Institutional Investor PLC.

Lovell, C. (2016, October 3). *IFRS "kills sale-and-leaseback" as an off balance sheet option*. Ishka Global. Retrieved from: <https://www.ishkaglobal.com/News/Article/5513/IFRS-16-kills-sale-and-leaseback-as-an-off-balance-sheet-option>.

Lovell, C. (2017, May 8). *Will Hong Kong's new tax rate lure lessors?* Ishka Insights by Ishka Global. Retrieved from: <https://www.ishkaglobal.com/News/Article/5613/Will-Hong-Kongs-new-tax-rate-lure-lessors>.

Lovell, C. (2018, January 16). *IFRS rules likely to cause currency volatility for airlines*. Ishka Global. Retrieved from: <https://www.ishkaglobal.com/News/Article/5742/IFRS-rules-likely-to-cause-currency-volatility-for-airlines>.

National Business Aviation Association (NBAA). *European Union aircraft importation*. (2018, June 8). Retrieved from www.nbaa.org: <https://www.nbaa.org/admin/taxes/intl/eu-importation/>.

O'Callaghan, B. (2017, December). *Balancing the books: IFRS 16 and aviation finance*. Retrieved from <https://www2.deloitte.com/content/dam/Deloitte/ie/Documents/FinancialServices/ie-Balancing-the-Books-IFRS-16-and-Aviation-Finance-Report_Dec2017-5.pdf>.

Osborne-Kinch, J., Coates, D., & Nolan, L. (2017). *The aircraft leasing industry in Ireland: Cross border flows and statistical treatment*. Central Bank of Ireland.

Price Waterhouse (PwC). *An industry focus on the impact of IFRS16-Airlines*. Price Waterhouse Website. (2016 April). Retrieved from: <https://www.pwc.com/gx/en/audit-services/ifrs/publications/ifrs-16/ifrs-16-implications-for-the-airlines-industry.pdf>.

Raghavan, S., & Zarb, B. (2018). Implications of the new accounting changes for aircraft leasing. *Journal of International Finance and Economics*, *18*(2), 49–58.

Schott, K. (2011). Germany. In R. Murphy, & N. Desai (Eds.), *Aircraft financing* (pp. 167–173). London: Euromoney Institutional Investor PLC.

Sheard, E., & Falkenburger, F. (2011). Brazil. In R. Murphy, & N. Desai (Eds.), *Aircraft financing* (pp. 132–139). London: Euromoney Institutional Investor PLC.

Singapore Economic Development Board. (2017). *Aircraft leasing scheme*. Singapore: Singapore Economic Development Board. Retrieved from https://www.edb.gov.sg/content/dam/edb/en/why%20singapore/Incentive-ALS.pdf.

Sivaramakrishnan, P. (2017, October 12). *Ireland as a hub for the aviation industry*. Cogency Global. Retrieved from: <https://www.cogencyglobal.com/blog/ireland-as-a-hub-for-the-aviation-industry>.

Stokes, D., & Runagall, M. (2011). Japan. In R. Murphy, & N. Desai (Eds.), *Aircraft financing* (pp. 177–184). London: Euromoney Institutional Investor PLC.

United States Security and Exchange Commission. *Delta Airlines Inc. Form. 10-K*. United States Security and Exchange Commission. (2017a, December 31). Retrieved from: <http://d18rn0p25nwr6d.cloudfront.net/CIK-0000027904/1b58e244-f144-431a-afb7-1aaceed67f10.pdf>.

United States Security and Exchange Commission. *Form 10-K, annual report, Spirit Airlines, Inc*. United States Security and Exchange Commission. (2017b, December 31). Retrieved from: <http://ir.spirit.com/static-files/7dfdf0dc-22cf-4cf4-8b8a-70118a4ecfaf>.

Valentin, C., & Perus, S. (2011). France. In R. Murphy, & N. Desai (Eds.), *Aircraft financing* (pp. 162–167). London: Euromoney Institutional Investor PLC.

CHAPTER

ENGINE LEASING

14

CHAPTER OUTLINE

Aircraft Leasing and Financing. DOI: https://doi.org/10.1016/B978-0-12-815285-0.00014-6

The engine(s) typically accounts for roughly 30% of an aircraft's total initial value. After 20 years, that same engine could take on 70% of the value, given it was properly maintained. Conversely, the airframe is likely to depreciate by 80%–90% over a 20-year utilization. This is why airlines and lessors are so focused on engine maintenance. Since the aircraft is the critical tool which airlines use to generate profit, they must have access to spare engines either by purchasing the spare engine or by leasing from an engine lessor to cover the engine shop visit (ESV) period. As a finance professional, it is important to understand the main factors that affect an engine's residual value, as this will lead to better decisions about engine management. There are also aftermarket service programs (e.g., TotalCare, True Choice) available from the OEMs to help airlines maximize their engine values and maintain a more accurate forecast of future maintenance events and expense.

PRINCIPLES OF JET ENGINE OPERATION

Newton's Third Law of Motion states that for every action there is an equal and opposite reaction. In other words, if object 1 exerts force on object 2, then object 2 exerts an equal force on object 1 but in the opposite direction. This is the underlying principle of jet propulsion. In fact, the term "jet" refers to a stream of matter that is discharged in the direction opposite that of motion. In a jet engine, air is the discharged matter, and the action/reaction is what produces the thrust necessary to propel the aircraft.

Jet thrust is produced via internal combustion, but unlike rocket engines, aircraft engines are air breathing. Gunpowder provided the original means for the earliest attempts at jet propulsion, but this resulted in a firework effect that simply could not sustain motion. It wasn't until the development of gas turbines that the technology became practical. In a gas turbine, external air enters an internal compressor before moving onto a combustion chamber where it is sprayed with fuel and ignited into high-temperature, pressurized gas. The turbine, which also powers the compressor, extracts this thermal energy, which ultimately transmits to thrust as it exists through the exhaust nozzle (Sonntag & Borrgnakke, 2007).

There are many types of turbine-powered jet engines, including ramjets, turbo props, turbojets, and turbofans. In a turbojet, for example, all the extracted air passes through the compressor, combustion chamber, and the turbine. However, the most common engine used on today's commercial aircraft is the turbofan.

THE TURBOFAN

Unlike a turbojet, which sends all the air through the compressor, a turbofan functions with an intake fan, as shown in the cross-section view in Fig. 14.1. Note that while the fan is powered by the turbine, it actually directs a large portion of the inlet air around the core. This flow of air bypasses the compressor and turbine and eventually meets the high-temperature gas at the exhaust nozzle. The result is twofold. First, this output has a higher mass per second, which equates to more thrust, and second, the bypass air does not ignite and therefore does not require any fuel.

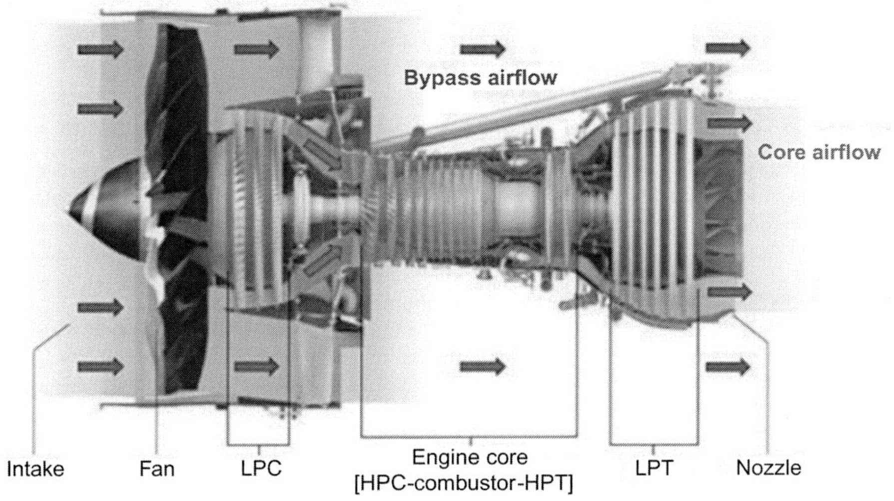

FIGURE 14.1

Turbofan engine.

Ackert (2011).

Thus, most commercial jets operate with turbofans due to the combined benefits of fuel efficiency and power (Mattingly, 2006).

Modules

Turbofan engines are constructed from six main assemblies, commonly referred to as modules. This modular design not only decreases turn time but also reduces the need to stock spare engines. Each module has an individual serial number, a limited lifetime rating, and a specific inspection threshold (Ackert, 2011).

1. *Fan/Low-Pressure Compressor (LPC)*—The first stage of the engine comprised fan blades, a compressor disk, and a compressor case. Again, the fan serves to direct some of the inlet air through the bypass ducts surrounding the core. Most fan blades are built with titanium, although some of the newer generation engines, such as the GE90, also incorporate advanced composite materials. Compression comprised several stages, beginning with the LPC. Note that all turbofan engines today operate with axial flow, meaning that air moves parallel (as opposed to radially) to the axel shaft as it flows through the engine (Ackert, 2011). Compression occurs via two main assemblies: moving rotor blades and stationary stator blades. Air passes through each row via alternating airfoils.
2. *High-Pressure Compressor (HPC)*—The HPC is the first component of the engine core, where air is further pressurized through additional stator and rotor assemblies before being sent to the combustor. While early jet engines used one set of compressor disks that rotated at one rate, most new models operate multiple rows of concentric disks, each rotating at a different rate.

This allows the engine to operate more efficiently under varying conditions and at different speeds.

3. *Combustor*—As the central part of the engine core, the combustor (or combustion chamber) sits between the compressor and the turbine. This is where high-pressure air is sprayed with fuel and ignited into thermal energy, which is then sent through the turbine and out the nozzle. Primary components of the combustor include inner and outer casings, fuel nozzles, and the high-pressure nozzle guide vanes. Most turbofan engines today are built with an annular or ring-shaped combustor.
4. *High-Pressure Turbine (HPT)*—The HPT connects to and powers the HPC by extracting thermal energy from the combustor and expanding it to a lower temperature and pressure. It's comprised several stages, each with one row of stationary airfoils (nozzles, stator vanes, or guides vanes) and one row of moving rotor blades. The number of stages depends on the torque required for each specific engine. Fundamentally, a turbine operates much like a pinwheel in that it rotates when air is blown against its inverted blades. The air flows first through the stator vanes that decrease pressure and increase tangential velocity. Think of a carousel horse spinning around and then suddenly detaching and flying off the ride. Once the air hits the rotor blades, the energy is absorbed, causing the turbine fan to rotate and generate power for the compressor. Depending on the engine type, this rotation might be as fast as 1500 ft/s. (Mattingly, 1996; Rolls-Royce, 1996).
5. *Low-Pressure Turbine (LPT)*—The LPT module sits downstream of the HPT and comprised a second series of stators and blades to further expand the high-temperature gas output. The nozzle stator case and turbine rear frame extract the remaining combustion thermal energy to drive both the intake fan and the LPC rotor assembly.
6. *Accessory Drive*—Mechanical energy produced from HPT and LPT is transferred by an accessory drive to power the auxiliary components, including the fuel pump, hydraulics, pneumatics, and electrical systems. The accessory drive functions via an external mounted gearbox, and on a high by-pass engine, requires up to 500 hp from the engine (Rolls-Royce, 1996).

The HPC, combustor, and HPT, are collectively known as the engine's hot section, whereas the intake fan and LPC make up the cold section. While this is the same for turbojets, the turbofan is further classified as low-bypass or high-bypass, depending on the mass flow bypassing the core relative to the mass flow passing through the core. This is known as the bypass ratio. Early turbofan models operated a ratio around 2:1, meaning 2 kg of bypass air for every 1 kg of air flowing through the core (Mattingly, 2006). However, as shown throughout this chapter, many turbofans today have much higher ratios, with the bypass air alone accounting for up to 85% of total engine thrust (Ackert, 2011).

ORIGINAL EQUIPMENT MANUFACTURERS

The first jet engine patent was on a ramjet in 1913. However, because heat-resistant material had not yet been developed, it was not manufactured until much later. Furthermore, this type of engine is more suitable toward weaponry and military application. The first gas turbine engine was patented in 1930 and served as the basis for manufactured models developed by a handful of companies, including Rolls-Royce (RR) Welland, Nene, Dart, and Derwent (Rolls-Royce, 1996). Today, nearly all jet airliners are powered by turbofans, specifically high-bypass models, although low-bypass models, turboprops, and turbojets are still being used on smaller aircraft and for many military applications.

As a financier involved in engine leasing, it is important to have at least a basic knowledge of engine mechanics and operation. Equally important is a familiarity with the original OEMs that are developing and selling the engines that power airlines' fleets. Table 14.1 displays a list of airframe models as well as a list of potential engine configurations.

Note from the table above that some airframes are manufactured to operate with several different engine models. An A330 operator, for example, has three different engine options from three different OEMs. Furthermore, just as Airbus, Boeing, and Bombardier dominate the airframe market, the civilian jet engine market today is heavily concentrated among a few key players.

GENERAL ELECTRIC

The General Electric (GE) company was founded in 1892 as a merger between the Edison GE Company (led by Thomas Edison) and the Thomas-Houston Electric Company (led by Charles Coffin), both headquartered in the Northeast United States. The business has since grown into an

Table 14.1 Engine Options for Commercial Aircraft

Aircraft Type	No. of Engines	Engine Option 1	Engine Option 2	Engine Option 3
A319/A320/A321	2	CFM56-5B	V2500	
A319neo/A320neo/A321neo	2	Leap-1A	PW1100G	
A330	2	CF6	PW4000	Trent 700
A330neo	2	RR Trent 7000		
A350	2	Trent XWB		
A380	2	GP7200	Trent 900	
737-300/400/500	2	CFM56-3B		
737NG (-600/700/800/900)	2	CFM56-7B		
737 Max (-7/8/9)	2	Leap-1B		
747-8	4	GEnx-2B		
757	2	RB211	PW2000	
767-300ER/300F	2	CF6	PW4000	RB211
777-200LR/300ER/F	2	GE90		
787 Dreamliner	2	GEnx-1B	Trent 1000	
ERJ 145 family	2	AE 3007		
E-170/175/190/195	2	CF34		
CRJ (all variants)	2	CF34-8		
Airbus A220	2	PW1500G		

Company websites.

international conglomerate covering many areas of industry, with a heavy focus on aviation, transportation, and energy. The company was and still is incorporated in New York but maintains its headquarters in Boston. GE is multibillion-dollar company that owns and operates a number of subsidiaries. In fact, Forbes Global named it the fourth largest company in world in 2000. GE established a presence in the aviation industry with the development of its first turbine engine (W.1) in 1941. The company expanded considerably during the early 1970s and has since become a key player in the jet engine manufacturing market. Today, GE Aviation's main engine products include the CF6, which powers the B767 and A330; the CF34, which powers the Bombardier CRJ and Challenger, the Embraer E-Jets, and the Comac ARJ21; GE90, which powers the B777; and the GE Next-Generation (GEnx), which powers the B787 and B747-8. GE also partners with several other manufacturers, including Pratt & Whitney (P&W) through the Engine Alliance (EA), as well as CFM International (FlightGlobal, 2016).

PRATT & WHITNEY

P&W is an aerospace manufacturer based in the Northeast United States. Frederick Rentschler founded the company in 1925 following his executive role at the original firm of the Wright brothers. P&W is actually a fully owned subsidiary of United Technologies, which manufactures a variety of industrial products, including heating, ventilation, and air conditioning (HVAC) systems, aerospace systems, elevators, and of course, aircraft engines. P&W entered the jet engine market in the 1950s, widely used in both civil and military aviation. P&W began producing commercial jet engines in the late 1950s, starting with its JT3 and JT4A models. These were designed for the Boeing 707 and Douglas DC-8. The company later unveiled the JT8D, which powered the first B727-100 flight. Later editions of this model featured up to 17,000 lb of thrust. Today, the company's main products include the PW2000, which powers the B757; the PW4000, which powers the B747, B767, B777, A300, A310, A330, and the MD-11; and the GTF engine, which was developed for the recent A320neo, Airbus A220, Embraer EJets E2, and Mitsubishi Regional Jet (MRJ). P&W also operates joint ventures with competitors, GE and RR. Together, these companies are commonly referred to as the "big three" aeroengine manufacturers (FlightGlobal, 2016).

ROLLS-ROYCE

RR is the only big-three manufacturer that was founded outside the United States. The company was developed from a 19th century engineering firm and was officially incorporated in England in 1906. Although the name is widely known for its presence in the luxury automotive market, this part of the company was eventually sold to auto-maker BMW. RR faced financial trouble in the early 1970s and, following a government buyout, restructured as RR Group plc. As of 2011, ownership falls under RR Holdings. Not only is the company one of the largest manufacturers of both civil and defense aircraft engines, but it is also a major player in marine products, nuclear services, reciprocating engines, and distributed energy systems (Rolls-Royce, 2017).

The company built its first aircraft engine in 1914 and has been consistently manufacturing since the 1950s. Today, RR engines can be found on more than 2000 commercial airplanes worldwide, and the company supplies to over 20 different airframe models, including narrowbody, widebody, and regional. Key products include the BR700, which powers regional and corporate jets; the

Trent series, which powers the A330, A330neo, A340, A350, A380, B777, and B787; and the AE 3007, which is found on the Embraer line. The company operates joint ventures with both GE and P&W (FlightGlobal, 2016).

CFM INTERNATIONAL

CFM international is a joint venture between France-based Safran and US-based GE. The venture was launched in 1974 for the purposes of developing the M56 engine model. However, CFM is most commonly known for its CFM56 turbofan, which first ran on demonstration at a GE facility in that same year. Today, the model is still in production and can be found on thousands of military and civilian aircraft, including the A320 and B737 lines. The second main product is the Leap turbofan engine. Specifications are shown in Table 14.2. This is CFM's latest development and is to be used on the Airbus 320neo, Boeing 737Max, and Comac C919, all of which are narrowbody aircraft. By March 2016, there were 1544 orders for CFM's Leap-1A versus 1312 orders for P&Ws 1100G-JM which, for the A320neo, is the only other engine choice (FlightGlobal, 2016). As of October 31, 2017, the Airbus 320neo line alone had amassed over 8000 orders from airlines and lessors around the globe.[1]

ENGINE ALLIANCE

In 1994, Airbus announced its plan to develop a very large airliner designated as A3XX and later named A380. At the same time, Boeing was considering its own new large aircraft to replace the 747. Neither P&W nor GE had an engine product with a high enough thrust range (70,000–85,000 lb). As a result, in 1996, GE and P&W began a joint venture known as the EA. Each company was already expecting a high global demand in this market segment, but neither could justify spending $1 billion to develop a new centerline engine. But a partnership appeared

Table 14.2 Features of the Leap1 Turbofan Engine Models

Model	Fan Diameter (in.)	Bypass Ratio	Static Thrust (lb)	Improvement in Fuel Consumption (Versus Previous Generation of Engines) (%)	Application	Entry into Service
LEAP-1A	78.7	11:01	24,500–32,900	− 15	A320NEO	2016
LEAP-1B	68.4	09:01	23,000–28,000	− 15	737 MAX	2017
LEAP-1C	75	11:01	27,980–30,000	− 15	COMAC C919	2016

Bank of America Merrill Lynch (2015) and CFM International (2017).

[1]www.aircraft.airbus.com/market/orders-deliveries.

less risky, allowing the companies to capitalize on the previous success of both the GE90 and the PW4000. The plan going forward was to develop a high-capacity, long-range aircraft engine—the GP7000. Today, this model powers the popular Airbus 380 aircraft and offers up to 81,500 lb of thrust. According to EA, it is also a more fuel-efficient option for this aircraft, saving up to $500,000 per year per aircraft comparing with RR Trent 900 engine (Engine Alliance, 2017).

INTERNATIONAL AERO ENGINES

International Aero Engines (IAE) launched in 1983 as a joint venture among RR, P&W, MTU Aero Engines, and Japanese Aero Engine Corporation. However, RR sold its share of the company in 2011. Today, IAE remains registered in Switzerland and has become an industry leader in the single-aisle market with its V2500 engine. The company focuses on continuous improvement and strives to be at the forefront of technology. The V2500 was chosen for the Embraer KC-390 and the MD-90 and currently powers 45% of all A320s currently in operation (International Aero Engines IAE, 2017).

In terms of market share, Fig. 14.2 displays the number of commercial aircraft equipped with engines produced by the manufacturers discussed above. While each OEM has a significant market presence, CFM maintains the largest share with over 11,300 aircraft flying with CFM engines and 4641 and 777 aircraft being on order and on option correspondingly.

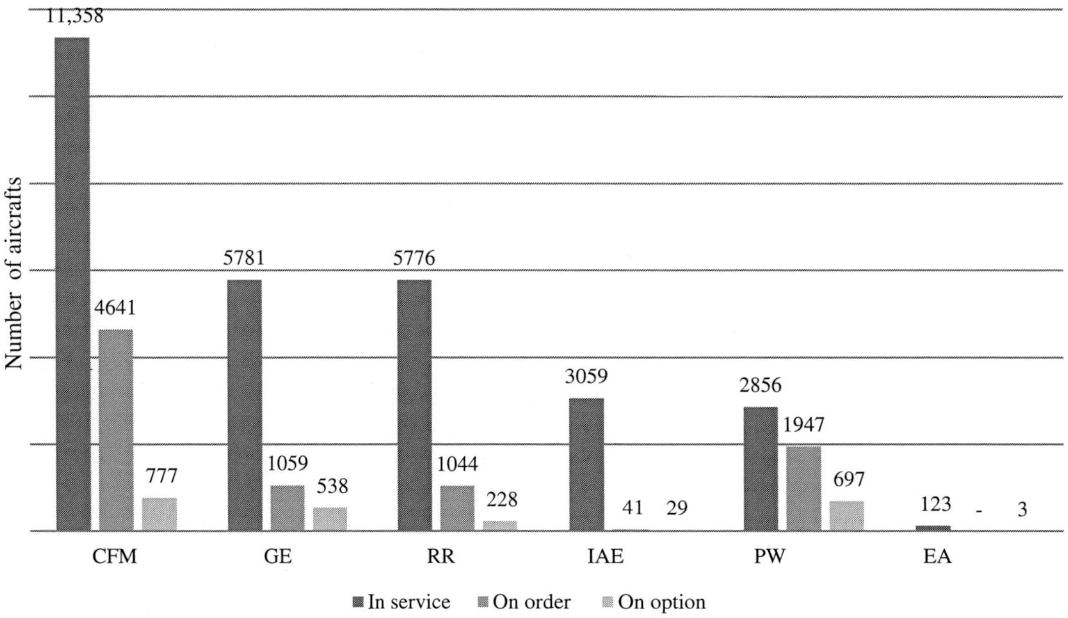

FIGURE 14.2

Commercial aircraft equipped with engines manufactured by different OEMs. *OEMs*, Original Equipment Manufacturers.

Compiled by the authors using data from FlightGlobal in April 2018.

NARROWBODY ENGINE MARKET

Historically, Boeing has dominated the narrowbody or single-aisle jet market with its 737 series, but Airbus is now a major contender with the A320. Together, the two companies have a 96% share of the narrowbody market. Similarly, the market share for qualifying engine models is concentrated among the major OEMs, namely, CFM, as shown in Table 14.3. Specifically, the CFM56 is the most popular engine in the narrowbody market (Fig. 14.3).

In this section, we detail the development and application of some of the top engines in the narrowbody market.

CFM56—CFM international

The CFM56 from CFM International is a high-bypass turbofan engine. The engine's LPC, combustor, and HPT are all manufactured by GE, while the inlet fan, gearbox, exhaust, and LPT are manufactured by Safran Snecma. CFM International is the exclusive supplier for the Boeing 737, whereas operators of the A320 family have the choice between the CFM56 and the V2500, which is produced by IAE.

The CFM56-5 series is specifically designed for the Airbus aircraft. In the series are three distinct sub-variants: 5A, 5B and 5C. The 5A series was originally designed for the short-to-medium haul Airbus 320 family, whereas the 5C was designed for Airbus' long-range A340. The 5C is the most powerful engine in the CFM56 lineup.

The 5B is a modified version of the 5A and is the most common engine supplied to Airbus. In fact, there are more than 3000 CFM56-5B series engines installed on Airbus aircraft in service today. As of 2017, the 5B had been selected to power roughly 60% of all A320s in operation around the world. In addition, there are nine variants within the 5B series, ranging from 5B1 to 5B9. Recently, the company also began developing a 10th variant, known as the CFM56-5BX/3. This is part of the Performance Improvement Program aimed at a technology standard to increase fuel efficiency by 0.5% and lower maintenance costs by 1%.

Next up is the CFM56-7B, which is the exclusive engine for Boeing's Next-Generation narrowbody aircraft and one of the best-selling models in commercial aviation. As of November, 2017, there were over 8000 CFM56-7B engines in service on B737s worldwide, half of which are

Table 14.3 Engine OEMs in the Narrowbody Market

	B737	B757	B737Max	A318	A319/320/321	A319/320/321Neo	Comac C919
RR		×					
P&W		×		×			
GE							
CFM	×		×	×	×	×	×
IAE					×		
EA							

RR, *Rolls-Royce;* P&W, *Pratt & Whitney;* GE, *General Electric;* IAE, *International Aero Engines;* EA, *Engine Alliance.*
FlightGlobal (2016).

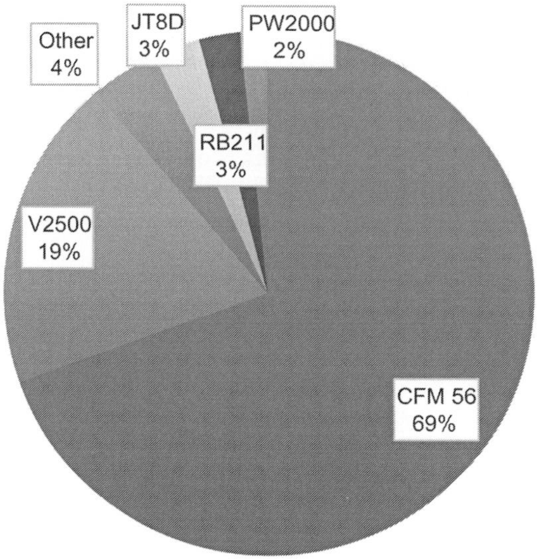

FIGURE 14.3

Engine OEM narrowbody market share. *OEM*, Original Equipment Manufacturer.

Compiled by the authors using data from FlightGlobal in April 2018.

737-800s. This success is due in large part to the fact that CFM is the sole source engine provider for the Boeing 737NG aircraft, but also due to the engine's reliability, reparability, and durability.

Like the 5B series, the 7B series has five variations—7B20, 7B22, 7B24, 7B26, and 7B27. The last two digits indicate the thrust rating in thousands of lb. There are also some sub-variants denoted with a suffix that stands for a new technology or upgrade feature. For instance, you might find an engine model called CFM56-7B27/2. The "/2" means that this engine is built with a dual annual combustor that could potentially reduce emissions by up to 40%.

CFM has also developed several improved build standards for the CFM56-7B, such as Tech Insertion and Evolution. The Tech Insertion program increases the engine's fuel efficiency by 1% and exhaust gas temperature (EGT) margins by 10°. This is achieved by upgrading both the high-pressure and LPT components and by redesigning the high-pressure combustor blades. An engine built to the Tech Insertion standard will be denoted with a "/3" suffix.

Table 14.4 displays a summary of the CFM56 engine line, including the thrust rating, bypass ratio, and application for each variant.

Overall, market demand for the CFM56-5B and -7B is relatively stable, although this may increase as more shop visits take place. Current market value is between $3.5 and $7 million, with lease rates ranging between $45,000 and $76,000 (Aircraft Commerce, 2016).

V2500—International Aero Engines

The IAE V2500 is a high-bypass turbofan engine that is installed on the Airbus 319, 320, and 321 models. It was also selected to power the Boeing MD-90 and the Embraer KC390.

Table 14.4 CFM56 Specs for Airbus and Boeing Aircrafts

Family	Model	Thrust (lb)	Bypass Ratio	Applicable Aircraft Model
CFM56-5	CFM56-5B3	33,000	5.4	A321
	CFM56-5C2	31,200	6.6	A340-200/-300
	CFM56-5B2	31,000	5.5	A321
	CFM56-5B1	30,000	5.5	A321
	CFM56-5B4	27,000	5.7	A320
	CFM56-5A3	26,500	6	A320
	CFM56-5A1	25,000	6	A320
	CFM56-5B5	22,000	6	A319
CFM56-7	CFM56-7B27	27,300	5.1	B737-800/-900/BBJ
	CFM56-7B26	26,300	5.1	B737-700/-800/-900
	CFM56-7B24	24,200	5.3	B737-700/-800/-900
	CFM56-7B22	22,700	5.3	B737-600/-700
	CFM56-7B20	20,600	5.5	B737-600/-700
	CFM56-7B18	19,500	5.5	B737-600

CFM International (2017).

The V2500-A5 series began service in 1993 after being developed from the V2500-A1 series. The main drawback of the A1 series was that the EGT margin was relatively low. As such, the engine was a poor fit for the A321, which required a much higher thrust configuration. Therefore, when developing the A5 series, IAE used a wider core diameter and a shroudless fan blade to increase efficiency and reduce the risk of foreign object damage (FOD) [International Aero Engines (IAE), 2017]. The engine also incorporates an extra stage to the LPC to improve its EGT margin.

Like the CFM56-5B and -7B, the V2500-A5 line was designed with several sub-variants to accommodate different build standards. The latest upgrade is the V2500-A5 SelectTwo, which greatly reduces fuel burn.

There have been several Airworthiness Directives (ADs) and Service Bulletins that have affected the V2500-A5 series, namely, some manufacturing errors on the HPT hub's No. 3 Bearing and the HPC 3–10 Drum. This has resulted in accelerated shop visits and replacement of LLPs and parts, which has not only impacted local operations, but has also delayed IAE manufacturing. There has been a significant increase in the demand for spare V2500-A5 engines as well as a sharp rise in value premiums of lease rate. Currently, the market for the V2500-A5 series is very strong, especially for the high-thrust models. Current market value for the V2500-A5 series engines ranges from $4.20 to $7.30 million, while lease rates are hovering between $50,000 and $90,000 (Aircraft Commerce, 2016).

There are more than 2800 V2500-A5 series engines installed on in-service aircraft around the world, half of which are powering the A320. There are five main variants within V2500-A5 series: V2522-A5, V2524-A5, V2527-A5, V2530-A5 and V2533-A5. The model number indicates the engine's takeoff thrust, which ranges from 22,000 to 33,000 lb. For instance, the thrust on an

V2522-A5 is 22,000 lb. Likewise, thrust on the V2527-A5 is 26,400 lb. The V2527-A5 is the only option for the A320 airframe, whereas as the A321 qualifies for either the V2530-A5 or the V2533-A5. IAE offers several options for the A319, including V2522-A5, V2524-A5, and V2527-A5 (Table 14.5).

Outlook for the narrowbody market

The narrowbody market remains the largest market both in value and size. After Airbus introduced the A320neo, Boeing introduced the 737 MAX series as a way to compete, with the first aircraft entering service in 2017. The situation is similar on the engine side, and there are several models being developed to stay ahead of the competition.

CFM International's LEAP engine is a high-bypass turbofan, with a thrust range between 23,000 and 30,000 lb, depending on the airframe. The engine also operates a 15% lower fuel burn than the current CFM56 series. The production ramp-up of the LEAP coincides with the ramp-up of the 737MAX in 2017–18 and the A320neo family in 2016–17. It was also selected to the power the COMAC C919 (CFM International, 2017).

The flagship Boeing 737 MAX will be powered by the LEAP-1B, but Airbus' A320neo can be powered by either the CFM's Leap-1A or the P&W's PW1100G-JM. The PW1000G family is another series of high-bypass turbofans designed to improve fuel efficiency. P&W claims a 16% reduction in fuel burn and plans to increase this by another 2% before 2019. The PW1500G has been selected as the exclusive engine for the Airbus A220, MRJ, Embraer's second gen E2-jets, and as an option on the Irkut MS-21.

Lessors' choice

Airbus received 4502 firm orders from 60 airlines and lessors, 63% of which have already announced their engine of choice. Leap-1A holds 54% of the market share versus the 46% belonging to the PW1100G-JM. Lessors represent a significant segment of the neo customer base and are thereby essential to the success of new narrowbody engine models. According to FlightGlobal's 2016 fleets analyzer database, 11 lessors represented a 22% share of 984 neo orders. Among neo

Table 14.5 V2500 Engine Specifications for Airbus and McDonnel Douglas

Series	Model	Thrust (lb)	Bypass Ratio	Applicable Airframe Model
V2500	V2533-A5	33,000	4.5	A321
	V2530-A5	31,300	4.6	A321
	V2528-D5	27,800	4.7	MD90
	V2527-A5	26,400	4.8	A320
	V2500-A1	25,000	5.4	A320
	V2525-D5	25,000	4.8	MD90
	V2524-A5	24,000	4.9	A319
	V2522-A5	22,000	4.9	A319

International Aero Engines (IAE) (2017).

customers, 34% have chosen the LEAP-1A, 28% have chosen the PW1100G-JM, and 38% remain undecided, as of 2016.

Like with airframe leasing, diversification is a common strategy for engine leasing. Many lessors are ordering a mix of engines from different manufacturers to keep up with the growing demand in the narrowbody market demand and to maximize the liquidity of their portfolios.

WIDEBODY ENGINE MARKET

The engine market for widebody airframes appears even more diversified than the engine market for narrowbody aircraft. When it comes to long-haul jet power, the dominant players are RR, GE and P&W, as shown in Table 14.6. Note that while CFM International and EA also manufacture models in this segment, they do so on a much smaller scale.

From Fig. 14.4, we see that half of all widebody commercial jets are being powered by the Trent (RR) or the CF6 (GE). In this section, we detail the development and application of these and other engines in the widebody market.

CF6—GENERAL ELECTRIC

The CF6 is a series of high-bypass turbofan engines. With a thrust range between 41,500 and 69,800, the engine is built to power widebody aircraft traveling long distances. Qantas Airlines, for example, uses four CF6 engines on the 747-400 to fly the 15-hour route from Dallas to Sydney—one of the longest non-stop flights in the world.

Table 14.7 details the operating specifications of the CF6 series. It initially entered service in 1971 on the DC-10 and was GE's first major turbofan engine for commercial aircraft. Today, the series powers the B747, B767, A300, A310, A330, DC-10, and the MD-11. The CF6-80C and -80E are considered mature fleet engines, whereas the CF6-50 and CF6-80A are already being retired from the market.

Table 14.6 Engine OEMs in Widebody Market

	B747	B767	B777	B787	A330	A340	A350	A380
RR	×		×	×	×	×	×	×
P&W	×	×	×		×			
GE	×	×	×	×	×			
CFM						×		
IAE								
EA								×

RR, *Rolls-Royce;* P&W, *Pratt & Whitney;* GE, *General Electric;* IAE, *International Aero Engines;* EA, *mean-time-between removals.*
FlightGlobal (2016).

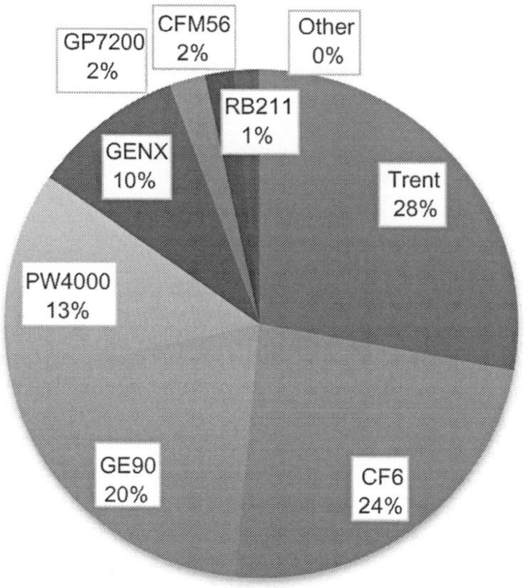

FIGURE 14.4

Engine OEM widebody market share. *OEM*, Original Equipment Manufacturer.

Compiled by the authors using data from FlightGlobal in April 2018.

Table 14.7 CF6 Engine Model Specifications

Series	Model	Thrust (lb)	Bypass Ratio	Applicable Airframe Model
CF6	CF6-80	48,000–69,800	5.2	Boeing 767, A310, 747, MD-11, A330
	CF6-50	51,500–54,000	4.2	DC-10, Boeing 747, A300
	CF6-6	41,500	5.2	DC-10

GE Aviation (2017).

GE90—General Electric

The GE90 is a product from the combined resources of GE Aviation, IHI of Japan, and FiatAvio of Italy. The engine was designed specifically for the Boeing 777 and was first introduced in 1995. The GE90 has a thrust rating ranging from 74,000 to 115,000 and powers some the longest flights in the world.

Not only is the GE90 considered one of the most powerful widebody engines, but it is also one of the most fuel efficient. Recall our earlier discussion on fan blades. The type of material used in construction has a large impact on performance, and the GE90 was the first engine to incorporate a composite fan blade (GE Aviation, 2017). This helps lower fuel consumption by 5–6% and lower NO_x emissions by 33%. The engine also runs quieter than comparable models.

Table 14.8 GE90 Engine Model Specifications

Series	Model	Thrust (lb)	Bypass Ratio	Applicable Airframe Model
GE90	GE90-94B	93,700	8.4	B777-200, B777-200ER
	GE90-115B	115,300	9	B777-200LR, B777-300ER

GE Aviation (2017).

Table 14.8 details the operating specification for the two main variants of the GE90 series, which are the GE90-94B and GE90-115B. Note again that the last 2 or 3-digit number indicates thrust, which is 93,700 and 115,300 lb, respectively. At one point in time, the Boeing 777 was the best-selling long-range large widebody aircraft. By 2007, the A350 XWB from Airbus and the 787 Dreamliner from Boeing became worthy alternatives to the B777. So, to make 777s more attractive to customers, Boeing developed the 777-300ER, which offered the capacity of the 300 and the range of the 200ER. This resulted in a 5000-lb maximum zero-fuel weight increase and a 1%–2.5% thrust enhancement for the increased weight during high-altitude takeoffs. The 777-300ER is one of the most common variants within the 777 family, and has also been one of the most successful. According to FlightGlobal, there were 757 777-300ERs in service as of April 2018, and all of them are equipped with the GE90-115B. Among all 777s in service, 80% are powered by the GE90 engine. The GE90 is also the most expensive engine. Market values for the GE90-115B hovered between $20.5 million and $22.9 million in 2016. Lease rates ranged from $210,000 to $260,000.

GEnx—General Electric

The GEnx is a high-bypass turbofan engine that was designed to replace the CF6. Today, it is the fastest selling high-thrust engine in the history of commercial aviation and is available in two models. The GEnx-1B is the option for the B787-8, B787-9, B787-10, while the GEnx-2B is the engine option for the B747-8 Intercontinental and Freighter (see Table 14.9 for specifications).

Like the GE90, the GEnx incorporates carbon fiber composites in the fan blades to reduce weight and improve fuel efficiency. Similarly, the LPT is fitted with titanium aluminum blades to further reduce overall engine weight (GE Aviation, 2017). Compared to the CF6, this series saves up to 15% on fuel and is built to stay on wing 30% longer. It also uses 30% fewer parts, which has a big impact on maintenance expenses for airlines and lessors. According to FlightGlobal, emissions from the GEnx series can be as much as are expected to 95% below regulatory limits.

In terms of price, the current market value of the GEnx-1B series engines ranges from $16.2 to $18.2 million, while lease rates sit between $210,000 and $280,000.[2]

GE9X—General Electric

According to Boeing, the 777X will be the largest and most efficient twin-engine aircraft in the world. This all-new airliner is built on the success of the 777 and 787 families and will be powered by all-new GE9X engine. GE believes that GE9X will be the most fuel-efficient jet engine GE has ever produced on a per-pound-of-thrust basis. It will achieve an approximate 10:1 bypass ratio, a

[2]Source: myairlease.com, July 2017.

Table 14.9 GEnx Engine Model Specifications

Series	Model Series	Takeoff Thrust (lb)	Bypass Ratio	Applicable Aircraft Model
GEnx	GEnx-1B	69,800–74,100	7.9–8.3 (top of climb)	B787-8, B787-9, B787-10
	GEnx-2B	66,500	7.4	B747-8

GE Aviation (2017).

60:1 overall pressure ratio, and 8-db margin to Stage 5 noise limits. The engine will be in the 100,000 pound thrust class and will have the largest front fan at 134 in in diameter (GE Aviation, 2017). Certification testing of the GE9X engine began in May 2017, flight testing began in March 2018, and certification is expected in 2019. As of March 2018 GE reports almost 700 GE9X on order (GE Aviation, 2017).

PW4000—Pratt & Whitney

P&W's PW4000 series is another line of high-bypass turbofan aircraft engines, with a thrust range of 52,000–99,040 lb. This was a development from the JT9D series engines and now is considered as one of the market's most mature products. Nonetheless, it is known for excellent performance retention, flexibility, and long on-wing time (Pratt & Whitney (P&W), 2017).

Today, the PW4000 powers the A300, A330, B747-400, B767 and B777 aircraft. Furthermore, the series comprised three sub-series according to fan tip diameter: 94-, 100-, and 112-in. The 94-in series powers the B747-400 and the B767-200/300 and has 11 different models ranging from PW4052 to PW4462. The 100-in series, on the other hand, was developed specifically for the Airbus A330 and offers between 64,500 and 70,000 lb of thrust. The 100-in engine comes in three models: PW4164/68/68A-1D, PW4168A, and PW4170. Finally, the 112-in family is an engine option for the B777-200/200ER and the B777-300. It also comes in three distinct models: PW4074/74D/77/77D, PW4084D/90/90-3, and PW4090/90-3. It is P&W's largest commercial jet engine, with a thrust capability of up to 98,000 lb (see Table 14.10 for specifications).

The PW4000 series dominates the B777-200 market, but only has a 20% share of the B777-200ER airframe segment. According to the FlightGlobal, the PW4000 is on over 820 aircraft in April 2018. Current market value for half-life PW4000 series engines ranges from $2.5 to $9.9 million, while lease rates hover between $40,000 and $160,000. The PW4090, in particular, accounts for the highest rates.[3]

Trent—Rolls-Royce

The Trent series from RR is a development of the RB 211. It comprised several versions of a triple-spool, high-bypass turbofan engines with a thrust range of 53,000–95,000 lb, and a bypass ratio of up to 10.1. Triple-spool engines are common on medium and long-haul engines, and compared to a double-spool configuration, they tend to have stronger shafts and optimized speed blades for better performance and efficiency. At takeoff, two Trent 1000 engines on a Boeing 787 Dreamliner are able to deliver a combined thrust of 150,000 lb, which equates to the power of

[3]Source: myairlease.com, July 2017.

Table 14.10 PW4000 Engine Model Specifications

Series	Model (in.)	Takeoff Thrust (lb)	Bypass Ratio	Applicable Airframe Model
PW4000	94	52,000–62,000	4.8–5.0	B747, B767, 747, MD-11, A300, A310
	100	64,500–70,000	5.0	A330-200, A330-300
	112	74,000–98,000	5.8-1–6.4-1	B777-200, B777-200/ER, B777-300

Pratt & Whitney (P&W) (2017).

roughly 1500 piston-powered cars. The blade tip itself rotates at over 900 mph (Rolls-Royce, 2017).

Trent engines are installed on the Airbus A330, A340, A380, and A350XWB as well as the Boeing B777 and B787. There are several iterations of the Trent, including 500, 700, 800, 900, 1000, XWB, and most recently, 7000. The Trent XWBs are designed specifically for the A350XWB, which Airbus developed to replace the A340 and compete with Boeing's Dreamliner and B777. There are three variations of the XWB engine, with three different thrust ratings: XWB-75, XWB-79 (A350-800), XWB-84(A350-900), and XWB-97(A350-1000). The benefit of the XWB is 15% better fuel efficiency, 20% lower CO_2 emissions, 60% lower NO_x emissions.

In 2014, RR launched yet another Trent model, the 7000. This was a competitive strategy to take some of the B787 share from GE, as the engine offers 3% lower fuel burn than GE's comparable GEnx model. Moreover, the Trent 7000 is the exclusive engine for the A330neo.

Outlook for the widebody market

While growth prospects in the aircraft and engine markets remain strong, nearly 70% of new deliveries are narrowbody airframes and their accompanying engines. This is due in large part to the growth among low-cost airlines. In 2017, the industry was forecasting nearly 30,000 narrowbody deliveries through 2036, compared to the 9100 expected widebody deliveries (Boeing, 2017).

Now that we have detailed the main jet engine models on the market, we pick up where the OEMs leave off. In the following section, we introduce key components and intervals and what lessors need to know about jet engine maintenance.

ENGINE MAINTENANCE

Engine maintenance requirements are dictated by the number of flight cycles (FCs), the number of flight hours (FHs), or by calendar months. In general, there are three main reasons to perform scheduled inspections and routine maintenance on an engine:

- To maintain a serviceable aircraft and thereby revenue
- To maintain engine value by minimizing deterioration
- To meet minimum regulatory standards

ENGINE OPERATING PARAMETERS

Recalling our introductory discussion on jet propulsion, OEMs manufacture each turbofan component to operate within certain parameters. Essentially, maintenance is largely about maintaining these parameters. Thus, there are several key measures that are used to diagnose and analyze the overall health of an engine:

Engine Bypass Ratio—The amount of intake air that goes around the engine relative to the amount of intake air that passes through the engine core. The inverse of this is called the core ratio. In newer turbofans, bypass air is responsible for the majority of thrust. Thus, a higher bypass ratio usually indicates a high-thrust engine that is also more efficient than a low-bypass engine. Moreover, the higher the bypass ratio, the larger the intake fan.

N1 Speed (Fan Speed)—The ratio between the rotation speed of the fan and its design rate per minute (RPM). A fluctuating N1 speed can be a sign of engine stall. A low N1 speed can be a sign of flame-out (Ackert, 2011).

Engine Pressure Ratio (EPR)—The ratio of the total pressure at the output (exhaust) to the total pressure at the intake (fan). Put another way, EPR is the total pressure ratio across the engine. In general, a high EPR means better efficiency, although some engine manufacturers use this as a measure of engine thrust.

EGT—The temperature measured at the exhaust. This is used to measure engine efficiency in terms of its design-level thrust. In other words, the higher the EGT, the larger the effect that wear and deterioration have on the life and performance of engine parts. A high EGT can also be a direct sign of deterioration.

EGT Margin—The difference between maximum permissible EGT and peak EGT during takeoff. EGT margin is used to evaluate and track engine health. Thus, margins are at their highest when the engine is new or newly refurbished. Note that EGT margin is particularly sensitive to changes in outside air temperatures (OATs). As OAT increases, EGT also increases for a given thrust setting. See example in Table 14.11.

Maintenance for minor damage and certain preventative measures in typically performed on site. This is often referred to as "on-wing" maintenance. For major damage or a complete refurbishment, however, an engine must be removed from the aircraft and sent to an engine maintenance facility for inspection and repair. This process is referred to as "off-wing" maintenance or an "engine shop visit".

Table 14.11 CFM56-3 EGT Margin Table

Mature CFM56-3 rate at 235,000 lb			**Standard EGT margin = 30°**		
Standard EGT margin = 30°					
OAT (°C)	0	10	20	30	40
Available EGT margin	126	94	62	30	0

OAT, *Outside Air Temperatures;* EGT, *Exhaust gas temperature.*
Aircraft Commerce (2006).

ON-WING MAINTENANCE

On-wing engine maintenance is known as line maintenance, for which the focus is monitoring the physical condition of the engine. For instance, the RR Trent engine has sensors strategically installed to remotely detect conditions and measure key parameters, such as EGT, EGT margin, N1 speed, pressure ratio, RPM, and more. This data can be quickly transferred from the air to a ground control center and then automatically uploaded to the RR aeromanager website where operators can easily view the health of an entire fleet.

Another key tool used in on-wing maintenance is the borescope. Each is equipped with a camera and flexible wiring that allows aircraft mechanics to inspect areas that are internal of the engine and otherwise inaccessible without disassembling the engine. Borescopes are commonly used to inspect various stages of the engine for defects, cracks, burning or foreign object damage (FOD).

Aircraft maintenance accounts for roughly 10%–15% of operating expenses for the average airline. Moreover, 35%–45% of annual maintenance expense is scheduled. In other words, this is standard work performed after a certain number of engine hours, engine cycles, and/or calendar months. Finally, 60%–70% of maintenance costs are typically tied to the high cost of necessary repairs for damages and the associated material used for such repairs.

OFF-WING MAINTENANCE

As previously mentioned, off-wing engine maintenance refers to an engine shop visit (ESV). The following are some of the primary reasons for removing an engine for an ESV.

1. EGT margin deterioration
2. Expiry of LLPs
3. Failing borescope inspection
4. Engine vibration

EGT margin deterioration

The EGT margin will reduce as the engine deteriorates, until it becomes zero. As shown in Fig. 14.5, EGT redline temperature is a warning stage, representing the temperature just below the point where damage is likely to occur. EGT margin deterioration is caused by gradual wear of the

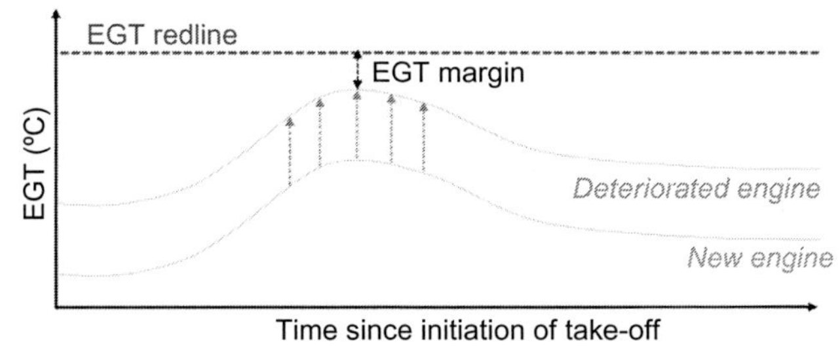

FIGURE 14.5

EGT margin deterioration. *EGT*, Exhaust Gas Temperature.

compressor and turbine blades. Even with a complete overhaul, the repaired engine's EGT margin never return to its initial value. At best, an overhaul might restore 70%–80%. Since the EGT margin is constantly monitored, it is possible to calculate an EGT margin deterioration rate and even predict the next ESV. Therefore, airlines often schedule periodic maintenance events to prevent accelerated damage (Ackert, 2011).

Expiry of life-limited parts (LLPs)

LLPs include the engine rotor and major static structural parts identified as such in the airworthiness limitations of the Instructions for Continued Airworthiness and are listed in the manufacturer's maintenance manuals as approved by the regulatory authority. The service life is specified by the OEM and is based on the maximum number of FC. Usually airlines remove the engine when the LLPs reach 90%–95% stub life (amount of unusable life remaining). For instance, if the LLP's engine stub life is rated for 10,000 FCs, then the engine will be removed and sent to a repair center once it reaches between 9000 and 9500 FCs. To illustrate, Table 14.12 shows how to calculate a 10% stub life rate for LLPs on a CFM 56-3 engine.

Table 14.12 LLP Stub Rate Calculation for the CFM56-3 Engine

LLP		Flight Cycle Limit	Cost ($)	$/Flight Cycle	10% Stub ($)
1	Fan and booster module	30,000	305,000	10.16	11.29
2					
3					
4	LPT	25,000	485,000	19.40	21.56
5					
6					
7					
8					
9					
10					
11	High-pressure compressor and turbine	20,000	755,000	37.75	41.95
11					
12					
13					
14					
15					
16					
17					
18					
19					
	Total cost		*1545,000*	*67.31*	*74.80*

LPT, *Low-Pressure Turbine.*
10% Stub rate = $Cost/(90% × FC limit).

Unfortunately, LLP replacement is relatively expensive. Consider the CFM 56-3, which contains 19 LLPs—three on the fan and booster module, seven on the LPT rotor module, and nine on the HPT rotor module. The total cost to purchase the replacement LLPs with new parts on the CFM 56-3 is roughly $1,500,000 (Ackert, 2011). However, used parts that are certified airworthy can be used instead of new parts provided that the life remaining (green time) complies with the minimum requirements of the lease.

Hardware deterioration

No engine component is immune to deterioration. As such, financiers and operators should know that every component has a point at which it is expected to fail. Common deterioration mechanisms include low- and high-cycle fatigue, thermomechanical, and elemental corrosion.

Other removal causes

As an example, an engine may be removed for an ESV to repair FOD damage caused by a bird strike or due to other causes such as high oil consumption or excessive vibration. Occasionally, an engine removal and ESV may be due to an AD requiring such removal, with the engine having reached its mandatory compliance time, even if there are no other defects.

SHOP VISIT RATE

ESV rate is a meaningful performance metric that measures the engine's overall reliability. It is used by airlines, engine lessors, and even the OEMs. From an airline's perspective, SVR is a key tool for predicting the number of spare engines to keep for its fleet. If it knows the shop repair turn time, the airline can use the SVR to maximize engine usage and avoid disrupting daily operations. Likewise, from a lessor's perspective, access to this data is a key factor in demand planning. Note that engine manufacturers usually guarantee a certain level of equipment reliability. In other words, the operator (and lessor) is protected from the cost of any unexpected shop visit, even beyond the initial warranty period. Here is an example of wording that can be found in a purchase agreement:

> OEM assures operator that by the end of warranty period commencing with the first commercial operation of aircraft powered by OEM engines, the cumulative engine Shop Visit Rate will not exceed a guaranteed rate of [****] per 1000 eligible engine flight hours. Under this guarantee, if the cumulative engine Shop Visit Rate exceeds the guaranteed rate, the engine OEM will credit operators account an amount of [****] U.S. Dollars for each Eligible Engine Shop Visit determined to have been more than the guaranteed rate.
>
> **Ackert (2015).**

Usually, the SVR is measured for a 12-month time period to achieve the cumulative analysis. The formula for SVR is

$$\text{SVR} = \frac{\text{Number of shop visits for the period} \times 1000}{\text{Number of engine operating hours for the period}}$$

Number of shop visits essentially means the number of times an engine was removed for maintenance.

Table 14.13 SVR Calculation

Fleet	Time-On-Wing	Removed
Engine No. 1	18,500 FH	×
Engine No. 2	18,900 FH	
Engine No. 3	21,000 FH	×
Engine No. 4	20,010 FH	
Engine No. 5	19,305 FH	
Engine No. 6	19,605 FH	
Engine No. 7	20,300 FH	×

An alternative engine reliability measure is mean-time-between removals (MTBR). MTBR is the reciprocal of total SVR:

$$\text{MTBR} = \frac{\text{Number of engine operating hours for the period}}{\text{Number of engine removals for the period}}$$

Again, airlines and lessors typically measure engine reliability across an entire fleet. To illustrate, assume Company A owns and leases the seven aircraft engines listed in Table 14.13. Each incurs a different number of flight hours for a given 12-month period. Furthermore, several of the engines were removed during the year for maintenance.

SVR for the engine fleet above is calculated as follows:

$$\text{SVR} = \frac{3 \times 1000}{18,500 + 18,900 + 21,000 + 20,010 + 19,305 + 19,605 + 20,300} = 0.0218$$

In a similar fashion, MTBR is calculated as follows:

$$\text{MTBR} = \frac{18,500 + 21,000 + 20,300}{3} = 19,933$$

A typical aircraft engine for a narrowbody aircraft will have three shop visits for performance restoration through its operational life (Fig. 14.6). The first shop visit typically occurs between 10,000 and 12,000 FCs. Following this first performance restoration, the second shop visit will be required after the next 6000–8000 FCs. Finally, the third shop visit occurs after another 5000–7000 FCs.

Notice above that the shortest FC interval is for the last shop visit. The older the engine, the more prone it is to deterioration. That is why mature engines must be monitored more frequently. Furthermore, over the course of the engine's life, its SVR stabilizes and becomes more accurate. The term "mature" ultimately means that the SVR rate is beginning to align with the average time on-wing (Ackert, 2015).

It is important to note that there are usually two SVR rates—a scheduled engine removal rate (SER) and an unscheduled engine removal rate (UER). In general, there are three main reasons for a scheduled engine removal:

1. Mandatory LLP replacement
2. AD compliance
3. Performance restoration

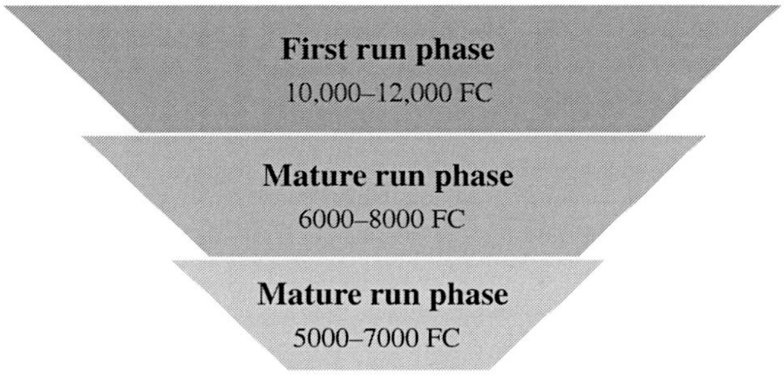

FIGURE 14.6

Engine life cycle.

Bank of America Merrill Lynch (2015).

The SER rate indicates how often the specific engine model is removed for required maintenance actions. This is usually detailed in the OEM maintenance manual, so operators and financiers can plan ahead to minimize service disruptions.

On the other hand, the UER measures how often an engine is removed for repair or refurbishment before the normal maintenance intervals are reached. Such a case is usually due to an unexpected engine anomaly that poses a risk to the operation. Therefore, whenever the frequency of unscheduled engine removals increases, the impact will have a direct adverse effect on operational reliability. If an engine OEMs implement product improvement packages or if they update recommended maintenance practices, then the UER will capture the expected improvements derived from these changes.

PARTS MANUFACTURER APPROVAL

As a final note on maintenance, it is important that lessors, operators, and technicians understand a few regulations. Not only do the regulatory authorities monitor when aircraft parts must be replaced, but they also monitor where those parts come from. In general, all replacement parts must be certified, but they do not necessarily have to come directly from the OEM. Alternatively, the regulatory authorities of the country of manufacture (FAA or EASA) grant Parts Manufacturer Approval (PMA) to third-party manufacturers.

PMA parts were widely accepted by airlines (although not by lessors) in the economic decline during 2001 when airlines were pressured to reduce operating costs on account of drastically decreasing revenues. Since then, they have become more widespread as an increasing number of parts are being manufactured under a PMA. The approval process, however, is often more difficult, as the PMA manufacturer must prove that a specific part is the same as or better than the OEM version. According to the FAA's (2008) Special Airworthiness Information Bulletin, all PMA applicants must

> Show that the design meets the applicable airworthiness standards by either of the following two ways: (1) Showing that the PMA part's design is identical to the design of a part that is covered under a TC, or (2) Using test and computation that shows the PMA part's design meets the airworthiness requirements that apply to the affected product.[4]

A supplemental type certificate (STC) is an approval by the regulatory authority for a modification that causes an aircraft to deviate from its type certificate (TC). It references the original TC and approves a modification as well as how that modification affects the original design. The FAA will determine the need for any additional approval, limitations, or other conditions to ensure that the STC is safely incorporated into the product.

Historically, OEMs have enjoyed high margins, which have created a pricing umbrella for PMA producers, whereby they can justify the costs to reengineer OEM parts and attain approval, while still offering the part at a discount. PMA manufacturer's state that their products are 30%–50% cheaper than those of the OEMs. To counter that claim, the OEMs argue that sticking to OEM parts will be cheaper in the long-run, based on the idea that PMA parts may pose a safety risk if manufacturing techniques differ from those that were intended. Recently, some PMA manufacturers have been targeting the CFM56, due to the high number of deliveries.

On the other end, the OEMs have been fighting to maintain their share of the spare part market with several methods:

- Long-term service agreements
- Better, higher tech engines with parts that are difficult to replicate
- Warranties that are invalidated by PMA parts

Nonetheless, the PMA market has a certain degree of uncertainty, particularly with the new FAA requirements about global qualification and influencing engine hardware. Furthermore, an engine lessor's ability to lease an engine with PMA parts installed, as well as the engine's resale value, may come into question if the operator has been using PMA parts.

ENGINE ECONOMICS

Maintenance is just one aspect, and there are many other economic factors that have an impact on an engine's value. As we discussed earlier, a mature engine requires closer monitoring, but it also refers to an aging technology. In general, we can categorize an engine as new, mature, or sunset, based on where it is in terms of age and life cycle. Table 14.14 illustrates these different stages and their implications on engine value.

Each of the stages above has its own advantages and disadvantages in terms of cost. For example, a sunset engine, such as the CFM56-3 and CF6-50, is nearing the end of its life cycle. Therefore, there is likely a surplus of available material and engine models. The same goes for Designated Engineering Representative (DER) repairs and PMA parts. However, the maintenance work will have shifted from a manufacturer-assigned maintenance, repair, and overhaul (MRO)

[4] FAA, 2008; Chapter 1, Fig. 14.1.

Table 14.14 Engine Economic Life Cycle

	New Engine	Mature Engine	Sunset Engine
Demand	High	Replacement technology rises; sub-fleets move to secondary operators	Low; out of production as technology gets replaced
Required maintenance	In good condition and covered by warranty; no shop visit needed	Installed on wing; requires performance restoration	Maintenance planning is critical to airworthiness
Spare engine demand	Low; slight increases as shop visits increase	Increases to cover overhauls and fleet transitions	High for green-time engines to avoid maintenance
Spare engine availability	Limited	Active trading market	Increased aircraft retirements increase engine supply
Engine value	OEMs escalate new prices; no added premiums	Slight depreciation; maintenance status is the main factor	Decreases exponentially; determined by "green-time" or as a part-out

Bank of America Merrill Lynch (2015).

service to a smaller, independent facility that specializes in sunset engines. Finally, the engine will have a relatively low leasing rate and residual value, especially if fuel prices are high. This is why many low-cost carriers, particularly those in developing countries, fly older planes.

Now, consider the life cycle of several engine models as of 2017. As shown in Table 14.15, the new Leap series comes with higher financing costs and a low used parts supply compared to the JT8D, which is nearing the end of its life cycle. Note also that newer engines are much more fuel efficient, which has always been a key technological factor in aircraft engine development (Tables 14.14 and 14.15).

According to AviTrader, the market share of new technology engines increased from 11% in 2000 to 47% by the end of 2010. During this period, sunset engines were either preserved and stored in hangars or sent off to an engine part-out facility, even though some had not yet reached the end of their technical lives. According to Germany-based MTU Maintenance, "airlines have emerged from the recent recession... more focused on efficiency than ever before, and the high price of oil means that fuel consumption represents a far higher percentage of direct operating costs (DOC) than in the past, and higher still for older aircraft carrying less fuel-efficient engines" (AviTrader, 2011). This holds true today and is precisely why the technical life cycle might not match its economic life cycle.

RESIDUAL VALUE

A common misconception about engine leasing is that the market is relatively small compared to the aircraft market as a whole. On the contrary, according to ICF International (2015), the total market value of the global commercial jet fleet is roughly $600 billion dollars, of which $258

Table 14.15 Engine Models and Different Life Cycles

	New Engine	Mature Engine	Sunset Engine
Representative engine	NB: Leap-1A/PW1000G WB: GE90nx, T1000	NB: CFM56-7/V2500-A5 WB:PW4000-94	NB: JT8D/CFM56-3 WB: JT9D/ CF6-50
Financing/leasing cost	High	Medium	Low
Maintenance costs	Medium	High	Low
Fuel efficiency	High	Medium	Low
MRO competition	High	Medium	High
DER/PMA availability	Low	Medium	High
Surplus/used parts	Rare	Medium	High
Major concern	Acquisition cost	MRO cost	Fuel consumption

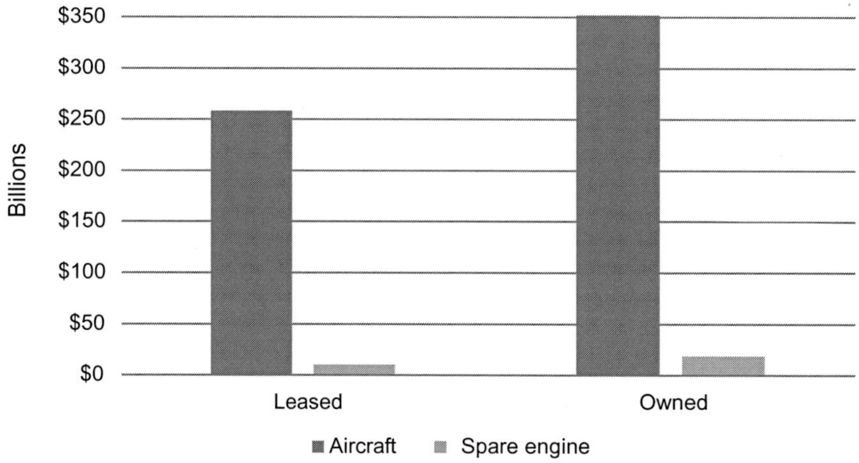

FIGURE 14.7

Total market value of commercial aircraft and spare engines.

billion represents leased aircraft and $352 billion represents airline-owned aircraft (Fig. 14.7). Similarly, total market value of spare engines is roughly $29 billion, of which $10 billion comes from leases. However, the perspective changes when we divide aircraft market value by airframe value and installed engine value (Fig. 14.8). In this light, the size of the engine market equals nearly 40% of the total market.

In terms of value, engine patterns differ significantly from that of airframes. For example, a 5-year old engine may have the same value as a 25-year old engine with a similar maintenance, whereas a 25-year old airframe holds only about 10%–20% of its original value. The reason for this is that an engine can be repeatedly restored to like-new condition. An airframe, on the other

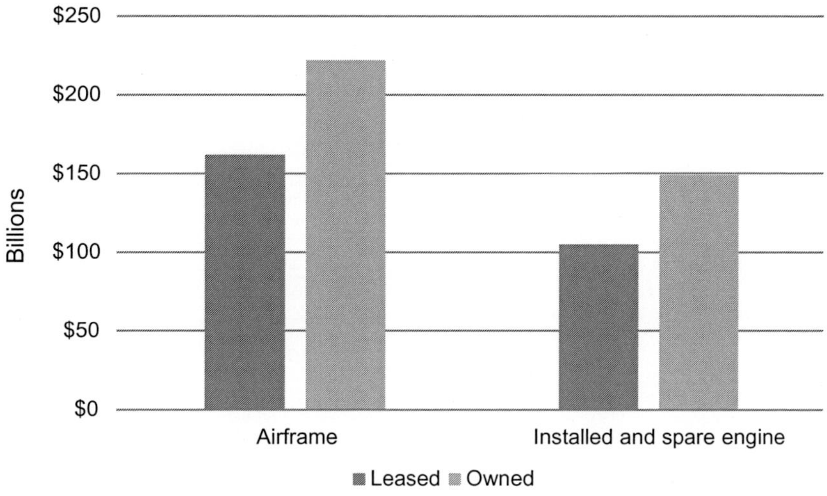

FIGURE 14.8

Value of commercial airframes and installed/spare engines.

hand, is a depreciating asset that continues to lose value over the course of its serviceable life, which is typically 25 years (Figs. 14.9 and 14.10).

As mentioned before, engine value is stable based on the assumption that it is well maintained. If not, the engine can lose over 60% of its value by the end of its lease or useful life. This is called residual value. In accounting terms, it means total value of an asset after it has been fully depreciated. For lessors, there are three main components that make up the total residual value of an engine:

1. *ESV Maintenance Value*—The time and capability an engine has before requiring a shop visit.
2. *LLP Maintenance Value*—Refers to the number of cycles that each LLP could operate before reaching the end of its life limit.
3. *Core Value*—Remaining engine value, including engine data plate and non-*LLP*s. Maintenance overhauls usually continue as long as the core value is higher than the salvage value. But, when the core value dips below the salvage value, the engine is normally disassembled for part-out.

One driver for sale or part out is whether or not the airline needs the engine as a replacement. If not, the operator would typically either repair and sell the engine or part it out and sell the parts. Some part-out specialists have been buying engines with sufficient life remaining and then turning a profit by leasing them out on short-term contracts before they reach a run-out condition. We are now seeing more part-out instances on high-liquidity engines like the CFM56-7B, in response to the high demand for spare parts. But, if the spare is still needed, the airline will make its decision by considering the costs of repair and the cost of leasing or acquiring an engine.

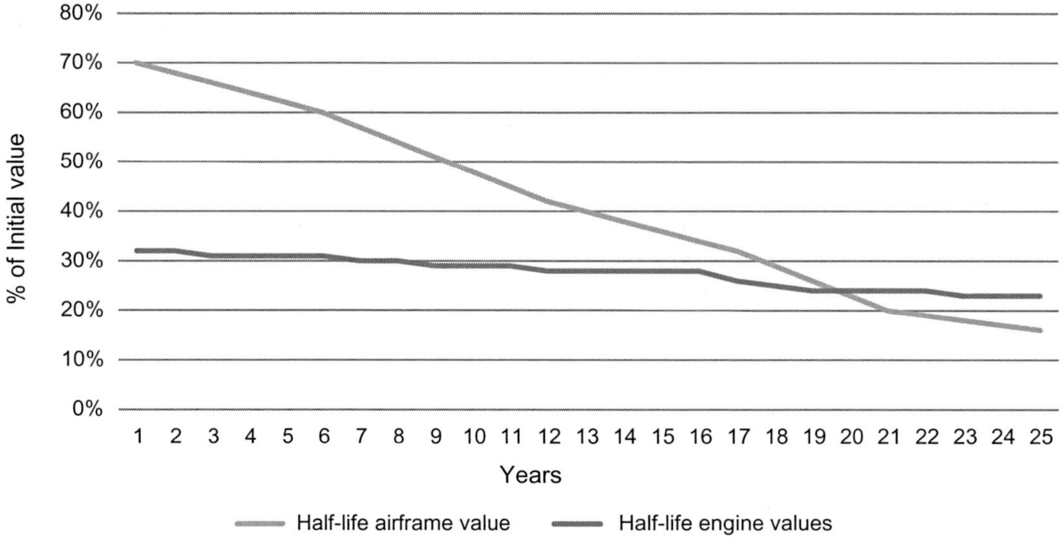

FIGURE 14.9

Airframe and engine value trends.

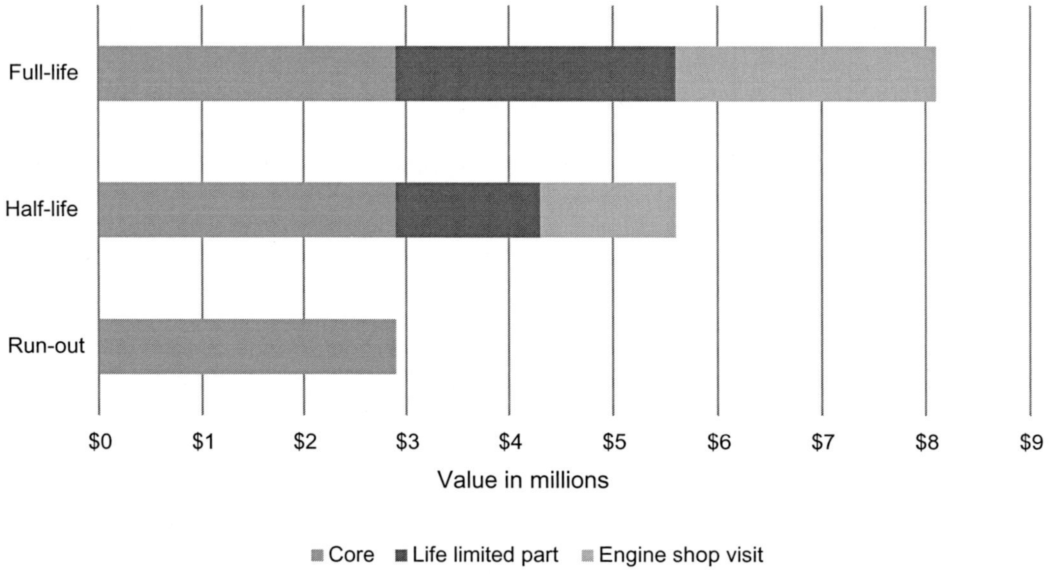

FIGURE 14.10

CFM56-7B engine value under different conditions.

ICF International (2015).

ENGINE LEASING CONCEPTS

Now that we have covered engine operation, maintenance, manufacturing, and engine economics, we can now detail the process of leasing an engine. In this final section, we cover key concepts for lessors, including original equipment sale, leasing business models, financing/leasing costs, return conditions, and aftermarket service programs.

ORIGINAL EQUIPMENT (OE) SALE

Airframe OEMs typically provide either a single-engine option or a multiple-engine option (usually 2) on the frontend. Airlines and lessors tend to benefit more from the two-engine option, because it allows them to be more flexible with their fleets. It also gives them more bargaining power with the engine OEMs. However, this must be balanced with a potentially lower residual value on the backend due to a more limited operator base for each engine type.

Single-engine option

Airframe manufactures may offer the single-engine option when they want to provide any performance/fuel consumption guarantees to their customers. In this case, the engine price will be included in the total airplane price. The airframe OEM will have negotiated prices with the engine OEM for a major part of the program or against a certain volume threshold. The airline will then negotiate the support contract separately with the engine provider, including the initial support package, spare engines, training, etc. A prime example of the single-engine option is the B737MAX. In this case, engine pricing is particularly critical because Boeing wants this aircraft to effectively compete against Airbus' A320neo.

Multiple-engine option

When it comes to multiple engines, the business model changes. In this case, airlines will negotiate with engine and airframe OEMs separately for a price on the engines and a price on the airframe. The benefit here is that the customer is free to negotiate the engine price with or without a support package attached to it. Of course, an airline can always request such support separately by inviting third-party maintenance providers to bid.

Airframe manufacturers generally prefer that customers (e.g., airlines, lessors) make an engine decision at least 2 years prior to the delivery of a widebody and at least 18 months prior to the delivery of a narrowbody. However, the engine is not usually delivered to the airframe until about 1–2 months before final delivery of the airplane to the customer.

ENGINE LEASING BUSINESS MODEL

Engines are expensive assets. As one lessor noted, "the sheer cost of new generation aircraft engines is making leasing more attractive. The GE90 engine built for the Boeing 777 costs $32.5 million. 20 years ago, when I started in the business, that's what you'd pay for a new aircraft. Cash-rich airlines like Singapore Airlines and Emirates can raise money fairly easily to buy their own engines, but for smaller companies and start-ups airlines, leasing seems to be a better option for them. That is why the engine leasing industry has been growing significantly over the last 20 years."[5] For airlines, leasing allows for the immediate use of high-priced assets with little cash outlay, or for capital to be freed up through the use of a sale-and-leaseback transaction. This concept is addressed in detail below.

Like the OEMs, engine lessors also offer multiple products. In general, there are two types of engine leases: short term and long term.

Short-term lease

Short-term leases range anywhere between 2 days and 9 months. Oftentimes, an airline will use a short-term lease to cover an unscheduled maintenance event or shop visit and thereby keep its aircraft from being grounded due to engine failure. The leased asset is simply returned once the original has been repaired. Alongside the lessors are the MROs, who also specialize in these short-term leases that cover shop visits for both scheduled and unscheduled maintenance.

Most lessors offer several options under a short-term contract, one of which may be access to multiple engines. This is known as an engine pool and includes not only the lessor's inventory but also those of participating airlines. Another option may be a 100% guarantee. This requires a separate contract and is generally offered to larger airlines with a greater need for spare engines. Once the agreement is signed, the lessor has the obligation going forward to supply rental engines within 24 hours of an aircraft being grounded. Next is volume lease days. Customers who purchase this option are given a designated number of lease days which can be used on several engines at the same time or within a certain time frame. Some lessors will even tailor this ad-on to help airlines phase out their older engines.

An engine lessor will charge either a daily lease rate or monthly lease rate (MLR). In general, short term-lease rates tend to be higher than long-term lease rates, although this depends to some degree on the engine type and situation. Lessees are also required to pay a maintenance reserve fee as well as a deposit. Maintenance reserve fees are based on the engine's thrust, hour-to-cycle ratio, and the LLP charge. A high thrust and a low hour-to-cycle ratio usually commands a higher reserve fee, although this may be waived for airlines with very strong credit profiles. In such case, the lessor would settle any accrued maintenance at end of the contract by charging for the use of hours and cycles. Deposits are usually in the form of cash or a letter of credit and will either be returned at the end of the lease or written off following redelivery.

Long-term lease

A long-term lease typically lasts anywhere between 1 and 10 years. Lessors rarely purchase engines without having a long-term contract in place. An airline can also purchase a spare engine directly from the OEM at a discounted rate as part of a broader aircraft acquisition, and then sell it to a leasing company at close to a full list price. In this case, the sale would come with a long-term lease agreement between the airline and the leasing company, whereby the operator maintains exclusive use of engine. This model is referred to as a sale-and-lease-back. The lessor would then

[5]John Sharp, President and CEO of Engine Leasing Finance Corporation.

receive monthly payment from the airline. Many lessors who favor long-term contracts might have upwards of 80% of their engines under sale-and-lease-back agreements.

When it comes to the long-term lease strategy, return conditions are critical and are usually a main element of the written agreement. Equally important are the maintenance reserve fee and lease deposit. Again, maintenance reserve fees are based on the thrust, hour-to-cycle ratio, and the LLP charge, and are usually highest for engines with higher thrusts and smaller ratios. An airline's credit profile is more critical for a long-term contract, but a lessor may still offer to waive the reserve fees for strong-credit customers. Alternatively, the airline can use an aftermarket service agreement (ASA) as a bargaining tool against paying reserves, but again, the lessor will still charge for used hours and cycles at the end of the lease.

SPARE ENGINE LEASING MODEL

At one point, most airlines kept spares for about 15% of their installed, in-services engines. This was meant to cover operations during engine overhauls. However, with new technology and OEM monitoring programs, this has been reduced to around 8%–10%. Furthermore, many of the growing low-cost carriers operate single-type fleets with large quantities of the same aircraft and at least one spare engine. This spare engine is usually kept in a hangar at the airline's hub airport. One spare engine can cover an airline for the first 5 years or so, since no ESV is required during this period, assuming no FOD or another unscheduled situation. However, as the first shop visit approaches, airlines begin to need more spare engines to cover the overhaul period, since they often take delivery of multiple aircraft in a short time period. In other words, many of the engines in a fleet will have logged the same number of cycles and hours.

One reason for an airline to lease a spare engine is that the lessor takes on the residual value risk. The airline still benefits from the asset, particularly when it is trying to retire an older fleet or transition to a new technology. Moreover, from a budgetary perspective, spare engine leasing makes it easier for airlines to forecast operating costs. Most develop their spare engine strategy according to the aircraft fleet plan, engine maintenance schedule, and any capital requirements. For those with MRO facilities and a strong balance sheet, leasing may be less attractive. For many small or less-profitable airlines, however, leasing helps drive the renewal strategy and secure new engine technology. This is typically done through a combination of sale-and-lease back, long-term, and short-term leasing. For many carriers, it is important to have not only long term leases but also access to a short-term engine pool. This helps them better handle unscheduled removals or peak maintenance periods.

LESSORS

Clearly, there is no universal engine leasing model. One lessor might focus on a particular region where credit risk tends to be high, while another company may choose to rent only one type of engine. Overall, every engine lessor has a unique strategy in terms of target market, inventory, and execution process.

Independent engine lessors

We often use the term "pure" when describing lessors who have no affiliation with an OEM. Two examples are California-based Willis Lease and Engine Lease Finance Corporation (ELFC) out of Ireland. Both companies have been around a since the 1980s. Since 2014, ELFC has operated as a subsidiary of Mitsubishi UFJ Lease & Finance Company Limited. With a portfolio of over 200 engines, it is the largest bank-owned engine financing and leasing company. ELFC favors the long-term business model, and most of its contracts are sale–lease-back transactions. Some lessors even operate their own part-out facilities, which allow them to support airlines that want to reduce the cost of retiring sunset engines.

Unlike ELFC, Willis Lease is not affiliated with any financial institution. The benefit here is more flexibility. While bank-backed lessors may have lower costs, they are often held to strict covenants. Willis pioneered the model of cooperative engine sharing pools, having first launched the program in China in 2003 and in North America in 2006. The Chinese program supports five major airlines and over 300 Boeing 737 Next Generation aircraft. Even larger is the North American program, which supports over 700 B737 Next Generation airplanes. Members include American Airlines, Southwest Airlines, and Delta Air Lines. Pooling allows airlines to work together to re-evaluate their spare engine plans, re-deploy capital, and realize better utilization. (AviTrader, 2011).

Finally, TES Aviation Service is an example of an engine risk management firm. Based in the United Kingdom, the company has been in the engine leasing industry since 2006. TES found a niche as a "green-time" lessor, specializing in mature engine types. Their strategy is to acquire and lease older engines that still have useful life remaining. As such, most of the company's contracts are short-to-medium term. Like other leasing companies and MROs, TES also offers a fleet management service by covering engine usage requirement during shop visits and supplying any necessary LLPs or other serviceable materials.

OEM-affiliated engine lessors

OEMs have been actively involved in engine leasing, MRO maintenance, and aftermarket service sectors for the past 10 years. The big-three—GE, RR, and P&W—all have engine leasing outlets and their own subsidiary engine leasing companies.

GE Engine Leasing (GEEL) is a wholly owned subsidiary of GE. With over 400 engines in its portfolio, it is one of the largest players in the leasing world. GEEL has a diversified set of engine models, not from its own line, but also from CFM International, RR, P&W and IAE. The subsidiary offers a variety of products, including one-day short-term agreements, long-term operating leases, sale-and-lease back transactions, engine exchanges, long-term financing options, and asset management. In addition, thanks to the scope and experience of its parent company, GEEL has the advantage of a huge global reach, the depth of experience and the reputation offered by its parent company GE capital.

Similarly, RR & Partners Finance (RRPF) is a joint venture between RR and US-based financier GATX. RRPF manages over 300 engines. Unlike GEEL, however, RRPF only leases RR and IAE models. According to vice president Bobby Janagan, "our superior technical knowledge of RR designed engines, and our extensive knowledge of customers who operator RR and IAE equipment and utilize RR's used parts trading division to exit from engines at the end of their investment period, allow us to source funding with relative ease and more cheaply than our competition" (AviTrader, 2011).

P&W Engine Leasing (PWEL) is the most recent comer to the market. P&W remained a pure warranty provider until about 12 years ago when it decided to enter the aftermarket by offering a comprehensive portfolio of services, including short-term engine leasing, long-term engine leasing, sale-and-lease-back, and asset trading. PWEL operates a 200 + engine portfolio that includes the PW4000, PW2000, V2500, CFM56, JT9D, and the JT8D. The company is also part of a global services partners' program.

Finally, Shannon Engine Support (SES) is a fully owned subsidiary of CFM International. The company is known for its 100% availability guarantee program (GAF), which is a type of insurance designed to help airlines reduce the risk of an AOG. Participants sign a contract for one or more engines, and pay an annual access fee based on the engine fleet's maintenance situation and demands. The main benefit of GAF is that engines are available within 24 hours. To achieve this, however, SES supports only one engine type—the CFM56 line. With over 250 engines and 12 pools on three continents, SES is the largest lessor of the CFM56 model.

As we have discovered, there are advantages and disadvantages for both independent lessors and OEM affiliates. When lessors are related to the manufacturing process, they can offer unique products like credits for future parts purchases or future maintenance as part of the overall sales proposition. They can also take advantage of maintenance facilities to store parts and inventory. On the other hand, some airlines have felt unfairly treated by OEMs and prefer to work with an independent company. In fact, some independent leasing companies win contracts simply because they are not tied to any OEM. Ultimately, it depends on the airline and the situation. Nonetheless, it is becoming more difficult for pure lessors to compete with their OEM-backed competitors.

ENGINE DELIVERY

When a lessor receives a request from a customer, the first thing to check for is an existing contract. If there are no signed contracts, the lessor will send a quote along with engine data to the customer. Once accepted by the potential lessee, the two parties move into the contract negotiation phase. After the customer signs the contract, the lessor will prepare for the engine delivery process. Prior to delivery, it is very important for the lessor to collect a deposit and the first month's rent. In addition, the lessor should obtain an insurance/reinsurance certificate, a process agent letter (if applicable), and an acceptance certificate. It is also a good idea to obtain a legal opinion with respect to the contract. After receiving the paperwork, the lessor can then deliver and release the engine to the customer with confidence. Below is a more detailed roadmap of how the process plays out (Fig. 14.11).

AFTERMARKET SERVICE AGREEMENTS

Our final discussion addresses the various ASAs currently offered by the manufacturer. As we mentioned in the previous section, an airline customer may already have a contract in place with the manufacturer regarding engine guarantees or perks. Generally speaking, these OEM-provided programs fall under one of two models: time and materials (TMs) or long-term agreements, also known simply as term agreements.

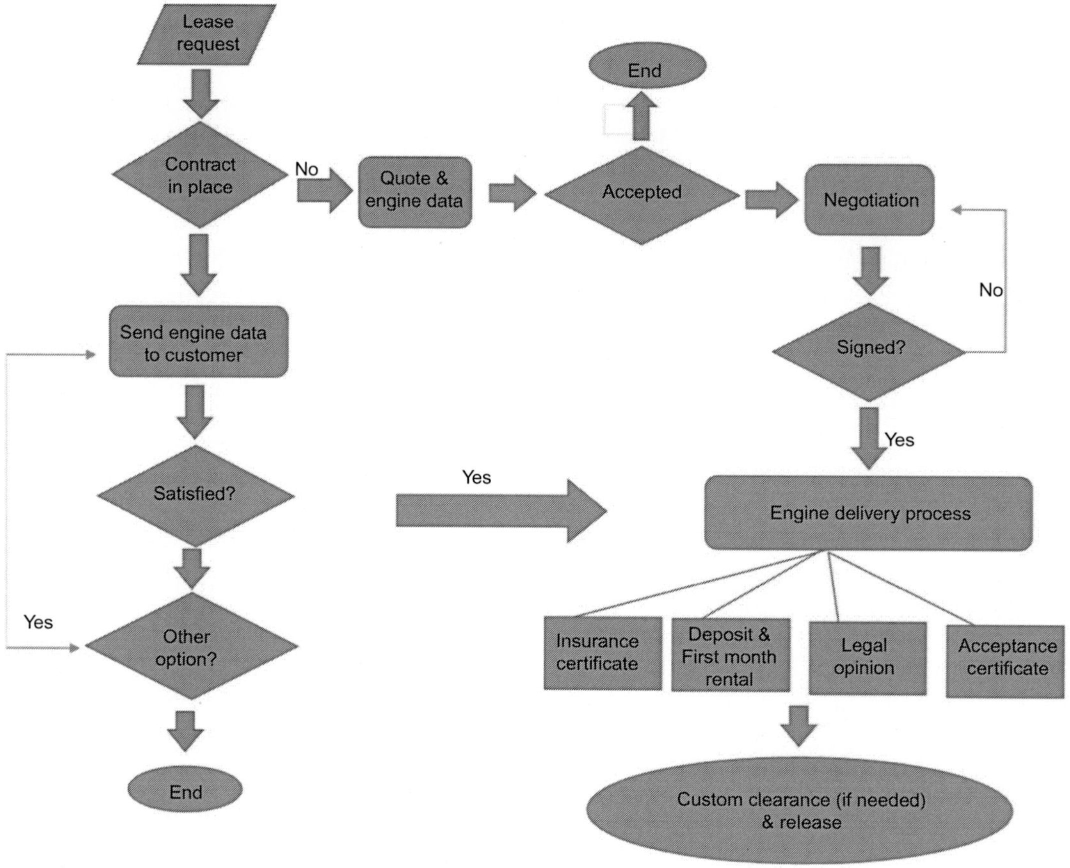

FIGURE 14.11

Engine delivery process.

Time and materials

A TM aftermarket contract model is the standard term given to contracts, whereby the engine operator pays for required engine maintenance and spares for each individual engine when that engine goes into the shop. The strategy behind this model is that the OEM could sell the new engine to an airline with a relatively even margin and then profit from spare parts sales. Typically, the revenue from spares is limited in the first 5–7 years and is highly dependent upon usage. For example, engines wear out more quickly on jets that are constantly flying short-haul routes. When it comes to the first major overhaul, the cost is typically \$2.5–\$3 million for narrowbody engines and \$5–\$6 million for widebody engines. The cost is estimated under the scenario that the shop visit is not required for LLPs replacement. Otherwise, this would double the cost. The next shop visit will then take place between 5 and 7 years.

Long-term agreements

Long-term ASAs are becoming more and more common. This is especially true for engine models that have just been released, since it takes time for new technology to build a reputation for reliability. In the mid-1990s, RR coined the "power-by-the-hour" concept with its TotalCare program designed to help streamline the customer's operation and budget. GE then mimicked this strategy with a program called On Point, and P&W followed with their version, known as Fleet Management Program. The following paragraphs summarize a few of the more noteworthy programs on the market today.

- *TotalCare*—A flagship brand for RR civil aerospace and is tailored to individual operators. It offers full asset management with a range of services, including line maintenance, initial provisioning, spare engines, lease engines, rotable assets, power plant engineering, engine overhauls, maintenance logistics fuel burn optimization. The cost depends on how many service models are chosen, and services are available worldwide. Essentially, the airline pays RR periodically for each hour or flight that the engines have completed. When the engine is removed for maintenance, RR fits the bill and returns a fully serviceable engine to the customer. The major benefits to airlines are the fixed maintenance costs, increased aircraft availability, and lower financial risk.[6]
- *TrueChoice*—A GE-provided program for airlines, lessors, and MROs that features a breadth of capabilities and customizations across the entire engine lifecycle. Within the program are four main products. TrueChoice Flight Hour provides flexible payment options for FOD coverage, technology upgrades, SD/AD coverage, scheduled and unscheduled engine removals, and guaranteed spare engine availability. TrueChoice Overhaul provides time and material shop visits with customized work scopes, while TrueChoice Material offers a range of new, used, and OEM-qualified parts. Finally, TrueChoice Transitions covers green time leases, exchanges, material buy-back, and custom work scopes with shorter builds, as well as products for lessors that can accommodate a change in ownership or operator. The program also incorporates digital solutions products designed to collect flight data, assess engine health, improve fuel efficiency, streamline invoicing, and benchmark fleet performance against operators worldwide.[7]

Pricing

Most airlines that lease aircraft from lessors are required to pay monthly maintenance reserves or settle the costs at end of the lease. However, if the engines are under an ASA, the airline might already be paying the OEM for these costs. To prevent the airlines from paying twice, OEMs offer a portable product, meaning that cash paid to the engine manufacturer by the airlines is transferable to aircraft lessors and their future lessees. With this portability, the lessor only pays a "top up" fee to cover the gap between the shop visit expense and the cash collected by the OEM through the service agreement. There are life-based and term-based pricing agreements.

---

[6]Rolls-Royce TotalCare™ https://www.rolls-royce.com/sustainability/performance/sustainability-stories/totalcare.aspx.
[7]GE Aviation, TrueChoice™ Transitions http://www.geaviation.com/commercial/truechoice-commercial-services/truechoice-transitions.

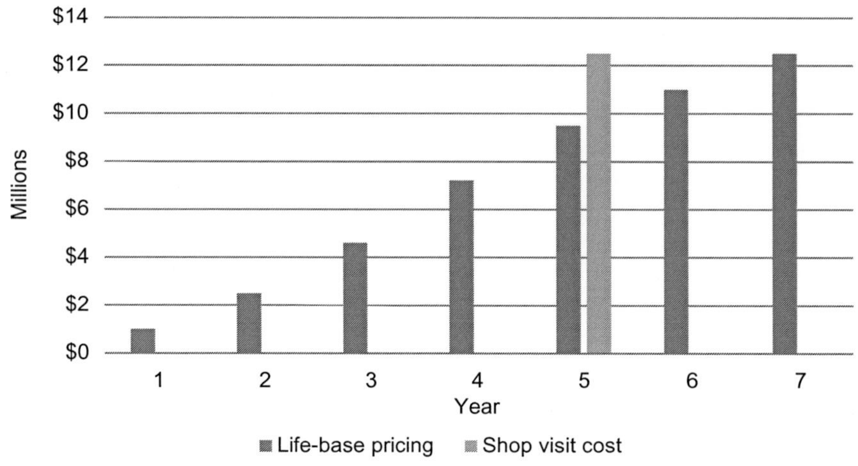

FIGURE 14.12

Term-base pricing.

It is important to note that for the term-based agreement (Fig. 14.12), lessors might not receive any funds from the previous lessee. This is because the purpose of term-based pricing is to collect enough money to cover specific time periods, which in most cases, is a lease term. Therefore, the shop visit is most likely to happen during the term and the maintenance costs will be collected during the lease term. It is highly possible that the engine manufacturer will not have collected funds equal to the cost of the work prior to the engine restoration; thus, the cost is averaged out over the entire lease term.

Life-based pricing is not designed for just a specific lease term of the service agreement. Instead, it is calculated based on the full engine life (usually around 25 years). The cost of the shop visit and date of engine performance restoration could be forecasted through historical data. The OEM will collect enough funds before the shop visit, after which the life-based pricing fee will decrease (Fig. 14.13).

Today, many new engines are under some form of long-term ASA, particularly the higher technology models. In fact, this is case for 80%–90% of Trent engines and 80%–85% of CFM LEAP engines. The recent demand for these programs can be attributed to range of valuable benefits they provide:

1. The technical and financial risks of maintenance shift from the airline to the OEM
2. Airlines have a more predictable cost base that is directly proportional to revenue
3. OEMs keep their repair and overhaul market share against PMA companies
4. Revenue streams for OEMs are less cyclical
5. Airline revenue is more resilient to recessions due to the constant cost/penalty
6. Interests align between OEMs and airlines
7. OEMs earn higher revenues over 10–15 years when compared to the T&M model
8. Lessors maximize asset value by guaranteeing the condition of the engine

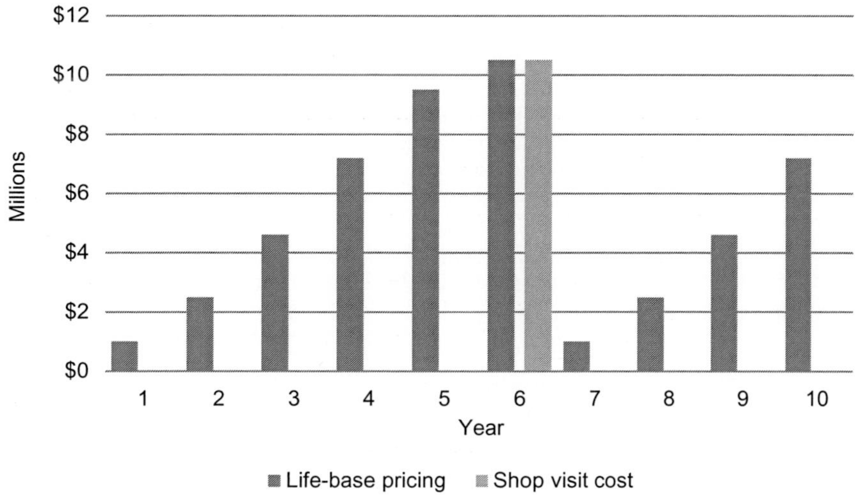

FIGURE 14.13

Life-base pricing.

Note that the benefits above are spread among airlines, lessors, and OEMs. RR, in particular, earned over 50% of its revenue in 2014 from service agreements. This is a good example of how an OEM can transform from a product company to a service provider. (AviTrader, 2011). Historically, OEMs profited from engine maintenance, but with power-by-the-hour programs, they no longer profit when engines fail. Thus, time-on-wing and life cycle costs are becoming more and more important since time in shop equals money, and this is where they generate a large portion of their revenue. That is why, under this business model, the objectives of airlines and OEMs are truly aligned.

CONCLUSION

Throughout this chapter, we have discussed how airlines procure spare engines in order to maintain full usage of their aircraft. One method is to purchase their own spare engines directly from OEMs. Alternatively, they may choose to lease via a sale-lease-back agreement from an engine lessor, and therefore only pay a monthly fee in addition to the maintenance costs. They could also sign a contract with the engine lessor and lease the engine to only cover the shop visit period, which is known as short-term leasing. Some leasing companies even specialize in engine green time leases to help the airlines manage their old fleet retirement. On the other hand, engines are getting more reliable and staying on-wing longer. Built-in sensors in the new engine types can provide more accurate operational data and improve reliability. However, the more reliable the engine is, the lower the demand is for spares. This is likely to have a bigger impact on lessors in the coming years. One positive trend is that airlines are not keen on acquiring the spare engines, as it is not a core business. As a result, more and more spare engines will be delivered under long-term lease financing.

Lessors previously charged maintenance reserves for engines, but nowadays, they are willing to compromise if the lessee has participated in the OEMs' aftermarket service program. In conclusion, engine leasing is dynamic market, and it is very important for lessors to adapt quickly and find their niche either in narrowbody or widebody, new technology, or sunset green-time.

CASE STUDY

Hawk Airline operates a hub on the West Coast of the United States. Presently, the airline has five Boeing 737-400 aircraft, each of which powered by two CFM56-3C1 engines, and each engine has a thrust of 23,500 lb. The fleet operates on average, 8.35 flight hours and five cycles per aircraft per day, giving an estimated annual utilization of 3157 flight hours and 1825 cycles. Based on historical data, the unscheduled removal shop visit rate is 0.029 per 1000 engine flight hours (engine flight hours to engine flight cycles (EFH-to-EFC) ratio is 1.67). This translates to a high probability of a shop visit occurring about once every 34,482 hours, which equates to once every 20,648 FCs. All engine flight hours, engine FCs, and cycles since overhaul are listed in Exhibit 14.1.

Exhibit 14.1: Engine Fleet Utilization since Overhaul

Engine	EFH	EFC	CSO	EGT Margin at OAT 20
1	19,720	13,185	1185	45
2	13,502	8194	8194	18
3	22,350	13,902	2200	41
4	26,780	20,600	5023	21
5	34,250	20,757	200	46
6	18,720	12,830	150	54
7	13,502	8194	8194	19
8	16,789	9875	9875	16
9	8830	5518	5518	22
10	8830	5518	5518	22

EFH, *engine flight hours*; EFC, *engine flight cycles*; CSO, *cycles since overhaul*; EGT, *Exhaust Gas Temperature*; OAT, *outside air temperature.*

There are two spare engines in the hub hangar to cover the ESV period. According to the engineer's report, one of these spares will soon be beyond economic repair (BER). It is important that Hawk's finance manager evaluate the various options in detail and plan for the replacement of the BER spare engine. The estimated utilization of the BER engine's replacement from the engineer's report is listed in Exhibit 14.2.

Exhibit 14.2: Estimated Utilization for the BER Spare Engine

Year	Flight Hour	Flight Cycle
1	650	430
2	700	467
3	900	600
4	700	467
5	400	267

Exchange Option: Since the CFM56-3C1 engine is no longer in production, it is impossible for Hawk to acquire a brand-new engine from the OEM. However, there is an exchanged half-life engine available from the OEM which has 9000 EFHs and 6000 EFCs remaining before any heavy maintenance or LLP replacements are required. The price for this exchange engine is $1.3 million.

Lease Option: Again, since the CFM56-3C1 is no longer in production, Hawk's second option is to lease a spare engine from an engine lessor as a long-term agreement. The MLR is $15,000 plus a maintenance reserve fee of $55 per EFH and $70 per EFC. This rate assumes that the leased engine will not experience any heavy maintenance during Year 5 of the contract term and will meet the return condition requirement by the end of Year 5. See Exhibit 14.3 for the long-term lease proposal.

Green-Time Option: The third option is for Hawk to purchase a green-time engine from the marketplace, assuming all the green-time engines in the market have around 3000 EFH and 1700 EFC left on before LLPs burn out or heavy maintenance is required. From Year 0 to Year 2, the current market value for a green-time engine is $0.6 million. After Year 2, the price for a green-time engine will drop to $0.55 million.

Exhibit 14.3: Long-Term Lease Proposal

Lease term	5 Years from the date of delivery
Monthly lease rental rate	$15,000, paid monthly
Deposit	3 months' rent, payable upon acceptance of the lease proposal and refundable upon the expiration of the lease
Maintenance reserve rates	Paid monthly
Per engine flight hour	$55
Per engine flight cycle	$70
Validity of maintenance reserve rates	Maintenance reserve rates are fixed for the entire lease term
Return condition 1	Certified serviceable, with at least 5000 hours until the next heavy maintenance
Return condition 2	Each LLP has at least 3000 cycles remaining

All estimations presume that the tax rate for Hawk Airlines is 35% and that the exchanged engine and green-time engine will be depreciated in 5 years with a $0.1 million residual value.

ADDITIONAL INFORMATION

B737-300/-400/-500 series are also known as Boeing 737 Classics. They are the second generation of the B737 aircraft and are targeted for the short-to-medium range, narrowbody market. CFM56-3 is the sole engine option for the 737 Classics. There are three engine variations for CFM56-3: -3B1, -3B2, and -3C1. The three main reasons leading to Hawk's engine removal during their shop visit are EGT margin deterioration, a high EFH:EFC ratio, and no remaining cycles on the LLPs.

According to previous data, the EGT erosion rate of a mature -3C1 engine, rated at 23,500 lb thrust power, that is operated on the West Coast where the average OAT is roughly 20°C. The EGT margin decreases by 12° during the first 1000 EFCs, by 6° during the second 1000 EFCs, and by 4° per 1000 EFCs thereafter. On this basis, the engine will be left with a EGT margin of about 44°C after 2000 EFCs (see Exhibit 14.4). The total expected on-wing EFC is about 13,000 before an engine performance restoration is required.

Exhibit 14.4: CFM56-3 EGT Margin Table

Mature CFM56-3 rate at 23,500 lb			Standard EGT margin = 30°		
Standard EGT margin = 30°					
OAT (°C)	0	10	20	30	40
Available EGT margin	126	94	62	30	0
EGT, *Exhaust Gas Temperature.* *Aircraft Owner's & Operator's Guide (2006). CFM56-3 Maintenance Analysis & Budget.*					

LLPs are another main factor to be considered when managing an engine. The CFM56-3C1 has 19 LLPs. There are three LLPs in the fan and booster modules, with life limits of 30,000 EFCs and a combined value of $305,000. Furthermore, there are seven LLPs in the LPT module with life limits of 25,000 EFCs and a combined value of $485,000. The remaining nine LLPs are found in the HPC and HPT modules, with life limits of 20,000 EFCs and a combined value of $755,000.

Question 1. What is the 10% LLPs reserve rate for the CFM56-3C1 engine?
Question 2. How many engine removals will occur within 5 years (calculate for all engines listed in Exhibit 14.1)?
Question 3. Calculate the cash flow for all three options within 5 years.

REFERENCES

Ackert, S. (2011). *Engine maintenance concepts for financiers: Elements of turbofan shop maintenance costs* (2nd ed.). Aircraft Monitor.

Ackert, S. (2015). *Keeping score: Analysis of an engine's shop visit rate*. Aircraft Monitor.

Aircraft Commerce. (2016). *The used market for regional & narrowbody engines*. Aircraft Commerce, Issue No. 109, December 2016/January 2017.

Aircraft Commerce. (2006). *CFM56-3 aircraft owner's and operator's guide: Maintenance analysis & budget*. Aircraft Commerce, Issue No. 45, April/May 2006.

AviTrader MRO. (June, 2011). *Engine life cycles: When to repair, when to replace.*

Bank of America Merrill Lynch. (June 9, 2015). Power on—Commercial aerospace engine primer. *Industry review: Aerospace and defense.*

Boeing. (2017). *Current market outlook: 2017–2036.*

CFM International. *Company Website: Engines.* (2017). From <https://www.cfmaeroengines.com/engines/> Retrieved November 13, 2017.

Engine Alliance. *Our Gp7200 Powers the A380. Empowering the operator.* Company Website. (2017). Retrieved from <http://www.enginealliance.com/gp7200/>.

FAA. (June 23, 2008). Parts manufacturing approval process. US Department of Transportation Federal Aviation Administration National Policy. Order 8110. 42C.

Flight Global. *Commercial engines 2016: TurboFan Focus.* Industry Reports. (2016). Retrieved from <https://www.flightglobal.com/resources/special-reports/>.

FlightGlobal. (2016). Engine selection trends on the A320neo. *FlightGlobal News*, March 22, 2016.

GE Aviation. Company Website: Commercial Engines. (2017). From <https://www.geaviation.com/commercial/engines/cf6-engine> Retrieved November 18, 2017.

ICF International. (2015). Engine residual values. In: *Presented at Aircraft and Engine Trading & Remarketing Day*. Shanghai, June 3, 2015.

International Aero Engines (IAE). Company Website: Company History. (2017). From <http://i-a-e.com/history.html> Retrieved November 13, 2017.

Mattingly, Jack D. (1996). *Elements of gas propulsion*. New York: McGraw Hill.

Mattingly, Jack D. (2006). Elements of propulsion: Gas turbines and rockets. *AIAA education series*. Reston, VA: American Institute of Aeronautics and Astronautics.

Pratt & Whitney (P&W). *Company Website: Products.* (2017). <http://www.pw.utc.com/PW400094_Engine> Retrieved November 18, 2017.

Rolls-Royce. Company Website: Products. (2017). From <www.rolls-royce.com/products-and-services.aspx> Retrieved November 18, 2017.

Rolls-Royce. (1996). *The jet engine.* (5th ed.). Derby, England: Rolls Royce plc.

Sonntag, Richard E., & Borrgnakke, Claus (2007). *Introduction to engineering thermodynamics*. Hoboken, NJ: J. Wiley & Sons.

Index

Note: Page numbers followed by "*f*," "*t*," and "*b*" refer to figures, tables, and boxes, respectively.

E

T

U

Printed in Australia by Griffin Press
an Accredited ISO AS/NZS 14001:2004
Environmental Management System printer.